THE ROCK
HISTORY READER

THE ROCK
HISTORY READER

edited by **Theo Cateforis**

Syracuse University

Routledge
Taylor & Francis Group
New York   London

Routledge is an imprint of the
Taylor & Francis Group, an informa business

Routledge
Taylor & Francis Group
270 Madison Avenue
New York, NY 10016

Routledge
Taylor & Francis Group
2 Park Square
Milton Park, Abingdon
Oxon OX14 4RN

International Standard Book Number-10: 0-415-97501-8 (Softcover) 0-415-97500-X (Hardcover)
International Standard Book Number-13: 978-0-415-97501-8 (Softcover) 978-0-415-97500-1 (Hardcover)

Library of Congress Cataloging-in-Publication Data

The rock history reader / [edited by] Theo Cateforis.
    p. cm.
  Includes bibliographical references.
  ISBN 0-415-97500-X -- ISBN 0-415-97501-8
  1. Rock music--History and criticism. I. Cateforis, Theo.

ML3534.R6333 2007
781.6609--dc22
                                                      2006031346

Visit the Taylor & Francis Web site at
http://www.taylorandfrancis.com

and the Routledge Web site at
http://www.routledge-ny.com

Contents

Preface

Rock music has been with us now, by one name or another, for more than half a century. It is an utterly familiar presence. We hear it in commercials, movie soundtracks, and political campaigns, and we are constantly reminded of its privileged cultural status through frequent lists of the "100 greatest rock songs of all time." The music even has its own Hall of Fame and Museum, populated by a cluster of towering icons, many of whom have had book-length academic studies devoted to their life and works. As it has become engrained in our environment, rock music has also become a subject deemed worthy of study in higher education. Browse the course listings for most universities and colleges and chances are good that you will find a "History of Rock" or "Rock Music" class listed somewhere in their catalog. Currently there are approximately half a dozen rock music textbooks in circulation, many of them on their fourth and fifth editions. Yet until recently instructors seeking an anthology of historically based readings as a supplement to these textbooks have looked in vain. This book aims to fill that gap.

The Rock History Reader is modeled after the types of annotated source reading collections that should be well familiar to scholars and teachers in the humanities. Within the realm of music history anthologies, the book follows most closely the purpose and design set forth by Oliver Strunk's *Source Readings in Music History* and Piero Weiss and Richard Taruskin's *Music in the Western World: A History in Documents*. These anthologies bring to life, via primary sources, the often contentious issues, arguments, conflicts, and creative tensions that have defined music as a social practice throughout the ages. I have, at one time or another, required both these collections in classes that I have taught, and as years of student testimonies have proven, such books are truly invaluable pedagogical tools.

Like these predecessors, the concern of *The Rock History Reader* lies not with simply reinforcing a canon of great artists and their creations, but rather, with introducing students to the various ways in which music has been explained and received throughout its history. The purpose of this anthology is twofold: on the one hand, it offers vivid and detailed eyewitness accounts that extend beyond the scope of what a textbook can reasonably provide; on the other hand, the selected readings are designed to encourage reflection, debate, and classroom discussions. To this end, in many places I have included multiple perspectives on the same subject: a critique of Elvis Presley followed by the singer's response, three different recollections of the Woodstock Festival, and a debate over Madonna's true significance for feminists. In other instances, such as Tipper Gore's analysis of violence in heavy metal music and Steve Albini's cynical assessment of alternative rock and the music industry, I have chosen readings whose deliberately polemical nature is intended to foster dialogue about rock's various meanings.

I am well aware that those who might use a book such as *The Rock History Reader* will likely come from an array of disciplinary backgrounds, a reality reflected in the variety of rock textbooks themselves, which range from the detailed music analyses of Joe Stuessy and Scott Lipscomb's *Rock and Roll: Its History and Stylistic Development* to David Szatmary's more sociologically oriented *Rockin' In Time: A Social History of Rock-and-Roll*. With this diversity in mind, I have employed a number of different criteria in selecting the *Reader's* contents. Many readings focus on the music of a specific artist or group, such as Chuck Berry, The Beatles, Brian Wilson, Bruce Springsteen, and Public Enemy, while others deal more broadly with an entire genre or style, such as Motown, punk, disco, grunge, and indie pop. In many cases I have chosen readings that directly address social and cultural issues such as censorship, race relations, youth subcultures, and the importance of identity as it relates to gender and sexual formations. And I have also sought readings that place an emphasis on rock's relationship with such technological formations as television, radio, video, and the Internet. On the whole, I have tried to maintain a balance in the book's content so that the readings are not overly centered on rock's "classic" first quarter century, but spread equally through its later decades as well.

Throughout the book I have taken several steps to present the readings as part of rock's specific historical narrative. All the readings are arranged chronologically by decade, and each selection is prefaced by a detailed introductory note that sets the background context, explains the significance of key figures in the reading, and highlights issues for discussion. In some cases I have also identified relevant readings of interest for further research. Readers will notice as well that there are various places within the reprinted texts where I have added explanatory footnotes. I have done so wherever I felt that certain terminology or references seemed to require further clarification. In order to avoid confusion with any notes that might belong to the original text, all my annotations are found as footnotes, while all original notes and citations are placed as endnotes at the conclusion of the appropriate selection.

* * *

The Rock History Reader is by no means the first attempt to present an anthology of writings about rock. I was inspired to undertake this project by a number of previous collections, and it is important that they be acknowledged here. The first is Jonathan Eisen's 1969 anthology *The Age of Rock: Sounds of the American Cultural Revolution*. An excellent survey of the first major wave of rock journalism, Eisen's book—which he quickly followed with two others, *The Age of Rock 2* (1970) and *Twenty-Minute Fandangos and Forever Changes: A Rock Bazaar (1971)*—was one of my first introductions to the golden age of late 1960s rock writing. Eisen's long out-of-print books are distinguished by their uniformly high quality, and I had to resist the temptation to fill my 1960s chapters with authors and material cribbed solely from his collections. I consider it a measure of great restraint that in the end only two such selections found their way into *The Rock History Reader*. Two later collections—Clinton Heylin's *The Penguin Book of Rock & Roll Writing* (1992) and William McKeen's *Rock and Roll is Here to Stay: An Anthology* (2000)—proved to be particularly helpful as well. Both these books venture beyond the realm of rock criticism, adding selections from fiction, autobiographies, and the efforts of rock historians like Charlie Gillett and Peter Guralnick. As such, they broadened my conception of what an anthology of rock writings could be.

In addition to these books, I found myself returning most often to two anthologies of source materials: one of them a collection of rock writings, the other a jazz history reader. The first, and probably lesser known of these, is Michael J. Budds and Marian Ohman's 1993 publication *Rock Recall: Annotated Readings in American Popular Music from the Emergence of Rock and Roll to the Demise of the Woodstock Nation*. A truly ambitious project, their book brings together a staggering total of more than 200 entries relating to the 1950s and 1960s, drawn primarily from the popular press and various autobiographies and biographies. Their extensive research paved a path for my own exploration into these decades, and in two cases I have reprinted selections that I initially encountered in their collection: Jeff Greenfield's "But Papa, It's My Music, I Like It" and Chester Anderson's "Notes for a New Geology."

The second of these anthologies, Robert Walser's *Keeping Time: Readings in Jazz History* (1999), is a text that I always require in my jazz history classes, and from which I have learned a great deal. For example, unlike many readers, Walser's book includes a number of rather substantial and lengthy entries. Readings like these are important for they enable students to see how an author develops a sustained commentary on a narrow topic. Following Walser's lead, I have incorporated similar such pieces into *The Rock History Reader* wherever possible. Part of what also distinguishes *Keeping Time* from other anthologies is Walser's willingness to include articles from academics. As with jazz, scholarly writings on rock contribute in significant ways to the music's history and discourse, and it is crucial that they be represented. I have tried, to the extent that I can, to do so in my own reader. One such selection comes from Walser himself, with his musicological examination of heavy metal virtuosity, "Highbrow, Lowbrow, Voodoo Aesthetics."

Lastly, an anthology that deserves special mention is David Brackett's collection *The Pop, Rock, and Soul Reader: Histories and Debates*, which appeared in 2005 midway through my own work on *The Rock History Reader*. Brackett's intentions are in many respects similar to mine, in that he designed his book specifically as a pedagogical tool, complete with detailed notes and annotations. I was well aware of Brackett's book project when I began compiling *The Reader*, and was even concerned that there might be significant overlap in our choices of materials. Given the vast amounts of rock literature out there, however, I should not have been surprised that those fears proved to be unwarranted. As it turned out, our books share only two selections between them.

As the editors of all the aforementioned anthologies would likely agree, the task of assembling a reader is an endeavor both rewarding and frustrating. What I assumed would be a finite project soon spiraled into a seemingly endless search for the best material available. In the end, I had to balance my impossible desire to examine every possible rock-related source with the inevitability of approaching publication deadlines. As a result, I cannot help but see *The Reader* as incomplete. Having fretted over its selections for so long, I am ever aware of its gaps, of the musicians missing from its pages, and of the absence or underrepresentation of certain genres. The rationale for these omissions runs the gamut. Some articles or essays that I desperately wanted to include were simply too lengthy to fit within the book's limited space. In other cases I encountered insurmountable copyright restrictions, and in some instances I was faced with prohibitive permission fees.

That a book of this nature should have holes, however, is to be expected. Rock's history at this point is so expansive and well chronicled that even were this book twice its length, I would still be voicing the same apologies. To this end *The Rock History Reader* is perhaps best considered not as a standalone document, but in concert with the larger wealth of writing about rock and its ever-changing history. My one hope is that what I have contributed to this discourse leaves the reader feeling informed, inspired, or even infuriated, but never bored. After all, a music as loud, vibrant, and colorful as rock deserves a group of writings as equally enjoyable and engaging.

Acknowledgments

There are many people without whom this book would not have been possible. Richard Carlin was the acting music editor when I first pitched the idea of *The Reader* in Routledge's direction, and his unflagging enthusiasm for the project and his prompt advice helped navigate the book through its initial stages. His successor at Routledge, Constance Ditzel, was just as crucial in seeing the book into its final production. Others at Routledge, including Samina Calin and especially Devon Sherman and Robert Sims, were always ready with assistance as needed and answers to my many queries. In addition, I would like to thank Maribeth Payne at Norton, whose initial encouragement for this project was critical as well.

Much of the research for this book was completed while I was in a visiting position at Carleton College, and then in my first year at Syracuse University. I bombarded the interlibrary loan departments at both institutions with long lists of requests, and their assistance in tracking down many obscure sources proved absolutely crucial to this book's completion. I would also like to thank Patty Falk at Bowling Green's Music Library and Sound Recordings Archive, who helped with some urgent last-minute reference questions.

I am especially thankful to various people at Syracuse University, who generously provided financial support that aided the book in its final stages. In particular, I would like to thank Beverly Allen and Ann Gold and the Tolley Humanities Grant, Gerry Greenberg in the College of Arts and Sciences, and especially Stephen Meyer and Wayne Franits in the Fine Arts Department for steering my requests in the right direction.

Along the way a number of colleagues, specifically within the International Association for the Study of Popular Music (IASPM) community, provided helpful advice and conversation and replied to my inquiries, in some cases offering suggestions for materials and sharing their own writings. I am indebted to David Brackett, Mark Butler, Barbara Ching, Norma Coates, Deborah Pacini Hernandez, Kevin Holm-Hudson, Mark Katz, Charles Kronengold, Steve Waksman, Jacqueline Warwick, and S. Louis Winant. Their help was instrumental in bringing this book to fruition. Most of all, I want to thank Peter Winkler, who provided my initiation into the world of popular music studies at SUNY Stony Brook, and years later passed along to me his collection of rock magazines just as I was leaving town for good. Although I could not have guessed it at the time, those magazines would prove to be invaluable to *The Rock History Reader*'s completion.

Whether they know it or not, my family are the ones most directly responsible for this book, for it is from them that I inherited not only my love of music, but more significantly the habit of clipping and saving music-related articles. It started with my grandfather, Raymond Baugh, an English teacher, choir director, and music aficionado, who invited me, as a young boy, to cut and collect whatever I wanted from his treasured stacks of old magazines. It continued with my mother,

Mary-Ann Cateforis, who to this day always has a pile of clippings awaiting me when I return home for a visit. And for many years my brother David has sent me articles of interest from various and sundry sources. It is only fitting then that one of this book's last selections should come courtesy of my father and longtime *Playboy* subscriber, Vasily Cateforis, who thought that I might be interested in a special feature on the music industry that the magazine had run in its October 2004 issue. To anyone who ever questioned my father's insistence that he has spent his time *reading* rather than just looking at his *Playboy* collection, I offer this article's inclusion here as evidence in his support.

Finally, I would like to save the last word of thanks for my wife Margaret Martin: First, for her patience and understanding during those times that the writing of this book threatened to swallow and consume me whole. Second, for her unfailing words of encouragement, proofreading expertise, and the many suggestions that made this book much better than it would have been otherwise.

Copyright Acknowledgments

Every effort has been made to trace and acknowledge copyright holders of the material appearing in this book. The following publishers and individuals have generously given permission to reprint articles and excerpts from longer works. Additions or amendments to this list are welcomed.

Arnold, Gina. Excerpts from *Route 666: On the Road to Nirvana*. St. Martin's Press, 1993. Reprinted by permission of the author.

Azerrad, Michael. "Punk's Earnest Mission," *New York Times*. New York Times Co., 2004. Reprinted with permission.

Bangs, Lester. "How to Be a Rock Critic." Reprinted from *Shakin' Street Gazette*, October 1974. Copyright by Lester Bangs. Used by permission of the Bangs estate.

"The Beatles Press Conference, Wash. DC." From Geoffrey Giuliano *The Lost Beatles Interviews*, 1994. Reprinted by permission of Cooper Square Press.

Berry, Chuck. Excerpts from *Chuck Berry: The Autobiography*. Isalee Publishing Co., 1987. Used by permission of Harmony Books, a division of Random House, Inc.

Bracker, Milton. "Experts Propose Study of 'Craze'," *New York Times*. New York Times Co., 1957. Reprinted with permission.

"Celebrity Rate-A-Record," *Hit Parader*, September 1983. Reprinted by permission of Hit Parader Publications, Inc. and the Enoble Media Group.

Dahlen, Chris. "My Week on the Avril Lavigne E-Team," http://www.pitchforkmedia.com, September 12, 2002. Reprinted by permission of the author.

Dancis, Bruce, Abe Peck, Tom Smucker, and Georgia Christgau. "Disco! Disco! Disco?: Four Critics Address the Musical Question," *In These Times*, June 6–12, 1979. Reprinted by permission of the publisher.

Delehant, Jim. "An Interview with Wilson Pickett," *Hit Parader*, April 1967. Reprinted by permission of Hit Parader Publications, Inc. and the Enoble Media Group.

Ferguson, Sarah. "The Comfort of Being Sad," *Utne Reader*, July/August 1994. Reprinted by permission of the author.

Fox, Ted. Excerpt from *In the Groove: The People Behind the Music*. St. Martin's Press, 1986. Reprinted by permission of the author.

France, Kim. "Feminism Amplified," *New York*, June 3, 1996. Reprinted by permission of the author.

Frith, Simon. "The Real Thing—Bruce Springsteen" from *Music for Pleasure: Essays in the Sociology of Pop*. Routledge Press, 1988. Reprinted by permission of the author.

Gary, Kays. "Elvis Defends Low-Down Style." Copyright owned by *The Charlotte Observer*, 1956. Reprinted with permission from *The Charlotte Observer*.

Gehr, Richard. "The MTV Aesthetic," *Film Comment*, July/August 1983. Reprinted by permission of the author.

Green, Abel. "A Warning to the Music Business," *Variety*, February 23, 1955. Reprinted with permission of Reed Business Information, a division of Reed, Elsevier Inc.

Greenfield, Jeff. "But Papa, It's My Music, I Like It!" *New York Times*. New York Times Co., 1971. Reprinted with permission.

Guevara, Rubén. Excerpt from the "View from the Sixth Street Bridge: The History of Chicano Rock," by Rubén Guevara, from *The First Rock and Roll Confidential Report*, edited by Dave Marsh. Duke & Duchess Ventures, Inc., 1985. Used by permission of Pantheon Books, a division of Random House, Inc.

Hansen, Barret. Excerpts from "The Country Boom," *Hit Parader*, November 1969. Reprinted by permission of Hit Parader Publications, Inc. and the Enoble Media Group.

Harrison, Barbara Grizzuti. "Can Madonna Justify Madonna?" © 1991 by Barbara Grizzuti Harrison. Originally appeared in *Mademoiselle*, June 1991. Reprinted by permission of Georges Borchardt, Inc., on behalf of the author.

Hebdige, Dick. Excerpts from *Subculture: The Meaning of Style*. Routledge Press, 1979. Reprinted by permission of the author.

Johnson, Linton Kwesi. "Roots and Rock: The Marley Enigma," *Race Today*, October 1975. Reprinted by permission of the author.

Kemp, Mark. "The Death of Sampling?" *Option*, March/April 1992. Reprinted by permission of the author and publisher.

Kopkind, Andrew. "Reggae: The Steady Rock of Black Jamaica," *Ramparts*, June 1973. Reprinted by permission of John Scagliotti and the Kopkind Colony.

Korall, Burt. "James Taylor: Sunshine and...," *Saturday Review*, September 12, 1970. Reprinted by permission of the author.

Landau, Jon. "A Whiter Shade of Black" from *The Age of Rock*. Vintage Books, 1969. Reprinted by permission of the author.

Martin, George and Jeremy Hornsby. Excerpts from *All You Need is Ears*. © 1994 by the authors and reprinted by permission of St. Martin's Press, LLC and Macmillan Publishers Ltd.

McNeil, Legs and Gillian McCain. "Why Don't We Call It Punk?" from *Please Kill Me: The Uncensored Oral History of Punk*. © 1996 by Legs McNeil and Gillian McCain. Used by permission of Grove/Atlantic, Inc.

Moon, Tom. "Public Enemy's Bomb Squad," *Musician*, October 1991. Reprinted by permission of the author.

Morrison, Joan and Robert K. Morrison. Excerpt from *From Camelot to Kent State: The Sixties Experience in the Words of Those Who Lived It*. © 1987 by Joan Morrison and Robert K. Morrison. Currently available in paperback from Oxford University Press.

Paglia, Camille. "Madonna—Finally a Real Feminist," *New York Times*, December 14, 1990. Reprinted by permission of the author.

Rabid, Jack. "The Big Takeover: The Punk Rock Years, 1980–81," *The Big Takeover*, 2000. Reprinted by permission of the author.

Regev, Motti. Excerpt from "Rock Aesthetics and Musics of the World." *Theory, Culture & Society Ltd.*, 1997. Reprinted by permission of Sage Publications Ltd.

Reynolds, Simon. "Radical Dance Fictions," *Monitor*, 1985. Reprinted by permission of the author.

Rockwell, John. Excerpts from "Art Rock" from *The Rolling Stone Illustrated History of Rock and Roll*. Rolling Stone Press, 1976, 1980. Used by permission of Random House, Inc.

Sanneh, Kelefa. "The Rap Against Rockism," *New York Times*. New York Times Co., 2004. Reprinted with permission.

Sheff, David and Rob Tannenbaum. "Rip. Burn. Die." *Playboy*, October 2004. © David Sheff and Rob Tannenbaum. All rights reserved. Reprinted by permission of the authors.

Siegel, Jules. "Goodbye Surfing Hello God!—The Religious Conversion of Brian Wilson." Originally published in *Cheetah*, October 1967. © 1967, 1972, 2005 by Jules Siegel. All rights reserved. Reprinted by permission of the author.

Sullivan, Kathleen. "2 Live Crew and the Cultural Contradictions of Miller," *Reconstruction*, 1990. Reprinted by permission of the author.

Sweeney, Joey. "We're the Younger Generation," http://www.salon.com, August 31, 2000. An online version remains in the Salon archives. Reprinted with permission.

Tate, Greg. "It's Like This Y'all," *Village Voice*, January 19, 1988. Reprinted by permission of the author.

Walser, Robert. "Highbrow, Lowbrow, Voodoo Aesthetics" from *Microphone Fiends: Youth Music & Youth Culture*. Routledge Press, 1994. Reprinted by permission of the author.

Walters, Barry. "The Arson Is Blowin' in the Wind: Why Woodstock '99 Devolved into a Frat-Style Free-for-All," *The Washington Post*, August 8, 1999. Reprinted by permission of the author.

Wesley, Jr. Fred. Excerpts from *Hit Me Fred: Recollections of a Sideman*. Duke University Press, 2002. All rights reserved. Used by permission of the publisher.

Williams, Paul. "Understanding Dylan," *Crawdaddy!*, August 1966. Reprinted by permission of the author.

Williams, Richard. "The Sound of Surprise," *Melody Maker*, August 21, 1976. Reprinted by permission of IPC+ Syndication.

Wolfe, Tom. "Cosmo's Tasmanian Deviltry" from *The Electric Kool-Aid Acid Test* by Tom Wolfe. © 1968, renewed 1996 by Tom Wolfe. Reprinted by permission of Farrar, Straus and Giroux, LLC.

Young, Jon. "Roll Over Guitar Heroes; Synthesizers Are Here," *Trouser Press*, May 1982. Reprinted by permission of the author.

I

THE 1950S

1

Chuck Berry
In His Own Words

Widely acknowledged as one of the early rock 'n' roll era's most important performers and song-writers, Chuck Berry (born 1926) blazed a path through the 1950s that paved the way for countless future rock musicians. In the excerpts that follow from his 1987 autobiography, Berry narrates in the voice of one of the many young African American musicians who were hoping to make a living off their craft at that time, only to be met with densely worded recording contracts, crooked managers, and harsh touring conditions. He begins by describing his entry into the rock 'n' roll business in 1955 via Muddy Waters (1915–1983), and the specific circumstances surrounding the genesis and recording of "Maybellene," his first hit single for Chicago's famed Chess Records. "Maybellene," which, as Berry explains, was inspired by the traditional song "Ida Red,"* was his first effort to "sing country-western," and the first of many songs that he intended as integrationist endeavors, deliberate attempts to appeal to rock 'n' roll's broad, diverse youth community. Along those lines, Berry, in his typically inventive language, concludes his autobiography by invoking the idealized image of a United States where "all races and nationalities" have merged into one "Americanese" people.†

It was a hot Friday typical of summer in the Gateway City. It was only May, but in Missouri the month doesn't matter. When it decides to be hot it just does it. Dad, Hank, and I had been disassembling an old frame bungalow in the suburbs of St. Louis but I'd asked for this day off because I had an urge to hit the road again in the new station wagon.

Ralph Burris, my high-school classmate and long-time friend, had agreed to take off with me to visit his mother in Chicago. We arrived at sundown in the equally hot but windy city and drove directly to Ralph's mother's home to pay our respects, ate a well-prepared supper, then hit the streets to paint Chicago's Southside. Starting on 47th Street at Calumet, we hit most of the blues joints, bar after bar, spending time only in those that had live music.

I saw Howlin' Wolf and Elmore James for the first time on 47th Street, a tour I'll never lose memory of. I didn't want to leave the place where Elmore James was performing but Ralph had seen these artists before and insisted that we try other places. At the Palladium on Wabash Avenue we looked up and found the marquee glowing with MUDDY WATERS TONIGHT. Ralph gave me the lead as we ran up the stairs to the club, knowing I sang Muddy's songs and that he was my favorite blues singer. We paid our fifty-cents admission and scrimmaged forward to the bandstand, where in true living color I saw Muddy Waters.

---

* Berry refers to the song both as "Ida Red" and "Ida May."
† *Source:* Chuck Berry, *Chuck Berry: The Autobiography* (New York: Harmony, 1987), pp. 97–109, 121–26, 141, 143–45.

He was playing "Mo Jo Working" at that moment and was closing the last set of the night. Once he'd finished, Ralph boldly called out from among the many people trying to get Muddy's autograph and created the opportunity for me to speak with my idol. It was the feeling I suppose one would get from having a word with the president or the pope. I quickly told him of my admiration for his compositions and asked him who I could see about making a record. Other fans of Muddy's were scuffling for a chance to just say hi to him, yet he chose to answer my question.

Those very famous words were, "Yeah, see Leonard Chess. Yeah, Chess Records over on Forty-seventh and Cottage." Muddy was the godfather of blues. He was perhaps the greatest inspiration in the launching of my career. I was a disciple in worship of a lord who had just granted me a lead that led to a never-ending love for music. It was truly the beginning as I continued to watch his most humble compliance in attempting to appease his enthused admirers. The way he communicated with those fans was recorded in my memory, and I've tried to respond in a similar way to fans of my own.

(Somewhere, somebody wrote in their column that on the occasion when I met Muddy he allowed me to play with his band. It has always hurt me when a writer replaces the truth with fictitious dramatic statements to increase interest in his story. I was a stranger to Muddy and in no way was I about to ask my godfather if I could sit in and play. He didn't know me from Adam on that eve and Satan himself could not have tempted me to contaminate the father's fruit of the blues, as pure as he picked it. Furthermore, I had wonders about my ability as a professional musician, singer, or anything else when in the presence of someone like the great Muddy Waters.)

I had planned to drive home to St. Louis that Sunday afternoon but, with anticipations of a chance at recording, I decided to stay over in Chicago until Monday. I couldn't believe I would be making connections with the Chess Record Company after being lucky enough to speak with Muddy, too.

Monday morning early I drove over to 4720 Cottage Grove Avenue to the Chess Record Company and watched from a store across the street for the first person to enter the door. After a lady entered, a man came in dressed in a business suit, so I ran across Cottage Grove to challenge my weekend dream. While I was posing just inside the office door, he looked up from scanning mail and said, "Hi, come on in," then left for a further office.

Before I started my well-rehearsed introduction, I saw a black girl receptionist (Adella, as I remember) and asked her if I could speak with Mr. Leonard Chess. I was getting more of the shivers as I glanced through the big window into the studio. She told me that the man I had followed in was himself Leonard Chess, and he reentered the outer office and beckoned me into his. He listened to my description of Muddy's advice and my plans and hopes, asking occasional questions regarding my expectations. Finally he asked if I had a tape of my band with me.

I had been taping at home on a seventy-nine-dollar, quarter-inch, reel-to-reel recorder that I'd purchased in contemplation of such an audition. I told him I was visiting from St. Louis, but could return with the tapes (which I hadn't truly made yet) whenever he could listen to them. He said he could hear them within a week and I left immediately for St. Louis. He had stood all the while I was talking to him with a look of amazement that he later told me was because of the businesslike way I'd talked to him.

After I traveled down from U.S. Highway 66, I contacted Johnnie Johnson and Ebby Hardy and began arranging rehearsals. Johnnie, Ebby, and I had been playing other people's music ever since we started at the Cosmo, but for this tape I did not want to cover other artist's tunes. Leonard Chess had explained that it would be better for me if I had original songs. I was very glad to hear this because I had created many extra verses for other people's songs and I was eager to do an entire creation of my own. The four that I wrote may have been influenced melodically by other songs, but, believe me, the lyrics were solely my own. Before the week had ended, I brought fresh recorded tapes to the ears of the Chess brothers in Chicago.

Chess was in the heart of the Southside of Chicago amid a cultural district I knew all too well. Leonard told me he had formerly had a bar in the neighborhood as well, which accounted for his easy relations with black people. When I carried the new tape up I immediately found out from a poster on the office wall that Muddy, Little Walter, Howlin' Wolf, and Bo Diddley were recording there. In fact, Bo Diddley dropped by the studio that day.

Leonard listened to my tape and when he heard one hillbilly selection I'd included called "Ida May," played back on the one-mike, one-track home recorder, it struck him most as being commercial. He couldn't believe that a country tune (he called it a "hillbilly song") could be written and sung by a black guy. He said he wanted us to record that particular song, and he scheduled a recording session for May 21, 1955, promising me a contract at that time.

I went back to St. Louis to more carpenter work with Dad but also with a plan to cut a record with a company in Chicago. Each time I nailed a nail or sawed a board I was putting a part of a song together, preparing for the recording session to come. At the Cosmo Club I boasted of the records we were going to make soon and we took the lead in popularity over Ike Turner's band, our main rivals at the time in the East St. Louis music scene.

Muddy Waters was in the St. Louis area one night around this time and visited the Cosmopolitan Club. Enthralled to be so near one of my idols, I delegated myself to chaperone him around spots of entertainment in East St. Louis. Ike Turner was playing at the Manhattan Club and since he was my local rival for prestige I took Muddy there to show Ike how big I was and who I knew. When we got to the Manhattan Club, Muddy preceded Johnnie, Ebby, and myself up to the box office and announced, "I'm Muddy Waters." The cashier said, "A dollar fifty." Muddy just reached in his pocket and forked it out with no comment. That incident remains on my mind unto this very day. From that experience I swore never to announce myself in hopes of getting anything gratis, regardless of what height I might rise to in fame.

I took Muddy to my house that night, introduced him to Toddy, who was a devout lover of his music long before I came into her life with mine, and took a photo of him holding my guitar.* May his music live forever, he will always be in first place at the academy of blues, my man, "McKinley Morganfield," Muddy Waters.

Finally the day came and I drove back to Chicago with my little band, on time, as I'd promised Leonard Chess. According to the way Dad did business, I was expecting Leonard to first take me into his office and execute the recording contracts. But instead he said he wanted to get "that tune" on tape right away. So we unloaded my seven-month-new red Ford station wagon and Phil Chess took the three of us into the studio and placed us around, telling us how we should set up for the session. I could see right away that Leonard was the brains of the company because he was busy making decisions and dictating to the five or six employees there. Phil ran around making friends and seeing that everybody was jockeyed into position for the flow of productions during the day.

I was familiar with moving in and away from the microphone to project or reduce the level of my voice but was not aware that in a studio that would be done by the engineer during the song. Having as much knowledge about recording as my homemade tapes afforded me was a big help, but I listened intently and learned much from the rehearsal of the tunes with Phil instructing us. I tried to act professional although I was as frightened and green as a cucumber most of the time.

The studio was about twenty feet wide and fifty feet long with one seven-foot baby-grand piano and about twelve microphones available. I had used only one for the tape I'd come to audition with

---

* "Toddy" is Berry's wife, Themetta "Toddy" Suggs.

and eight were used for our four-piece session. There was a stack of throw rugs, a giant slow-turning ceiling fan, and two long fluorescent lights over a linoleum tile floor. Leonard Chess was the engineer and operated the Ampex 403 quarter-inch monaural tape recorder. Through the three-by-four-foot studio control-room window we watched him, or sometimes his brother Phil, rolling the tape and instructing us with signs and hand waving to start or stop the music.

The first song we recorded was "Ida May." Leonard suggested that I should come up with a new name for the song, and on the spot I altered it to "Maybellene."

Leonard had arranged for a lyricist/musician, Willie Dixon, who'd written many of Muddy's tunes, to sit in on the session, playing a stand-up bass to fill out the sound of the music. Electric bass instruments were yet to come and Willie, stout as he was, was a sight to behold slapping his ax to the tempo of a country-western song he really seemed to have little confidence in.

Each musician had one mike, excepting the drummer, who had three. I had one for the guitar and one for my vocal, which I sat down to sing because a chair was there and I thought that was how it was supposed to be done. We struggled through the song, taking thirty-five tries before completing a track that proved satisfactory to Leonard. Several of the completions, in my opinion, were perfectly played. We all listened to the final playback and then went on to record the next song which was "Wee Wee Hours." By then it was midafternoon. Around eight-thirty that night we finished the recording session. "Maybellene," "Wee Wee Hours," "Thirty Days," and "You Can't Catch Me" were the songs completed. Leonard sent out for hamburgers and pop and we lingered an hour picnicking, an ordeal that became a ritual with Leonard bearing the tab.

It was nearly ten o'clock when we went into Leonard's office and sat down for the first time to execute the contract he'd promised. The recording contract he handed me seemed to be a standard form, having no company-name heading at the top. It was machine printed on one side of the single sheet of paper. The other paper he gave me was a publishing contract, a segment of the music business I was totally ignorant of. It was printed on a double sheet, but I didn't understand most of the terms and arrangements of publishing either. I did see the word *copyright* several times as I read through it and thus figured if it was connected with the United States government, it was legitimate and I was likely protected. I remembered when I was a child, Dad had talked about getting a patent for a perpetual-motion apparatus that he'd invented, telling us nobody could take your achievements from you when they're patented and copyrighted.

Anyway, I read it word for word. Some of the statements were beyond my knowledge of the record business, such as the "residuals from mechanical rights," the "writer and producer's percentages," and the "performance royalties and publisher fees," but I intentionally would frown at various sections to give the impression that a particular term (I actually knew nothing of) was rather unfavorable. From the white of my eyes I could detect Leonard watching my reaction closely all the while I was reading, which made me think I was being railroaded. In fact, the corner of my left eyeball was checking out his response to my reaction, yet still knowing full well I'd sign the darn thing anyway. I slowly read on, finally signing it at last. I took my single-page copy, shook hands, and bade happy farewells to what was now "my" record company, loaded up, and drove off into the night with Johnnie and Ebby to St. Louis.

As we drove home through the black night more songs were sprouting in my head. As easy as it seemed now that the session was over, another four were bound to come forth.

Back home I continued to enjoy the local action at the Cosmo Club. The immediate future looked stable enough to support the little family I'd started. Melody was approaching two years old, Ingrid was nearing four, and I had been married nigh six years, a veteran at paying monthly bills. Toddy and I were looking forward to Ingrid being enrolled in grade school that September. I was feeling no pain, playing three nights a week at the Cosmo Club and, except for the half day I took off to go to Poro College of Cosmetology to study hairdressing, I was working with Dad during the day. Our bank account had risen to fourteen hundred dollars, with the Ford station wagon payments paid to date and the house installment note one month ahead.

Days and weeks passed with no word from anyone about the recording session. No mail or phone calls followed to reveal any results of the contract I had with the Chess Company. I sat and waited, wondering if all the time and effort was in some trash can or did it actually take a lifetime to organize these things.

Ike Turner was sizzling at the Manhattan Club in East St. Louis just a couple of blocks from the Cosmopolitan Club. By then Ike had recorded "I'm Tore Up," and it was just beginning to be heard making its air way back toward the ears of the home folks. People were asking when was our record coming out and we had nothing to answer. Albert King, another artist from the St. Louis area who sported a left-hand guitar, began climbing to the Ike and Chuck level.

Suddenly from the mouths of babes came remarks that they'd heard "Maybellene" on the radio and shortly after I picked it up while driving home from Dad's house in the station wagon. There is no way to explain how you feel when you first hear your first recording for the first time in your first new car. I told Toddy as soon as I reached home and we celebrated as you can imagine how!

Johnnie told me that while coming home from the Cosmopolitan Club one hot night he was tuning the radio for some blues and on station WGN in Chicago heard the unmistakable rhythmic bounce of "Maybellene" being played over and over. WGN was a big rock station, bringing a linked-up program by a New York disk jockey.

On July 19, a phone call came from Leonard Chess informing me to expect a visit from a Mr. Jack Hook, an affiliate of his, who was bringing a contract from the Gale Booking Agency for me to sign. I picked up this mediator at the St. Louis airport, brought him home, discussed the booking-agency contract, and signed it, keeping my copy. The exciting thing in the contract was that the Gale Booking Agency was to assure me of forty thousand dollars' worth of work each year for three years!

I was feeling so good about the way things were falling in place, I began wondering if I would die in a few weeks. I couldn't believe I had the chance to earn such a sum in such a short period. Themetta and I stayed up until 4 a.m. reading over the contract for flaws and mistakes, but found none. Plus it had no obligation on my part that I felt I could not uphold. I would be earning the money if only I got to the concert, played, and sang. I knew I'd make it to them on time even if I had to hire a police escort.

So now we knew the session was processed and records made. Would they sell? What was next? When would we see them on the jukebox?

What had happened was that Leonard Chess had sent our recordings to one of his promotion affiliates, Alan Freed, a big disk jockey in New York whose program was on the network going to major cities of the U.S. It was sent to him as a test run to determine which of the four tunes got the best response.* "Maybellene" took priority over not only the four Chuck Berry songs, but over all the records sent from other record companies for play that week. The phone lines from Alan Freed's radio audience were jammed with repeated requests for "another spin" of "Maybellene." Alan Freed was unknown to me at that time, but I was to become a distinct disciple. Leonard released "Maybellene" as a single, with "Wee Wee Hours" on the flip side.

I showed the Gale Agency contract to my folks, who wished me well. The fulfillment of the contract, traveling and performing, would put an end to the ritual of carpenter work with Dad. During

---

* For his services, Chess listed Freed as one of "Maybellene"'s coauthors, guaranteeing him a slice of the song's royalties.

the following days, up to the last day working with Dad, people would often mention that they'd heard a song and ask if I was the "Berry" who recorded it. Rapidly "Maybellene" rose to number one on the charts and there were many phone calls from Gale and Chess telling me what to expect in the coming weeks.*

One such call from Leonard Chess culminated in an opportunity to go and play three thirty-minute shows with the trio on the fifth, sixth, and seventh of August 1955 at the Peacock Lounge in Atlanta, Georgia, for a total of five hundred dollars. I swallowed the opportunity, not letting on that I'd walk down to Georgia and play all week for half that bread. The Ford station wagon was loaded three days before we left and without tricks, treats, or trouble, I pulled my red wagon up in front of the Royal Peacock Lounge. The marquee on the front of the building blazed with names from the show, reading, the FOUR FELLOWS, MISS WIGGLES, and CHUCK BERRY. Seeing my name there reminded me that my mother had once predicted that "Maybe someday your name will be in lights."

We registered at Mr. B. B. Beaman's Savoy Hotel on Auburn Avenue, shaved, shivered, and shot over to the gig to find out when and what we were supposed to do. Evidently we were liked and enjoyed since they requested "Maybellene" six times one night, and we played it as many. When the club owner paid me the five hundred dollars, it reminded me of making the down payment on 3137 Whittier, our little home, which was the largest amount I'd handled up to then.

That was our first professional road gig and after it we returned to the Cosmo and twenty-one dollars a night. A farewell party for our little combo was held there on August 14, the eve of our departure for a week-long gig in Cleveland. The entire family, including my dad, was present. My brother Paul, without a drop in him (he doesn't drink either), made his debut singing "On Top of Old Smokey" along with me during the country-western segment of the program. It was the first time my dad had ever chosen to be in such unholy surroundings and to date, as far as I know, it was his last. Nevertheless his attitude while there would have never given light to his indifference. "When in Rome," Dad always told the children, "do as the Romans." He seemed to be happy for my prospects but I could sense he had reservations about my ability to handle the wicked world he envisioned me headed into.

Then it was on the road, going to Cleveland and Gleason's Bar in the little red wagon. The bar was a jazz hangout and I thought we didn't go over too well, particularly with "Maybellene." At Gleason's Bar I received telegrams from the Gale Agency telling us to continue on around the lake to Vermilion and Youngstown, Ohio; Lynn and Roxbury, Massachusetts; and to Linden, New Jersey, doing two shows in each city, with the exception of Youngstown, where three nights were booked. We did it in great spirit, learning as we went how to manage the traveling.

A big entry, near to four hundred pounds, a friend of Jack Hook's named Teddy Roag, came into my ventures on this swing.† Teddy was organized by Jack Hook to arrange my schedules and assist my trio while traveling up the New England coast. The tour itself was a great education for me as to what a "concert" was, what a box office was actually for, and how to register into a hotel. I was unaccustomed to hotels, having never up to then experienced any out-of-town sleeping accommodations other than rooming houses. I also learned about percentages of gross-attendance income. My nightly fee then was 60 percent of the gross box-office intake with a minimum guarantee of $150. Teddy Roag, my acting manager, somehow always managed to see to it that the attendance was just at the brink of entering the 60 percent range, never into it.

---

* "Maybellene" was no. 1 on the R&B chart. It reached no. 5 on the pop singles chart.
† Teddy Roag is Chuck Berry's poetic pseudonym for his manager Teddy Reig (1918–1984), who is characterized in the book by his corrupt "rogue"-like tendencies.

I was a fair wizard at math in high school and could eyeball the dance houses to estimate attendance. Most nights I determined that there was enough attendance to carry into percentages, but when I mentioned this once I was told I'd have to prove it, so I didn't question anymore. I couldn't think of any way to support my judgment or monitor the attendance. The figures that Roag would return with, after sometimes over an hour of counting the gross paid attendance, would reach me on a handwritten statement and would usually show us just a few dollars under the amount that would have started my overage payable. Teddy had a habit of snapping his fingers and saying, "Damn, we almost made it."

Before I came to realize Teddy's tactics, he had been for weeks advising me that I needed his expert management and that he was available for the job. I should have known the big beer-bellied bully did not like rock 'n' roll enough to be traveling along without any compensation but the prospect of the job he hoped to get. I'd heard of managers for Marian Anderson and Joe Louis and thought having one was the professional thing to do, so I agreed and accepted him, signing him as my manager while still wondering about his integrity. Almost immediately after I signed him he stopped showing up at most concerts except when we'd be playing near where he lived.

After a concert in Lynn, Massachusetts, in 1955, he handed me a hundred-dollar bill, but without the usual written statement, saying, "How's that?" That night the crowd had to number over twelve hundred and the admission was $1.50 so it must have grossed at least $1,500 excluding freebies. We should have earned near to $750 aside from the guarantee of $150, but I could not have proved it. I pondered dearly how to overcome being vulnerable to such swindles. Since I had no other way to know the attendance I had to trust the promoters and my manager, who all knew each other very well.

* * *

Forgive me for using my own word, *hospitaboo,* which is meant to represent *hospitality* with *taboo* or in other words *how do you do but don't-you-dare.* I feel that the greatest hospitality on the entire globe is found in the Southland of the United States. There is no other place, at least that I've been, where friendliness and consideration for others are perpetuated more. But be that as it may, when it comes to matters of race the type of hospitality practiced by most southern people seems to fit the compound word I've improvised.

Remember that my view, the only true view I can see with, is through the black eyes that I have. As I toured far from St. Louis, I saw and I wondered, then reasoned and felt, then realized and believed. But I don't know any truths about racial matters but what I have seen.

Two buses were parked at the stage door of the Apollo when we closed the two-week engagement on September 16, 1955. Teddy Roag had given me a list of cities that the Gale Booking Agency had lined up for me as part of a tour that included Arthur Prysock; the Four Fellows; the Spaniels; the Cleftones; a comedian, Clay Tyson; Queenie Owens; an upside-down dancer known as Miss Wiggles; my group; and Buddy Johnson and his orchestra, featuring Ella Johnson. We all felt pretty much at home since all of the acts were black and there weren't likely to be any internal racial problems.

My heart sang when I viewed the list because I had been to only a couple of the cities listed. The instructions informed us that a bus ride plus hotel reservations would be provided, which left me only to ride, get dressed, sing, and peep then eat, meet fans, hide and sleep. It was for sure going to be exciting to be on the road with all of these recording stars who, just a month before, I had only heard sing on radio and records. Now I was going to be practically living with them.

At 3:30 a.m. the buses rolled across the George Washington Bridge and down the New Jersey Turnpike. Buddy's eighteen-piece orchestra, the roadies, the valets, and the equipment occupied the second bus and I was with the rest of the artists on the leading bus. I saw things going on among them that I had never known about a month before. I saw my first live gambling, a bold and blazing crap game in the aisle of the bus that carried on until dawn. When I woke up at the announcement of a breakfast stop, only three were left in the game and maybe twenty thousand dollars had changed hands in the aisle.

On we rode, snacking, arguing, singing, and still sleeping half the day until we reached the auditorium in Youngstown, Ohio, where the tour was to begin. We went directly to a hotel where I learned fast to rush to be first checking in to get the better rooms of those reserved collectively. At eight o'clock that evening the Buddy Johnson Show opened the Nu Elms Ballroom in Youngstown.

Many of the places we played on that first tour did not have enough dressing rooms or toilets for such a large show. Things were just getting started with rock 'n' roll and a lot of places weren't prepared for shows on a grand scale. This ballroom was one such and we all had to share the few dressing rooms. The fans were not restricted from freely coming backstage, visiting the artists, and whatnot. Whatnots were real nice then, since the management knew not what would be going on backstage. I thought the older artists knew all the fans who would come backstage and chat with them so I would leave the room when chats became whisperingly soft.

All first shows are bummers as far as everybody getting tight with the orchestra and getting coordinated with the time schedule of the show itself. Considering all, the Youngstown date went well with a near full house in attendance. After the final act of the show that night, everybody who knew the ropes let their hair down and the good times rolled in the hotel rooms.

I found that the custom of travel was to lay over on a night after we had traveled a long way that day. The following noon took us south to the Municipal Auditorium in Charleston, West Virginia; then we traveled on to the Skating Rink in Kyle, Virginia, and to the City Auditorium in Raleigh, North Carolina, where we began to bump into bits of biased behavior. The danger deferred any desire for drumming up any dilly-dally down in Dixie. Up to then I had never spent much time in the southern states, though I had constantly heard of things that occurred there from my father. Now I was traveling through the Heart of Dixie, where heeding his advice would behoove me to behave better than a Baptist bishop.

We played the Recreation Center in Kingston, North Carolina, on September 20, followed by Columbia, South Carolina, then the Duval Armory in Jacksonville, Florida. That is where southern habit hit home. My memory of how it went down remains vivid. We had to stay in a private boardinghouse and dined collectively on soul food. The conditions were good, I might add, except that they were the only legal accommodations available.

Once we got to the Duval Armory that evening, the conditions radically changed. "You boys this" and "You boys that" was the language used until an elderly stagehand started to address one of the band members with his customary term. It wasn't a nice or necessary name for a neatly dressed black guy, but then the addressee was hip to the old man's concept. After the obvious readdressing of the slip-lipped word to "ni-boy," the trombone player replied, "Yahzza, we need da platform over 'ere."

Just before they were to open the doors for the spectators, four of the maintenance guys came out and roped off the armory with white window cord. They looped and tied it to each seat down the center aisle, making it an off-limits zone that neither coloreds nor whites could tread. They didn't, we didn't, no one else didn't during the entire show although the armory was jam-packed with standing room sold as well. That six-foot-wide aisle, holding the choicest views in the place, stayed clear as a whistle.

At the close of the show, twice as many young whites as blacks rushed toward the stage, climbed on, and began socializing with us. After mumbling to ourselves the whole evening about the conditions we performed under, we overwelcomed them, extending hugs and some kisses. We knew the authorities were blazing angry with them for rushing on stage and at us for welcoming them, but they could only stand there and watch young public opinion exercise its reaction to the boundaries they were up against. Almost as if it was rehearsed they hugged, kissed, greeted, or shook a hand and filed off to the exits untouched by the helpless, amazed security.

I'd been hearing of this sort of racial problem for years from my father, except his stories were more severe. The difference that I could conceive between his stories and my observation showed that some progress had taken place in race relations.

On to Mobile, where the same attitudes prevailed. We were determined, at least I was, to bring those southerners to accept us for what we thought we were: northern artistic performers and not Yankee black lord-knows-what. When my turn came, I skipped on stage and belted out my song, "Maybellene." I put everything I had into it: a hillbilly stomp, the chicken peck, and even ad-libbed some southern country dialect.

Contrary to what I expected, I received far greater applause from the white side of the ropes than the black side, where I noticed only a chuckle or two. Okay, I thought, with my mind on getting next to my brethren and sisteren. There was truth showing up in what Leonard Chess had told me about "Wee Wee Hours," which was on the B side, selling mostly in the rhythm-and-blues market. On the other hand, "Maybellene" had hit in the pop charts, identifying the popular or the white market. When songs were so posted in the trade charts it seemed to serve as a guide to help disk jockeys and merchants direct their respective businesses. Thanks to the trade magazines, by the time any new recording reached the broadcasting or merchandising market, it had already been "Anglopinion-ated," my own word for being "white worthy" of broadcasting.

Determined to retaliate, I bowed longer to the bored black side than I lingered on the left, let my fingers crawl into the introduction, and poured out the pleading guitar passage of "Wee Wee Hours," hoping to pierce the perfect passion of my people. It seemed to be going homeward as I continued to pour on the profound pleadings. I began hearing the "uhmms" and "awws" as I approached the kissing climax and how beautifully the black side began to moan. I knew I was getting next to them. It was just like we were all then boarding da' ol' ribba-boat, about to float into a land of flawless freedom.

The palms of black and white were burning as the producer signaled me to exit. My act was scheduled for only two songs and my ad-libbing during "Wee Wee Hours" had carried me over-time, which was frowned at in such a regulated show. But I was thrilled and dragged my feet walking off stage as the applause simmered.

That night when the concert ended, it seemed the whole police force had surrounded our bus. Over a dozen patrolmen were lined up forming a path for the show people to walk through. The isolation ignited ill feelings in the fans as well as the artists, who vented their feelings by ridiculing the conditions in disguised voices. My father's stories came to mind as I watched the officers taking the abuse and I thought, do in Rome as the Romans do. Fear that the police would reciprocate led me to board the bus. As it turned out, nothing happened except bragging on the bus as we continued the tour westward.

* * *

I have been asked many times, "Where did you get the idea to write that song, Chuck?" Off hand, I wouldn't know, but I always refer to the story within the song, which usually recalls my inspiration. Or sometimes the melodic lines bring me in sync with the time and place where the tune got its origin. The embarrassing thing is that sometimes when I have been asked about a song's origin I have made up a reason that is dramatic enough to get by the question. But the origins have varied under different circumstances or with different interviewers.

"Maybellene" was my effort to sing country-western, which I had always liked. The Cosmo club-goers didn't know any of the words to those songs, which gave me a chance to improvise and add comical lines to the lyrics. "Mountain Dew," "Jambalaya," and "Ida Red" were the favorites of the Cosmo audience, mainly because of the honky-tonk gestures I inserted while singing the songs.

"Maybellene" was written from the inspiration that grew out of the country song "Ida Red." I'd heard it sung long before when I was a teenager and thought it was rhythmic and amusing to hear. I'd sung it in the yard gatherings and parties around home when I was first learning to strum the guitar in my high-school days. Later in life, at the Cosmo Club, I added my bit to the song and still enjoyed a good response so I coined it a good one to sing.

Later when I learned, upon entering a recording contract, that original songs written by a person were copyrighted and had various rewards for the composer, I welcomed the legal arrangement of the music business. I enjoyed creating songs of my own and was pleased to learn I could have some return from the effort. When I wrote "Maybellene" I had originally titled it "Ida May," but when I took the song to Chess Records I was advised to change its title. That was simple because the rhythmic swing of the three syllables fit with many other names. The music progression itself is close to the feeling that I received when hearing the song "Ida Red," but the story in "Maybellene" is completely different.

The body of the story of "Maybellene" was composed from memories of high school and trying to get girls to ride in my 1934 V-8 Ford. I even put seat-covers in it to accommodate the girls that the football players would take riding in it while I was in class. Just to somehow explain the origin of the lyrics of "Maybellene," it could have been written from a true experience, recalling my high-school days thus:

> As I was watching from the windowsill,
> I saw pretty girls in my dream De Ville
> Riding with the guys, up and down the road
> Nothin' I wanted more'n be in that Ford
> Sittin' in class while they takin' rides
> Guys in the middle, girls on both sides
>
> Oh Pretty girl, why can't it be true
> Oh Pretty girl, that it's me with you
> You let football players do things I want to do
>
> Girls in my dream car, door to door
> My Ford bogged down wouldn't hold no more
> Ring goes the last school bell of the day
> Hurrying outside, see 'em pullin' away
> Backseat full even sittin' on the hood
> I knew that was doing my motor good
>
> Oh Pretty girl, why can't it be true
> Oh Pretty girl, that it's me with you
> You let football players do things I want to do
>
> The guys come back after all that fun
> Walking with the pretty girls, one by one
> My heart hangin' heavy like a ton a lead
> Feelin' so down I can't raise my head
> Just like swallowin' up a medicine pill
> Watching them girls from the windowsill

These lines were written just to provide an example of the true depiction of an event. This differs from the improvised writing of a song, which does not necessarily, if ever, coincide with a true story but mostly just goes along the pattern or close to the train of events. I have never, in my life, met or even known of any woman named "Maybellene." The name actually was first brought to my knowledge from a storybook, when I was in the third grade, of animals who bore names. Along with Tom the cat and Donald the duck, there was Maybellene the cow. Not offending anybody, I thought, I named my girl character after a cow. In fact, the girl was to be two-timing, so it would have been worse if I had used a popular name.

2

R&B

A Danger to the Music Business?

Abel Green

There is little doubt that one of the appeals of R&B in the early 1950s was its sometimes coarse and earthy depiction of sexuality, often approached through cleverly deployed slang. While young fans may have flocked to these songs, many detractors within the industry saw R&B "leer-ics" as a dangerous and intrusive presence. *Variety*'s ominously titled "A Warning to the Music Business," issued under the name of editor-in-chief Abel Green, asks that the music business claim a self-policing responsibility for its products. The editorial is purposefully vague, mentioning neither any specific songs nor artists, nor even R&B itself. But for any reader who had been following other articles and letters within the magazine's pages, it was clear that the perceived threat extended to renegade disc jockeys, payola, the influence of BMI, and tacitly, R&B's obvious racial dimension. *Variety*'s "Warning" proved to be wildly influential, as wire services picked up the editorial, turning it into a national news item. It was followed by two further *Variety* editorials that helped set the stage for the controversies that would accompany rock 'n' roll's explosion the following year in 1956.[†]

Music "leer-ics" are touching new lows and if the fast-buck songsmiths and musicmakers are incapable of social responsibility and self-restraint then regulation—policing, if you will—will have to come from more responsible sources. Meaning the phonograph record manufacturers and their network daddies. These companies have a longterm stake rather than a quick turn-around role. It won't wash for them to echo the cheap cynicism of the songsmiths who justify their "leer-ic" garbage by declaring "that's what the kids want" or "that's the only thing that sells today."

What are we talking about? We're talking about "rock and roll," about "hug," and "squeeze," and kindred euphemisms which are attempting a total breakdown of all reticences about sex. In the past such material was common enough but restricted to special places and out-and-out barrelhouses. Today "leer-ics" are offered as standard popular music for general consumption, including consumption by teenagers. Our teenagers are already setting something of a record in delinquency without this raw musical idiom to smell up the environment still more.

The time is now for some serious soul-searching by the popular music industry. This is a call to the conscience of that business. Don't invite the Governmental and religious lightning that is sure to strike. Forget the filthy fast buck. Nor is it just the little music "independents" who are heedless of responsibility.

---

[*] See Abel Green, "A Warning to the Music Business," *Variety*, February 23, 1955, p.2.

[†] *Source*: Abel Green, "A Warning to the Music Business," *Variety*, February 23, 1955, p. 2.

The major diskeries, with the apparently same disregard as to where the blue notes may fall, are as guilty. Guiltier, perhaps, considering the greater obligation—their maturer backgrounds—their time-honored relations with the record-buying public.

The most casual look at the current crop of "lyrics" must tell even the most naive that dirty postcards have been translated into songs. Compared to some of the language that loosely passes for song "lyrics" today, the "pool-table papa" and "jellyroll" terminology of yesteryear is polite palaver. Only difference is that this sort of lyric then was off in a corner by itself. It was the music underworld—not the mainstream.

For the music men—publishers and diskeries—to say that "that's what the kids want" and "that's the only thing that sells nowadays," is akin to condoning publication of back-fence language. Earthy dialog may belong in "art novels" but mass media have tremendous obligation. If they forget, they'll hear from authority. Seemingly that is not the case in the music business.

Before it's too late for the welfare of the industry—forgetting for the moment the welfare of young Americans—VARIETY urges a strong self-examination of the record business by its most responsible chief executive officers. A strong suspicion lingers with VARIETY that these business men are too concerned with the profit statements to take stock of what's causing some of their items to sell. Or maybe they just don't care. A suspicion has been expressed that even the network-affiliated and Hollywood-affiliated record companies brush things off with "that's the music business." This is illogical because it is morally wrong and in the long run it's wrong financially.

Today's "angles" and sharp practices in the music business are an intra-trade problem. Much of it, time-dishonored. The promulgation and propagation of a pop song, ever since there was a Tin Pan Alley, was synonymous with shrewdness, astuteness and deviousness that often bordered on racketeering in its subornation of talent, subsidy, cajolery and out-and-out bribery.

In its trade functions no trade paper, VARIETY included, wants to be accused of "blowing the whistle." But the music business is flirting with the shrill commands of an outer influence if it doesn't wake up and police itself.

This is not the first time VARIETY has spotlighted the pyramiding evils of the music business as it operates today. One of the roots is the payola. If some freak "beat" captures the kids' imagination, the boys are in there quick, wooing, romancing, cajoling the a&r men.

Here is where the responsible chief officers of the major diskeries should come in. They can continue to either blind themselves, as apparently seems to be the case, or they can compel their moral obligations to stand in the way of a little quick profit. This has an accumulative force, because their own radio outlets can limit the exploitation of this spurious stuff. Not only the commodities of their own affiliation, but others.

Some may argue that this is a proposal of "censorship." Not at all. It is a plea to ownership to assume the responsibilities of ownership and eliminate practices which will otherwise invite censorship. In short, chums, do it yourself or have it done for you. You're not going to get or have it done for you.

3

Elvis Presley and "The Craze"

John Crosby

When Elvis Presley (1935–1977) rocketed into the national spotlight in 1956 on the wings of the rock 'n' roll phenomenon, his popularity and notoriety were aided in no small part by his numerous television appearances. Presley performed with his group six times on the Dorsey Brothers' CBS Stage Show between January and March, helping to send his first RCA single, "Heartbreak Hotel," to the top of the charts. But it was not until Presley's June 5 appearance on NBC's Milton Berle show that the young singer from Memphis drew the ire of incredulous and indignant television critics. Abandoning his guitar for the first time and engaging in a series of exaggerated motions and dance steps, Presley playfully gyrated his way through a burlesque version of "Hound Dog" that the band had worked up during a brief stint playing in Las Vegas. The reaction came swift from influential critics like John Crosby of the *New York Herald Tribune*, who bemoaned both the faddish appeal of Presley's music as well as the negative effects that his suggestive bodily movements were having on a nation of impressionable teenagers. Critics have voiced similar concerns throughout other eras of American history. From the ragtime and close-contact "animal dances" of the 1910s to the "freak dancing" of the 1990s, youth dance crazes have long served as the very center of indecency debates. At their roots, all of these instances have arisen as responses to the importation of African American musical forms and dances into white society.[*]

One thing about Elvis Presley, the convulsive shouter of rock 'n' roll songs—if that's what they are: this may be the end of rock 'n' fall and just conceivably a return to musical sanity. I mean where do you go from Elvis Presley?

The best description of Presley's performance on the Milton Berle show came from the chairman of the music department of Bryant High School, Harry A. Feldman, who wrote Berle: "The guest performer, Elvis Presley, presented a demonstration which was in execrable taste, bordering on obscenity. The gyrations of this young man were such an assault to the senses as to repel even the most tolerant observer.

"When television entrepreneurs present such performers to millions of viewers and pronounce them great, when such deplorable taste is displayed in the presentation of primitive, shoddy and offensive material, one begins to understand the present day attitude of our youth. We in the classroom can do very little to offset the force and impact of these displays in our efforts to stem the tide toward a cultural debacle."

About the only guy who ever summed up Elvis "The Pelvis" any better than that was the California policeman who, after watching him writhe around a stage, commented: "If he did that on the street, we'd arrest him."

---

[*] *Source:* John Crosby, "The Craze," *New York Herald Tribune*, June 18, 1956, Section Two, p. 1.

The last appearance of this unspeakably untalented and vulgar young entertainer brought forth such a storm of complaints both from press and public that I imagine any entertainer would hesitate to try him again on television. Even gentle old Ben Gross of "The Daily News" of New York blew his top over this one. I doubt that in the thirty odd years he's been writing that column Ben has ever gotten quite so angry.

But, as I say, where do you go from Elvis, short of open obscenity which is against the law? Popular music has been in a tailspin for years now and I have hopes that with Presley it has touched bottom and will just have to start getting better.

Where did the degeneration of popular music start? You'd probably get a dozen different answers from a dozen different people. My own theory is that it started just before the war when the radio networks battled ASCAP over the price they were asked to pay for the use of songs. ASCAP pulled its music off the air and, since every composer of note was a member, music on the air consisted either of stuff in the public domain or perfectly dreadful new music.

Everyone and his Aunt Agatha thinks he can write songs and during that deplorable period, they all trotted them out. Songs that ordinarily would not have got past the receptionist at any reputable music publishers were not only published but played on the air. The public, particularly the teen-age public, got a taste for bad music that it hasn't lost to this day. The good composers—Irving Berlin, Rodgers and Hammerstein and the like—had their songs forced off the air and with a few exceptions their songs are still off it.

I am heartened by the fact that television is beginning to make fun of this absurdity. The other night "The Hit Parade" did an unavoidable version of "Heartbreak Hotel"—after all, it was *on* the hit parade—with all the singers dressed as Charles Addams monstrosities.

That same evening Goodman Ace on the Perry Como show wrote a very nice piece for his announcer. He enunciated a rock 'n' roll lyric—than which there is nothing more inane—without benefit of music (if that's what it is) in the style of a commencement address. It went something like this.

> "Digga boom
> "Digga boom.
> "Digga
> "Boom."

And Bob Hope came out with a blistering little parody on hillbilly music which I found very entertaining. If there's anything that will knock this craze into oblivion, it's laughter—and the laughter has started.

4

"Elvis Defends Low-Down Style"

KAYS GARY

Elvis Presley weathered a tremendous storm of criticism in the immediate wake of his controversial June 5, 1956, appearance on the Milton Berle television show. As such, it was perhaps to be expected that the singer would eventually defend himself in the press. That moment finally occurred three weeks after the Berle show, when Presley, who was on tour in Charlotte, North Carolina, opened up in an interview conducted with the local newspaper. To the charges of obscenity that John Crosby of the New York Herald Tribune and others had thrown at him, Presley responded by calling attention to the double standard that allowed the sexual objectification of actress Debra Paget, who had been on the Berle show as well, to pass without comment. As to the music itself, Presley acknowledged his debt to the blues and musicians like Arthur "Big Boy" Crudup (1901–1974), establishing a mark of authenticity that doubtless held little sway with his critics. On a different note, Presley also expressed his interest in the ballad style of Eddie Fisher and Perry Como, a path that he would pursue on his very next hit, the romantic title song to his 1956 film debut, *Love Me Tender.*

Elvis Presley is a worried man. Some, that is, for a man with four Cadillacs and a $40,000 weekly pay check. Critics are saying bad things about him. It has been especially rough during the past three weeks. And that is why he bucked his manager's orders to stay away from newsmen in Charlotte Tuesday until showtime. That is why he refused to stay in the seclusion of his hotel room. At 4:10 he couldn't stand it any longer, and with "Cousin Junior" left the room.†

He walked quickly to a restaurant a few doors away for a barbecue, flirtation with a few women and a 30-minute round of pool next door.

"Sure I'll talk. Sit down. Most of you guys, though, been writin' bad things about me, man!"

His knees bounced while he sat. His hands drummed a tattoo on the table top. Eyes, under long lashes, darted from booth to booth, firing rapid winks at the girls who stared at him. "Hi ya, baby," he breathed. And she flopped back in the booth looking like she'd been poleaxed.

"This [John] Crosby guy, whoever he is, he says I'm obscene on the Berle show. Nasty. What does he know?"

"Did you see the show? This Debra Paget is on the same show. She wore a tight thing with feathers on the behind where they wiggle most. And I never saw anything like it. Sex? Man, she bumped and pooshed out all over the place. I'm like Little Boy Blue. And who do they say is obscene? Me!"

"It's because I make more money than Debra. Them critics don't like to see nobody win doing any kind of music they don't know nothin' about."

---

* *Source:* Kays Gary, "Elvis Defends Low-Down Style," *The Charlotte Observer*, June 27, 1956, p. 1B.
† "Cousin Junior" is Presley's cousin, Junior Smith, who was accompanying him on the trip.

And he started to eat. The waitress brought his coffee. Elvis reached down and fingered the lace on her slip.

"Aren't you the one?"

"I'm the one, baby!"

Presley says he does what he does because this is what is making money. And it is music that was around before he was born.

"The colored folks been singing it and playing it just like I'm doin' now, man, for more years than I know. They played it like that in the shanties and in their juke joints, and nobody paid it no mind 'til I goosed it up. I got it from them. Down in Tupelo, Mississippi, I used to hear old Arthur Crudup bang his box the way I do now, and I said if I ever got to the place where I could feel all old Arthur felt, I'd be a music man like nobody ever saw."

Yep, some of the music is low-down.

"But, not like Crosby means. There is low-down people and high-up people, but all of them get the kind of feeling this rock 'n' roll music tells about."

Elvis says he doesn't know how long rock and roll will last.

"When it's gone, I'll switch to something else. I like to sing ballads the way Eddie Fisher does and the way Perry Como does. But the way I'm singing now is what makes the money. Would you change if you was me?"

Investments? "I haven't got to the place for investments. I put it in the bank, man, because I don't know how long it will last." How about the Cadillacs? "Yeah, that's right, I got me four Cadillacs. I keep two at home and two with me. One pink and one white." He never reads his fan mail. "I got nine secretaries in Madison, Tenn., to do that. If I meet somebody on the road I want to keep knowing I give 'em my home address."

Little Rosie Tatsis walked up to the booth and held out a trembling hand. Elvis gave her an autograph. "Look, I'm shaking all over," she tittered. And the grown-up girls in the next booth swapped long, searching looks.

Elvis fingered the collar of his shirt, opened half-way down his chest.

"Some people like me. There's more people than critics." The people who like him, he said, include Eddie Fisher, Como, Liberace, Kate Smith, Bob Hope and Guy Lombardo. And there are more. Lots more.

"When I sang hymns back home with Mom and Pop, I stood still and I looked like you feel when you sing a hymn. When I sing this rock 'n' roll, my eyes won't stay open and my legs won't stand still. I don't care what they say, it ain't nasty."

5

"Experts Propose Study of 'Craze'"

MILTON BRACKER

Among the public events that brought widespread notoriety to rock 'n' roll were Alan Freed's stage shows. When more than 15,000 teenagers descended upon midtown Manhattan on February 22, 1957, to attend Freed's all-day Washington's Birthday extravaganza at the Paramount Theatre, there was little doubt that the sizable crowds would draw the media's attention. As the day's events unfolded and reports surfaced of unruly youth, damaged storefront property, and the efforts of police to control the crowd, Freed's spectacle mushroomed into a full-blown sensationalized story. During the mid-1950s newspapers routinely trotted out "stylized and stereotypical" depictions of these events, bolstered by the pronouncements of authority figures and diagnoses of "socially accredited experts"—all of which fed a growing "moral panic" among parents.* For their own coverage of the Paramount show and rock 'n' roll "craze," the *New York Times* called on the "expert" opinion of Doctor Joost A. M. Meerloo, a Columbia University instructor of psychiatry and author of books on mass delusion and totalitarian brainwashing.† Given Meerloo's interests, it comes as little surprise that he characterizes rock 'n' roll's effects on youth in terms of a contagious disease, drug addiction, Fascist mind control, and social depersonalization. As reports of rock 'n' roll riots continued to proliferate in the media, such portrayals became more and more common.‡

Psychologists suggested yesterday that while the rock 'n' roll craze seemed to be related to rhythmic behavior patterns as old as the Middle Ages, it required, full study as a current phenomenon.

One educational psychologist asserted that what happened in and around the Paramount Theatre yesterday struck him as "very much like the medieval type of spontaneous lunacy where one person goes off and lots of other persons go off with him."

A psychopathologist, attending a meeting of the American Psychopathological Association at the Park Sheraton Hotel feared that this was just a guess.

Others present noted that a study by Dr. Reginald Lourie of Children's Hospital, Washington indicated in 1949 that 10 to 20 per cent of all children did "some act like rocking or rolling." The study went into detail on the stimulating effects of an intensified musical beat.

Meanwhile, a parallel between rock 'n' roll and St. Vitus Dance has been drawn by Dr. Joost A. M. Meerloo, associate in psychiatry at Columbia University in a study just completed for publication.

---

* Stanley Cohen, *Folk Devils and Moral Panics: the Creation of the Mods and Rockers* (London: MacGibbon and Kee, 1972), p. 9.

† See specifically *Delusion and Mass-Delusion* (New York: Nervous and Mental Disease Monographs, 1949) and *The Rape of the Mind: The Psychology of Thought Control, Menticide, and Brainwashing* (Cleveland: World Publishing

‡ *Source*: Milton Bracker, "Experts Propose Study of 'Craze'," *New York Times*, February 23, 1957, p. 12.

Dr. Meerloo described the "contagious epidemic of dance fury" that "swept Germany and spread to all of Europe" toward the end of the fourteenth century. It was called both St. Vitus Dance (or Chorea Major), he continued, with its victims breaking into dancing and being unable to stop. The same activity in Italy, he noted was referred to as Tarantism and popularly related to a toxic bite by the hairy spider called tarantula.

"The Children's Crusades and the tale of the Pied Piper of Hamelin" Dr. Meerloo went on "remind us of these seductive, contagious dance furies."

Dr. Meerloo described his first view of rock 'n' roll this way: Young people were moved by a juke box to dance themselves "more and more into a prehistoric rhythmic trance until it had gone far beyond all the accepted versions of human dancing."

Sweeping the country and even the world, the craze "demonstrated the violent mayhem long repressed everywhere on earth," he asserted.

He also saw possible effects in political terms: "Why are rhythmical sounds and motions so especially contagious? A rhythmical call to the crowd easily foments mass ecstasy: 'Duce! Duce! Duce!'" The call repeats itself into the infinite and liberates the mind of all reasonable inhibitions … as in drug addiction, a thousand years of civilization fall away in a moment."

Dr. Meerloo predicted that the craze would pass "as have all paroxysms of exciting music." But he said that the psychic phenomenon was important and dangerous. He concluded in this way: "Rock 'n' roll is a sign of depersonalization of the individual, of ecstatic veneration of mental decline and passivity.

"If we cannot stem the tide with its waves of rhythmic narcosis and of future waves of vicarious craze, we are preparing our own downfall in the midst of pandemic funeral dances.

"The dance craze is the infantile rage and outlet of our actual world. In this craze the suggestion of deprivation and dissatisfaction of deprivation and dissatisfaction is stimulated and advertised day by day. In their automatic need for more and more, people are getting less and less."

"The awareness of this tragic contradiction in our epoch," Dr. Meerloo said, "must bring us back to a new assessment of what value and responsibility are."

6

The Rock 'n' Roll Audience
"But Papa, It's My Music, I Like It"

JEFF GREENFIELD

One of the ways in which the media asserted control over rock 'n' roll in the 1950s was through its depictions of the music's young audience. Often presented as a homogenous crowd, or simply a haven for delinquency, rock 'n' roll fans rarely were accorded any agency within the mainstream press. Jeff Greenfield's 1971 reminiscences of his experiences as an adolescent in New York City during the late 1950s, offers a more personalized account of rock 'n' roll's impact on its young fans. Greenfield, a New York mayoral speechwriter who would later go on to a distinguished career as a political commentator, touches on a number of points. Most notably he describes the ways in which radio and live performances served to create an imagined community, unifying a disparate group of young rock 'n' roll fans, separated by class, race, and ethnicity. Much of Greenfield's article describes the important role of Alan Freed (1921–1965), the disc jockey often credited with popularizing the phrase "rock and roll." Freed's live shows at both the Brooklyn and New York Paramount Theaters routinely drew crowds of 4000 to 5000 teenagers (and many more who could not be admitted). The first performance that Greenfield attended, during "Washington's Birthday of 1957," was part of a ten-day marathon run of shows that attracted a total of 65,000 spectators. These shows, which as Greenfield describes, involved the destruction of property and demonstrative dancing, drew extensive media coverage and acted as lightning rods for the mounting concerns about rock 'n' roll's supposedly pernicious effects.*

TERROR. Perhaps you think you can define it. It is sitting in a jet fighter cockpit, plummeting to a crash landing in a hostile country. It is losing footing on a mountain ledge in the midst of a blizzard. It is walking down a deserted city street in the dead of night, with the sudden, certain sound of footsteps behind you.

No, that is not terror. I will tell you what terror is. Terror is waiting on line at 6:30 in the morning on a school holiday in 1957 for the Brooklyn Paramount to open for Alan Freed's rock and roll revue.

You have been up since 5:30 on your first day of vacation, Christmas or Easter (Hanukkah or Passover in my set). You have staggered into the darkness, found your friend Alan (another normal, neurotic Jewish kid) and weaved your way into the subway. There you pass interminable time, speeding past unfamiliar stops, emerging into the sullen dawn in downtown Brooklyn (down-town *Brooklyn*?). There, about a block away, is the Brooklyn Paramount, a huge movie palace built to hold the thousands who do not go out to movies anymore. On the marquee are big red letters: "Ten Days Only! Alan Freed's All-Star Rock 'n' Roll Revue!"

---

* *Source:* Jeff Greenfield, "'But Papa, It's My Music, I Like It'," *New York Times*, March 7, 1971, pp. HF1, 6.

You walk to the theater, past the shuttered luncheonettes and cheap clothing stores. There is already a knot of kids waiting on line, even though the doors will not open for 2 hours and 45 minutes. And now you will begin to learn the meaning of terror.

These people are different. They do not look the way I do. They do not talk the way I do. I do not think they were born the same way I was. All of the males are six feet, seven inches tall. The last six inches is their hair, carefully combed into a pompadour. They are lean, rangy, even scrawny (except for one who is very, very fat). They have the hard faces of the children of the working poor. They read auto specs at night, not college catalogues. They wear St. Christopher medals, white T-shirts with their cigarette packs held in the left sleeve which is rolled up to the muscles. They have muscles.

The girls are all named Fran. They have curlers in their hair and scarves tied around their heads. They chew gum. They wear jeans and sweaters, and their crucifixes bounce on their breasts, some of which are remarkable examples of stress under pressure.

The conversation is guttural, half-sentences and grunts, with innuendos and veiled hints of lubricity. "Eh, that party, eh, Fran? Remember, heh, heh? Nah, she don' remember nuthin.'" Fran is giggling, blushing. There is about these people an overwhelming sense of physical force, the same sense exuded by the students of Ascension High who chased the Jews home from school every afternoon: they hit other people a lot. Every joke, every insult, every question, is followed by open-handed jabs to the face, punches on the arm, slaps which barely miss being punches. It is like watching Leo Gorcey and Huntz Hall in the Bowery Boys movies.

At this point, there is only one stark thought in my mind: what in God's name am I doing here? These people are going to kill me and steal my five-dollars and I will not be found for days. Consequently, the strategy of waiting on line at the Paramount is clear. You do not talk with your friend about your grades on the Social Studies test. You do not talk about where you are going to college. You do not engage in precocious arguments about socialism. You keep your big mouth shut.

The vow of silence makes time go slowly, so you look at the posters over the theater entrance: the pictures of the stars blown up on cardboard, the names spelled out in letters glittering from the gold and silver dust. There is Buddy Holly and the Crickets; the Cleftones, in white dinner jackets and red slacks; Jo-Ann Campbell, "the blonde bombshell" who wears high-heeled shoes and very tight skirts, and whose biggest hand comes when she turns her back to the audience.

If you talk at all, it is in grunts to the others. "Yeah, Frankie Lyman, I saw him—seen him—last year. You heard the new Fats Domino?" You wait for the doors to open, for the sanctuary of the dark theater, for the Terror to go away.

What were we waiting for, those dark mornings? The singers and their songs, yes; but there were shows that were clinkers. Alan Freed paid mediocre fees to his talent, splitting the net with his partners and himself. Sometimes he could not pull in the big names, and he was left with headliners who had recorded a single hit that everyone knew would not be repeated. No, it was something else. We waited for Alan Freed and what he was for the children of the 1950's. And waited because of something in each of us: an unspoken, undetected yearning for a sense of unity; an urge to join and celebrate this music that was ours as a community; an impulse that a decade later swept our younger brothers and sisters out of mainstream America.

Alan Freed had come out of Middle America in the mid-1950's, rising from $43-a-week obscurity in New Castle, Pa., to regional prominence in Akron, Ohio, and later Cleveland. He took music that had been played only on black radio stations and sold in black neighborhoods—race music, it was called—and played this black music for white kids.

Freed played this music with an infectious on-the-air spirit, emphasizing the heavy afterbeat by slamming a telephone book with the palm of his hand, shouting encouragement to the frenzy of a tenor saxophone, clanging a cowbell. And somewhere between Akron and Cleveland, he chose to label the sound with a term heard again and again in the bluntly sexual lyrics of rhythm and blues, in titles like "My Baby Rocks Me With a Steady Roll,"* or "All She Wants to Do Is Rock." He called it rock and roll. It had a good beat. You could dance to it.

The country was finding out in 1954 that Alan Freed knew what the kids wanted to hear. Rock and roll conquered young white America that year. Slowly at first, then regularly, rhythm and blues songs began selling outside the racial barriers, winning places on mainstream pop music charts. "I Understand" by the Four Tunes; "One Mint Julep" by the Clovers; "Gee" by the Crows; "Cryin' in the Chapel" by Sonny Till and the Orioles—all sold well. All were copied—"covered" is the polite music term—by white artists who imitated the distinctive arrangements note for note: a legal if shady practice, since arrangements could not be protected by copyright. But despite the imitations, the kids were often buying the original versions. Because those were the versions with the beat.

The first Alan Freed show in New York was during Christmas of 1954, at the Brooklyn Academy of Music. It grossed $150,000—an unheard-of sum for live shows. But it was nothing compared to his Labor Day show in 1955 which pulled in $254,000. Freed, now a $75,000-a-year disk jockey on WINS, had gone into partnership with the station—which may account for its indifference to his plugs over his radio show—and the 10-day affair netted $125,000. Disk jockeys all over the country began promoting rock and roll stage shows, and in New York, the seasons were marked by the Brooklyn Paramount—Christmas, Easter, Labor Day, Christmas.

Each night, sprawled on my bed on Manhattan's Upper West Side, I would listen to the world that Alan Freed created. To a 12- or 13-year-old, it was a world of unbearable sexuality and celebration; a world of citizens under 16, in a constant state of joy or sweet sorrow.

Freed would read "dedications" to the songs from faraway places with strange-sounding names: Bayside, New Dorp, Huntington, Erasmus, Riverdale.

"To John from you-know-who. I want you, but you want her. Listen to the words of this song— and go back to her."

"To Mike from Fran. Going steady for six weeks … and forever."

"To the kids of Miss Epstein's class. Good luck—and may our friendships never be broken."

Somewhere, somewhere there really were candy stores with juke boxes, where the kids ate Pop's hamburgers and danced after school the way they did in those Jane Withers movies. Somewhere, there were parties with close dancing (Bill Haley and the Comets cut a song called "Dim, Dim the Lights" which had more sexual implications than "I Am Curious (Yellow)"). Somewhere there were kids who spent their time with each other, touching and laughing and running around to all this music…

"Turn that damn thing down!"

My father has always been a fair and gentle man, but in the face of Little Richard or Fats Domino he abandoned himself to rage.

"You're going to turn your brain to mush!"

Francis of Assisi become Spiro Agnew. My adolescence is a continuing re-play: the door swinging open, the dark, furrowed brow, the flash of anger, the sullen retreat. Like a river of troubled water, rock and roll music was the boundary of a house divided.

Worse, there was a fifth column, a corner of my mind which told me: you know, of course, they're right. It is crap and your brain is turning to mush. One of the authentic scars of my life—far more vivid than a broken date or a broken zipper—is buying a rock and roll album with my parents during a shopping trip to Union Square. We walked into a record store, and there it was, on Specialty Records: "Here's Little Richard." On a yellow background, a tight shot of a Negro face bathed

---

* Greenfield is most likely referring to the blues standard "My Daddy Rocks Me (with One Steady Roll)," originally recorded in 1922 by Trixie Smith.

in sweat, the beads of perspiration clearly visible, mouth wide open in a rictus of sexual joy, hair flowing endlessly from the head.

"Oh my God," my mother said.

Come on, I thought, let's just buy it and get out of here, come on…

"We better play it first," my father said.

The saleslady smiled indulgently. From the phonograph, ripping through the store, came the shouted opening to "Long Tall Sally": "Gonna tell Aunt Mary 'bout Uncle John! Says he got the misry but he has a lotta fun! Oh baby, who-o-ooh baby…"

"Jesus Christ," my father said.

I muttered something vague about "authentic gospel roots … tradition of Afro-American … folk…" but what I was saying inside was something else: look, it's my music, I like it, and you're not supposed to listen to it anyway.

And that, after all, is what I was doing on line outside the Brooklyn Paramount on a chilly dawn, surrounded by six-foot, seven-inch hoodlums who were going to kill me. It was a refuge from ridicule, a liberated zone where everyone else liked the same crap I did. In those days before the Beatles, before scholarly studies of rock in Partisan Review, before even Presley, Ed Sullivan was not presenting rock and roll stars. They were rarely seen on television outside local teen bandstand shows, and when they did appear it was an embarrassment. They did not belong there, vulnerable to our elders' outrage. They belonged here—apart from Them and with Us.

This whole sense of self-defense was part of the magic attraction of rock and roll. Night after night, Alan Freed would indignantly answer editorials in the Brooklyn Tablet or the Daily Mirror that accused rock and roll of filth or fostering juvenile delinquency—the latter an accusation heard with more frequency after "The Blackboard Jungle" reached the screen, opening with the music of "Rock Around the Clock."

"It's the one per cent of the bad kids who are making it rough for the 99 per cent of the good kids." Freed would say, and the theme became part of our cause. When Freed began to make rock and roll movies in the mid-1950's—with plots out of the I've-got-a-great-idea-let's-put-on-a-dance-and-build-the-new-gym school—he stressed this theme that goods kids liked rock and roll music. But the adult anger, the fury, the ban on rock shows in Boston and Bridgeport and New Haven, pulled us into a kind of sect. To journey to Brooklyn was not simply going to a show: it was an act of faith.

Of course, nobody knew that or talked like that at the time. There was no self-conscious Wood-stock spirit, no notion that that this was a way we could live out our lives. We knew we had to grow up sometime, to be like Them, We were here because … well, it had a good beat and you could dance to it.

Actually, my first journey was not out to Brooklyn, but to the safer regions of the New York Para-mount on Times Square. Alan Freed had taken a big gamble, breaking the four-month cycle to put on a show during Washington's Birthday of 1957. To shorten the odds on conquering the citadel of Dorsey, Goodman, and Sinatra, Freed had booked two big acts: Frankie Lyman and the Teenagers, and the Platters. And he chose this occasion for the premiere of his movie, "Don't Knock the Rock," with Bill Haley and the Comets and Little Richard.

My friend Alan and I got there about 6:30 a.m. The line already went past McBride's Ticket Service's plate glass window, down 43rd street toward the offices of The New York Times. By the time the doors opened, the line was blocks long. The show broke all of Sinatra's records. It also broke McBride's plate glass window. The kids danced in the aisles. They stomped so hard to the beat that the Fire Department evacuated the balcony. They cheered the good-guy grown-up in the movie who said, "I don't see anything wrong with the music. I kinda like it." They told Middle America—through pictures in Life magazine—that the conquest was complete.

At about 9 a.m. at the Brooklyn Paramount, a ticket-taker, alone and afraid in a world he never made, edges into the booth. The line begins to rock, slowly, ominously. The doors open. Ushers flank the line, chanting "Admission is $1.50. Have your money ready please. Admission is…"

The enormous, cavernous theater is filled as it has not been since television. The horrible Western or mystery movie begins. The movie ends. Cheers. The newsreel comes on. Groans and boos. The newsreel ends. Cheers. *Another* newsreel—a feature on pet shows or women's fashions—comes on. Boos and shouts. The newsreel ends. Cheers. The lights go out. There is movement behind the curtain. Anticipatory shrieks. The announcer: "And now—the Brooklyn Paramount is proud to present—Alan Freed and his Rock and Roll Revue!" Yaaaayyyy!

The lights go on, red and blue and yellow, as the Alan Freed All-Star 18-piece orchestra plays "Night Train," one of Freed's trademarks. The band—as Freed has told us innumerable times—has great stars, sax men Sam the Man Taylor, Big Al Sears, Panama Francis. The song ends and Freed comes out to enormous cheers, grinning widely from a slightly misshapen face, permanent reminder of an auto crash in 1954 and the plastic surgery. His voice is raspy, electrically charged.

"Hiya!"

"Hiiii!"

"This is Alan Freed, the ol' king of rock 'n' roll."

The acts. In a sense, they are all the same. Four or five singers, outlandishly dressed, in flaming red dinner jackets, purple pants, yellow shirts. There are always two mikes—one for the lead singer, one for the rest of the group, including (always) a bass singer who supplies the do-bobba, doo-bobba line, one falsetto, to surround the reedy lead voice with logistical support.

The steps. They defy description. In a tribute to symmetry, the guy on the right puts out his right hand, the guy on the left puts out his left hand, the guy in the middle puts out both hands. Fingers snap and wave, in mirror-image perfection. Now the hands switch, the feet shuffle in tempo. The tenor sax break begins. The singers whirl around; they do splits. They gesture with the words.

"You know"—point out

"In my heart"—point to the heart

"I pray"—hands together in prayer

"We'll never part"—hands separate, heads shake no

No group, no matter how big, did more than six or seven songs (although Little Richard, in his last show before a four-year retirement, was on-stage for 40 minutes). It kept the shows short enough to do six or seven a day, which hiked the grosses. But nobody minded. Few of the groups had been in existence long enough to have a long string of songs, and the more groups that appeared, the better the shows.

And all the while, back at the radio show, a constant hype was kept up by Paul Sherman—the solid, straight, square d.j. who subbed for Freed. Sherman, whose voice went up 20 decibels during his stint on Freed's slot, would tell us endlessly that "Alan's at the Brooklyn Paramount theater right now, in an un-be-*liev*-a-ble show, you've just got to go see it." If you were home listening, if you hadn't seen the show, you felt like everybody in the world was at a party except you.

Alan Freed was driven off the air in 1959 in the wake of the payola scandals. He had given himself authorship credit—and a royalty share—on many songs he hadn't really written and, as the best-known jockey, Freed was the scapegoat. He left New York for the West Coast, where he found and lost several jobs. In early 1965, as the Beatles first swept America, Freed was indicted for perjury. He died at 43 of a liver ailment before the month was out.

The Brooklyn Paramount is no longer a theater. It's part of Long Island University. There is nothing there to remind anybody that Alan Freed once existed.

In late 1969, I went to the shiny new Felt Forum in Madison Square Garden for a Fifties rock and roll revival. As I approached the entrance, I felt the Terror. The Others were there, a little plumper, a turtleneck or two where T-shirts used to be, but with the pompadours, the grunts, the hostility still in place. They had all married Fran. A lot of them wore American flags and Honor America buttons. I hid my peace button instinctively. Terror does not die easily.

But we went in together and when the M.C. announced that this show was being dedicated to Alan Freed we applauded together, and when the Five Satins came out and sang "In the Still of the Night," we sang with them and stood together and cheered together until they sang it again.

7

Leiber & Stoller

TED FOX

As songwriters and "independent producers" for artists ranging from The Coasters and The Drifters to Big Mama Thornton and Elvis Presley, Jerry Leiber (born 1933) and Mike Stoller (born 1933) were responsible for many of the rock 'n' roll era's most enduring hits. In this 1985 interview conducted by music writer and current Buckwheat Zydeco manager Ted Fox, the two songwriters discuss their formative years and the stories behind some of their most famous songs, giving insight along the way into the creative process behind many R&B and early rock 'n' roll recordings. As Fox points out, Leiber and Stoller's situation also throws the unusual racial dynamics surrounding 1950s rock 'n' roll into sharp relief. Songs like "Kansas City" and "Hound Dog" are often taken to be forms of "authentic" black musical expression, yet their authors were two nineteen-year-old white Jewish teenagers, both of whom felt a powerful attraction to the culture and music of African Americans. Much like Johnny Otis (born 1921), the white musician, producer, and author of "Willie and the Hand Jive," whose immersion among African Americans led him to feel "black by persuasion," Leiber and Stoller's experiences prove that notions of race in America have been informed as much by culture as they have by the color of one's skin.˙

Let's talk about how you got together.

Leiber: I was writing songs with a drummer, and going to Fairfax High School in Los Angeles. The drummer lost interest in writing songs and suggested I call Mike Stoller, whom he had worked with in a pickup dance band. I called Mike. He said he was not interested in writing songs. I said I thought it would be a good idea if we met anyway.

Mike, you were really into jazz and modern classical at that time, no?

Stoller: I was a very big modern jazz fan really. At the time Jerry called me, 1950, I was very into Charlie Parker and Thelonious Monk and Dizzy. And through modern jazz I got interested in Stravinsky and Bartók. When I lived in New York—before I moved to California when I was sixteen—I used to hang out on 52nd Street.

Didn't you take piano lessons with James P. Johnson?

Stoller: I did when I was ten or eleven. Four or five lessons. That was my earliest love, boogie-woogie and blues piano. But the thing that cemented our relationship was when Jerry showed me his lyrics and I saw that they were blues in structure. Most of them had a twelve-bar structure—a line, then ditto marks, then the rhyming line. So it wasn't

* *Source:* Ted Fox, *In the Groove: The People Behind the Music* (New York: St. Martin's Press, 1986), pp. 157–69.

difficult for me to relate to it and go back to my first love, which was Pine Top Smith and Meade Lux Lewis, and Albert Ammons.

Jerry, were you more rhythm and blues oriented?

Leiber: Boogie-woogie, rhythm and blues. I was working in a record shop on Fairfax Avenue after school. But actually I was exposed to boogie-woogie when I was a little kid in Baltimore. My mother had a grocery store just on the border of the black ghetto. She had many black customers.

It seems like an almost fateful encounter. You were both so heavily into black culture.

Stoller: We were, but my background was a bit different. I went to an interracial summer camp, which was very unusual in those days. Starting in 1940, I went there every summer for eight years. I heard the older black kids playing the upright piano in the barn. A couple of them played very good boogie-woogie. I tried to emulate what I'd heard.

When you first started, were there songwriters you tried to emulate or whom you admired?

Leiber: I was trying to imitate certain styles—sounds that I heard on records. Some of the writers I was imitating, I found out later were actually the performers.

You both were totally into the black scene in L.A. at that time. You had black girlfriends, and would go to the black clubs.

Leiber: Oh yeah. We lived a kind of black existence. I'd say eighty percent of our lives were lived that way. It's an interesting thing. I sometimes look back on it and I think, why did I do that? I think that somehow or other I was alienated from my own culture and searching for something else. My father died when I was five. My mother was a refugee from Poland. I don't know what fragments of tradition there were left in my family, but they were so slight, there was little to go on.

Did you feel that way, too, Mike?

Stoller: No, not exactly. My family life was very warm, very emotionally comfortable. My mother and father were very supportive. My mother in particular was very supportive of me, and later of Jerry as well. But I must have felt somewhat alienated from my white peers. I felt there was something more special about not only the music I heard, that came from black people, but the black people themselves who made the music. I belonged to a social club in Harlem when I was about thirteen or fourteen.

Leiber: The black neighborhood was groovy, and I was accepted there right away. Part of it was my mother's doing. Her store was the only store within ten blocks of the ghetto that extended credit to black families. So I was a welcome person in the black neighborhood.

This translated itself immediately and automatically into the stuff you were writing, didn't it? Your songs became authentic black songs of the period.

Leiber: Leroi Jones, writing about us in the sixties, said that we were the only authentic black voices in pop music. [Laughs.] He changed his tune a few years later when he became [Amiri] Baraka. We were flattered. Actually I think we wanted to be black. Being black was being great. The best musicians in the world were black. The greatest athletes in the world were black, and black people had a better time. As far as we were concerned the worlds that we came from were drab by comparison.

Jerry Wexler said in his interview with me that he supported the separation of black and white music into the pop and rhythm and blues charts because he felt that created more opportunity for black artists. How do you feel about that?

Stoller: I never thought about it that way. I always felt that it was sad, in the early days especially, that artists like Ray Charles and Lloyd Price and Big Mama Thornton weren't exposed to a wider audience.

Leiber: If they had had exposure on the major stations, then Georgia Gibbs wouldn't have been able to make all those covers of all those great records by Ruth Brown and LaVern Baker.

Stoller: And Pat Boone, who was covering Fats Domino records and Little Richard records…

Leiber: …wouldn't have happened. If Richard was played on all the Top 40 stations, nobody could have sold another record of anything he made. Could anybody cover Elvis Presley?

Stoller: The point is that today people are still buying and listening to Little Richard, Fats Domino, and Laverne Baker. Nobody is buying their songs in a cover version by Pat Boone. Nobody wants to hear a Georgia Gibbs' record or The Crew Cuts' record [of The Chords' original "Sh-Boom"]. What I imagine Jerry Wexler meant was that within a smaller and separate pool you could support more new fish. But I think the black fish in that smaller pool were being denied an ocean in which they could have very well survived.

Let's talk about how you two worked together as songwriters.

Leiber: Often, in the early days, I'd stalk around Mike's room. There'd be an upright piano against one of the walls. I'd just walk around and smoke and mumble, and he would jam until I would just get struck by some notion. Then I'd start yelling some kind of line. If Mike dug it, he would pick it up somewhere. Sometimes Mike would yell out some lines, too.

Stoller: It was like spontaneous combustion, like Jackson Pollock. You threw a lot of paint at the canvas. I would just play riffs and Jerry would shout lines, almost like automatic writing.

Mike, it's been said you had an almost encyclopedic grasp of musical styles, and you could throw out ideas from everything you'd digested over the years.

Stoller: I think that's somebody else's description.

Leiber: I think it is true, although I don't think he was conscious of it. We used to just use shorthand after a while, sort of make signs. I'd say, "More Fats" [Domino] or "More Richard" [Little Richard] or "More Amos" [Milburn], "More Charles" [Ray Charles]. All these were signals for different styles pianistically. If I was talking about Toussaint [Allen Toussaint], it meant New Orleans.

Stoller: If he said Fats, it generally meant triplets.

Leiber: Hard triplets, at a certain tempo.

Stoller: But we're talking about the way we used to work. Our mode of working has changed through the years, and also the type of work that we do has changed.

Leiber: The songs for the Peggy Lee album were written in a different way.* A number of songs were written where the lyrics came first, and Mike set them to music.

Stoller: On others I wrote the music first and then Jerry wrote the words.

---

* They are referring to Peggy Lee's 1969 album *Is That All There Is?*.

Leiber: So it wasn't the same kind of spontaneous combustion that occurred with the early writing. This [later] stuff was much more complex. Much more deliberately worked out, structurally.

Stoller: The early things were almost written as if it were an improvisation.

It sounds like a maturation to a more traditional method of writing.

Stoller: We've talked about the kind of music which brought us together, the thing that really got us going, the propelling force—different styles of black music. But at the same time, we were not unfamiliar with...

Leiber: ...many other forms....

Stoller: George Gershwin's music, and Rodgers and Hart and so on. There's a thing we used to say to each other, we said that what we wrote were records and that these records were like newspapers or magazines in that they'd last for a month and then they'd be gone.

Leiber: We didn't think we were writing songs that would last.

Stoller: All the standards had already been written, we thought. We were writing songs that we loved and that we were compelled to write. But we didn't think they had any lasting value.

You didn't think you were in the league of someone like Cole Porter?

Leiber: Absolutely no   We never thought so.

Stoller: The type of music that we write now is different.

Leiber: It requires different working habits.

Is it not as much fun now?

Leiber: No. It's not as much fun. And yet, it is sometimes, finally, more gratifying.

Better product?

Leiber: Different. I hope it's better. We play what we feel are some of the finest songs that we have ever written and some people say, "You know what? You'll never write a better song than 'Hound Dog.'" The people we admire most and the people we want to be most admired by are our fellow songwriters. I remember Johnny Mercer coming up to me one day and saying, "Kid, you finally wrote a good song." It was "Is That All There Is?" [for Peggy Lee]. I think that was the greatest compliment I've ever received.

Stoller: That's out of a different tradition than our earlier work. It no longer holds my attention to work in the format of the traditional three- or four-chord blues that we used to work in. So I choose to write something other. At that time I was absolutely happy with the basic colors in my paint box.

Let's pick up now with the chronology. Lester Sill was the guy who...

Leiber: ...introduced us to everybody—the Bihari Brothers of Modern Records, the Mesner Brothers who owned Aladdin, and Ralph Bass....

Stoller: Lester took us to New York and introduced us to Ralph Bass, who was with King and Federal Records. Ralph then moved to California and we started to work with him out there.

Leiber: Ralph was a friend of Lester's. Lester was the national sales promotion man for Modern Records.

How did you meet Lester?

Stoller: Jerry was selling records in Norty's Record Shop after school....

Leiber: He came in one afternoon to check the sales on certain records. We got to talking. He asked me what I was going to do with my life. I told him I was interested in becoming a songwriter. I sang him some lyrics. He was very encouraging.

Stoller: He introduced us to a disc jockey named Gene Norman. Gene Norman ran a series of concerts called Just Jazz, like Norman Granz' Jazz at the Philharmonic. But he also had an annual blues jamboree at the Shrine Auditorium. He gave us the names of the artists who were going to appear on his 1950 blues jamboree and he told us where they were staying. Jerry and I went down to the Dunbar Hotel to see artists like Wynonie Harris, Percy Mayfield, Helen Humes, and so on. We had one song performed at that concert—"Real Ugly Woman"—and Jimmy Witherspoon sang it. It was our first public performance. What a thrill!

When you went around to the record companies with Lester Sill, would you play piano and sing to demonstrate the songs?

Leiber: We would play and sing our songs to the record company owners, and if they were accepted, we'd teach them to the artist.

Let's talk about "Kansas City." Wasn't it first titled "K.C. Loving?"

Stoller: It was written for Little Willie Littlefield. We called it "Kansas City," but Ralph Bass came to us and said, "You know, 'K.C.' is the hip thing, so I'm going to change the title of your song to 'K.C. Loving.'" We said "Okay. Just put it out!"

It's so authentic sounding, but different, it's not just a twelve-bar blues.

Stoller: Actually it *is* a twelve-bar blues, but it's a *melodic* one, as opposed to a traditional blues melody, which is basically just a series of inflections. I wanted to write something that, if it was played on a trumpet or a trombone, people could say it was a particular song, instead of that's a blues in E flat or F. I wanted something you could listen to instrumentally, and say, "I know that song."

Most people then, and probably to this day, think the song is traditional. How do you feel about that?

Stoller: At first when that happened we felt we had achieved something, that we had written something good enough to be thought of as traditional.

Leiber: At the time we were writing it, Mike and I had a little bit of an argument, and Mike turned out to be right. I didn't want it to have a melody. I wanted it to have a traditional straight blues contour, that any blues singer would sing in his own style with just the changes and the words. Mike said, "I don't want to do that, I want to write a melody. I want this to have a real identity." I said, "The other way it's much more flexible." He said, "Well, man, you're writing the words and I'm writing the music, and I'm going to write the music the way I hear it." [Laughter.]

At this point, and until the "Hound Dog" session with Big Mama Thornton in 1952, your records were being produced by other people....

Stoller: Yeah. In the case of "Kansas City" we went out to Maxwell Davis' house. He was an A&R man, producer, arranger, songwriter, horn player. And he was the house musical director for Aladdin Records. He also made records for Modern, Specialty, and other labels, including Mercury.

Leiber: If he were alive today, he'd be making a million dollars a second. He was wonderful. There were four or five guys around the country at this time who had this ability.

Stoller: Like Jesse Stone, who worked for Atlantic, or Bumps Blackwell, who worked for Specialty. But up until that time, after we performed a song for an artist, we frequently went to the studio. At first it was like, "You guys can stay here, but be quiet." Later we began to express some ideas to whomever was running the session. Sometimes they'd use some of the ideas. After all, when you're working with the blues, which is pretty repetitive, you need as many ideas as you can get to make it a little different. We would be invited to the studio with songs after a while. Ralph would call us to bring songs to the studio. We would run them down with artists like Little Esther or Bobby Nunn or Little Willie Littlefield with Johnny Otis' band, and discuss how they ought to go. They would be worked out on the session. Sometimes we'd bring three songs with us and write a fourth during the session. When we did "Kansas City," it was the first time we had the opportunity to really spend time before the session laying out the ideas with an arranger who actually wrote down the ideas, as opposed to the way we had worked with Johnny Otis, where the charts were head arrangements done on the spot.

During this time when your material was being produced by others, were you happy with the way it was coming out?

Leiber: A lot of the stuff was misinterpreted. So we started to involve ourselves more and more in the making of arrangements and the running of sessions until we got to a point where we could run our own sessions. After a while they were calling us to produce records.

Stoller: "Hound Dog" was the first record we produced, although unofficially. Johnny Otis had played drums at the rehearsal. He had the snares turned off and was playing some old Southern, Latin-sounding kind of beat. On the actual recording date, he had his road drummer playing because Johnny was supposed to be running the session for Don Robey of Peacock Records. It wasn't happening. So Jerry said, "Johnny, get on the drums the way you were." Johnny said, "Who's gonna run the session?" and we said, "We will." Jerry went into the booth and directed from there. I stayed on the floor and worked with the musicians. There were only two takes, and both of them were good, but the second was better than the first.

You were known, along with Jerry Wexler and Ahmet Ertegun at Atlantic, for doing as many takes as necessary to get the song right, and for rehearsing your artists before entering the studio with them. That was pretty unusual in rhythm and blues at that time, wasn't it?

Stoller: I think so.

Leiber: We took a lot more time than the Biharis's and the Mesners' did. They'd do two, three, four, five takes and good-bye. We'd lay in there for two hours on a side if we had to. But we almost always got four sides in the allotted three hours—two A sides and two B sides. In fact, "Searchin'," which we did in the last six minutes of a session as a B side, was the fourth song of the session and we just *had* to get it.* I mean if we had come out of a session with only three sides, we'd have felt like failures. We were very thorough. We would rehearse for three weeks before a session, eight hours a day. Every lick was planned. The only thing we would leave to chance on the session was the feel, and the tempo. Sometimes Mike would take a note or two out of a bass pattern because it was too cluttered, or add a note or two. We knew what kind of a beat the drummer was going to lay down because we knew the drummer. We knew more or less how the piano player was going to play because Mike was playing piano. So we knew pretty much what to expect. The

---

* "Searchin'" is from a 1957 session with The Coasters. It resulted in the group's first hit on the pop singles chart.

only thing we were looking for was that magic, that thing that comes together when everything is cooking.

Stoller: I used to write out some kind of road map for all the musicians. When it came to The Coasters, it took lots of preparation. Harmony was not their forte, and I used to rehearse them for weeks till they could remember who had which note.

Were the musicians available for this kind of extended rehearsal?

Stoller: No, no. We never rehearsed the musicians, only the vocal group. The musicians came to the studio where we had these little charts written out for them so that they wouldn't have to start learning from scratch what the bass pattern was, whether we had a four- or eight-bar intro, or where the break chorus came.

You had been working for a number of record companies, then you and Lester decided to start Spark Records late in 1953.

Stoller: It lasted about a year and a half.

Leiber: We didn't know what to do in terms of promotion. Well, we knew in a sense. Lester [Sill] knew that we couldn't get past the Rockies.

Stoller: We were underfinanced. We couldn't afford to send Lester on a trip. We were selling 100,000 singles in Los Angeles and nothing in the rest of the country.

And Lester was quite a promotion guy, quite a character, wasn't he?

Leiber: Fantastic. He'd do a sand dance—take some sand out of his pocket, throw it on the floor and dance to a record…

Stoller: …in the record store, to show the store owner what a great danceable record it was. Anyway, Atlantic liked our records very much. They convinced us, which wasn't very hard to do, that they were better in selling product, or records, I should say. I hate that word, product. They took our last release, the Robins' "Smokey Joe's Cafe," and put it on one of their labels, Atco. They sold a quarter of a million after we'd sold 100,000 in L.A.

What was the deal that Ahmet and Jerry made you at Atlantic?

Leiber: Two cents a record. And we arm-wrestled over getting our names on the records as producers. Jerry Wexler said, "What do you mean? You're getting the money. What do you need? We don't put our names on the records." I said, "Yeah, but you own the label."

Stoller: He said, "Well, you have your names on as writers." And he said, "Man, we tell everybody that you made the record!"

Leiber: He said, "We told [Waxy] Maxy, and Henry Stone knows, man. Who else do you want to know about it?" [Laughter.]

Stoller: Actually, although we kept this argument up for a number of years, it only began to make sense to them when we started producing songs that we hadn't written.

Leiber: We got good at producing, and we started doing other people's songs. We would give assignments to Doc Pomus and Mort Shuman, Bacharach and David, Mann and Weill, Goffin and King. Sometimes we wouldn't write for the sessions, we just wouldn't feel it. If we were doing a Drifters' date, we'd write a song, but we weren't going to write *four* songs. We would try to get the best song from each team.

Stoller: Then we would concentrate on ideas for orchestral coloration.

Leiber: It actually varied the work. We didn't feel like writing all the time. So we'd devote some weeks to writing, and sometimes just devote time to producing or producing in another style other than that which we were writing.

Until you came along, records were generally made by staff producers. You were really the first inde-
pendent producers, weren't you?

Stoller: Jerry Wexler told me that we were, so I assume we were.

Leiber: There were people doing independent record dates with their own money, like Buck
         Ramm. But we were the first independent producers ever, as I understand it, formally
         contracted by a label to make records.

Stoller: [Laughs.] We were record company owners who were persuaded to give up their com-
         pany and become producers on a royalty basis.

It was a new job title.

Stoller: And a misnomer which we didn't invent ourselves—producer.

Leiber: It should have been director. The producer has always been the money raiser and the
         manufacturer.

Stoller: Like the producer of a film or a show. We were the supervisors, the directors.

8

The History of Chicano Rock

Rubén Guevara

Singer and songwriter Rubén Guevara (born 1942) is perhaps best known for his doo-wop and R&B group Ruben & the Jets, who gained a measure of notoriety in the 1970s through their association with Frank Zappa. But Guevara has also been one of the most active historians of Chicano Rock, producing a variety of musical exhibitions and album releases that draw on his own Mexican American heritage. His 1985 essay, "A View from the Sixth Street Bridge," was a landmark essay and remains one of the few attempts to sketch a detailed social and musical history of Chicano contributions to the history of rock.[*] As Guevara describes, the emergence and blossoming of Chicano Rock in the years between World War II and the British Invasion resulted from both the strong Mexican presence in Los Angeles and a distinctive cultural intermingling. Similar to New York's Spanish Harlem, Mexicans and African Americans in southern California found themselves in close proximity, settling together in affordable neighborhoods and sharing their music with one another. Meanwhile, white disc jockeys like Hunter Hancock (1916–2004) helped spread the new sounds over the airwaves of stations like KFVD and KGFJ, and entrepreneurs like Billy Cardenas (born 1938) looked to promote artists as part of a "Chicano Motown" sound.[†]

ROOTS

What is Chicano rock? First we have to understand "Chicano": as a word, a concept, an expression of a people's history. Nobody is sure of the exact genesis of the term, although it can be traced back to the state of Chihuahua in Mexico, where the upper classes used it as a term of contempt for the poor. But "Chicano!" as an epithet was transformed into "Chicano!" as a statement of pride and defiance by student activists in the sixties. Where *Hispanic, Mexican-American,* and *Latino* are neutral, purely descriptive words—census talk—*Chicano* not only says what you are but that you're proud to be it. It doesn't mean Latino in general but the Southwest in particular. The best of many worlds rolled into one.

Los Angeles, City of the Angels, was founded in 1781 by Felipe de Neve and initially settled by Mexicans, blacks, Anglos, and the local Gabrielino Indians. The Mexicans who "immigrated" to L.A. didn't have to cross an ocean or a continent, only an invisible line on a map that separates

---

[*] See also Steven Loza, *Barrio Rhythm: Mexican American Music in Los Angeles* (Urbana: University of Illinois Press, 1993) and David Reyes and Tom Waldman, *Land of a Thousand Dances: Chicano Rock 'n' Roll from Southern California* (Albuquerque: University of New Mexico Press, 1998).

[†] *Source:* Rubén Guevara, "The View from the Sixth Street Bridge: The History of Chicano Rock," in Dave Marsh, ed., *The First Rock & Roll Confidential Report* (New York: Pantheon, 1985), pp. 113–21.

regions that once were one, still irreversibly connected by longstanding familial, historical, and cultural ties. L.A.'s roots run deep and the roots are Mexican.

The first great wave of immigrants came in the 1870s from Sonora, Mexico, settling in what is now Chinatown. The area was called Sonora-town and eventually grew into what is now called The Flats along the L.A. River. Around the turn of the century, Mexicans moved into Boyle Heights, which was mostly Jewish, and into Lincoln Heights, which was mostly Italian. Then came the second great wave during the Mexican Revolution of 1910. By 1923, Whittier Boulevard had been built, and by 1930 there were over 100,000 Mexicans living in Los Angeles.

In what was to become a constant pattern of push/pull, immigration/deportation, open/shut, during the Depression 64,000 residents—one third of whom were U.S. citizens—were removed from their homes and jobs and sent back to Mexico. This was called "repatriation." Depressing times for real, but at least there was music. In the mid-thirties, teens would go to party at playgrounds and parks. The music was usually traditional Mexican folk, boleros, and mariachi. Later in the decade, dance halls became popular. There was the Bowery Ballroom downtown at Ninth and Grand, where Sal's Deluxe Big Band, probably the first Chicano dance band, used to play. It was a horn band playing swing, jitterbug, and traditional Mexican music—sort of like Bob Wills from the other side of the Rio Grande. Two of the other popular house bands at the Bowery, the George Brown Band and the Irwin Brothers, were black. But since there were still very few blacks in L.A., the crowd was mostly Chicanos.

The Forties: You Might As Well Jump

In East L.A., as in so many other places, the link between swing and early R&B and rock & roll was jump blues. Jump evolved in the thirties from Harlem bands like those of Cab Calloway and the Kansas City groups of Count Basie and Louis Jordan. In Los Angeles the leading early practitioners were Roy Milton and the Solid Senders. When it became financially impossible to maintain a big swing orchestra, Milton cut his band down to ten pieces. Singer-turned-drummer-turned-conductor Roy Milton instructed his drummer to accent the 2 and 4 beats of a bar. Thus, the back beat of rock was born. By the end of the war it was being heard across the country as the Kansas City refugee reached national prominence with his 1945 hit "R. M. Blues," on Specialty Records.

Zoot Music, Zoot Riots

Although thousands of Mexican families had called the City of Angels home for four generations, East L.A. remained separate and most unequal from the dominant mainstream Anglo parts of the city. This was due to social and economic discrimination, the language barrier, and the need for new arrivals from Mexico to have an area where they had some chance to escape the long arm of immigration officials. Such environments force people to build a protective shell from behind which they can secure, preserve, and expand their music, art, and culture.

One expression of that in East Los was the emergence of the Pachuco in the early forties. Pachucos were Chicano gang members who wore the outlandish zoot suit as a statement of defiance to the Anglo establishment. Pachucos originally came from El Paso (El 'Chuco) and were identifiable by a small cross with three dots or rays tattooed on the left hand between the thumb and first finger.

Pompadoured, in his tailored "drapes," strutting with his girlfriend, and swinging his long gold chain, he cut a most impressive figure. The girls—Pachucas—would wear their hair stacked and sported modified zoot coats called "fingertips." The Pachuco was L.A.'s first modern rebel, the epitome of cool. Unfortunately, he was too cool.

With the outbreak of World War II, southern California was thrown into a state of hysterical paranoia. The war against Japan was perceived by many as a war against all people of color, at home and abroad. In 1942, following the shipment of hundreds of thousands of Japanese-Americans to internment camps, the tension between white servicemen stationed in California and Pachucos began to increase. As Luis Rodriguez wrote in the *L.A. Weekly,* "By mid-1943, anti-Chicano sentiment in Los Angeles reached its height, spurred on by newspaper articles about a 'huge Mexican crime wave,' 'zoot suit gangsters,' and a new breed of 'scum' known as Pachucos. In June, sailors rampaged out of L.A. Harbor and into Chicano neighborhoods, where they grabbed and beat lone 'zooters,' leaving them in bloody heaps to be arrested by the police. As a result, whole neighborhoods on the Eastside turned into armed camps, battles ensued, and there were an estimated 112 casualties.

"The riots were 'officially' stopped when the naval officer in charge ordered the sailors back to base. By then the Chicanos had gained support from black, Filipino, and even a few Anglo brothers."

The bitter irony of the event was that the U.S. government, with the advent of the war, had stopped deporting Mexicans and instead began drafting them into the armed forces, where they won more medals per capita than any other nationality.

While East L.A. was and is an enclave, the isolation of the community was only one side of the story of the development of Chicano rock. The flip side was the impact of technological change, reflected in the development of an unlikely pair: modern farming and the radio. It was the advent of modern methods of agriculture in the early 1940s that drove millions of blacks off the land in the South, and many were attracted to California by the relatively well-paying jobs in the burgeoning war industries.

The blacks settled in Mexican neighborhoods in East and South Central L.A. because that was where they could afford to live. Conversely, Anglos who lived nearby moved out because they could afford to. Blacks and Chicanos, isolated together, began to interact and, in large numbers, they listened to the same radio stations. For instance, there was Hunter Hancock ("Ol' H.H.") on KFVD. He had a show on Sundays called "Harlem Matinee," which featured records by Louis Jordan, Lionel Hampton, and locals Roy Milton, Joe and Jimmy Liggins, and Johnny Otis.

Johnny Otis moved to L.A. in 1943 from Tulsa, via Oakland, and by the end of the war was a mover and a shaker on the jump blues scene. When Johnny first played the Angelus Hall in 1948, introducing black jump blues to the Eastside, he caused quite a sensation. His swing didn't just swing. It jumped! And the Eastside jumped right along with him. Chicano jump bands began to form—the first was the Pachuco Boogie Boys, led by Raul Diaz and Don Tosti. They had a local hit, "Pachuco Boogie," which consisted of a jump-type shuffle with either Raul or Don rapping in *Galo* (Pachuco street slang: half Spanish, half English) about getting ready to go out on a date. Very funny stuff and another candidate for the title of the first rap record.

Pioneer record companies that would later help to spread R&B around the world were formed right and left in L.A. in the forties. Among them were Art Rupe's Specialty Records, Jules Bihari's Modern, and 4 Star, Exclusive, Aladdin, and Imperial.

East Coast musicians such as Tito Puente and Machito made appearances in Los Angeles in the mid-forties, introducing Afro-Cuban dance music that would later evolve into salsa. However, these out-of-towners performed mostly for Anglo show biz audiences in Hollywood clubs. Few Chicanos attended, not only because of the economic barrier a night on the town presented, but because the Latin musical traditions of countries such as Mexico, which didn't have slavery, are very different from those, such as Cuba or Brazil, that did.

The Fifties: At the Pachuco Hop

The fifties brought the Korean War, the Bracero Program (importation of temporary farm labor from Mexico), and the arrest and deportation of Mexican union and community organizers. In 1954 alone over a million Chicanos were deported. This continued a pattern that is still very much a part of life in the Southwest. When times are good, Mexican workers are allowed across the border into the United States, where they form a pool of cheap and easily controlled labor. But when times are hard, their contribution is forgotten and they are rounded up like animals and sent packing. But the fifties also saw the merging of diverse currents into something called rock & roll. This took place not only in Memphis, Chicago, and New Orleans, but in East L.A. as well.

DJs in L.A. played an important part in the development of local and regional sounds that often became a part of national hits. In 1952, Hunter Hancock broke a smokin' sax instrumental called "Pachuco Hop" by a black musician who lived on the Eastside, Chuck Higgins. A few years later, Hancock moved to KGFJ, which was the first local station to broadcast an all-black playlist seven days a week. A massive audience in East L.A. tuned in on each and every one of those days. At about the same time, DJs like Art Laboe and Dick "Huggy Boy" Hugg started playing jump and doo-wop on the radio.

Black jump sax players heard on the radio, such as Joe Houston, Big Jay McNeely, and Chuck Higgins, were a big influence on Chicano jump sax kingpins Li'l Bobby Rey and Chuck Rios. In the mid-fifties, a record came out on Laboe's Starla label entitled "Corrido Rock," by the Masked Phantom Band, which featured Rey. It's an instrumental with a couple of saxes playing a harmony Norteño riff over a fast rockin' back beat, predating Los Lobos by better than twenty years. Li'l Bobby went on to record "Alley Oop" with the Hollywood Argyles, while Chuck Rios and the Champs had a national hit in 1958 with the instrumental "Tequila."

In 1956 Johnny Otis discovered Li'l Julian Herrera, a singer who was Hungarian by birth but had been raised by Chicano parents. Herrera, heavily influenced by Jesse Belvin and Johnny Ace, was the first Eastside R&B star. With Johnny Otis, he cowrote "Lonely Lonely Nights," which became a major local hit. It's an elegant and beautiful doo-wop ballad, very much in the black style, but something about it—the accent, the voice, the *attitude*—made it different. It was Chicano rock. Otis introduced Li'l Julian to his growing audience at the legendary El Monte Legion Stadium, which became *the* dance hall in the late fifties and early sixties.

A typical weekend dance at the Legion would pack in crowds that were 90 percent Chicano, 10 percent Anglo. The dancers sported khaki pants with a Sir Guy shirt and a charcoal gray suit coat, one button roll, and spitshined French-toed shoes. The girls had stacked hair and wore white shoes called "bunnies," black tight short skirts, and feathered earrings. A lot of Anglo kids copied not only the styles but the dances, the most popular of which were the Pachuco Hop, Hully Gully, and the Corrido Rock.

Of all the dances, the Corrido was the wildest, sort of an early form of slam dancing. Two or three lines would form, people arm-in-arm, with each line consisting of 150 to 250 people. With the band blasting away at a breakneck rocking tempo, the lines took four steps forward and four steps back, eventually slamming into each other (but making sure that no one got hurt). The *corrido* is an old Mexican traditional folk story/song and dance that goes back to at least the mid-1800s, still very popular at weddings and dances today.

An evening at the Legion always ended with tight, slow dancing, called scrunching, usually to ballads by locals like "Handsome" Mel Williams or Vernon Green and the Medallions. After the dance, it was out to the parking lot for the grand finale. Where's the party? *Quien tiene pisto? Mota?* Who's got the booze? Weed? Rumors would fly all night as to which gangs were going to throw *chingasos*—come to blows. The Jesters Car Club from Boyle Heights, which dominated the Eastside, would parade around the parking lot in their lavender, maroon, or gray primered cars, wearing T-Timer shades (blue- or green-colored glass in square wire frames). In what was an inviolable ritual every weekend, the police would eventually break everything up and we'd caravan back to the Foster's Freeze at Whittier and Mott or to John-nies' at Whittier and Ditman.

The Sixties: The Golden Age of the Eastside Sound

The success of Ritchie Valens, a seventeen-year-old kid from the barrio in Pacoima, with "La Bamba" and "Donna" in 1958 sent a strong signal to aspiring Chicano musicians, myself included, that we could make it, too. It served to convince several independent producers that it might be worth their while to help us. By the early 1960s, bands were forming left and right and East L.A.'s golden age had begun.

Frequent "Battle of the Bands" shows held at East L.A. College were the focus of the action. The Motown sound was a very heavy influence on Eastside bands in spite of the fact that the relatively friendly relations between blacks and Chicanos that had existed in the immediate postwar era had been deteriorating for some time. The civil rights movement had, in some ways, awakened us to the reality that our two cultures were very different. Neighborhoods began to separate on the basis of race. Towards the late 1950s, serious gang problems began to surface between blacks and Chicanos, and in the 1960s affirmative action programs often wound up pitting us against each other for jobs. But one thing did unite us: Motown. Whether it was Marvin Gaye, the Temptations, or Mary Wells, it sounded good at the end of a day of hard work or no work, regardless of the color of your skin. There were even a few Eastside bands, such as the Mixtures and Ronnie and the Pomona Casuals, composed of blacks, whites, and Chicanos.

Independent producer Billy Cardenas envisioned a "Chicano Motown" label. To that end, he brought the Premiers to the attention of Eddie Davis, the most important Eastside producer. The collaboration resulted in a remake of the Don and Dewey chestnut "Farmer John," which reached Number 19 on the national charts in 1964. As Cardenas expanded his promotion of dances featur-ing Eastside bands to several different ballrooms (including the Shrine, which later would become the rough equivalent of the Fillmore), the pace began to quicken. Cannibal and the Headhunters became a staple on the ballroom circuit and then had a national Top 30 hit with their version of Chris Kenner's "Land of a Thousand Dances" in April of 1965. Later that year they opened for the Beatles on their American tour, with King Curtis backing them up.

Cannibal and the Headhunters' arch rivals at the battles of the bands were Thee Midniters. Fronted by the dynamic Li'l Willie G (Garcia), who drew his inspiration from James Brown, Thee Midniters recorded "Land of a Thousand Dances" before either Cannibal or Wilson Pickett, reach-ing Number 67 on the *Billboard* chart. They peaked later in the year when they released their anthe-mic instrumental "Whittier Boulevard" and appeared at the Rose Bowl before 38,000 people along with the Turtles, Herman's Hermits, and the Lovin' Spoonful.

Several other Eastside bands, such as Ronnie and the Pomona Casuals and the Salas Brothers, had local and regional hits. The big records from the Eastside became hits because they were dance tunes, party tunes, keeping right up with Motown's dance-oriented records, but without the slick-ness. Billy Cardenas did succeed artistically with his "Chicano Motown" concept, but not commer-cially. He was unable to build a commercial enterprise that could guarantee national distribution and promotion, and that limited the Eastside sound to a regional phenomenon. It was in some ways parallel to what happened with surf music. The more polished Beach Boys had across-the-board success, but very talented but looser bands with more emphasis on the local aspects of the subculture, like Dick Dale and the Del-Tones or the Challengers, never built any base of popularity outside southern California. Although there was little contact between surfers and the Eastside (except for fights at the beaches), there is no denying that almost all surf instrumentals are based on "Malagueña."*

The golden age of the Eastside sound was nearly as short-lived as Ritchie Valens' career. Nineteen sixty-four and 1965 were a brief but glorious high point, but we were done in not only by a lack of polish or promotion but also by the British invasion, which, ironically, exerted quite an influence on later records by groups like Thee Midniters. I well remember a night in late 1965 when my band and I were booed at the Hullabaloo, an important Hollywood club. The audience wanted to hear Beatles hits and nothing else. My experience was all too typical.

Another factor was the escalation of the war in Vietnam. Many Eastside musicians were drafted, a true irony when you consider that Ringo Starr has attributed the success of the British Invasion to the end of the draft in England, which allowed British kids to pursue careers as musicians.

Finally, the rock & roll business was becoming more nationally organized as the independent labels and producers that gave birth to the music got swallowed up by the major record companies. In turn, the majors began to merge with each other. This meant that decisions about who would be signed and who would tour and be promoted were made at a national level. The increasing rigidity of radio formats began to blur the local and regional distinctions on the dial and, as a result, made it much harder for a local act to build a base on hometown radio as a stepping-stone to the stars. In a country where most media executives continue to doubt the existence of the massive Latin market, success was made just that much more elusive for us.

The golden age of the Eastside sound was over well before the Tet offensive of 1968 put the Vietnam War on the minds of all Americans, including a million-plus East Los Angelenos.

---

* Composed by Cuban pianist and songwriter Ernesto Lecuona in 1927, "Malagueña" is a popular Latin music standard that has been recorded by numerous surf bands.

II

THE 1960S

9

Phil Spector and the Wall of Sound

RONNIE SPECTOR

Sandwiched between rock 'n' roll's supposed decline at the end of the 1950s and the rejuvenating arrival of the Beatles on America's shores in 1964, the explosive rise in popularity of early 1960s girl group music has often been trivialized and overlooked within mainstream histories of rock. And to the extent that rock histories have celebrated girl groups like the Ronettes, it has often been to praise the innovations of their Svengali-like male producers or the songwriting teams that provided them with their hits.[*] Lead singer Ronnie Spector of the Ronettes speaks from the perspective of the performer in the two following passages from her 1990 autobiography *Be My Baby*, offering a little seen window into the complex creative processes and inordinate power relationships behind the girl group phenomenon. In the first excerpt, Spector describes the genesis of the group's breakout hit, "Be My Baby," recorded in 1963 at Gold Star Studios in Los Angeles. The second excerpt rejoins the Ronettes in 1965, at which point their career was already in a state of decline (they would break up the next year). Reading these two passages from *Be My Baby*, it is hard to believe that Ronnie Spector (born Veronica Bennett, 1943) and her producer, Phil Spector (born 1940), were separated in age by only three years. Even though the two were romantically involved during the Ronettes' meteoric rise to success, Spector held a firm control over the young singer, inserting her as the final jigsaw puzzle piece in his celebrated "wall of sound." Ronnie would eventually marry Spector in 1968 only to divorce him in 1974.[†]

When we returned from California, the Ronettes went right back to work. Even though our Colpix singles had all flopped, we were always in demand as a live group. By 1963, all three of us were out of high school and playing with rock and roll variety shows like Clay Cole's Twisterama Revue. The following we developed at those shows—along with the fans we made at Murray the K's Brooklyn Fox revues—were all that kept us going before we met Phil.

Even before we ever had a hit record, we had a hard core of fans who followed us from show to show, and for some reason, a lot of them seemed to be gay men or lesbians. I'm not sure why. Maybe it was because we were half-breeds, and the gay crowd sensed that the Ronettes were outsiders just

---

[*] In recent years there have been many attempts to redress this imbalance as scholars have directed more emphasis to how girl groups and their singers provided a strong point of identification for adolescent female audiences. See in particular, Susan J. Douglas. "Why The Shirelles Mattered," in *Where The Girls Are: Growing Up Female With the Mass Media* (New York: Times Books, 1994), 83–99, and Jacqueline Warwick, *Girl Groups, Girl Culture: Popular Music And Identity In The 1960s* (New York: Routledge, forthcoming).

[†] *Source:* Ronnie Spector with Vince Waldron, *Be My Baby: How I Survived Mascara, Miniskirts, and Madness or My Life as a Fabulous Ronette* (New York: Harmony Books, 1990), pp. 49–55, 104–8.

like they were.* Whatever the reason, there was something about our style that spoke to a lot of gay people, because they've always been there for us. Even today I meet gay guys who saw the Ronettes at the Cafe Wha or the Bazaar in the Village, and they can still name every song we did at a show that happened twenty-five years ago.

In that long stretch before "Be My Baby," our live shows were the only place our fans could hear us. Even after Phil recorded our first song out in California, he refused to release it. When I asked him when "Why Don't They Let Us Fall in Love" was coming out, he answered without missing a beat.

"Never," he said.

I was shocked. I thought it was a pretty good record. But Phil just shook his head. "It's a good song," he told me. "But it's not a number-one record."

By this time I really believed that Phil actually could predict a number-one song, and I thought that was fantastic. "I'm still working on your first million-seller," he teased, "and it's almost finished. If you're a real nice girl, I might let you come over to my house to hear it."

I'd never been in a penthouse before—Phil's or anyone else's. So naturally, when I walked in I couldn't resist peeking into all the closets and poking around behind all the closed doors. I opened one door and was surprised to find a bedroom where six or seven pairs of women's shoes were scattered all over the floor. When I asked Phil who they belonged to, he nearly turned pink.

"Will you stop snooping around where you don't belong?" he snapped. I think it was the first time I ever saw Phil lose his temper.

"Okay, honey," I said. "I'm sorry." He must've noticed the hurt look in my eyes, because he softened his tone immediately.

"Those are my sister Shirley's shoes," he explained. "She stays here sometimes when she's in New York. Now," he said, changing the subject, "why don't you go into the other bedroom and watch TV? Jeff and Ellie are going to be here any minute to work on the song, and we don't want to be disturbed."

Phil was still very hush-hush about our relationship at that point, and he didn't want his writing partners to know I was there.† I didn't complain. I was too thrilled. I thought it was the greatest thing in the world to be sitting in the bedroom while my boyfriend wrote my first hit record in the next room. But what did I know? I also believed those were his sister's shoes spread out all over the floor.

If I had any doubts, I was too busy listening to what was going on in the living room to worry about them. I put my ear to the wall and tried to hear what Phil, Ellie Greenwich, and Jeff Barry were singing. It was hard to hear the words over Ellie's piano playing, but when they came around to the chorus, I could hear all three of them loud and clear. "Be my, be my baby," they sang. "Be my baby, now." I thought it was catchy, and I couldn't help wondering if that was what a number-one record sounded like.

Phil and I rehearsed that song for weeks before he would let me fly out to California to record it. But when that morning came, I knew the words to "Be My Baby" backwards and forwards.

I got up really early so my mother and I could catch the plane. Since I was going to sing lead, Phil wouldn't need Estelle and Nedra to do their backgrounds until later, so they stayed behind in New York for a few more weeks. I remember the morning I left, Estelle stuck her head out from under the sheets and said, "Don't forget to fill out the airplane insurance forms when you get to the airport." Airport insurance was a big thing with my family. Whenever one of my uncles would drop me off at the airport, it was always straight to the insurance stands.

---

* Throughout her autobiography Spector refers to all of the Ronettes (herself, her sister Estelle, and their cousin Nedra Talley) as half-breeds. Spector's mother was part "black and Cherokee," and her father was white; Nedra's father was Spanish.

† At that time Spector was still married to his first wife, Annette Merar.

My mother and I got in a cab, and I sang "Be My Baby" all the way out to LaGuardia. I wanted to be so perfect, I couldn't rehearse it enough. I even made my mother wait in the airport bathroom with me while I sang through it a few times more. We must've stayed in there a little too long, because by the time we got out we'd missed our plane.

Then my mother did something I'd never seen her do before. She sat down and sighed. Right there in the airport waiting room, she just let out a big sigh like she was real tired all of a sudden. "Ronnie, sit down here with me," she said, patting the brown cushion of the airport couch. "I think you're at the age where you can go out there and sing "Be My Baby' all by yourself now, so I don't think I'm gonna go all the way out there to California with you this time." Then I kissed her good-bye and got on the next plane all by myself.

When I landed in California, Phil picked me up at the airport in his big limousine and drove me straight to Gold Star Studios. Gold Star's Studio A was old and really tiny, but that was the only place he ever recorded anymore, because he knew he could get sounds out of that room that he couldn't get anywhere else. It had something to do with the acoustics. The room was so small, the sound seemed to bounce off the walls, creating a natural echo that made every song recorded there sound fuller.

And Phil loved that, because he was always experimenting with ways to make his sound as big as possible. Instead of having one guitarist playing rhythm, he would have six. Where someone else might use one piano, Phil would have three. He'd have twin drum sets, a dozen string players, and a whole roomful of background singers. Then he'd record everything back on top of itself to double the sound. Then he'd double it again. And again. And again and again, until the sound was so thick it could have been an entire orchestra. That's what Phil was talking about when he told a reporter that his records were like "little symphonies for the kids."

Watching Phil record the background music for "Be My Baby," I finally understood what he meant when he stopped me that time and said, "That's it! That's the voice I've been looking for." He knew from the first second he heard me that my voice was exactly what he needed to fill in the center of this enormous sound. Phil had been trying to construct this giant wall of sound ever since he got started in the record business, and when he heard me, he knew my voice was the final brick.

I was always surprised at how much Phil used me when he had singers like Fanita James and Darlene Love around. When I'd hear them singing with those great big gospel voices, I'd start to wonder what was so special about my little voice. But I have to give Phil credit. He loved the way I sang, and he knew exactly what to do with my voice. He knew my range. He knew my pitch. He even knew which words sounded best coming out of my mouth. He knew that "Be My Baby" was a perfect song for me, so he constructed the whole record around my voice from the ground up.

It took about three days to record just my vocals for "Be My Baby." I was so shy that I'd do all my vocal rehearsals in the studio's ladies' room, because I loved the sound I got in there. People talk about how great the echo chamber was at Gold Star, but they never heard the sound in that ladies' room. And, between doing my makeup and teasing my hair, I practically lived in there anyway. So that's where all the little "whoa-ohs" and "oh-oh-oh-ohs" you hear on my records were born, in the bathroom at Gold Star.

Then, when I finally did go into the studio, I'd hide behind this big music stand while I sang, so Phil and Larry Levine wouldn't see me with my mouth all popped open when I reached for a high note. I'd keep the lyric sheet right in front of my face, and then, after I finished a take, I'd peep out from behind my music stand and look through the window to see how Phil and Larry liked it. If they were looking down and fooling with the knobs, I'd know I had to do it again. But if I saw they were laughing and yelling "All right!" or "Damn, that little girl can really sing!" I'd know we had a take. Since my approach to each song was completely up to me, watching Phil and Larry react afterward was the only real feedback I ever got.

Recording at Gold Star in those days was like one big party. Phil always got the best musicians in town to play at his sessions, guys like Hal Blaine, Nino Tempo, Leon Russell, Barney Kessel, and Glen Campbell. Jack Nitzsche did all of our early arrangements, and the guy was a genius. Then there was Larry Levine, who engineered all our songs. Phil had so many good people working for him that it really was a joy to go into work.

But the biggest fun of all came when it was time to lay down the background vocals, because Phil always invited everyone in the whole studio to join in. If you were standing around and could carry a tune, you were a background singer in Phil's wall of sound. And everybody Phil knew seemed to show up the day we did the backgrounds for "Be My Baby." Darlene Love was there, and we had Fanita James from the Blossoms, Bobby Sheen from Bob B. Soxx and the Blue Jeans, Nino Tempo, Sonny Bono—who was Phil's gofer in those days—and Sonny's girlfriend, who was a gawky teenager named Cher.

I have to be honest—the first time I saw Cher, I thought she was a hooker. It was in a hotel room where I was supposed to meet Phil for a rehearsal. She and Sonny were already in the room sitting at the piano when I walked in. And when I saw this skinny young kid with her long black hair and thick mascara, I just assumed she was a call girl from the hotel. Then Sonny introduced her as his girlfriend, and I was so embarrassed, I just had to laugh. After a few minutes I could tell that she was really just a sweet kid, and we got to be friends.

We would meet in the bathroom at Gold Star to tease our hair. Sitting over the sink, we would share black eyeliner and gossip. We were about the same age, and we both had stars in our eyes, so it was only natural that we would hit it off. I had fun with Darlene and Fanita and the other girls who sang for Phil, but I never felt like I could talk to them the way I did with Cher. I was probably closer to her than to anyone outside of my family in those days. And as time went on, Cher and I began to see that we had a lot more in common than just bangs and makeup.

Sonny always acted extremely jealous of Cher. And when I got out to California, I started to notice that Phil could get pretty possessive of me, too. Neither of them liked for us to go off on our own. But Phil seemed to trust Cher, so she and I spent a lot of time together while Phil and Sonny worked in the studio. We'd go shopping together, or we'd spend the day at the movies. Other days we'd just drive around in Cher's little red MG, looking at all the strange sights of Hollywood.

As soon as we finished "Be My Baby," I flew right back to New York, where the Ronettes were scheduled to start a two-month tour of the East Coast with Joey Dee and the Starliters. One of our first stops was Wildwood, New Jersey. I'll always remember that town, because that was where we heard "Be My Baby" for the first time. It was one of those moments that changes your life forever.

Nedra, Estelle, and I were sleeping late in our motel room on the Saturday morning after our first show in Wildwood. In those days all three Ronettes would share one big bed, and Mom or Aunt Susu would usually sleep in the other one. By the time I woke up that morning, Mom had already gone out to get breakfast, so I walked over and turned the TV on to find "American Bandstand," which we woke up to every Saturday, just like every other teenager in America. You would turn it on even if you were still half-asleep, because you didn't want to miss the latest records.

Even though I was barely awake, I could hear Dick Clark talking about how this next record was guaranteed to be the hit of the century. I couldn't wait to hear what this thing could be. Then I heard "boom-ba-boom-boom"—the drumbeat that starts off "Be My Baby." Even though I was sitting up in bed, I was convinced that I'd fallen back asleep and was only dreaming that Dick Clark was playing our record on "American Bandstand." But if I was dreaming, Estelle and Nedra were having the same dream, because they sprang upright in bed and started staring at the TV, same as me. After that I nearly passed out right there in that motel room.

We sat there for about a minute watching all those happy teenagers dancing to our record. Then Nedra and I ran out to the terrace to tell Joey Dee and the guys, who were all swimming around in the pool.

"Hey, guys!" I yelled. "Get up here. Dick Clark's playing our record!"

It was like we couldn't really believe that this was happening unless we had witnesses.

Joey and the guys ran up the stairs just in time to catch the end of our song. Then they hugged us, and we hugged them. And then we all laughed and sang and enjoyed what it feels like to be on top of the world.

A few minutes later Phil was on the phone. He was as surprised as we were to see the record taking off so fast—or so he said. He told us the Ronettes would have to leave Joey Dee's tour immediately so we could get back to New York to promote the record. Of course, Joey Dee wasn't very happy to hear that. But he didn't want to stand in our way, so he finally did let us out of the tour.

* * *

Even after the Ronettes' slump began in 1965, I didn't get too concerned. Phil had just scored the biggest smash of his career with "You've Lost That Lovin' Feeling," by the Righteous Brothers, and he was still as hot as ever. So I figured it was just a matter of time before he turned his attention back to my career.

It wasn't like he could ignore me. I'd practically been living with him since he moved into the mansion on La Collina. Whenever I came out to California, that is. Which actually wasn't that often in 1965, since the Ronettes had personal appearances booked solid throughout the year.

And I was having so much fun onstage with the Ronettes, I didn't have time to worry about our failing recording career. I still had my audience, and I could tell by their applause that they still loved me. Before long, though, I think Phil even grew jealous of them.

We did one of our biggest shows ever in late November, when Phil put us in *The Big T.N.T. Show,* which was a concert he produced in Hollywood that was being filmed for release as a movie. Phil was the orchestra leader for a lineup that included some of the biggest names in rock, including Ray Charles, the Byrds, and the Ike and Tina Turner Revue. Of course, Phil had to be in complete control whenever he produced anything, and this show was no exception.

When the technicians asked us to do some of our act during rehearsal, we ran through our routine just to give the camera guys a basic idea of what we did. We didn't give them a full performance, because we wanted to save that for the show. But Phil was in charge—and he wanted to make sure everyone knew it–so he stopped us in the middle of the rehearsal and started barking out orders at us like we were in the chorus or something.

"Hold it, girls," he commanded. "You're just walking through it. I'd like you to start again, and this time, I want you to do it just like you're going to do it tonight."

That was ridiculous. We'd been doing the same basic routines ever since we started at the Brooklyn Fox, but our act always changed a little bit each night, depending on the audience response. The only thing you could be sure of was that we never ever did exactly the same show twice. But Phil insisted, so we went ahead and played our entire act to this empty theater.

"That wasn't so hard, was it?" he called out after we finished. "Do it *exactly* like that tonight."

That night we did our act the same way we always did it—flat out crazy. I shimmied around the stage and danced wherever the feeling took me. The crowd was up for grabs, but I think it was too much for Phil.

The director and all the cameramen told us how exciting it was, and the other acts all said the nicest stuff. But Phil hated it. He came up to me after the show, steaming mad. "What did you think you were doing out there?" he shouted. I hated it when Phil got like that, but I knew the only thing I could do was humor him until the mood passed.

"What's wrong?" I asked. "Was there something wrong with our routine?"

"It was all wrong," he snapped. "It looked completely different tonight than it did this afternoon."

"But there was no audience then," I explained. "You know I always play the house."

"*Play the house?*" he exclaimed. "You were all over the place. Out of control." That was a big thing with Phil. If I lost control in front of a crowd, he hated it because that meant that I was out of *his* control.

"And on top of everything else, you came in off key!" He could only ever criticize my singing for technical reasons, because he knew I didn't read music, so I couldn't argue. "Don't bother coming to the party after the show," he ordered. "I don't want to see you there!"

I went straight back to my hotel room and cried. I suppose I could've gone to the party anyway, but I never even considered it. I just couldn't go against Phil's wishes in those days. I was like a little Japanese geisha girl walking five paces behind her master. Phil couldn't control what I did once I got out onstage, but that wasn't a problem he had in our personal life.

Of course, he dominated me most of all in the recording studio. After the hamburger incident with Sonny Bono, I knew Phil didn't want me getting too friendly with the other singers and musicians at Gold Star.* He never really came out and said so—he didn't have to. He had more charming ways of getting me to do what he wanted.

Once when I was doing backgrounds with a bunch of people at Gold Star, this big fat singer named Olla got me laughing. She was always saying something that cracked me up, and this time I was doubled up with laughter when I happened to catch a peek at Phil, who was smiling at me from behind his glass window in the control room. "Ronnie," he said, waving me into the booth. "Come on in here."

When I got there, Phil pulled up an old wooden stool and motioned for me to sit down on it. Then he turned back to work at the mixing board. "Uh, Phil?" I asked. "What was it you wanted?"

"Nothing, really," he admitted, looking a little embarrassed. "I just felt like I could use some inspiration in here."

It was such a sweet thing to say, and so flattering. Up until then, Phil had always tried to keep up the illusion that our relationship was purely professional. But by inviting me to sit next to him in the control booth, he was admitting to the whole world that I was someone special. I sat straight up on that rickety old stool and felt like a queen.

From then on I always sat in the booth with Phil. He seemed to really enjoy having me in there with him, and it made me feel like a privileged character. Phil would make jokes about whoever happened to be standing on the other side of the glass, and they were especially funny because no one could hear them but me and Larry Levine.

And I also got to watch Phil at work, which was always a thrill. He would sit there in his booth with the speakers blasting so loud I thought he must have been going deaf. But then he would hear something in the mix that no one else could, and he would motion for Larry to stop the tape. One time I saw him point to the end violinist in a row of ten and say, "You. Sounds like you're a little flat. Check your A string." The guy checked his tuning, and Phil was right. It was amazing.

A lot of people have asked me how Phil created his wall of sound, but to understand Phil's sound, you have to understand Phil. The wall of sound was really just a reflection of his own

---

* Ronnie had left to get a hamburger with Sonny Bono during a lull in a recording session without informing Spector. In her absence, Spector proceeded to go into a rage and trash Gold Star Studios.

personality, which was very extravagant. When Phil made a record, he might start out with the same basic tracks as everyone else—drums, guitars, bass, and vocals. But then he'd always add in more sounds, because he wanted his records to be as extravagant as he was. He didn't have any use for a record unless it was at least ten times bigger than life. Phil was one guy who believed that *more* is more.

When he walked into a recording studio, Phil was always looking for a new rule he could break. He wasn't afraid to try anything. I remember there was this little meter on the tape machines that told you how loud the volume was, and it had a needle that would go into the red zone whenever the sound got too loud or distorted. Well, everyone in the record business lived in fear of making that needle go into the red—but not Phil. Sometimes I think he was only really happy when he was in that red zone.

After being in the studio with Phil for a time, it was only natural that you'd get caught up in his madness. Everyone who worked for him did. With Phil as our inspiration, we'd try to push ourselves as hard as he pushed himself. When I'd sing a lyric, I'd close my eyes and try to feel the truest emotion I could find. And I'd keep pushing myself until I got there. Then Phil would add that sound to the sounds of all the other singers, musicians, and engineers. And the result would be a wonderful combination of textures and personalities and genius that people started calling the wall of sound. You can say what you want about Phil Spector, but no one who was there at Gold Star can ever forget the music we made. No one had ever heard anything like it before, and they'll never hear anything like it again.

As much as I loved hanging around the booth with Phil, it wasn't long before I started to miss being out in the studio with the crowd. But the first time I tried to leave the booth and join in on the fun in the studio, Phil made it clear that my place was with him and only him.

"Where are you going, Ronnie?" Phil asked when I got up from my stool.

"I'm just going out to sing a few of these backgrounds with the guys."

"No, no, no," he said. "I don't want you doing that anymore."

"But, Phil," I argued. "Everybody sings backups."

"Not you, Ronnie," he said. "Your voice is too distinctive. It comes right through."

"Well," I suggested, "maybe I could just go 'oooh,' real low." But Phil wouldn't budge. So while everyone else was laughing and joking and smoking cigarettes, I'd sit there watching them in silence from behind my glass wall.

10

The Beatles, Press Conference, 1964

The Beatles arrived at New York's Kennedy Airport on February 7, 1964, officially sparking the British Invasion that would drastically reshape the face of rock music in the mid-1960s. From their very first steps off the plane, the band found themselves the subjects of intense public scrutiny. While much of their success stemmed from their recordings, it was also the group's charm, wit, and absurdist, self-deprecating humor that endeared the Beatles to the American media. They were the first rock group to use the press conference as their own personal platform, both establishing and playfully mocking their distinctive personas. Historically, Paul was known as the "cute" one, John the "smart" one, George the "quiet" one, and Ringo the "funny" one.[*]

Question: Do any of you have any formal musical training?

John: You're joking.

Question: What do you think of President Johnson?

Paul: Does he buy our records?

Question: What do you think of American girls and American audiences?

John: Marvelous.

Question: Here I am, surrounded by the Beatles, and I don't feel a thing. Fellas, how does it feel to be in the United States?

John: It's great.

Question: What do you like best about our country?

John: You!

Question: I'll take that under advisement. Do you have any plans to meet the Johnson girls?

John: No. We heard they didn't like our concerts.

Question: Are they coming to your performance tonight?

Paul: If they do, we'd really like to meet them.

Question: You and the snow came to Washington today. Which do you think will have the greater impact?

John: The snow will probably last longer.

Question: One final question. Have you ever heard of Walter Cronkite?

Paul: Nope.

John: *NBC News*, is he? Yeah, we know him.

Question: Thanks, fellas. By the way, it's *CBS News*.

George: I know, but I didn't want to say it as we're now on ABC.

---

[*] *Source:* "The Beatles, Press Conference, Washington, DC, February 11, 1964," in Geoffrey Giuliano, ed., *The Lost Beatles Interviews* (New York: Plume, 1994), pp. 12–14.

Question: This is NBC, believe it or not.

John: And you're Walter?

Question: No, I'm Ed.

John: What's going on around here?

Question: What do you think of your reception in America so far?

John: It's been great.

Question: What struck you the most?

John: You!

Ringo: We already did that joke when we first came in.

George: Well, we're doing it again, squire!

Question: Why do you think you're so popular?

John: It must be the weather.

Question: Do you think it's your singing?

Paul: I doubt it. We don't know which it could be.

Question: Where'd you get the idea for the haircuts?

John: Where'd you get the idea for yours?

Paul: We enjoyed wearing our hair this way, so it's developed this way.

Question: Well you save on haircutting at least.

Paul: Roar...

John: I think it costs more to keep it short than long, don't you?

Paul: Yeah, we're saving our money.

Question: Are you still number one in Europe?

George: We're number one in America.

Question: Where else are you number one then?

John: Hong Kong and Sweden...

Paul: Australia, Denmark, and Finland.

Question: And you haven't any idea why?

Ringo: We just lay down and do it.

John: In Hong Kong and these other places, suddenly you're number one years after putting out your records. Even here, we've got records we've probably forgotten.

Question: You call your records "funny records"?

John: "Funny," yeah, the ones we've forgotten.

George: It's unusual because they've been out in England for over a year. Like "Please, Please Me" is a big hit over here now, but it's over a year old.

Question: Do you think they're musical?

John: Obviously they're musical because it's music, isn't it! We make music. Instruments play music. It's a record.

Question: What do you call it, rock and roll?

Paul: We try not to define our music because we get so many wrong classifications off it. We call it music even if you don't.

Question: With a question mark?

George: Pardon?

John: We leave that to the critics.

Question: Okay, that's it. Have a good time in America.

John: Thank you. Keep buying them records and look after yourself.

11

"Beatlemania Frightens Child Expert"

DR. BERNARD SAIBEL

From its etymological roots in "madness" and "lunacy" to its more current usage in psychiatry as a hyperactive mental disorder, the word "mania" has long served as a marker for irregular and potentially destructive behavior. Given this history, it should come as little surprise that the arrival of Beatlemania in the United States—punctuated by large demonstrative crowds of hysterically sobbing and screaming teenage girls—aroused the attention of numerous sociologists, pop psychologists, and behavioral specialists.[*] In keeping with this spirit, the *Seattle Daily Times* arranged for its own child expert, Dr. Bernard Saibel (the supervisor of the Washington State Division of Community Services) to attend and report on the Beatles' August 21, 1964, concert at the Seattle Center Coliseum. Saibel's alarmed response, fearful of the sexually charged "orgy" that was unfolding before him, demonstrates the degree to which Beatlemania was indeed perceived as a *mania*, and one that thrust into the media spotlight the moral concerns surrounding teenage female sexuality.[†]

The experience of being with 14,000 teen-agers to see the Beatles is unbelievable and frightening. And, believe me, it is not at all funny, as I first thought when I accepted this assignment.

The hysteria and loss of control go far beyond the impact of the music. Many of those present became frantic, hostile, uncontrolled, screaming, unrecognizable beings. If this is possible—and it is—parents and adults have a lot to account for to allow this to go on.

This is not simply a release, as I at first thought it would be, but a very destructive process in which adults allow the children to be involved—allowing the children a mad, erotic world of their own without the reassuring safeguards of protection from themselves.

The externals are terrifying. Normally recognizable girls behaved as if possessed by some demonic urge, defying in emotional ecstasy the restraints which authorities try to place on them.

The hysteria is from the girls and when you ask them what it is all about, all they can say is: "I love them."

Some, restrained from getting up on the stage after the Beatles left, asked me to touch the drums for them.

---

[*] See, for example, A.J.W. Taylor, "Beatlemania—A Study of Adolescent Enthusiasm," *British Journal of Social and Clinical Psychology* 5 (September 1966): 81–88. For an insightful analysis of the Beatlemania phenomenon and female sexuality in the 1960s, see Barbara Ehrenreich, Elizabeth Hess, and Gloria Jacobs, "Beatlemania: Girls Just Want to Have Fun," in *The Adoring Audience: Fan Culture and Popular Media*, edited by Lisa A. Lewis (New York: Routledge, 1992), 84–106.

[†] *Source:* Dr. Bernard Saibel, "Beatlemania Frightens Child Expert," *Seattle Daily Times*, August 22, 1964, p. 1.

There are a lot of things you can say about why the Beatles attract the teen-age crowd.

The music is loud, primitive, insistent—strongly rhythmic and releases in a disguised way (can it be called sublimation?) the all too tenuously controlled, newly acquired physical impulses of the teen-ager.

Mix this up with the phenomena of mass hypnosis, contagious hysteria and the blissful feeling of being mixed up in an all-embracing, orgiastic experience and every kid can become "Lord of the Flies" or the Beatles.

What is it all about?

Why do the kids scream, faint, gyrate and in general look like a primeval, protoplasmic upheaval and go into ecstatic convulsions when certain identifiable and expected trademarks come forth such as "Oh, yeah!," a twist of the hips or the thrusting out of an electric guitar?

Well, this music (and the bizarre, gnome like, fairy tale characters who play it) belongs to the kids and is their own—different, they think, from anything that belongs to the adult world.

Every time a teen-ager screams over this music he thumbs his nose with impunity and with immunity at an adult or several adults.

Besides, kids, like the other separate and distinct parts of humanity, are competitive. If there is a youngster who can scream loudly, there is one who can scream louder.

If there is one who belongs to the cognoscenti (those in the know), there is one who is more sensitive and more appreciative of this art than any of the others. And to prove it, she faints and all can see how much more affected she is, because she has to be carried out on a stretcher — a martyr, a victim of her capacity for deep understanding and overwhelming emotion.

Regardless of the causes or reasons for the behavior of these youngsters last night, it had the impact of an unholy bedlam, the like of which I have never seen. It caused me to feel that such should not be allowed again, if only for the good of the youngsters.

It was an orgy for teen-agers.

12

George Martin
On the Beatles

Often referred to as "the fifth Beatle," producer George Martin (born 1926) was instrumental in the group's development and success, especially after the Beatles ceased touring in 1966 and became solely studio recording artists. Martin not only worked with the Beatles on all their arrangements (scoring their orchestral parts, for example), but he also performed crucial keyboard lines on songs like "In My Life" and many others. In the following excerpts from his autobiography, the producer describes The Beatles' evolution from the one-day recording session in 1963 that resulted in *Please, Please Me* to the elaborate studio collaborations in 1966 and 1967 that would lead to the release of *Sgt. Pepper's Lonely Heart's Club Band*. Along the way, Martin sketches out how rock music expanded across the middle of the decade from a compact, singles-oriented style to a more ambitious, self-consciously experimental medium. Martin also spends considerable time discussing the intersections between popular music and art music practices, and how these figured into the songwriting tendencies of both John Lennon (1940–1980) and Paul McCartney (born 1942).*

After the success of 'Please Please Me' I realised that we had to act very fast to get a long-playing album on the market if we were to cash in on what we had already achieved. Because, while a single which sells half a million doesn't reap all that great a reward, half a million albums is big business. I knew their repertoire from the Cavern, and I called the boys down to the studio and said: 'Right, what you're going to do now, today, straight away, is play me this selection of things I've chosen from what you do in the Cavern.† There were fourteen songs in all, some by the Beatles, some by the American artists whom they liked to copy. We started at ten that morning, with Norman Smith as the balance engineer, and recorded straight on to twin-track mono. By eleven o'clock at night we had recorded the lot, thirteen new tracks, to which we added the existing recording of 'Please Please Me'.

All we did really was to reproduce the Cavern performance in the comparative calm of the studio. I say 'comparative', because there was one number which always caused a furore in the Cavern—'Twist and Shout'. John absolutely screamed it. God alone knows what he did to his larynx each time he performed it, because he made a sound rather like tearing flesh. That *had* to be right on the first take, because I knew perfectly well that if we had to do it a second time it would never be as good.

Like its namesake single, the album rapidly went to number one, and because of the popularity of 'Twist and Shout' (which was not actually a Beatles song) we issued an EP with that and three

* *Source:* George Martin with Jeremy Hornsby, *All You Need Is Ears* (New York: St. Martin's Griffin, 1979), pp. 130–33, 137–40, 199–202, 205–6.
† The "Cavern" is the Cavern Club in Liverpool, where the Beatles played on a regular basis between 1961 and 1963.

other titles. It too went to number one in the singles charts, the first time an EP had done so. The boys were elated with their success. I asked them for another song as good as 'Please Please Me', and they brought me one—'From Me to You'. I said, 'I want more.' Along came 'She Loves You'.

There seemed to be a bottomless well of songs, and people have often asked me where that well was dug. Who knows? To begin with, they'd been playing about at writing songs since they were kids, and had a large amount of raw material which simply needed shaping. A lot of the songs we made into hits started life as not very good embryos. When they had first played me 'Please Please Me', it had been in a very different form.

The way that Lennon and McCartney worked together wasn't the Rodgers-and-Hart kind of collaboration. It was more a question of one of them trying to write a song, getting stuck, and asking the other: 'I need a middle eight. What have you got?' They were both tunesmiths in their own right, and would help each other out as the need arose. In the early days, that was a matter of necessity. But as they developed their art, each moved on to writing songs entirely on his own. Collaboration became rare, apart from the odd word or line: it was either a John Lennon song or a Paul McCartney song. We established the working format that whoever wrote the song generally sang it, and the others would join in. If it were John's song, he would sing it, and when we came to the middle eight – the section in the middle of a song where the tune changes—Paul would sing thirds above or below, or whatever; if a third part were needed, George would join in. It was a very simple formula.

I would meet them in the studio to hear a new number. I would perch myself on a high stool, and John and Paul would stand around me with their acoustic guitars and play and sing it—usually without Ringo or George, unless George joined in the harmony. Then I would make suggestions to improve it, and we'd try it again. That's what is known in the business as a 'head arrangement', and we didn't move out of that pattern until the end of what I call the first era. That was the era which lasted through 'Love Me Do', 'Please Please Me', 'From Me to You', 'She Loves You', and 'I Want to Hold Your Hand', which were the first batch of recordings.

At that point there wasn't much arranging to do. My function as producer was not what it is today. After all, I was a mixture of many things. I was an executive running a record label. I was organising the artists and the repertoire. And on top of that, I actually supervised the recording sessions, looking after what both the engineer and the artist were doing. Certainly I would manipulate the record to the way I wanted it, but there was no arrangement in the sense of orchestration. They were four musicians—three guitarists and a drummer—and my role was to make sure that they made a concise, commercial statement. I would make sure that the song ran for approximately two and a half minutes, that it was in the right key for their voices, and that it was tidy, with the right proportion and form.

At the beginning, my speciality was the introductions and the endings, and any instrumental passages in the middle. I might say, for instance: "'Please Please Me' only lasts a minute and ten seconds, so you'll have to do two choruses, and in the second chorus we'll have to do such-and-such." That was the extent of the arranging. Again, the way they first sang 'Can't Buy Me Love' was by starting on the verse, but I said: "We've got to have an introduction, something that catches the ear immediately, a hook. So let's start off with the chorus." It was all really a matter of tidying things up. But that record was the point of departure for something rather more sophisticated.

With 'Yesterday' we used orchestration for the first time; and from then on, we moved into whole new areas. The curious thing is that our relationship moved in two different directions at once. On the one hand, the increasing sophistication of the records meant that I was having a greater and greater influence on the music. But the personal relationship moved in the other direction. At the start, I was like a master with his pupils, and they did what I said. They knew nothing about recording, but heaven knows they learned quickly: and by the end, of course, I was to be the servant while they were the masters. They would say, 'Right, we're starting tonight at eight o'clock,' and I would be there. It was a gradual change of power, and of responsibility in a way, because although at the end I still clung to putting in my two cents' worth, all I could do was influence. I couldn't direct.

* * *

I have often been asked if I could have written any of the Beatles' tunes, and the answer is definitely no: for one basic reason. I didn't have their simple approach to music. Of the four, Paul was the one most likely to be a professional musician, in the sense of learning the trade, learning about notation and harmony and counterpoint. At that time he was friendly with Jane Asher, who came from a musical family. Her mother was a fine musician, a freelance teacher who by sheer coincidence had taught me the oboe when I was at the Guildhall. I think that that family must have had quite an influence on Paul.

Soon after we got together he started taking piano lessons. I, on the other hand, bought myself a guitar and started to teach myself that. There was good reason for both: in the early stages there was a certain lack of communication, and we had to find common ground in which to talk about music. If I suggested a particular complicated chord or harmony to them, and they didn't know it, I would go and play it on the piano and say: 'Look, this kind of thing.' Then they would get their guitars and start trying to find the same notes on them. But they wouldn't get it very readily, because although they could see my fingers on the piano, that didn't mean much to them. All they could try to work out was the sounds they were hearing. But if I played the chord on the guitar myself, they would be able to look at my fingers and say: 'Oh, yes. It's that kind of shape.' With both the guitar and the piano you can learn a great deal from the shape of the player's fingers. But the two instruments are very different, and there's no way of extrapolating from one to the other—which is why I started the guitar. John and Paul, however, learned the piano far more quickly than I could master their instrument. So I dropped the guitar.

But at least we now had a rapport, and could talk to each other about particular notes. There's no doubt that Lennon and McCartney were good musicians. They had good musical brains, and the brain is where music originates—it has nothing to do with your fingers. As it happened, they could also play their own instruments very well. And since those early days they've all improved, especially Paul. He's an excellent musical all-rounder, probably the best bass-guitar player there is, a first-class drummer, brilliant guitarist and competent piano-player.

But those accomplishments didn't affect their extremely practical approach to music. They simply couldn't understand the need for complication. For example, John once came to me while I was working in the studio with a saxophone section, overdubbing one of his tunes. 'Look,' he said, 'I like what you've done there, but I think it would be a good idea if the saxes did such-and-such...', and with that he picked up his guitar and played me some notes.

'Yes, that's quite easy,' I said. 'It'll be a good idea for the saxes to reinforce that.' I quickly wrote out the notes, turned to the saxophone players and said, 'O.K., chaps, these are the notes you play.'

'No,' said John, 'they're not those notes. These are the notes they play – look...' and he proceeded to play them to me all over again.

'I know, John,' I explained. 'They're the notes that you're playing. But I'm giving them the notes for their instruments that will correspond to what you're playing.'

'But you've given them the wrong names of the notes!'

'No, I haven't,' I said. 'Because their instruments are in different keys. That's an E flat saxophone, and that's a B flat saxophone. When you play a C on that one, it sounds in B flat. When you play a

C on the other saxophone it plays an E flat. So I've got to work out other notes to compensate for that. Do you see?'

'That's bloody silly, isn't it?' he said in disgust.

'Yes, I suppose it is.'

He turned and walked away and left me to it. He just couldn't understand one of those silly little facts of life. Equally, I think that if Paul, for instance, had learned music 'properly'—not just the piano, but correct notation for writing and reading music, all the harmony and counterpoint that I had to go through, and techniques of orchestration—it might well have inhibited him. He thought so too. (And after all, why should he bother, when he had someone around who could do it for him?) Once you start being taught things, your mind is channelled in a particular way. Paul didn't have that channelling, so he had freedom, and could think of things that I would have considered outrageous. I could admire them, but my musical training would have prevented me from thinking of them myself. I think, too, that the ability to write good tunes often comes when someone is not fettered by the rules and regulations of harmony and counterpoint. A tune is a one-fingered thing, something that you can whistle in the street; it doesn't depend upon great harmonies. The ability to create them is simply a gift.

There have been many great musicians who couldn't write a pop tune to save their lives. Equally, the pop world in particular has seen many who have known nothing of music but could write great tunes. Lionel Bart, for example, can't play an instrument. I believe he just whistles his tunes as he thinks of them. Irving Berlin couldn't read music, and could only play the piano in the key of G flat, which is all the black notes. He only played on the black notes. It was the only way he knew. Once he had some success, he could afford to have a special piano built for him. It had a lever at the side, like a fruit-machine, and if he wanted to change key while keeping his fingers on the same notes, he just pulled that.*

*   *   *

The time had come for experiment. The Beatles knew it, and I knew it. By November 1966 we had had an enormous string of hits, and we had the confidence, even arrogance, to know that we could try anything we wanted. The sales we had achieved would have justified our recording rubbish, if we had wanted to. But then, we wouldn't have got away with foisting rubbish on the public for long.

The single of 'Yellow Submarine' and 'Eleanor Rigby', and the album *Revolver*, had been issued in August that year. So it was several months since we had been in the studio, and time for us to think about a new album. 'New' was certainly how it was to turn out.

I suppose the indications were already there. 'Eleanor Rigby' and 'Tomorrow Never Knows', from *Revolver*, had been strong hints for those with ears to hear what was to come. They were fore-runners of a complete change of style. Even I didn't realise at the time how significant it was, nor the reasons for it. Flower Power and the hippy and drug revolution had been taking place, affecting the boys in front of my very eyes, yet my own brand of naïvety had prevented me from seeing the whole thing for what it really was. I hardly knew what pot smelled like, although it was right under my nose! But I did realise that something was happening in the music, and that excited me.

Strangely, the *Sergeant Pepper* album originated with a song which was never on it, 'Strawberry Fields'. That November John came into the studio, and we went into our regular routine. I sat on my high stool with Paul standing beside me, and John stood in front of us with his acoustic guitar and sang the song. It was absolutely lovely. Then we tried it with Ringo on drums, and Paul and George on their bass and electric guitars. It started to get heavy—it wasn't the gentle song that I had first

---

* A "fruit machine" is the British name for a slot machine.

heard. We ended up with a record which was very good heavy rock. Still, that was apparently what John wanted, so I metaphorically shrugged my shoulders and said: 'Well, that really wasn't what I'd thought of, but it's O.K.' And off John went.

A week later he came back and said: 'I've been thinking about it, too, George. Maybe what we did was wrong. I think we ought to have another go at doing it.' Up to that time we had never remade anything. We reckoned that if it didn't work out first time, we shouldn't do it again. But this time we did. 'Maybe we should do it differently,' said John. 'I'd like you to score something for it. Maybe we should have a bit of strings, or brass or something.' Between us we worked out that I should write for cellos and trumpets, together with the group. When I had finished we recorded it again, and I felt that this time it was much better. Off went John again.

A few days later he rang me up and said: 'I like that one, I really do. But, you know, the other one's got something, too.'

'Yes, I know,' I said, 'they're both good. But aren't we starting to split hairs?'

Perhaps I shouldn't have used the word 'split', because John's reply was: 'I like the beginning of the first one, and I like the end of the second one. Why don't we just join them together?'

'Well, there are only two things against it,' I said. 'One is that they're in different keys. The other is that they're in different tempos.'

'Yeah, but you can do something about it, I know. You can fix it, George.'

John always left this kind of thing to me. He never professed to know anything about recording. He was the least technical of the Beatles. He had a profound faith in my ability to cope with such problems, a faith which was sometimes misplaced, as I certainly felt it was on this occasion. He had presented me with an almost insuperable task. But I had to have a go. I listened to the two versions again, and suddenly realised that with a bit of luck I might get away with it, because, with the way that the keys were arranged, the slower version was a semitone flat compared with the faster one.

I thought: If I can speed up the one, and slow down the other, I can get the pitches the same. And with any luck, the tempos will be sufficiently close not to be noticeable. I did just that, on a variable-control tape machine, selecting precisely the right spot to make the cut, to join them as nearly perfectly as possible. That is how 'Strawberry Fields' was issued, and that is how it remains today—two recordings.

The next song we recorded was 'When I'm Sixty-Four'; that was much simpler. It was the kind of vaudeville tune which Paul occasionally came up with, and he said he wanted 'a kind of tooty sound'. So I scored it for two clarinets and a bass clarinet. I remember recording it in the cavernous Number One studio at Abbey Road, and thinking how the three clarinet players looked as lost as a referee and two linesmen alone in the middle of Wembley Stadium.

Following that came 'Penny Lane', which started life as a fairly simple song. But Paul decided he wanted a special sound on it, and one day, after he had been to a concert of Bach's Brandenburg Concerti, he said: 'There's a guy in them playing this fantastic high trumpet.'

'Yes,' I said, 'the piccolo trumpet, the Bach trumpet. Why?'

'It's a great sound. Why can't we use it?'

'Sure we can,' I said, and at that he asked me to organise it for him. Now, the normal trumpet is in B flat. But there is also the D trumpet, which is what Bach mostly used, and the F trumpet. In this case, I decided to use a B-flat piccolo trumpet, an octave above the normal. To play it I engaged David Mason, who was with the London Symphony Orchestra. It was a difficult session, for two reasons. First, that little trumpet is a devil to play in tune, because it isn't really in tune with itself, so that in order to achieve pure notes the player has to 'lip' each one.

Secondly, we had no music prepared. We just knew that we wanted little piping interjections. We had had experience of professional musicians saying: 'If the Beatles were real musicians, they'd know what they wanted us to play before we came into the studio.' Happily, David Mason wasn't like that at all. By then the Beatles were very big news anyway, and I think he was intrigued to be playing on one of their records, quite apart from being well paid for his trouble. As we came to each little section where we wanted the sound, Paul would think up the notes he wanted, and I would write them down for David. The result was unique, something that had never been done in rock music before, and it gave 'Penny Lane' a very distinct character.

Then came Christmas, and we agreed to get together again after they had written some more material. But in the meantime EMI and Brian Epstein had told me that they needed another single, since they hadn't had one for a while. I said: 'O.K. It means we'll have to find extra material for the album, but let's couple the best two we have so far—'Strawberry Fields' and 'Penny Lane'—and issue them as a double-A-sided record.' To this day I cannot imagine why that single was beaten to the number one spot, because for my money it was the best we ever issued. But there it was, and now we were left with 'When I'm Sixty-Four' on its own for the new album.

We started work again in February 1967, and the boys began bringing in the various songs they had written. But 'Sergeant Pepper' itself didn't appear until halfway through making the album. It was Paul's song, just an ordinary rock number and not particularly brilliant as songs go. Nor was there anything difficult or special about the recording of it. But when we had finished it, Paul said, 'Why don't we make the album as though the Pepper band really existed, as though Sergeant Pepper was making the record? We'll dub in effects and things.' I loved the idea, and from that moment it was as though *Pepper* had a life of its own, developing of its own accord rather than through a conscious effort by the Beatles or myself to integrate it and make it a 'concept' album.

* * *

Compared with Paul's songs, all of which seemed to keep in some sort of touch with reality, John's had a psychedelic, almost mystical quality. 'Lucy in the Sky with Diamonds' was a typical John song in that respect, and a lot of analysts and psychiatrists were later to describe it as the drug song of all time. They were talking rubbish, but the tag stuck. I was very offended recently when I saw a television programme about the drug raid, Operation Julie, in which some major world suppliers of LSD were rounded up. The programme was prefaced with 'Lucy', as though it were *the* drug song—a 'fact' which people have taken as finally proven simply because 'Lucy', 'Sky' and 'Diamonds' happen to start with the letters LSD.

The gospel truth of the matter is that Julian, John's young son, came home from school one day carrying a picture of a little girl in a black sky with stars all round her. John asked if he had done the picture, and when Julian said he had, John asked him, 'What is it, then?'

Julian's best friend at school was a little girl called Lucy, and he replied, 'It's Lucy, in the sky, with diamonds.'

John's imagery is one of the great things about his work—'tangerine trees', 'marmalade skies', 'cellophane flowers'. I hope it doesn't sound pretentious, but I always saw him as an aural Salvador Dali, rather than some drug-ridden record artist.

On the other hand, I would be stupid to pretend that drugs didn't figure quite heavily in the Beatles' lives at that time. At the same time they knew that I, in my schoolmasterly role, didn't approve, and like naughty boys they would slope off into the canteen, lock the door and have their joints. Not only was I not into it myself, I couldn't see the need for it; and there's no doubt that, if I too had been on dope, *Pepper* would never have been the album it was. Perhaps it was the combination of dope and no dope that worked, who knows? The fact remains that they often got very giggly, and it frequently interfered with our work.

13

"Understanding Dylan"

Paul Williams

One of the first major rock critics, Paul Williams launched the influential *Crawdaddy!* magazine in 1966, while still a freshman at Swarthmore College. At the time, serious examinations of rock music were rarely to be found in the popular press. One of Williams's first significant articles, "Understanding Dylan" tackles the subject of rock's most opaque poet, a figure whose complex lyrics virtually begged to be analyzed. What do we gain, Williams asks, from scrutinizing the songs of Bob Dylan (born Robert Zimmerman, 1941), specifically those from his then most recent release, *Blonde on Blonde*? Are we searching for some hidden significance that we can attach to Dylan's biography or some clue to the music's cultural context? Williams's stance is clear throughout. Such undertakings, he argues, are misguided; Dylan's music is an art form that should be experienced, not interpreted. Williams's opinions are radical and debatable, even more so because they echo almost to the word, contentious sentiments that had been bubbling over in the world of art and literary criticism, most notably in philosopher Susan Sontag's provocative 1964 essay "Against Interpretation."* By aggressively digging at a text to unearth its meaning, Sontag believed that modern critics were becoming numb to art's more immediate formal properties. What was instead needed, she argued, was an "erotics of art," one that would restore the primacy of art's sensory experience while celebrating its surface transparency. Similarly Williams insists that if we are to "understand" the substance of Dylan's rock 'n' roll poetry, we must approach it on an experiential level.†

Perhaps the favorite indoor sport in America today is discussing, worshiping, disparaging, and above all interpreting Bob Dylan. According to legend, young Zimmerman came out of the west, grabbed a guitar, changed his name and decided to be Woody Guthrie. Five years later he had somehow become Elvis Presley (or maybe William Shakespeare); he had sold out, plugged in his feet, and was rumored to live in a state of perpetual high (achieved by smoking rolled-up pages of *Newsweek* magazine). Today, we stand on the eve of his first published book (*Tarantula*) and the morning after his most recent and fully realized LP (*Blonde on Blonde*), and there is but one question remaining to fog our freshly minted minds: what in hell is really going on here?

Who is Bob Dylan, and—this is the question that is most incessantly asked—what is he really trying to say? These are not, as such, answerable questions; but maybe by exploring them we can

---

* Susan Sontag, "Against Interpretation," *Evergreen Review*, 8, no. 34 (December 1964): 76–80, 93; Reprinted in *Against Interpretation and Other Essays,* (New York: Farrar, Straus & Giroux, 1966), 3–14.

† *Source:* Paul Williams, "Understanding Dylan," *Crawdaddy!*, August 1966. Reprinted in *Outlaw Blues: A Book of Rock Music* (New York: E.P. Dutton, 1969), pp. 59–69.

come to a greater understanding of the man and his songs. It is as an approach to understanding that I offer you this essay.

Everyone knows that Dylan came east from the North Country in 1960, hung around the Village, and finally got a start as a folksinger. If you're interested in biographical information, I recommend a book with the ridiculous title of *Folk-Rock: The Bob Dylan Story*.* The authors' attempts at interpretations of songs are clumsy, but the factual portion of the book is surprisingly reasonable (there is no such word as "accurate"). The book perpetuates a few myths, of course (for instance, the name Dylan actually comes from an uncle of Bob's and *not* from Dylan Thomas); and it has its stylistic stumblings. But for just plain (irrelevant) biographical info, the book is worth your 50 cents.

There are a few things about Dylan's past that *are* relevant to understanding his work (or to not misunderstanding it), however, and these appear to be little known. His roots are deep in country music and blues: he lists Percy Mayfield and Charlie Rich among the musicians he admires most. But he did not start out as a "folksinger," not in the currently accepted sense. From the very beginning his desire was to make it in the field of rock and roll.

In 1960, however, rock and roll was not an open field. The songs were written in one part of town, then sent down to the recording companies in another part of town where house artists recorded them, backed by the usual house bands. A country kid like Dylan didn't stand a chance of getting into rock and roll, and it did not take him long to find that out. The only way he could get anyone to listen to him—and the only way he could keep himself alive—was to start playing the coffeehouses. This got him a recording contract and an interested audience, as well as a reputation as a folksinger, and it was one of the luckiest things that ever happened to him. First of all, it put him under pressure to produce; and nothing better can happen to any young writer. Secondly, it made him discipline his songwriting, and though he may have resented it at the time, it was this forced focusing of his talents that made them emerge. You have to learn some rules before you can break them.

But it was inevitable that "folk music" would only be a temporary harbor. "Everybody knows that I'm not a folk singer," he says; and, call him what you will, there is no question that by the time *Another Side of Bob Dylan* appeared he was no longer thinking his songs in terms of simple guitar accompaniments (to a certain extent, he never had been). He was straining at the bit of folk music's accepted patterns, and fearing, perhaps rightly so, that no one was interested in what he wanted to say any more. But then "Tambourine Man" caught on, and people began responding to him as a man and not as a politician. The light was green: he'd been working very hard on a very important song, and he decided he was going to sing it the way he heard it. That was "Like a Rolling Stone," and its success meant that from now on he could do a song any way he wanted. "I knew how it had to be done," he says; "I went out of my way to get the people to record it with me."

It was a breakthrough. He was into the "rock and roll field" for real now, but of course he is no more a rock and roll singer than a folksinger. He is simply an artist able to create in the medium that for him is most free.

I have gone into this background only because there continues to be so much useless misunderstanding, so much talk about "folk-rock," so much discussion of "the old Dylan" and "the new Dylan." Until you, as a listener, can hear *music* instead of categories, you cannot appreciate what you are hearing. As long as people persist in believing that Dylan would be playing his new songs on a folk guitar instead of with a band, except that recording with a band brings him more money, they will fail to realize that he is a creator, not a puppet, and a creator who has reached musical maturity. Dylan is doing his songs now the way he always wanted to do them. He is a bard who has

---

* Sy and Barbara Ribakove, *Folk-Rock: The Bob Dylan Story* (New York: Dell Publishing Co., 1966).

found his form, no more, no less; and if you're interested in what he's saying, you must listen to him on his own terms.

It is my personal belief that it is not the artist but his work that is important; therefore, I hesitate to go too deeply into the question of *who* Bob Dylan is. Owl and Churchy once had a fantastic fight over whether a certain phrase actually fell from the lips of Mr. Twain, or Mr. Clemens.* And someone has pointed out that nobody knows if the *Odyssey* was written by Homer or by another early Greek poet of the same name. Perhaps I don't make myself clear. I only want to point out that if we found out tomorrow that Bob Dylan was a 64-year-old woman who'd changed her sex, and a proven Communist agent, we might be surprised, but the words to "Mr. Tambourine Man" would not change in the slightest. It would still be the same song.

I will say, to dispel any doubts, that Mr. Dylan is not a 64-year-old woman or an agent of anything. I met him in Philadelphia last winter; he is a friendly and straightforward young man, interested in what others are saying and doing, and quite willing to talk openly about himself. He is pleased with his success; he wanted it, he worked for it honestly, and he's achieved it. We talked about the critics, and he says he resents people who don't know what's going on and pretend they do. He named some names; it is my fervid hope that when this article is finished, and read, my name will not be added to the list.

It is difficult to be a critic; people expect you to *explain* things. That's all right if you don't know what's going on … you can make up almost any clever-sounding explanation, and people will believe you. But if you do understand a poem, or a song, if it is important to you, then chances are you also understand that you're destroying it if you try to translate it into one or two prose sentences in order to tell the guy next door "what it means." If you could say everything that Dylan says in any one of his songs in a sentence or two, then there would have been no point in writing the songs. The sensitive critic must act as a guide, not paraphrasing the songs but trying to show people how to appreciate them.

One problem is that a lot of people don't give a damn about the songs. What interests them is whether Joan Baez is "Queen Jane," or whether or not Dylan dedicated "Tambourine Man" to the local dope peddler. These people, viewed objectively, are a fairly objectionable lot; but the truth is that all of us act like peeping toms now and then. Dylan himself pointed this out in a poem on the back of *Another Side*. He wanders into a mob, watching a man about to jump off the Brooklyn Bridge; "I couldn't stay an' look at him/because I suddenly realized that/deep in my heart/I really wanted/to see him jump." It is a hard thing to admit that we are potential members of the mob; but if you admit it, you can fight it—you can ignore your curiosity about Dylan's personal life and thoughts, and appreciate his generosity in offering you as much as he has by giving you his poems, his songs. In the end you can know Bob Dylan much better than you know your next door neighbor, because of what he shows you in his songs; but first you have to listen to his songs, and stop treating him as though he lived next door.

Another problem, and in a way a much more serious one, is the widespread desire to "find out" what Dylan's trying to say instead of listening to what he is saying. According to him: "I've stopped composing and singing anything that has either a reason to be written or a motive to be sung.... The word 'message' strikes me as having a hernia-like sound." But people go right on looking for the "message" in everything Dylan writes, as though he were Aesop telling fables. Not being able to hear something, because you're too busy listening for the message, is a particularly American

---

* Owl and Churchy are two characters from the satirical comic strip *Pogo*. Mark Twain was the pen name of Samuel Clemens.

malady. There's a tragic lack of freedom in being unable to respond to things because you've been trained to await the commercial and conditioned to listen for the bell.

Take a look at a great painting, or a Polaroid snapshot. Does it have a message? A song is a picture. You see it; more accurately, you see it, taste it, feel it ... Telling a guy to listen to a song is like giving him a dime for the roller coaster. It's an experience. A song is an experience. The guy who writes the song and the guy who sings it each feel something; the idea is to get you to feel the same thing, or something like it. And you can feel it *without knowing what it is*.

For example: you're a sixth grader, and your teacher reads you Robert Frost's "Stopping by the Woods on a Snowy Evening." The poem sounds nice; the words are perhaps mysterious, but still powerful and appealing. You don't know what the poem "means," but you get this feeling; the idea of having "miles to go before I sleep" is a pretty simple one, and it means a lot to you. The poet has reached you; he has successfully passed on the feeling he has, and now you have it too.

Years later you read the poem again, and suddenly it seems crystal clear that the poem is about death, and the desire for it. That never occurred to you as a sixth grader, of course; does that mean you originally misunderstood the poem? Not necessarily. Your teacher could say "We want the peace death offers, but we have responsibilities, we are not free to die"; but it wouldn't give you anything. It's a sentence, a platitude. You don't even believe it unless you already know it's true. What the poet does is something different: walking through the woods, he gets a feeling that is similar to the idea your teacher offered you in a sentence. But he does not want to tell you what he believes; that has nothing to do with you. Instead, he tries to make you feel what he feels, and if he succeeds, it makes no difference whether you understand the feeling or not. It is now a part of your experience. And whether you react to the poem as a twelve-year-old, or an English professor, it is the feeling you get that is important. Understanding is feeling ... the ability to explain means nothing at all.

The way to "understand" Dylan is to listen to him. Listen carefully; listen to one song at a time, perhaps playing it over and over to let it sink in. Try to see what he's seeing—a song like "Visions of Johanna" or "Sad-Eyed Lady of the Lowlands" (or almost any of his more recent songs) is full of pictures, moods, images: persons, places and things. "Inside the museums," he sings, "infinity goes up on trial." It doesn't *mean* anything; but you know what a museum feels like to you, and you can see the insides of one, the particular way people look at things in a museum, the atmosphere, the sort of things that are found there. And you have your image of a trial, of a courtroom: perhaps you don't try to picture a lazy-eight infinity stepping up to the witness chair, but there's a solemnity about a trial, easily associable with the image of a museum. And see how easily the feeling of infinity slips into your museum picture, endless corridors and hallways and rooms, a certain duskiness, and perhaps the trial to you becomes the displaying of infinity on the very walls of the museum, like the bones of an old fish, or maybe the fact that museums do have things that are old in them ties in somehow ... there's no *explanation*, because the line (from "Visions of Johanna," by the way) *is* what it is, but certainly the line, the image, can turn into something living inside your mind. You simply have to be receptive ... and of course it is a prerequisite that you live in a world not too unlike Dylan's, that you be aware of museums and courtrooms in a way not too far different from the way he is, that you be able to appreciate the images by having a similar cultural background. It is not necessary that you understand mid-century America and the world of its youth in order to understand Dylan; but you do have to be a part of those worlds, or the songs will lose all relevance. This is true of most literature, in a way; and of course Dylan has his elements of universality as well as his pictures of the specific.

I *could* explain, I suppose. I could say that "Memphis Blues Again" is about displacement, and tell you why Dylan would think of a senator as "showing everyone his gun." But the truth is, that wouldn't give you anything. If you can't feel it, you can't get anything out of it; you can sneer and say "It's commercialism" or "It's about drugs, and I'm above it," but not only are you dead wrong, you're irrelevant.

In many ways, understanding Dylan has a lot to do with understanding yourself. For example, I can listen to "Sad-Eyed Lady of the Lowlands" and really feel what the song is about, appreciate it; but I have no idea why "a warehouse eyes my Arabian drums" or what precise relevance that has. Yet it does make me feel something; the attempt to communicate is successful, and somehow the refrain "Now a warehouse eyes my Arabian drums" has a very real relevance to me and my understanding of the song. So it isn't fair to ask Dylan what the phrase means, or rather, why it works; the person I really have to ask is the person it works on—me. And *I* don't know why it works—i.e., I can't explain it. This only means I don't understand me; I do understand Dylan—that is, I appreciate the song as fully as I believe is possible. It's the example of the sixth grader and Robert Frost all over again.

If you really want to understand Dylan, there are perhaps a few things you can do. Read the poems on the backs of his records; read his book when it comes out; read the brilliant interview that appeared in last April's *Playboy*.* But above all listen to his albums; listen carefully, and openly, and you will see a world unfold before you. And if you can't see his songs by listening to them, then I'm afraid that all the explaining in the world will only sink you that much deeper in your sand trap.

We have established, I hope, that art is not interpreted but experienced (whether or not Dylan's work is art is not a question I'm interested in debating at the moment. I believe it is; if you don't, you probably shouldn't have read this far). With that in mind, let's take a cursory look at *Blonde on Blonde*, an excellent album which everyone with any admiration for the work of Bob Dylan should rush out and buy at once.

Two things stand out: the uniform high quality of the songs (in the past Dylan's LPs have usually, in my opinion, been quite uneven) chosen for this extralong LP; and the wonderful, wonderful accompaniments. Not only is Dylan's present band, including himself on harmonica, easily the best backup band in the country, but they appear able to read his mind. On this album, they almost inevitably do the right thing at the right time; they do perfect justice to each of his songs, and that is by no means a minor accomplishment. *Blonde on Blonde* is in many ways—the quality of the sound, the decisions as to what goes where in what order, the mixing of the tracks, the timing, etc.—one of the best-produced records I've ever heard, and producer Bob Johnston deserves immortality at least. Certainly, Dylan's songs have never been better presented.

And they really are fine songs. It's hard to pick a favorite; I think mine is "Memphis Blues Again," a chain of anecdotes bound together by an evocative chorus ("Oh, Mama, can this really be the end, To be stuck inside of Mobile with the Memphis blues again?"). Dylan relates specific episodes and emotions in his offhand impressionistic manner, somehow making the universal specific and then making it universal again in that oh-so-accurate refrain. The arrangement is truly beautiful; never have I heard the organ played so effectively (Al Kooper, take a bow).

"I Want You" is a delightful song. The melody is attractive and very catchy; Dylan's voice is more versatile than ever; and the more I listen to the musicians backing him up the more impressed I become. They can't be praised enough. The song is lighthearted, but fantastically honest; perhaps what is most striking about it is its inherent innocence. Dylan has a remarkably healthy attitude toward sex, and he makes our society look sick by comparison (it is). Not that he's trying to put down

---

* The *Playboy* interview to which Williams is alluding (and which appeared in the March 1966 issue) is reprinted in *Bob Dylan: A Retrospective*, edited by Craig McGregor (New York: William Morrow & Company, 1972), pp. 124–45. Like many of his interviews from this period, Dylan comes across as a deliberately evasive subject, responding to journalist Nat Hentoff's straightforward queries with nonsensical, absurdist answers.

anybody else's values—he simply says what he feels, and he manages to make desire charming in doing so. That is so noble an achievement that I can forgive him the pun about the "queen of spades" (besides, the way he says, "I did it ... because time is on his side" is worth the price of the album).

"Obviously Five Believers" is the only authentic rock and roll song on the record, and it reflects Dylan's admiration of the early rock and rollers. Chuck Berry and Larry Williams are clear influences. "I'd tell you what it means if I just didn't have to try so hard," sings Bob. It's a joyous song; harp, guitar, vocal, and lyrics are all groovy enough to practically unseat Presley retroactively.

"Rainy Day Women #'s 12 & 35" (the uncut original) is brilliant in its simplicity: in a way, it's Dylan's answer to the uptight cats who are searching for messages. This one has a message, and it couldn't be clearer, or more outrageously true. *Time* magazine is just too damn stoned to appreciate it.

I could go on and on, but I'm trying hard not to. The album is notable for its sense of humor ("Leopard Skin Pillbox Hat" and "Pledging My Time" and much else), its pervading, gentle irony (in "4th Time Around," for example), its general lack of bitterness, and above all its fantastic sensitivity ("Sad-Eyed Lady of the Lowlands" should become a classic; and incidentally, whoever decided it would sound best alone on a side, instead of with songs before it and after it, deserves a medal for good taste).

"(Sooner or Later) One of Us Must Know" is another favorite of mine: in its simplicity it packs a punch that a more complex song would often pull. "Visions of Johanna" is rich but carefully subdued ("The country music station plays soft but there's nothing really nothing to turn off" ... I love that); Dylan's world, which in *Highway 61* seemed to be bubbling over the edges of its cauldron, now seems very much in his control. Helplessness is still the prevalent emotion ("Honey, why are you so hard"), but chaos has been relegated to the periphery. Love (and sex, love's half-sister) are all-important, and love, as everyone knows, has a certain sense of order about it, rhyme if not reason. No one has to ask (I hope) what "I Want You" is about, or "Absolutely Sweet Marie." Or "Just Like a Woman," which I want to cut out of the album and mail to everybody. The songs are still a swirl of imagery, but it is a gentler, less cyclonic swirl; more like autumn leaves. The nightmares are receding.

Blonde on Blonde is a cache of emotion, a well-handled package of excellent music and better poetry, blended and meshed and ready to become a part of your reality. Here is a man who will speak to you, a 1960's bard with electric lyre and color slides, a truthful man with X-ray eyes you can look through if you want. All you have to do is listen.

14

Motown
A Whiter Shade of Black

JON LANDAU

Diana Ross and The Supremes, Stevie Wonder, Smokey Robinson and the Miracles—Motown's famed roster virtually defined the height of pop sophistication in the 1960s. Modeling his label's sound on the successful assembly-line production of Detroit's Ford Motor Company, Berry Gordy (born 1929) fashioned a durable hit single formula. The songwriting team of Eddie Holland (born 1939), Lamont Dozier (born 1941), and Brian Holland (born 1941) provided a host of memorable melodies, the Funk Brothers contributed their propulsive rhythm section arrangements, and soulful singers like Levi Stubbs of The Four Tops added their voice and image. The author of "A Whiter Shade of Black," music journalist Jon Landau, would later go on to greater fame in the 1970s as Bruce Springsteen's manager and producer. In this 1967 article, originally published in *Crawdaddy!* magazine, Landau examines the Motown style as a form of musical crossover designed to appeal equally to white and black audiences. Like many other observers, he also contrasts Motown with the more "hard core" sounds of the Stax-Volt label. Landau identifies many of Motown's most characteristic elements, from song forms to details of instrumentation. What he outlines is nothing less than a formula for success, and one whose features have been replicated throughout rock's history, from the 1970s Philadelphia soul explosion to the various regional hip-hop production teams that have dominated popular music in the 2000s.[*]

Traditionally there have been three types of Negro musicians in pop music. The first consists of artists who for either aesthetic or financial reasons have chosen to sever their ties with specifically Negro music and instead work in the general field of pop. Richie Havens, as an exponent of the contemporary urban ballad in the Ochs-Dylan-Paxton tradition, and Jimi Hendrix, as an exponent of freaking out, are good examples. The second class consists of performers who are still working in one of the basic Negro musical forms but who seek to alter their approach enough to make it appealing to a large part of the white audience. Motown is the ideal example, but someone like Lou Rawls also falls into this category. Finally there is the hard core: performers who won't or can't assimilate, and therefore just continue to do their thing. If the white audience digs what a performer in this group is doing, it's just gravy; the performer never expected it. This category contains all of the independent R&B labels, most importantly the Stax-Volt group in Memphis, Tennessee.

Obviously the first group identified above is irrelevant in a discussion of Negro music because performers in this group are working in musical idioms which are not distinctively Negro. Motown,

[*] *Source:* Jon Landau, "A Whiter Shade of Black," *Crawdaddy!*, October 1967. Reprinted in Jonathan Eisen, ed., *The Age of Rock: Sounds of the American Cultural Revolution* (New York: Vintage Books, 1969), pp. 298–306.

as the basic representative of the second group, seeks a white audience but maintains a basically Negro identity, and is a logical starting point for any survey of Negro pop.

Motown is two things above all. It is a place and a form. By the first I mean that it is a community, obviously tightly knit, made up of a group of people all aiming at the same thing. By the second I mean that the music that this community makes is stylized to express precisely what Motown wants it to by use of recurring techniques, patterns, and other devices. In the evolution of Motown the community clearly came first, and a brief look at how Motown began will help us clarify what the Motown form is, and why it takes the form that it does.

When Motown began is not altogether clear. Legend has it that Berry Gordy, Jr., the man who runs the place, quit a job on a Detroit assembly line nine or ten years ago, borrowed some money, and began his rise to success instantly. The history of Motown shows us that it was not all that simple. It is a fact that almost a decade ago Berry Gordy was already in the music business writing for one of the greatest of all Motown performers, although he has never recorded on a Motown label, Jackie Wilson. (Wilson, who was clearly a major influence on Smokey Robinson, has always recorded for Brunswick.) The first records that Gordy produced for his own labels were written by himself, starting around 1960, perhaps earlier. Two of the earliest Motown tunes were Barrett Strong's "Money" and the Contours' "Do You Love Me?" Both of these songs seem remarkably unsophisticated compared to what the typical Motown song-writing team of today throws out, even for flip-side material. Both of these records were in fact indistinguishable from the general R&B of the day. "Do You Love Me?"—the later of the two—even has the old-fashioned twist drumming, a rarity on the oldest of Motown records.

It appears that the first major move Gordy made in his attempt to build Motown was to bring William "Smokey" Robinson into the picture. At first Gordy collaborated with Smokey in writing tunes for Smokey's legendary Miracles. After four or five duds, their joint labors resulted in the spectacular "Shop Around." This was one of the early big ones for the Motown organization and it was not only a financial success but an aesthetic one, with Robinson's faultless lead earmarking the Miracles as something far above the rank and file of R&B vocalists.

Smokey gradually moved up in the organization. But while he was struggling to make a name for the Miracles, other talent was being brought into the picture. Mary Wells, Marvin Gaye, the Marvelettes, Little Stevie Wonder, and the Supremes were all gradually added to the roster. When back-up vocalists were needed for records by big stars, a former Motown secretary named Martha Reeves organized a trio—Martha and the Vandellas. Motown soul records with big booming commercial arrangements were making it into the pop charts. Marvin Gaye put two straight blues, "Wonderful One" and "Can I Get a Witness," right up there, and a little twelve-year-old kid named Stevie Wonder sold a million copies of one of the freakiest Motown records ever, "Fingertips, Pt. II." The community was clearly developing at breakneck speed in the early sixties, but there was still no form. Individual successes were common but they were not based on any specific Motown style. Motown was still just an electric grouping of artists not readily distinguishable from the rest of souldom except by virtue of the fact that they generally did what they did better than anyone else around.

The Motown form came in 1963–64, with the advent of the Supremes. During the pre-Supremes era a Motown vocalist named Eddie Holland had been occasionally releasing singles, mostly poor imitations of Jackie Wilson. Over a period of time he, Brian Holland, and Lamont Dozier formed a song-writing-and-producing team. They had their first significant opportunities to develop their style with Martha and the Vandellas, and they wrote and produced many of the girls' early hits: "Come and Get These Memories," "Quicksand," "Livewire," and "Heatwave."

Apparently the Vandellas could only go so far. Martha has a straight, tough, soul voice and probably was not the right type for the more commercial records being planned. So attention was soon turned to the Supremes. The one advantage Diana Ross had over Martha, on a record, was her cooling sexy voice. This was coupled with the consummated Holland-Dozier-Holland writing-producing concept, and the result, after a few failures, was fantastic financial success. There can be no doubt that "Where Did Our Love Go" and the follow-up, "Baby Love," set the direction for the future of Motown. With these two records, H-D-H and the Supremes had created the Motown definition of success. Each of these records was the product of a carefully thought out, highly distinctive musical form that had been a long time in coming. When the formula paid off, Motown lost no time in refining the form, stylizing it, and imposing it on all of their artists, one way or another.

What then is this Motown style? It is a distinctive approach to all facets of record making, especially rhythm, melody, instrumental sound, and vocal arranging. With regard to rhythm the most important thing is Motown drumming. Up until the time of H-D-H the most common pattern of drumming was for the drummer to hit the snare on the second and fourth beats of every measure. That was changed to the drummer hitting the snare on every beat. While this aspect of the style was not present on the earliest H-D-H productions, with the Vandellas and the Supremes, it soon became a Motown staple to the point where it would be safe to say that seventy-five percent of the records recorded in a Motown studio since "Baby Love" have this style of drumming. In addition, over a period of time production techniques were developed to give added emphasis to the drums, and to give them a distinctive sound. Tambourines were added on some records and in general anything that would deepen or solidify the effect of the beat was thrown in. The Motown beat was to become the key to public identification of the Motown sound.

Motown changed things around melodically as well. Prior to the Supremes there were two basic pop music forms: the blues form and the ballad form. Motown changed all that. Repetition was the new order. "Baby Love" is a circle of repetition. Its form is very close to a-a-a-a. Motown writers were among the first to realize that they were writing for the car radio and they learned early in the game to keep it simple. By and large the songwriting chores were turned over to a select number of teams such as H-D-H or the team of Stevenson-Gaye ("Dancing in the Streets"), all of whom stuck to the basic credo of keeping the melodic structure relatively simple and easy to follow. However, it must be added that within easy-to-follow melodic structures Motown has often produced melodies and chord progressions of surprising sophistication for a pop song.

Perhaps the part of a Motown record that is easiest to recognize is the overall instrumental background. In addition to the distinctive beat, already discussed, Motown has always presented the public with highly regimented, stiff, impersonal back-up bands. Even the solos so common on Motown singles are totally lacking in spontaneity. It's easy to see where the charge of black Muzak comes from. Of course this approach succeeds commercially because it keeps things simple, predictable and danceable, and besides, lots of the basic arrangements are pretty. (Like on "Stop in the Name of Love.")

Equally as important as the instrumental back-up style is the vocal back-up. Here Martha and the Vandellas can take full credit for stylizing the pattern of beginning sentences with high-pitched "Ooh's" and ending them with "di-doo-doo wah's" You can hear them do it perfectly on Marvin Gaye's "Stubborn Kind of Fellow" or throughout their own Dance Party album.

Such is the fourfold path to the Motown sound. However one other thing not strictly a part of the musical form must be mentioned. It is the Motown approach to the lead vocal. I haven't included this as one of the basic characteristics of the Motown sound because I feel there is too great a variation among the Motown lead vocalists and because I don't believe vocals can be stylized in the same way that other aspects of pop music can.

In discussing Motown vocals the first thing to realize is that Berry Gordy, Jr., knows that you can give a singer everything, but if the guy can't sing he won't sell any records. Therefore Motown makes damn sure that everybody who they sign has the basic raw material. Motown takes these vocalists and of course tries to give them a style. But most of the successful Motown artists have retained a strong degree of individual identity.

Within the context of many individual vocal styles, two basic approaches can be identified. One is symbolized by Diana Ross (of the Supremes), one of the most successful vocalists of all time. Diana's approach is to stick closely to the form. She rarely steps out on her own, seldom improvises, and never gets in the way. She restrains herself so as to fit perfectly into the prerecorded instrumental tracks that she dubs her voice into. Consequently she is the least jarring of Motown vocalists, the least disturbing, and the most able to reach a car-radio audience. I wouldn't deny for a second that she has a fantastic voice for what she is doing, that she oozes sex, and that she is a fine vocalist. But she seldom goes beyond what was planned for her by the production team.

The other type of Motown vocalist is seen in Levi Stubbs (lead singer of the Four Tops). His thing is breaking through the barrier that the regimented background sticks him with. All his shouting, his frenzy, his individuality, is something that Motown can't quite control or make predictable. He is an artist who can be told what to say only within certain limitations—once within them he is on his own and there is no telling what he will do. The dichotomy between Levi's style and Diana's is simply this: Diana strives for unity whereas Levi creates conflict. Diana's approach is to roll with the given version of the Motown sound she is to record. She will try to fit snuggly into the overall framework. A very commercial, good record will then be produced, but one without much artistic merit because it contains no tension. It becomes too smooth. The best example of this is Diana's performance on "You Can't Hurry Love." The alternative to this approach is Levi's method of attacking the song, and in the process creating his own dynamic. Levi's style is based on creating tension between the lead vocal and everything else that happens on the record. It is the same dynamic that Stevie Wonder creates when he sings "Uptight," and that David Ruffin creates when he sings "I'm Losing You." When the artist chooses this path the record as a whole improves because the background and the beat no longer have to stand on their own but can act as counterweights to the vocal. And when a record is created in which all the different parts are interacting in this fashion then the listener is suddenly able to appreciate individual excellence on the part of the musicians as well as the vocalists, and you may find yourself digging the fantastic thing the bass is doing on "Bernadette," or the fact that the drummer is socking it to you on "Uptight." This is Motown at its finest.

Having gone this far in identifying a Motown style, it should be noted that things do not remain pat or static within the context of the basic sound. Refinements are constantly taking place and there are always some limited forms of experimentation going on. For example, Smokey's "Tracks of My Tears," one of the classic Motown lyrics, also was notable for the un-Motown-like use it made of the guitars. The Four Tops have been doing songs which have clearly been influenced by the Dylanesque technique of incessant repetition, as Richard Goldstein correctly noted some time ago. However, one thing Motown will never do is go against the grain of its highest value—success. It may dabble here and there in electric variations on its style, but if these variations don't sell records, forget it. Smokey Robinson's activities as songwriter and producer have recently been curtailed, presumably for that reason.

Of course, since the Supremes era began, success has never really been in question at Motown. They have the style and they have the talent, and by God, they sell the records. But success means many things to many people, and here is the rub. The head of the Motown corporation picked up some pretty perverse notions as to what constitutes success, somewhere along the line. It hasn't been enough to just break out of the soul charts and radio stations. It hasn't been enough to outsell the top pop stars in every field. Berry Gordy's idea of success is to be able to put each one of his groups into the big nightclub scene. As I write this the Temptations are at the Copa wowing them with "Swanee," according to the latest issue of Variety. As a result of this philosophy Motown has weighed down its artists with absurd album material (Would you believe the Four Tops singing "Strangers in the Night" on their On Broadway album?) and absurd live nightclub acts. There is no sense in laboring the point, because things are going to get worse before they get better. But it should be pointed out that such a policy may put big Motown stars into high-paying clubs but lose them some of their hard-core, record-buying audience in the process.

It has been suggested that Berry Gordy's experience as an auto worker in Detroit before his entrance into the music business has given him too rigid an idea of how to run a record company, and it is certainly true that he likes to run things in assembly-line-like fashion. The Temptations are going to do the Copa bit because that is what Motown stars are expected to do when they reach a certain level of success. And the fact that David Ruffin doesn't sound good singing "The Best Things in Life Are Free" isn't going to keep him from doing it.

This rigidity in management is particularly evident in the Motown album approach. Motown policy here is not hip to the concept being developed by the big pop stars that an album is a whole thing, not just your latest hits and some junk. As a result the best Motown albums are in the "Greatest Hits" series, because such albums at least retain the uniform high quality of Motown singles. They also sell quite well. The best of these is The Temptations' Greatest Hits. Only a few Motown albums outside this series are listenable. Dance Party is certainly one of these, but I don't know how many others could be named. This is a quick-money policy based on the concept that a few hits will sell an album. But as the Doors and the Airplane have recently proven, an album which builds up a reputation of being good unto itself doesn't need big hits on it to sell. Both Surrealistic Pillow and The Doors sold extremely well before any of the album cuts made it as singles. And Sgt. Pepper doesn't have any singles on it at all.

In general, Motown must base its reputation on singles. "Reach Out I'll Be There" is certainly the best record the Four Tops ever made and probably the best record ever produced at Motown. There are simply no flaws. No dumb instrumentals. A beautiful lyric and a very sophisticated chorus. Perfect tension between artist and orchestra. Fantastic use of verbal repetitions in the vocal backup. It's a record that cuts through, that transcends all the limitations of the recorded rock form. In my opinion if there is any one thing that makes the difference on this record it is the power and absolute conviction of all four vocalists. When Levi sings you know he is not kidding. His voice literally drives that band through the floor of the record ... And the rest of the Tops push even Levi that one step further with their perfectly timed responses to him, and their "Aahs" at the beginning of each verse.

As manufacturers of single records Motown is unparalleled in both artistic and financial success. From the Supremes on there has always been an abundance of first-rate Motown records. "Shotgun," "Ooh, Baby, Baby," "Heatwave," "Ain't That Peculiar," "Tracks of My Tears," "Baby I Need Your Loving," "Uptight," "Dancing in the Streets": it's positively remarkable what this company has achieved within the limited form they have chosen to produce their music in. And in the last year important steps have been made to broaden that form. Increased virtuosity, particularly of the rhythm instrumentalists, is being featured. The level of songwriting for singles is fantastically high. (Just off the charts: "I Was Made to Love Her," "Ain't No Mountain High Enough," and "More Love.") New production people are being added who are doing good things, like Harvey Faqua.

The night before I started this article I saw Stevie Wonder on Joey Bishop's late-night show. He performed "Alfie," which I think is a decent song, on the harmonica. As they were introducing him

I got upset thinking to myself that this was going to be dreadful. Stevie played it beautifully; he really did. And that—right there—showed me the power, the freedom the artist has to transcend the ephemeral, like the particular song he is playing, or the particular band he is working with. And after writing all this if I had to say what makes Motown work, when it does work, I would say it is the combination of the limitations that are imposed on Motown's artists, and their capacity, which manifests itself only occasionally, to shatter them with some little nuance that no one could have predicted. Motown is the transcendence of Levi saying "Just look over your shoulder." And the beautiful thing is that the way Levi says that—that could never be formalized or stylized. The beauty of Motown is that it gives great artists something to work with and against. It gives them salable good songs and a beat and a producer and musicians and supervisors. But it doesn't give its vocalists their voices, their talent, or their soul. When Smokey sings "This is no fiction, this is no act, it's real, it's fact," or when Stevie sings "No one is better than I/ And I know I'm just an average guy," we are no longer listening to a thing called Motown. We are participating in the transcendence of a particular artist, we are drawn into an individual vision of reality. From every aesthetical point of view possible it can truly be said that when these moments occur there is no longer Motown, but only music.

15

"An Interview with Wilson Pickett"

JIM DELEHANT

From Motown to Seattle grunge, rock styles have often been connected with specific regions and sounds. In the mid-1960s, few regional styles enjoyed more success than the "Memphis sound," which was associated most of all with Stax Records and the rise of soul music. In his interview with Wilson Pickett (1941–2006) *Hit Parader* editor Jim Delehant encourages the soul singer to discuss the differences between Stax—where Pickett had recorded his popular hits "In the Midnight Hour" and "634-5789 (Soulsville U.S.A.)"—and the Motown sound. If Motown envisioned itself as a crossover style, then the Memphis sound seemed to be linked more directly with African American culture, as evidenced through the music's gospel roots and the expressive verbal language of soul. In actuality, however, the creative forces behind '60s soul reflected the cooperative interactions of an interracial environment. The Stax house bands—composed of Booker T. and the MGs and the Markey Horns—who backed Pickett and other singers such as Otis Redding and Sam and Dave in the studio were integrated ensembles, all of which adds a certain poignancy to Delehant's observation, in the midst of the Civil Rights era, that the Stax people "seem like one big family."*

As we walked into Wilson Pickett's dressing room at the Apollo in New York, two shady characters were in the process of selling a freshly acquired amplifier to the singer himself. "What am I going to do with that little Mickey Mouse amp," said Wilson. "Those speakers wouldn't even fill my bathroom," and he asked one of his friends to show the gentlemen to the door. Then, after Wilson and his buddies roared with laughter over a private joke about "the Reverend Solomon Burke selling motions, notions and potions," he settled back for the following interview.

JD: *Would you say that the many years of shouting have given you that rough voice?*

Wilson: When you sing loud like I do, you develop a hard voice.

JD: *Does that type of singing ever irritate your vocal chords?*

Wilson: No. Singing doesn't do that. Just when I get a cold.

JD: *Do you record in Memphis or New York?*

Wilson: Memphis, Tennessee. I did my last LP in Muscle Shoals, Alabama, at the Rick Hall Studio. They mostly use the musicians from Memphis.

JD: *What's the big difference between the Memphis sound and the Motown sound?*

Wilson: Memphis is real soul. But Motown is mostly pop.

JD: *Both of them seem to have strong emphasis on bass and drums.*

---

* *Source:* Jim Delehant, "An Interview with Wilson Pickett," *Hit Parader*, April 1967, p. 47.

Wilson: I don't think Motown has as much accent on the drums as Stax. Stax people deal strictly with R&B. There's a big difference in the R&B beat and the Motown beat.

JD: *Do you think we're experiencing a comeback of old blues?*

Wilson: I don't think it'll ever go back to the real low-down blues, the stuff John Lee Hooker does. My blues aren't low down. I think the R&B sound has developed quite a bit in the last three years. It used to be that you couldn't get an R&B record played on a pop station. Now it's changed so much, that it's hard to figure out the blues from a pop record.

JD: *Why do you think that is?*

Wilson: I really don't know. I skuffled for a break for a long time. The blues was smothered then. But suddenly it broke out.

JD: *Do you think the British singers had something to do with it?*

Wilson: Definitely, when I go to England, all I hear is blues tunes. All they play is American blues records. People like Otis Redding, and the people in America like the English sounds. Every night club I went to in England played American records. I really loved it in England.

JD: *What kind of band did you have in England?*

Wilson: I had a group called the Stateside, an English group. They had my songs down pat. I only took one guitar player with me from America. But those British guys learned all my songs from records.

JD: *The Stax people in Memphis seem like one big family.*

Wilson: I'll tell you right now they live with that studio. They stay in there all day and all night.

JD: *Does Booker T. play piano on your records?*

Wilson: No. He's not on any of them. Just the Markeys. I can't think of the piano player's name, but he's with the Stax firm. Those guys really feel what each other plays.

JD: *The band you worked with at the Apollo today was nothing like the one on your records.*

Wilson: It's hard to get that feeling. It sounds like a fifty-piece band on the record. Actually, there are only about nine pieces on my records.

JD: *When you sang gospel were you a shouter?*

Wilson: I don't understand what you're talking about.

JD: *Were you more subdued or were you as hard as you are now?*

Wilson: The gospel sound is much more powerful than the stuff I'm doing now. All of the strong voices come out of gospel.

16

James Brown
Soul Brother No. 1

<small>FRED WESLEY, JR.</small>

The self-proclaimed "hardest working man in show business," James Brown (born 1928 or 1933 [date disputed]) had already been a major R&B and soul star for nearly a decade and a half by the time trombonist Fred Wesley, Jr. (born 1944) joined his group in 1968. Wesley was an experienced sideman, having played with Ike and Tina Turner and Hank Ballard. As he reveals in his autobiography, however, nothing could have prepared him for Brown's dynamic stage show and the dictatorial tactics by which he kept his performers within his grip of power. The two passages excerpted here from Wesley's book capture the trombonist's induction into Brown's world, when the singer was at the height of his success in the mid-late 1960s. In Wesley's eyes the musicians deserved the majority of the credit for crafting and perfecting Brown's trademark sound. At the same time he concedes that were it not for Brown's demanding star presence and controlling, manipulative personality, the music would have been far less remarkable. Wesley's initial stay with Brown was relatively short, as he quit in early 1970, following in the footsteps of disgruntled, departed musical director Alfred "Pee Wee" Ellis and countless other former band members. Wesley was soon back with Brown, however, rejoining the band as its musical director in December 1970 and remaining in that position through 1975. During that time Wesley was one of the main architects behind Brown's influential early '70s funk grooves.*

Maceo, Pee Wee, and I became and have remained close friends, with Waymon being the connection and catalyst between us.† Joe Dupars and St. Clair Pinckney completed the horn section at that time. The other James Brown horn players, who I had known before, Brisco Clark and Mack Johnson, were long gone. For reasons that became clear to me later, there was high turnover in the James Brown horn section. As we sat around between the dressing room and the bus, Waymon, Pee Wee, and the other guys told stories of Brisco's drinking, Mack's insubordination, and other confrontations with the Boss. Jabo, Bernard (who for some reason was known as "Dog" in this band), Junior Gunther, Kenny Hull, and the local stage crew went about setting up the stage.

At about six or seven o'clock, Mr. Brown and an entourage of about four people arrived in what looked to be a rental car. Mr. Brown didn't ride the bus. He would station himself at a central point, in this case Miami, and fly in his private Lear jet back and forth to gigs in the area. Mr. Brown exited the driver's seat, went straight to the stage, and began fooling around with the Hammond B-3 organ

---

* *Source:* Fred Wesley, Jr., *Hit Me, Fred! Recollections of a Sideman* (Durham: Duke University Press, 2002), pp. 88–99, 106–7.
† Tenor saxophonist Maceo Parker and Trumpeter Waymon Reed.

that had been the first thing to be set up. He was much shorter than I had imagined him to be from seeing him on stage. Ms. Sanders* and the people who were busy on the stage greeted him respectfully. I and the other guys were out of sight on the bus and just kind of observed the arrival.

A beautiful, well-built, light-skinned girl got out of the car and went directly into Mr. Brown's dressing room without saying anything to anyone. The guys told me that she was Marva Whitney, the featured singer on the show, and hinted that she also had a more personal relationship with Mr. Brown. A stockily built guy with what looked like a hairdryer in his hand followed closely behind Ms. Whitney. This, I was told, was Henry Stallings, the hairdresser. Although he sported a nice "do," he looked like anything but a hairdresser. His demeanor also wasn't what you'd expect of a hairdresser. He had the loud, gruff, profane way of speaking you would more likely attribute to a gangster. A big, tall, black, rough-looking dude got out of the car last. He was scuffling with getting the luggage out of the car. This was Baby James, who *was* a gangster. His job was bodyguard, general enforcer, and whatever else Mr. Brown needed done that required brute strength and not a lot of brainpower. Actually, all of the nonmusical employees of the James Brown show sort of fit that description, except for Mr. Bell, the fourth person in the entourage, who was a middle-aged white man who piloted the James Brown Lear Jet.

After an afternoon of meeting people, reacquainting myself with old friends, and generally getting to know my new gig, it was finally time for the show. Unlike the Ike and Tina Turner show and the Hank Ballard show, I didn't go right onstage. I was told that I had to watch, go through a few rehearsals, and be fitted with some uniforms before I could go onstage.

I didn't know what kind of show to expect. I had only seen a small part of the show back in 1962 at the Howard Theater. The Orlando Sports Arena was hardly a theater. This place was more suited for rodeos and stock shows. (There were actually some live animals corralled in the back of the place.) However, the stage was set up with a somewhat elaborate sound system. All of the backline amplifiers were by vox, as were the drums and guitars. In fact, I think the entire sound system was by vox. Conspicuously missing, though, was a monitor system. When I had visited the show in Huntsville, I had seen the four sets of drums onstage, but I still hadn't seen how more than one drummer at a time operated during a show. The multiple-drummer concept was the subject of much discussion and speculation among musicians throughout the world. I was anxious to see firsthand what it was all about.

The horns were positioned on the left of the stage (from the audience's point of view) and in front of the organ. Jabo's drums were positioned upstage, left of center. Clyde's drums were also positioned upstage, but right of center. The bass player—Bernard or Buddy or Dog, whatever you want to call him—was parallel to and between Jabo and Clyde. A little to the right and behind Jabo was Country Kellum on rhythm, and I do mean *rhythm*, guitar. A little to the right and behind Clyde was Jimmy Nolen, the lead guitar player. On an elevated platform, stage left, angled to face center stage, were the three violins, each plugged into their own sound-enhancing amplifier, also by vox. There were two mikes for the horns—one for the saxes and one for the trumpets and trombone. A single mike was at center stage. On a high riser in the center of the stage behind the band was the lone JB Dancer. Although this was a rodeo arena, the James Brown stage had a big-time, professional, showbiz theater look about it.

It was finally show time. The place was packed. There were chairs set up on a portable floor over the ground, which was the real floor of the arena, but most of the crowd was standing all around the arena. The house lights went down and the band took the stage. After an involved musical introduction that included some really hip jazz licks, some funky rhythms, and some real hard bebop-type

---

* Gertrude Sanders, Brown's "wardrobe mistress."

runs by the horns that melted into a dramatic drumroll, an offstage voice announced, "L-A-DIES AND GENTLEMEN, THE JAMES BROWN ORCHESTRA." Under the direction of Mr. Alfred "Pee Wee" Ellis, the band did a set, about six tunes. The only ones I remember are "Hip Hug-Her," a then-current hit by Booker T. and the MGs, and "Why Am I Treated So Bad," a current hit by the Staple Singers. All the tunes were very interestingly arranged by Pee Wee, immediately convincing me of his musical genius. Maceo and Waymon played most of the solos, with a couple by St. Clair on tenor sax and Pee Wee himself on alto sax.

I was very impressed with the band. Although it wasn't a jazz band, they played jazz very well. It wasn't the Jazztet, but it was far more musical than I had expected. So far, I was happy about being on this gig. The people seemed to be people I could deal with. Some I already liked a lot. And the music seemed to be reasonably challenging. I would be happy if I had to play straight-up blues all night after the band's opening set. I was sure that associating with musicians like Pee Wee and Waymon would make the whole thing worthwhile.

But wait. There was more to come. Suddenly, the stage went black. The band played a grandiose, almost symphonic intro/fanfare type of thing, complete with strings and what I swear sounded like timpani and French horns. When this bodacious introduction decrescendoed, the lights hit center stage and there was James Brown. There he was. Sitting on a stool. Not just an ordinary stool, but a stool of carved, highly polished oak, with a padded leather back, more like a big high chair. He was dressed in a beige, mohair, three-piece suit, with a three-quarter-length coat, a turtleneck shirt, and the baddest burgundy alligator boots I have ever seen. He calmly sang Tony Bennett's "If I Ruled the World." Bear in mind, I'm expecting a screaming and hollering, fast-dancing little sissy to come out and sweat all over the place. Instead, I'm seeing a real cool man, milking one of my favorite ballads dry. The band went out of "If I Ruled the World" into a smooth swing version of Sinatra's "That's Life." The arrangements were absolutely fantastic. Sinatra and Nelson Riddle couldn't have performed the songs any better. I was totally surprised and amazed.

But that's not all. At the end of "That's Life," James Brown pushed the mike forward in a military-rifle-salute type move, accented by a rim shot from Jabo, and the band hit a descending drag triplet riff and went directly into a heartstopping Mobile, Alabama, blues type shuffle. Before I could get straight from the shock, James Brown was deep into "Going to Kansas City." The band was clicking like a funk machine, everything hitting in the right place. Jimmy Nolen, Country, Dog, and—leading the pack—Jabo, doing what nobody in the world can do like him. A hard-driving shuffle. They did several verses and choruses, increasing the intensity of the groove until it spilled over into a vamp that had the rhythm driving wide open, horns screaming in a frenzy, and James Brown, still basically cool, giving us a glimpse of the fury that was to come, with a little mash here and a split there, suddenly leaving the stage as abruptly as he had appeared. Danny Ray, still offstage, promised, "JAMES BROWN WILL BE BACK."

The audience went crazy. I went with them. I don't even remember exactly how it happened, but when I looked up again the lovely Ms. Marva Whitney was onstage singing some song I'd never heard before. It must have been an original. The highlight of her set was a beautiful arrangement of "People." Obviously, the genius of Pee Wee Ellis had struck again.

As she left the stage, the lights went out again, and the spotlight that followed her off followed James Brown back on, as the band hit the intro to "Man's World." This time James was wearing a pantsuit with a formfitting shirt that had bloused sleeves and alternating navy-blue and white pleats. The pants were navy-blue velvet bell-bottoms. This time a pair of navy-blue lizard boots adorned his little fast feet. He was center stage by the time the violins finished their famous run. There was a pause. He sang, in his familiar voice, the familiar line, *"This is a man's world."* The audience and I went berserk again. Even I, a jazz person, was familiar with that hit song. I can't say that

I had liked it before. It made so little sense to me. He did the song all the way through. "Man made the car," "Man made money, to buy from other man," and all that. The words were usually silly to me, but seeing it performed, in person, now, was thrilling. He went straight into a ten-minute vamp in which he did a complete production number that included everything from horn "hits"—one, two, three, and four times—to tricks with the mike and drops to his knees, all held together by a steady "motion of the ocean" groove by Jabo and the rhythm section. He finally turned us loose— just before everybody died from ecstasy—and left the stage again. Once again, Danny Ray, offstage, assured us: "JAMES BROWN WILL BE BACK."

The band left the stage, and Danny Ray made himself visible for the first time and made a few announcements about souvenir items on sale in the front of the arena. I had noticed a big fat man set up at a table, selling merchandise. This was the intermission. The band went into the stalls that served as dressing rooms and proceeded to change clothes. The place was littered with clothes bags, hangers, irons, shoes, shoetrees, socks, bow ties, belts, and accessories. After about fifteen minutes of furious activity, the band emerged, dressed in lime-green suits with white satin lapels, bow ties, and patent-leather shoes. The look was absolutely stunning. A startling contrast to the ordinary black tuxedos in which they had opened the show. Each band member looked as if he had just left home in fresh clothes straight out of the laundry. The Army would have been proud of the spit and polish of this band. They stood around, ready, waiting, I guessed, for Mr. Brown to come out of his dressing room.

After a while, Henry Stallings came out of the man's dressing room and in a gruff voice said, *"He's ready."* Everyone moved out immediately and took their positions on stage. I'm standing on the side of the stage now. The band started a quiet, bluesy-jazz vamp that went on until Danny Ray took center stage. The groove was cut off abruptly, and Ray went into his legendary introduction of James Brown. "*The hardest working man in show business,*" "*The man who made 'Try Me,' 'Out Of Sight'....*" Each of his phrases was accented by hits and riffs from the band. He continued: "*The amazing Mr. 'Please, Please, Please' himself . . . JAAAAAAMES BROWN.*" With that, James—whom I could see framed in his dressing-room door, prancing and bucking like a race horse in the starting gate—stormed onto the stage and proceeded to do an hour-and-a-half medley of his repertoire. He did songs like "I Got the Feeling," "I Got You," and "I'll Go Crazy," going from tune to tune via clever segues and intros. The groove remained intense, even through all the tempo changes. Most of the things were fast and funky, with the exception of "Try Me" and another long production performance of "Lost Someone."

Mr. Brown was exactly as advertised. His dancing was unbelievable. He did things that seemed impossible for the human body to do. How he could sing with that much energy and dance at the same time was amazing. His rhythm and soulful attitude and demeanor epitomized what black music was all about. The band was now literally a funk machine. Overpowering and relentless. I got the sense that James was plugged into the band, and it was generating energy directly to his body. At times, the band was totally musical, with beautiful chords and melodies mixing with the constant funky grooves. But, at other times, things happened that totally defied musical explanation. There were chords that were just sounds for effect and rhythms that started and ended wherever they started or ended, not in accord with any time signature or form. Through it all, the band was tight, doing all the complicated dance routines and the music at the same time. Everything conspired in exactly the right way to make for an extraordinarily entertaining show that was sometimes directed by Pee Wee, but mostly signaled by the same man who was also doing all the singing and dancing. The sounds, the sights, and the relentlessly intense feeling of that funky groove were completely thrilling and mesmerizing.

By the time the show climaxed with "Please, Please, Please" and the famous act in which James Brown collapses to his knees and is covered sympathetically with a cape by Danny Ray, the audience was completely fucked up, responding to any and everything that James or the band did. After his third drop to his knees and covering by a third, spectacularly designed cape, James Brown left the stage as the band opened up and went all the way crazy. We were all thoroughly entertained, all funked up, wanting more but satisfied, when all of a sudden he was back and giving us what we had forgotten was missing: Mr. Brown's then-current hit, "I Can't Stand Myself." This encore was like a climax on top of an already all-consuming climax. The encore must have lasted another thirty minutes. The crowd—and that included me—was completely satiated. I felt guilty for not having bought a ticket. This was the most completely thrilling, spectacular, hypnotizing, soulful, incredible, unbelievable, entertaining, and satisfying show I had ever seen or heard of.

After the show was over and I had caught my breath, I could barely keep myself from raving to the guys in the band about how thrilled I was with the show. I was very anxious to get onstage and be a part of what had to be the greatest show on earth. It was clear now why they needed another trombone player. All during the show Rasbury* was going back and forth between the box office and James's dressing room, and every now and then he would grab his horn, which was a valve trombone, and go onstage for a little while. I didn't miss his part, but it would definitely become a fuller brass sound with me onstage. When they cooled down and changed out of their suits, which were soaking wet with sweat, Waymon and Pee Wee took me to meet "The Man."

We went to the dressing room door and waited and waited until finally Ms. Sanders told us we could come in. As we entered the dressing room, I was amazed that what was probably supposed to be a storeroom had been transformed into a very comfortable dressing room, complete with a rug on the floor, racks of clothes hanging around, shoes lined up in a very orderly manner, an ironing board, a table with a large mirror and make-up on it, and, indeed, a professional looking hairdryer. This room had all the comforts of home. Ms. Sanders even offered us a soda from the cooler that was there.

Mr. Brown was sitting at the table in a robe, rubbing his face with a make-up sponge. He was still dripping sweat from his hair, which Henry was carefully rolling up as Brown talked in his fast, assured way to Rasbury—not leaving any space for Rasbury to get a word in edgewise—about how good the show was and how much the people enjoyed it. Brown seemed amazed and even relieved that the audience had accepted and enjoyed the show as much as they had. This surprised me. At that time, I didn't know if this was a new show that had not been audience tested or if the great James Brown was so insecure that he never took pleasing the audience for granted. I learned later that most true stars are never sure or confident about their performances. Mr. Brown was a glaring example of this insecurity, although he put up a self-confident and cocky, if paper-thin, façade.

After a long time of listening to him rant and rave about how big he was, how well his records were selling, and how much the people loved him, he finally allowed Waymon to say, "Mr. Brown, I'd like you to meet the new trombone player, Fred Wesley." He seemed unimpressed. He didn't turn around from the mirror. Instead, he kept on fussing with his make-up and wiping sweat, then glared at me through the mirror and asked, "Can you dance?" Taken aback, I paused and collected myself, then said, "Yeah." Then I realized that he had probably noticed that I was a little chubby and thought that dancing might be a problem for me. At the same time, I realized that I'd said "Yeah," not "Yes, sir," as everyone else was saying. So I quickly got myself together and started assuring him that dancing was not a problem for me. I said, "Yes, sir, I can dance. I can dance very well." I might have even given him a little step or two. I didn't want anything to keep me from getting this gig.

---

* Levi Rasbury, trombonist who also doubled as a road manager.

He told me that I was on probation and would be watched and evaluated over the next few days to see if I would fit in. I assured him that I was the right man for the job and that he would not have a problem with me. He still seemed unconvinced but said, "Okay. We'll see."

The next few days found me adjusting to the day-to-day routine of the James Brown system. We worked almost every night, making that $225-a-week, work-or-no-work salary, not so great when you considered that the "work-or-no-work" clause was in favor of management. The salary covered anything that came up. Sometimes we did more than one show in the same place, two cities in the same day, recording sessions, and TV shows—all covered by the same weekly salary. I found out that what I had thought was security for a musician was really just a guarantee of cheap labor for James Brown. Most road musicians get paid by the show, making off days detrimental to their income. With bands like Hank Ballard or Bobby Bland or even a jazz group like Art Blakey, a guaranteed weekly salary was a good thing, because you were covered for those off days, and hardly any big stars worked seven days a week, three hundred days a year like James Brown did.

I figured out that James could make anywhere from $350,000 to $500,000 a week, but his payroll remained at about a paltry $6,000 a week. And he acted like he didn't want to give you that. I had to almost beg for a draw during that first week I was out there. It soon became clear that there was no set payday. It was supposed to be Sunday, but it never happened on time. You knew the money was there. You could plainly see bags and even cardboard boxes full of money being loaded into the rented car every night. It was now clear why there was such a high turnover rate in the band.

After my probation period, my salary shot up to $350 a week, so even with paying my own hotel and food out of that, I was able to get enough money home to support my family at least as well as that milkman job would have. Also, although there was a serious discrepancy between the money you were helping to generate and the percentage you were being paid, the salary was still just a little above what you could make in a year with most of the other bands working regularly. Still, like me, most of the guys must have had ulterior motives for staying on the gig; it was clear that none of the James Brown sidemen would ever get rich.

I'm sure that some of the old-timers felt that they were lucky to have a gig on this level and weren't about to take a chance on trying to get another gig even this good somewhere else. Others saw the James Brown show as a stepping-stone to bigger and better things. I'm sure that was the case with guys like Pee Wee and Waymon. And some were there simply because of the glamour and the opportunity to have fun and score exotic and beautiful women, who were always around big-time shows like this.

Whatever their reasons were, Mr. Brown took full advantage of them all and ruled his empire with an iron hand, using all they had to offer for his own benefit, giving back as little as possible in return. He had a knack for knowing how much to take and how much to give to keep his show operating. He knew who he could yell at without getting the hell knocked out of him. He knew how much to pay each individual to keep him hanging on. He also knew who and how to humiliate and insult in order to demonstrate his power and keep everyone on their toes. He would chastise and counsel his employees in front of certain disc jockeys, reporters, and local politicians to make himself look benevolent and merciful, so many people actually thought him to be a leader and father figure. He was a master of manipulation. I more than once saw him talk his musicians into getting into big debt with a house or a car only to fire them, watch them suffer for a while, then hire them back at a lower salary and at his complete mercy. Some of these people actually loved and respected him, no matter how horribly he treated them. It didn't take me long to realize that I was involved with a man unique among performers and among human beings in general. James Brown was a great performer, probably the greatest to ever live, but I had to be careful—this was a man with the power and will and, it seemed, the need to control not only the career but the whole life of every person who worked for him.

It wasn't long before I was onstage, playing and dancing right along with everyone else. I was onstage before my uniforms arrived. I did the gig at the Regal Theater wearing Jimmy Nolen's coat, standing behind the organ speaker to hide my pants. The Regal Theater in Chicago was the site of my first "James Brown Horror Rehearsal." This was a punishment rehearsal. A rehearsal that James called when he felt his grip on somebody or everybody slipping. This type of rehearsal was generally called at the most inopportune time. This particular one was called right after we had done three shows to sold-out Regal Theater audiences. The weather was abominable—there was a Chicago blizzard. Everyone was exhausted. James came out of his dressing room, still in his robe and slippers, and said that we had to get "Please, Please, Please" right. According to him, what we had been doing for weeks was, all of a sudden, all wrong. Of course, that was just his way of keeping us away from what we wanted to be doing after the show. This was the last day of a three-day stint in Chicago, and there was much to be done, like pack after being in the same place for three days. Also, when we stayed in one place for any length of time, many of the guys brought in their wives and loved ones. Brown knew that. He really seemed to hate any distraction or diversion from the show. At the time, I took the rehearsal as his way of letting me know, personally, because I was new, how he could control my life if and when he wanted to. But I now realize that his absolute commitment to the show drove him to want everyone else to have that same commitment.

This type of rehearsal was completely unnecessary musically. "Please, Please, Please" or "Try Me" were always the songs rehearsed because they were the only songs that he could almost make anyone believe he really knew. And it became clear to me right off that he didn't know those two songs either. I know it's hard to believe, but it would have been impossible for James Brown to put his show together without the assistance of someone like Pee Wee, who understood chord changes, time signatures, scales, notes, and basic music theory. Simple things like knowing the key would be a big problem for James. So, when James would mouth out some guitar part, which might or might not have had anything to do with the actual song being played, Jimmy or Country would have to attempt to play it simply because James was still in charge. We all had to pretend that we knew what James was talking about. Nobody ever said, "That's ridiculous" or "You don't know what you're talking about." The whole James Brown Show depended on having someone with musical knowledge remember the show, the individual parts, and the individual songs, then relay these verbally or in print to the other musicians. James Brown could not do it himself. He spoke in grunts, groans, and la-di-das, and he needed musicians to translate that language into music and actual songs in order to create an actual show.

So we just stood and took it while he went through changing little things that didn't need changing, adding things that didn't need adding, going over and over some little phrase and never being satisfied with it. He would tell the horns "It's not ladaladadida, it's ladalada*di*da." We would go ladalada*di*da, and he would say, "No, I said lada*la*dadida." Over and over it continued, until you wanted to just scream. He would get mad and chew out certain individuals (the ones he knew he could get away with chewing out) and do anything else to take up time. After a few hours of this misery or after he finally got tired, he would appear to be pleased and say things like, "Noooooow, we finally got it right. Noooooow, we have an arrangement." The truth of the matter was that nooooow the stuff was so confused that Pee Wee would have to have a real rehearsal to bring the songs back to any semblance of recognizability. That's why, even today, it's hard to recognize some of the songs during the James Brown live performances.

The Chicago rehearsal lasted right up until almost time to get on the bus and go to the next gig. No time to spend with your loved one. Hardly enough time to pack or get some breakfast. Any chance to take care of any business in a large city was gone. All you had time to do now was get on the bus.

Another time in Hollywood, California, at Modern Music Rehearsal Studios, he called one of those rehearsals. Here we are in beautiful Hollywood, full of distractions and diversions, and we have a horror rehearsal. This one was especially memorable because not only did we go through the ladaladadidas and the usual random humiliations, but Brown also created a new and very time-consuming wrinkle. The premise was that if you really knew the show you could recite the song titles really fast. So he had someone write the order of songs down, including the segues, interludes, and introductions. He would then go around the band and have each person recite the order as fast as they could from memory. In the first place, everyone had his own way of remembering the show. I, for one, didn't think of titles. I went more by my part. This is where I play the high B, or this is the song in which I play this rhythm or do this routine, for example. I had many different ways of cueing myself. It was very interesting, the different cues people made for themselves. And the fact is that they all worked, and the show went on. Having to identify each tune by title was automatically confusing and, the real point of the exercise, time-consuming. To an outside observer, it must have been hilarious. Here were people standing around holding instruments and saying rapidly: "There Was a Time Try Me Got the Feeling Cold Sweat Lost Someone Brand New Bag Intro Brand New Bag Please Please Please Can't Stand Myself...."

At first he went around the band in order for a few hours until most everybody got it, but he wasn't satisfied. He then sprang on people at random and actually timed us with a stopwatch, just draaaging the thing out. If you hesitated, you didn't know the show. If you missed something, you didn't know the show. If you didn't do it fast enough, you didn't know the show. We were in agony, but Brown never tired over hours and hours. I've seen people like Ike Turner and Ray Charles try stuff like this, but after a while they would get physically tired and stop. You, me, Ike, Ray, and any other normal human being would eventually grow weary or at least have something else to do. But, in Hollywood, California, James Brown, world-famous entertainer, with all the money in the world, could find nothing better to do than torment his band. I heard him say one time, "That's what makes me *me*."

When you were in the midst of one of those horror rehearsals or recording sessions or self-proclaiming conversations with James Brown, you felt pain, excruciating fatigue, and intense boredom, which led to suppressed anger and hate. I wonder to this day why nobody ever bolted, telling him to his face how ridiculous those rehearsals were and just walking out. And to my knowledge, nobody ever did. I came close many times, but there was always some reason—economic, political, or psychological—that I didn't. Sometimes, oddly, I think that I simply didn't want to risk hurting his feelings. He was so definite in the way he spoke to you that you got the feeling that he really believed the ridiculous stuff he was saying and you didn't want to embarrass him. Also, the few times I did challenge what he had said, he got so loud and so much farther away from reality that I gave up, because I knew he would never admit to seeing my point. It was like being held hostage by real strong, loud, unbeatable ignorance. The kind of ignorance that can make you look crazy if you continue to confront it. To my mind, I am intelligent enough to know that such manipulation and torture is unnecessary to the creation of an act as exciting as the James Brown Show. But, on the real side, there has never been a show that exciting, that tight, that completely entertaining. There also has never been a man so dedicated, so determined, so focused. I reluctantly have to admit that the things he did that seemed so stupid to me were, indeed, what made him *him*, the greatest entertainer in the world. Conversely, the intelligent things that I do are what make me *me,* the greatest sideman in the world.

* * *

My first recording session with Mr. Brown was also during that trip to L.A. The whole band was loaded into some station wagons and transported to the vox recording studios somewhere in the Los Angeles area. We set up and Pee Wee proceeded to put together a song—with no written music. He started by giving Clyde a simple drumbeat. Clyde started the beat and held it steady while Pee Wee hummed a bass line to Charles Sherrell, a bass player from Nashville recently hired onto the show. When the bass line had become clear to Charles and locked with the drumbeat, Pee Wee moved to Country, the rhythm guitar player, and began to choose a chord that would fit with the bass notes. A B-flat 9 was finally settled on and a chunky rhythm was matched up with the bass line and the drumbeat. I was, so far, amazed at how this song was coming together. Jimmy Nolen was allowed to find his own thing to fit the developing groove. He came up with sort of a womp-womp sounding, single-string thing that seemed to really pull all of the other parts together. At this point, we, once again, have that washing-machine thang going. That was the best way to describe the various sounds and rhythms, each in its own space, each in its own time, occurring in just the right places, to make for a funky groove. With the rhythm section solidly in place, Pee Wee proceeded to hum out horn parts. We were given some strategic hits with carefully voiced chords and a melodic line that happened whenever it was signaled. Of course, the reeds played a version of the James Brown horns' signature ladidadidat. With this groove firmly in place, Pee Wee started putting together a bridge.

Before he got started on it good, the Boss walked in. Everything went silent. He walked to Pee Wee and said, "Let me hear it." Pee Wee counted it off, and we played what we had been rehearsing for the last two hours. James listened intently, walked over to Clyde and said something to him as we all kept playing. Clyde then started playing a pop-pop every now and then. Brown made similar adjustments to all the parts and, sporting a little grin, started to dance a little bit and kind of winked at us and said "Nooooow *that's* a groove." James and Pee Wee continued to make up a bridge. The whole band did sort of an ensemble stop rhythm on an E-flat major chord, with Jimmy Nolen doing a little doodit solo lick on top. After James was satisfied that everything was in place, he pulled some scraps of paper out of his pocket and started reading what sounded like grunting and groaning, mostly to himself, as the band played on. We had been playing now for about fours hours straight, and I, for one, was getting tired. I mean, how many times can you go da daaaa da dot da dot da da without getting a cramp in your lip? I was young, all right, but I wanted to live to get old.

Just then, Mr. Bobbit, the road manager, and a bunch of people, mostly kids, walked into the studio. We stopped playing, and Mr. Brown went over and greeted them like he had expected them. I had no idea what they had to do with this recording. James was over on one side of the studio, talking and waving his hands with the kids. After this went on for a while, he came back to us and counted the tune off again. When the groove settled, he yelled to the kids, "Say it loud!" The kids responded, "I'm black and I'm proud!" He instructed the kids to say their line on cue and gave us cues to do the bridge and other things. With all the cues and signals in place, we were ready to record. All the time we were getting the groove together, engineers were in and out of the control room, setting mikes, adjusting amplifiers, placing baffles, and the like. They were ready, and we were ready. Mr. Brown was in control now. Pee Wee took his place in the reed section, and James counted it off. The groove was already strong, but when James counted it off and began to dance and direct, it took on a new power. All of a sudden, the fatigue I had been feeling was gone. The kids were doing their chant with a new energy. In fact, the energy level in the whole studio was lifted. James went straight through the whole tune and that was it. After about four hours of preparation, "Say It Loud, I'm Black and I'm Proud" went down in one take.

17

"Goodbye Surfing Hello God!—The Religious Conversion of Brian Wilson"

Jules Siegel

Along with the Beatles, Brian Wilson (born 1942) of the Beach Boys was one of the driving forces behind rock music's mid-1960s transformation from a fad almost exclusively associated with teenagers into a more ambitious medium. Originally known for their surf music style, intricate vocal harmonies, and glorification of the southern California lifestyle, the Beach Boys gained critical acclaim for their lush and lavish studio experimentation on their 1966 album *Pet Sounds*. The follow-up single, "Good Vibrations," was an unprecedented mammoth recording event, one that spanned six months and approximately fifteen separate sessions at four different studios. Wilson eventually was forced to whittle away more than ninety hours of studio tape to arrive at the three-and-a-half-minute finished product, a song which he famously referred to as his "pocket symphony." Jules Siegel's 1967 article describes Wilson's work on his next project, the ill-fated *Smile* (which would lay dormant until Wilson finally completed it in 2004). Siegel portrays a musician struggling with the daunting implications that go with the label of "genius," a word that conjures images of a tortured artist imbued with otherworldly gifts. Siegel's depiction of Wilson certainly fits this bill. The author also paints Wilson as a religious individual, and one who believes in the spiritual power of music. Such portraits were commonplace during the nineteenth century, when critics heralded Romantic era composers for both their genius and the spirituality of their musical creations. To what extent can we reasonably speak of rock music, such as that of the Beach Boys, as part of a spiritual practice, or as fulfilling a spiritual purpose?[*]

It was just another day of greatness at Gold Star Recording Studios on Santa Monica Boulevard in Hollywood. In the morning four long-haired kids had knocked out two hours of sound for a record plugger who was trying to curry favour with a disc jockey friend of theirs in San José. Nobody knew it at that moment, but out of that two hours there were about three minutes that would hit the top of the charts in a few weeks, and the record plugger, the disc jockey and the kids would all be hailed as geniuses, but geniuses with a very small g.

Now, however, in the very same studio, a Genius with a very large capital G was going to produce a hit. There was no doubt it would be a hit because this Genius was Brian Wilson. In four years of recording for Capitol Records, he and his group the Beach Boys, had made surfing music a national craze, sold 16 million singles and earned gold records for 10 of their 12 albums.

---

[*] *Source:* Jules Siegel, "Goodbye Surfing Hello God!—The Religious Conversion of Brian Wilson," *Cheetah*, October 1967, pp. 26–31, 83–87.

Not only was Brian going to produce a hit, but also, one gathered, he was going to show everybody in the music business exactly where it was at; and where it was at, it seemed, was that Brian Wilson was not merely a Genius—which is to say a steady commercial success—but rather, like Bob Dylan and John Lennon, a GENIUS—which is to say a steady commercial success and hip besides.

Until now, though, there were not too many hip people who would have considered Brian Wilson and the Beach Boys hip, even though he had produced one very hip record, *Good Vibrations*, which had sold more than a million copies, and a super-hip album, *Pet Sounds*, which didn't do very well at all—by previous Beach Boy sales standards. Among the hip people he was still on trial, and the question discussed earnestly among the recognized authorities on what is and what is not hip was whether or not Brian Wilson was hip, semi-hip or square.

But walking into the control room with the answers to all questions such as this was Brian Wilson himself, wearing a competition-stripe surfer's T-shirt, tight white duck pants, pale green bowling shoes and a red plastic toy fireman's helmet.

Everybody was wearing identical red plastic toy fireman's helmets. Brian's cousin and production assistant, Steve Korthoff, was wearing one; his wife, Marilyn, and her sister, Diane Rovelle—Brian's secretary—were also wearing them, and so was a once dignified writer from the *Saturday Evening Post* who had been following Brian around for two months trying to figure out whether or not this 24-year-old oversized tribute to Southern California who carried some 250 pounds of baby fat on a 6 foot 4 inch frame, was a genius, Genius or GENIUS, hip, semi-hip or square—concepts the writer himself was just learning to handle.*

Out in the studio, the musicians for the session were unpacking their instruments. In sport shirts and slacks, they looked like insurance salesmen and used-car dealers, except for one blonde female percussionist who might have been stamped out by a special machine that supplied plastic mannequin housewives for detergent commercials.

Controlled, a little bored after twenty years or so of nicely paid anonymity, these were the professionals of the popular music business, hired guns who did their job expertly and efficiently and then went home to the suburbs. If you wanted swing, they gave you swing. A little movie-track lushness? Fine, here comes movie-track lushness. Now it's rock & roll? Perfect rock & roll, down the chute.

"Steve," Brian called out, "where are the rest of those fire hats? I want everybody to wear fire hats. We've really got to get into this thing." Out to the Rolls-Royce went Steve and within a few minutes all of the musicians were wearing fire hats, silly grins beginning to crack their professional dignity.

"All right, let's go," said Brian. Then, using a variety of techniques ranging from vocal demonstration to actually playing the instruments, he taught each musician his part. A gigantic fire howled out of the massive studio speakers in a pounding crush of pictorial music that summoned up visions of roaring, windstorm flames, falling timbers, mournful sirens and sweating firemen, building into a peak and crackling off into fading embers as a single drum turned into a collapsing wall and the fire engine cellos dissolved and disappeared.

"When did he write this?" asked an astonished pop music producer who had wandered into the studio. "This is really fantastic! Man, this is unbelievable! How long has he been working on it?"

"About an hour," answered one of Brian's friends.

"I don't believe it. I just can't believe what I'm hearing," said the producer and fell into a stone silence as the fire music began again.

---

* The *Saturday Evening Post* writer to whom Siegel is referring is himself. The *Post* ultimately rejected his piece, however, and Siegel ended up publishing "Goodbye Surfing" in *Cheetah* magazine.

For the next three hours Brian Wilson recorded and re-recorded, take after take, changing the sound balance, adding echo, experimenting with a sound-effects track of a real fire.

"Let me hear that again." "Drums, I think you're a little slow in that last part. Let's get on it." "That was really good. Now, one more time, the whole thing." "All right, let me hear the cellos alone." "Great. Really great. Now let's *do it!*"

With 23 takes on tape and the entire operation responding to his touch like the black knobs on the control board, sweat glistening down his long, reddish hair on to his freckled face, the control room a litter of dead cigarette butts, Chicken Delight boxes, crumpled napkins, Coke bottles and all the accumulated trash of the physical end of the creative process, Brian stood at the board as the four speakers blasted the music into the room.

For the 24th time, the drums crashed and the sound effects crackle faded and stopped.

"Thank you," said Brian, into the control room mike. "Let me hear that back." Feet shifting, his body still, eyes closed, head moving seal-like to his music, he stood under the speakers and listened. "Let me hear that one more time." Again the fire roared. "Everybody come out and listen to this," Brian said to the musicians. They came into the control room and listened to what they had made.

"What do you think?" Brian asked.

"It's incredible. Incredible," whispered one of the musicians, a man in his fifties, wearing a Hawaiian shirt and iridescent trousers and pointed black Italian shoes. "Absolutely incredible."

"Yeah," said Brian on the way home, an acetate trial copy or "dub" of the tape in his hands, the red plastic fire helmet still on his head. "Yeah, I'm going to call this 'Mrs. O'Leary's Fire' and I think it might just scare a whole lot of people."*

As it turns out, however, Brian Wilson's magic fire music is not going to scare anybody—because nobody other than the few people who heard it in the studio will ever get to listen to it. A few days after the record was finished, a building across the street from the studio burned down and, according to Brian, there was also an unusually large number of fires in Los Angeles. Afraid that his music might in fact turn out to be magic fire music, Wilson destroyed the master.

"I don't have to do a big scary fire like that," he later said. "I can do a candle and it's still fire. That would have been a really bad vibration to let out on the world, that Chicago fire. The next one is going to be a candle."

A person who thinks of himself as understanding would probably interpret this episode as an example of perhaps too-excessive artistic perfectionism. One with psychiatric inclinations would hear all this stuff about someone who actually believed music could cause fires and start using words such as neurosis and maybe even psychosis. A true student of spoken hip, however, would say *hang-up*, which covers all of the above.

As far as Brian's pretensions toward hipness are concerned, no label could do him worse harm. In the hip world, there is a widespread idea that really hip people don't have hang-ups, which gives rise to the unspoken rule (unspoken because there is also the widespread idea that really hip people don't make *any* rules) that no one who wants to be thought of as hip ever reveals his hang-ups, except maybe to his guru, and in the strictest of privacy.

In any case, whatever his talent, Brian Wilson's attempt to win a hip following and reputation foundered for many months in an obsessive cycle of creation and destruction that threatened not only his career and his future but also his marriage, his friendships, his relationship with the Beach Boys and, some of his closest friends worried, his mind.

---

* "Mrs. O'Leary's Fire" appears on Wilson's 2004 version of *Smile* under the name of "Mrs. O'Leary's Cow." The songs take their name from the urban legend that a cow owned by Mrs. O'Leary started the Great Chicago Fire of 1871 by kicking over a lantern in a barn.

For a boy who used to be known in adolescence as a lover of sweets, the whole thing must have begun to taste very sour; yet, this particular phase of Brian's drive toward whatever his goal of supreme success might be began on a rising tide that at first looked as if it would carry him and the Beach Boys beyond the Beatles, who had started just about the same time they did, into the number-one position in the international pop music fame-and-power competition.

"About a year ago I had what I considered a very religious experience," Wilson told Los Angeles writer Tom Nolan in 1966. "I took LSD, a full dose of LSD, and later, another time, I took a smaller dose. And I learned a lot of things, like patience, understanding. I can't teach you or tell you what I learned from taking it, but I consider it a very religious experience."

A short time after his LSD experience, Wilson began work on the record that was to establish him right along with the Beatles as one of the most important innovators in modern popular music. It was called *Good Vibrations*, and it took more than six months, 90 hours of tape and 11 complete versions before a 3-minute 35-second final master tape satisfied him. Among the instruments on *Good Vibrations* was an electronic device called a theremin, which had its debut in the soundtrack of the movie *Spellbound*, back in the '40s. To some people *Good Vibrations* was considerably crazier than Gregory Peck had been in the movie, but to others, Brian Wilson's new record, along with his somewhat earlier release, *Pet Sounds*, marked the beginning of a new era in pop music.

"THEY'VE FOUND THE NEW SOUND AT LAST!" shrieked the headline over a London *Sunday Express* review as "Good Vibrations" hit the English charts at number six and leaped to number one the following week. Within a few weeks, the Beach Boys had pushed the Beatles out of first place in England's *New Musical Express*' annual poll. In America, "Good Vibrations" sold nearly 400,000 copies in four days before reaching number one several weeks later and earning a gold record within another month when it hit the one-million sale mark.

It was an arrival, certainly, but in America, where there is none of the Beach Boys California-mystique that adds a special touch of romance to their records and appearances in Europe and England, the news had not yet really reached all of the people whose opinion can turn popularity into fashionability. With the exception of a professor of show business (right, professor of show business; in California such a thing is not considered unusual) who turned up one night to interview Brian, and a few young writers (such as the *Village Voice*'s Richard Goldstein, Paul Williams of *Crawdaddy!*, and Lawrence Dietz of *New York* magazine), not too many opinion-makers were prepared to accept the Beach Boys into the mainstream of the culture industry.

"Listen man," said San Francisco music critic Ralph Gleason who had only recently graduated from jazz into Bob Dylan and was apparently not yet ready for any more violent twists, "I recognize the LA hype when I hear it. I know all about the Beach Boys and I think I liked them better before, if only for sociological reasons, if you understand what I mean."

"As for the Beach Boys," an editor of the *Post* chided his writer, who had filed the world's longest Western Union telegram of a story filled with unrelieved hero worship of Brian Wilson, "I want you to understand that as an individual you feel that Brian Wilson is the greatest musician of our time, and maybe the greatest human being, but as a reporter you have got to maintain your objectivity."

"They want me to put him down," the writer complained. "That's their idea of objectivity—the put-down."

"It has to do with this idea that it's not hip to be sincere," he continued, "and they really want to be hip. What they don't understand is that last year hip was sardonic—camp, they called it. This year hip is sincere."

"When somebody as corny as Brian Wilson starts singing right out front about God and I start writing it—very *sincerely*, you understand—it puts them very up tight.

"I think it's because it reminds them of all those terribly sincere hymns and sermons they used to have to listen to in church when they were kids in Iowa or Ohio.

"Who knows? Maybe they're right. I mean, who needs all this goddamn intense sincerity all the time?"

What all this meant, of course, was that everybody agreed that Brian Wilson and the Beach Boys were still too square. It would take more than *Good Vibrations* and *Pet Sounds* to erase three-and-a-half years of *Little Deuce Coupe*—a lot more if you counted in those J. C. Penney-style custom-tailored, kandy-striped short shirts they insisted on wearing on stage.

Brian, however, had not yet heard the news, it appeared, and was steadily going about the business of trying to become hip. The Beach Boys, who have toured without him ever since he broke down during one particularly wearing trip, were now in England and Europe, phoning back daily reports of enthusiastic fan hysteria—screaming little girls tearing at their flesh, wild press conferences, private chats with the Rolling Stones. Washed in the heat of a kind of attention they had never received in the United States even at the height of their commercial success, three Beach Boys—Brian's brothers, Dennis and Carl, and his cousin, Mike Love—walked into a London Rolls-Royce showroom and bought four Phantom VII limousines, one for each of them and a fourth for Brian. Al Jardine and Bruce Johnston, the Beach Boys who are not corporate members of the Beach Boys enterprises, sent their best regards and bought themselves some new clothing.

"I think this London thing has really helped," said Brian with satisfaction after he had made the color selection on his $32,000 toy—a ducal-burgundy lacquered status symbol ordinarily reserved for heads of state. "That's just what the boys needed, a little attention to jack up their confidence." Then, learning that he wouldn't be able to have his new car for three months, he went out and bought an interim Rolls-Royce for $20,000 from Mamas and Papas producer, Lou Adler, taking possession of the automobile just in time to meet his group at the airport as they returned home.

"It's a great environment for conducting business," he explained as his friend and former road manager, Terry Sachen, hastily pressed into service as interim chauffeur for the interim Rolls-Royce, informally uniformed in his usual fringed deerskins and moccasins, drove the car through Hollywood to one of Brian's favorite eating places, the Pioneer Chicken drive-in on Sunset Boulevard.

"This car is really out of sight," said Brian, filling up on fried shrimp in the basket. "Next time we go up to Capitol, I'm going to drive up in my Rolls-Royce limo. You've got to do those things with a little style. It's not just an ordinary visit that way—it's an arrival, right? Wow! That's really great—an *arrival*, in my limo. It'll blow their minds!"

Whether or not the interim Rolls-Royce actually ever blew the minds of the hard-nosed executives who run Capitol Records is something to speculate on, but no one in the record industry with a sense of history could have failed to note that this very same limousine had once belonged to John Lennon; and in the closing months of 1966, with the Beach Boys home in Los Angeles, Brian rode the *Good Vibrations* high, driving forward in bursts of enormous energy that seemed destined before long to earn him the throne of the international empire of pop music still ruled by John Lennon and the Beatles.

At the time, it looked as if the Beatles were ready to step down. Their summer concerts in America had been only moderately successful at best, compared to earlier years. There were ten thousand empty seats at Shea Stadium in New York and 11 lonely fans at the airport in Seattle. Mass media, underground press, music-industry trade papers and the fan magazines were filled with fears that the Beatles were finished, that the group was breaking up. Lennon was off acting in a movie; McCartney was walking around London alone, said to be carrying a giant torch for his sometime girl friend Jane Asher; George Harrison was getting deeper and deeper into a mystical

Indian thing under the instruction of *sitar*-master Ravi Shankar; and Ringo was collecting material for a Beatles museum.

In Los Angeles, Brian Wilson was riding around in the Rolls-Royce that had once belonged to John Lennon, pouring a deluge of new sounds on to miles of stereo tape in three different recording studios booked day and night for him in month-solid blocks, holding court nightly at his $240,000 Beverly Hills Babylonian-modern home, and, after guests left, sitting at his grand piano until dawn, writing new material.

The work in progress was an album called *Smile*. "I'm writing a teen-age symphony to God," Brian told dinner guests on an October evening. He then played for them the collection of black acetate trial records which lay piled on the floor of his red imitation-velvet wallpapered bedroom with its leopard-print bedspread. In the bathroom, above the wash basin, there was a plastic color picture of Jesus Christ with trick effect eyes that appeared to open and close when you moved your head. Sophisticate newcomers pointed it out to each other and laughed slyly, almost hoping to find a Keane painting among decorations ranging from Lava Lamps to a department-store rack of dozens of dolls, each still in its plastic bubble container, the whole display trembling like a space-age Christmas tree to the music flowing out into the living-room.

Brian shuffled through the acetates, most of which were unlabelled, identifying each by subtle differences in the patterns of the grooves. He had played them so often he knew the special look of each record the way you know the key to your front door by the shape of its teeth. Most were instrumental tracks, cut while the Beach Boys were in Europe, and for these Brian supplied the vocal in a high sound that seemed to come out of his head rather than his throat as he somehow managed to create complicated four and five part harmonies with only his own voice.

"Rock, rock, Plymouth rock roll over," Brian sang. "Bicycle rider, see what you done done to the church of the native American Indian ... Over and over the crow cries uncover the cornfields ... Who ran the Iron Horse ... Out in the farmyard the cook is chopping lumber; out in the barnyard the chickens do their number ... Bicycle rider see what you done done..." A panorama of American history filled the room as the music shifted from theme to theme; the tinkling harpsichord sounds of the bicycle rider pushed sad Indian sounds across the continent; the Iron Horse pounded across the plains in a wide open rolling rhythm that summoned up visions of the old West; civilized chickens bobbed up and down in a tiny ballet of comic barnyard melody; the inexorable bicycle music, cold and charming as an infinitely talented music box, reappeared and faded away.

Like medieval choirboys, the voices of the Beach Boys pealed out in wordless prayer from the last acetate, thirty seconds of chorale that reached upward to the vaulted stone ceilings of an empty cathedral lit by thousands of tiny votive candles melting at last into one small, pure pool that whispered a universal amen in a sigh without words.

Brian's private radio show was finished. In the dining-room a candle-lit table with a dark blue cloth was set for 10 persons. In the kitchen, Marilyn Wilson was trying to get the meal organized and served, aided and hindered by the chattering suggestions of the guests' wives and girlfriends. When everyone was seated and waiting for the food, Brian tapped his knife idly on a white china plate.

"Listen to that," he said. "That's really great!" Everybody listened as Brian played the plate. "Come on, let's get something going here," he ordered. "Michael—do this. David—you do this." A plate-and-spoon musicale began to develop as each guest played a distinctly different technique, rhythm and melody under Brian's enthusiastic direction.

"That's absolutely unbelievable!" said Brian. "Isn't that unbelievable? That's so unbelievable I'm going to put it on the album. Michael, I want you to get a sound system up here tomorrow and I want everyone to be here tomorrow night. We're going to get this on tape."

Brian Wilson's plate-and-spoon musicale never did reach the public, but only because he forgot about it. Other sounds equally strange have found their way on to his records. On *Pet Sounds*, for example, on some tracks there is an odd, soft, hollow percussion effect that most musicians assume is some kind of electronically transmuted drum sound—a conga drum played with a stick perhaps, or an Indian tom-tom. Actually, it's drummer Hal Blaine playing the bottom of a plastic jug that once contained Sparklettes spring water. And, of course, at the end of the record there is the strangely affecting track of a train roaring through a lonely railroad crossing as a bell clangs and Brian's dogs, Banana, a beagle, and Louie, a dark brown Weimaraner, bark after it.

More significant, perhaps, to those who that night heard the original instrumental tracks for both *Smile* and the Beach Boys' new single, "Heroes and Villains," is that entire sequences of extraordinary power and beauty are missing in the finished version of the single, and will undoubtedly be missing as well from *Smile*—victims of Brian's obsessive tinkering and, more importantly, sacrifices to the same strange combination of superstitious fear and God-like conviction of his own power he displayed when he destroyed the fire music.

The night of the dining-table concerto, it was the God-like confidence Brian must have been feeling as he put his guests on his trip, but the fear was soon to take over. At his house that night, he had assembled a new set of players to introduce into his life game, each of whom was to perform a specific role in the grander game he was playing with the world.

Earlier in the summer, Brian had hired Van Dyke Parks, a super-sophisticated young songwriter and composer, to collaborate with him on the lyrics for *Smile*. With Van Dyke working for him, he had a fighting chance against John Lennon, whose literary skill and Liverpudlian wit had been one of the most important factors in making the Beatles the darlings of the hip intelligentsia.

With that flank covered, Brian was ready to deal with some of the other problems of trying to become hip, the most important of which was how was he going to get in touch with some really hip people. In effect, the dinner party at the house was his first hip social event, and the star of the evening, so far as Brian was concerned, was Van Dyke Parks' manager, David Anderle, who showed up with a whole group of very hip people.

Elegant, cool and impossibly cunning, Anderle was an artist who had somehow found himself in the record business as an executive for MGM Records, where he had earned himself a reputation as a genius by purportedly thinking up the million-dollar movie-TV-record offer that briefly lured Bob Dylan to MGM from Columbia until everybody had a change of heart and Dylan decided to go back home to Columbia.

Anderle had skipped back and forth between painting and the record business, with mixed results in both. Right now he was doing a little personal management and thinking about painting a lot. His appeal to Brian was simple: everybody recognized David Anderle as one of the hippest people in Los Angeles. In fact, he was something like the mayor of hipness as far as some people were concerned. And not only that, he was a genius.

Within six weeks, he was working for the Beach Boys; everything that Brian wanted seemed at last to be in reach. Like a magic genie, David Anderle produced miracles for him. A new Beach Boys record company was set up, Brother Records, with David Anderle at its head and, simultaneously, the Beach Boys sued Capitol Records in a move designed to force a renegotiation of their contract with the company.

The house was full of underground press writers; Anderle's friend Michael Vosse was on the Brother Records payroll out scouting TV contracts and performing other odd jobs. Another of Anderle's friends was writing the story on Brian for the *Saturday Evening Post* and a film crew from CBS-TV was up at the house filming for a documentary to be narrated by Leonard Bernstein. The Beach Boys were having meetings once or twice a week with teams of experts, briefing them on corporate policy, drawing complicated chalk patterns as they described the millions of dollars everyone was going to earn out of all this.

As 1967 opened it seemed as though Brian and the Beach Boys were assured of a new world of success; yet something was going wrong. As the corporate activity reached a peak of intensity, Brian was becoming less and less productive and more and more erratic. *Smile*, which was to have been released for the Christmas season, remained unfinished. "Heroes and Villains," which was virtually complete, remained in the can, as Brian kept working out new little pieces and then scrapping them.

Van Dyke Parks had left and come back and would leave again, tired of being constantly dominated by Brian. Marilyn Wilson was having headaches and Dennis Wilson was leaving his wife. Session after session was cancelled. One night a studio full of violinists waited while Brian tried to decide whether or not the vibrations were friendly or hostile. The answer was hostile and the session was cancelled, at a cost of some $3,000. Everything seemed to be going wrong. Even the *Post* story fell through.

Brian seemed to be filled with secret fear. One night at the house, it began to surface. Marilyn sat nervously painting her fingernails as Brian stalked up and down, his face tight and his eyes small and red.

"What's the matter, Brian? You're really strung out," a friend asked.

"Yeah, I'm really strung out. Look, I mean I really feel strange. A really strange thing happened to me tonight. Did you see this picture, *Seconds*?"

"No, but I know what it's about; I read the book."

"Look, come into the kitchen; I really have to talk about this." In the kitchen they sat down in the black and white hounds tooth-check wallpapered dinette area. A striped window shade clashed with the checks and the whole room vibrated like some kind of pop art painting. Ordinarily, Brian wouldn't sit for more than a minute in it, but now he seemed to be unaware of anything except what he wanted to say.

"I walked into that movie," he said in a tense, high-pitched voice, "and the first thing that happened was a voice from the screen said 'Hello, Mr. Wilson.' It completely blew my mind. You've got to admit that's pretty spooky, right?"

"Maybe."

"That's not all. Then the whole thing was there. I mean my whole life. Birth and death and rebirth. The whole thing. Even the beach was in it, a whole thing about the beach. It was my whole life right there on the screen."

"It's just a coincidence, man. What are you getting all excited about?"

"Well, what if it isn't a coincidence? What if it's real? You know there's mind gangsters these days. There could be mind gangsters, couldn't there? I mean, look at Spector, he could be involved in it, couldn't he? He's going into films. How hard would it be for him to set up something like that?"

"Brian, Phil Spector is not about to make a million-dollar movie just to scare you. Come on, stop trying to be so dramatic."

"All right, all right. I was just a little bit nervous about it," Brian said, after some more back and forth about the possibility that Phil Spector, the record producer, had somehow influenced the making of *Seconds* to disturb Brian Wilson's tranquility. "I just had to get it out of my system. You can see where something like that could scare someone, can't you?"

They went into Brian's den, a small room papered in psychedelic orange, blue, yellow and red wall fabric with rounded corners. At the end of the room there was a jukebox filled with Beach Boys singles and Phil Spector hits. Brian punched a button and Spector's *Be My Baby* began to pour out at top volume.

"Spector has always been a big thing with me, you know. I mean I heard that song three and a half years ago and I knew that it was between him and me. I knew exactly where he was at and now I've gone beyond him. You can understand how that movie might get someone upset under those circumstances, can't you?"

Brian sat down at his desk and began to draw a little diagram on a piece of printed stationery with his name at the top in the kind of large fat script printers of charitable dinner journals use when the customer asks for a hand-lettered look. With a felt-tipped pen, Brian drew a close approximation of a growth curve. "Spector started the whole thing," he said, dividing the curve into periods. "He was the first one to use the studio. But I've gone beyond him now. I'm doing the spiritual sound, a white spiritual sound. Religious music. Did you hear the Beatles album? Religious, right? That's the whole movement. That's where I'm going. It's going to scare a lot of people.

"Yeah," Brian said, hitting his fist on the desk with a large slap that sent the parakeets in a large cage facing him squalling and whistling. "Yeah," he said and smiled for the first time all evening. "That's where I'm going and it's going to scare a lot of people when I get there."

As the year drew deeper into winter, Brian's rate of activity grew more and more frantic, but nothing seemed to be accomplished. He tore the house apart and half redecorated it. One section of the living-room was filled with a full-sized Arabian tent and the dining-room, where the grand piano stood, was filled with sand to a depth of a foot or so and draped with nursery curtains. He had had his windows stained gray and put a sauna bath in the bedroom. He battled with his father and complained that his brothers weren't trying hard enough. He accused Mike Love of making too much money.

One by one, he canceled out the friends he had collected, sometimes for the strangest of reasons. An acquaintance of several months who had become extremely close with Brian showed up at a record session and found a guard barring the door. Michael Vosse came out to explain.

"Hey man, this is really terrible," said Vosse, smiling under a broad-brimmed straw hat. "It's not you, it's your chick. Brian says she's a witch and she's messing with his brain so bad by ESP that he can't work. It's like the Spector thing. You know how he is. Say, I'm really sorry." A couple of months later, Vosse was gone. Then, in the late spring, Anderle left. The game was over.

Several months later, the last move in Brian's attempt to win the hip community was played out. On July 15, the Beach Boys were scheduled to appear at the Monterey International Pop Music Festival, a kind of summit of rock music with the emphasis on love, flowers and youth. Although Brian was a member of the board of this non-profit event, the Beach Boys canceled their commitment to perform. The official reason was that their negotiations with Capitol Records were at a crucial stage and they had to get "Heroes and Villains" out right away. The second official reason was that Carl, who had been arrested for refusing to report for induction into the army (he was later cleared in court), was so upset that he wouldn't be able to sing.

Whatever the merit in these reasons, the real one may have been closer to something another Monterey board member suggested: "Brian was afraid that the hippies from San Francisco would think the Beach Boys were square and boo them."

But maybe Brian was right. "Those candy-striped shirts just wouldn't have made it at Monterey, man," said one person who was there.

Whatever the case, at the end of the summer, *Heroes and Villains* was released in sharply edited form and *Smile* was reported to be on its way. In the meantime, however, the Beatles had released *Sergeant Pepper's Lonely Hearts Club Band* and John Lennon was riding about London in a bright yellow Phantom VII Rolls Royce painted with flowers on the sides and his zodiac symbol on the top. In *Life* magazine, Paul McCartney came out openly for LSD and in the Haight-Ashbury district of San Francisco George Harrison walked through the streets blessing the hippies. Ringo was still collecting material for a Beatles museum. However good *Smile* might turn out to be, it seemed somehow that once more the Beatles had outdistanced the Beach Boys.

Back during that wonderful period in the fall of 1966 when everybody seemed to be his friend and plans were being laid for Brother Records and all kinds of fine things, Brian had gone on a brief visit to Michigan to hear a Beach Boys concert. The evening of his return, each of his friends and important acquaintances received a call asking everyone to please come to the airport to meet Brian, it was very important. When they gathered at the airport, Brian had a photographer on hand to take a series of group pictures. For a long time, a huge mounted blow-up of the best of the photographs hung on the living-room wall, with some thirty people staring out—everyone from Van Dyke Parks and David Anderle to Michael Vosse and Terry Sachen. In the foreground was the *Saturday Evening Post* writer looking sourly out at the world.

The picture is no longer on Brian's wall and most of the people in it are no longer his friends. One by one each of them had either stepped out of the picture or been forced out of it. The whole cycle has returned to its beginning. Brian, who started out in Hawthorne, California, with his two brothers and a cousin, once more has surrounded himself with relatives. The house in Beverly Hills is empty. Brian and Marilyn are living in their new Spanish Mission estate in Bel-Air, cheek by jowl with the Mamas and the Papas' Cass Elliott.

What remains, of course, is *Heroes and Villains*, a record some people think is better than anything the Beatles ever wrote. And there is also a spectacular peak, a song called *Surf's Up* that Brian recorded for the first time in December in Columbia Records' Studio A for a CBS-TV pop music documentary. Earlier in the evening the film crew had covered a Beach Boys vocal session which had gone very badly. Now, at midnight, the Beach Boys had gone home and Brian was sitting in the back of his car, smoking moodily.

In the dark car, he breathed heavily, his hands in his lap, eyes staring nowhere.

"All right," he said at last, "Let's just sit here and see if we can get into something positive, but without any words. Let's just get into something quiet and positive on a nonverbal level." There was a long silence.

"OK, let's go," he said, and then, quickly, he was in the studio rehearsing, spotlighted in the center of the huge dark room, the cameraman moving about him invisibly outside the light.

"Let's do it," he announced, and the tape began to roll. In the control room no one moved. David Oppenheim, the TV producer, fortyish, handsome, usually studiously detached and professional, lay on the floor, hands behind his head, eyes closed. For three minutes and 27 seconds, Wilson played with delicate intensity, speaking moodily through the piano. Then he was finished. Oppenheim, whose last documentary had been a study of Stravinsky, lay motionless.

"That's it," Wilson said as the tape continued to whirl. The mood broke. As if awakening from heavy sleep the people stirred and shook their heads.

"I'd like to hear that," Wilson said. As his music replayed, he sang the lyrics in a high, almost falsetto voice, the cameras on him every second.

"*The diamond necklace played the pawn,*" Wilson sang. "*...A blind class aristocracy, back through the opera glass you see the pit and the pendulum drawn.*

"*Columnated ruins domino.*" His voice reached upward; the piano faltered a new set of falling chords.

In a slow series of impressionistic images the song moved to its ending:

I heard the word:

Wonderful thing!

A children's song!" On the last word Brian's voice rose and fell, like the ending of that prayer chorale he had played so many months before.

"That's really special," someone said.

"Special, that's right," said Wilson quietly. "Van Dyke and I really kind of thought we had done something special when we finished that one." He went back into the studio, put on the earphones and sang the song again for his audience in the control room, for the revolving tape recorder and for the cameras which relentlessly followed as he struggled to make manifest what still only existed as a perfect, incommunicable sound in his head.

At home, as the black acetate dub turned on his bedroom hi-fi set, Wilson tried to explain the words.

It's a man at a concert," he said. "All around him there's the audience, playing their roles, dressed up in fancy clothes, looking through opera glasses, but so far away from the drama, from life—*Back through the opera glass you see the pit and the pendulum drawn.*"

"The music begins to take over. *Columnated ruins domino.* Empires, ideas, lives, institutions—everything has to fall, tumbling like dominoes.

"He begins to awaken to the music; sees the pretentiousness of everything. *The music hall a costly bow.* Then even the music is gone, turned into a trumpeter swan, into what the music really is.

"*Canvas the town and brush the backdrop.* He's off in his vision, on a trip. Reality is gone; he's creating it like a dream. *Dove-nested towers.* Europe, a long time ago. *The laughs come hard in Auld Lang Syne.* The poor people in the cellar taverns, trying to make themselves happy by singing.

"Then there's the parties, the drinking, trying to forget the wars, the battles at sea. *While at port a do or die.* Ships in the harbor, battling it out. A kind of Roman Empire thing.

"*A Choke of grief.* At his own sorrow and the emptiness of his life, because he can't even cry for the suffering in the world, for his own suffering.

"And then, hope. *Surf's up! ... Come about hard and join the once and often spring you gave.* Go back to the kids, to the beach, to childhood.

"*I heard the word*—of God; *Wonderful thing*—the joy of enlightenment, of seeing God. And what is it? A *children's song!* And then there's the song itself; the song of children; the song of the universe rising and falling in wave after wave, the song of God, hiding His love from us, but always letting us find Him again, like a mother singing to her children."

The record was over. Wilson went into the kitchen and squirted Reddi-Whip direct from the can into his mouth; made himself a chocolate Great Shake, and ate a couple of candy bars.

"Of course that's a very intellectual explanation," he said. "But maybe sometimes you have to do an intellectual thing. If they don't get the words, they'll get the music, because that's where it's really at, in the music. You can get hung up in words, you know. Maybe they work; I don't know." He fidgeted with a telescope.

"This thing is so bad," he complained. "So Mickey Mouse. It just won't work smoothly. I was really freaked out on astronomy when I was a kid. Baseball too. I guess I went through a lot of phases. A lot of changes, too. But you can really get into things through the stars. And swimming. A lot of swimming. It's physical; really Zen, right? The whole spiritual thing is very physical. Swimming really does it sometimes." He sprawled on the couch and continued in a very small voice.

"So that's what I'm doing. Spiritual music."

"Brian," Marilyn called as she came into the room wearing a quilted bathrobe, "do you want me to get you anything, honey? I'm going to sleep."

"No, Mar," he answered, rising to kiss his wife goodnight. "You go on to bed. I want to work for a while."

"C'mon kids," Marilyn yelled to the dogs as she padded off to bed. "Time for bed. Louie! Banana! Come to bed. Goodnight, Brian. Goodnight, everybody."

Wilson paced. He went to the piano and began to play. His guests moved toward the door. From the piano, his feet shuffling in the sand, he called a perfunctory goodbye and continued to play, a melody beginning to take shape. Outside, the piano spoke from the house. Brian Wilson's guests stood for a moment, listening. As they got into their car, the melancholy piano moaned.

"Here's one that's really outasight from the fantabulous Beach Boys!" screamed a local early morning Top-40 DJ from the car radio on the way home, a little hysterical, as usual, his voice drowning out the sobbing introduction to the song.

"We're sending this one out for Bob and Carol in Pomona. They've been going steady now for six months. Happy six months, kids, and dig! *Good Vibrations! The Beach Boys! Outasight!*"

18

Rock and the Counterculture

CHESTER ANDERSON

A science fiction novelist and founding member of the Underground Press Syndicate, Chester Anderson (1932–1991) was also an integral presence in the 1960s San Francisco countercultural scene. Anderson's essays appeared in many places, including the *San Francisco Oracle*, whose twelve-issue run from 1966–1968 established the paper as the leading publication of the Haight-Ashbury District (the home of groups like the Jefferson Airplane and the Grateful Dead). The descriptions he sets forth in his "Notes for the New Geology" are a far cry from what rock 'n' roll had signified a mere decade before and hint at a broad generational shift. Anderson evokes a dizzying array of "principles" that situate rock as more than just music; it is a cultural, participatory phenomenon, intimately linked with psychedelic drugs, tribal rituals, and the "aesthetic of discovery." Most of all he sees rock as the greatest realization of Marshall McLuhan's 1960s media age, a synaesthetic technological experience that renders obsolete the "typeheads" (those still rooted in the power of "the word") of an older era.[*] Anderson also evokes what at first glance may seem to be an unusual comparison between rock and Baroque music. Yet as musicologist Richard Middleton has noted, there is a "high syntactic correlation" between rock and Baroque that does not apply as strongly to other historical art music periods.[†] Both use rather formulaic and repetitive harmonic progressions, "strongly marked beats," and fairly limited formal ideas. Procol Harum made this connection explicit in 1967 with their Top 10 hit, "A Whiter Shade of Pale," which derived its harmonic and melodic material from Johann Sebastian Bach's *Cantata BWV 140*, "Sleepers Awake."[‡]

I

Rock's the first head music we've had since the end of the baroque.[§] By itself, without the aid of strobe lights, day-glo paints & other sub-imaginative copouts, it engages the entire sensorium, appealing to the intelligence with no interference from the intellect. Extremely typographic people are unable to experience it, which—because TV didn't approach universality till 1950—is why the rock folk are so young, generally. (Most of the astounding exceptions are people, like the poet Walter Lowenfels, who have lived a long time but have not become old.)

---

[*] Among Marshall McLuhan's many publications, his most widely read and influential book of the 1960s was *Understanding Media: The Extensions of Man* (New York: McGraw-Hill, 1964.)
[†] Richard Middleton, *Studying Popular Music* (Philadelphia: Open University Press, 1990), 30–31.
[‡] *Source:* Chester Anderson, "Notes for the New Geology," *San Francisco Oracle* I (1967), pp. 2, 23.
[§] "Head" music was conventional slang for music associated with psychedelic drugs or the psychedelic experience.

II

Some Principles:

- That rock is essentially head (or even psychedelic) music.
- That rock is a legitimate avant garde art form, with deep roots in the music of the past (especially the baroque & before), great vitality, and vast potential for growth & development, adaptation, experiment, etcetera.
- That rock shares most of its formal/structural principles with baroque music (wherein lie its most recent cultural roots), and that it & baroque can be judged by the same broad standards (the governing principles being that of mosaic structure of tonal & textural contrast: tactility, collage).
- That rock is evolving Sturgeonesque *homo gestalt* configurations:*
  - the groups themselves, far more intimately interrelated & integrated than any comparable ensembles in the past;
  - super-families, like Kerista & the more informal communal pads;
  - and pre-initiate tribal groups, like the teenyboppers; all in evident & nostalgic response to technological & population pressures.
- That rock is an intensely participational & non-typographic art form, forerunner of something much like McLuhan's covertly projected spherical society.
- That far from being degenerate or decadent, rock is a regenerative & revolutionary art, offering us our first real hope for the future (indeed, for the present) since August 6, 1945; and that its effects on the younger population, especially those effects most deplored by typeheads, have all been essentially good & healthy so far.
- That rock principles are not limited to music, and that much of the shape of the future can be seen in its aspirations today (these being mainly total freedom, total experience, total love, peace & mutual affection).
- That today's teenyboppers will be voting tomorrow and running for office the day after.
- That rock is an intensely synthesizing art, an art of amazing relationships (collage is rock & roll), able to absorb (maybe) all of society into itself as an organizing force, transmuting & reintegrating what it absorbs (as it has so far); and that its practitioners & audience are learning to perceive & manipulate reality in wholly new ways, quite alien to typeheads.
- That rock has reinstated the ancient truth that art is fun.
- That rock is a way of life, international & verging in this decade on universal; and can't be stopped, retarded, put down, muted, modified or successfully controlled by typeheads, whose arguments don't apply & whose machinations don't mesh because they can't perceive (dig) what rock really is & does.
- That rock is a tribal phenomenon, immune to definition & other typographical operations, and constitutes what might be called a 20th century magic.
- That rock seems to have synthesized most of the intellectual & artistic movements of our time & culture, cross-fertilizing them & forcing them rapidly toward fruition & function.
- That rock is a vital agent in breaking down absolute & arbitrary distinctions.
- That any artistic activity not allied to rock is doomed to preciousness & sterility.
- That group participation, total experience & complete involvement are rock's minimal desiderata and those as well of a world that has too many people.

---

* This is a reference to science fiction writer Theodore Sturgeon's 1953 novel *More Than Human*, in which a group of psychically gifted individuals join together their powers to form a single "*homo gestalt.*"

- That rock is creating the social rituals of the future.
- That the medium is indeed the message, & rock knows what that means.
- That no arbitrary limitations of rock are valid (i.e., that a rock symphony or opera, for example, is possible).
- That rock is handmade, and only the fakes are standardized.
- That rock presents an aesthetic of discovery.

III

Marshall McLuhan makes no sense at all, not as I was taught to define *sense* in my inadequately cynical youth. He's plainly no Aquinas. And yet, somehow, he embarrassingly manages to explain to perfection an overwhelming array of things that used to make even less sense than he does and were somewhat threatening as well: things like pop, op & camp (which sounds like a breakfast food); the psychedelic revolution, the pot & acid explosion; the Haight-Ashbury community, and especially what we'll keep on calling Rock & Roll until we can find some name more appropriate for it. (I nominate Head Music, but I don't expect it to catch on.)

Not that McLuhan mentions any of these things. He simply gives the clues. Synthesis and synaesthesia; non-typographic, non-linear, basically mosaic & mythic modes of perception, involvement of the whole sensorium; roles instead of jobs; participation in depth; extended awareness; preoccupation with textures, with tactility, with multisensory experiences—put 'em all together & you have a weekend on Haight Street.

The electronic extension of the central nervous system, the evolutionary storm that's happening right now (which is having, slowly, exactly the same effect on the whole world as acid has had on use) makes everything else make sense; and McLuhan taught us how to see it. He doesn't *have* to make sense.

IV

We're still so hooked on mainly visual perception that the possibilities of our other senses are almost unimaginable. We still interpret highs in visual terms, for instance: though acid is mainly tactile, spatial, visceral & integrative; whilst pot affects mostly hearing & touch. It's all a matter of conditioning: we'll learn.

The things a really imaginative engineer could accomplish by working on our many senses, singly & in orchestrated combinations, are staggering. Imagine: sensory counterpoint—the senses registering contradictory stimuli & the brain having fun trying to integrate them. Imagine *tasting* g minor! The incredible synaesthesiae!

Rock & roll is toying with this notion.

Though we've been brought up to think of music as a purely auditory art, we actually perceive it with the whole body in a complex pattern of sympathetic tensions & interacting stimuli.

Melodies—and especially vocal melodies or tunes in the vocal range—affect the larynx. It follows the tune, subvocalizing. As the line ascends, the larynx tightens, and as the line descends it relaxes, responding sympathetically to the tension of the tones. (The larynx also tightens in response to strong emotion, just before the tears begin.) That's what makes an unexpected high note such an emotional event, because the part of the brain in charge of such things can't tell one kind of tension from another. That's also much of what makes melodies work. Whether you want to or not, you participate.

Meanwhile, low notes—especially on the bass, and most acutely if it's plucked & amplified—are experienced in the abdomen as localized vibrations, an amazingly private sensation impossible to resist. The deeper the note, furthermore, the lower down on the trunk it seems to be felt. A properly organized R&B bass line is experienced as a pattern of incredibly intimate caresses: still more unavoidable participation.

(The same visceral perception yields a sense of musical space.)

A steady bass line in scales induces something like confidence and/or well-being. A jagged, syncopated bass can range you from nervous exhilaration to utter frenzy. (Old Bach knew all about this.) The possibilities are next to endless.

Rhythms, meanwhile, affect the heart, skeletal muscles & motor nerves, and can be used to play games with these pretty much at will. Repeated patterns (ostinati) & drones induce an almost instant light hypnosis (just like grass), locking the mind on the music at hand & intensifying all the other reactions. Long, open chords lower the blood pressure: crisp, repeated chords raise it.

And this is only the beginning, the barest outline of our physical response to music, but data enough for me to make my point. An arranger/composer who knew all this, especially if he had electronic instruments to work with, could play a listener's body like a soft guitar. He could score the listener's body as part of the arrangement, creating an intensity of participation many people don't even achieve in sex. (So far this seems to have happened mainly by accident.) And there's no defense but flight: not even the deaf are completely immune.

19

"The Electric Kool-Aid Acid Test"

TOM WOLFE

Along with writers like Norman Mailer and Joan Didion, Tom Wolfe's works of the mid-1960s ushered in the age of "new journalism," a term that Wolfe (born 1930) himself coined. His celebrated best-selling novel, *The Electric Kool-Aid Acid Test*, broke with many of the conventions to which reporters and journalists typically adhered. Rather than simply describing from an objective standpoint the adventures of author/LSD guru Ken Kesey (1935–2001) and his coterie, The Merry Pranksters, Wolfe positions himself as an anonymous, informed insider who narrates the group's exploits in exaggerated, sensational detail. This fantastical approach is accompanied by a turn to fictional literary devices, whether it be Wolfe's penchant for inventive grammatical constructions or his tendency to flesh out the narrative through the imagined dialogue and thought processes of the story's central characters. In the passage featured here, Wolfe recounts two of the early "acid tests" or LSD experiments, the first at Big Nig's house (December 4, 1965) and the second at Muir Beach (December 11, 1965). Both of these gatherings would provide the impetus for the large-scale Trips Festival held in San Francisco in January 1966, one of the first events of the emerging counterculture to draw nationwide media attention. Jerry Garcia (1942–1995) and the Grateful Dead were integral components of the acid tests and they figure prominently in Wolfe's descriptions. Their live music performances were at the center of a barrage of light designs, film projections, electronic sound manipulations, and experimental drugs, all of which fused together to make the acid test a truly mixed media event. Wolfe's book remains widely read precisely because it captures the LSD experience in such vibrant language, a fact made all the more remarkable by Wolfe's claim that he never ingested any of the drugs himself.[*]

The first Acid Test ended up more like one of the old acid parties at La Honda, which is to say, a private affair, and mostly formless.[†] It was meant to be public, but the Pranksters were not the world's greatest at the mechanics of things, like hiring a hall. The first one was going to be in Santa Cruz. But they couldn't hire a hall in time. They had to hold it out at Babbs' house, a place known as the Spread, just outside of Santa Cruz in a community known as Soquel.[‡] The Spread was like a rundown chicken farm. The wild vetch and dodder vines were gaining ground every minute, at least where the ground wasn't burnt off or beaten down into a clay muck. There were fat brown dogs and broken vehicles and rusted machines and rotting troughs and recapped tires and a little old farmhouse with linoleum floors and the kind of old greasy easy chairs that upholstery flies hover

---

[*] *Source:* Tom Wolfe, "Cosmo's Tasmanian Deviltry," from *The Electric Kool-Aid Acid Test* (New York: Farrar, Straus & Giroux, 1968), pp. 208–18.

[†] La Honda was the site of Ken Kesey's house, where many of the previous acid parties had been held.

[‡] Babbs is Ken Babbs, one of the major members of the Merry Pranksters

over in nappy clouds and move off about three-quarters of an inch when you wave your hand at them. But there were also wild Day-Glo creations on the walls and ceilings, by Babbs, and the place was private and tucked off by itself. In any case, they were stuck with the Spread.

About all the advertising they could do was confined to the day of the Test itself. Norman Hartweg had painted a sign on some cardboard and tacked it onto some boards Babbs had used as cue signs in the movie, and put it up in the Hip Pocket Bookstore. CAN *YOU* PASS THE ACID TEST? The Hip Pocket Bookstore was a paperback bookstore that Hassler and Peter Demma, one of the Prankster outer circle, were running in Santa Cruz. They left word in the store that afternoon that it was going to be at Babbs'. A few local bohos saw it and came out, but mainly it was the Pranksters and their friends who showed up at the Spread that night, including a lot of the Berkeley crowd that had been coming to La Honda. Plus Allen Ginsberg and his entourage.

It started off as a party, with some of the movie flashed on the walls, and lights, and tapes, and the Pranksters providing the music themselves, not to mention the LSD. The Pranksters' strange atonal Chinese music broadcast on all frequencies, à la John Cage. It was mostly just another La Honda party—but then around 3 a.m. a thing happened … The non-involved people, the people just there for the beano, the people who hadn't seen the Management, like the Berkeley people, they had all left by 3 a.m. and the Test was down to some kind of core … It ended up with Kesey on one side of Babbs' living room and Ginsberg on the other, with everybody else arranged around these two poles like on a magnet, all the Kesey people over toward him and all the Ginsberg people toward him—The super-West and the super-East—and the subject got to be Vietnam. Kesey gives his theory of whole multitudes of people joining hands in a clump and walking away from the war. Ginsberg said all these things, these wars, were the result of misunderstandings. Nobody who was doing the fighting ever *wanted* to be doing it, and if everybody could only sit around in a friendly way and talk it out, they could get to the root of their misunderstanding and settle it—and then from the rear of the Kesey contingent came the voice of the only man in the room who had been within a thousand miles of the war, Babbs, saying, "Yes, it's all so *very obvious.*"

It's all so very obvious…

How magical that comment seemed at that moment! The magical eighth hour of acid—how clear it all now was—Ginsberg had said it, and Babbs, the warrior, had certified it, and it had all built to this, and suddenly everything was so … very … clear…

The Acid Test at the Spread was just a dry run, of course. It didn't really … reach out into the world … But! soon … the Rolling Stones, England's second hottest pop group, were coming to San Jose, 40 miles south of San Francisco, for a show in the Civic Auditorium on December 4. Kesey can see it all, having seen it before. He can see all the wound-up wired-up teeny freaks and assorted multitudes pouring out of the Cow Palace after the Beatles show that night, the fragmented pink-tentacled beast, pouring out still aquiver with ecstasy and jelly beans all cocked and aimless with no flow to go off in…* It *is* so very obvious.

For three or four days the Pranksters searched for a hall in San Jose and couldn't come up with one—naturally—it really seemed natural and almost right that nothing should be definite until the last minute. All that was certain was that they *would* find one at the last minute. The Movie would create that much at least. And what if the multitudes didn't *know* where it was going to be until the last minute? Well, those who were meant to be there—those who were in the pudding—they would get there.† You were either on the bus or off the bus, and that went for the whole world, even in San

---

* The Beatles had played at the Cow Palace (a large San Francisco event center) on August 31, 1965.
† Someone who is in "the pudding" is part of the crowd that has adopted the acid test mentality.

Jose, California.* At the last minute Kesey talked a local boho figure known as Big Nig into letting them use his old hulk of a house.

Kesey had hooked up with a rock 'n' roll band, The Grateful Dead, led by Jerry Garcia, the same dead-end kid who used to live in the Chateau in Palo Alto with Page Browning and other seeming no-counts, lumpenbeatniks, and you had to throw them out when they came over and tried to crash the parties on Perry Lane. Garcia remembered—how they came down and used to get booted out "by Kesey and the wine drinkers." *The wine drinkers*—the middle-class bohemians of Perry Lane. They both, Kesey and Garcia, had been heading into the pudding, from different directions, all that time, and now Garcia was a, yes, beautiful person, quiet, into the pudding, and a great guitar player. Garcia had first named his group The Warlocks, meaning sorcerers or wizards, and they had been eking by playing for the beer drinkers, at jazz joints and the like around Palo Alto. To the Warlocks, the beer drinker music, even when called jazz, was just square hip. They were on to that distinction, too. For Kesey—they could just play, do their thing.

The Dead had an organist called Pig Pen, who had a Hammond electric organ, and they move the electric organ into Big Nig's ancient house, plus all of the Grateful Dead's electrified guitars and basses and the Pranksters' electrified guitars and basses and flutes and horns and the light machines and the movie projectors and the tapes and mikes and hi-fis, all of which pile up in insane coils of wires and gleams of stainless steel and winking amplifier dials before Big Nig's unbelieving eyes. His house is old and has wiring that would hardly hold a toaster. The Pranksters are primed in full Prankster regalia. Paul Foster has on his Importancy Coat and now has a huge head of curly hair, a great curly mustache pulling back into great curly mutton chops roaring off his face. Page Browning is the king of face painters. He becomes a full-fledged Devil with a bright orange face and his eyes become the centers of two great silver stars painted over the orange and his hair is silver with silver dust and he paints his lips silver with silver lipstick. This very night the Pranksters all sit down with oil pastel crayons and colored pens and at a wild rate start printing handbills on 8½ x II paper saying CAN *YOU* PASS THE ACID TEST? and giving Big Nig's address. As the jellybean-cocked masses start pouring out of the Rolling Stones concert at the Civic Auditorium, the Pranksters charge in among them. Orange & silver Devil, wild man in a coat of buttons—Pranksters. Pranksters!—handing out the handbills with the challenge, like some sort of demons, warlocks verily, come to channel the wild pointless energy built up by the Rolling Stones inside.

They come piling into Big Nig's, and suddenly acid and the worldcraze were everywhere, the electric organ vibrating through every belly in the place, kids dancing not *rock* dances, not the frug and the—what?—*swim*, mother, but dancing *ecstasy*, leaping, dervishing, throwing their hands over their heads like Daddy Grace's own stroked-out inner courtiers—yes!—Roy Seburn's lights washing past every head, Cassady rapping, Paul Foster handing people weird little things out of his Eccentric Bag, old whistles, tin crickets, burnt keys, spectral plastic handles.† Everybody's eyes turn on like lightbulbs, fuses blow, blackness—wowwww!—the things that shake and vibrate and funnel and freak out in this blackness—and then somebody slaps new fuses in and the old hulk of a house shudders back, the wiring writhing and fragmenting like molting snakes, the organs vibro-massage the belly again, fuses blow, minds scream, heads explode, neighbors call the cops, 200, 300, 400 people from out there drawn into The Movie, into the edge of the pudding at least, a mass closer and higher than any mass in history, it seems most surely, and Kesey makes minute adjustment, small toggle switch here, lubricated with Vaseline No. 634-3 diluted with carbon tetrachlo-

---

* "On the bus" is a reference to the refurbished school bus Furthur, which the Merry Pranksters famously had driven cross country to New York in 1964.

† Cassady is Neal Cassady, another of the Pranksters' inner circle, most noted for serving as Furthur's bus driver on the Pranksters' cross-country trip.

ride, and they *ripple*, Major, *ripple*, but with meaning, 400 of the attuned multitude headed toward the pudding, the first mass acid experience, the dawn of the Psychedelic, the Flower Generation and all the rest of it, and Big Nig wants the rent.

"How you holding?"

How you holding—

"I mean, like, you know," says Big Nig to Garcia. "I didn't charge Kesey nothing to use this place, like *free*, you know? and the procedure now is that every cat here *contributes*, man, to help out with the rent."

With the rent—

"Yeah, I mean, like"—says Big Nig. Big Nig stares at Garcia with the deepest look of hip spade soul authority you can imagine, and nice and officious, too—

Yeah, I mean, like—Garcia, for his part, however, doesn't know which bursts out first, the music or the orange laugh. Out the edges of his eyes he can see his own black hair framing his face—it is so long, to the shoulders, and springs out like a Sudanese soldier's—and then Big Nig's big earnest black face right in front of him flapping and washing comically out into the glistening acid-glee red sea of faces out beyond them both in the galactic red lakes on the walls—

"Yeah, I mean, like, for the *rent*, man," says Big Nig, "you already *blown* six fuses."

Blown! Six fuses! Garcia sticks his hand into his electric guitar and the notes come out like a huge orange laugh all blown fuses electric spark leaps in colors upon the glistening sea of faces. It's a freaking laugh and a half. A new star is being born, like a lightbulb in a womb, and Big Nig wants the rent—a new star being born, a new planet forming, Ahura Mazda blazing in the world womb, here before our very eyes—and Big Nig, the poor pathetic spade, wants his rent.

A freaking odd thought, that one. A big funky spade looking pathetic and square. For twenty years in the hip life, Negroes never even *looked* square. They were the archetypical soul figures. But what is Soul, or Funky, or Cool, or Baby—in the new world of the ecstasy, the All–one ... the *kairos*....

If only there were the perfect place, which would be a place big enough for the multitudes and isolated enough to avoid the cops, with their curfews and eternal hassling. Shortly after that they found the perfect place, by acci—

By *accident*, Mahavira?

The third Acid Test was scheduled for Stinson Beach, 15 miles north of San Francisco. Stinson Beach was already a gathering place for local heads. You could live all winter in little beach cottages there for next to nothing. There was a nice solid brick recreation hall on the beach, all very nice—but at the last minute that whole deal fell through, and they shifted to Muir Beach, a few miles south. The handbills were already out, all over the head sections of San Francisco, CAN *YOU* PASS THE ACID TEST, advertising Cassady & Ann Murphy Vaudeville and celebrities who *might be* there, which included anybody who happened to be in town, or might make it to town, the Fugs, Ginsberg, Roland Kirk. There were always some nice chiffon subjunctives and the future conditionals in the Prankster handbill rhetoric, but who was to deny who *might be* drawn into the Movie...

Anyway, at the last minute they headed for Muir Beach instead. The fact that many people wouldn't know about the change and would go to Stinson Beach and merely freeze in the darkness and never find the right place—somehow that didn't even seem distressing. It was part of some strange analogical order of the universe. Norman Hartweg hooked down his LSD—it was in the acid gas capsules that night—and thought of Gurdjieff. Gurdjieff wouldn't announce a meeting until the last minute. We're gonna get together tonight. The people that got there, got there; and there was message in that alone. Which was, of course: *you're either on the bus or off the bus.*

Those who were on the bus, even if they weren't Pranksters, like Marshall Efron, the round Mercury of Hip California, or the Hell's Angels ... all found it. The cops, however, never did. They were apparently thrown off by the Stinson Beach handbills.

Muir Beach had a big log-cabin-style lodge for dances, banquets, and the like. The lodge was stilted up out in a waste of frigid marsh grass. A big empty nighttime beach in winter. Some little log tourist cabins with blue doors on either side, all empty. The lodge had three big rooms and was about 100 feet long, all logs and rafters and exposed beams, a tight ship of dark wood and Roughing It. The Grateful Dead piled in with their equipment and the Pranksters with theirs, which now included a Hammond electric organ for Gretch and a great strobe light.*

The strobe! The strobe, or stroboscope, was originally an instrument for studying motion, like the way a man's legs move when he is running. In a darkened chamber, for example, you aim a bright light, flashing on and off, at the runner's legs as he runs. The light flashes on and off very rapidly, maybe three times as fast as a normal heartbeat. Every time the light flashes on, you see a new stage in the movement of the runner's legs. The successive images tend to freeze in your mind, because the light flashes off before the usual optical blur of the motion can hit you. The strobe has certain magical properties in the world of the acid heads. At certain speeds stroboscopic lights are so synched in with the pattern of brain waves that they can throw epileptics into a seizure. Heads discovered that strobes could project them into many of the sensations of an LSD experience without taking LSD. *The strobe!*

To people standing under the mighty strobe everything seemed to fragment. Ecstatic dancers—their hands flew off their arms, frozen in the air—their glistening faces came apart—a gleaming ellipse of teeth here, a pair of buffered highlit cheekbones there—all flacking and fragmenting into images as in an old flicker movie—a man in slices!—all of history pinned up on a butterfly board; the *experience*, of course. The strobe, the projectors, the mikes, the tapes, the amplifiers, the variable lag Ampex—it was all set up in a coiling gleaming clump in the Lincoln Log lodge, the communal clump, Babbs working over the dials, talking into the microphones to test them. Heads beginning to pour in. Marshall Efron and Norman, Norman already fairly zonked ... Then in comes Kesey, through the main door—

Everyone watches. His face is set, his head cocked slightly. He is going to *do* something; everyone watches, because this seems terribly important. Drawn in right away by the charismatic vacuum cleaner, they are. Kesey heads for the control center, saying nothing to anyone, reaches into the galaxy of dials, makes ... a single minute adjustment ... yes! one toggle switch, double-pole, single-throw, double-break, in the allegory of Control...

Babbs is there, bombed, but setting up the intricate glistening coils of the tapes and projectors and the rest of it. Each of the Pranksters, bombed, has some fairly exacting task to do. Norman is staring at the dials—and he can't even see the numbers, he is so bombed, the numbers are wriggling off like huge luminous parasites under a microscope—but—*function under acid*. Babbs says, "One reason we're doing this is to learn how to function on acid." Of course! Prepare for the Day—when multitudes, millions, civilizations are on acid, seeking satori, it is coming, the wave is spreading.

The heads are all sitting around on the floor, about 300 of them. Into the maelstrom! Yes. At Big Nig's in San Jose, a lot of the kids the Pranksters had corralled coming out of the Rolling Stones show did not take LSD that night, although there were enough heads at Big Nig's stoned on various things to create that sympathetic vibration known as the "contact high." But this is different. Practically everybody who has found the place, after the switch from Stinson Beach, is far enough

---

* Gretch is Gretchen Fetchin, the Prankster code name for Paula Sundsten, Ken Babbs' girlfriend (and future wife).

into the thing to know what the "acid" in the Acid Test means. A high percentage took LSD about four hours ago, rode out the first rush and are ready … now to groove … The two projectors shine forth with The Movie. The bus and the Pranksters start rolling over the walls of the lodge, Babbs and Kesey rapping on about it, the Bus lumping huge and vibrating and bouncing in great swells of heads and color—Norman, zonked, sitting on the floor, is half frightened, half ecstatic, although something in the back of his mind recognizes this as his Acid Test pattern, to sit back and watch, holding on through the rush, until 3 or 4 A.M., in the magic hours, and then dance—but so much of a rush this time! The Movie and Roy Seburn's light machine pitching the intergalactic red science-fiction seas to all corners of the lodge, oil and water and food coloring pressed between plates of glass and projected in vast size so that the very ooze of cellular Creation seems to ectoplast into the ethers and then the Dead coming in with their immense submarine vibrato vibrating, *garanging*, from the Aleutian rocks to the baja griffin cliffs of the Gulf of California. The Dead's weird sound! agony-in-ecstasis! submarine somehow, turbid half the time, tremendously loud but like sitting under a waterfall, at the same time full of sort of ghoul-show vibrato sounds as if each string on their electric guitars is half a block long and twanging in a room full of natural gas, not to mention their great Hammond electric organ, which sounds like a movie house Wurlitzer, a diathermy machine, a Citizens' Band radio and an Auto-Grind garbage truck at 4 A.M., all coming over the same frequency … Then suddenly another movie

THE FROGMAN

Babbs and Gretch and Hagen made it down in Santa Cruz, the story of Babbs the Frogman, arising from the Pacific in black neoprene Frogman suit from flippers to insect goggles, the pranking monster, falling in love with the Princess, Gretch, with floods of frames from elsewhere—the Bus Movie?—brittering in stroboscopically Frogman woos her and wins her and loses her to the Pacific Chohans in submarinal projection

BABBS! GRETCH!

Norman has never seen a movie while under acid before and it deepens, deepens, deepens in perspective, this movie, the most 3-D movie ever made, until they are standing right before him, their very neoprene fairy tails and the Pacific is so far in the distance and black out beyond the marshes around the Muir Beach lodge until Babbs and Gretch are now in the room in the flesh in two separate spots, here before me on the beach and over here in this very room in this very lodge on the beach, Babbs at the microphone and Gretch nearby at the new Hammond organ—such *synch!* that they should narrate and orchestrate their own lives like this, in variable lag, layer upon layer of variable lags

HEEEEEEEE

into the whirlpool who should appear but Owsley.* Owsley, done up in his $600 head costume, has emerged from his subterrain of espionage and paranoia to come to see the Prankster experiment for himself, and in the middle of the giddy contagion he takes LSD. They never saw him take it before. He takes the LSD and

RRRRRRRRRRRRRRRRRRRRRRRROIL

the whirlpool picks him up and spins him down into the stroboscopic stereoptic prankster panopticon in full variable lag

SUCH CREATURES

Hell's Angels come reeling in, shrieking Day-Glo, then clumping together on the floor under the black light and then most gentle Buddha blissly passing around among themselves various glittering Angel esoterica, chains, Iron Crosses, knives, buttons, coins, keys, wrenches, spark plugs, grokking

---

* Stanley Owsley, who supplied many of the psychedelic drugs for the acid tests.

over these arcana winking in the Day-Glo. Orange & Silver devil gliding through the dancers grinning his Zea-lot grin in every face, and Kesey crouched amid the gleaming coils, at the

CONTROLS

Kesey looks out upon the stroboscopic whirlpool—the dancers! flung and flinging! *in ecstasis!* gyrating! levitating! men in slices! in ping-pong balls! in the creamy bare essence and it reaches a

SYNCH

he never saw before. Heads from all over the acid world out here and all whirling into the pudding. Now let a man see what

CONTROL

is. Kesey mans the strobe and a twist of the mercury lever

Up

and they all speed up

Now

the whole whirlpool, so far into it, they are. Faster they dance, hands thrown up off their arms like confetti in the strobe flashing, blissful faces falling apart and being exchanged, for I am you and you are me in Cosmo's Tasmanian deviltry. Turn it

DOWN

and they slow down—or We turn down—It—Cosmo—turns down, still in perfect synch, one brain, one energy, a single flow of intersubjectivity. It is *possible*, this alchemy so dreamed of by all the heads. It is happening before them

CONTROL

Curiously, after the first rush at the Acid Test, there would be long intervals of the most exquisite boredom. Exquisite, because it was so unsuspected after the general frenzy. Nothing would happen, at least not in the usual sense. Those who were … not on the bus … would come to the realization that there was no schedule. The Grateful Dead did not play in *sets;* no eight numbers to a set, then a twenty-five-minute break, and so on, four or five sets and then the close-out. The Dead might play one number for five minutes or thirty minutes. Who kept time? Who *could* keep time, with history cut up in slices. The Dead could get just as stoned as anyone else. The … non-attuned would look about and here would be all manner of heads, including those running the show, the Pranksters, stroked out against the walls like slices of Jello. Waiting; with nobody looking very likely to start it back up. Those who didn't care to wait would tend to drift off, stoned or otherwise, and the Test would settle down to the pudding. The Prankster band started the strange Chinese cacophony of its own, with Gretch wailing on the new electric organ. Norman got up and danced, it being that time. He even fooled about a bit with a little light projection thing of his own, although he didn't think it was good enough, but the magic hours were coming on like electric velvet. Kesey spoke softly over the microphone. They were into the still of the hurricane, the pudding.

20

"The Country Boom"

Barret Hansen

From the 1950s rockabilly strains of Elvis Presley and Carl Perkins to the more recent alt-country sounds of Wilco and Ryan Adams, rock has long been infused with a strong country music presence. In the following excerpt from his 1969 article "The Country Boom," *Hit Parader* writer Barret Hansen (better known as radio personality Dr. Demento) details one of the key moments in the ongoing relationship between country and rock, surveying then recent releases of Bob Dylan, The Byrds, and the Flying Burrito Brothers. At precisely that moment in the late 1960s when rock musicians like John Lennon were turning away from rock's experimentations toward the more simplified structures of the blues, artists like Dylan and The Byrds were seeking a similar inspiration in country music. In his article, Hansen takes as a given that there are inherent differences that separate country from rock, whether it be in terms of instrumentation, expressive content, or the music's audience formations. Such boundaries serve a twofold purpose for Hansen: to denote an authentic sense of country music symbolism and musical practice, and to judge those rock musicians who cross over into country's territory. It is worth asking, however, why Hansen and many fans in general find these notions of purity and authenticity to be so useful. What do we gain from embracing authenticity as an evaluative measuring stick?*

Country music has been making a lot of news lately. Thanks to The Tube, Glen Campbell is now heard and seen every week by more people than the legendary Jimmie Rodgers played for in his whole lifetime.† Meanwhile, the Nashville sound is being heard everywhere, as all kinds of pop people flock to take advantage of country music's studio techniques.

The country-music industry, as they like to call it, has publicized itself with a zeal and success unmatched anywhere else in the music world. Yet, with all this happening, the music itself has become stagnant. Whereas country music in the 1950's and before was righteously anti-Establishment, the C&W industry of the 1960's is 100% commercial, tempted more and more every day by the big money of the "easy listening" market.

But if the country music establishment seems determined to shuck the most meaningful parts of its heritage in order to reach those big-spending city people, there are a lot of *other* city people picking up on that heritage. Within the last year, a whole new breed of country music has made its appearance. By combining the gentleness, warmth, and natural feeling of country music with the broad-minded imagination of modern rock, these young musicians are creating a beautiful

---

* *Source:* Barret Hansen, "The Country Boom," *Hit Parader*, November 1969, pp. 22–23, 25.

† Country & Western singer Glen Campbell had begun hosting his own TV variety show, *The Glen Campbell Good Time Hour* in 1969.

alternative to the Nashville assembly line. And in the process, they have created what will be, for many people, an alternative to the excesses of rock as well.

Bob Dylan has led the way, as he has so many times before in contemporary music. Dylan, of course, was deeply into country music even before he decided that Bobby Zimmerman wasn't the most appropriate name for himself. His first album is liberally laced with old-time country sounds. There was a time (*Bringing It All Back Home)* when he seemed to be leading the world *away* from country-folk into city-rock. No other American musician of the 1960's has made a larger contribution to the rock scene, and what it is today, than Bob Dylan.

Shortly before a motorcycle accident interrupted his career, Dylan had recorded an album in Nashville, *Blonde on Blonde.* Though this album was stylistically an extension of its predecessor, *Highway 61 Revisited,* and not really in a country bag, his choice of recording location gave a clue to his future direction. As soon as he had recovered sufficiently from his accident to record, he went back to Nashville, and recorded *John Wesley Harding.* That album, truly one of the unclouded bright spots among 1968's plethora of disappointments, marks the beginning of the new breed of country music.

All the songs in *John Wesley Harding* represent a trend toward simplicity of expression, and greater melodic character, as compared with *Blonde on Blonde.* But it is primarily the last two songs in the album, "Down Along the Cove" and "I'll Be Your Baby Tonight," that contain the germ of the new country music. These two tunes both feature Pete Drake, one of the most prominent of Nashville's famous studio side-men, on steel guitar. Now the "steel" has been a staple of country music for over thirty years, but many rock people have never seen one. The modern steel guitar is a descendant of the Hawaiian guitar, in which the strings are not fretted with the fingers, but instead played with a steel bar; hence the name. The modern steel, relying solely on electronic amplification, does away with the traditional guitar shape; the strings are strung on a table-like surface. Often there are several sets, each tuned to a different chord. The volume is controlled by a pedal, and there are other pedals to change the harmonies. The "steel" is one of the most electronic of all instruments, and it is a little surprising that it did not find a place in rock long ago.

It is the "steel" that makes the soaring countermelodies on "I'll Be Your Baby Tonight;" the sound is much more flowing, less jagged, than standard guitar lines with their inevitable sharp attacks. But there is a lot more to "Baby."

The words are remarkably free of the mixed metaphors and other poetic intricacies that had been a Dylan trademark since "A Hard Rain's Gonna Fall." Like the rare best of modern C&W, it deals with personal relationships on a very down-to-earth level, communicating honest thoughts in plain language. It doesn't call attention to its literary technique, or force you to puzzle out the meaning word by word, as does (for instance) "Gates of Eden." You get the message first, and then admire the poetry, rather than the other way around.

It's really more similar to "I Walk the Line" or "Your Cheatin' Heart" than to most of Dylan's earlier work. If it strays at all from the guidelines of taste country music has evolved for itself, it may be just a little *too* direct, too earthy … "Bring that bottle over here," etc. We of the rock world would view such touches as superbly subtle examples of Dylan's genius, breaking through needless restrictions to make his expression more eloquent. A conservative country fan would see it as a breach of taste, period. Now we're not implying that all country-and western people are that conservative, but therein lies the gulf between the traditional country audience and the rock audience. As we go along we will see some of the problems this gulf has created.

It was only appropriate that the Byrds, who did so much to spread the Dylan gospel back in 1965, became the first group to expand the new-breed country concept into a whole album. This was *Sweetheart of the Rodeo,* released in mid-1968.

Once the most celebrated group in all America, the Byrds had seen better days. *Sweetheart,* however, was hailed by all as a new beginning. Gene Clark, Mike Clark and David Crosby were gone, but drummer Kevin Kelley and singer-guitarist-songwriter Gram Parsons were ready to take their places. Amid much high expectation, the group went to Nashville, appeared on the *Grand Ole Opry* (country music's most revered institution) and recorded part of their album there, the rest being done in L.A.

Sweetheart contains two Dylan songs, a couple of originals by Gram Parsons, Woody Guthrie's "Pretty Boy Floyd," the old hymn "I Am A Pilgrim" and several songs from the modern C&W repertoire. It's a good assortment. The new Byrds were an appealing blend of the old and the new—the vocal sound that had remained constantly recognizable through all the Byrds' changes, and a country instrumental sound with plenty of steel guitar, banjo and the like.

The album begins beautifully. Dylan's "You Ain't Goin' Nowhere" is harmonized exquisitely. The steel guitar, right in there from the beginning, sets a mood as fresh as a Tennessee springtime. "I Am A Pilgrim" is also superb; they do it in very traditional country style, very simply and nobly, with nary a hint of rock's tension or sophistication.

For their third song they chose a modern gospel song by the Louvin Brothers, "The Christian Life." The accompaniment, featuring steel, is beautiful. But suddenly the vocal ceases to ring true. Something goes wrong with the accent, which becomes more country than country—in other words, a put-on.* The lyric of the Louvin Brothers' song, we should point out, is a little backwoods sermon; it makes no attempt to stay cool. It's impossible to escape the suspicion that the Byrds treat it as a little camp classic. It clashes most unfortunately with the nobility of "I Am a Pilgrim," immediately preceding it on the album.

Country music was created by people who hold many attitudes that city musicians have a little trouble handling. Even though they may have loved country music since childhood, city people are so used to making fun of the sincere sentiment of country folk, that they have serious troubles making certain types of country songs come out right. The trouble is compounded by their efforts to please both city and country audiences with the same performance. Dylan has learned to surmount these difficulties, probably through years of hard knocks. The Byrds were not so fortunate.

* * *

So far, the Burrito Brothers have been the most successful; their album, *The Gilded Palace of Sin* has won them a fair amount of national recognition.

In terms of musicianship, the Burrito Brothers come off a good deal better than the Byrds did on *Sweetheart.* The singing is generally stronger (though still hardly in Buck Owens' league) and Sneeky Pete does very nice things with his steel guitar. In addition to doing the exquisite whines and howls that make up the contemporary C&W steel style, Pete can transform the instrument into a brilliant rock-&-roll lead guitar. As he rips off single-string runs, it's easy to forget that it's a steel guitar—until he throws in a bend or two that would only be possible on the four-legged guitar. The result is a very exciting expansion of lead guitar sound.

This is a group that can play for the hip and pseudo-hip at the Whisky-a-Go-Go on Sunset Strip one night then buzz out to North Hollywood the next night and please the people at the Palomino Club—strictly C&W. They can be very country and very hip. All this is an impressive accomplishment. The only thing wrong with the Flying Burrito Brothers and their careful country-rock blend

---

* Gram Parsons had originally sung "The Christian Life" during the initial recording sessions, but Roger McGuinn substituted his own lead vocal for the final album release (an act which drew Parsons' bitter complaints in later interviews). The 1997 reissue of *Sweetheart* includes both McGuinn's and Parsons's versions.

is that they work too hard at it. Instead of just doing their thing, they seem intent upon constantly reminding us that they are trying so hard to bring these two unlike things together. Like the combination of shaggy hair and custom-tailored C&W clothes; like having their cover picture taken in front of an outhouse; and like inserting an obnoxious rock guitar, sounding like last year's Blue Cheer, into the gentle and fresh country sounds of "Christine's Tune."

There's an awful lot that's good about the Burrito Brothers, and it's a real dirty shame that a few slips in taste have the cumulative effect of making them look very Hollywood and plastic. What ought to be the most genuine music in the country becomes a cheap novelty.

21

Woodstock Nation

Joan and Robert K. Morrison

The Woodstock Music and Arts Fair and Aquarian Exposition, which took place on Max Yasgur's farm in upstate New York between August 15 and 18 of 1969, has passed into rock mythology as the canonizing statement of the late 1960s counterculture. As memorably captured in the Academy Award-winning 1970 documentary, Woodstock brought together many of the era's top performers and united thousands of youths in peaceful solidarity, a sharp contrast to the Rolling Stones' disastrous Altamont Speedway concert that would end in chaos and murder a mere four months later. As the cultural memory of Woodstock grows to be more a part of rock's distant history, there is a tendency to celebrate the festival and its participants as part of a monolithic, unifying event. In the decades since Woodstock, however, various histories have surfaced in print and on the Internet that have served both to confirm and contradict the popular myths and perception of Woodstock.*
The following passage, excerpted from Joan and Robert Morrison's mid-1980s oral history of the 1960s, contributes to this historicizing process, drawing together divergent viewpoints from three of the festival's attendees, one of whom elects to remain anonymous.†

JASON ZAPATOR

In the summer of 1969, the Woodstock Music and Art Fair and Aquarian Exposition drew hundreds of thousands of young people to a farm in upstate New York to hear dozens of the top rock bands of the time. In spite of rain, mud, and overburdened facilities, the crowd was remarkably good-natured throughout the three days of the festival. Jason Zapator describes it as one of the most important experiences of his life. Now married and raising a family, he works in advertising sales and spends his free time writing and playing music. When interviewed, he was putting together an album of original compositions.

I turned nineteen at Woodstock on Friday, August 15, 1969, and that was a very interesting coming of age. I was into what was happening at the time, the whole gigantic social kaleidoscope of events, ideas, feelings, and music—everything that contributed to me going out on Route 46 in New Jersey, sticking my thumb out, and putting a sign around my neck that said "Woodstock."

---

* See, in particular, Robert Spitz, *Barefoot in Babylon: The Creation of the Woodstock Music Festival*, 1969 (New York: Viking Press, 1979) and Andy Bennett, ed., *Remembering Woodstock* (Burlington: Ashgate Press, 2004).
† *Source:* Joan and Robert K. Morrison, eds., *From Camelot to Kent State: The Sixties Experience in the Words of Those Who Lived It* (New York: Oxford University Press, 1987), pp. 197–204.

Personally I didn't even know how to get there, but I just started picking up rides, one right after another, like a chain reaction. I don't think I waited more than five minutes between rides. It was like there was an energy in the air that just kind of carried me up there. There was a sense of community that stretched from down here all the way up there.

Somebody picked me up in a van, and there were all kinds of strange, long-haired creatures in it, myself included. It turned into a caravan of cars and vans, and there came a point where everything came to a standstill, and everybody just parked their cars. The police were there, trying to wave people on, but the cars couldn't go anyplace, and it didn't matter. There was a camaraderie, even with the state troopers who were directing traffic that was amazing. People were smoking marijuana and doing things like that, and the state troopers weren't batting an eye. I had never seen anything like it.

I got out of the van and started walking where I saw everybody else was going. Pretty soon I got to the gates. There were these nominal ticket booths there, and some people were buying tickets for a while, but that didn't last very long. Everybody kind of felt like we were going to get in, finally they made an announcement that from here on it's a free concert, and everybody just went right through. There were no more barriers.

I guess you could say love was in the air. There was a lot that we put up with for those three days, because at times it was packed like sardines. The valley was filled with people just trying to get around. I mean, it took me two days to get to the bathroom. Maybe it wasn't two days, but it seemed like it. But there was a mutual feeling of wanting to have a good time, of everybody being for each other. What it was is basically I think the way anything works: Everybody agrees on it. And when we were at Woodstock, we just made up our minds that this was the way it was going to be. As long as nobody was getting hurt, and everybody was having a good time, nothing was open to question. Peace was the ideal.

Even the Hell's Angels were cool. Of course, anyplace the Hell's Angels wanted to go, they went, and they went right to the front of the stage. They had front-row seats. But they didn't do anything bad. In fact, they were almost like the police, the security forces, making sure everybody would stay cool. They appointed themselves, and nobody gave it a second thought. Nobody had to say it, because we understood that's what they were doing. Well, everybody has something in them that's good if they want to concentrate on it. It just so happened at Woodstock that everybody was aware of it. Even the Hell's Angels understood it.

I just brought me and the clothes on my back, but it didn't matter, because everything was freely shared. It didn't matter whether the thing was food or if it was smoke or if it was conversation or if it was attention, or whatever it was that humans do with each other, whatever kind of intercourse it was. There wasn't really a second thought about, "Well, I'd better hold on to this," because everybody was all there together anyway.

If you wanted to get something to eat, you'd go to the top of the hill, where there was a commune from California called the Hog Farmers, and they had all kinds of things going. Anybody that needed something to eat was welcome to eat for free. And there was a lot of free living going on. People weren't particularly uptight about wearing clothes. There were a lot of beautiful ladies there, and you got to see a lot of their beauty.

As for drug use, it wasn't a thing where all of a sudden, "Oh, now there's nobody here to stop us, we're all going to go crazy." It wasn't really like that. If somebody wanted something to smoke, it was there. If they didn't want to smoke, it didn't matter. Everybody took it in stride.

The music was another whole thing altogether. So many great bands played there—forty, fifty bands—one right after another. There were times when there was some rain, but then as soon as the weather broke; it would be going on again. It didn't matter what time of day it was. We're talking like two o'clock in the morning, five o'clock in the morning. Something was going on constantly.

The music wasn't just something that you listened to. It was something that you felt inside. It would be as though it could come out of you, out of everybody who was there. I remember the night when Melanie came out and sang that song, "Lay down, lay it all down." What is it? … "Let your white bird smile…" Something like that—a very peace-oriented song. It was beautiful. Everybody lit up candles, and the whole valley looked like a sea of stars in the dark.

I also remember when the Who came out and played, especially Peter Townshend playing guitar, because he jumps all over the place when he's playing. But what he did that day I'll never forget. It was like in the middle of a song, and he was playing and strumming really, really aggressively, and then he took the guitar and threw it up in the air. It went end over end at least twenty feet in the air, and it came back down end over end, and he caught it right in the exact position he needed to make that chord that came in at the right time. He just grabbed it *exactly right*. Not only was it a spectacular performance, but it was excellent musicianship.

And the way he was bending the neck as he was squeezing the strings, it was like he was wrenching the sound out of the guitar, and it was echoing all over the valley. Finally he put it over his head until the feedback finally died out, and then he took the guitar, and he threw it out into the audience. And some lucky guy or girl out there ended up with it. Everybody loved it.

The grand finale I was waiting for was when Jimi Hendrix came out. There were rumors, a sense of expectation that, "Okay, Hendrix is coming, Hendrix is coming." Everybody just kind of knew it. They brought him in a helicopter, and as soon as he came off and hit the stage, he just took over everything. He was wearing his turquoise shirt with all the streamers hanging from it and a headband and he was very, very serene. And everybody just focused on him.

He was playing so fast at times, it looked as though his hand was passing through the guitar neck and going out the other side. He was playing on his back. He was playing with his teeth. He was playing upside-down. He held the guitar in the air and played with one hand. He did everything. But the way he was doing it, it was just part of his natural way of playing.

He played for a total, I think, of two-and-a-half hours. I remember I got a pair of binoculars from someone and I was looking at him, and his eyes were closed just about all the way through. It seemed like he was from another world, and it was immaterial whether his body was there or not.

When he played "The Star Spangled Banner," it was incredible. I don't know if anything quite equaled it. I mean, it was ringing and echoing all over. It was like it filled the entire valley—a bowl of sound that stretched for miles around your hearing range. It just electrified everything.

It was probably the truest rendition of that song I've ever heard, because Hendrix was using sound effects through the guitar to complement the lyrics. I mean, you definitely *heard* the bombs bursting in air, you definitely *heard* the rockets going off when he played.

At the time, of course, if you were thinking of war, you were thinking of Vietnam, so Hendrix was calling up revolutionary feelings in us. His playing was reminding everybody that "the rockets' red glare" and "the bombs bursting in air" was really the napalming of the villages. Like this was the supreme irony that the lyrics and the song were supposed to be about the defense of freedom.…

Of course, after Woodstock people became very radical. It was like we finally made our statement for peace and love, but now it became a thing of putting your fist in the air. The next concert up in that area, about a year later in Connecticut, was called Powder Ridge, appropriately so. A lot of the same kind of bands played there, but you didn't get the feeling it was like Woodstock. People were flying American flags upside down, and it felt like an armed camp. Everybody was ready to go to war.

I took a long journey, and I ended up going all the way out West. I was getting involved with a lot of Eastern religions—Hinduism, Buddhism. I was looking into the American Indians, their beliefs. I was looking into ancient mythologies. And I went through a period when I got into Christianity, where the only thing I looked at was the Bible. Only the Bible—everything else, forget it.

I guess I've come full circle now to the Woodstock way of thinking and conducting myself: sharing, banding together. That's really where my heart is. And I'd like to do something that will bring about a constructive way of life for others.

What I'm doing now is preparing for my final statement before I depart this scene. I earn a living like anybody else, but I've been working on my music a lot, putting it down on tape. Right now I have a drummer I'm working with regularly. I've been doing all the other parts. Like I'll lay down the bass line, and then I'll lay down the guitar line, and then I'll put down the vocals and the harmonies, and the drummer plays the drums, and we're able to build the album piece by piece.

We hope to have that wrapped up in the studio before too long. I'm going to share artistically what I've been given, as much as I can, with everybody, and hopefully I'll leave it here after I'm gone. Just like Jimi Hendrix isn't here, but his music is. That's the way to really live.

DAVID MALCOLM (NOT HIS REAL NAME)

He is an editorial writer for a medium-sized suburban daily newspaper.

I went to Woodstock. It was not the new millennium. It was not the new society. It was a lot of shit. It was three days in a muddy cow pasture with the toilets blocked up.

I did drugs and I smoked grass and I wore my hair a lot longer than I wear it now, but I was not a hippie by any means. I never wore beads or adopted that sort of wide-eyed naive ethic of the hippies. I was always completely turned off by this kind of Dionysian spirit of the times, you know, where they said, "Turn your mind off and let your emotions run free." I never said, "Oh, wow." Also, hippies were sloppy. I'm a very neat person.

In some ways I was more redneck than the worst rednecks. I was more hostile to the hippies than the worst pot-bellied Southern sheriff. I did not admire the generation of the Sixties very much, or anyone who was stupid enough to think that Woodstock was a blueprint for modern society. I mean, there were people who lived in a pasture for three days without toilets or food. This is not a new society. This is a bunch of people wallowing in the mud. It was sick.

I remember running into some woman, some space cadet, and she told me she was going to San Francisco. So I said, "Well, what are you going to do there?" She looked at me like I was crazy. She said, "I'm going to *live*." I thought that was ridiculous. I thought that was really stupid. I'd decided that people were on the world to do things, not to just exist. You know, we aren't just sort of flowering plants.

So we'd lie on bales of hay and listen to them play music. The music was all right. It helped. But I don't think that music has held up terribly well nowadays. I mean, if you put Janis Joplin on the record player today, it's lousy stuff. I think Jimi Hendrix is unlistenable today. Let's put it this way: I'd rather go to the Metropolitan Opera.

KEVIN COMPTON

He was a student in high school when he made the trip to Woodstock. Now in his forties, he continues to enjoy the music and occasionally attends a rock concert with his son.

I remember them telling us at one point that we were then, at three or four hundred thousand, the third largest city in New York State. They got a big cheer out of that. That was the first time, I think, that we actually knew how widespread the countercultural movement was. Most of us came from rather small towns where long hair was the exception instead of the rule, fashionwise. To see that many people who looked like us—or worse—from all over the country was very striking.

I had already experienced a lot of prejudice because of that, having the greasers or jocks back at the high school or in town pick on you and try to start fights, just because you had long hair. They'd say things like, "Are you a boy or a girl?" It got to the point where, "God, can't you guys think of anything else?"

And this was not just kids, but adults in authority. I remember I got pulled over a lot of times for having my license-plate light too dim. Even my physical education teacher threatened me physically, pushed me up against a locker, and said, "You'd better get a haircut." Even if you believed in rock music and love, peace, and understanding, that many people putting you down was going to give you some doubts.

Woodstock made you think. This counterculture has taken a lot of knocks, but it really looks like it's capable of great things. Some of the artists would come on and talk about how large groups like this show that it's possible to get together and to do things without violence and without hatred.

I think there was a certain leftover glow after Woodstock, a camaraderie, although that didn't last too long. We very quickly realized that you couldn't tell whether another person thought the same as you did just by virtue of their hair or anything like that. We had plenty of occasion to find that out.

III

THE 1970S

22

James Taylor, Singer-Songwriter

BURT KORALL

Of all the musical developments that marked the transition from the 1960s to a new decade, few were more pronounced than the emergence of the singer-songwriter genre. If the rock group, with its collective membership, had symbolized a certain communal countercultural ideal, then the singer-songwriter as solo artist heralded the arrival of what Tom Wolfe would famously label the "Me Decade." Singer-songwriters like James Taylor (born 1948) increasingly turned towards their own feelings and inner turmoil for inspiration. Setting their personal experiences directly to song, their music became a form of autobiography. In Taylor's case, his acknowledged bouts with depression and drug dependency formed the basis for his first hit single, "Fire and Rain." Music journalist Burt Korall's 1970 essay for the *Saturday Review* offers an overview of the traits that would make Taylor the genre's most visible star, eventually landing him on the cover of *Time* magazine the following year. Korall mentions that part of Taylor's success rests on the fact that young audiences "seek artists who personify themselves." If this is true, what are we to make of Taylor's well-publicized privileged background (his father was the dean of the University of North Carolina medical school, and Taylor had received treatment for his depression at an exclusive Harvard-affiliated psychiatric institution)? Are such details significant to understanding Taylor's appeal or that of the singer-songwriter genre in general?[*]

The pop music business has many aspects of a high-pressure con game. Almost constant saturation bombardment of hyperbolic claims, concerning a seemingly endless number of faceless artists, progressively suspends one's capacity for belief. Every now and then, however, reality and publicity are consonant with one another. A surprising experience, it provides reassurance that, indeed, there *is* real talent out there.

James Taylor is the genuine article. The young songsmith-singer-guitarist brings to bear a substantial gift and admirable artfulness in the creation and performance of songs. Endearingly musical, he pairs memorable melodic lines with words that fit their contours tightly and well and document a singularity of vision. A fund of feelings, buoyantly lyrical and light on the one hand and darkly reflective on the other, mingle in his monologues. One cannot remain indifferent for long. His songs, though highly personal in content and delivery, are relevant to a large sampling of people on both sides of the invisible, yet almost tangible, age-thirty dividing line.

A product of his time, Taylor has much on his mind. Songs, it would seem, are a form of therapy, a way of getting feelings out where he can look at them. Like a number of his contemporaries, he avails himself of a variety of musical sources and means, both as a performer and songwriter.

[*] *Source:* Burt Korall, "James Taylor: Sunshine and…," *Saturday Review*, September 12, 1970, p. 83.

Taylor juggles and blends blues and folk, jazz inflection, and the open, almost naïve flavor of country music, What emerges is simultaneously literate and formal and relaxed and unpretentious. The thrust is rather direct, yet each one of Taylor's stories of love, loneliness, anguish, and puzzlement is open to interpretation. He always leaves the listener that option.

Tall, angular, with longish locks and an interesting face, James Taylor makes decisive in-person contact. His essentially young audience immediately links up with him. Inner turbulence and the searching quality expressed in his songs provide common ground. In a homespun yet persuasive manner he reaches out, and his audience responds to his warmth. Like Dylan, Taylor has all the trappings of a central figure who can speak for the young constituency, allay fears, and, through music, temporarily terminate connection with arbitrary, distasteful surroundings. The only difference: Taylor is not political. His central concern is living life—and feeling.

As in times past, youngsters today seek artists who personify themselves, performers who can serve the dual function of leader and tranquilizer. The old-time security sources—family and country, church and school—don't seem to work as well. So, the fast-maturing, alienated, sometimes self-indulgent postwar spawn turn to music makers. Dylan, the Beatles, the Stones, Joan Baez, for example—figures who either have something to say or spew on the so-called Establishment from a great height, with admirable disdain.

What about James Taylor? He has the look: the piercing blue eyes, high cheekbones, imposing height. He has the credentials: the crucial combination of vulnerability and underlying strength, the suggestion of mysticism and inner agitation. Most important, he possesses talent in abundance. He could very well fit the bill.

23

"Cock Rock: Men Always Seem to End Up on Top"

As feminists throughout the 1970s addressed issues ranging from reproductive rights to equal pay, the women's movement emerged as one of the decade's most dynamic forces for social change. Musically the results could be seen reflected in the formation of Olivia records and the independent "women's music" industry as well as strong-willed singer-songwriters like Carole King and Joni Mitchell. Yet these performers were in many respects separate from the mainstream, male-dominated rock world, where it often seemed as if the aggressive attitudes of groups like the Rolling Stones allowed little agency for women outside the thrill-seeking adventures of groupies.* One of the first articles to address the contradictory allure and repulsion of rock music from a woman's perspective, "Cock Rock" originally appeared in the New York-based underground feminist publication *Rat* magazine.† The article is cast in a decisively downbeat tone, no doubt influenced by the passing of one of rock's few female icons, Janis Joplin (1943–1970), who had died from a heroin overdose mere days before the essay was published. Like many of the writings in *Rat*, "Cock Rock" appeared without an attributed author, an anonymity that served to reflect the communal solidarity of the women's movement itself. The article was later anthologized, however, under the pseudonym of Susan Hiwatt, a playful allusion to a British line of guitar amplifiers favored by groups like The Who and Pink Floyd.‡§

I. THIS WAS THE WORLD THAT ROCK BUILT

I grew up on Peter Trip, the curly-headed kid in the third row (an AM D.J. in New York City in the late '50s). I spent a lot of time after school following the social life of the kids on *American Bandstand*. Then in high school I spent most of my time in my room with the radio, avoiding family fights. Rock became the thing that helped fill the loneliness and empty spaces in my life. The sound became sort of an alter-world where I daydreamed—a whole vicarious living out of other people's romances and lives. "Sally Go 'round the Roses." "Donna."

In college, rock was one of the things that got me together with other people: hours spent in front of a mirror learning how to dance, going to twist parties—getting freakier—tripping off the

---

* Susan Hiwatt, "Cock Rock," in Jonathan Eisen, ed., *Twenty-Minute Fandangos and Forever Changes: A Rock Bazaar* (New York: Random House, 1971), 141–47.

† For an alternative view of the Rolling Stones, see Karen Durbin, "Can a Feminist Love the World's Greatest Rock and Roll Band," *Ms.*, October 1974, pp. 23–26.

‡ *Rat* appeared under various titles throughout its brief publication run, including *Rat Subterranean News* and *Women's LibeRATion*.

§ *Source:* "Cock Rock: Men Always Seem to End Up On Top," *Rat*, October 15–November 18, 1970, pp. 16–17, 26.

whole outlaw thing of "My Generation" and "Satisfaction." I was able to dance rock and talk rock comfortably in a college atmosphere when other things were mystified and intellectualized out of my comprehension and control. You didn't have to have heavy or profound thoughts about rock—you just knew that you dug it.

A whole sense of people together, behind their own music. It was the only thing we had of our own, where the values weren't set up by the famous wise professors. It was the way not to have to get old and deadened in White America. We wore hip clothes and smoked dope and dropped acid. Going to San Francisco with flowers in our hair.

For a couple of years, when I was with a man, I remember feeling pretty good—lots of people around, a scene I felt I had some control over, getting a lot of mileage off being a groovy couple. For as long as I was his woman, I was protected and being a freak was an up because it made me feel like I had an identity.

When I split from him a whole other trip started. It got harder and harder to be a groovy chick when I had to deal with an endless series of one-night stands and people crashing and always doing the shitwork—thinking and being told that the only reason I wasn't being a freak was because I was too uptight. Going to Woodstock all but bare-breasted somewhere in the middle of all that and thinking I was fucked up for not being able to have more fun than I was having. In a world where the ups were getting fewer and fewer, rock still continued to turn me on.

Then I connected to the women's movement and took a second look at rock.

II. CRASHING: WOMEN IS LOSERS

The Sound of Silence

It took me a whole lot of going to the Fillmore and listening to records and reading *Rolling Stone* before it even registered that what I was seeing and hearing was not all these different groups, but all these different groups of men. And once I noticed that, it was hard not to be constantly noticing: all the names on the albums, all the people doing sound and lights, all the voices on the radio, even the D.J.'s between the songs—they are *all* men. In fact, the only place I could look to see anyone who looked anything like me was in the audience, and even there, there were usually more men than women.

It occurred to me that maybe there were some good reasons, besides inadequacy, that I had never taken all my fantasies about being a rock musician very seriously. I don't think I ever told anyone about them. Because in the female 51 percent of Woodstock Nation that I belong to, there isn't any place to be creative in any way. It's a pretty exclusive world.

There are, of course, exceptions. I remember hearing about some "all-chick" bands on the West Coast, like the Ace of Cups, and I also remember reading about how they were laughed and hooted at with a general "take them off the stage and fuck them" attitude. And how they were given the spot between the up-and-coming group and the big-name group—sort of for comic relief. Or the two women I saw once who played with the Incredible String Band. They both played instruments and looked terrified throughout the entire concert (I kept thinking how brave they were to be there at all). The two men treated them like backdrops. They played back-up and sang harmony, and in fact, they were introduced as Rose and Licorice—no last names. The men thought it was cute that they were there and they had such cute names. No one, either on stage or in the audience, related to them as musicians. But they sure were sweet and pretty.

It blew my mind the first time I heard about a woman playing an electric guitar. Partly because of the whole idea we have that women can't understand anything about electronics (and we're not even supposed to want to), and also because women are supposed to be composed, gentle, play soft songs. A guy once told my sister when she picked up his electric guitar that women were meant to play only folk guitar, like Joan Baez or Judy Collins, that electric guitars were unfeminine. There are other parallel myths that have kept us out of rock: women aren't strong enough to play the drums; women aren't aggressive enough to play good, driving rock.

And then there is the whole other category of exception—the "chick" singer. The one place, besides being a groupie, where the stag club allows women to exist. And women who make it there pretty much have to be incredible to break in, and they are—take, for example, Janis Joplin and Aretha Franklin. It's a lot like the rest of the world where women have to be twice as good just to be acceptable.

Words of Love

Getting all this together in my head about the massive exclusion of women from rock left me with some heavy bad feelings. But still there was all that charged rock energy to dig. But what was that all about, anyway? Stokely Carmichael once said that all through his childhood he went to movies to see westerns and cheered wildly for the cowboys, until one day he realized that being black, he was really an Indian, and all those years he had been rooting for his own destruction. Listening to rock songs became an experience a lot like that for me. Getting turned on to "Under My Thumb," a revenge song filled with hatred for women, made me feel crazy. And it wasn't an isolated musical moment that I could frown about and forget. Because when you get to listening to male rock lyrics, the message to women is devastating. We are cunts—sometimes ridiculous ("Twentieth Century Fox"), sometimes mysterious ("Ruby Tuesday"), sometimes bitchy ("Get a Job") and sometimes just plain cunts ("Wild Thing"). And all that sexual energy that seems to be in the essence of rock is really energy that climaxes in fucking over women—endless lyrics and a sound filled with feeling I thought I was relating to but couldn't relate to, attitudes about women like put-downs, domination, threats, pride, mockery, fucking around and a million different levels of women-hating. For some reason, the Beatles' "rather see you dead, little girl, than see you with another man" pops into my head. But it's a random choice. Admittedly, there are some other kinds of songs—a few with nice feelings, a lot with a cool *macho* stance toward life and a lot with no feelings at all, a realm where, say, the Procol Harum shines pretty well at being insipid or obscure ("A Whiter Shade of Pale"). But to catalog the anti-women songs alone would make up almost a complete history of rock.

This all hit home to me with knock-out force at a recent Stones concert when Mick, prancing about enticingly with whip in hand, suddenly switched gears and went into "Under My Thumb," with an incredible vengeance that upped the energy level and brought the entire audience to its feet, dancing on the chairs. Mass wipeout for women—myself included.

Contrast this with the songs that really do speak to women where our feelings are at, songs that Janis and Aretha sing of their own experience of being women, of pain and humiliation and the love. And it's not all in the lyrics. When Aretha sings the Beatles' "Let It Be," she changes it from a sort of decadent-sounding song to a hymn of hope. A different tone coming from a different place.

The Great Pretenders

The whole star trip in rock is another realm where *macho* reigns supreme. At the center of the rock universe is the star—flooded in light, offset by the light show and the source of incredible volumes of sound. The audience remains totally in darkness: the Stones kept thousands waiting several hours, till nightfall, before they would come on stage at Altamont. The stage is set for the men to parade around acting out violence/sex fantasies, sometimes fucking their guitars and then smashing them, writhing bare-chested with leather fringe flying, while the whole spectacle is enlarged a hundred times on a movie screen behind them. And watching a group like the Mothers of Invention perform is a lesson in totalitarianism—seeing Frank Zappa define sound and silence with a mere gesture of his hand. There is no psychic or visual or auditory space for anyone but the performer. Remember Jesse Colin Young of the Youngbloods turning to his audience with disdain and saying, "the least you could do is clap along"? First you force the audience into passivity and then you imply that they are fucked up for not moving.

Smile On Your Brother

Something else about the audience. Even after I realized women were barred from any active participation in rock music, it took me a while to see that we weren't even considered a real part of the listening audience. At first I thought I was being paranoid, but then I heard so many musicians address the audience as if it were all male: "I know you all want to find a good woman," "When you take your ol' lady home tonight . . ." "This is what you do with a no-good woman," etc., etc. It was clear that the concerts were directed only to men and the women were not considered people, but more on the level of exotic domestic animals that come with their masters or come to find masters. Only men are assumed smart enough to understand the intricacies of the music. Frank Zappa laid it out when he said that men come to hear the music and chicks come for sex thrills. Dig it!

It was a real shock to   ut this all together and realize rock music itself—all the way from performing artist to listener—refuses to allow any valid place for women. And yet I know there would never be rock festivals and concerts if women weren't there—even though we have nothing to do with the music. Somehow we're very necessary to rock culture.

Women are required at rock events to pay homage to the rock world—a world made up of thousands of men, usually found in groups of fours and fives. Homage paid by offering sexual accessibility, orgiastic applause, group worship, gang bangs at Altamont. The whole rock scene (as opposed to rock music) depends on our being there. Women are necessary at these places of worship so that, in between the sets, the real audience (men) can be assured of getting that woman they're supposed to like. Well, it's not enough just to be a plain old cunt. We have to be beautiful and even that's not enough: we've got to be groovy, you know, not uptight, not demanding, not jealous or clinging or strong or smart or anything but loving in a way that never cuts back on a man's freedom. And so women remain the last legitimate form of property that the brothers can share in a communal world. Can't have a tribal gathering without music and dope and beautiful groovy chicks.

For the musicians themselves there is their own special property—groupies. As one groupie put it: "Being a groupie is a fulltime gig. Sort of like being a musician. You have two or three girl friends you hang out with, and you stay as high and as intellectually enlightened as a group of musicians. You've got to if you're going to have anything to offer. You are a non-profit call girl, geisha, friend, housekeeper—whatever the musician needs."

This total disregard and disrespect for women is constant in the rock world and has no exceptions. Not even Janis Joplin, the all-time queen of rock. She made her pain evident in all her blues—that's what made them real. And the male rock world made her pay for that vulnerability in countless ways. Since women don't get to play the instruments, it means they're always on stage with nothing to relate to but the microphone, and nothing between them and the audience but their own bodies. So it is not surprising that Janis became an incredible sex object and was related to as a cunt with an outasight voice. Almost everyone even vaguely connected to rock heard malicious stories about how easy she was to fuck. This became part of her legend, and no level of stardom could protect her because when you get down to it, she was just a woman.

And Who Could Be Fooling Me?

And who ever thought this was all the brothers were offering us when they rapped about the revolution? Why do we stick with it? Women identified with youth culture as the only alternative to our parents' uptight and unhappy way of life. We linked up with rock and never said how it fucked us over. Partly this was because we had no sense of being women together with other women. Partly because it was impossible to think of ourselves as performing as exhibitionists in *macho* sex roles, so we didn't wonder why there weren't more of us on stage. Partly because we identified with the men and not other women when we heard lyrics that put women down. And a lot because we have been completely cut off from perceiving what and who really are on our side and what and who don't want to see us as whole people.

In a world of men, Janis sang our stories. When she died, one of the few ties that I still had left with rock snapped. It can't be that women are a people without a culture.

24

The Art of the Hard Rock Lifestyle

DAVID LEE ROTH

The 1970s, when the band Van Halen first formed and worked their way toward a contract and enormous success with Warner Brothers records, are generally viewed as rock's most hedonistic era. It was during this decade that the spectacle of stadium rock and its attendant macho posturing, groupies, drugs, and hotel room decadence became synonymous with what Robert Pattison has memorably termed "the triumph of vulgarity."* Few musicians have embraced the "vulgar" rock star lifestyle more fully and spoken more frankly about its excesses than Van Halen's former lead singer, David Lee Roth (born 1954). Like many celebrities, Roth's autobiography emerged mostly from spoken transcripts (some 1200 pages) that with the help of an editor were then whittled down into a 360-page book. The resulting conversational tone mirrors Roth's outrageous, outspoken style and allows for a litany of offbeat references and narrative diversions. The three passages selected from *Crazy from the Heat* detail the various stages through which Van Halen ascended from a suburban southern California backyard party band in the mid-1970s to international superstars in the 1980s. Large outdoor youth parties such as the ones Roth describes were much more common in the 1970s when many states lowered the drinking age to match the voting age of 18 (it would not be raised to 21 again until 1984 with the passage of the National Minimum Drinking Age Act). Roth depicts the 1970s as a less regulated, more promiscuous era. Still for all of the band's wild and spectacular allure, he is careful to stress their dedicated and carefully planned attention to the proper fashion, equipment, presentation, and daily rituals.†

Backyard parties developed into an art form. J. C. Agajanian, the famous auto-racing promoter, had a nephew who lived in a house with five bedrooms and a big pool, and lots of space. So when his folks would split, two, three times a year, there'd be a *massive* party. Well over two hundred people would show up. This was right about the time, going to one of these parties, that I first saw the Van Halens. It's the brother and the brother, you know, the guitar player and the drummer, with the bass player, doing note for note, *verbatim* renditions of The Who, *Live at Leeds*, or Deep Purple, "Smoke on the Water," or shit from Woodstock, when Alvin Lee comes out and plays "Goin' Home" faster than any known human being on earth, or at least up until that time—Edward could do *that* lick. You know, it was *amazing* stuff.

---

* Robert Pattison, *The Triumph of Vulgarity: Rock Music in the Mirror of Romanticism* (New York: Oxford University Press, 1987).
† *Source:* David Lee Roth, *Crazy from the Heat* (New York: Hyperion, 1997), pp. 59–63, 73–84, 150–57.

Playing at those parties got competitive fast. 'Cause I got into a band the last year of high school, right in there, '72, and we made the impossibly forward-thinking move of *renting* a little stage from Abbey Rents. It was about nine inches tall, with little risers, like they do at union meetings.

We set up the band on this little stage. Oh, nobody'd *ever* seen anything like this, God. We took some of the money from the proceeds, and rented a little PA system. Altec Lansing 15/20s, I think. With a horn and a fifteen-inch speaker in each cabinet. Well, a horn and a fifteen-inch speaker on either side is what Dr. Dre is sitting on when he takes off down Whittier Boulevard today. But back then it was impossibly cutting edge—we had upped the ante.

I got into a band called the Red Ball Jets, named after a sneaker. We played "Johnny B. Goode" for twenty-five minutes at a time, some Rolling Stones songs. And our musicianship level, our musicality, between a one and a ten, was a solid five, a solid six on a good night. There was no signature sound to it, but we *had* a helluva show. 'Cause I was already Diamond Dave. I had pants with the pleats and the little sweater, little sleeveless sweater that just goes right to the top of the pants, you could see a little bit of belly button, maybe some suspenders—that was a little bit aggressive, but can you dig what I'm sayin'? Shag haircut that I drove down to Balboa Island to get, little Cuban heels—not two-toned shoes in a gangster sense, but a stripe that ran right down the middle, from the laces to the toe. Blue and tan.

Halfway through singing at a party, I'd take my suspenders down and let 'em hang around my butt, and that really showed I was workin'. We were a pretty big hit on the backyard circuit. We entered into *immediate* competition with the Van Halens, who at the time were called Mammoth, a typical kind of rock band name—nondescript. (It would be my idea to call the band Van Halen. They wanted to call the band Rat Salade, named after a Black Sabbath song. I said, "No." I felt the name Van Halen was like the name Santana.)

There was conflict and rumormongering between bands. During their set, the Van Halens stood around like the guys in Nirvana. They wore Levi cords with the boxer shorts stickin' out and a T-shirt, and just sort of stood there, but their music was spectacular. Chain-smoked Camel filters. They had girlfriends, Alex's girlfriend would sit behind him on a little packing case while he played drums.

We Red Ball Jets were in belligerent competition with Mammoth.

We'd compete for whose parties were the best and the biggest. There were a couple little park gigs, in the public park. The Youth Community Center, the recreation center of the Pasadena Youth Organization, would have some bands playing. People would gather on the field at sundown, and some rock bands would play—just beginning rock bands, you know, high school, junior college. But these gigs were to be *fought* over venomously.

That was the first stage of "I'm gonna be somebody!" I was bound and determined to go places. Playing at the Agajanian's party was the first place you had to get to.

Youth Club dances … they weren't an alternative, they were chaperoned, they were screened and controlled. People were watching you—they would follow you outside to see if you were smoking Marlboros. You weren't allowed to kiss the girls and make them cry.

All those gals from Alverno Heights and Saint Francis, the Catholic girls' schools, the thoroughbreds, I suddenly had entree to. If I could perform in a band, at one of these parties, well, *all* those girls were in attendance. Suddenly, it became what later on, during the Gulf War, was known on CNN as "a target-rich environment."

Okay now, I'm leaping ahead here, in the party schism, because I didn't actually join the Van Halens until probably late '74. But we began to play the backyard parties, as well as dance clubs, Top 40 coverband, dance clubs or whatever. But the first critical step, first base, was to play the backyards.

In Van Halen, we were the first to get lights. We'd go and steal floodlights from the lawns of little apartment complexes all over Pasadena, at one in the morning. You know, those little red and blue and amber and green floodlights that sit in those little Formica cones? The ones that shine on two palm trees or against the wall where it said something like Winston Apartments. You would take an Ironboy work glove, 'cause the lamp would be really hot by one in the morning; you could unscrew it manually. You'd carry a paper bag to put it in.

We made three boxes that would accommodate five colors: Red, blue, yellow, green, and off. "Off" being the most important color, because then you knew it was the end of the song. You *knew*, man, 'cause we'd hit a note … boom! Very cool.

Your color green served as white; you'd throw that light on, you'd know you were into the next little episode, the next little segment. This was run by a foot switch that the bass player, Mike Anthony, worked. As well as doing backup vocals, he ran the foot switch for the lights.

We would stack these, two banks of each, on either side of the stage, on the little PA system, on this little bar stage. Nobody had ever seen anything like this. This was full-scale production value. Talk about bang for your buck!

* * *

Back to early Van Halen:

When I first joined the band, tried to sing some of the songs, there was Grand Funk Railroad, as well as Black Sabbath. The music was pretty alien to me. I didn't even own those records. I had to go to the Thrifty Drugstore to buy them. Did my best, which was awful, at the time, and the Van Halens were shocked and horrified. There was a conflict from the beginning. Now I perceive it as par for the course.

When Zeppelin got together, Jimmy Page *hated* Robert Plant, couldn't wait for him to be out of the band, figured that the band would be over in two albums. That's how they did it then. There's always constant shift and change, because all of your cool players, like the Jimmy Pages and Jeff Becks, were session guys as well. That's how they fed themselves, that's how they paid for their— ooh, here's a good group therapy word—proclivities. Show me a couple of yours and I'll show you one or two of mine. By the way, how do you finance yours?

These guys were all working sessions. The most you would expect was two albums, and then they're gonna be off somewhere because of schedule difficulties, going on the road, which is considerably more wearying than anybody lets on. It's a magnificent magic trick, and yes, it is absolutely the Emerald City times Henry Miller and Kiki's Paris with a Helmut Newton photograph and the Bee Gees on the stereo. At the same time you better learn to sleep in your clothes. Enough said for the time being.

Anyway, a couple of albums with the band, a couple of tours, hey, it's going to take you a couple of tours' worth to recover whatever is left of your medical constitution. A lot of these guys are running on fumes and that may be what fuels their music, that desperate kind of "put your belts on, I think we can make it, but I'm not really sure"-ism.

I'm certain it's fueled some of my favorite rock epics, regardless. Zeppelin got together, they hated each other. Clash of the Titans. Mick and Keith? Their constant to-and-fro and reconciliations are a matter of history. It is part of the breakfast discussion. If you're important enough, you wind up at the breakfast table with everybody in the world. "So what do you think about such-and-such and—Roth?" And everybody knows what you're talking about. That's how you know you're breathing that rarefied air.

So, cut right from the classic stone, we had conflict right away. We were suspicious of each other, not exactly accepting, the sound was not there but the look was. Jesus, how do we get this all to match up? A lot of very opinionated cats, at least three of us.

Had an original bass player named Mike Stone, was more academically set to go to school and follow a more dependable path. But between the two Van Halens and me, we were very opinionated. A *lot* of argument. Created a competitive atmosphere. We really wanted to just have everybody undeniably go, "Okay, wow." When you got one of those happening into the air and up and surfing, everybody's egos were big enough and strong enough to also say, "Okay, that's—that's a wow." I mean, we accepted each other's "Hey, dude, that's a wow," more often than not.

Went in to play the parties. It was the first time I really became aware of how possessive an audience could really be about a given artist or a given band. Way beyond "this is great music," it was almost as if it was football team time. "Hey, this is our band, they represent *us*." I came from another side of town, so to speak. The first time I sang with the band in a backyard party the audience hated it! So unanimously in fact that I knew I was onto something big.

They didn't have a singer before, really. Ed Van Halen sang the traditional tunes. Black Sabbath, Deep Purple, Grand Funk Railroad, et cetera. And he held down the fort fairly well. I remembered seeing him at youth club dances, you know, high school things. Singing was just an addition, just to get it up and going.

When I got into the band, I was ridin', I was up. I went ballistic right off. Completely confounded, confused and baffled and amazed and stunned and astonished their backyard party audience, which was large. A good backyard party would easily pull six hundred kids. Charge a dollar at the door, band would get one hundred and twenty-five bucks. Kegs of beer. You knew right about ten o'clock, you got a little tired of playing, you just turned the volume up a tad, the police would show up with the new helicopter part of their "Eye in the Sky" program. Wow. A lot of police officers were vets, and so things were particularly athletic, but there was never any serious injuries or conflicts, just a lot of running after and being chased by. Eleven cop cars show up parked in a line, all with the flashing lights and a lot of flares. It was all very exciting and kind of scary, and you might go to jail, and your parents might have to come get you out, and even maybe pay for a friend or two. It was great.

One night, the Van Halens are playing in a pool of beer, and we had rented a Trooperette spotlight. You'd plug it into a wall, didn't require a generator, little Trooperette, it was fifty-five dollars for the night. We'd put it on top of the workshed, which is on the other side of the swimming pool, and shine it down on us. You'd open it up wide enough that you've got the whole band until there was some singing or a solo or something like that, then you would make the spot smaller so you could bring some focus to the proceedings.

We had the PA hooked up where you would tape the microphone to the stand that held the snare drum, and if you got it tuned up just right it would pick up the sound of all the other drums so you actually had drums in the PA system. All of this never before seen in backyard parties.

The actual party commenced at about two, three o'clock that afternoon, 'cause you'd have to show up and you'd set up. That's when the first kegs were cracked. And everybody hung out and, you know, the band would tune up and play a few songs, and that was very cool.

Much, much later the helicopter would fly in with the spotlight, and the cops made big announcements about unlawful assembly and order to disperse, and everybody would be running. The cops would come bursting in, in a great big line, kind of like football style, onto the field. They would run in and split into a "surround and pound" strategy, you know, surround everybody, move everybody out but also contain everybody.

We would all sit up on the stage and say, "Man, we're with the band. This is our equipment. We don't know nothing about this, man. We were just hired to play what we thought was going to be a normal party. There's nothing fucking normal about this party at all. All we want is out. We're with you, man." So they would leave us alone. We also said: "And she's with me, man. And so is she."

The cops would clear the place out, and they'd all be outside on the street cleaning up the kids, making the neighborhood safe for whatever. We would wait till everybody was gone, then break out our flashlights that we kept specifically for this purpose. Big plastic flashlights with the giant lens that had more throw.

We'd fan out and go over the backyard inch by inch and pick up all the loose joints and unopened little bottles of booze and stuff everybody had thrown down when the cops charged in. We'd come up with little baggies of pot and papers and pipes, whatever your "proclivity" was. We had roadies by then, of a sort, people who would lend us their truck or drive a pickup to help us get the PA and the amplifiers and extra drum stands and help us set up.

After combing the grounds, we would sit up on that stage till four in the morning just samplin' everything.

It became an art form to strategize for the parties, and when we would play them and schedule them so that we had a routine. I had determined early on that there was to be a campaign.

I had read a book called *The Advance Man* by Jerry Bruno. He was an adviser to JFK during the 1960 election campaign. I read this book in maybe 1964, sixth grade at the latest.* It made an impression on me.

It explores the idea of continuity, what people would call "exposure," routines, just to be there, to be available. Like on some of my favorite Latino radio stations in Miami, where I get to hear the song "Siempre"—very aptly named, it means "always"—every twenty-eight minutes.

If you're good enough, people will tell friends and they'll want to come back and see you. And then you must be available. You have to be there to be seen. And, yes, that does take strategy. That does take thinking academically or sportingly. It's like playing chess. And one of my fortes in the band was to provide that manner of thinking.

There was certain rituals that were critical to the success of the show. First was sharing Camel filter cigarettes; that's what we all smoked in the band. That was important. You had to share 'em.

We had to drink Schlitz malt liquor, 'cause that was Alex's favorite. For a while there Budweiser malt liquor was still around but it was like a designer toy. Schlitz malt liquor was much more direct.

Once we started playing parties and clubs in Hollywood, Pink's chili dogs became part of my ritual. I would have to stop and buy one with extra mustard and onions on the way to every Gazzari's gig or every Starwood gig. As a direct result, I went on to sell over fifty million records and traveled the world. Just kidding.

Backstage at these little beer bars and clubs became one of my favorite places on earth to be. It was a clubhouse. It was a tree house. It was always some little back room with a couple of filthy couches and cigarette burns in the rug and graffiti on the walls. And that was your place, that's where you hung around, that's where you held court. I was part of what you were working for.

The greatest backstage of all was at the Whisky-A-Go-Go. By the time Van Halen started playing there, which was right around 1975, they had not yet erased all of the graffiti that covered every inch of the ceiling in the famous main dressing room upstairs. You had poems by Jim Morrison written on the ceiling, complete paragraphs, Morrison's signature, and the signature of everybody in The Doors. The signatures of everybody from Led Zeppelin to Johnny Winter to ZZ Top, Alice Cooper, Jethro Tull, the Mahavishnu Orchestra, Jeff Beck, Santana, Janis Joplin, Jimi Hendrix, and on and on. They covered every square inch. You could spend—and I did—many, many hours just checking out each little quote.

It wasn't until probably the early eighties when they painted it over and commenced the tradition anew, but by then the Whisky had changed. This was one of the first landing spots on the West

---

* Roth's recollection is slightly off. *The Advance Man* was first published in 1971.

Coast for any band. And when we in VH first started playing there, that was the first testimonial that we had arrived. We were going to write on the walls, right next to the guy in Led Zeppelin, somewhere in between him and Aretha Franklin.

What made Van Halen's backyard parties different from anybody else's backyard parties was that we really perceived them as little concerts, and we advertised them as little concerts. We put out flyers, we started to take the profits, whatever it was that we could barely make, and use it to rent a little stage and get a little better PA system. There was this store in the Monterey Park–Alhambra area, which is south of Pasadena, called Johnny Roberts Music.

Johnny Roberts Music was the coolest place that you could ever go to rent or buy your equipment. They had little pictures of everybody who had been through town from the late sixties to the early seventies: a picture of Jimmy Page buying a guitar, or maybe Tina Turner buying a microphone ... nah, you wouldn't have seen that, Ike was in charge of the equipment.

Coming up with a better and better PA system was an important issue because we were pulling more and more people, so you need more and more volume just to get the music across. Bought some big Altec Lansing speakers—it's a big horn, a fifteen-inch speaker, and it put out great sound. And we started dressing up a little bit. What was popular then were the bell-bottoms.

The bondage element was just kicking in, and there was one little store in Hollywood that custom-made all of this leather gear. I don't think any of us were really sure exactly what bondage was, we just knew that the leather belts looked cool. You'd get a black leather belt with some studs on it and a big silver belt buckle, that was your prize of the three-month period, whatever it took to afford the thing. You had to wear it low, gunslinger style.

There weren't many places that you could buy black leather pants. It was still a left-of-center statement. You had to go to some underground place, who would custom-make them for you. I had a pair of black leather pants with drawstrings in the front and the back made super low-cut. You could never sit down in them; you'd pop right out. They would dye my legs purple black. They were unlined, just raw leather. Some little guy with a Marlon Brando motorcycle hat and a handcuff belt made these for me. He had some little slave working for him behind the counter, with his little dog collar and everything, the guy that did all the sewing and shit.

These damn pants stained my legs every time I'd go to sing, 'cause I'd sweat in them, and I couldn't get the dye off. I went to more than one doctor, because at first I was terrified. I thought, wow, I'm going to have some kind of toxic chemical reaction to something in the leather. Now I'm permanently tattooed.

If I stopped wearing the pants, then all the dye would come off on the hotel room sheets in four day's time. It would be okay for me to drop trou in front of you with the lights on, four days later. Till then, we didn't turn on the lights. I looked like the Toxic Avenger, about to put the triple whammy on you.

I was black—except where my little underwear was, from my legs to up above my belly, all you'd see is my little wiener glowing in the dark because of the contrast. Look at the first Van Halen album, on the back cover, I'm wearing those damned pants. Every morning on tour I'd have to bundle up the sheets, put them in the corner of the bathroom so housekeeping wouldn't see the dye had come off. The sheets looked like the Shroud of Turin.

Anyway, Edward and I picked up the gauntlet first, and we eventually became as much fun to look at as to listen to.

We started to improve on the production. We painted a sign on a bed sheet, and *this* had never been done before. The bass player at the time, Mike Stone, knew the way to make a gridwork on the sheet so that the lettering would be right, and then we taped it off with adhesive tape and spray-painted it. It was the first of many signs to be hung behind the band. Whoa, this was *amazing*. This wasn't a sign, it was a *backdrop*.

The banners that we hung behind the stage merely showed the name of the band, Van Halen. But it was an *effort at production*. And production was always a part of Van Halen, that it would look like it sounded. Alex would spruce up his drum stage, you know, figure out things to hang in front so it wasn't just milk cartons. We went on to build backdrops made out of plywood and pieces of mirror and such that we found.

A very important part of the Van Halen show were smoke pots, which were completely illegal, and I certainly don't recommend fooling with them. You get little empty tins, say, cat food cans, and you bolt them to a little piece of two-by-four. You run a plug, a double-headed plug, up the middle of it, and you run an electric wire over to a little switch system. Next you go down to the local gun store and buy a can of 4F black gunpowder; this is for people who load their own bullets. They would only sell you two cans of 4F per person, especially if you're a nineteen-year-old long-hair. So we would each take turns and go down and buy our allotment of 4F powder until we had eight cans. Put a little gunpowder in the tins, and then when you hit the foot switch, it sparks it off and you get a great big colorful "fooomm!"—a smoke bomb.

We would set them up on top of the PA and on the sides of the drums and behind the ampli-fiers. I would scream, "Ladies and gentlemen, please welcome the amazing Van Halen," and we'd hit the first note and fire off half the smoke pots. It looked like Tiananmen Square. People would be running, gasping, crying from all the smoke. If it was an indoor dance and we'd miscalculated the ventilation, it was like playing in a cloud. You couldn't see three feet in front of you. All of which was immensely cool. It was all too much, it was all over the top. And then, of course, at the end you would fire off the rest of the smoke pots to signify the big finish.

Just setting up and loading the smoke pots took hours. And we would get burned. You'd have a few beers, you're dancing around, you say, "Hey, thank you, have a good night!" and somebody would fire off the smoke pots, and you'd be leaning a little too far to the left and blow off half of your haircut, take off an eyebrow, lose a sleeve, what the hell. Regularly, something on stage would catch fire and have to be put out.

We became known for it; that with Van Halen you got a full-blast show, a real show. This, of course, all carried on into bigger and bigger elements. Once we started to play on the road, we took all of this stuff with us. It was all fiercely illegal. Otherwise, you'd need a fireman and a court-appointed expert in pyrotechnics.

But in the seventies things were looser. People weren't screwed down quite as tight. Vietnam had just ended, nobody even thought of all of these party favors as addictive, you didn't have AIDS, you didn't have Moms Against Drunk Drivers with AIDS, you didn't have Ethiopians with AIDS, whatever. There was sort of a big long halftime going on.

Pretty soon, the smoke pots alone took up half the car. They were all run by the bass player, who also ran the lights. Had a lot of foot switches that boy, *and* backup vocals. Sometimes, of course, just like the Space Shuttle, you go for the lights and hit the smoke bomb. Somebody would lose a sideburn and their sense of humor, but only briefly.

I think you can hear elements of our most classic smoke-pot caper on a bootleg tape of Van Halen's last real show before we went on to make a record and go on the road in 1977 at the Pasadena Civic. We saved all the smoke pots for the grand finale, hit the last song and fired off all twenty-five at once—in a forty-five-hundred-person exhibition hall with the windows closed, and it just smoked the place out. It looked like the Tet Offensive, from what I read. I was afraid to move because I thought I would fall off the stage. I couldn't see two feet in front of me, the smoke was so acrid and thick.

And it, of course, set off all of the smoke and fire sensors in the building, and fire departments from seven cities showed up. It was like right out of the movies. All the doorways flew open all at once, and all you can see was those rolling red lights on top of the fire trucks and all of these guys with gas masks and hoses and full-blast fire boots and gear—from the movie *Brazil*—bursting through the door to throw forty-five hundred of our closest friends out of the building. "Hey, I'm with the band, man. And so is she. And her, too."

One of the vice presidents from Warner Brothers had heard of the band, came down to see the show, sat behind the amplifiers and watched. When those firemen showed up, I knew we had it in the bag.

* * *

You set up for a tour and you've got eighty people and six tour buses. They all pull into port, usually in front of the "Riot House," the Hyatt House on Sunset Boulevard. Everybody shows up just like at the docks, kiss their significant others good-bye, there's tears, there's waving. Then there's those of us who are streaming out of the bars, or waking up next to Juanita Somebody and going, "Jesus, it's first bell."

The ultimate guys show up with barely a belly pack, wearing a pair of shorts, some tennis shoes and a T-shirt. In the pack is a jacket and a pair of long jeans. That's about it. Some cigarette lighters, a toothbrush. You'll get your hair conditioner and shampoo at the hotel, those little bottles in every bathroom. Ultimately everybody is wearing free promotional merchandise.

In the late seventies, up until the mid-eighties, there was a lot more throwaway cash before Reaganomics—that's a quickie way to say it. It means that we all ran out of money. But up until then, Jesus, we'd all come walkin' in wearing a merchandising hat with the name of the band. Pair of sunglasses that had been supplied by the guy from Hawaiian Tropic because he got free tickets. A T-shirt that came from the record company. You got a tour jacket on. Pair of shorts featuring the last promoter's logo.

Every band would have a Nike or a Converse representative show up, a fan, and say, "Hey, I'm coming to the show in St. Louis. Do any of you guys need tennis shoes?"

"Oh, you bet." And he would show up literally with seventy pairs of tennis shoes.

Want to throw a little salt in the rice? You send a runner out to the local Harley-Davidson shop, which exists in every major city of the free earth, and invite the whole staff to the show, and you start your collection of Harley-Davidson shirts from city to city. 'Cause every Harley shop has their own variation, you know, the "Ride to Live," "Live to Ride," or whatever. And if you go through an entire tour like this, you're going to have three hundred Harley-Davidson shirts in infinite variety, all of them on black material.

This is how we all looked. It was something like from a Terry Gilliam movie. It was the wildest ragtag army, as all great armies are. Think of the great American Indian warriors and how they would dress. Traditional Indian breastplate with a top hat, a colonel's wool jacket and a loincloth and buckskin. The spoils of war.

So it's off to war. Everyone on the bus!

Low end of the bus spectrum was the first time Van Halen went to tour Europe and we opened for Black Sabbath. Literally twenty-two cities in twenty-eight days. I never knew there *were* that many cities in England. England, three television channels in 1978, two of them BBC. A lot of documentaries.

We got a "tour bus," which was for tourists; windows all the way down, two seats and an aisleway and two seats. But wasn't meant for sleeping. The armrests were bolted into the floor, and the way that you would go to sleep—'cause you would travel all night after the show to the next city—you put your head down on your shoulder, slid your bottom leg under the armrests, across the aisleway, onto the other seat under the armrest. You're on your side, you put your upper leg on top of the armrests across the aisleway, and lay there on your side, like so. You're done, right? Wrong. 'Cause your right arm's hanging off the edge of the seat. So we all started wearing suspenders so that you could gaffer-tape your arm to the suspenders and keep it from hanging down off of the seat. And every set of seats had a body sleeping like this, all the way down.

Sometimes when we'd go into a bigger city from Peoria to Paris, a number of the road crew would get on our bus, the band bus, because we would leave sooner, and they wanted to get there earlier and shop. They would sleep head-to-toe on the floorboards underneath, all the legs going across the seating. It was like climbing into an Apollo module. Took a while to get in position. First you would arrange the little net piece that sits on the back of a bus seat, you know, to put your map or your cigarettes, your water, your sunglasses. I remember somebody saying, "Look, there's Edinburgh Castle," and it was too much trouble to get out of the capsule. I opened one eye and there it was reflected upside down in my mirror sunglasses.

If you had to use the toilet in the back, you had to monkey down on top of the seats over all the bodies. And if the bus hit a bump or took a weird turn—and Britain is not known for its straight-line construction—you'd crash down and if somebody was sleeping on the floor, there would be a five-guy pileup.

High end of the bus world is what I call Dolly Parton's bathroom. You'd get these huge Eagle buses that travel America and, you know, the country western crew spend so much of their time out there, they really do the insides of their buses. They can sleep fourteen comfortably in bunks, with a video, microwave, refrigerator, freezer, grill stove, hot and cold water, bathroom, shower, back room in the back with its own stereo and TV video system. Hanging plants, pink tile on the floors, this kind of thing. Dolly Parton's bathroom.

But nevertheless you're in a forty-foot aluminum tube, eighteen feet wide, with all these other guys. On this last tour I looked down the gangway from the back of the bus. It had the appearance of being round, cylindrical, because of the doorways. You'd see various arms hanging out of bunks and off of couches and one little bulb, red, hanging in the ceiling up front. It was right out of *Das Boot*.

Touring is intensely difficult work, and you will always bus it until you're playing nothing but stadiums. And even then all your road crew and front office and so forth are going to be on disco submarines. It becomes your home. It's like living on a yacht. Your own time zones, you wake up and go to sleep according to your own schedule.

German U-boats had no space for storing food or gear. Everything had to be stuck in and around the equipment, the engines and the men. Tour bus, same thing. Here you have the mighty Van Halen touring behind twenty million record sales already, halfway through the career, you're still finding nooks and crannies to stuff your paperback or your cigarette lighter, you're still finding little corners to tuck your extra shoe.

Take your bags onto the bus, spend the first couple of hours coordinating all your shit, set your space up and everything, because that's going to be your home for probably the next year. If things go really well, you'll be out for two years. And you get road burn within two weeks, terminal fatigue, but you're used to it. Everybody talks in a slower cadence. Lots of body language suffices. Everybody gets worn down and simplifies.

The only people who didn't simplify were the security teams. We would have maybe eight guys working security for the hall, the band, the hotel, merchandise, et cetera, and they traveled with us. They all had walkie-talkies, and they'd have call names. At the beginning of every tour it would be "Doctor to Lawyer, this is Indian Chief. Over." Within four weeks, "Butcher to Hacker, this is Paladin. Over." And Hacker was a little Woody Allen–type guy.

Just like on a boat, during the summer you'd stop wearing a shirt. And because you traveled self-contained, it's not like you're going to airports every day. People think, oh, you fly from gig to gig. You do if you're foolish. Sabbath did on that first tour in America. Jesus, you got to get up an hour and a half early, you get into some rent-a-cars, you get lost, you find the airport, you wait, the plane's delayed, you're in the public, you land, you get rent-a-cars, you get lost on the way to the hotel.

Or you walk out of the hotel wrapped in a bedsheet, get on your boat, and you're there. After a few weeks you see guys who haven't worn a shirt in a week. They eat all their meals backstage. Half the time the road crew doesn't even stay in a hotel. They drive right to the next gig. They're going to finish tearing down at six in the morning, drive six hours and begin to set up again.

Get used to sleeping in your clothes. You come up with little tricks because always during the summer they fire up the air-conditioning, it goes hog wild, you're sweaty and overheated and tired, maybe just ate late. Your body temperature's up, two hours later your body temperature drops a few degrees, and you wake up coughing and snotting and hacking like a stripper on a Sunday morning. So I learned: sleep in your clothes, always wear a ski hat, stabilize your temperature. Just like my sherpa Wong Chu told me at twenty-some thousand feet in the Khumbu Icefall. "Wong Chu, how will I know when I'm dressed right for up here?" He said, "Dave, when you can lay down anywhere on the glacier at any time and fall asleep, comfortable and warm and dry, you're there."

Same thing on a tour bus. And this doesn't matter if you're brand new to the groove or if you're Madonna's backup band on the way to a stadium. Sleep in your clothes, socks included. Pull a hat over your eyes so you can lose all the light. Earplugs block out ambient noise. You can go to sleep anywhere, at any time.

After twenty years of this, I still basically sleep in my clothes. I think nothing of it. My girlfriends have thought something of it. It's like decompression shock. Hard to let go, you know, it's part of my routine. I don't even think about it till somebody asks. My last girlfriend, I'd come back from biz or work or from downstairs, she would have made the bed and put my little ski hat on the pillow. That was so cool, to me. She realized I had a series of experiences that were way different. You just don't get it out of your system.

* * *

Trashing hotels was an art form that you learned about. It wasn't like you invented it. It was something that you had to read about. You read about the drummer from The Who driving a Cadillac into the hotel swimming pool. He went on to recite about how he was lucky—that he had heard somewhere that if you ever drove your car into a lake that you have to open the window and let the car fill up with water, otherwise you won't be able to open the door. These were great lessons in life.

We in Van Halen took it to a new level. On the second album it says, "Special thanks to the seventh floor—" I think it was Sheraton Inn in Madison, Wisconsin. Something amazing happened … well, maybe nothing happened. There were festivities, room to room, carryings on and it's a college town so there's a lot of carrying-onners to be found. You've got to understand, rock 'n' roll is a lot like God took the map of the United States and tilted it, and everybody loose and unscrewed down rolled into my business.

Well, we've heard about throwing a television out of a window. How about getting enough extension cords out of one of the trucks parked in back of the hotel so that the television can remain plugged in all the way down to the ground floor? I don't know, it's just kind of abstract. But that's what made it aesthetic.

Or taking everything that you could possibly find in the given hotel room and jamming it in the closet and the bathroom. That includes the bed frame, the television set, the stand, the dressers. Those colorful armoires and easy chairs are going to have to be disassembled.

Then wait outside the door once your victim comes back. You can even make it a little more poetic if you take the door off the hinges. That way you can hear the response that much better from down the hall.

The science of hydraulics is taught in agricultural seminars in every major university in the world; it's part of engineering, it's part of bridge building, heavy construction, and it's a very important part of rock 'n' roll on the road. What happens when you jump on a toilet? What can we expect when you disassemble a sink? What happens if we do both at the same time in the same bathroom? Is it twice as much hydraulic force or is it exponential? Is it geometric? Is it four times, eight times as much? Well, I can tell you. These things all come into play!

We'd play a game called "Maybe it's in here." And you'd get way into somebody's room and go, "Damn it, I knew Bobby had that new *Playboy* issue in here somewhere. Maybe it's in here. No, it's not on the roof. Maybe it's in here. Nope, not behind the wallpaper. I know, he's clever, he knows I'm on to his game. Maybe it's under the sink. Nope, nothing under here but a bunch of nuts and bolts and . . . a lot of water," and on and on.

25

"How to Be a Rock Critic"

Lester Bangs

Nearly a decade after the rock press had first taken shape via the pages of *Crawdaddy!*, *Rolling Stone,* and other magazines, the mid-'70s "rock critic" had become a recognized music industry career occupation, an alluring bohemian profession for scores of young music fans. Among the many influential critics of the era, Lester Bangs (1948–1982) stands out as arguably the most notorious and revered of them all. While Bangs's tastes in music could be eclectic, he is especially remembered for championing the "authentic" rock primitivism of then unfashionable styles like heavy metal and punk. Fired from *Rolling Stone* in 1973 for "being disrespectful to musicians," Bangs joined the staff of the irreverent Detroit-based rock magazine *Creem*, where for many years he served as both a writer and editor. Bangs's writings are instantly recognizable, steeped in the subjective style of New Journalists like Tom Wolfe and Hunter S. Thompson, yet mixed with equal doses of his own unique cynical attitude, corrosive wit and expressive insights. For many, this intense, self-reflexive approach signified an unparalleled level of integrity in rock journalism. Offered in the form of a humorous MadLib, "How to be a Rock Critic" is typical of Bangs's famed off-the-cuff "first draft" style.*

Lately I've noticed a new wrinkle on the American landscape: it seems as if there's a whole generation of kids, each one younger than the last, all of whom live, breathe and dream of but one desire: "I want to be a rock critic when I grow up!"

If that sounds condescending let it be known that I was once just like them; the only difference was that when I held such aspirations, the field was relatively uncluttered—it was practically nothing to barge right in and commence the slaughter—whereas now, of course, it's so glutted that the last thing anybody should ever consider doing is entering this racket. In the first place, it doesn't pay much and doesn't lead anywhere in particular, so no matter how successful you are at it, you'll eventually have to decide what you're going to do with your life anyway. In the second place, it's basically just a racket in the first place, and not a particularly glorious one at that.

It almost certainly won't get you laid. (Rock critics are beginning to get groupies of a sort now, but most of them are the younger, aspiring rock critics—like the kind on Shakin' Street—of one sex or another.) It won't make you rich: the highest-paying magazine in the rock press still only pays thirty bucks a review, and most of the other magazines fall way below that. So you'll never be able to make a living off of it. Nobody will come up to you in the street and say, "Hey, I recognize you!

* *Source:* Lester Bangs, "How to be a Rock Critic: A Megatonic Journey with Lester Bangs," *Shakin' Street Gazette,* October 10, 1974. Reprinted in Jim DeRogatis, *Let It Blurt: The Life & Times of Lester Bangs, America's Greatest Rock Critic* (New York: Broadway Books, 2000), pp. 247–60.

You're Jon Landau! Man, that last review was really far out!" A lot of people, in fact, will hate you and think you're a pompous asshole just for expressing your opinions, and tell you so to your face.

On the other side of the slug, though, are the benefits. Which are okay, if you don't get taken in by them. The first big one is that if you stay at this stuff long enough you'll start to get free records in the mail, and if you persevere even longer you may wind up on the promotional mailing lists of every company in the nation, which will not only save you a lot of money on payday and ensure that you'll get to hear everything and anything you want, but help to pay the rent on occasion when you sell the albums spilling into your bathroom to local used records stores, at prices ranging from $.05 to over a dollar apiece. Plus on Christmas you don't have to buy anybody any presents if you don't want to: just give your mother the new Barbra Streisand album Columbia sent you because Barbra's trying to relate, your big sister one of the three copies of the new Carole King that you got in the mail, your little sister that Osmonds double live LP you never even opened because you're too hip...all down the line, leaving you with enough money saved to stay fucked up on good whiskey over the holidays this year.

Another fringe benefit which will sooner or later accrue if you hew steadily on this jive ass scrawl, is that you will be invited to press parties for the opening of new acts in town. It helps to live in places like L.A. and New York, because they have more of them there; I know some people, in fact, who have almost literally kept themselves from starving for months at a time by eating dinner at a different press party every night. (I know other people who have made entire careers out of attending these things, but that's a different story.) The food's usually pretty good to magnificent, unless it's some bluejeaned folkie and the company's trying to be with-it by serving organic slop unfit for the innards of a sow; even in such an extreme case as that, though, you can content yourself with sopping up the booze, which is plentiful and usually of high quality. So even if you live at home or haven't had any trouble lately keeping the wolf from the door, you can get drunk free a lot and that's always a pleasure, even if you do usually have to sit through some shit like John Prine or Osibisa just for a few glasses of gin. Sure you're prostituting yourself in a way, but so are they, and what are most modern business, social or sexual relationships if not a process of symbiotic exploitation? It's the same tub of shit no matter where it perches, so you might as well kick back and enjoy yourself while you can.

The next big step up after press parties is that you'll start receiving invitations to concerts, events and record company conventions in distant cities. Free vacations! The record companies will pay your plane fare, put you up in a swank hotel with room service (usually), and wine and dine you like mad for the duration of your stay, all just because they want you to write about some act they're trying to break. This is where things get a little cooler and less of a hustle, because once you've had enough stuff published that they're willing to drop a few hundred smackeroos to get you to do a story on somebody in their stable, you can pretty much pick and choose who you want to write about. Well, not totally, but everybody finds their own level, and it finds them. Like if you're a red-hot flaming-eared heavy metal fanatic, they'll call you up one day and offer to fly you to Chicago or New York to see, oh, the Stooges, maybe. Or at least Jukin' Bone.

The final benefit (and for some people, the biggest) is that during most of these stages and at an increasingly casual level as time goes on, you'll get to hobnob with the Stars. Backstage at concerts, in the dressing room drinking their wine, rapping casually with the famous, the talented, the rich and the beautiful. Most of 'em are just jerks like everybody else, and you probably won't really get to meet any real Biggies very often since the record companies don't need publicity on them so why should they inflict you on 'em, but you will become friends with a lot of Stars of the Future. Or at least also rans.

Okay, so that's the rosy vista. I painted it for true, and if you want it, it's yours, becuz after almost five years in this racket I finally decided I'm gonna break down and tell the whole world how to break in. I could get a lotta dough for this if I wanted to—some of us have talked for years about starting a Famous Rock Critics' School—but fuck it, I'm too lazy to take the time to set up some shit like that, and besides it's about time everybody got wind of the True Fax of Rock 'n' Roll Criticism. Listen well, and decide for yourself whether you wanna bother with it.

The first thing to understand and bear in mind at all times is that the whole thing is just a big ruse from the word go, it don't mean shit except exploitatively and in the zealotic terms of wanting to inflict your tastes on other people. Most people start writing record reviews because they want other people to like the same kind of stuff they do, and there's nothing wrong with that, it's a very honest impulse. I used to be a Jehovah's Witness when I was a kid so I had it in my blood already, a head start. But don't worry. All you gotta do is just keep bashin' away, and sooner or later people will start saying things to you like "How do you fit the Kinks into your overall aesthetic perspective?"

Well they won't really talk that jiveass, but damn close if you travel in the right (or wrong, as the case may be) circles. Because that old saw is true: most rock critics are pompous assholes. Maybe most critics are pompous assholes, but rock critics are especially—because they're working in virgin territory, where there's absolutely no recognized, generally agreed on authority or standards. Nor should there be. Anything goes, so fake 'em out every chance you get. Rock 'n' roll's basically just a bunch of garbage in the first place, it's noise, it's here today and gone tomorrow, so the only thing that can possibly trip you up is if you begin to reflect that if the music's that trivial, can you imagine how trivial what you're doing is?

Which actually is a good attitude to operate from, because it helps keep the pomposity factor if check. Half the rock critics in the country, no, 90% of the rock critics in the world have some grand theory they're trying to lay on each other and everybody else, which they insist explains everything in musical history and ties up all the loose ends. Every last one of 'em has a different theory and every last one of the theories is total bullshit, but you might as well have one as part of your baggage if you're going to pass. Try this: ALL ROCK 'N' ROLL CULTURES PLAGIARIZE EACH OTHER. THAT IS INHERENT IN THEIR NATURE. SO MAYBE, SINCE WHAT ROCK 'N' ROLL'S ALL ABOUT IS PLAGIARISM ANYWAY, THE MOST OUT-AND-OUT PLAGIARISTS, THE IMITATORS OF THE PRIME MOVING GENIUSES, ARE GREATER AND MORE VALID THAN THOSE GENIUSES! JUST CHECK THIS OUT: THE ROLLING STONES ARE BETTER THAN CHUCK BERRY! THE SHADOWS OF KNIGHT WERE BETTER THAN THE YARDBIRDS! P.F. SLOAN'S FIRST ALBUM WAS A MASTERPIECE, WAY BETTER THAN BLONDE ON BLONDE (I know one prominent rock critic in Texas who actually believes this; he's a real reactionary, but so are most of 'em!)!

Pretty pompous, huh? Well, that just happens to be one of my basic theories, although I don't really believe all the stuff I said in there (not that that makes a diddley damn bit of difference), and you can have it if you want it to bend or mutate as you please. Or come up with your own crock of shit; anyway, it's good to have one for those late-nite furious discussions leading absolutely nowhere. See, the whole thing's just a big waste of time, but the trappings can be fun and you always liked to whack off anyway. Like, look, you can impress people you wanna fuck by saying impressive things like "John Stewart Mill couldn't write rock 'n' roll, but Dylan could have written 'An Essay On Human Understanding'. Only he would have called it 'Like a Rolling Stone!'" (Dave Marsh of *Creem* magazine actually said that to me, and everybody else who lived with us, and everybody he talked to on the phone for the next month, once.) Just imagine laying that on some fine little honey—she'd flip out! She'd think you were a genius! Either that or a pompous asshole. But in this business, like any other, you win some and you lose some. Persevere, kid.

Where were we? Ah yes, you should also know that most of your colleagues are some of the biggest neurotics in the country, so you might as well get used right now to the way they're gonna be writing you five and ten page single spaced inflammatory letters reviling you for knocking some group that they have proved is the next Stones. It's all very incestuous, like this great big sickoid club full of people who were probably usually the funny looking kid in class, with the acne and the big horn rims, all introverted, and just sat home every night through high school and played his records while the other kids yukked and balled it up. Tough luck, genius is pain. Or frustrated popstars, all rock critics are frustrated popstars and you should see 'em singing to themselves when nobody else is around. Boy, do they get corny! Melodramatic? Whooo!! Some of them actually go so far as to invest their entire life savings in trendy popstar wardrobes, and others are so monomaniacal as to go beyond that to the actual steps of forming a band of their own.* And you can rest assured that all of them write songs, and have constant daytime and nightdaze fantasies of big contracts with ESP-Disk at least.

Speaking of investing your life savings, another good way of letting on to everybody on the block that you're a rock critic is to go out and waste a lot of money buying old albums in bargain bins. They have these turd-dumps in most drugstores or supermarkets, full of last year's crap and older stuff at prices ranging from as low as a quarter all the way up to $2.50 and more. If you patronize these scumholes regularly, you will soon begin to build a Definitive Rock 'n' Roll Albums Collection, which is of course a must for anybody who's into this way of life really seriously. The object is simple: you gotta have EVERYTHING, no matter how arcane or shitty it is, because it all fits into the grand bulwark of Rock. So just go out there and throw all your money away, it's a good investment. You'll be filling your room with mung, but so what: how many other people do you know who have the Battered Ornaments album? Right. They don't know what they're missing.

I know one rock critic who actually drew out his life's savings and drove from St. Louis, where he lived, to New York and back, by way of Chicago, Detroit and New Jersey, AND STOPPED AT EVERY BARGAIN BIN ALONG THE WAY. That was the entire purpose of the trip, to visit bargain bins. Now this guy is obviously a real doofus and totally out of his mind, but you can see where this business can lead you if you're lucky and apply yourself: *down blind alleys.*

Speaking of this same doofus reminds me of another riff that is essential to have if you're gonna be a hotshit rock critic. You gotta find some band somewhere that's maybe even got two or three albums out and might even be halfway good, but the important thing is the more arcane it is the better, it's gotta be something that absolutely nobody in the world but you and two other people (the group's manager and one member's mother) knows or cares about, and what you wanna do is TALK ABOUT THIS BUNCH OF OBSCURE NONENTITIES AND THEIR RECORD(S) LIKE THEY'RE THE HOTTEST THING IN THE HISTORY OF MUSIC! You gotta build 'em up real big, they're your babies, only you alone can perceive their true greatness, so you gotta go around telling everybody that they're better than the Rolling Stones, they beat the Beatles black and blue, they murtelyze the Dead, they're the most significant and profound musical force in the world. And someday their true greatness will be recognized and you will be vindicated as a seer far ahead of your time.

Sometimes this scheme can really pay off, like if you happen to pick a Captain Beefheart or Velvet Underground way before they get widely known, although they're not really eligible because this group has gotta be so obscure that they can put out all kindsa albums and nobody pays any attention to 'em but you, they're just off mouldering in a cutout rack somewhere if not for your devoted efforts.

---

* Bangs would form his own band three years later in 1977.

Doofus (of the preceding paragraph) came up with a lulu in this department, couple of 'em in fact: All he ever talks about is Amon Düül II, Bang and Budgie. Ever heard of any of 'em? That's what I thought. And you probably never will except if he's around to pester you about them. Amon Düül II are this psychedelic experimental avant-garde chance music free jazz electronic synthesizer space rock group from Germany. They got all kinds of albums out over there, there's even two groups with the same name, Amon Düül I and Amon Düül II, but they only got three albums out here and hardly anybody ever heard of 'em, although a whole shitload of people sure will if Doofus keeps up his one-man propaganda campaign on their behalf! They happen to be real good, but that's beside the point. And Bang and Budgie, his other two pet monomanias, are a couple of Black Sabbath imitations, one from Florida and one from England, one pretty good and one not so hot. So he and this other critic from Texas (also previously mentioned) send big long hate letters back and forth to each other telling each other what morons they are, because the Texan don't like Budgie or something like that. Get the idea?

Also I turned Doofus onto Can, another German psychedelic schnozz-ball that has lotsa 17-minute electroraga jams, and he listens to one side of their album one time and sez to me: "Don't you think Can are better than the Stooges?" See what I mean? When all week he's been asking me things like "Don't you think Amon Düül II are the greatest group in history?" and "Don't you think *Dance of the Lemmings* (one of their albums, featuring such standards as "Dehypnotized Toothpaste," "Landing in a Ditch" and "A Short Stop at the Transylvanian Brain Surgery") is the greatest album of all time?" and I keep saying no, but he won't take no for an answer, he's a man with a Plan! A crusader on behalf of Neglected Genius. So you see the key: *persistence*. Make a total nuisance of yourself, and people will begin to take you seriously. Or at least stop regarding you as not there. And if he wants to continue on this obscuro roller-coaster ride, there are zillions of German bands: take Guru Guru or Floh de Cologne, for example—these qualify as two of the finest choices in the Arcane Masterpiece department in history, indeed they do, because both are imports and you can't even find a single Floh de Cologne or Guru Guru album anywhere in the United States except by ordering it special from Germany! *Nobody* knows what it sounds like so they gotta listen to Doofus. So as you can see Doofus copped himself a real hot item, but chances like that come only once in a lifetime.

That pretty much takes care of the qualifications. Like what you see? Wanna give it a try? Well, get ready, because the big time is just around the corner. The only thing left to mention before you embark on your career as a rock critic is that talent has absolutely nothing to do with it, so don't worry if you don't know how to write. Don't even worry if you can't put a simple declarative sentence together. Don't worry if you can only sign your name with an X. Anybody can do this shit, all it takes is a high level of unconsciousness (and you just got done reading an unconsciousness expanding session) and some ability to sling bullshit around. Also the bullshit is readymade, you don't even have to think it up, all you gotta do is invest in a slingshot. All the word-type stuff you need has already been written anyway, it's in old yellow issues of *Shakin' Street, Rolling Stone, Creem* and all the rest; just sit around reading and rereading the damn things all day and pretty soon you'll have whole paragraphs of old record reviews memorized, which is not only a good way to impress people at parties and girls you're trying to pick up with your erudition, but allows you to plagiarize at will. And don't worry about getting caught, because nobody in this business has any memory and besides they're all plagiarists too and besides that all record reviews read the same. I learned to write 'em outta *Down Beat*, and it's the same shit in *Rolling Stone*; it's the same shit all over. Just stir and rearrange it every once in awhile. Take one riff and staple it to another; and if you get tired of thinking about how you're a rock critic, remember William Burroughs and the cutup methods and think about being avant-garde. I do it all the time.

Okay, now it's time for you to write YOUR VERY FIRST ORIGINAL RECORD REVIEW. It's easy, all you gotta do is point. First, pick a title for the album:

A. *Oranges in Exile*
B. *Outer City Blues & Heavy Dues*
C. *Cajun Sitar Dance Party*
D. *Hungry Children of Babylon*
E. *Eat Your Coldcream*

Got it? Okay, the next part's just as easy. Just fill in the blanks: This latest offering from_____

A. Harmonica Dan and His Red Light District
B. The Armored Highchair
C. Ducks in Winter
D. The Four Fat Guys
E. Arturo de Cordova

is _____

A. a clear consolidation of the artistic moves first tentatively ventured in his/her/their/its last album.
B. a real letdown after the masterpiece album and single that carried us all the way through the summer and warmed us over in the fall.
C. important only insofar as it will delineate the contours of the current malaise for future rock historians, if there are any with all the pollution around now.
D. definitely the album of the year.
E. a heap of pig shit.

(How you doin' so far? See how easy it is!) Onward! Choose one of the following for the next sentence: _____

A. In dealing with such a record, the time has come at last to talk about the responsibilities, if any, which any artist making rock 'n' roll bears to his audience, and specifically how those responsibilities relate to the political situation which we, all of us, and perforce rock 'n' roll, are compelled to come to terms with by dint of living in the United States of America today.
B. I don't really think these guys/this dude/the chick in question/a singing dog can defend musical output which has proven increasingly shoddy by referring to such old handles as "personal expression," "experimentalism," "a new kind of artistic freedom," or any other such lame copout.
C. It's such a thrill that this album finally came, that I am finally actually holding it in my hands, looking at the fantastically beautiful M. C. Escher drawing on the cover whilst trembling all over to the incredible strains of the music on the record from inside it which even now are wafting from the old Victrola, that I really don't know if I am going to come or cry.
D. It's so goddam fucking boring to have to open all these pieces of shit every day, you waste your time, you break your fingernails, half the time it's just a repeat of an album that came yesterday, that I can hardly bring myself to slit open the shrinkwrap once I get 'em outta

the cardboard (which piles up in a big mess all over the house after it gets dragged outta the corner by all my asshole friends!), and I really can just barely stand to put the goddam things on the turntable after that. I wish it would break anyway so I wouldn't have to listen to 'em anymore. (Good one, huh, more than one sentence in this one!) But anyway, I put this piece of shit on just like all the others except the ones I never get around to, and right now I'm listening to it and you know what? I was right. It is a piece of shit!

E. I don't remember how I got here, whose house this is or where this typewriter came from, but anyway this new album is by the greatest fucking rock 'n' roll band in the whole wide world/most talented, sensitive balladeer of his generation whom many of us are already calling the New Dylan/sweetest songbird this side of the Thames has saved my life again just like all the others did, so I don't even care where I am, I don't care if I got rolled last night, I don't care if this place gets busted right now, I don't care if the world comes to an end because the cosmic message of truth and unity which this music is bringing to me has made me feel complete for the first time since 1968.

(Well, that wasn't hard at all, was it? A whole paragraph written already! But this is no place to stop: the most fun's yet to come. Tally ho!)

The first song on side one _____

A. "Catalina Sky"
B. "Death Rays in Your Eyes"
C. "I Wish I Was a Rusty Nail"
D. "Lady of Whitewater"
E. "Nixon Eats"

(choose again) _____

A. is a rousingly high spirited opener in march tempo.
B. starts things off at an extremely high energy level.
C. sets the pace and mood of the album most atmospherically.
D. won't win any Grammies this year.
E. reminds me of my Grandmother puking up her sherry into the bathtub the night we had fish that had gone bad for dinner when I was three years old.

The first thing you notice is _____

A. the vicious, slashing guitar solo.
B. the deep, throbbing bass lines.
C. how mellowly the sensitive, almost painfully fragile vocal is integrated with the mesmerizing Spanish chords from those four fine hollow-body Gibson guitars.
D. the cymbals aren't miked right.
E. that the entire mix is a washout and this album has what is probably the worst production of the year.

The full impact of what's going on in this cut may not reach you the first time, but if you keep listening a couple of times a day for a week or two, especially through headphones, it will come to you in a final flash of revelation that _____

    A. you were wasting your time.

    B. you are listening to a masterpiece of rock which so far transcends "rock" as we have known it that most people probably won't recognize its true worth for at least ten years.

    C. the instruments are out of tune.

    D. you should have bought the Band instead.

    E. you're deaf in one ear.

Cut two is _____

    A. a nice change of pace

    B. more of the same phlegm

    C. a definite picker-upper

    D. interesting, at least

    E. insulting to the human ear (my dog didn't like it either)

by virtue of the fact that _____

    A. it was produced by Phil Spector's cousin from Jersey.

    B. it's only two seconds long.

    C. the lyrics say more, and more concisely, about what we have done to our natural environment than anything else written in the past decade.

    D. Bobby Keyes, Jim Price and Boots Randolph sit in for a real old time "blowing session."

    E. I spilled Gallo Port in the grooves and it made it sound better.

In spite of that, I feel that the true significance of its rather dense and muted lyrics can only be apprehended by_____

    A. the purchase of a hearing aid.

    B. reading the sheet enclosed with the record.

    C. going back and listening to "Memphis Blues Again," *then* come back to this and see if it doesn't blow you out the door!

    D. taking a course in German.

    E. throwing the incoherent piece of pig shit in the trash and going out for a beer, where something good is probably on the jukebox.

(Time for paragraph three already! Smooth sailing, bunky! You're almost there.) This record has inspired such_____

    A. ambivalent feelings

    B. helpless adoration

    C. bile and venom

    D. total indifference

    E. a powerful thirst

in me that I can't bring myself to describe the rest of the cuts. Track by track reviews are a bore anyway, and the album only costs $4.97 at the right stores, so go down and get it and find out for yourself whether you'll like it or not. Who am I, who is any critic or any other sentient being on the face of the earth, to tell you what a piece of music sounds like? Only your ears can hear it as only your ears can hear it. Am I right or am I wrong? Of course I am. I do know that I will _____

    A. go on listening to this album till I drop dead of cancer.
    B. walk out into the backyard and toss this offense unto mine eyes into the incinerator soon as I finish typing this spew.
    C. never forget the wonderful chance I've had here in the pages of *Fusion* to share this very special record, and my own deepest dredged sentiments about it, with you, who whether you know it or not are a very special person whom I love without qualification even if we've never seen each other, I don't even know your name, and am so righteous that I don't even care if you look like a sow.
    D. break this elpee over the head of the very next Jesus Freak or Hare Krishna creep I see in the street, just for thrills!
    E. go to sleep now and awaken upon a new morning in which I may be able to appreciate this unabridged poetic outpouring with fresh ears.

So before I sign my name at the bottom of this page and pick up the check from the cheap kikes that run this rag who will never pay me anyway, I would like to leave you with one thought:_____

    A. Today is the first day of the rest of your life.
    B. There are many here among us who feel that life is but a joke.
    C. The red man lost this land to you and me.
    D. Rock 'n' roll is dead. Long live rock 'n' roll.
    E. Since these assholes that're stupid enough to print this stuff don't pay me anything, why don't you? I've probably turned you on to a lot of good records over the years, and what do I get out of it? Nothing but a lot of grief! A lot of abuse from cretins who can't understand that rock 'n' roll IS the Revolution! A lot of cheap bloodsuckers like hellhounds on my trail! I got "Yer Blues"! I've paid my body and soul! So send me some $$$, goddammit, or I'll never write a word again as long as I live!

Your faithful correspondent, _____

    You did it! You really did it! There, you see, that wasn't so hard, was it? Now YOU TOO are an officially ordained and fully qualified rock critic, with publication under your belt and everything. Just cut out the review, if you're finished filling in all the blanks, and send it to the rock magazine of your choice with a stamped, self-addressed envelope! If they send it back, send it to another one! Be persistent! Be a "go getter"! Do you think Jon Landau ever let rejection slips get him down? No! And if you send it to all the rock mags in America, one of them is bound to print it sooner or later because most of them will print the worst off the wall shit in the world if they think it'll make 'em avant-garde! You could send 'em the instruction booklet on how to repair your lawn mower, just write the name of a current popular album by a famous artist at the top of the cover, sign your name at the bottom of the last page, and they'll print it! They'll think you're a genius!

    And you are! And when all the money you asked for in this review starts pouring in from your fans, you'll be rich! David Geffen will invite you out to his house in the Catskills for the weekend! Miles Davis will step aside when you walk down the street! Seals of Seals & Crofts will tip his hat to you and sing "Bah'aii!" as you walk down the street! David Peel will write songs about you! So will John Lennon! So will everybody! Andy Warhol will put you in his movies! You'll tour with David

Bowie, Leon Russell and Atomic Rooster, reading your most famous reviews to vast arenas full of rabid fans! You'll be an international celebrity and die at 33! You made the grade! You are now a rock critic, and by tomorrow you will be one of the most important critics in America! You'll make *Esquire*'s Heavy Hundred in 1974!

Congratulations, and welcome to the club!

Your pal,
R. J. Gleason*

---

* One of the foremost jazz and rock critics of the 1960s, Gleason was also a cofounder of *Rolling Stone*, the magazine that had fired Bangs back in 1973.

26

"Reggae: The Steady Rock of Black Jamaica"

Andrew Kopkind

Reggae artists enjoyed a smattering of popularity outside of Jamaica throughout the late 1960s and early 1970s, but it was not until 1972 and the release of the film *The Harder They Come* and its accompanying soundtrack that the music seemed primed to cross over into the American market. A number of articles on reggae appeared in the film's wake, among them Andrew Kopkind's report for the radical Berkeley-based magazine *Ramparts*. Given the publication's leanings, it should come as little surprise that Kopkind highlights reggae's revolutionary role in the Jamaican political landscape and its significance as the voice of Jamaica's oppressed people. The article also draws attention to reggae's distinctive rhythmic grooves, what singer Jimmy Cliff (born 1948) calls a type of "rock turned over." Taking stock both of reggae's musical and cultural allure, Kopkind expresses his misgivings about its possible exploitation as the "next big thing," a forecast that would be realized over the course of the next three years with Bob Marley's rise as reggae's first international star.[*]

The bleached white tourists at the Holiday Inn Reef Club, the Banana Boat and the Jamaica Hilton still request "Day-O" and gasp with the joy of recognition when a crooner starts "I Left a Little Girl in Kingston Town." And at the $12-a-head beach parties the Jamaica Tourist Board throws for the swinging set, short-haired frat boys still shove their giggling girlfriends under the limbo stick in time to the latest 1957 Belafonte hits. In the same vein but on the other hand, heavy American freaks under the palms at Negril keep the natives at bay with blasts of strong *ganja* and hard rock from hidden hi-fi's. But the time-encapsulated world of winter-week visitors to the Caribbean sands is particularly absurd in Jamaica this year, because an entirely new style of popular culture—soon to be mass-marketed in North America—is growing in native groves alongside the stands of tourists. The new form (new to us up North) is called reggae: at bottom a percussive beat and a melodic line of music, but by extension a social and artistic movement that expresses the special Jamaican mood of suffering, blackness and heavenly peace.

Reggae sounds have been drifting into the U.S. off and on for several years, and the music is well-known in Britain with its large West Indian communities. Desmond Dekker's "The Israelites" was a kinky hit of sorts; Paul Simon's "Mother and Child Reunion" presented Jamaican reggae overlaid with L.A. kitsch; and Johnny Nash made it biggest last year with a reggae single, "I Can See

[*] *Source:* Andrew Kopkind, "Reggae: The Steady Rock of Black Jamaica," *Ramparts*, June 1973, pp. 50–51.

Clearly Now." But the industry called all that "novelty." Now, the Anglo-American music moguls are hyping reggae into a commercial craze, and their rock stars are flying off to Kingston to record personal versions. The Rolling Stones have already been and gone (Mick Jagger hired a reggae band to play at his wedding); Cat Stevens came soon thereafter; the Jefferson Airplane went down to check it out; Roberta Flack is reported en route. J. Geils recorded a reggae number safely in white America, while Paul McCartney did it in England. Jimmy Cliff, the first Jamaican multi-media reggae star (Johnny Nash comes from Texas), has been signed by Warner Brothers Records for an upcoming album, and his Jamaican-made film, "The Harder They Come," is seeking provincial bookings after its *succes d'estime* in New York.

"We took the *ts-ts-ts*—the syncopation—out of jazz," Cliff explained, by way of a definition and a history of reggae, when we talked not long ago in a Warner Brothers office in New York. "The guitar rhythm is out of calypso, the percussion part of it is Latin and West African. The drumming is like the reverse of rock, it's rock turned over: rock drumming is off the beat, reggae drumming is right on the beat—and the bass goes in between." However obscure that exegesis may be, the sound is obvious after the first hearing. It is danceable and whistleable like the best old rhythm & blues before rock ran it into the ground.

In its purely musical form, reggae (also called rock steady) is an outgrowth of ska, a Jamaican style popular in the early '60s. For years before that, Jamaicans had fed on American R&B records; when the rock-and-roll boom slowed R&B exports, Jamaicans began going it alone. Ska put a West Indian flavor into black North American Music. Later—in the mid-'60s—reggae developed as a Caribbean counterpart of soul, with more than a few echoes of fundamentalist church gospel singing and African chants. You can hear a kind of unself-conscious reggae flowing from any church in Jamaica every Sunday: as you can hear pre-commercial soul in any rural black church in America.

But the content of reggae music—lyrically and melodically—is strikingly different from most North American black pop music today, even though the forms have resulted from the cross-pollenization of all the same Afro-American strains. Reggae lyrics are rarely macho and violent in the manner of Shaft or Super Fly; rather, they say something about the pain of the world and the hope for a sunnier future—sentiments that sound naive and perhaps primitive to cool Americans, but replicate exactly the visual tones of Jamaican shantytown poverty against the agonizing beauty of the Caribbean sea-sky.

"Sixty percent of reggae is the frustration of oppressed people," Jimmy Cliff said with the calm and kindly honesty that softens the hard edge of Jamaicans' anger—in person and in music. "They're just fighting to get out from under that heavy weight. They know that pie-in-the-sky is a fake. But still, 40 percent of it is fantasy. The music is happy; we sing a happy melody, but it's sad underneath. You can sing a happy song and underneath you're really hungry. The Prime Minister once said that if you want to know what's going on in Jamaica, look at what's on the charts, listen to the words of the songs."

In fact, the Jamaican Prime Minister, Michael Manley, is said to prefer European classical music to reggae, but his advice is sound enough. His political party, the reformist Peoples National Party, upset the decade-long rule of the Jamaica Labour Party last year by riding an insurgent campaign style off which reggae and "The Harder They Come" seemed to be in the cultural vanguard. The conservative Labour Party Government closed down the movie set several times during production because of the insurrectionist attitudes the film was bound to convey to Jamaicans (although it seems somewhat less revolutionary in the U.S.; politics rarely survives a sea journey). Cliff plays a country boy who comes to Kingston to make it as a pop singer, suffers humiliation from a music industry boss, a horny, authoritarian clergyman, and a mocha middleclass lady (played by Prime

Minister Manley's wife), and drifts into the *ganja* trade. He almost gets to the top smuggling dope to the U.S. market, but he falls hard in the end—a political conclusion, written into the script, with which Cliff disagrees. All this after offing a spectacular array of uniformed and civilian pigs, with the universal approval of the island populace, on-screen and off.

The movie scored an historic success in Jamaica, and its implicit political messages, Cliff said, contributed to the PNP's electoral victory: an ambiguous outcome, he thought, because "if the Jamaica Labour Party had been returned, there would have been a revolution." There are no significant whites in "The Harder They Come," no long shots of manicured beaches and planted palms. It was made in a Jamaica that tourists simply do not see. "It is not," Jimmy Cliff said emphatically, "a tourism promotion film." By its concentration on black and poor Jamaicans, the movie takes some kind of a stand against the pervasive Anglo-American penetration of the island—even, contradictorily, while the imperial entertainment industry is making plans for the biggest cultural rip-off since Calypso.

Reggae is the only "fresh" music around today, as Jimmy Cliff claims, and more than that it's the only true *popular*—that is to say, people's—music capable of commercial success. Reggae is still close to spontaneous folk forms, a professionalized version of common rhythms and harmonies that you can hear in the beeping of automobile horns and the cry of fruit vendors. Jamaican kids tap distinctive reggae rhythms when they idly and unconsciously hit a stick against a rock in play.

North American "folk" is mostly intellectualized and commercialized; rock is degenerating into rococo repetitions of itself; and Lenox Avenue soul is on a sex-'n-violence trip that destroys itself and its cultural context. The David Bowie-Lou Reed gender-fuck idea, which was so promising in its beginning (see RAMPARTS, March 1973) is already being blown by hype into fatuous fraudulence.

That leaves reggae as the next exploitable number. The music industry is looking for a really big gimmick "like Presley or the Beatles," an RCA publicity person said the other day. It's doubtful that reggae could fill the bill: it is too fragile, too vulnerable, too honest to withstand the massive assaults on its authenticity that the collective corporate shuck would mount. Jimmy Cliff may translate some of his Jamaican success into American—although few other artists from Kingston will be so lucky—but he'd better watch out for the American music monster. Naturally, he is optimistic. "We've been kicked and licked and repressed," he said at the end of our talk, in a line which is equally honest as his song lyric and a political philosophy, "and we'll stand the test."

27

"Roots and Rock: The Marley Enigma"

Linton Kwesi Johnson

Jamaican born poet and activist Linton Kwesi Johnson (born 1952) first rose to prominence during the 1970s in England, where his politically charged writings and reggae dub poetry performances earned him great critical acclaim. In the decades since, he has remained one of the most visible social commentators and compelling voices for black British culture. In his 1975 essay "Roots and Rock," which originally appeared in the London-based journal *Race Today*, Johnson addresses Bob Marley's rise to fame and his crowning within the American and British music press as the "new king of rock." Marley (1945–1981), and his group the Wailers, were pivotal in bringing reggae to a larger international audience. As Johnson points out, much of Marley's success hinged upon the generalized appeal of his Rastafarian lifestyle, and a rebellious image that seemed to fit seamlessly within rock's prescribed set of heroic values. Johnson has provided the *Rock History Reader* with his own introduction (in italics below), which further places the article in its proper historical context.[*]

I wrote "Roots and Rock: The Marley Enigma" as a fan of the Wailers, after the group had broken up, and Bob Marley was declared the new "King of rock" following the release of "Natty Dread". In 1975 when I wrote the article, I was a young consumer, collector and student of reggae music. The departure of Peter Tosh and Bunny Wailer from the Wailers and the appropriation of Bob Marley as the new hero of rock music felt like a double blow. It led me to consider the commodification and commercialisation of the music. Today I recognise the genius of Bob Marley and the enormous contribution he has made to popular culture the world over. © Linton Kwesi Johnson, June 2006.

So Bob Marley has made it and the Wailers too, what's left of them—after eleven years of musical devotion and changing emotions. The 'little brown man' from down a St. Ann is now a big big man, albeit a musical one. Now everyone is singing Marley's song—even Johnny Nash, once called 'the king of reggae' by the white music culture—vultures. The rock critics of Europe and North America now hail Bob Marley the new king of rock and protest, the new King Emperor Haile I/King Selassie I/King of kings. They speak of the new Hendrix, the new Dylan, the musical messiah of the rockers, the hippies, the beatniks, the trendies and the drop outs. But the 'I yah' man knows that:

> *The rise of the 'rasta rebel from Trench Town'*
> *who likes to wear a frown*
> *is not fulfilment of prophecy,*
> *but the realisation of a commercial dream*

---

[*] *Source:* Linton Kwesi Johnson, "Roots and Rock: the Marley Enigma," *Race Today* 7, no. 10 (October 1975), pp. 237–38.

a capitalist scheme.

To be sure, the coming of the new musical messiah had been long awaited in Europe and North America, since the departure of Hendrix, who could not stand the 'purple haze'. Dylan, the lyrical propagandist of the campus revolutionaries, seems to have died with the 'hippies' and their sit-in revolution. There was a vacuum of vogue until

> *Marley let riddim drop*
> *and it was not*
> *or rather, it was not until*
> *the capitalists sighted the gap*
> *Sought and found*
> *The right man with the right sound*
> *who was not black but brown.*

Truly, it was a capitalist affair. What a sensation, Bob Marley, the talk of the musical nations/The standing ovations/The long citations. The man behind it all? Chris Blackwell, descendant of slave masters and owner of Island records, continuing the tradition of his white ancestors. Blackwell puts his vision of Marley for capital thus: 'I think that generally rock music has become a bit stale and I think Bob's music has an energy and a fresh feel to it.' Indeed.

The energy of which Blackwell speaks, is the dynamism of the culture of the urban unemployed, the sufferers, the oppressed of Jamaica. The 'fresh feel' is the soul and rock elements which have been incorporated into the music of the Wailers. But this alone with Marley's lyrical excellence could not spell success. The commodity is not complete and it is commodities that the capitalist deals in, not music per se. There had to be an angle, an image. And what better image than that of the Rasta rebel (the long haired rasta rebel).

From the very beginning, it could be seen, Marley was destined for fame; destined to become the chosen one. For it is a unique set of experiences and circumstances that has shaped Marley's music the son of an Afro-Jamaican woman and an Englishman. His experiences are rooted within the sufferers of Jamaica. He celebrated the rudi 'rebellion' of the 60's and defended 'rudi' in tunes like, 'Let Them Go'. Living in America for a while, Marley was very much influenced by American rhythm and blues and soul music. By 1969 'reggae' had superseded 'rock steady' and ska as the new musical mode of Jamaica. Bob and the Wailers came back on the scene after a short impasse as the new 'soul rebels'. 'I am a rebel/soul rebel', sang Marley, 'I am a capturer soul adventurer' in Temptations style. By this time Marley's lyrical excellence had been acknowledged by the sufferers in the ghettoes, at least. His persecution by babylon lent a new style of rhetoric to his lyricism; this was the rhetoric not of protest but of defiance and rebellion. And the language was that of Rastafarai.

This is the image that is used to sell Marley, the image of the rasta rebel, and god only knows the eroticism and romanticism that this image invokes in the mind of his white fans. And this is where the ironies multiply. The 'image' is derived from rastafarianism and rebellion, which are rooted in the historical experience of the oppressed of Jamaica. It then becomes an instrument of capital to sell Marley and his music, thereby negating the power which is the cultural manifestation of this historical experience. So though Marley is singing about 'roots' and 'natty', his fans know not. Neither do they understand the meaning or the feeling of dread. And there is really no dread in Marley's music. The dread has been replaced by the howling rock guitar and the funky rhythm and what we get is the enigma of 'roots' and rock.

28

Dub and the Sound of Surprise

RICHARD WILLIAMS

During the 1970s, *Melody Maker*, along with the *New Musical Express* and *Sounds*, was one of Britain's three main rock-oriented weekly music magazines. Addressing a mainstream audience, rock critic Richard Williams presents an overview in this 1976 article of one of reggae's most influential offshoots: dub. As he describes, the placement of dub remixes on the B-sides of reggae singles allowed producers like Lee "Scratch" Perry (born Rainford Hugh Perry, 1936) and King Tubby (Osbourne Ruddock, 1941–1989) to assert themselves through the mixing board as active "composers," reimagining a familiar song in a new, surprising way. Williams proposes that dub may also be understood as an "aesthetic," one that could have a broader application and influence the direction of future musical styles. Since its emergence in the 1970s, dub has indeed expanded well beyond its specific associations with reggae music. It has become, in short, a familiar technique, where one isolates vocals and instrumental layers in the mix, shifting them in and out of the texture, or even "shrouding them in echo." Nowhere is dub's legacy outside of reggae more apparent than in rap and hip-hop, where producers have completely absorbed the essence of dub's studio manipulations and tricks.*

How can I persuade you not to laugh when I say that the technique of dub may well be the most interesting new abstract concept to appear in modern music since Ornette Coleman undermined the dictatorship of Western harmony almost two decades ago?

First, I'm assuming that you're aware of dub's existence. For those who unaccountably aren't, the briefest of rundowns: It's what you find on the flip side of most reggae singles, where the producer has taken the A-side and fed it through various equalisation facilities (sound-modification devices) available on his mixing board.

Vocals and instruments appear and disappear with what at first seems a bewildering anarchy, often shrouded in echo or distorted beyond recognition.

It's completely bizarre, and yet among Jamaicans the dub records are usually more popular than the straight versions of the same tunes. It's not abnormal for several dubs of the same basic track to appear, and prerelease dub albums sell at enormous prices in considerable quantities.

What I want to discuss, however, is not necessarily dub in its present application, interesting though that may be.

---

* *Source:* Richard Williams, "Dub is the Nearest Aural Equivalent to a Drug Experience," *Melody Maker,* August 21, 1976, p. 21.

It strikes me that there are possibilities inherent in this aberrant form which could perhaps resonate through other musics in the years to come; this may seem wild prophesy, but it could change the nature of some areas, and the nature of the ways in which we both play and apprehend music.

THE ROOTS OF DUB

Dub had its beginning in the mid-sixties, when Jamaican disc jockeys first started making funny noises through their microphones in time to the records they played; this eventually found its way onto the records themselves. A primitive and popular example would be Prince Buster's hit "Al Capone," where a voice provides a curious and persistent quasi-percussive accompaniment.

A few years later, gathering courage, jocks like U-Roy started making up impromptu verse on top of the records, and when this too was reproduced in the studio, the original singer's voice was frequently faded in and out around the overdubbed chanting (or "toasting," as it became known).

The next step was to muck around with the sound of the instruments themselves, and with the whole arrangement of the track.

Producers like Lee Perry (the rawest), King Tubby (the most innovatory), and Jack Ruby (the most sophisticated) vied with each other to create the most eccentrically ear-bending effects.

A couple of years ago dub had become so popular that an album called "King Tubby Meets the Upsetter" (a kind of "battle of the boards" between Tubby and Perry) bore, on the rear of its sleeve, large pictures of the mixing consoles used by the two protagonists. Not a human in sight.

Currently, and perhaps most interesting of all, certain reggae bands are beginning to duplicate dub in live performance.

As yet they haven't managed to reproduce the full panoply of bass and drum techniques, but the use of heavy sporadic echo on lead instruments like harmonica and guitar is being featured.

THE AESTHETICS OF DUB

One's overriding impression, on initial exposure to dub at the high volume for which it is intended, is that this is the nearest aural equivalent to a drug experience, in the sense that reality (the original material) is being manipulated and distorted.

I have no doubt that this was an important motivation in dub's development, whether consciously or otherwise. That's quite interesting but ultimately insignificant when compared with its other and more sophisticated effects on the listener.

Because it's most often applied to an already-familiar song or rhythm track, dub has a uniquely poignant quality: memories are revived, but rather than being simply duplicated (as when we hear a "golden oldie" from our youth on the radio) they are given subtle twists. Memory is teased rather than dragged up, and is thereby heightened.

It is, above all, the supreme sound of surprise, whether that of an anguished, Echoplexed scream, or a rimshot mechanically flared into a facsimile of thunder, or a steady bass riff suddenly and mysteriously disappearing in the middle of a bar (with an effect like that of stepping into an empty lift shaft).*

Ideally, therefore, no dub performance should be heard more than once.

Its evanescence and randomness make it perhaps the most existential of musics, and its most stunning implication comes with the realisation that no dub track is ever "correct" or "finished": it can always be done again a thousand different ways, each one as "correct" as any other.

---

* The Echoplex was an electronic device that created a tape delay.

For the nonaligned (i.e., non–West Indian) listener to cope with this, some values must be adjusted in order to accept and enjoy the constant sense of shock it provides when the hands of a Lee Perry or a Tappa Zukie are at the controls. Once assimilated, though, it can have the invigorating effect of the best so-called Free Music.

Does it, can it, have a wider implication? I think so, and we may already be on the road. Two examples:

(1) When Roxy Music was formed, it was Brian Eno's function—him again!—firstly to introduce relevant sound effects (the standard and expected sirens, bleeps, whooshes, and so on), and secondarily to modify the form and content of what the musicians onstage were playing. (In the early days, Eno's synthesizer and tape machines were positioned at the mixing desk.)

A couple of weeks ago Phil Manzanera was quoted in this paper as saying that, then, he was never sure how his guitar would sound once Eno had finished interfering with its output.

As Roxy Music became more conventional, stripping away one by one the original experimental factors in a curious instance of success actually inhibiting exploration, Eno became more of a "player" in his own right and less of a modifier … and then he left. A missed opportunity.

(2) Late last year one of the young groups currently fashionable on the punk rock scene recorded a song which purposely employed elements of dub: repeat-echo on harmonica, delay and superimposition of rhythm guitars, and the occasional tweak on the lead vocal.

Although it has yet to be released, the track was a complete artistic success: the tension which resulted from these devices was wholly congruous, thoroughly in keeping with the spirit and atmosphere of such music.

Looking elsewhere, one can spot other signs. Ever since "What's Going On," Marvin Gaye has been developing a kind of sound-stratification which allows for a certain randomness within the overall texture.

This is slightly misleading, because Gaye's records (I'm thinking particularly of "Let's Get It On" and "I Want You") must be the result of many hours of forethought and care and patience, all of which would appear to be inimical to the crucial spontaneity of dub.

Miles Davis's last release, the in-concert "Agharta," displayed an almost dublike nonchalance and disregard of "planning," but here the difference is that all the musicians are left to their own devices, unhindered.

I have sometimes felt, too, that the loud and apparently arbitrary synthesizer interjections which Joe Zawinul is prone to perpetrate during Weather Report concerts (but not their records) have something of the spirit of King Tubby—although that is perhaps being too lenient.

THE POLITICS OF DUB

In its present "natural" state, dub has no inbuilt politics; were it to be utilised by nonreggae musicians, though, these would arise and create controversy, for one of its major principles is the denial of the right of the musician to control completely his own output.

While advocating its study and wider use, I am not of course suggesting that it would benefit everyone. Only a fool would maintain that the formal purity of a Joni Mitchell or the majestic poise of a John Coltrane could be improved by meddling.

But, in the hands of adventurous groups and composers, it could be a fascinating tool. It seems to me to be a gripping and revolutionary idea that an outside agency—in other words, the man at the mixing desk—could control the actual content of a live performance, choosing exactly what he wanted to be heard, so that while (say) a bassist might be playing throughout a piece, only an unpredetermined proportion of his contribution would be heard. And he'd be as surprised as anybody by what did (and what didn't) come out.

Rather than the performers serving as an interface between composer and audience, therefore, the composer himself would assume that function, standing very relevantly between the players and the listeners.

(Another precedent comes to mind: anyone who's seen Gil Evans conducting an orchestra will know the way he seems to draw out punctuations and colours at will.)

At the lesser end of the scale, Dub offers a range of new playing and recording gimmicks which could be plagiarised and thereby enliven all kinds of styles, from Chinn-and-Chapman to Anthony Braxton. At the limit of its potential, it proposes nothing less than a new kind of composing.

29

Art Rock

JOHN ROCKWELL

British progressive or "art rock" bands like Emerson, Lake and Palmer were among the most popular stadium and recording acts of the 1970s, raising the level of virtuosity and spectacle in rock music to previously unseen levels. At the same time, their elevated borrowings of classical music, eclectic stylistic pastiche, and fascination with ornate synthesizer technology rarely endeared them to critics.[*] For a generation of rock journalists who had been raised on the revolutionary, rebellious values of the 1960s American counterculture, progressive rock's upper-class pretensions seemed an ill fit. John Rockwell echoes many of these populist sentiments in his "art rock" chapter summary for the 1976 *Rolling Stone Illustrated History of Rock & Roll*. As an art music critic for the *New York Times*, Rockwell (who reviewed rock music as well) is particularly suspicious of what he sees as a "pillaging" of the classical music canon. Rockwell is far less critical, however, when he turns to the avant-garde works of musician and producer Brian Eno (born 1948), whose ambient leanings show a deeper connection with trance music and minimalism. In the case of Eno, Rockwell draws explicit connections between art rock and the experimental drugs and compositional styles of the 1960s, in the process grounding his music in an accepted countercultural authenticity.[†]

There is a morphology to artistic movements. They begin with a rude and innocent vigor, pass into a healthy adulthoood and finally decline into an overwrought, feeble old age. Something of this process can be observed in the passage of rock and roll from the three-chord primitivism of the Fifties through the burgeoning vitality and experimentation of the Sixties to the hollow emptiness of much of the so-called progressive or "art" rock of the Seventies.

The whole notion of art rock triggers instinctive hostility from those who define rock in terms of the early-middle stages of its morphology. Rock was born as a street rebellion against pretensions and hypocrisy—of Fifties society, Fifties Tin Pan Alley pop, and high art in general ("Roll Over Beethoven"). Thus the very idea of art rock strikes some as a cancer to be battled without quarter, and the present-day reversion to primitivism is in part a rejection of the fancier forms of progressive rock. The trouble is, once consciousness has intruded itself onto the morphological process, it's impossible to obliterate it (except maybe with drugs, and then only temporarily). And so even primitivism, self-consciously assumed, becomes one of the principal vehicles of art rock.

The Beatles' *Sgt. Pepper's Lonely Hearts Club Band* (1967) is often cited as the progenitor of self-conscious experimentation in rock. It was the album that dramatized rock's claim to artistic

---

[*] For an examination of progressive/art rock's critical reception in the 1970s, see John J. Sheinbaum, "Progressive Rock and the Inversion of Musical Values," in Kevin Holm-Hudson, ed., *Progressive Rock Reconsidered* (New York: Routledge, 2002), 21–42.

[†] *Source:* John Rockwell, "Art Rock," in Jim Miller, ed., *The Rolling Stone Illustrated History of Rock & Roll*, (New York: Random House, 1976), pp. 322–25.

seriousness to an adult world that had previously dismissed the whole genre as blathering teen entertainment. The Beatles aspired to something really daring and new—an unabashedly eclectic, musically clever (harmonies, rhythms and, above all, arrangements) mélange that could only have been created in the modern recording studio.

One inevitable implication of the whole notion of art rock, anticipated by *Sgt. Pepper*, is that it parallels, imitates, or is inspired by other forms of "higher," more "serious" music. All young artists, it is said, begin by imitating those they admire, and the good ones eventually break loose on their own. Since mature rock musicians are mostly young and tend to be technically limited, their imitations are often blatant. Sometimes, their very lack of technical facility makes their copies bad ones, and hence leads inadvertently to originality.

On the whole imitative art rock has tended to emulate classical music, primarily the 18th- and 19th-century orchestral sorts. The pioneers in this enterprise were the Moody Blues, whose million-selling 1968 album *Days of Future Passed* paired the group with the London Festival Orchestra. Although Moody Blues devotees seemed to think they were getting something higher toned than mere rock, they were kidding themselves: Moody Blues records are mood music, pure and regrettably not so simple. There's nothing wrong with that, of course, except for the miscategorization into something more profound.

The vast majority of the bands that pillage traditional classical music come from Britain. Why British bands feel compelled to quote the classics, however tongue-in-cheek, leads into the murky waters of class and nation analysis. In comparison with the British, Americans tend to be happy apes. Most American rockers wouldn't know a Beethoven symphony if they were run down by one in the middle of a freeway. One result of such ignorance is that American art (music, painting, poetry, films, etc.) can develop untroubled by lame affectations of a cultured sensibility. In Britain, the lower classes—the source of 99% of all British rockers—enjoy no such isolation. The class divisions and the crushing weight of high culture flourish essentially untrammeled. One result is that in London there is a far closer interchange between establishment contemporary classical composers like David Bedford or even Peter Maxwell Davies and the rock world. It also means that rockers seem far more eager to "dignify" their work, to make it acceptable for upper-class approbation, by freighting it with the trappings of classical music. Or, conversely, they are far more intent upon making classical music accessible to their audiences by bastardizing it in a rock context. Or, maybe, they feel the need to parody it to the point of ludicrousness. In all cases, they relate to it with a persistence and intensity that American groups rarely match.

The principal examples here are acts like the Nice; Emerson, Lake and Palmer; Deep Purple; Procol Harum; Renaissance; Yes; and Rick Wakeman. Much of what these groups do is just souped up, oversynthesized, vaguely "progressive" rock of no particular interest or pretensions. But at one time or another all of them have dealt in some form of classical pastiche. Wakeman, classically trained as a pianist at the Royal Academy, is as good an example as any. After serving time as a session pianist for the likes of David Bowie and Cat Stevens, he joined Yes, helping to lead the group into a convoluted pop mysticism. He eventually left Yes, in 1974, to pursue a solo career devoted to such elaborate, portentously titled orchestral narratives as *Journey to the Centre of the Earth* and *The Myths and Legends of King Arthur and the Knights of the Round Table*. These ice-skating epics have their elements of elephantine humor, I suppose. But his classical excursions are dispatched with such a brutal cynicism as to be genuinely appalling.

Even when such groups aren't busily ripping off Grieg their music is operatically arty in the bad sense, through their ponderous appeal to middle-class sensibility and their lame reliance on electronically updated 19th-century vaudeville stage tricks. Too often these pastiches are further burdened by the seemingly irresistible weakness certain sorts of loud, arty British bands have for science fiction art and "poetry." Yes's album covers make the point as well as anything, but such puerile mythologizing—Tolkien for the teenyboppers—pervades much of British pop poetry, and lapses over with insufferable affectation into much of the British electric folk-rock camp, too; think only of Jethro Tull and Cat Stevens.

Classical borrowings don't have to be limited simply to quotations, however, nor do they have to be bad by definition. The whole craze for "rock operas" of the Kinks/Who variety has produced some fascinating work. Similarly, some of the fairly straightforward heavy-metal groups have colored their music with the judicious application of nonrock styles, to telling effect (the use of Middle Eastern modes and instrumental accents in Led Zeppelin's "Kashmir," for example).

Such use of classical and other nonrock styles and formal ideas blends imperceptibly into all-purpose stylistic eclecticism—the free and often febrile switching among different styles within the same piece. Eclecticism has been more prominent in London than anywhere else, and, at its best, it stops being lamely imitative and enters the realm of creativity.

Numerous British bands fall into the eclectic art rock camp: Genesis, King Crimson, Electric Light Orchestra, Queen, Supertramp, Sparks, 10cc, Gentle Giant, and Be-Bop Deluxe. There are continental bands like Focus, and even some American groups like Kansas that fit here also. Certainly there are differences between these groups, large differences—and there are many more groups that could be listed. But they all share a commitment to unprepared, abrupt transitions from one mood to another. Sometimes the shifts are between tempos, sometimes between levels of volume, sometimes between whole styles of music. The effect in any case is violent, disruptive and nervously tense, and as such no doubt answers the needs of the age as well as anything. At their best (or at their most commercially successful), these groups never lose sight of older rock basics, as with Queen's best work or with Bill Nelson's extraordinary guitar playing in any style you can think of on Be-Bop Deluxe's albums.

The leader of this particular pack, Roxy Music, is discussed elsewhere. But Brian Eno, one of Roxy's original members, merits special attention here. Aside from the quality of his music, which is considerable, Eno is interesting from two points of view: his command of the synthesizer and his relation to others on the London experimental scene.

The synthesizer is a much-abused, much-misunderstood instrument. When played like a souped up electric organ by people like Keith Emerson, Jon Lord (of Deep Purple) or Rick Wakeman, it can sound simply flashy and cheap. If the obligatory drum solo used to be the bane of any self-respecting rock-concert goer's life, the obligatory synthesizer solo, preferably with smoke bomb and laser obbligato, is the current curse. If synthesizers aren't regarded as newfangled organs, they are taken literally, as something that "synthesizes," and we are subjected to Walter Carlos's and Isao Tomita's synthesized versions of the classics (not rock, or even art rock, technically, but certainly appealing to the same market).

What the synthesizer really is, is an instrument with its own characteristics, and those characteristics are just beginning to be explored by rock musicians. When played with the subtlety and discretion of a Stevie Wonder or a Garth Hudson, it can reinforce conventional textures superbly. And when somebody like Eno or Edgar Froese of Tangerine Dream gets hold of it, the synthesizer can create a whole world of its own. Eno's *Discreet Music* (1975), with its title-track first side full of soothing, hypnotic woodwindish sounds, or *No Pussyfooting* (1975) and *Evening Star* (1976), two collaborations with Robert Fripp, ex-King Crimson guitarist, are masterly examples of genuine rock avant-gardism. Of course, they aren't really "rock" in any but the loosest sense: there is no reference back to a blues base, even in attenuated form. But it is music produced by a rock sensibility aimed at a rock audience.

* * *

Michael Oldfield fits here to a certain extent, although his work—particularly after his best-selling *Tubular Bells* (1973), which did admittedly have a bland appeal as a reduction of California composer Terry Riley's ideas—is lame beyond recall.

Much of this work, from Oldfield to Eno and even Riley, is head music, and relates to a rather interesting form of avant-garde trance music, which brings us to the subject of drugs. The avant-gardism in rock of the Sixties and Seventies, for all its ultimate debts to surrealism and other vanguard movements from earlier in the century, owes its primary debts to the proliferation of drugs in the Sixties. It would be misleading to overstress this, but just as false to repress it. Marijuana, LSD and other psychedelics, and methedrine or speed, have all had a profound effect on how music in general, and art rock in particular, was made and perceived. This is not to say that you have to be stoned to play or enjoy this music. But it does mean that the climate and stylistic preoccupations of many varieties of present-day art are built in part on perceptions analogous to the drug experience. Sometimes it only takes a single trip, as with acid, to give you a whole other fix on the world. Certainly for many people, the state of mind of a marijuana high is something that can be meditatively evoked without an actual joint to inhale.

30

"Why Don't We Call It Punk?"

Legs McNeil and Gillian McCain

"Lurid, insolent, disorderly, funny, sometimes gross, sometimes mean and occasionally touching"—in the words of the *New York Times* review, Legs McNeil's and Gillian McCain's punk rock history *Please Kill Me* is a book its utterly befitting of the musical phenomenon it seeks to describe. Published in 1996, twenty years after New York punk icons the Ramones released their groundbreaking self-titled debut album, *Please Kill Me* was one of the first oral histories of American punk rock drawn from the scene's participants.[*] Like any oral history or filmed documentary, the editors were forced to stitch together a story from a variety of different sources, including original testimonies and previously published materials. The narrative sketched out in the passage below centers on the formation of *Punk* magazine, and comes primarily from one of its founders, Legs (Eddie) McNeil (born 1956), and contributing writers, Mary Harron (born 1956).[†] Along the way appearances from the four original Ramones (Joey, Johnny, Dee Dee, and Tommy), an inadvertent cameo from former Velvet Underground front man Lou Reed (born 1942), and the storied Bowery Avenue club CBGB's provide the appropriate local New York City color.[‡§]

Leee Childers: The first time I went to CBGB's was with Wayne County. There were six people in the audience. We ate the chili, which, years later, Bebe Buell was horrified to learn. She said, "You ate the chili? Stiv told me the Dead Boys used to go back in the kitchen and jerk off in it."

I said to her, "So what? I've had worse in my mouth."

So the first time I went to CBGB's, we ate chili, which tasted horrible. The whole place stunk of urine. The whole place smelled like a bathroom. And there were literally six people in the audience and then the Ramones went onstage, and I went, "Oh ... my ... God!"

And I knew it, in a minute. The first song. The first song. I knew that I was home and happy and secure and free and rock & roll. I knew it from that first song the first time I went to see them. I was the one who called Lisa Robinson and said, "You won't

---

[*] Other oral histories of punk have included John Lydon, *Rotten: No Irish, No Blacks, No Dogs* (New York: Picador Press, 1994) and Marc Spitz and Brendan Mullen, *We Got the Neutron Bomb: The Untold Story of L.A. Punk* (New York: Three Rivers Press, 2001).

[†] Harron has since gone on to an acclaimed directing career with such films as *I Shot Andy Warhol* and *American Psycho.*

[‡] The full name is CBGB's OMFUG (Country Bluegrass Blues & Other Music for Uplifting Gormandizers).

[§] *Source:* Legs McNeil and Gillian McCain, *Please Kill Me: The Uncensored Oral History of Punk* (New York: Grove/Atlantic, 1996), pp. 201–8.

believe what's going on!" and she said, "Oh, what are you talking about? Oh, the Bowery, ugggghhhhh!!!"

I said, "Just come."

Danny Fields: I was editing *16* magazine and writing a column in the *SoHo Weekly News,* and I was always gushing about the wonderfulness of Television and how exciting their performances were.

I rarely wrote about the Ramones. I hadn't seen them, I didn't know who they were. I was always writing about Television and Patti Smith. They came first, chronologically, of that bunch. And Johnny Ramone would say to Tommy, "You're supposed to be in charge of publicity. Why doesn't Danny Fields write about us?"

I could just hear it happening. I wasn't there, but I can just imagine the conversations. So Tommy would call me at *16* magazine and say, "Please, why don't you ever write about us?" I always had the feeling that someone was prodding in the background, like he better deliver on this or else. And the Ramones were doing the same thing to Lisa Robinson as they were doing to me. That's when Lisa and I decided to divide up. There was some other band who was harassing both of us at that time and we decided to kill two birds in one night. I would go see the other band and Lisa would see the Ramones. I don't remember the other band, they must have left me cold. The next day Lisa called me up all excited about the Ramones, saying, "Oh, you'll love them. They do songs one minute long and it's very fast and it's all over in less than a quarter of an hour. And it's everything you like and you'll love it. And it's just the funniest thing I've ever seen."

And she was right. I went down to see them at CBGB's, and I got this seat up front with no problems. In those days I don't think anybody packed it in. And they came on and I fell in love with them. I just thought they were doing everything right. They were the perfect band. They were fast and I liked fast. Beethoven quartets are supposed to be slow. Rock & roll is supposed to be fast. I loved it.

I introduced myself to them afterwards and I said, "I love you so much, I'll be your manager."

And they said, "Oh good, we need a new drum set. Do you have money?" I said I was going down to see my mother in Miami. When I got to Miami, I asked my mother for three thousand dollars and she gave it to me. That's how I started managing the Ramones. I bought myself into being their manager.

Legs McNeil: When I was eighteen, I was living in New York, working at some hippie film commune on Fourteenth Street, making this horrible movie about a stupid advertising executive who takes acid and drops out and becomes sexually, emotionally, and spiritually liberated. It was just crap.

This was 1975, and the idea of taking acid and dropping out was just so lame—like ten years too late. And the hippie film commune was just as lame. I hated hippies.

Anyway, summer came, and I went back to Cheshire, Connecticut, where I grew up, and made this Three Stooges comedy—sixteen millimeter, black and white film—with two high school friends of mine, John Holmstrom and Ged Dunn.

John Holmstrom was a cartoonist, and Ged Dunn was a business guy, so at the end of the summer we decided we were going to work together. We had all worked together before when we were in high school—Holmstrom had put together this theater group called the Apocalypse Players, which was Eugène Ionesco meets Alice Cooper. We even had the police close down one of our shows when I missed throwing a pie and hit somebody in the audience.

But when John and Ged and I regrouped, it was kind of undetermined just what we were going to do—films, comics, some sort of media thing.

Then one day we were riding in the car, and John said, "I think we should start a magazine."

All summer we had been listening to this album *Go Girl Crazy* by this unknown group called the Dictators, and it changed our lives. We'd just get drunk every night and lip-sync to it. Holmstrom had found the record. He was the one who really followed rock & roll. He was the one who turned Ged and I on to the Velvet Underground, Iggy and the Stooges, and the New York Dolls. Up until then I just listened to Chuck Berry and the first two Beatles records, and Alice Cooper.

But I hated most rock & roll, because it was about lame hippie stuff, and there really wasn't anyone describing our lives—which was McDonald's, beer, and TV reruns. Then John found the Dictators, and we all got excited that something was happening.

But I didn't understand why Holmstrom wanted to start a magazine. I thought it was a stupid idea.

John said, "But if we have a magazine, people will think we're cool and stuff and want to hang out with us."

I didn't get it. Then he said, "If we had a magazine, we could drink for free. People will give us free drinks."

That got me. I said, "Okay, then let's do it."

Holmstrom wanted the magazine to be a combination of everything we were into—television reruns, drinking beer, getting laid, cheeseburgers, comics, grade-B movies, and this weird rock & roll that nobody but us seemed to like: the Velvets, the Stooges, the New York Dolls, and now the Dictators.

So John said he wanted to call our magazine *Teenage News,* after an unreleased New York Dolls song. I thought it was a stupid title, so I told him that. And he said, "Well, what do you think we should call it?"

I saw the magazine Holmstrom wanted to start as a Dictators album come to life. On the inside sleeve of the record was a picture of the Dictators hanging out in a White Castle hamburger stand and they were dressed in black leather jackets. Even though we didn't have black leather jackets, the picture seemed to describe us perfectly—wise guys. So I thought the magazine should be for other fuck-ups like us. Kids who grew up believing only in the Three Stooges. Kids that had parties when their parents were away and destroyed the house. You know, kids that stole cars and had fun.

So I said, "Why don't we call it *Punk?*"

The word "punk" seemed to sum up the thread that connected everything we liked—drunk, obnoxious, smart but not pretentious, absurd, funny, ironic, and things that appealed to the darker side.

So John Holmstrom said, "Okay. Well, I'm gonna be the editor." Ged said, "I'm gonna be the publisher." They both looked at me and said, "What are you gonna do?" I said, "I don't know." I had no skills.

Then Holmstrom said, "You can be the resident punk!" And they both started laughing hysterically. Ged and John were both like four years older than me. And I think half the reason they hung out with me was because I was always getting drunk and into trouble and Holmstrom found it constantly amusing. So it was decided I would be a living cartoon character, like Alfred E. Neuman was to *Mad* magazine. And Holmstrom changed my name from Eddie to Legs.

It's funny, but we had no idea if anybody besides the Dictators were out there. We had no idea about CBGB's and what was going on, but I don't think we cared. We just liked the idea of *Punk* magazine. And that was all that really mattered.

Mary Harron: I met Legs when I was working as the cook for Total Impact, the hippie film commune on Fourteenth Street. Legs came in and was the only one who said this movie sucks and these people are crazy. So I asked him what he was doing. Legs said he was just doing some part-time work on the movie, and he asked me what I did. I said I wanted to be a writer and he said, "We're starting a magazine. It's called *Punk*."

I thought, What a brilliant title! I don't know why it seemed so brilliant, because this was before there was punk, but it was obviously so ironic.

I mean there was something in it, you know, because if somebody said that they're starting a magazine, you think, Oh, a literary magazine. But *Punk,* it was so funny, bratty—it was so unexpected—and I thought, Well, that's really great. So I said, "Oh, I'll write for you," even though I didn't know what it was about.

A few nights later I was in the kitchen of the horrible film commune, I was washing the floor, being a Cinderella, and doing the dishes. Legs and John came in and said they were going to go to CBGB's and I thought, Okay.

We all went to CBGB's to hear the Ramones and that was the night everything happened.

Legs McNeil: We talked our way into CBGB's, and then we were walking down the length of the bar, when I saw this guy with really short hair and sunglasses sitting at a table and I recognized him as Lou Reed. Holmstrom had been playing Lou Reed's *Metal Machine Music* for weeks. That was Lou's two-album set of nothing but feedback. It was awful, just noise, which Holmstrom loved and proclaimed the ultimate punk album. We were always having big fights about John playing the record: "Come on, take off that shit!" That's how I knew who Lou Reed was.

So when I spotted Lou at the table, I went up to Holmstrom and said, "Hey, there's that guy you're always talking about. Maybe we should interview him too?" I was thinking, you know, as long as we were there. So I went up to Lou and I said, "Hey, we're gonna interview you for our magazine!" You know like, "Aren't you thrilled?" I had no idea of what we were doing. Then Holmstrom said to Lou, "Yeah, we'll even put you on the cover!" Lou just turned around, real deadpan, and said, "Oh, your circulation must be fabulous."

Mary Harron: I was horrified when Legs and John went up to Lou Reed and told him they wanted to interview him. I thought, Oh my god, what are they doing?

Because Lou was a famous person and I thought, Oh that's so rude. What do they think is going to happen?

I think I was in awe of Lou much more than John or Legs were. I knew quite a lot about Andy Warhol, because I'd had a complete Warhol obsession, and I was a fan of the Velvet Underground. So I was cringing.

Legs McNeil: Just as we were talking to Lou Reed the Ramones hit the stage and it was an amazing sight. Four really pissed-off guys in black leather jackets. It was like the Gestapo had just walked into the room. These guys were definitely not hippies.

Then they counted off a song—"ONE, TWO, THREE, FOUR!"—and we were hit with this blast of noise, you physically recoiled from the shock of it, like this huge wind, and before I could even get into it, they stopped.

Apparently they were all playing a different song. The Ramones had a mini-fight onstage. They were just so thoroughly disgusted with each other that they threw down their guitars and stomped off the stage.

It was amazing. It was like actually seeing something come together. Lou Reed was sitting at the table laughing.

Joey Ramone: That was the first night we met Lou Reed. Lou kept telling Johnny Ramone that he wasn't playing the right kind of guitar, that he should play a different kind of guitar. It didn't go over so favorably with Johnny. I mean when John found his guitar he didn't have much money—he bought his guitar for fifty dollars. And Johnny liked the idea of the Mosrite because nobody else used a Mosrite—so this would be his sort of trademark. So Johnny thought Lou was a real jerk.

Legs McNeil: Then the Ramones came back, counted off again, and played the best eighteen minutes of rock & roll that I had ever heard. You could hear the Chuck Berry in it, which was all I listened to, that and the Beatles second album with all the Chuck Berry covers on it. When the Ramones came offstage we interviewed them, and they were like us. They talked about comic books and sixties bubble-gum music and were really deadpan and sarcastic.

I really thought I was at the Cavern Club in 1963 and we had just met the Beatles. Only it wasn't a fantasy, it wasn't the Beatles, it was *our* band—the Ramones. But we couldn't hang out with them that long, because we had to go interview Lou Reed, who was old, and snotty, and like someone's cranky old drunken father.

Mary Harron: We all went off to the Locale and none of us had any money and we couldn't order food. I remember Lou Reed ordered a cheeseburger because I was so hungry. Lou was with Rachel, who was the first transvestite I'd ever met. Very beautiful, but frightening. But I mean definitely a guy: Rachel had stubble.

Legs and John were chatting with Lou so I sat next to Rachel, and I asked her what her name was—him, what his name was—and he said, "Rachel."

I thought, Right. That kind of shut me up for a bit. I think I actually sort of tried to make conversation with him, but Rachel wasn't talkative. I think that was the sum total of our conversation.

I was quite startled because of the way Legs and John would ask the questions. It was quite amateurish. They would ask, "What kind of hamburgers do you like?" Like student journalism, and I thought, Oh god, who are these guys? What are they doing? What are you asking these stupid questions for?

Then Lou Reed started showing some of his famous nastiness. He was mean to Legs. Very mean. And I was very upset by that, actually. I thought he was quite devastating really. But Legs and John didn't seem to mind.

But the night was very exciting, you know—seeing the Ramones, meeting Lou Reed ... I remember thinking, Oh my god, wait till I tell people back home I've met Lou Reed! That was really going through my head—Wait until I tell people...

But then, somehow, because of Lou lashing out or getting bored or whatever, it had ended on this rather sour note. Lou started getting so hostile. I can't remember why. He got very mad at Legs, he just hated him.

But when we got out in the street, John Holmstrom was jumping around being ecstatic and I was thinking, I don't really understand this. Why he's so happy?

I couldn't understand why he was so excited, ecstatic. Because what did we get? Lou Reed being rude to us really.

Legs McNeil: Holmstrom kept jumping up and down, saying, "We got Lou Reed for the cover! We got Lou Reed for the cover!" I didn't know what he was so excited about. I just said, "Yeah, but did you see that chick he was with?"

Mary Harron: When I finished writing the Ramones article it was late and I still had no money, so I walked that night all the way across town to deliver the article to the "Punk Dump," the *Punk* magazine office on Tenth Avenue. It must have been ten avenues—you know, one side of the city to the other.

It was *Taxi Driver* time, you know, steam coming out of the manholes. It was really a beautiful kind of weird New York night—and the Punk Dump was an incredible place. It looked like something out of *Batman*. It was a storefront under the train tracks on Tenth Avenue with the windows painted black—like a cave. So I found the door and the light was on and John Holmstrom was there at his desk, his glasses on, and he was doing the artwork for the cover, for the Lou Reed interview—the first issue of *Punk*.

He showed it to me, and it was a *cartoon!* I read the Lou Reed interview quickly, and I could see that everything that was humiliating, embarrassing, and stupid had been turned to an advantage. And that's when I knew that *Punk* was going to work.

Legs McNeil: The next thing we did was go out and plaster the city with these little posters that said, "WATCH OUT! PUNK IS COMING!" Everyone who saw them said, "Punk? What's punk?" John and I were laughing. We were like, "Ohhh, you'll find out."

Debbie Harry: John Holmstrom and his living cartoon creature, Legs McNeil, were two maniacs running around town putting up signs that said, "Punk is coming! Punk is coming!" We thought, Here comes another shitty group with an even shittier name.

James Grauerholz: I was living at the Bunker, John Giorno's loft at 222 Bowery, which became William Burroughs' home in New York City. I'd had an affair with William, and when that ended I started working for him. But at that time William was not as well known. I mean, he was the world-famous William Burroughs, but only a tiny minority knew anything about who that was. William was kind of considered to be a little bit of a has-been in some ways. He was revered, but his works had gone out of print. So I began to see myself as the impresario of William and we began to see ourselves as kind of a symbiotic partnership.

In late 1975, I used to go to Phoebe's a lot. Phoebe's was the off-off-Broadway theater hangout, a restaurant up the street from the Bunker. Phoebe's was a real mainstay. So on my little route from the Bunker to Phoebe's, I would pass these street poles, right outside my house, with posters glued up: "PUNK IS COMING!"

And I loved it, from the first moment I saw that sign I thought, punk is coming! I thought, What is this gonna be? A band or what?

But "punk!"—I loved it, because it meant to me a derisory word for a young, no-count piece a shit. And then from Burrough's *Junky*—you know, there's that great scene where William and Roy, the sailor, are rolling the lushes in the subway and there's two young punks. They cross over and they give Roy a lot of shit and Roy says, "Fucking punks think it's a joke. They won't think it's so funny when they're doing five twenty-nine on the island." You know, five months and twenty-nine days.

"Fucking punks think it's a joke."

So I knew that punk was a direct descendant of William Burroughs' life and work. And I said, "We've gotta put these two things together for the benefit of all parties." And that's what I did.

William Burroughs: I always thought a punk was someone who took it up the ass.

31

The Subculture of British Punk

Dick Hebdige

The academic study of popular music took a quantum leap in the mid-1970s thanks to the influential research emanating from the University of Birmingham Centre for Contemporary Cultural Studies (CCCS). Turning their gaze toward Britain's diverse youth groups, CCCS sociologists like Dick Hebdige attempted to unravel the layered meanings of the teddy boys, mods, skinheads, rastafarians, rude boys, and other subcultures, framing them as "resistant" social formations. Pitted against the dominant, or "parent," culture's ordered "systems of beliefs" and "use of objects and material life," the subculture was seen to fashion their own set of values, so as to "significantly differentiate them from the wider culture."[*] One of the first book-length studies to put these theories to test, Hebdige's 1979 *Subculture: The Meaning of Style* takes as its subject a broad crosssection of British subcultures. Much of his attention, however, is devoted to the appearance of punk in 1976. In regard to this "spectacular subculture," Hebdige asks what types of meaning we can glean from a style that deliberately seems to signify disorder. To this end he introduces the concept of *bricolage*, taken from the writings of anthropologist Claude Levi-Strauss, while borrowing liberally from other intellectual traditions as well. While *Subculture*'s scholarly tone would have a profound impact on the rise of academic-based popular music studies, it also received favorable publicity and reviews in the mainstream rock music press as well. As such, it was a landmark book that signified an important crossover moment in the study of popular music.[†]

April 3, 1989, Marrakech

The chic thing is to dress in expensive tailor-made rags and all the queens are camping about in wild-boy drag. There are Bowery suits that appear to be stained with urine and vomit which on closer inspection turn out to be intricate embroideries of fine gold thread. There are clochard suits of the finest linen, shabby gentility suits ... felt hats seasoned by old junkies ... loud cheap pimp suits that turn out to be not so cheap the loudness is a subtle harmony of colours only the very best Poor Boy shops can turn out.... It is the double take and many carry it much further to as many as six takes (William Burroughs, 1969)

---

[*] John Clarke, Stuart Hall, Tony Jefferson, and Brian Roberts, "Subcultures, Cultures and Class: A Theoretical Overview," *Resistance Through Rituals: Youth Subcultures in Post-War Britain*, edited by Stuart Hall and Tony Jefferson (London: Hutchinson, 1976), 10, 14.
[†] *Source*: Dick Hebdige, *Subculture: The Meaning of Style* (New York: Methuen, 1979), pp. 23–26, 100–108.

HOLIDAY IN THE SUN: MISTER ROTTEN MAKES THE GRADE

The British summer of 1976 was extraordinarily hot and dry: there were no recorded precedents. From May through to August, London parched and sweltered under luminous skies and the inevitable fog of exhaust fumes. Initially hailed as a Godsend, and a national 'tonic' in the press and television (was Britain's 'curse' finally broken?) the sun provided seasonal relief from the dreary cycle of doom-laden headlines which had dominated the front pages of the tabloids throughout the winter. Nature performed its statutory ideological function and 'stood in' for all the other 'bad news', provided tangible proof of 'improvement' and pushed aside the strikes and the dissension. With predictable regularity, 'bright young things' were shown flouncing along Oxford Street in harem bags and beach shorts, bikini tops and polaroids in that last uplifting item for the *News at Ten*. The sun served as a 'cheeky' postscript to the crisis: a lighthearted addendum filled with tropical promise. The crisis, too, could have its holiday. But as the weeks and months passed and the heatwave continued, the old mythology of doom and disaster was reasserted with a vengeance. The 'miracle' rapidly became a commonplace, an everyday affair, until one morning in mid-July it was suddenly re-christened a 'freak disorder': a dreadful, last, unlooked-for factor in Britain's decline.

The heatwave was officially declared a drought in August, water was rationed, crops were failing, and Hyde Park's grass burned into a delicate shade of raw sienna. The end was at hand and Last Days imagery began to figure once more in the press. Economic categories, cultural and natural phenomena were confounded with more than customary abandon until the drought took on an almost metaphysical significance. A Minister for Drought was appointed, Nature had now been officially declared 'unnatural', and all the age-old inferences were drawn with an obligatory modicum of irony to keep within the bounds of common sense. In late August, two events of completely different mythical stature coincided to confirm the worst forebodings: it was demonstrated that the excessive heat was threatening the very structure of the nation's houses (cracking the foundations) and the Notting Hill Carnival, traditionally a paradigm of racial harmony, exploded into violence. The Caribbean festival, with all its Cook's Tours connotations of happy, dancing coloured folk, of jaunty bright calypsos and exotic costumes, was suddenly, unaccountably, transformed into a menacing congregation of angry black youths and embattled police. Hordes of young black Britons did the Soweto dash across the nation's television screens and conjured up fearful images of other Negroes, other confrontations, other 'long, hot summers'. The humble dustbin lid, the staple of every steel band, the symbol of the 'carnival spirit', of Negro ingenuity and the resilience of ghetto culture, took on an altogether more ominous significance when used by white-faced policemen as a desperate shield against an angry rain of bricks.

It was during this strange apocalyptic summer that punk made its sensational debut in the music press.[1] In London, especially in the south west and more specifically in the vicinity of the King's Road, a new style was being generated combining elements drawn from a whole range of heterogeneous youth styles. In fact punk claimed a dubious parentage. Strands from David Bowie and glitter-rock were woven together with elements from American proto-punk (the Ramones, the Heartbreakers, Iggy Pop, Richard Hell), from that faction within London pub-rock (the 101-ers, the Gorillas, etc.) inspired by the mod subculture of the 60s, from the Canvey Island 40s revival and the Southend r & b bands (Dr Feelgood, Lew Lewis, etc.), from northern soul and from reggae.

Not surprisingly, the resulting mix was somewhat unstable: all these elements constantly threatened to separate and return to their original sources. Glam rock contributed narcissism, nihilism and gender confusion. American punk offered a minimalist aesthetic (e.g., the Ramones' 'Pinhead' or Crime's 'I Stupid'), the cult of the Street and a penchant for self-laceration. Northern Soul (a genuinely secret subculture of working-class youngsters dedicated to acrobatic dancing and fast

American soul of the 60s, which centres on clubs like the Wigan Casino) brought its subterranean tradition of fast, jerky rhythms, solo dance styles and amphetamines; reggae its exotic and dangerous aura of forbidden identity, its conscience, its dread and its cool. Native rhythm 'n blues reinforced the brashness and the speed of Northern Soul, took rock back to the basics and contributed a highly developed iconoclasm, a thoroughly British persona and an extremely selective appropriation of the rock 'n' roll heritage.

This unlikely alliance of diverse and superficially incompatible musical traditions, mysteriously accomplished under punk, found ratification in an equally eclectic clothing style which reproduced the same kind of cacophony on the visual level. The whole ensemble, literally safety-pinned together, became the celebrated and highly photogenic phenomenon known as punk which throughout 1977 provided the tabloids with a fund of predictably sensational copy and the quality press with a welcome catalogue of beautifully broken codes. Punk reproduced the entire sartorial history of post-war working-class youth cultures in 'cut up' form, combining elements which had originally belonged to completely different epochs. There was a chaos of quiffs and leather jackets, brothel creepers and winkle pickers, plimsolls and paka macs, moddy crops and skinhead strides, drainpipes and vivid socks, bum freezers and bovver boots—all kept 'in place' and 'out of time' by the spectacular adhesives: the safety pins and plastic clothes pegs, the bondage straps and bits of string which attracted so much horrified and fascinated attention. Punk is therefore a singularly appropriate point of departure for a study of this kind because punk style contained distorted reflections of all the major post-war subcultures.

STYLE AS INTENTIONAL COMMUNICATION

> I speak through my clothes. (Eco, 1973)

The cycle leading from opposition to defusion, from resistance to incorporation encloses each successive subculture. We have seen how the media and the market fit into this cycle. We must now turn to the subculture itself to consider exactly how and what subcultural style communicates. Two questions must be asked which together present us with something of a paradox: how does a subculture make sense to its members? How is it made to signify disorder? To answer these questions we must define the meaning of style more precisely.

In 'The Rhetoric of the Image', Roland Barthes contrasts the 'intentional' advertising image with the apparently 'innocent' news photograph. Both are complex articulations of specific codes and practices, but the news photo appears more 'natural' and transparent than the advertisement. He writes—'the signification of the image is certainly intentional ... the advertising image is clear, or at least emphatic'. Barthes' distinction can be used analogously to point up the difference between subcultural and 'normal' styles. The subcultural stylistic ensembles—those emphatic combinations of dress, dance, argot, music, etc.—bear approximately the same relation to the more conventional formulae ('normal' suits and ties, casual wear, twin-sets, etc.) that the advertising image bears to the less consciously constructed news photograph.

Of course, signification need not be intentional, as semioticians have repeatedly pointed out. Umberto Eco writes 'not only the expressly intended communicative object ... but every object may be viewed ... as a sign' (Eco, 1973). For instance, the conventional outfits worn by the average man and woman in the street are chosen within the constraints of finance, 'taste', preference, etc. and these choices are undoubtedly significant. Each ensemble has its place in an internal system of differences—the conventional modes of sartorial discourse—which fit a corresponding set of socially prescribed roles and options.[2] These choices contain a whole range of messages which are transmitted through the finely graded distinctions of a number of interlocking sets—class and status, self-image and attractiveness, etc. Ultimately, if nothing else, they are expressive of 'normality' as opposed to 'deviance' (i.e., they are distinguished by their relative invisibility, their appropriateness, their 'naturalness'). However, the intentional communication is of a different order. It stands apart—a visible construction, a loaded choice. It directs attention to itself; it gives itself to be read.

This is what distinguishes the visual ensembles of spectacular subcultures from those favoured in the surrounding culture(s). They are *obviously* fabricated (even the mods, precariously placed between the worlds of the straight and the deviant, finally declared themselves different when they gathered in groups outside dance halls and on sea fronts). They *display* their own codes (e.g., the punk's ripped T-shirt) or at least demonstrate that codes are there to be used and abused (e.g., they have been thought about rather than thrown together). In this they go against the grain of a mainstream culture whose principal defining characteristic, according to Barthes, is a tendency to masquerade as nature, to substitute 'normalized' for historical forms, to translate the reality of the world into an image of the world which in turn presents itself as if composed according to 'the evident laws of the natural order' (Barthes, 1972).

As we have seen, it is in this sense that subcultures can be said to transgress the laws of 'man's second nature'.[3] By repositioning and recontextualizing commodities, by subverting their conventional uses and inventing new ones, the subcultural stylist gives the lie to what Althusser has called the 'false obviousness of everyday practice' (Althusser and Balibar, 1968), and opens up the world of objects to new and covertly oppositional readings. The communication of a significant *difference*, then (and the parallel communication of a group *identity*), is the 'point' behind the style of all spectacular subcultures. It is the superordinate term under which all the other significations are marshalled, the message through which all the other messages speak. Once we have granted this initial difference a primary determination over the whole sequence of stylistic generation and diffusion, we can go back to examine the internal structure of individual subcultures. To return to our earlier analogy: if the spectacular subculture is an intentional communication, if it is, to borrow a term from linguistics, 'motivated', what precisely is being communicated and advertised?

STYLE AS *BRICOLAGE*

> It is conventional to call 'monster' any blending of dissonant elements.... I call 'monster' every original, inexhaustible beauty. (Alfred Jarry)

The subcultures with which we have been dealing share a common feature apart from the fact that they are all predominantly working class. They are, as we have seen, cultures of conspicuous consumption—even when, as with the skinheads and the punks, certain types of consumption are conspicuously refused—and it is through the distinctive rituals of consumption, through style, that the subculture at once reveals its 'secret' identity and communicates its forbidden meanings. It is basically the way in which commodities are *used* in subculture which mark the subculture off from more orthodox cultural formations.

Discoveries made in the field of anthropology are helpful here. In particular, the concept of *bricolage* can be used to explain how subcultural styles are constructed. In *The Savage Mind* Levi-Strauss shows how the magical modes utilized by primitive peoples (superstition, sorcery, myth) can be seen as implicitly coherent, though explicitly bewildering, systems of connection between things which perfectly equip their users to 'think' their own world. These magical systems of connection have a common feature: they are capable of infinite extension because basic elements can be used in a variety of improvised combinations to generate new meanings within them. *Bricolage* has thus been described as a 'science of the concrete' in a recent definition which clarifies the original anthropological meaning of the term:

> [Bricolage] refers to the means by which the non-literate, non-technical mind of so-called 'primitive' man responds to the world around him. The process involves a 'science of the concrete' (as opposed to our 'civilised' science of the 'abstract') which far from lacking logic, in fact carefully and precisely orders, classifies and arranges into structures the *minutiae* of the physical world in all their profusion by means of a 'logic' which is not our own. The structures, 'improvised' or made up (these are rough translations of the process of *bricoler*) as *ad hoc* responses to an environment, then serve to establish homologies and analogies between the ordering of nature and that of society, and so satisfactorily 'explain' the world and make it able to be lived in. (Hawkes, 1977)

The implications of the structured improvisations of *bricolage* for a theory of spectacular subculture as a system of communication have already been explored. For instance, John Clarke has stressed the way in which prominent forms of discourse (particularly fashion) are radically adapted, subverted and extended by the subcultural *bricoleur*:

> Together, object and meaning constitute a sign, and within any one culture, such signs are assembled, repeatedly, into characteristic forms of discourse. However, when the bricoleur relocates the significant object in a different position within that discourse, using the same overall repertoire of signs, or when that object is placed within a different total ensemble, a new discourse is constituted, a different message conveyed. (Clarke, 1976)

In this way the teddy boy's theft and transformation of the Edwardian style revived in the early 1950s by Savile Row for wealthy young men about town can be construed as an act of *bricolage*. Similarly, the mods could be said to be functioning as *bricoleurs* when they appropriated another range of commodities by placing them in a symbolic ensemble which served to erase or subvert their original straight meanings. Thus pills medically prescribed for the treatment of neuroses were used as ends-in-themselves, and the motor scooter, originally an ultra-respectable means of transport, was turned into a menacing symbol of group solidarity. In the same improvisatory manner, metal combs, honed to a razor-like sharpness, turned narcissism into an offensive weapon. Union jacks were emblazoned on the backs of grubby parka anoraks or cut up and converted into smartly tailored jackets. More subtly, the conventional insignia of the business world—the suit, collar and tie, short hair, etc.—were stripped of their original connotations—efficiency, ambition, compliance with authority—and transformed into 'empty' fetishes, objects to be desired, fondled and valued in their own right.

At the risk of sounding melodramatic, we could use Umberto Eco's phrase 'semiotic guerilla warfare' (Eco, 1972) to describe these subversive practices. The war may be conducted at a level beneath the consciousness of the individual members of a spectacular subculture (though the subculture is still, at another level, an intentional communication) but with the emergence of such a group, 'war—and it is Surrealism's war—is declared on a world of surfaces' (Annette Michelson, quoted Lippard, 1970).

The radical aesthetic practices of Dada and Surrealism—dream work, collage, 'ready mades', etc.—are certainly relevant here. They are the classic modes of 'anarchic' discourse.[4] Breton's manifestos (1924 and 1929) established the basic premise of surrealism: that a new 'surreality' would emerge through the subversion of common sense, the collapse of prevalent logical categories and oppositions (e.g., dream/reality, work/play) and the celebration of the abnormal and the forbidden. This was to be achieved principally through a 'juxtaposition of two more or less distant realities'

(Reverdy, 1918) exemplified for Breton in Lautréamont's bizarre phrase: 'Beautiful like the chance meeting of an umbrella and a sewing machine on a dissecting table' (Lautréamont, 1970). In *The Crisis of the Object*, Breton further theorized this 'collage aesthetic', arguing rather optimistically that an assault on the syntax of everyday life which dictates the ways in which the most mundane objects are used, would instigate

> ...a *total revolution of the object*: acting to divert the object from its ends by coupling it to a new name and signing it.... Perturbation and deformation are in demand here for their own sakes.... Objects thus reassembled have in common the fact that they derive from and yet succeed in differing from the objects which surround us, by simple *change of role*. (Breton, 1936)

Max Ernst (1948) puts the same point more cryptically: 'He who says collage says the irrational'.

Obviously, these practices have their corollary in *bricolage*. The subcultural *bricoleur*, like the 'author' of a surrealist collage, typically 'juxtaposes two apparently incompatible realities (i.e., "flag": "jacket"; "hole": "teeshirt"; "comb: weapon") on an apparently unsuitable scale ... and ... it is there that the explosive junction occurs' (Ernst, 1948). Punk exemplifies most clearly the subcultural uses of these anarchic modes. It too attempted through 'perturbation and deformation' to disrupt and reorganize meaning. It, too, sought the 'explosive junction'. But what, if anything, were these subversive practices being used to signify? How do we 'read' them? By singling out punk for special attention, we can look more closely at some of the problems raised in a reading of style.

STYLE IN REVOLT: REVOLTING STYLE

> Nothing was holy to us. Our movement was neither mystical, communistic nor anarchistic. All of these movements had some sort of programme, but ours was completely nihilistic. We spat on everything, including ourselves. Our symbol was nothingness, a vacuum, a void. (George Grosz on Dada)

> We're so pretty, oh so pretty ... vac-unt. (The Sex Pistols)

Although it was often directly offensive (T-shirts covered in swear words) and threatening (terrorist/guerilla outfits) punk style was defined principally through the violence of its 'cut ups'. Like Duchamp's 'ready mades'—manufactured objects which qualified as art because he chose to call them such, the most unremarkable and inappropriate items—a pin, a plastic clothes peg, a television component, a razor blade, a tampon—could be brought within the province of punk (un)fashion. Anything within or without reason could be turned into part of what Vivien Westwood called 'confrontation dressing' so long as the rupture between 'natural' and constructed context was clearly visible (i.e., the rule would seem to be: if the cap doesn't fit, wear it).

Objects borrowed from the most sordid of contexts found a place in the punks' ensembles: lavatory chains were draped in graceful arcs across chests encased in plastic bin-liners. Safety pins were taken out of their domestic 'utility' context and worn as gruesome ornaments through the cheek, ear or lip. 'Cheap' trashy fabrics (PVC, plastic, lurex, etc.) in vulgar designs (e.g., mock leopard skin) and 'nasty' colours, long discarded by the quality end of the fashion industry as obsolete kitsch, were salvaged by the punks and turned into garments (fly boy drainpipes, 'common' miniskirts) which offered self-conscious commentaries on the notions of modernity and taste. Conventional ideas of prettiness were jettisoned along with the traditional feminine lore of cosmetics. Contrary to the advice of every woman's magazine, make-up for both boys and girls was worn to be seen. Faces became abstract portraits: sharply observed and meticulously executed studies in alienation. Hair was obviously dyed (hay yellow, jet black, or bright orange with tufts of green or bleached in question marks), and T-shirts and trousers told the story of their own construction with multiple zips and outside seams clearly displayed. Similarly, fragments of school uniform (white bri-nylon shirts, school ties) were symbolically defiled (the shirts covered in graffiti, or fake blood; the ties left undone) and juxtaposed against leather drains or shocking pink mohair tops. The perverse and the abnormal were valued intrinsically. In particular, the illicit iconography of sexual fetishism was used to predictable effect. Rapist masks and rubber wear, leather bodices and fishnet stockings, implausibly pointed stiletto heeled shoes, the whole paraphernalia of bondage—the belts, straps and chains—were exhumed from the boudoir, closet and the pornographic film and placed on the street where they retained their forbidden connotations. Some young punks even donned the dirty raincoat—that most prosaic symbol of sexual 'kinkiness'—and hence expressed their deviance in suitably proletarian terms.

NOTES

1. Although groups like London SS had prepared the way for punk throughout 1975, it wasn't until the appearance of the Sex Pistols that punk began to emerge as a recognizable style. The first review of the group which, for the press at least, always embodied the essence of punk, appeared in the *New Musical Express*, February 21, 1976. The most carefully documented moment of this early period was the Sex Pistols' performance at the Nashville in West Kensington in April, during which Johnny Rotten allegedly left the stage in order to help a supporter involved in a fight. However, it wasn't until the summer of 1976 that punk rock began to attract critical attention, and we can date the beginning of the moral panic to September 1976, when a girl was partially blinded by a flying beer glass during the two-day punk festival at the 100 Club in Soho.
2. Although structuralists would agree with John Mepham (1974) that 'social life is structured like a language', there is also a more mainstream tradition of research into social encounters, role-play, etc. which proves overwhelmingly that social interaction (at least in middle-class white America!) is quite firmly governed by a rigid set of rules, codes and conventions (see in particular Goffman, 1971 and 1972).
3. Hall (1977) states: '...culture is the accumulated growth of man's power over nature, materialised in the instruments and practice of labour and in the medium of signs, thought, knowledge and language through which it is passed on from generation to generation as man's "second nature"'.
4. The terms 'anarchic' and 'discourse' might seem contradictory: discourse suggests structure. Nonetheless, surrealist aesthetics are now so familiar (though advertising, etc.) as to form the kind of unity (of themes, codes, effects) implied by the term 'discourse'.

BIBLIOGRAPHY

Althusser, L. and Balibar, E. (1968), *Reading Capital*, New Left Books.
Barthes, R. (1972), *Mythologies*, Paladin.
Breton, A. (1924), 'The First Surrealist Manifesto', in R. Seaver and H. Lane (eds.), *Manifestos of Surrealism*, University of Michigan Press, 1972.
———. (1929), 'The Second Surrealist Manifesto', in R. Seaver and H. Lane (eds.), *Manifestos of Surrealism*, University of Michigan Press, 1972.
———. (1936), 'Crisis of the Object', in L. Lippard (ed.), *Surrealists on Art*, Spectrum, 1970.
Burroughs, W. (1969), *The Wild Boys*, Caldar & Boyers.
Clarke, J. (1976), 'Style' in S. Hall, *et al.* (eds.), *Resistance Through Rituals*, Hutchinson.
Eco, U. (1972), 'Towards a Semiotic Enquiry into the Television Message', *W.P.C.S. 3*, University of Birmingham.
———. (1973), 'Social Life as a Sign System', in D. Robey (ed.) *Structuralism: The Wolfson College Lectures 1972*, Cape.
Ernst, M. (1948), *Beyond Painting and Other Writings by the Artist and His Friends*, ed. B. Karpel, Sculz.
Hawkes, T. *Structuralism and Semiotics*, Methuen.
Lautréamont, Comte de (1970), *Chants de Maldoror*, Alison & Busby.
Levi-Strauss, C. (1966), *The Savage Mind*, Weidenfeld & Nicolson.
Lippard, L. (ed.) *Surrealists on Art*, Spectrum.
Reverdy, P. (1918), *Nord-Sud*.

32

Disco

Four Critics Address the Musical Question

The disco explosion that swept through the recording industry in 1978 was a true musical and cultural phenomenon symbolized by the unprecedented success of the *Saturday Night Fever* soundtrack, an album whose international sales of 30 million copies made it the best-selling record in history at that time. Disco's popularity ensured that it was instantly polarizing, especially to numerous rock fans who saw disco's orchestrated and synthesized style of dance music as the antithesis to rock music's 'naturalized' mode of authentic expression. The four music critics assembled to discuss disco's "musical question" by the Chicago-based "independent socialist newspaper" *In These Times* highlight the tensions surrounding the movement, from its unabashed commercialism to its roots in urban gay audiences. Not long after this article was published, the vilification of disco reached an apex in July 1979 when Chicago rock radio DJ Steve Dahl organized a "Disco Demolition Night" at Comiskey Park as part of a between-game exhibition stunt for a White Sox baseball doubleheader. With nearly 50,000 frenzied fans looking on, Dahl exploded a pile of disco records, inciting the crowd to swarm the field to thundering chants of "disco sucks." Years later, disco has assumed a more privileged place in popular music history. The notorious exploits of nightclubs like Studio 54 have passed into myth as one of the last bastions of pre-AIDS-awareness hedonistic abandon and disco has been reevaluated as a pivotal moment in the developing history of the disc jockey and various electronic music styles.[*][†]

1. BY BRUCE DANCIS[‡]

"Disco," like "rock," is too large a type of popular music to characterize easily with one pithy phrase. The best disco—songs by Sister Sledge, Gloria Gaynor and the Atlantic Starrs—strikes me as being as good as the best current soul music. Similarly, the worst disco—Madleen Kane and the tackily discofied versions of "Tuxedo Junction" and "McArthur Park"—equals or sinks beneath the most mindless rock.

But disco bears two additional burdens that weigh down much of the genre. Dominated by producers much more than rock, disco too often reflects business or commercial viability over artistic

---

[*] See for example, Bill Brewster and Frank Broughton, Last Night a DJ Saved My Life: The History of the Disc Jockey (New York: Grove Press, 2000) and Tim Lawrence, Love Save the Day: A History of American Dance Music Culture, 1970–1979 (Durham: Duke University Press, 2004).

[†] *Source:* Bruce Dancis, Abe Peck, Tom Smucker, and Georgia Christgau, "Disco! Disco! Disco?: Four Critics Address the Musical Question," *In These Times*, June 6–12, 1979, pp. 20–21.

[‡] Dancis is the only one of the four critics whose affiliations are not listed in the article. At the time, he was the main contributing music critic to In *These Times*.

vitality. Although imaginative auteurist producers have always existed in rock music, for the most part producers reign when musicians have least to say.

Disco also suffers from its predominant function as a dance music. The insistent beat, which is never allowed to vary, constrains even the most boisterous group. A good example is Atlantic Starr's "(Let's) Rock 'n' Roll," on their *Straight to the Point* album (A&M Records). Excellent vocals and a solid band seem to be chained awkwardly, struggling to break out of the rigid rhythm. In addition, for dancing purposes disco songs tend to be extremely long—eight to ten minute album cuts are the norm. In the history of rock music, *no one,* with the exception of Bob Dylan, has been able to sustain excitement and tension beyond 2–4 minutes. To me, this says more about the vitality of concentrated power than it does about any death of creativity.

Much of the across the board dismissal of disco borders on homophobia and racism, the product of insecure and defensive rock fans flailing away at this strange beast that suddenly came to dominate the singles charts. (Why people are so freaked out is a surprise to me; since the British invasion of the mid '60s, the Top 40 has seldom reflected the most compelling trends.)

Still, there is something sleazy about the ease, no, the desire of many disco stars to toady up to the worst creeps in the music industry. The day that Graham Parker appears in a suit and tie on the cover of *Fortune*—as the Bee Gees did in the April 23 issue is the day this rockophile hangs up his headset.

2. BY ABE PECK

Besides the sheer exuberance of freaking, spanking, rocking or simply stomping out, what interests me most about disco music is its current universality. Disco music includes both the fiery rhythms of Parliament-Funkadelic, Instant Funk—you get the idea—*and* the icily technocratic music of *Midnight Express,* which won an Oscar for producer Giorgio Moroder, even though nobody can name a musician who played on the album. It includes calculated excursions of the Rolling Stones and Rod Stewart, *and* the hilariously crass attempts best exemplified by the late Percy Faith, who gave the world the disco version of "Hava Nagila."

The clubs have the same range: from the Snub Sado-Masochism of New York's Studio 54 to the funky ambience of the haunts where the next new dance will be born. And who goes? Blacks and whites, gays and straights, sybaritic boogie children snorting coke off glass table tops and working-class Tony Maneros feverishly transcend the daily grind out there on the Saturday Night dance floor.*

Disco seems to bridge the cusp between the American Way and the Great Outside. Visit a disco on, say, the island of Jamaica. One minute a local reggae song explodes out of a bank of Stateside speakers, and the Visitors from the North left foot the oddly syncopated reggae movements the locals have down pat. Then the music smoothly segues into some stateside disco tune, and the dancing assumes equal axes, natives and visitors checking each other out for new moves.

Even in the U.S. of A., "mainstream" and "outside" coexist in a way they never did even during the supposedly egalitarian heyday of rock 'n' roll. The Village People's disco jingles appeal both to those who think "Y.M.C.A." is the most wholesome song since the Mormon Tabernacle Choir's last release and those who wink knowingly at its gay appeal. Black artists conquer the pop charts in a way they never did even during the height of rhythm and blues.

But any music that satisfies so broadly runs the risk of ultimate superficiality. Like rock before it, disco has moved from the outside to pop cult status to its current mass culture position. It's already an $8 billion business, and the truly giant record companies, Columbia and Warner Brothers, have just gone disco to retain control of the grooves.

---

* Tony Manero is the lead character played by John Travolta in *Saturday Night Fever.*

It's apt that one current funk/disco group is called Mass Production; the minimal music that is much of disco offers only so many variations on a theme. Many black musicians complain they've had to jump on the disco bandwagon or be trampled by it. Many whites hope that New Wave or some other music will reassert rock—which wouldn't hurt disco creatively (every "Miss You" has been countered by a score of misses), but would sap its music-industry bankroll.

What does the next flash of the strobe augur? Before we know it, we could be saying, "Forget disco, here's the Next Big Thing."

But that's what they said would happen last year.

Abe Peck, Chicago *Sun-Times* feature writer, wrote the Village People cover story for *Rolling Stone*'s recent disco issue.

3. BY TOM SMUCKER

It's a little late to debate the merits of disco music as if it were something that we could think out of existence if we want to. Particularly in the pages of a paper like *In These Times*, which expresses an interest in where the American public is at, not just where it should be at. Because disco has become one of *the* dominant forms of American and trans-Atlantic pop music.

Nevertheless, let me list what I think are some of disco's selling points, reasons besides its incredible popularity that should make it interesting to readers of *ITT*.

First: disco is the first pop music in a long while with a multiracial appeal. Elvis may have topped the pop, country, and black charts when he started, but that was 25 years ago. Since then there's been borrowing between black and white music, and some crossing-over of performers from one audience to another, but the lines of racial segregation could always be drawn. Disco, however, is sung, produced, danced and listened to by whites and blacks (as well as Latins, but that's a more complicated case).

There is, naturally, disco music that appeals more to one audience or another, and none of this signals the end of racism. But disco has created a common cultural ground for whoever wants to use it, even if just to throw a successful dance party or disco fund-raiser for black and white friends or fellow workers—something that would have been hard with the segregated music of five years ago.

Second: disco is the first pop music with an openly gay component. It originated in the urban gay subculture and the trendsetters and taste-makers of disco continue to be gay. This doesn't end sexual repression, but it does mean that an interesting, even encouraging space exists that includes both straight and gay.

Finally: disco, like punk rock, encourages energetic public action, unlike the music of the laid-back singer songwriters who dominated the early and mid-'70s. For every beautiful people gossip column gold mine like Studio 54, we should keep in mind the hundreds of discos and disco parties where the rest of us escape our work-a-day lives. Whether this leads to stupor or euphoria is still an open question, but it beats nodding off in private. A culture that tries for some sort of public ecstasy, if only on Saturday night, is at least aroused enough to respond to alienation in a group. That's a first step.

There's a connection, largely ignored, between the return to dance and the return to mass public demonstrations. People have energy again. No matter how tentative that connection is, one would guess that populist left-wingers would try to make it as strong as possible, the way the anti-war movement tried to connect to rock'n'roll.

Yet many leftists feel free to dismiss disco as "mindless," or "watered down," or "plastic," and leave it at that, using the same narrow minds their leftist parents used to dismiss swing music and their leftist older siblings used to dismiss rock'n'roll.

It's just pop music and there's no reason to feel obligated to enjoy disco if you don't. But any political person should be interested in the space and energy it creates.

**Tom Smucker writes on popular music for the *Village Voice*
and a variety of other publications.**

4. BY GEORGIA CHRISTGAU

Disco never needed me. Since its earliest—say the Trammps' "Where the Happy People Go," it celebrated itself, its fans, its milieu. It could be superficial ("More, More, More") or up-front ("Push, Push in the Bush"); either way, it lacked subtlety, and didn't take well to the page. Since it happened "underground"—gay bars, black and Latin communities—I and most of my peers had little experience with it. Then the Bee Gees wrote a monster hit for a white, or white enough, working-class hero in *Saturday Night Fever,* and disco became a phenomenon. And here we are, writing about it after it had already parodied itself with The Village People.

Anti-disco rock'n'rollers never needed me, either. They come complete with their own spectrum, from the bleeders at punk clubs to the fans of platinum-sellers like Bob Seger who sings, "Don't take me to no disco," to cheers from people who've never been inside one, either.

Three progressive FM rock stations in New York run anti-disco campaigns. It's not hard to do—radio is already segregated black from white. At a sellout show of Twisted Sister, a local group with a white following, a banner displayed from the balcony read, "We hate disco because it sucks." This isn't opinion, it's willful ignorance, racism feeding on paranoia: where will rock'n'rollers go now that "boogie" has become "boogie down"?

If the Beatles turned on the world to Chuck Berry, the Bee Gees are inspired by the Sylistics, or at least revive the memory of Smokey Robinson. Disco carries on a tradition in American music of integration, a synthesis of sharing as well as antagonism. People my age, white and black, can swoon to Sam and Dave or the Righteous Brothers, but some of them haven't made the disco connection. Polyester suits, strobe lights and mirrored floors threaten the flannel and jeans lifestyle. One powerful image cancels out the other; much money has been invested promoting the disco way of life, money that must see a return.

Me, I try to ignore the promo-hype. I enjoy disco without going to Studio 54, and have never purchased a whistle or sniffed amyl nitrate. I listen to enough disco to stay interested in its history. 1974's "Rock Your Baby" sounds like a garage band compared to 1978's "Supernature." Partial to southern rhythm and blues, I dance to Candi Staton, KC and the Sunshine Band, and Betty Wright—who've all had huge disco "crossover" hits. A sucker for extremes, I'm taken with Grace Jones, and fascinated by disco deejays, new superstars who know how to make the music never stop. For dancing, I rely on some version of the L.A. Hustle a friend from Detroit learned on vacation in Miami, which still holds up on the floor after five years. Do I really love disco? No, But when Blondie hits big with "Once had a love, it was a gas/Soon turned out to be a pain in the ass," I celebrate disco, too. It's the same old song.

Georgia Christgau writes on music for the *Village Voice* and other publications.

33

"The Confessions of a Gay Rocker"

Adam Block

Since its very beginnings rock music has been extolled for its liberating and empowering qualities. It has provided a space wherein performers and fans have explored identities and played with societal conventions of gender and sexuality. In the early 1970s, for example, musicians from David Bowie and Lou Reed to the New York Dolls delved into androgyny and role-playing, sparking the glitter and glam rock movement. Yet as music critic Adam Block points out in his essay written for gay lifestyles magazine *The Advocate*, rock musicians have rarely embraced an openly homosexual, public identity. Block's essay is essentially a travelogue examining the relationship between rock and gay identity, taking the reader through rock's first quarter century, stopping at the point where MTV was beginning to introduce American audiences to a new wave of British musicians such as Soft Cell and Pete Shelley. Had Block written his article a year or two later he might have mentioned Culture Club's cross-dressing Boy George or Frankie Goes to Hollywood's gay anthem "Relax." Still, even considering these examples, and the many more that have followed, it is worth reiterating Block's comments and complaints even today, more than two decades later. To what extent has rock served as an expressive medium for gay performers? And in what ways has rock spoken to gay audiences?*

JOHNNY ARE YOU QUEER?

In 1971 I was a teen-ager struggling with coming out. The scary part wasn't my family, and shucks, I knew I liked boys. The scary part was my music. "You can't be a homo," I kept thinking, "Homos don't like rock 'n' roll."

How was a kid raised on The Rolling Stones, The Animals and The Who supposed to relate to a world where the reigning deities seemed to be Judy Garland and Barbra Streisand, where polite conversation required a fascination with the minutiae of show tunes and opera? I figured you could always spot a homo by his record collection, and mine was a disgrace.

I had this nightmare: I would bring a male date home, and the mischievous tough would crouch on his haunches and flip casually through my LPs. Then he would cock his head suspiciously and demand, "You slumming or something, bub? I *know* you ain't gay. You don't even have a copy of *Stoney End*."† Irrefutable.

---

* *Source:* Adam Block, "The Confessions of a Gay Rocker," *The Advocate*, April 15, 1982, pp. 43–47.
† He is referring to Barbra Streisand's 1971 album release, *Stoney End*.

Rock was more than the soundtrack of my youth. It was a shared secret language that linked me to every other fan. It was unnerving and invigorating: the sound of lust and revolt, passion and humor—a public triumph over my private fears and aspirations. The problem was that rock, for all its daring celebrations, stopped short at the ultimate taboo: Boys don't kiss boys. That had me spooked…

If homos didn't like rock, I couldn't swear that the feeling wasn't mutual. The only performers my friends agreed were fruits were Liberace and Wayne Newton. Hardly inspirational role models.

Despite my panic, I took the plunge. At first it looked as if none of this was a very big deal. The post-Stonewall baby boom hitting the bars in San Francisco in '71 didn't seem to know or care whether we were taken for hippies or homos. Our only demand of the music was that it be danceable, and from Loggins and Messina to "Brown Sugar," from Janis Joplin to "Shaft's Theme," that covered a lot of territory.

There *seemed* to be plenty of gay rockers out there, but you could look in vain for an openly gay rock star. Rock was still a part of mainstream culture: a place, as Vito Russo said of the movies, "where one learned to pass for straight, where one learned the boundaries of what America would accept as normal." The next year, I was in London and thinking about the ways that rock and gay lib touched each other, when those boundaries began to stretch to the breaking point.

MY OBSESSION, YOUR OBSESSION: WALKIN' IT LIKE YOU TALK IT

In the summer of '72 the British press was full of David Bowie, an admitted bisexual who was releasing his *Ziggy Stardust* LP and inspiring young boys to pile on the make-up and glitter. I read an account of a 16-year-old who said he felt strange getting a hard-on while he watched Mick Jagger perform. That made me grin.

"I think that teen-ager's hard-on says more about rock as gay lib than Bowie's notoriety," I told a fellow writer. "Bowie may be claiming the form, but a hard-on, that's *function*."

In fact, both said a lot. If the Gay Revolution never took hold in rock, that said as much about gay lib as it did about music. Rock's strongest appeals have always been more implied than overt: sly promises in a shared, secret language—ambiguous in the same way that sexual ambivalence can be. Forthright celebrations and denunciations were folkie tools that often preached to the converted. Rock was more shadowy and subversive; the walk often was the talk.

The fact is that to this day I can't think of one rock artist who has been gay and proud, erotic and liberating—seizing the airwaves and giving the boys boners. Many who claim to be bi or straight have touched on the subject in exciting ways, but the fear and resentment of gays and gay impulses run deep, and hip rock is no exception. I began to look for music that expressed those fears and even dismantled them. Rock was built by voices that wreaked havoc with a nation's notion of deviance and decency. I watched to see the impulses of rock cross paths with the fact of being gay.

IT'S THE SINGER, NOT THE SONG

That same summer of '72, Little Richard appeared at a rock revival show at Wembley Stadium. Mascaraed to the tits, under a lacquered bouffant, the self-proclaimed Georgia Peach was grotesque and a little magnificent. Though he was acting like an outrageous queen in the '70s, Little Richard had been an apparition in a zoot suit in '55—the man was beyond camp, beyond macho—he was rock 'n' roll.

Greil Marcus has written, "He disrupted an era, broke rules, created a form. Little Richard gave shape to a vitality that wailed silently in each of us until he found a voice for it…. I can only marvel at his arrogance, his humor, his delight: Delivering a new vision of America with music, and more people than anyone can count are still trying to live in it."

Arrogance, humor and delight have always been our most effective weapons against despair and censure. Little Richard danced over the abyss and that will stand.

Some racy novelty numbers featured gay players in the '30s and '40s (collected on Stash Records' *AD/DC Blues*), but gays were invisible in the rock and pop of the '50s and early '60s. Gays could stake a claim only on the unconscious camp of the girls and girl groups: Lesley Gore's "It's My Party and I'll Cry If I Want To," covered by a coolly fey Brian Ferry in '74; The Angels' "My Boyfriend's Back," recently released with a lisp by the Bee Jays; or The Crystals' "He's a Rebel," which would reemerge in '81 as an obscure gay novelty, "He's a Rabbi," by David Roter.

These camp readings were subversions of the aggressively heterosexual fantasies of the time: acts of comic revenge (enacted well after the fact) that inserted a gay presence into a territory that had carefully excluded us. Gays had to reinvent the songs if they were going to find a place in them. That began to change as the shock troops started arriving from the United Kingdom.

THE BRITISH INVASION

A decade after Little Richard burst upon the scene, a major rock band, The Rolling Stones, appeared in drag on a record sleeve. Camp and drag were comic traditions in England, but the rockers were willing to make them threatening.

Ray Davies, the ever fey and tough leader of The Kinks (get it?) was regularly limp-wristed and loony. His early ballad "See My Friends," sounded to some like a subtle homo lament, but it was *mighty* subtle and was never a hit. In 1970, however, he scaled the Top 10 with his music-hall celebration of an innocent seduced by a transvestite.* It was the first gay rock song; the first time I'd ever heard us perverts mentioned, let alone celebrated, on the radio.

Some of the gay input was coming from bands' managers. British critic Simon Frith writes, "The sharp, college-educated music pushers were, unusually often, homosexuals; their stars were given a surly, sensual, leather-boy appeal." None more so than The Rolling Stones.

Mick Jagger invented himself in a way that embodied contradictions: the middle-class student of economics playing leather tough; a white Brit singing black American music, a heterosexual who liked to flirt with boys. He made those juxtapositions exciting and liberating.

The Stones' gay manager, Andrew Loog Oldham, pushed the bad-boy image, fueled by sexual ambiguity. Oldham wrote a song (with guitarist Keith Richards) called "I'd Much Rather Be with the Boys," which was a bit much even for the danger boys. It was eventually released in '75 on *Metamorphosis*.

Jagger outdistanced even Oldham with his 1971 song "Cocksucker Blues," in which he crowed, "I need to get my cock sucked. I need to get my ass fucked." It is probably the greatest gay rocksong ever recorded, but you're not liable to hear it. It was written to be unreleasable, in order to settle a contractual obligation to a party whom Jagger had no intention of helping. Jagger's song spotlighted the phobia that he knew would prevent either release or success for the cut.

Brian Epstein, who discovered, groomed and managed The Beatles, was a middle-class homo. The band knew his predilections. When he mentioned to the lads that he was writing an autobiography and asked if they had any suggestions for a title, John Lennon cracked laconically, "Yeah, how about *Queer Jew*?"

Epstein, closeted and unhappy, never mentioned his sexual bent in the memoir. A few years later he was dead from an overdose of sleeping pills. It's a shame that Epstein never lived to see the post-Stonewall era, when all those Beatle fans began to come out and demand a bit more breathing space.

---

* The song described here is "Lola."

In 1965 Tom Robinson was a schoolboy going quietly to pieces over his infatuation with another lad. He heard The Beatles on the radio sing: "Everywhere people stare,/Each and every day./I can see them laugh at me,/and I hear them say, 'Hey,/you've got to hide your love away.'" The song seemed to be addressed to him, just one more proof to Robinson that he was losing it. Years later he would learn that Lennon had written the song after a vacation in Spain with Epstein, and that Lennon considered it his first "serious piece of songwriting." Maybe Lennon had been singing Epstein's song, reaching out a hand to a gay friend. At the time it was only a glimmer to Robinson, who was institutionalized after he fell apart. Ten years later he would remember the incident, when he made a bid to be the first openly gay rock star.

In '67 some gays were finding a glimmer of recognition in The Rolling Stones' "Sitting on a Fence." Jagger sang: "There is one thing I could never understand:/Some of the sick things that a girl does to a man./So, I'm just sitting on a fence." You could decide for yourself whether the fence-sitter was a bisexual or just a misogynist refusing to plunge in to marriage. But the Stones looked to be forever plunging.

The Stones aren't a gay group, but they have played with the fear and allure of faggotry with more wit and panache than anyone else in rock. Jagger's marriage of camp to macho expressed an ambivalence that wasn't willing to choose one over the other. Nevertheless, Jagger never exposed any male liaisons. He got married and had a kid.

For that matter, so did David Bowie. But Bowie *admitted* to sleeping with boys. In '72 he seemed poised to do the unthinkable—to bring rock and gay lib together. Bowie brought Lou Reed over to England to produce an LP for him and Reed promptly announced that he too was gay, though he too would later marry—twice.

The fact is that Bowie's sexuality has always been as cool and costume-like as the rest of his act. I saw him in his glitter heyday, when he was flirting with his lead guitarist and giving the instrument head. I saw the master of masks perform Brel's "My Death" in Dietrich drag, but as Bowie's ambitions grew, the gay trappings would fall steadily away.

GLITTER IN THE U.S.A.

I was back in the states by '73, primed to watch glitter-rock sweep the continent. Lou Reed scored with "Take a Walk on the Wild Side," and suddenly there were addicts, transvestites and hustlers lounging in the Top 20. Ziggy Stardust toured, while critics raved about the outrageous androgyny of the New York Dolls. Fourteen-year-old boys were filching their mommies' mascara as Bowie sang, "Rebel, rebel how could they know? Hot tramp, I love you so."

If gay lib and rock had seemed poised for an alliance in those heady days (gay libbers even asked Bowie to write them an anthem), well, the moment passed. It wasn't just that glitter-rock failed to penetrate the heartland, or that what did get through was more costume than conviction. The rub was that gays weren't dancing to "Rebel, Rebel," which peaked at #64 in the pop charts, but to "Don't Rock the Boat" by The Hues Corporation, which hit #1. While Bowie had been busy making waves, gays were nailing down a luxury suite on the ark.

In the first flush of Bowie's success American record companies rushed out to sign their own house homos. There was Jobriath (the American Bowie), Sylvester (as black glitter-rocker) and Steven Grossman (the gay James Taylor). All came out of the closet and headed straight for the bargain bins.

As gay glitter was consumed in its own glare, I was unnerved by this rear-flank attack. Gays, blacks and Latins hadn't tried to attack the mainstream—they were building a scene on the fringes: a place to meet and dance. Disco side stepped the world of rock prophets and celebrities. The artists were faceless, the stars were on the dance floor. Why worry about when the first rock star would come out on the radio? Boys were kissing boys in the clubs.

SECRET STRATEGIES

By 1975 I was feeling a bit schizophrenic. By day I was writing about rock, but at night the clubs were locked down by that divinely enforced rhythm track that even a spastic on two quaaludes could follow. Disco seemed like some secret gas—turn the stuff on and suddenly you were in a queer bar. I never brought it home. If my heart was in rock, well, at least my crotch was in the discos.

Pop music came on aggressively straight, but I was learning that that image masked significant gay input. I found that being gay was giving me the leap on pop culture. The catch was that you'd almost have to be in the know already to see how gays were making stars.

Because gays were outsiders, they could sidle up to a risky talent, inspire it, celebrate it and let it roll on out to the suburbs. The trick seemed to be that America loved the gay spirit of outrageousness for its entertainment value, as long as the sex part didn't intrude. Boys still didn't kiss boys.

—HERE IS YOUR THROAT BACK, THANKS FOR THE LOAN – BOB DYLAN

Three voices I'd first encountered as gay cult figures went national in '75. I had first heard Labelle in Paris in '72, where gay discos spun "Moonflower" with a vengeance.* In '75, the group swept to the #1 spot in the U.S. pop charts with "Lady Marmalade" and a glitter-disco stageshow.

In '75 Patti Smith released her debut LP, *Horses*, which opened with her lesbo-erotic version of "Gloria" and featured the explicit, poetic rape of schoolboy Johnny up against a gym locker, by a pretty tough. Smith became the bohemian darling of the rock press, and broke the pop Top 50.

Meanwhile, gay discos were alive with a Euro-import single by an unknown named Donna Summer. By the time "Love to Love You, Baby," was beginning its climb towards #2 in the pop charts, Summer had already been crowned as gay royalty: the Queen of Disco.

It wasn't just happenstance that these "gay discoveries" were all women. That was the tradition. Gay men could identify with the raptures women were allowed to indulge. The women could even impersonate and give voice to male fantasies, while remaining straight themselves. Even "liberated gays," who seemed uncomfortable with men singing openly to other men, offered scant encouragement to male artists who might be so inclined.

Labelle, Smith and Summer were early signals of two scenes developing on the margins, punk and disco. Gays were midwives to both. Each promised to lend us some visibility and maybe free some people from their soul-sucking fear of homosexuality. What I *hadn't* counted on was the punk and disco scenes developing into opposing armed camps.

DISCO DETENTE

By 1976, there seemed to be nothing *but* disco in gay bars, and I found that more than a little irritating. The ugly thing about disco was that it seemed to announce and enforce an overwhelming conformity. I'd always thought that the liberating secret of coming out was, "Hey, it's OK to be different": it hadn't occurred to me that homos might create a society as intolerant as the one they had escaped from.

---

* Block most likely means Labelle's version of Cat Stevens's "Moonshadow."

Put simply, gays discovered disco while they were discovering one another. People came out to that split 4/4 beat in unprecedented numbers. The rhythm was reassuring, indomitable and dance-able. After all the agony and hurt, all disco insisted on was seamless celebration.

Disco boasted an upfront gay star in Sylvester, who scaled the charts with "You Make Me Feel" six years after he had flopped as a glitter-rock wonder. Syl didn't get invited on by Merv and Johnny to talk about being gay, although he never concealed his homosexuality. Nevertheless, his songs made little direct reference to the subject.

If disco had any allegiance to gay liberation, you'd hardly have known it from the lyrics, unless you would settle for: "If it feels good, do it." Tell it to a fag-basher. I didn't hate disco, but it did set me to wondering if maybe I'd been right—that homos really *didn't* like rock 'n' roll.

Critic Ellen Willis wrote, "The difference was that rock and roll as a musical language was always on some level about rebellion, freedom, and the expression of emotion, while disco was about cool-ing out as you move up, about stylizing and containing emotion."

Disco did in fact represent a kind of rebellion. But if punk was out to rip off the emperor's clothes, disco intended to outdress the mother. Both wanted to subvert the social order; it was just that disco intended to beat society at its own game: flaunting the rewards that ads had always prom-ised as the hallmarks of success (luxury, beauty, sex), while refusing to pay the price of abandoning faggotry. The fruits of capitalism and celebrity were celebrating and adorning the fruits themselves. As William Burroughs puts it, "Money is what the other guy has got."

PUNK IT UP

While disco was busily announcing a society of "insiders" appropriating the emblems of success, the punk scene emerged as a society of "outsiders" attacking those emblems. Disco perverted legiti-macy. Punk made perversity legitimate. Homos who had grown up in the '60s flocked to both scenes. But if disco was upwardly mobile and coolly hedonistic, punk was downwardly mobile and aggressively nihilistic. Though both developed in alternative "fringe" music scenes, they came to view each other as the enemy. The diverse motley of homos that I had met in the bars in the early '70s were facing off against one another five years later. And a lot of the punks were as insufferably insular as their disco counterparts.

In 1978 Andrew Kopkind reported, "No one hates punk worse than a gay disco purist, and no one has more venom for disco than a gay punk."

When I had to pick a side, it was with the underdog punks who insisted that music could still be a scary brand of fun. Gay punks were rejecting both the mainstream rock and mainstream gay scenes. They were creating an arena that welcomed sexual ambiguity, revolt. They were also a dec-laration against mainstream gay stereotypes.

The Ramones, the original intentional cartoon of a three-chord garage band, kicked things off with "53rd & 3rd," the account of a gay hustler turned fag-basher. A Frenchman, Plastique Ber-trand, had a hit with a punk-novelty number called "Ca Plane pour moi," Freely mistranslated by a Brit who called himself Elton Motello, it became "Jet Boy, Jet Girl," a savagely playful bit of homo-erotica that made Bowie's "Rebel, Rebel" sound touchingly chaste. The maniacal British band 999 roared in with a tune that insisted, "Let's face it—the boy can't make it with girls."

None of these songs were hits, and only "Jet Boy, Jet Girl" even gained much notoriety, but they spotlight an aggressive brand of honesty that was missing from both mainstream rock and disco. It was a message even more clearly stated in the rage, music and humors than in the lyrics.

The scene was a haven for the musically and socially disenfranchised. Many of the band managers, club owners, D.J.'s and critics who helped create this alternate scene were gay. But it only produced one openly gay artist who made that fact unavoidable in his music.

Tom Robinson emerged in '78, when his embittered anthem "Sing If You're Glad to be Gay" became a surprise hit in the United Kingdom. Touring the United States during the height of Briggs & Anita Fever,* he got a lot of interest from the press, but even in San Francisco he failed to draw crowds. Neither gays nor rockers turned out in force. Robinson was more earnest folkie than erotic rocker, and you couldn't dance disco to the anthems.

After a second LP, his band broke up, and Robinson cut a single with his own money—all proceeds to go to London's Gay Switchboard. Robinson even tried disco. Elton John wrote the music, a weak retread of "Philadelphia Freedom," and Robinson sang to a hot boy: "You know I hate to be salacious,/But it's hard to fight the feeling./Lechery can be such fun," while black girls chanted, "Sexist, Sexist." Who'd ever heard of a *rocker* worrying that horniness might not be politically correct? Let alone a disco queen? The noble failure nearly bankrupted the singer.

A subsequent band, Sector 27, put the politics on a back burner but failed to find an audience. He is currently working up material with his original guitarist. "Whenever I get depressed about the career," Robinson told me. "I can think about the letters I got—like the one from this kid in Ohio who was literally at the point of suicide when he heard "Glad to Be Gay" on the radio. Saving a life, that's something."

THE PATRICIA NELL WARREN OF POP?

In the late '70s songs written by and for straights, but specifically about homos, began to show up in mainstream pop. Rod Stewart's "Ballad of Georgie" arrived seven years after "Lola" broke the Top 10.

The most forthright and tender of the lot wasn't even written by a man. It wasn't rock or new wave. It wasn't even disco—just a waltz with a piano accompaniment. In the last verse she sang about two boys, "holding each other as young lovers do … The altar boy and the thief,/grabbing themselves some relief."

"The Altar Boy and the Thief" was on an LP, released in '77, called *Blowin' Away*. It was intended as a big commercial bid for Joan Baez. Unfortunately it didn't sell. God knows what the "Kumbayah" crowd would make of it. I guess it was inevitable that a woman would be the one to write it, but it still astonished me.

I GIVE IT A 90. IT'S GOT A GOOD BEAT. I CAN'T DANCE TO IT

By the end of the decade, new wave and disco were occupying the same chart in Billboard. It was called the Disco Chart, but they might as well have labeled it the Gay Page because the queer bars were calling the shots in dance music. New-wave artists had kicked a hole in the bell jar of disco and staked a claim on the dance floor, and if many disco purists were as ferociously defensive as ever, and if lots of gay new-wavers still claimed that their knees locked when a disco tune came on, well there were artists breaking through in both camps. Prince, Grace Jones, The Go Gos, The Jacksons, Soft Cell and Pete Shelley were all showing up on any play-list that wasn't hermetically sealed in

---

* Conservative California legislator John Briggs had launched an initiative to ban gays and lesbians from teaching in public schools; Florida-based celebrity Anita Bryant created the "Save Our Children" campaign to contest Dade County's newly passed gay rights ordinance.

'81. If categories weren't exactly exploding, there was some hope that they could soon become too hopelessly confused to prove useful to anyone.

RADIO REVELATION AND TEEN-AGE PANIC

It was one of those hazy days late last summer, and I was propped up on my tar-and-pebbled San Francisco roof, feeling as Mediterranean as the circumstances allowed. The radio was tuned to KUSF. They were playing the latest new wave and I wasn't really listening. A bright girl-group came on. They were singing about high-school heartbreak.

"When you asked for a date, I thought that you were straight. Johnny are you queer?" the girl demanded. I squinted at the radio, unbelieving. I hiked the volume. Then I laughed out loud.

The song was talking in the gum-chewing cadences of suburban teens, and it was admitting, plaintively and playfully, that homos in the high schools were confusing their girlfriends.

"Johnny Are You Queer," is a novelty—one silly, shocking bolt from the blue. But I hope that song reaches some kid off in Dubuque, feeling scared and baffled as he cranks up AC/DC and Van Halen on his radio and I hope it makes *him* grin. Because the song is also an anomaly. In 1982, rock and gay lib still rarely join forces on public airwaves. Ten years ago there weren't *any* high-school homos in rock, and I was the kid by the radio.

I'VE GOT SILENCE ON MY RADIO

The final irony may be that in the last decade rock has lost much of its significance as a shared voice, its power to define a passionate conspiracy among its young listeners. Today's teens seem more excited by a new video game than a new LP, and the current crop of stadium supergroups look to be competing with the ersatz firepower of the Asteroids Experience. Maybe I should be hoping for a gay Space Invaders, instead of a homo Springsteen.

Besides, the whole notion of a homo Springsteen sometimes seems hopelessly at odds with both gay and rock traditions. Both cultures favor innuendo—the suggestive attitude or lyric that makes the listener a conspirator in determining meaning. For gays, the choice has been camp over candor; for rockers, sly sexy promises over overt declaration.

Ambiguity forces the listener to think twice, to consider the alternatives.

Two current artists are combining these traditions in a way that just may disarm their mutual distrust. Soft Cell, a male duo who sound fabulously queer, scored with the song "Tainted Love"; and Pete Shelley (who casually admitted his bisexuality a couple of years back when he was with The Buzzcocks) beat all odds with the astonishing gay-inflected "Homosapien." Neither song became a radio hit, but they came close.

So with the kids becoming video zombies, and many gays and straights being shell-shocked after a decade of fashion wars, we may finally find a voice. It may not be bellowing the truth—just taking it for granted with arrogance, wit and delight. Turn it up.

IV

THE 1980S

34

Punk Goes Hardcore

JACK RABID

Information about independent and local punk rock bands and culture circulated in the late 1970s via networks well off the radar of the mainstream music industry. One of the most important forms of punk journalism emerged in the shape of numerous fanzines written and produced by young, devoted fans. Punk fanzines were essentially small, self-published magazines, which were often printed as Xerox copies and distributed either for free or sold with a nominal cover charge. Musician and punk fan Jack Rabid started the *Big Takeover* (named after a Bad Brains song) in June 1980 as a modest two-page New York City publication. Since then it has grown into an internationally renowned biannual magazine totaling more than 200 pages in length. In this excerpt from an issue celebrating the magazine's twentieth anniversary, Rabid takes a retrospective look at *Big Takeover* nos. 4 & 5 from 1981. The original fanzine text is presented in italics. Rabid's commentary, as well as reminiscences from former New York punk fan Geoff Hutchinson, is presented in plain type. Rabid details the emerging early '80s "hardcore punk" scene—a louder/faster version of the older punk sound, complete with a new type of slam dancing—as it developed on the West Coast and illustrates the glaring differences between punk in New York and Los Angeles.*

THE BIG TAKEOVER, ISSUE FOUR, FEBRUARY 1981 – JACK RABID

*The first concert I saw out in L.A. was **Black Flag** at the Starwood. This band really deals in distortion. Their concerts are all potential riots. They are very imposing looking. **Greg** (guitar), **Chuck** (bass), **Robo** (drums), and **Dez** (vocals, succeeding **Keith Morris** and **Ron Reyes**) played all the songs off their two EPs. Their best song is 'Depression,' which can be found on* Decline of the Western Civilization, *a live compilation LP just released.† Next I saw **The Circle Jerks**. They're the best band in California as of now, which is amazing considering they just started less than a year ago. Their 14-song LP* Group Sex, *out this week, takes 15 minutes to play, but it's 15 minutes of superb, lightning-quick rock. (If you thought no one was as fast as* The Bad Brains, *check out "Red Tape" and "What's Your Problem.") I think they might even be better than **The Dead Kennedys** (see their "California Über Alles" single) and **The Germs**, whose singer, **Darby Crash**, just committed suicide last month. I saw many lesser known bands—**Gears, China White, Fear, Adolescents,***

* *Source:* Jack Rabid, "The Big Takeover: The Punk Rock Years, 1980–81," *The Big Takeover*, no. 47 (2000), pp. 53–55, 164.

† Rabid is referring to *The Decline of Western Civilization*, the soundtrack to the 1981 L.A. punk documentary.

UXA, etc.—all very exciting. It's super to see so many loud, fast bands in one city/area. Punk dead, indeed!

The night before I returned home, I went to the Polish Hall to see Mad Society, The Runs, The Hits, and The Assassins. Upon arrival, I saw 1000 kids (!) milling about outside unable to get in because it was already filled. Every color of hair, all dressed to kill. It was almost frightening. Black Flag made a surprise appearance to open the show at 9PM, but there were still more kids outside than in. Back outside, I was talking to my friend, photographer Glen Friedman from New York [he of the My Rules *punk books since], when I saw a bunch of youths smashing the back windows. They would not be denied. Hundreds hurled themselves into the room through the broken glass. I re-entered the front just as the LAPD riot squad poured through the back entrance, clubs raised. This is when the violence really started, as the police began to club the kids. There was a stampede out the front to rival the Who concert, but I got out to see angered kids throwing chairs, stones, bottles, and bricks at the hall.* Within minutes, the place was surrounded by maybe 200 police cars, with a helicopter overhead lighting the area. I thought I was safe where I was: two blocks away, but I was wrong. The riot squad stormed around the corner, and one of the police brought his club crashing down on my head. I hit the ground and he started to kick me, a savage look on his face as he repeatedly screamed, 'Get out of here!' I took his advice.*

Saturday, January 31, I went to Washington, D.C. to see an incredible Bad Brains/Stimulators gig at the 9:30 Club. Washington is a very California-type scene. There are many similarities in attitude and dress, as well as musical taste. I have never seen so many young punks in one place on the East Coast before. I felt that these kids also had been studying California audiences. With the first notes of 'Run, Run, Run,' these kids went wild, slamming into each other like L.A. They even hop onto the stage to dive bomb back in the crowd, like out there. At times, there were eight or ten people on the stage, leaping over one another and singer Patrick. I talked to as many people as I could. All told me that there are few things worth seeing in D.C., so when something like this happens they come from all over the region. The Bad Brains are the leading band, but new bands like S.O.A. and Minor Threat are emerging. The Bad Brains' show was exciting as only they can be. H.R., Darryl, Dr. Know, and Earl are really loved by the fans. They turned over the house for a second show with these two bands, which I was told is an unusual occurrence for D.C. Even the DJ was good (a first). He must have played six songs from Stiff Little Fingers' Inflammable Material *LP.*

Geoff Hutchinson, 2000

"In the summer of 1977 I had a camp counselor who was also a DJ at a college radio station. He was a bit aloof, and quite cool. At the end of the summer I asked him to name me one band that he thought was the best thing going, he said **Talking Heads**. As soon as I got home I bought *Talking Heads '77*. This was the start. Two months later my brother got a new stereo for his birthday, with a receiver. We soon discovered WFMU college radio of Upsala college in N.J.; we heard **Television, Patti Smith, Sex Pistols,** everything! Our lives were transformed. At that time you either liked **Led Zeppelin, Grateful Dead, Jethro Tull, Yes** or **E.L.P.** And your friends were the same as you."

"My friends and I liked **David Bowie,** that made us freaks! Kids yelled 'freaks!' at us in the halls of our high school."

"We suffered for our taste, but we really didn't care, we didn't like those dumb jocks anyway. The first show we saw was (except for Bowie), Patti Smith. I remember the power, it was scary to me.

---

* There had been a stampede at The Who's December 3, 1979, concert at Cincinnati's Riverfront Stadium that resulted in eleven deaths.

The intensity, the chords, Patti did a few monologues, she suggested getting really high, and then reading the book of *Revelations*! I tried it. It's very trippy."

"Soon after that we discovered the New York scene. The group that you always wanted to see was **Johnny Thunders' Heartbreakers**. There was such drama! You waited for hours for them to get sufficiently high to get on-stage, and then it finally happened. It always started with this recording of bombs, and third Reich speeches and marching troops (*see the band's* Live at Max's *LP, though that's just an excerpt—Rabid*). We instantly tossed the tables of Max's to the sides, and began pogo-ing. The energy was ecstatic. A bunch of freaks dancing. For me, a kid from the lily white suburb of Summit NJ, this was paradise. There were gays, blacks, transsexuals, artists, everyone all dancing together. It was real freedom."

"In those days there were so few people interested in this new music, that when you saw someone dressed like you, you had an instant friend. We made lots of new friends that way. Riding the train in to New York, if you saw others dressed like you, you knew you could talk to them. That's how small the scene was. You knew you had a friend by sight, and we made lots of friends that way.

This egalitarian system lasted only for a few years, however. The dance at that time was the pogo, which was supposedly created by **Sid Vicious** (*still unsubstantiated, but very possibly true—ed.*). This dance was, as I viewed the scene, an all-inclusive dance. There was no skill, no violence. If you fell, everyone was there to help you up, and back in. Everyone could participate, and that was what it was about. Later, when slam dancing came about, people who didn't want to risk injury, especially girls, couldn't dance anymore. That to me was a death."

"As punk became more popular, non-freaks came into the scene. The Mudd Club was born. The Mudd Club was the first 'punk' club to have a red velvet rope at the door. Before the Mudd Club, if you knew about the event, then that was enough, you were cool enough to get in. I remember trying to see a show there, and not being let in by some self important asshole, who made some judgment about maybe my 'coolness' or something. I felt then that the truth had gone out of the scene."

"There are always people out here who are interested in creating a real reality, there was once a collective group called punks who had a dream together of creating a new society, but as things get popular, they get absorbed, or stolen by the general media. Things that are pure like that was, last only for a short time. I still look for them..."

Jack Rabid, 2000

[Issue No. 4 of the *Big Takeover*] contains the first small seeds of my disillusionment with the punk scene I'd been so excited about, seeds that would grow into an embittered divorce from it in less than two years. Los Angeles was my first glimpse of the future doom of a scene that had spawned so many tantalizing offshoots in a million different directions, from The Cramps and Suicide to Talking Heads to Ramones.

It is perhaps important to note that the New York scene I had literally grown up in was a smaller one and an older one. We as teens were *encouraged* to come up to the higher intellectual and creative level of veteran scene members in their 20s and 30s, and that was part of the excitement. (We in turn gave our teenage zeal and burgeoning knowledge and record collections.) The Stimulators, Mad, and Bad Brains shows had drawn 100-300 people at small clubs like Max's, Tier 3, CBGB, One Under, Botony, and Hurrah, while the newer young bands like our Even Worse, The Offals, Nastyfacts, and later The False Prophets drew maybe 40-50 friends.* The local bands we were following were lucky to even have a single out. There were no labels for them, and the local buzz and

---

* Even Worse was a punk band that Rabid had started shortly before he began his fanzine.

bigger label attention had long since passed punk bands–even the *New York Rocker* and *Trouser Press* didn't cover them.

So to see audiences in L.A. in the thousands, all kids even younger than I, was bewildering, to say the least. True, it was also enticing to see hot local punk rock bands of little renown drawing *huge crowds*–it was like some kind of alternative universe! (Even famous first-wave punk bands had played to small crowds prior to this, as noted in recent excellent books such as *Please Kill Me, From the Velvets to the Voidoids*, and *Make the Music Go Bang!*)

But at the same time, the violence, immaturity, and mob-mentality of the L.A. scene disgusted me. The riots, club and hall-destruction, and thuggish police beatings at the Whiskey Black Flag/D.O.A. show, and at Baces Hall and Vex had been chronicled throughout 1980 in *Damage*. Meanwhile, our contingent in New York were unable to understand how that could happen, since the New York cops never took any notice of us, and we never broke anything of note or caused any mayhem worthy of arrest. When I saw the incessant fights, slam-dancing, and wanton destruction of the venues for myself, and got beaten indiscriminately by the government's brightest crisis team to boot, it was more of an eye-opener than I had bargained for.

I remember driving back by myself to Santa Barbara that night in my parents' little Chevette, my head bleeding all over the seats, being as much revolted by the punks' blockheaded conduct (no wonder no clubs would let punk groups play there any more, as the Germs' manager lamented in the *Decline* movie—their "fans" were breaking every window, urinal, or chair they could smash), as I was over the brownshirt tactics of a helmeted police force with shields beating the hell out of skinny, unarmed 16-year-olds, *and really getting off on it*. My ribs ached from the boot-kicking, my head was woozy from the blow to the back of the head, and the shirt I had used as a towel was as much crimson as much as white.

Seeing me hurt, my usually punk-despising parents actually felt sympathy for me. The next day, the two-paragraph story in the *L.A. Times* said something like, "Five Officers Hurt in Punk Riot." Looking at the bloody shirt, I remember thinking, "Nice job of reporting, that" and even my folks had to allow from my eye-witness accounts the *Times's* story was a gross distortion.

The next day, I was on a plane home, thinking, "It's a good thing this stuff only happens in California, we have a much better scene back East!" It was like I was returning from barbarity to civilization, as strange as that sounds in reference to mean-streets-era New York. Yet only three weeks later I would discover, via that trip to D.C., that the L.A. scene *had* crossed the continent. Inaugural Dischord band Teen Idols had gone to L.A., seen the slam dancing and stage diving, and brought it back to D.C. with them. I had met Henry Rollins and Ian MacKaye at a Sham 69 show at Hurrah in December 1979, and had thought them as being just like me–part of the united U.S. punk scene. So it felt only natural to pass on news of their newer, as yet unrecorded bands, S.O.A. and Minor Threat in issue four. And though the 9:30 show *was* a blast, again, it seemed bizarre that they could get 300 *kids*, with nary a hint of post-college adults, for a show. Again, I was glad that our scene was more diverse and older. Even at 18, I knew I wanted to go to the next level, to the next course, not wallow in what I'd already passed through.

But this diversity and maturity connected to underground punk scenes was not to last, as becomes more plain in subsequent issues. The D.C. kids and the soon-to-be-touring L.A. bands would change punk to hardcore and then to thrash; would scare away all the open-minded older folks with more varied interests who had also supported punk; would soon even scare away punk fans like me, and would finally pave the way for a scene that resembled the worst aspects of junior high school, in place of the post-grad art school madness and sexual/creative smorgasbord it had once been.

I saw the fetid future coming for the first time at the Whiskey, at the Starwood, at Polish Hall, and at 9:30, though I'd somehow thought it would never come to roost in my town. Fortunately, there were at least two years left before the rot would set in completely and altogether engulf this great scene. I was still taking pride in the frowning stares I got from the passengers on the Greyhound from Easton to D.C. and back–a miserable journey otherwise. It was nice, then, to think you could really shake someone up by daring to dress as you pleased, and I thought it was wonderful to surprise people who'd made up their minds, by being well-spoken. It added to my later sorrow in seeing something noble become a self-parodying mirror of the media's image of it.

In any case, this somewhat emotional issue four also marked the first grain of an editorial comment in *BT*. On the next issue I would feel compelled to break into the first actual editorial. From now on, as thorns began appearing among the roses, I would find myself driven to address these issues as well as the music that still inspired the publication.

Donald typed up issue four and printed it in on yellow paper, and I signed it, as I had the previous two issues. It seemed like a good arrangement, but it wasn't to last. All I was doing after writing the issues was taking the copies wherever I went, to clubs and stores, leaving little stacks of the them on the jukebox at Max's or at 99 Records, and giving them to folks I knew. It was a lot easier than the weeks of distribution efforts these days! Come to think of it, it takes a little longer than one day to write the mag these days now, too.

THE BIG TAKEOVER, ISSUE FIVE, MARCH 1981

*Sat. March 14, was the New York debut of **Black Flag**, at Peppermint Lounge. Seeing them here was considerably different than seeing them at the Starwood or the Polish Hall in L.A. They were much looser here. **Mission of Burma** from Boston opened, the less said of them the better (a great band that played like shit! … expected more). [Note: they played 1000 times better at subsequent New York shows, removed from the hardcore context, blowing everyone away.] Black Flag came out and started with "Damaged." But first they spent a long time tuning. They made a lot of noise with their big amps, and they played loud and trebly.*

*There were a lot of people at the **Black Flag** show from Washington, D.C. there, many I recognized from the **Bad Brains/Stimulators** show at the 9:30 Club in January. I must admit I was a little upset at their attempts to turn the dance floor into the mess that it is in L.A. C'mon fellas, this was the Peppermint Lounge, not Hollywood, and the so-called "hippies" (basically anyone who wasn't dancing, and a few who were) did not get in your way. It seems to me pretty ridiculous that people should be attacked for the crime of dancing with the wrong outfit or haircut, and moreover, people have the right to stand off to the side and just watch if they so choose, and to go out of your way to bother them is a stupid, macho, phony trip. Dancing in front of the stage where I could watch the singer, **Dez**, I was and am more interested in seeing the band than in seeing how many people I could annoy, injure, etc. I enjoyed the band and I hope they come back soon, but I hate to see this kind of fake toughness going on. As one person stated, 'If you're so tough, go take on a Hell's Angel, their hair is longer than yours.' If you guys insist on this bullshit attitude then we may as well forget all the positive aspects of our scene and chuck the whole thing out the window. And may a "hippie" beat the living shit out of you.*

Jack Rabid, 2000

Well, there you have it, the very first *Big Takeover* editorial! A one-paragraph rant. I've always been happy in retrospect that it was on the malignant evil of slam dancing, and was penned only two days after its first sighting in New York. I'm proud of being on record as despising this squalid practice right from the first moment it raised its foul head here, and recognizing from the first its potential to destroy a vibrant underground music scene just beginning to get a national footing.

To this day, nothing has done more to hurt the spread and growth of underground music of any real aggression. Idiotic slam-dancing turns off people who 1) have brains, 2) are over the age of 19, 3) just want to see a band and dance and have fun, as we had for years at "punk" shows before then, and 4) are women or smaller men who want to stand anywhere near a stage. (I might add that all-male shows are pathetic and unappealing. Going to punk gigs since 1983 has ever felt like a testosterone-addled circus.) It's a loathsome, immature, inconsiderate, gig-ruining anti-sport that is grievously still with us 19 years later; though thankfully it's *finally* much in decline in nightclubs (though still in full force at giant shows for macho jocks and angry suburban kids).

Thus, March 14, 1981 was the day the once valiant punk rock scene of New York City was infected with a fatal virus. It was initially an annoying trifle, but over those next two years the disease grew and punk went from a profound inspiration to a childish exercise not worth defending. There were (and still are) great bands that were worth getting excited about. And as fans and as a magazine, we have always tried to separate great bands from the dull-witted supporters they've drawn. But something that was once so "unhealthily fresh" (to borrow a Howard Devoto phrase) was now worse than a seventh grade fist-fight where everyone surrounds the combatants and yells "fight, fight!" instead of breaking it up. The music and its message disappeared that day in the melees in front of Black Flag … It became just background music to the fracas.

This was also the first incidence of large numbers of "skinheads" (most from D.C.) at a New York gig. Until then, most punks in the East had hair of varying length. There was no uniformity in dress, hairstyles, or tastes. This also vanished. Though not all members of the human race with extreme crew cuts in punk rock garb were or are dolts, it's a prejudice that's been hard to shake since. To think that it was the D.C. skinheads, some of whom would go on to underground fame and to repudiate such inherently gangish, violent behavior who were going out of their way to slam into anyone that didn't fit their purist punk rock parameters. Talk about your "Star-Belly Sneetches."

Not surprisingly, the dance floor at this show was ugly: Dozens of "long-hair" (ha!) New Yorkers who'd never heard of West Coast slam-dancing were quite surprised to have people viciously hurtling into them out of nowhere. The New Yorkers responded with angry fists, so fights broke out all over the dance floor of the Pep. It was something out of The Ruts' "Staring at the Rude Boys." Going home covered in bruises (even though I'd retreated to the balcony after a few songs), I remember being more upset than I had even three months before when I'd been clubbed by the L.A. SWAT team. This was home, not some foreign war theater.

As slamming was to catch on (particularly after Fear played *Saturday Night Live* seven months later, with these same D.C. kids slamming their sad brains out), and a new breed of much younger kids made it a staple, it was sad to see an entire cluster of 20 and 30-year-olds *vanish* from punk rock shows, making subsequent punk gigs seem even more like a high school field trip for the worst elements of the school. And with this aging-down came the inevitable dumbing down. I am glad I spotted it right from the first, and said so in print.

A cultural force that surrounded the most feral rock 'n' roll in history was now in the process of being lost, after a nice six-year run, 1976–1982. The music has survived since, but only barely.

35

College Rock
"Left of the Dial"

GINA ARNOLD

R.E.M., The Replacements, Camper Van Beethoven: by the end of the 1980s it was not uncommon to find alternative bands like these lumped together under the generic label of "college rock." As one can surmise from Gina Arnold's *Route 666*, this association reflected not only the popularity of these bands among college-aged audiences, but also the crucial exposure they had received from college radio airplay. Arnold, a prominent rock critic whose work has appeared everywhere from the *Los Angeles Times* to *Rolling Stone*, approaches the topic from a personal perspective, beginning her narrative as a teenager listening to KSAN-FM, San Francisco's legendary, progressive station. KSAN, however, would eventually be swallowed up by Metromedia Inc., an act which prompts Arnold to symbolically pass the "progressive" torch along to the numerous college stations that since the late 1970s have represented one of the last bastions of free-form radio. Arnold portrays college radio as a social setting populated by outcasts and adventurous souls, unrestricted by formatting concerns and rigid playlists. Reflecting on her own experiences as a DJ during the 1980s, she describes the typical college station record library as a vast reservoir filled with the latest American underground bands, all of them connected in some way to a thriving network of regional scenes spread across the entire country.*

Once upon a time, radio was a sound salvation. It played all the time, in the kitchen, in the bedroom, on the pool deck, in the car. The tinny pop chug-a-lug wired the air around it with bright-minded echoes of retro romance and fakey fun, filling up the empty blue space that envelops all suburbia with the simplest of all possible remedies for boredom: a beat. You had your little radio on all the time, night and day, and it brought you something rich and nimble: dumb ideas and wacky fantasies, pretty pieces of movable furniture for your headroom, private and possibly ridiculous visions of a lovesexy life. I even used to like the way songs were repeated over and over all week long in high rotation: they changed so gradually, like the seasons, till suddenly, months later, you noticed you never heard your favorite anymore. Oh, when television was static and unreal and movies so hard to belong to, there was always the radio to light up your inner life. Inside its plastic confines, song followed sweet song, day in and day out. You turned each other on.

But one day the radio died. Disco killed it. In Frederic Dannen's book *Hitmen*, he describes the complex record company machinations that led to a monetarily based system of radio formatting so constipated and corrupt that any new record of merit or imagination without a large budget behind it would have no way of being played.

---

* *Source:* Gina Arnold, *Route 666: On the Road to Nirvana* (New York: St. Martin's Press, 1993), pp. 21–25, 61–63.

Add to that the mechanization that developed in the late seventies and early eighties: auto-programming, which eliminated the fine art of disc jockeying. Then there was a simultaneously disturbing rise of personality radio, plus the demographic polarization of the charts into the separate worlds of Black (Urban), AOR (Album-Oriented Rock, or seemingly, Always on the Radio), and CHR (Contemporary Hit Radio). Rock 'n' roll radio was ruined. To quote Abba, who shut down around the same time, no more carefree laughter. Silence ever after.

Throughout the seventies my brother and sister and I listened to two stations: KFRC-AM, the trashy top-forty station that was the only one we could get in our mother's dumb Barracuda, and KSAN-FM, the ground-breaking free-form AOR station that had, once upon a time, led American radio out of a thicket of quick hits and, in 1977, jerked our attention toward punk rock.

We loved KSAN so much. Its deejays (Bonnie Simmons, Tony Kilbert, Beverly Wilshire), its music (from Bruce Springsteen to Bob Marley to the Clash to the Talking Heads), its spirit, its live broadcasts from the Savoy Tivoli and Winterland, and its unspoken conviction that rock 'n' roll music still had meaning in this world, in spite of the marketplace. It was the soundtrack to San Francisco: to Armistead Maupin's *Tales of the City,* which we read serialized in the *Chron* every morning, to the free Pearl Harbor and Tubes shows we'd periodically see at Embarcadero Center, to tooling up Columbus Avenue after an afternoon spent browsing at Tower Records on Bay.

Always, my favorite deejay—my whole family's favorite deejay—was Richard Gossett. Vocally, he was almost a stereotype of the laid-back FM deejay made fun of on "Saturday Night Live" and the movie *FM:* a low, even boy's voice, muttering into the night. He was funny, in a dry sort of way, and often sounded stoned (or so my brother, who knew about such things, postulated gleefully). But what I liked best about Richard was his music. It was on his show—weeknights, six to ten—that I first heard Elvis Costello, the Jam, the Police, Television, Talking Heads, and the Clash. He played a lot of Michael Jackson, Graham Parker, and Toots and the Maytals. And there was a long time when his favorite song was "You're the One That I Want," by John Travolta and Olivia Newton-John. He used to segue it into "Rockaway Beach" by the Ramones all the time, thus unwittingly teaching me everything I needed to know about the magic art of radio programming. Rule number one: there are no real borders between genres and artists, only pretend ones, born of stupid snobbery and fashion. Rule number two: act on that principle alone, and you'll be all right.

When I went away to college in Los Angeles, I used to irritate my entire dorm by talking incessantly about how great KSAN was: how much better was its musical taste, how superior were its deejays, how much more fun it was to listen to in general than the bland white sound of L.A.'s monster rock stations. I couldn't walk into a room that had KMET or KLOS on its dial (inevitably playing tracks from Supertramp's *Breakfast in America,* an LP I can't hear without thinking of that time) without starting in on my long sad story: KSAN this, KSAN that, and how in San Francisco the Ramones play for free in Embarcadero Center … information to which everyone at UCLA's unanimous response was, *So?*

But by the time I came home, KSAN sounded different from what I remembered: more staid, less adventuresome, filled with a new, oppressive atmosphere that permeated its offices and came right through the receiver. It seemed that while I'd been away, they'd been sold to an entertainment conglomerate, Metromedia, Inc., which had instituted a number of changes, including a stiff playlist. Rumor had it that Richard Gossett was fired for not adhering to it: one day, in defiance of it, he played the Clash's "Complete Control," and that was the end of that. (If this rumor's not true, please don't ever tell me.) You know, it's right what they say about how you can't go home again.

KSAN struggled on as a corporate giant for a couple of years before turning into a country-and-western station. Richard Gossett got various shifts in one or two other places, but wound up getting a job at the Anchor Steam Brewery. And instead of sticking to the stiff new formats that were emanating from the corporate ogre, I, like so many other people in those fateful years, turned to the left of the dial.

College radio stations had, of course, always existed in some form or another—as a training ground for electrical engineers and as an extracurricular activity for campus-bound newsies, sportifs, and queers. By the mid-seventies, following the trend of the post-hippie music world, many such stations boasted late-night radio shows hosted by collegiate music fiends who delighted in playing the longest tracks off albums by obscure British art bands: Pink Floyd, Gentle Giant, Caravan. But when mainstream radio lost its grip on music, then the long-dormant airwaves of the college radio stations (reserved for years for *um*-ridden play-by-plays of intercollegiate football games) at schools ranging from the University of Texas and the University of Kansas to Upsala College in Orange, New Jersey, and to the University of San Francisco and U.C. Berkeley, where I was, began simultaneously to create new music programs that dealt more competently with the rest of radio's insufficiencies.

And suddenly—not gradually at all, but quite suddenly—those stations became an invaluable American network, linking the nascent punk rockers of each city to one another, and providing all the bands within a community with a way in which to prosper. Years later, while dining at an industry conclave with R.E.M. and a bunch of record company VIPs, Peter Buck asked the collected party how many had worked in college radio. Every single person present at the table—twenty-five or so, ranging from journalists and mainstream deejays to industry execs, record store clerks, and musicians, including a couple of Buck's own friends—raised a hand.

In some ways, the story of college radio has been like a fairy tale come true—or, at the very least, a made-for-TV movie: the geekiest, most unpopular nerds at the college decide to barricade themselves into a closet and start a gonzo radio station, alienating their more popular peers and professors by blaring out noisome, underproduced garage rock featuring the F word and worse. But the radio station struggles on, the geeks grow up and prosper, and *voilà!*, the records they've been playing—by U2, the Cure, R.E.M.—go platinum! The deejays get hired to positions of influence by major record companies! The airwaves have been won back by the righteous, and rock 'n' roll will rule again.

Oddly enough, that's almost exactly how it happened. For a while there in the early eighties, college radio really was our sound salvation. It, after all, still played free-form radio, nipping expertly from James Brown to James Chance, from Fairport Convention to the Slits, soundtracking not just the hits of the moment but the history of rock, giving it some context, teaching its listeners its secrets, creating an interior world of newfound glamour and romance and escape. And they provided an outlet for all the record nerds and frustrated musicians to meet each other, enabling them to form a community of misfits, maybe twenty people per town, generally just enough people to tempt bands to the area, to play whichever VFW hall or old-man bar was willing to allow them on the premises. And lastly, the stations, such as they were, became the inevitable conduit for all the independently released records to be given their due. They played the unheard music.

The college radio effect happened at the same time in obscure tiny towns all over America—at Oberlin in Ohio, at Florida State, at Evergreen in Olympia, Washington … anyplace where there was a bunch of bored and frustrated white kids with large record collections, and one kid in particular with the will to make things happen. But Boston was the city where this all happened in the most concentrated manner, and where the significance of college radio began to take on a larger meaning. Thanks to a predominance of colleges—some, like Harvard and MIT, containing far more than their share of record geeks and electrical whizzes—plus a proximity to New York City, it became a hotbed of punk rock early on. As early as 1976, WTBS (later called WMBR) at MIT had begun running the first punk rock show in America. And then, not surprisingly, since Boston is a city overrun with hypercompetitive overachieving white kids, Harvard's college station, WHRB, followed suit. Pretty soon, every significant college station in Boston—Harvard, MIT, Emerson, and Boston College—had its own resident punk rock show.

Scott Becker was a freshman at Tufts University in Boston when he tuned in to "Shakin' Street," the late-night proto-punk program on Harvard's WHRB, in 1977.* "I remember I heard the New York Dolls, and then the Ramones, for the very first time on the radio, and it shocked the hell out of me. That guy got the Pistols' import 45's first of everybody. Shortly after that, Oedipus, who back then had pink hair and a 45 adaptor tattooed on his shoulder, started doing a punk rock show on MIT's station, and pretty soon, every college in Boston had a punk rock show on their station.

"Before that, when I was in high school in Connecticut in the mid-seventies, the AOR station seemed so hip," recalls Becker. "But then suddenly it started to dawn on me that it wasn't that hip at all. It was punk rock that did it. It was just clear that there was the whole new scene and all these new labels and exciting new records, and commercial radio just rejected it, totally."

Becker describes himself as a high school recluse. "I just loved radio, way more than TV. I don't know what other kids did after school, maybe played football or smoked pot, but I ran home and listened to the radio for hours and hours and hours." When he applied to Tufts, one of his main concerns was the on-campus station, WMFO. But as a freshman, he found himself too shy to volunteer. "I went to a couple station meetings, but everybody knew each other and I was too out of it."

Happily, as a sophomore, his next-door neighbors were involved. By the end of the year, he was music director and, he recalls laughingly, part of an embattled cabal, immediately tied up in a serious intrigue. His first priority at the station was to emphasize and add records such as those from the nearby Rounder Records label—a specialty label featuring bluegrass, blues, and a new record by George Thorogood and the Destroyers—to the playlist. "We were ten watts, no guidance, no faculty advisor, no money, and no one got paid, and whenever we asked the student council for money, they'd go, 'Well, don't you get free records?' For us to just be on the air was really an accomplishment. We went from trying to imitate an AOR station to making our own."

Tufts's station wasn't as punked out as larger Boston college stations (though, Becker recalls, there was a gradual shift: "'Less Dead—more Ultravox' was our rallying cry"). Instead, its main concern, Becker recalls, was remaining free-form. "That didn't mean a person could play anything they wanted," he notes, "it meant playing a broad mix of different kinds of music. That was the ongoing philosophical debate of the era. We'd get into these big arguments with the student body 'cause they thought the music we played was weird. There was always a lot of politicking and intrigue around the station management. Someone was always trying to boot the general manager and put someone else in his place. But our main point of argument was specialty programming. We had an all-Portuguese hour, which served a really large local Portuguese-speaking community, and the student body was always going, 'But no one here speaks Portuguese!' And we had an R & B show that was real alien to white middle-class kids, that played the worst kind of disco and 'quiet storm' stuff."

These kinds of debates are still going on at college stations around the country, though in these trying times, merely getting funding for something as anachronistic as radio is difficult enough without adding in the trials of keeping programming consistent.

* * *

By the time I started working at a college radio station in late 1983, R.E.M. had two and a half records out, the EP *Chronic Town* and two LPs, *Murmur* and *Reckoning*, on the independent label IRS. Me, I'd just crawled back from college, having just spent every penny I ever managed to scrape

---

* Becker would go on to publish the influential alternative music magazine *Option* from 1985 to 1998.

together on bumming around Europe, and now I had to live in my old bedroom and be perse-cuted by the specter of adulthood and feel incredibly embarrassed and inadequate because I did not have a life. (This is my mom: "Honey, have you ever considered technical writing? My friend's daughter has a degree in English from Stanford and she's making thirty grand at Apple!") Instead of something proper like that, I had a stupid job stage-managing *Peter Pan* at the local children's theater, putting on the Indians' makeup and making all the Lost Boys hush.

So just for fun, I volunteered at the college radio station, putting together their little program guide, and deejaying four-hour fill-in shifts beginning at midnight. But I was never a very good deejay. I was almost entirely ignorant of everything between the Buzzcocks and Howard Jones. I could play the Ruts, but Wire had passed me by. It was only newfound love of R.E.M. that made it all right that I didn't know any songs by Freur, that I didn't understand why people thought the Birthday Party were a good band, that I had never heard of the Minutemen. The only thing I knew about was circa 1978 punk rock—The Clash, the Jam, the Ramones, and the Undertones—plus a little Elvis Costello, the Pretenders, Television, and T Heads, stuff like that. I wasn't adventurous enough with the new stuff, plus I hated the sound of my own voice, I'd be OK for an hour or two, playing my favorites by Gang of Four and XTC, but the last ninety minutes would be sheer hell, searching among the C library, pulling out "Burning for You" by Blue Oyster Cult or something by Stiff Little Fingers, Then I'd get pretty darn slipshod, hurling the headphones down on old album covers, or throwing the longest song I knew, "Marquee Moon" by Television, on the turntable in order to finish up some novel or the new *Rolling Stone*.

That's what I was doing the day I had my great Amerindie revelation; hunching up on the deejay stool, monitor on loud, headphones off, seven or so minutes into the great masterpiece by Televi-sion. I was reading *Record* when I came across a quote from Peter Buck in an article about R.E.M. that completely turned around my way of thinking about rock. He said: "I guarantee that I have more records from 1983 in my collection than any other year. I mostly buy independent records by American bands, and there's a lot of good ones. All over the country we go, and every town has at least one really top-notch group. Maybe they're too uncompromising or maybe they're all not pretty boys, or maybe they're just weird. From Los Angeles, which has a million good bands now—Dream Syndicate, Rain Parade, Black Flag, Channel 3, Minutemen—to the Replacements and Hüsker Dü from Minneapolis, Charlie Burton and the Cutouts from Nebraska, Charlie Pickett and the Eggs from Ft. Lauderdale, Jason and the Scorchers from Nashville, there are good bands all over America doing exciting things, and no one really hears them."

Well, there I was, surrounded by all the records he mentioned. What would you have done? I leapt off my stool and shoved aside my boring old punk rock picks—a song by X Ray Spex, the new one by the Smiths ("Jeane"). I scrabbled frantically among the vinyl. Headphones on, I carefully re-cued. And the next minute I was on the air, reading the above-mentioned paragraph aloud, before bopping the button, before turning up the news. *Don't know what to do when pink turns to blue...*"

That winter Hüsker Dü played a benefit for the station in the cafeteria, and before I knew what had happened, I'd suddenly become an Amerindie devotee, shunning all things British, dreaming of a world full of kudzu and mimosa and people who shopped at the Piggly Wiggly. Then suddenly it was spring, and me and my friend Francesca, renamed Jane from Occupied Europe and Divine Discontent, began hosting an early-morning show once a week that was entirely devoted to the American underground. Midwest and South, the Northeast and Texas, portions of the country we'd never thought about in our California cloud, took on all this significance in our poor little geographically deprived brains. No longer did we long to go to Paris or Tahiti; instead we pined for Athens and Minneapolis and Boston, creating in our minds' eyes a new America where every small town contained exactly four cool people and one large garage. Elvis Costello went by the wayside in our fury to follow Buck's advice. We played everything he'd told us to and then some, ranging from across the map of the United States with exactly the same results he'd foretold. From Boston, Mission of Burma and the Lyres and the Neats. From the New York/New Jersey area, the Feelies and the Bongos and the Individuals and the Dbs. From Ohio, Pere Ubu and Human Switchboard. The Violent Femmes, from Milwaukee, Wisconsin. The Windbreakers, from Mississippi. Defenestration and the Embarrassment, both from Lawrence, Kansas. We played the Woods and Let's Active and the Dbs and the Young Fresh Fellows, the Wipers and the Fastbacks and the Pontiac Brothers and more. We played Savage Republic and Redd Kross and the Meat Puppets, Camper Van Beethoven and 10,000 Maniacs, TSOL, Minor Threat, Black Flag, Soul Asylum. We played everything that came our way as long as it was American, and Buck was right: it was all really, really good.

And so, girls and boys alike, from coast to coast, we were spoken to not by the band's members, but by its music, heard live, heard not in our brains but deep down in our souls. Listening to R.E.M. was like watching the landscape flicker by on a train from the inside, not the sexual rock'n'roll churning of Aerosmith, Jeff Beck, and Muddy Water's "Train Keep A Rolling,"* but the prismatic impressionism of "Driver 8" and everything that came before it: Television, the Velvet Underground, Tom Petty, the Byrds. "Come on aboard, I promise you, we won't hurt the horse," sang Stipe on a B side called "Bandwagon," and that welcoming gesture, that basic ethic of hospitality was what really distinguished R.E.M. from both its predecessors and its peers. Throughout the early eighties, other alternatively oriented artists talked incessantly about avoiding the bandwagon: busting trends, keeping clean, not selling out and just generally being hipper than the masses. R.E.M. just invited everyone to come along for the ride.

---

* Arnold most likely has in mind Tiny Bradshaw's version of "Train Kept A Rollin," covered most notably by the Yardbirds and Aerosmith.

36

"Roll Over Guitar Heroes; Synthesizers Are Here"

Jon Young

A paradigm, as philosopher and popular music studies scholar Theodore Gracyk explains, is "an exemplary case or body of work around which a community organizes its practices and beliefs."* In the case of rock music, paradigms can emerge through specific artists (the Beatles), recordings (the Ramones' first album), or even entire genres or styles (disco). At the time of its greatest popularity in the early 1980s, few paradigms rivaled the growing use of synthesizers associated with the rise of important new wave groups like Depeche Mode and Soft Cell, both of whom had jettisoned guitars and drums entirely in favor of the new technology. Exploring the attitudes and aesthetics of the new synthesizer bands, Jon Young's article for *Trouser Press*—one of the only magazines of the era with a specific new wave orientation—provides a thorough overview of the newly emerging style. As Young points out, synthesizers had already been established in the 1970s through such virtuoso progressive rock keyboardists as Keith Emerson and Rick Wakeman. The new generation of musicians that Young profiles, however, had generally renounced the "synthesizer solo" as an outmoded venue of expression, turning instead for inspiration to punk's DIY ethos and the more minimal sounds of creative experimentation of groups like Kraftwerk. Like many paradigms, the prominence of synthesizers in rock began to wane by the beginning of the 1990s, only to appear once more in the 2000s as various groups looked back to the 1980s as a point of musical inspiration.†

Not a day goes by when you don't press a button, whether it's for a cup of coffee or to turn on the stereo or video. People are so surrounded now by electronics, of course there's electronic music.

—David Ball of Soft Cell

When Devo first sputtered onto the scene in 1978 they were fond of announcing in interviews that eventually they would give up guitars and switch over to synthesizers exclusively. Devo's provocative, revolutionary idea, however, was already accepted in England: the Human League, Gary Numan, Orchestral Manoeuvres in the Dark and other daring souls had begun mounting projects that would disregard the guitar's long dominance in rock in favor of a box of wires that made strange sounds.

Of course, the synthesizer wasn't invented in 1978 to amuse Gary Numan. Throughout the '70s the instrument slowly infiltrated pop music as knowledge of its unique qualities spread. Such

---

* Theodore Gracyk, *I Wanna Be Me: Rock Music and the Politics of Identity* (Philadelphia: Temple University Press, 2001), p. 69.

† *Source:* Jon Young, "Roll Over Guitar Heroes; Synthesizers Are Here," *Trouser Press*, May 1982, pp. 22–27.

major creative forces as Todd Rundgren, Stevie Wonder and Brian Eno (with and without Roxy Music) successfully integrated synth into their songs and encouraged others to do the same—and Kraftwerk's whimsical robotics and Tangerine Dream's ethereal oozings were available long before the emergence of Britain's latest chart sensations.

But today everyone from Abba to Public Image Ltd. uses synthesizers as a matter of course. So what actually did change?

One very significant thing. Pure, unadulterated synthesizer sound now appears on (more or less) conventional pop tunes. The instrument doesn't call attention to itself, as it had with Kraftwerk and their ilk; machine and song now meet on equal terms. In Britain, at least, the public has signaled its approval. Current UK charts are studded with synthesizer bands like Soft Cell, Human League and Orchestral Manoeuvres in the Dark, as well as groups heavily dependent on the instrument, such as Ultravox (the link between Roxy Music and Gary Numan).

What is a synthesizer, anyway? Guitars, drums and so forth are easy to comprehend, but these newfangled contraptions seem forbiddingly alien. Never fear. Scott Simon of Our Daughter's Wedding, a New York City trio that is one of the American alternatives to UK synth bands, offers a layman's explanation of how the thing works.

"The sound of a synth comes from a noise generator, which is an oscillator that puts out a signal with a wave shape. That's sent via circuit boards through filters that change the wave shape and pitch of the initial signal. *That* goes into a triggering system—the keyboard. A few different things happen to the signal as it goes through the process. What makes a synth complicated is what happens between the oscillator and keyboard."

Those options, Simon goes on to explain, include being able to store exact sounds in the synth's memory bank (a dead giveaway that computers are involved), the ability to change the shape or pitch of a note, and flexibility in setting the decay, or rate at which a note drops off. The sequencer, beloved to Who fans after *Who's Next*, "stores notes and puts them out the same way they're put in. You can alter their shape and speed at which they're sent back out, but the notes will always be in the order you put them in."

OK? Technology buffs will find more sophisticated insights into the workings of this modern electronic wonder in next month's TP.*

Daniel Miller is regarded as an elder statesman of the British synth-pop scene. In 1978 he inaugurated his Mute Records with a single by the Normal ("TVOD"/"Warm Leatherette"), which was actually Miller working alone. He went on to release an album of novelty synthesizer tunes as the Silicon Teens, and in 1981 signed and produced Depeche Mode, now a major UK chart success. He spoke to TP while in New York to mix sound on Depeche Mode's US tour.

Miller's involvement with the instrument is typical of current synthesizer musicians. "I was a fan of German bands [Can, Faust, Neu, Tangerine Dream] in the early '70s and I thought a lot about the possibilities of electronic music for someone like me, who's not a very good musician but likes playing music. I used to play guitar in really bad groups when I was at school. It was frustrating—I knew what I wanted to play but I practiced and still couldn't." Instead Miller saved up his money and purchased a synthesizer and tape recorder around the time the punk movement exploded.

Others experienced similar dissatisfaction. Scott Ryser of San Francisco's Units recalls, "I'd played in rock bands before and I got really sick of the people, of the whole scene." Vocalist Keith Silva of Our Daughter's Wedding was bored with stereotypic new wave bands when he took up the synth. Andy McCluskey of Orchestral Manoeuvres remembers that he and Paul Humphreys simply

---

* Dominic Milano, "Man Meets Machine: The Whys and Wherefores of Synthesizers," *Trouser Press*, June 1982, 31–33.

tired of writing parts for guitars and drums in their Liverpool band: "We wanted to do our songs exactly how we wanted to do them—just myself, Paul and a tape recorder."

Punk galvanized these malcontents. Anyone who suffered through the long reign of flashy progressive bands like Yes or Emerson, Lake and Palmer may find the connection between oft-overused synthesizers and punk's refreshing simplicity hard to grasp. However, David Ball of Soft Cell feels that "synthesizer bands now have got a lot to thank the punk bands of '77 for. The punk thing gave anybody a chance to get up and do it. It didn't matter how well you played as long as it was fast and energetic and exciting."

"I was very interested in punk as it was nonelitist," Daniel Miller says. "It started me doing my own things. I heard a link between the Ramones and Kraftwerk. If you analyze the music they're quite similar."

OMD's Andy McCluskey makes the connection more explicit. "In some ways it's quite strange that synthesizers were so hated in the punk era. They're the ideal punk instrument if you believe in the ethic of 'anybody can do it.' Someone who's been playing synth for 10 minutes can easily sound as good as someone who's been playing for years, provided the ideas are there.

"I think a lot of English bands would say one reason they use synths is because they're easy to play."

You'll get no argument on that count from the overly modest youths in Depeche Mode. Andy Fletcher looks back on their early days two years ago and remarks, "We couldn't play hardly at all then; we can't play very well now." Not that they undervalue their work. Singer Dave Gahan notes, "In pop music nowadays you don't need technical ability, you need ideas and the ability to write songs. That's the main thing."

Easy access to synthesizers has given them a bad image as a stale, monotonous instrument. Since practically anybody can play one, a lot of dullards have gotten involved. Andy Fletcher observes that "because you can get such good sounds on the synth you can get away with murder. You can have an awful song and make it sound quite good. Quite a lot of bands do that."

Some "sophisticated" musicians also don't understand how their own equipment works. "We're not Kraftwerk," Andy Fletcher says, acknowledging the obvious. "Kraftwerk built their own computers and keyboards." Dave Gahan adds, "If someone gave us a computer and said, 'Use that,' we wouldn't know what to do with it."

Andy McCluskey laughs at the situation. "We and a lot of other bands who use synths have this technological image that few bands actually deserve. For Kraftwerk, it's a total ideology; it's the way they work. The fact that they use synths is important to them. But as for a lot of new English bands—we don't understand how the hell the things work! Paul [Humphreys] did study electronics, so he knew the principles behind it, but I had to learn by hit and miss."

Those not deterred (or bothered) by electronic complexity find other attractions in addition to the synthesizer's pleasing sound and ready availability. Small, cheap synthesizers used by a beginning band are invariably more mobile than the guitars and cumbersome amplifiers necessary for even the most rudimentary rock bands. (A synthesizer can be plugged directly into the house p.a.) Our Daughter's Wedding boasts that at first their synths were carry-on luggage on airplanes.

Depeche Mode's Dave Gahan says the logistics of getting to London gigs from their home town of Basildon 25 miles away was a determining factor in their switch from guitars to synths. Andy Fletcher adds "Until about six months ago we used to go to and from gigs by train. The audience would see us play and they'd see us on the train afterward with our instruments!"

The band also raves about how easy it is to conduct a pre-show soundcheck. Once Depeche Mode's three players tune their instruments to a synthetic drum tape it's all systems go. Andy Fletcher says the process usually takes no more than an hour. By comparison, he notes, "When we supported Ultravox at the Rainbow, they were soundchecking for about five hours."

"I couldn't stand being in that sort of group." Soft Cell's David Ball cringes at the thought of playing in a "traditional" rock band. The instrumental half of Soft Cell (Marc Almond furnishes vocals) usually needs no more than an hour to get ready for a show.

Both Depeche Mode and Our Daughter's Wedding held early practice sessions in small suburban bedrooms. Since they didn't need amps, it was a simple matter to plug headphones directly into the synth and commence creating. (And no nasty noises to annoy Mom!) By the same token, Depeche Mode doesn't even use the big room in a recording studio; the band just plugs directly into the control room console. How's that for simple?

All well and good, you say, but what about the sound of synthesizers? Anyone who's been exposed to Gary Numan's whiny drone [*Singing or playing?—Ed.*] for more than three minutes may well conclude the synthesizer is an evil menace to rock, designed to eviscerate all feeling.

Rachel Webber, who shares the Units' synthesizer duties with Scott Ryser, probably speaks for the wary American public when she voices reservations about the current crop of British synth bands. "In general—'cause I like Orchestral Manoeuvres—those bands can get pretty similar. I don't like the Gary Numan type of scene."

Scott Ryser adds, "It doesn't seem like there's much depth to it. I like it for dancing, but it's hard to take very seriously."

Webber feels a lot of groups "just get a basic sound they know will work. Those cute little squiggles do work, as far as what people like, but it's not very challenging."

Don't blame the poor old inanimate synthesizer for appearing on a lot of boring records. Blame the musicians. Layne Rico of Our Daughter's Wedding observes, "A lot of people are against synthesizers and say, 'All you have to do is press a button'—which in a way is quite true. It's all down to how each individual plays the instrument."

Bandmate Keith Silva adds, "Some people use only what's easy to get out of it, but if you search there's a lot you can do."

The "new romantic" movement, with its watery dress-up ideology and simplistic dance motifs, has probably done a lot recently to give synths a bad name. Tedious stuff is being ground out with the aid of synthesizers—but what else is new? There are plenty of mediocre guitarists too.

Andy McCluskey recognizes the dangers. "Over the last 20 years or so kids who've wanted to be musicians have decided, 'I've gotta be a guitar player. I wanna be an axe hero.' They'd adopted what were new ways of playing at the time, but because they were copying they'd just start adopting clichés.

"In the last 10 years it seems like there have been very few new methods of playing guitar. Everybody's just trotting out the same old clichés, pulling the same faces, striking the same old rock 'n' roll poses.

"The synthesizer now has a history and there are already clichéd ways of playing it. You can sound like Gary Numan on a Polymoog. You can do lead solos like Billy Currie on an ARP Odyssey—that wailing, no-melody type of riffing. There are popular guidelines for playing synthesizer laid down by people who were around before.

"Recently I talked to a young guy from Liverpool who played us a demo. I asked him why it was so unmelodic and discordant; he refused to play melodies. He said, 'The trouble is, every time you play a melody on synthesizer you sound like Orchestral Manoeuvres!'"

McCluskey laughs, no doubt thankful he got there first.

Despite his reservations, McCluskey does not share Rachel Webber's skepticism about the current wave of English synth-pop groups. He sees great diversity among the bands, and frowns on efforts to lump them all together because of their choice of weapon.

"People from outside Britain see all bands that play synthesizer as part and parcel of the same movement or ideology, which is far from the truth. The music we and other bands make, and the reasons behind the making of the music, are actually quite different from each other.

"A few examples: That Human League plays synthesizers is almost unimportant. It's pop music for the '80s. The lyrical content is very traditional: 'I love you and you love me' or 'I love you and you don't love me.' When we write a love song it tends to be more offbeat. Depeche Mode is a very young thing, the sound of young boys. The lyrical content of Heaven 17 is fairly radical."

Some synth bands try to minimize the mechanical aspect of their electronic instruments. Keith Silva says that Our Daughter's Wedding avoids sequencers whenever possible. "To me it makes the music a little too sterile. I prefer the actual physical attack of playing a note yourself. I think the feeling actually changes when you use sequencers."

The rhythm section in a synth group tends to be its weakest component. Those tinny, ticking rhythm boxes used to sound pretty feeble coming out of Lowery organs; their descendants don't fare much better trying to drive a loud battalion of synths. Depeche Mode deals with the problem by taping all their percussion one element at a time. The sight of a big Teac reel-to-reel machine onstage where a drummer should be comes as a shock, but the output is, Dave Gahan says, "really clear and punchy." The band's tape consists of a bass drum sound from Daniel Miller's old ARP, the snare drum sound of a rhythm machine, and various sequencer bits.

On their five-song EP, *Digital Cowboy*, Our Daughter's Wedding used ace drummer Simon Phillips instead of a rhythm box. Onstage Layne Rico augments the mechanical beat with a Synare synth, which can produce either percussive or melodic tones.* The Units recently enlisted a percussionist and a drummer. On *Architecture & Morality* Orchestral Manoeuvres combine acoustic and synthetic drums for a hybrid sound.

Soft Cell and producer Mike Thorne concocted an intriguing approach for *Non-Stop Erotic Cabaret.* As David Ball reveals, "We took the output of an electronic snare and put it through a little speaker, which we laid face down on top of a snare drum; then we miked that up. So we were getting a real snare sound, but it was triggered by a drum machine. I think it gives a slightly richer sound."

There's no reason for any two synthesizer bands to sound alike if they've got talent and aren't too rigid in their outlook. Paul Humphreys believes synths are "*the* most versatile instrument—but there are things you can't do on a synthesizer, like get the power and rawness of strumming a guitar." That's why *Architecture & Morality* features OMD's first use of guitar, as well as horns, piano and saxes.

"Very often the mainstay of a song is not synthesizers but sound ideas in general," Andy McCluskey observes. OMD's recent single "Joan of Arc" employs a glockenspiel "which gives it springiness, and I did two different vocal takes. One has all these little voices—I'm trying to follow a synthesizer I'd set on D. On the other one I sing high-pitched, almost falsetto harmonies."

"Souvenir" resulted from equally ingenious procedures. Humphreys took tapes of an eight-member church choir singing scales and made up the tape loops that give the song its wobbly, shifting quality.

In other words, smile when you call Orchestral Manoeuvres a synth band. "They're not our number one priority," McCluskey states. "We're not on some electronic crusade; we're not interested in the synthesizer as an image. We have a load of them onstage because that's what we play. We just use them as a means to an end."

A close look reveals that, in one sense, most of these bands aren't all that different from traditional rock groups. Our Daughter's Wedding, the Units and Depeche Mode all dole out responsibilities for melody, bass and percussion to different members, just like the good old days. In most cases the material could be rearranged to accommodate implements of yore like guitars and drums. Our Daughter's Wedding recalls Sparks. Orchestral Manoeuvres sometimes suggests a smarter Beach

---

* The Synare was an electronic drum that consisted of synthesizer pads one played with sticks.

Boys. Soft Cell's massive UK smash "Tainted Love" was originally an obscure '60s soul recording by Gloria Jones.

"We've just worked up a James Brown tune ['It's a Man's, Man's, Man's World'], so I guess a guitar band could work one of ours up," the Units' Ryser says. (He originally wanted the Units to be "real brash and hard, the Iggy Pop of synthesizers.") David Ball would like to hear an orchestra tackle one of Soft Cell's songs.

Keith Silva even goes so far as to label Our Daughter's Wedding a rock band: "We're all keyboards but we still feel we're a rock band. It takes people a while to figure out, 'Hey, these guys just play good music and it rocks.'" Layne Rico adds that "'Lawnchairs' or 'Target for Life' could be done by Van Halen or any other band. It's just music."

If you were looking forward to a bloody shoot-out in the charts between guitars and synths, forget it. "There's room for everything," David Ball remarks. "Synthesizers are just another option. If people want to play guitars, that's great. You should be able to play any instrument you like."

Rachel Webber says, "There's supposed to be this big rivalry between synthesizers and guitars, which I think is pretty weird. I don't think people are sick of guitars, I just think they're looking for something different. If anything, guitars have gotten stronger."

The search for alternative means of expression may eventually lure synth bands into trying out guitars. Depeche Mode has already considered such a move.

"I think the guitar is a beautiful instrument," Layne Rico of Our Daughter's Wedding says. "When everybody thinks we're going too electronic, we might do a big circle and come onstage with guitars."

Made possible by the onward march of science, synthesizers and synthesizer bands will continue to change with the technology. Layne Rico is anxiously awaiting a set of hexagonal electronic drums. "They're made of the same material as football players' helmets. Playing them is like hitting a drumstick against a barstool. These drums are only about two inches deep; they look like hexagonal pie pans. We'll finally be able to break away from the rhythm machines a bit."

On a less sophisticated front, basic synthesizers have dropped in price so much that anyone with $200 can become at least a fledgling artiste.

Soon a generation that grew up on Gary Numan and the Human League, rather than the Stones and Led Zeppelin, will be ready to enter the musical job market. Andy Fletcher knows seven- and eight-year-olds who can play melodic lines on the synth; tomorrow's musicians will test the instrument's capabilities without treating it as a futuristic aberration. Sooner or later a bona fide synthesizer genius steeped in the early electronic bands may come along and revolutionize the field, just as Jimi Hendrix absorbed the blues and early rock guitar styles before emerging as staggeringly original.

David Ball has no doubts that synthesizers have arrived. "When electric guitars were first used I'm sure people were saying, 'Do you really think this is gonna last?' Electric guitars have been with us for years now, and I think it will be the same with synths. People have accepted it as a conventional instrument rather than a freak of science."

"I think synthesizers are here to stay," Daniel Miller sums up, "regardless of what they're playing now. A lot of things I thought were gonna happen a few years ago have happened.

"England has a basis for synthesizer music. I don't think it's a fad, because it's lasted. Since Gary Numan there's always been synthesizer music in the English charts. It's gone through all the different fashions and it's still there.

"The synthesizer's such a flexible instrument. You can play anything on it. It's not a kind of music; it's a way of making music."

Synthesizers now have the potential to become the next classic rock 'n' roll instrument. Keep your ears open. Who knows—in a few years the sequel to this piece may even star you!

37

"The MTV Aesthetic"

RICHARD GEHR

On August 1, 1981, when the cable network MTV—Music Television—aired its first broadcast in select U.S. markets, cable television was for many homes a luxury item. Radio remained the most crucial medium in "breaking a hit" and the music video was still a relatively unknown quantity. Within two years, however, MTV and cable had expanded nationally and become a driving force within the industry, helping to push various artists and their songs up the charts. Richard Gehr's 1983 article "The MTV aesthetic," which originally appeared in *Film Comment* as part of a larger overview of the MTV phenomenon, offers a rather cynical take on the new video style. Given that Gehr is writing for a journal of film criticism, it is perhaps to be expected that he relates MTV to cinematic conventions and models, an approach that others would later adopt as well.* Gehr also stresses the similarities between music videos and the standard language of advertising, another theme that would become common in the analysis of MTV. Most of all, he emphasizes the "discontinuity and disjunction" of the video, often seen as a dizzying melange of depthless surfaces and signs, as one of MTV's most typical traits. Without defining it as such, Gehr essentially describes the music video aesthetic in the terms of postmodernism, a label that would become attached to MTV with growing frequency throughout the 1980s. On the whole, how many of the tropes and techniques that Gehr observes are still common in music videos today?†

One of the reasons why rock has been the most vital form of popular culture in the last twenty years is that it has expressed so clearly the struggle involved: rock has been used simultaneously as a form of self-indulgence and individual escape and as a source of solidarity and active dissatisfaction.

—**Simon Frith in** *Sound Effects*

The myth of the rock "brotherhood," although long dispelled in the minds of all but the most voracious Grateful Dead fans, is laid to rest once and for all with the rise of MTV. The (idealized) reciprocity that was presumed to exist between audience and performer has evaporated, or at least become as cynical a communication as occurs with any Vegas glitterpuss and his audience. Taking MTV as a measure of rock's lowest common denominator proves that rock has lost the "struggle." The only dissatisfactions expressed over the network concern the inability to achieve satisfaction or individual escape. Time is no longer on Mick Jagger's (or anyone else's) side, if the Rolling Stones' videos

---

* See especially E. Ann Kaplan, *Music Television, Postmodernism & Consumer Culture* (London: Metheun, 1987).

† *Source:* Richard Gehr, "The MTV Aesthetic," *Film Comment*, July/August 1983, pp. 37–40.

are any indication. And the poor boy whose only recourse once was to play in a rock 'n' roll band is now apparently doomed to careering as a second-rate actor in a two-dimensional showcase.

The increasing influence of MTV as a marketing tool and necessary evil can well be compared to the way in which cinema supplanted theater as a form of popular entertainment in the early part of this century. Cinema did indeed change the way audiences perceived themselves in relation to entertainers: the direct communality between performer and audience was replaced in the cinema by a different form of communality (most films are still watched in crowded rooms). Now comes a new, more crucial change. MTV is not only altering relationships between spectators and musicians in live performances, it is also changing the way in which we hear records and radio.

MTV is a self-reflecting medium for narcissists of a limited age bracket (12- to 34-year olds). The symbiotic relationship that exists between audience and performer (he's one of us, with our desires and frustrations) with MTV becomes one-sided. Every image is directed, specifically and utterly, *at* the viewer.

The beginning of the Rolling Stones' *Going to a Go-Go* video consists of concert footage even worse than that found in Hal Ashby's *Let's Spend the Night Together*. Jagger struts his ambisexual, ambiracial body about the perimeter of an extended stage in a large, open arena. The camera dwells on his performance, with only a few of those occasional glimpses we have come to savor of the very bored Bill Wyman and Charlie Watts (who in the *Start Me Up* vid look even *more* weary of the whole charade, if that is possible). The concert footage is intercut with shots of a young woman's legs entering a house aglow with golden light. Then Jagger, rather menacingly, enters the house and ends up in a screening room where the continuing concert footage, still mainly of him, is being projected. He observes himself with obvious enjoyment, a pleasure enhanced by the presence of others in the room participating in an orgy.

The cooler, suaver Brian Ferry, however, watches himself with no movement whatsoever in Roxy Music's video of *The Main Thing*. The relationship of star to group is different with Roxy Music, in that a core trio (Ferry, guitarist Phil Manzanera, and saxophonist Andy Mackay) is all that remains of the group's original, six-man line-up in this video. This may be misleading, but it's economical. In *The Main Thing* the trio performs in front of a colorful, hazy background; then the camera pulls back to reveal Ferry, arm draped across a chair, in a screening room, again watching his own performance.

These two MTVideos epitomize the drift toward absolute self-consciousness by the star; the viewer is left only with a means of connecting to an elaborate self-obsession. First: the rock star is so impressed with his own performance, he must impress us with the seriousness of the distance between his stage persona and the "real" Jagger and Ferry. Second: rather than identifying with the camera, as when watching a movie, the audience identifies with the star watching himself. We become Jagger watching *Jagger*, Ferry watching *Ferry*; that is, we don't identify with the performance or the performer.

On the other hand, I think the most effective performance you'll find on MTV is Prince's straightforward rendition of "Little Red Corvette," a powerful, economical synopsis of the most distinctive elements of Prince's performing repertoire. The febrile young black lip synchs a pretty good rock ditty with self-assured conviction of his place in a rock pantheon that, on radio and especially on MTV, is reserved almost exclusively for white performers. Prince uses no particularly fancy stage design, symbolic imagery, or narrative crutch (this ain't no "concept" video), yet manages to equate himself with such as Jagger and Ferry.

Other than Prince, the most "genuine," least assuming acts on MTV are the numerous heavy metal groups (Def Leppard, the Scorpions, Blackfoot, April Wine) that populate the network. These acts usually align themselves with their audience on the levels of sexuality, power, and aggression, manifesting a brute force that would be nowhere as seductive if it were merely tethered to representational imagery.

The rest of rock-vid land consists of subtler come-ons, designed to tart up the music with imagery calculated to evoke the appropriate emotions. Apart from "rockumentaries" (in which, we note, audiences are hardly ever shown), MTV segments are either narrative "concepts," free-form potpourris of manipulated imagery, or straight in-studio performances.

Concept videos—sung stories—consist of one of more members of a group singing and playing as part of, or exterior to, a narrative that is attached to the song. The narrative is rarely unadulterated; that is, there are almost always moments in the three-minute fantasy when the band just plays (lip-synchs). The story may or may not have anything to do with the song's lyric content; indeed, it usually doesn't. What's important is the imagery associated with the group, the image the members wish to project. Greg Kihn's *Jeopardy*, Joe Jackson's *Steppin' Out*, Rick Springfield's *An Affair of the Heart*, ZZ Top's *Gimme All Your Lovin'*, and many others spin a small tale that has little if anything to do with content.

What these videos do is to transform a musician into a fictional character. The musical careers of Elvis Presley, Frank Sinatra, and the Beatles all changed radically once they became film stars. The Monkees, on the other hand, were created for television and were *always* perceived in that context.

An example of the way image is *added* to music is found in Kihn's popular *Jeopardy* video. Kihn himself is an unimpressive musician and actor, but this video is loaded with imagery guaranteed to touch the quivering adolescent heart of any man associating marriage with a castrating loss of liberty, or, for that matter, with the inevitable tragedy of growing up. Kihn plays a reluctant groom who develops cold feet at the altar and hallucinates that the entire bridal party, fiancée included, has turned into *Night of the Living Dead* ghouls anxious to add him to their ranks by way of holy matrimony.

Kihn is a clean-looking, ordinary Joe who suffers the smug blandishments of his future in-laws and the mocking of his pals on the way to the altar. While taking his vows he imagines that the older married couples in attendance are shackled together by both handcuffs (playing on teenagers' fear of police) and flesh. Once the ring is placed on the bride's finger, she turns into a rotting corpse and the wedding members become ghouls. As Kihn escapes from the chapel, he's grabbed back by a tinfoil monster (the "ironic" low-budget touch) and pretends to play guitar using a piece of pew with which he has killed the tinfoil (the obligatory connection with performance). His escape from the chapel dissolves into a home-movie of the "real" exit of bride and groom being shown in a room inhabited by the decayed corpses of the young marrieds. The video cuts back to the groom dressing for the wedding (this has been a fantasy), who then grabs a champagne bottle and vamooses out the church's back door. As he jumps into his car, the bride-not-to-be runs down the church steps and joins him in redemptive freedom from the ritual transformation into adulthood. David Cronenberg Meets *The Graduate*.

Imbedded in this one mundane video are numerous elements that can be repeatedly observed in dozens of others (death, fear of the loss of freedom, pursuit by authority figures, beautiful women), even though it lacks the surreal, high-gloss sheen of such videos as Joe Jackson's. One video maker (Richard Casey) claims that the haste and informality of production prevents videos from being compared with commercials. I'd argue the opposite: that because videos are relatively spontaneous reflections of what's on the mind of the performer—of how he wishes to be represented—they display a revealing free-association of the way the performer perceives himself, his audience, and the relationship between the two.

David Bowie's *Let's Dance*, which he co-directed, was made more or less during the course of a single day in Australia. The rapidity of its production may therefore account for the manner in which it resembles a synthesis of Roeg's *Walkabout* and *The Man Who Fell to Earth*, both in look and content. Once again, the video's concept (a comment on discrimination against aborigines) has nothing to do with the song's lyrics (Bowie wants us to dance), and neither has anything to do with the subject of the video (Bowie relaying his healthy Aryan liberality).

Bowie at least makes a stab at investing more than adolescent angst into his work. Since videos are now more or less obligatory for success in the marketplace, what we are now seeing is the strategy of the refined sell-out. MTV is, after all, jointly owned by Warner Communications and American Express, and it's amusing to see such one-time would-be iconoclasts as Pete Townsend and Kevin Rowland shuckin' and jivin' for the network. In fact, some viewers have reported a diminished respect for a few of their favorite artists after having observed the manner in which they've seen fit to despoil themselves. Dexy's Midnight Runners, ABC, Bowie, and the Clash come to mind.

If any one trope sums up the rhetoric of rock video, it's that of discontinuity and disjunction. Gestures, actions, and intentions are nearly always divorced from a systematic context, which is why so many rock-vids look as if they were made in homage to Jean Cocteau. In the previous history of music on film, from Cab Calloway shorts through Richard Lester's *Ring a Ding Rhythm* (1962; a.k.a. *It's Trad Dad*) and up to and including *Flashdance*, music was always comfortably framed by a story. MTV is a context that seems to abolish context, removing the freedom of the record listener to edit his or her experience, or the radio listener to imagine the music as playing some indirect part of his life. Michael Jackson's song "Billie Jean," for example, tells the story of a woman who is accusing the singer of paternity. The *Billie Jean* video features a magical, godlike Jackson being followed by a detective in scenes that refer to Jackson rather than the song. Another kind of discontinuity, dishonest as to means of production, is found in Prince's videos in which he is seen performing with a band. The music that is heard, however, was recorded by Prince alone.

The imagery of the typical rock-vid is usually generated by a single word or phrase: Bowie's *Let's Dance* centers around the aborigine couple's relationship to a symbolic pair of red shoes, stemming from the lyric "Put on your red shoes and dance the blues." In *Billie Jean* the word "eyes" in the song signals a cut to—what else?—Michael Jackson's eyes. And in Blue Oyster Cult's *Burnin' for You* vid, the group performs the song while a car burns in the background. Such abject literalness makes the music and imagery swerve even further apart, once again signalling through a form of free-association the simplicity of the intentions of all concerned. Martin Fry of ABC sings "I hope and I pray that maybe someday you'll walk in the room with my heart," evoking nothing more from the director than a cut to a woman holding a little plastic heart. At moments like these one realizes how *guarded* reasonably intelligent artists can be when forced to generate imagery through this medium and how lame their concessions turn out.

It sometimes appears on MTV that each group is handed a menu of images and is then told to pick five to be used in their video. The list includes beautiful Caucasian women, cars, high-heeled shoes, hotel rooms, fog, leather, snow, detectives, and beautiful Oriental women—the comic-book fantasies of adolescent males and James Bond fans. Many of the same elements are found in *film noir*; rock-vids, like *film noir*'s *femmes fatales*, are literally eye-catchers. They seduce the gaze as if to fill a lack in the viewer, his unspoken desires. They play to, and play with, his isolation, frustration, and loneliness.

Always heavily cosmeticized, the MTV women are made, not born, in the image of rock 'n' roll men. In Eddie Money's *Think I'm in Love*, the woman turns against Money, who is portrayed as a vampire: she is herself one. Men are constantly being deserted by women on MTV, which makes Daryl Hall lonely and miserable in Hall and Oates's *One on One* video, and leaves other men with the blues in the Scorpions' *No One Like You* and Dave Edmunds's *Slippin' Away*. But who cares?

Three minutes of angst will pass and then we're on to something else. The song existed before the video; the emotion is already cold and once more removed. Any emotional sympathy the listener might experience from hearing the music over the radio is dissipated by the spurious imagery that is made to represent the song's meaning.

Jean-Pierre Oudart once wrote of the "suturing" of viewer to narrative that takes place as the camera cuts from face to face in a filmed conversation. In this way the spectator is lured into the story, identifies with the camera, and participates in the cinematic web. No such intercutting takes place in rock videos, because there is no narrative as such within which the viewer can "find" himself. The suturing of a rock-vid stitches the evocative imagery first to the performer, then to the song being performed and to the album from which the song is derived, next to the record company that produces and markets the record, and finally to the world of entertainment and leisure activity as a whole. As the identity of the performer is transferred from actor to musician, he or she is ultimately revealed as pure commodity, no longer as a participant in a collective struggle, but merely a diversion.

Another variety of rock video consists of a continuous stream-of-self-consciousness imagery that accompanies the music without benefit of narrative concept. Two examples from this phylum are Bow Wow Wow's *Do You Wanna Hold Me?* and Wall of Voodoo's *Mexican Radio*. Both of these employ a grab bag of backdrops, costumes, multi-tracked imagery, and auxiliary watchables to beef up the song.

While both of these look as if they might have been cranked out during the course of an afternoon, the former displays rather more respect for the audience than the latter. Bow Wow Wow takes its visual cues from a couple of lines in the song about hanging out in California, "Where Mickey Mouse is as big as a house." Lead singer Annabella Lwin is costumed in various versions of Disneylandia (Peter Pan, Pinocchio, a Mouseketeer), and the other band members wear funny clothes, too. Cartoon images creep across close-ups of the musicians cramming junk food into their mouths, and the whole thing is punctuated by insert shots of equally unappetizing food products. It's about Consumption, get it? The viewer can decide for his or her self which is worse, consumption as portrayed here or the consumption of this video and the record it advertises.

Wall of Voodoo also uses the notion of food spoiling in *Mexican Radio*. Here the group ridicules Mexico with stereotypically (hip) racist imagery that includes bullfights, body shops, and Mexican food, all of which are not dwelled upon, but subliminally make their appearance through rapid insertions.

Although rapid cutting and a host of other camera and editing techniques are used during the relatively short length of time the average rock-vid lasts (usually about three minutes), they're not as similar to commercials (although that is in fact what they are) as you might expect. First, commercials are anything but discontinuous. The combination of sound and image is meticulously and expensively calculated to subliminally seduce the consumer into purchasing action. Rock-vids, on the other hand, are only subconsciously calculating, are relatively inexpensive, and probably don't do nearly as effective a job. What is true, however, is that the same kind of imagery used to sell a man a car is also frequently employed to sell a teenager a record: speed, power, girls, and wealth. Both Budweiser and Miller beers currently run commercials on MTV that in almost every way resemble rock videos.

As with most television, MTV usually serves as electronic wallpaper. MTV stands for *Music Television*, but in actual practice it often becomes the opposite when the sound is turned down and it's just a moving painting in the corner of a room, saying nothing until a song comes on that the viewer cares for. When the picture is erased from MTV, what remains is an AOR radio station complete with commercials and intermittent music news from deejays operating at a low level of commitment.

We refer to most TV as "commercial" television; actually only MTV can lay claim to that title because that is precisely what it is: ersatz commercials punctuated with "real" ones. Not only is it changing the way we listen to music, it is also beginning to change the way we perceive movies; the musical numbers from both *Flashdance* and the upcoming sequel to *Saturday Night Fever, Stayin' Alive*, were both filmed with the translation of musical numbers to MTV in mind. See the video, buy the album, see the movie—first in fragmented form, then as a whole.

There's nothing inherently evil in MTV; it's no better or worse than any aspect of the record industry has ever been. Nor is it without interest; it is simply being used to hype vinyl and little else. In its almost three years of existence, it is only just solidifying into a commercial force to be reckoned with. One of the more unfortunate consequences will be that a performer's success will probably depend on his or her appearance and acting ability more than ever before. On the other hand, we can only hope that the struggle against rock's corruption that has always been waged by a nervy handful will continue on this front, and that MTV will be considered a challenge to be subverted if it is not to remain a few hazy images, a fashion show, a synthesized beat.

38

Post-Punk's "Radical Dance Fictions"

SIMON REYNOLDS

Before beginning his career as an influential journalist for *Melody Maker* and other publications, Simon Reynolds first ventured into music criticism in the mid-1980s via the pages of his independent fanzine *Monitor*. In his 1985 article "Radical Dance Fictions," Reynolds examines the British post-punk movement of the early 1980s, a topic to which he would return in his 2005 book *Rip It Up and Start Again* (London: Faber and Faber). Unlike the punk explosion of 1976 and 1977, which had been firmly situated in the rhetoric of garage bands and pub rockers, the post-punk period of 1978–1984 saw an experimental turn to styles such as funk, disco, dub, and soul for inspiration. Focusing on a number of then-current bands, Reynolds addresses two dimensions in particular: the allure that blackness and black dance music holds for white post-punk musicians, and the ways in which the music's appropriations (and misappropriations) figure into the movement's radical, politicized agenda. Throughout, he weaves his critique with allusions to Norman Mailer's exoticized "White Negro," the "menace" of black funk, and a consideration of musical semiotics.* As with many discussions of race and rock music, it is interesting to see how notions of authenticity ultimately play into Reynolds's analysis, and to what degree he is critical of post-punk's practices.†

1985, and a gaggle of groups plough a well-furrowed, increasingly barren field. Its perimeters are staked out by Cabaret Voltaire, Shriekback, Clock DVA, 23 Skidoo, A Certain Ratio, and somewhere beneath it all lurks the notion that there is something radical about black dance music, that it is the appropriate base for experiments and polemic. 1985, and with Chakk's lazy talk of a "spirit of funk," perhaps it's time to delve into the history of this new orthodoxy. Gradually, late in the 70s, funk was valorised, it became a positive term, somehow more progressive than rock. Part of the reason for this minor revolution is bound up with the 'cultural economy' of youth music—the structural requirement for new input; not simply, simplistically, in order to maintain profits and preserve careers, but because the self-respect of musicians and journalists depends on their self-conception of themselves as, respectively, innovators and discoverers. And because youth culture, and all the hopes invested in its myths, depends on a constancy of rhetorical efflorescence, of a sense of happening(s), of revolution(s). With punk dying, there was a sense that rock was archaic and debased. At similar moments of entropy, black music has functioned as an alluring Outside for white bohemian youth—the old notion of the Black as Other, incarnation of sexuality and the forbidden. Alienated white youth has traditionally aspired to "white nigger" status, desiring both the

---

* Norman Mailer, "The White Negro: Superficial Reflections on the Hipster," *Dissent* 4, no. 3 (Summer 1957), 276–93.
† *Source:* Simon Reynolds, "Radical Dance Fictions," *Monitor*, no. 2 (1985), pp. 2–5.

oppression/exclusion blacks suffer, and their symbolic 'resolution' of their problems, their victory over environment, in style and music. But whereas, previously, identification with geographically proximate black subcultures was the influence, in the late 70s there was a dissemination of certain ideas of blackness through the media, a borrowing from the files of pop history. Rhythm/roots/radicalism—this cluster's perceived identity, was what lay behind the post-punk drive for a reinfusion of blackness. 'Funk' became a cipher, something to be cited or claimed; but crucially, it was an empty term into which varying kinds of power were read (in the face of rock's impotence).

For an element in the "post-punk vanguard"—overtly political groups like Gang of Four, Au Pairs, Pop Group—the clenched feel of funk, its tightness, was the appropriate rhythmic base for militancy and commitment and rigour of thought. The idea of funk as menace, probably stemmed from the idea of "bad-ass" as personified by James Brown, Sly Stone, George Clinton et al. Brown's music, in particular, has functioned as a crucial bridge between trad white rock culture and 80s disco—he weaned white ears onto other, softer, blacker music. Brown's peculiar appeal and influence lie in his exaggeration of r'n'b into a pure, precise pulse of male assertion/sexuality, a surface music of arid, cold textures, fleshless and soulless. (Which was why JB's collaboration with Afrika Bambaata and electro was so appropriate and so dreary.) Really, the funk of the agit-prop groups was no more than an acceptable form of masculine hardness and aggression (where rock as such was now embarrassing). Generally, they reduced funk to riffing, to guitars, bass and drums, unaware of the role of voices and production in black music.

Other groups 'found' different properties in funk. A genre developed based on a profound perversion of funk's sexual tension into a different sort of het-up charge, one of unease and dread. The disco backbeat became the given, the 'natural springboard for these experimentalists with their collages of industrial decay and social fragmentation. One reason was the neutrality of disco—it wasn't loaded with the associations that rock was, it was outside pop history, so it could be used as an element in 'futurist' music. The idea was simple—marry technology and savagery, control and madness, the cerebral and 'feel'. Music embodying both the system of industrial society and the breaking free (into violence, debauchery, excess) of instincts suppressed by the system. The musicians' ambivalent feelings towards control and collapse (attracted to both) is bound up with the old egghead problem/project—how to think yourself past thought, or as Talking Heads put it—"help us lose our minds," "stop making sense." *Jam Science*, the Shriekback LP title, is the most succinct, distressingly pat expression of the goal. Blackness was read as wildness, or unrepression, and so the "spirit of funk" was basically invested with a danger it does not really possess. Chakk and Hula are two current outfits who reveal both the extent and the limits of what can be achieved in this genre. The obvious musical strands—found voices; distorted, FX-ridden vocals; trails of discordant sax; sombre swathes of synth; filched ethnic noises; basslines and drum patterns that bear a formal resemblance to funk but are fatally drained of sex and soul—are strung around the familiar concepts and content: cut-up theory; the ambivalent obsession with religious/jingoist fanaticism, atrocity, psychosis (J. G. Ballard); totalitarianism (William Burroughs' "control"). Even the titles instill a sense of deja-vu—"Delirium," "Cut the Dust," "Tear Up," "Out of the Flesh," "Pleasure Hates Language." Hula's *Murmur* LP (Red Rhino Records) and Chakk's recent Peel session contain music that can emote and excite, but both groups make worthy additions to a pre-existing field, rather than enlargements or developments of it. The rhetoric of provocation, the claims to be "disturbing," seem misplaced. What strikes is the inarticulacy of the music, despite its sensual surface and the intelligence that goes into the play with sound: nothing is imparted, nothing resolved. It exists as entertainment, not challenge, for a converted, stable audience—all those withdrawn young men who 'groove' on this angst-funk disco noir.

Direct imitation of black music, rather than mutation or bricolage, seems to dominate today's music scene. Late in '83, X. Moore wrote in *Harper's and Queen* (!) that 1984 would see a new "revolt into style", an "upful" music, "brassy" and full of defiant hope, by groups steeped in Stax, Atlantic, Wilson Pickett, etc.* Apart from being a slightly embarrassing fantasy of future success for his own group, the Redskins, it was quite an accurate prognosis. Groups like the Style Council, Kane Gang, Special AKA and Redskins subscribe to the current orthodoxy that black music alone is the legitimate base for protest. Allied with the sort of journalist whose every other word is "pride" and "dignity", they have invested black music—60s and 70s soul, rap, African, jazz—with qualities like 'realism', a certain out-going 'health', and (a specifically political) positivism. Hence the Redskins' crusade against "miserabilism" (introspective rock groups like Joy Division, Bunnymen, Cocteau Twins, Smiths) a.k.a. "Reds Against the Blues," with its underlying notion that unemployment and oppression are more fitting subjects for pop than love, loss and the more existential forms of alienation. Hence the Style Council/Respond strategy of clean, smart clothes, sunny videos, freshness, beatnik sleevenotes, French flirtations—the idea of optimism as resistance, of 'style' and 'youth' as some sort of weapon or victory in itself. Weller has dropped the Who as model for political songs, in preference for ... early 70s disco (Curtis Mayfield's "We've Got to Have Peace," O'Jays' "Love Train"); likewise Kane Gang's ideal in agit-pop is ... the Staple Singers.† In the Style Council/Redskin musical universe, funky tightness ("Soul-Deep," "Money-Go-Round"), brassiness ("Keep on Keepin' On"), even strings (the fake Philly "Shout to the Top") have become ciphers for rebellion, just as powerchord guitar and vocal snarl were for another generation. The soul preacher has merely taken the exact place of the rebel rocker. Really, the summit of it all, the last word (let's hope) is "Shout It to the Top," with it sleevenotes:

> "Say
> Yes! to the thrill of the romp
> Yes! to the Bengali Workers Association
> Yes! to a nuclear free world
> Yes! to all involved in animal rights
> Yes! to fanzines
> Yes! to belief"

What use or interest is this hope, pride and joy? Why has so much threat been claimed for this affirmation?

What drives them all into the dead end that is the "return to blackness"; the path of imitation is littered with failures (ABC, Dexys, The Questions). Leave black music to the visionaries and the naturals—Womack, Jackson, Chaka—who can turn the banal into the paradisical. What seems more productive now is a rereading of white rock heritage—groups who commit violence to the texts of such as the Doors, Byrds, Velvets, Birthday Party, garage punk and psychedelia. We're talking about music at third or fourth remove from the r'n'b source, perversions of perversions. It's music that chafes at the tenet that black music alone has a hold on desire or rhythm; music ignorant of questions of responsibility, social conscience and the imperative of "upfulness" (a very narrow view of what black music "is all about"), made by groups who see themselves as artists rather than propagandists, who deal in poetry rather than reportage.

---

* *New Musical Express* music journalist and musician X. Moore (Chris Dean) of The Redskins was also a member of the British Socialist Workers Party. Reynolds inserts the exclamation point after *Harper's and Queen* to highlight the irony that Moore would be spouting socialist rhetoric in an upscale fashion magazine.

† Prior to forming the Style Council, Paul Weller had been the lead member of The Jam, whose admitted 1960s mod fascination earned them many comparisons with The Who.

39

Molly Hatchet
Celebrity Rate a Record

For decades music magazines from *Down Beat* to *Melody Maker* have taken the "celebrity record review" as an opportunity to offer its readership a more personal glimpse into the worlds of their favorite artists. Cast as critics, musicians can reinforce the taste hierarchies of the genre(s) to which they most closely belong, or they can use the review platform to reveal an unexpected depth and breadth in their listening habits. Invited by the heavy metal/hard rock magazine *Hit Parader* in the summer of 1983 to review the latest batch of 7-inch vinyl singles (45s), vocalist Danny Joe Brown (1951–2005) and lead guitarist Dave Hlubek (born 1952) of the southern rock band Molly Hatchet accomplish a little of both. As their brutally blunt comments make clear (it is difficult to imagine such a review being published today), a genre like southern rock or heavy metal is defined as much by exclusion as it is by inclusion. Taken as a whole, the range of music they encounter serves as a reminder that at any given moment rock can consist of an astonishingly diverse array of styles.*

We gave Molly Hatchet's Dave Hlubek and Danny Joe Brown a stack of recent 45s and asked them to give us their first impressions. The pair pulled no punches when it came to analyzing the product.

I Eat Cannibals. **Total Coelo**

Dave Hlubek: (looking at the picture sleeve) Is she squatting to take a leak?
Danny Joe Brown: Let's hear ZZ Top. Fuck this cannibal shit.
DH: They look like real pros. There's Kansas' fiddle player. Is he squatting on it too? And they say our careers are in trouble! Duane Allman is going to rise from his grave and slap these bitches. (Breaks the record.)

Electric Avenue, **Eddy Grant**

DH: It's a poor copy of Men At Work, those faggots from Australia. Rate-A-Record? A one.
DJB: A six on a scale of 100.

Living On The Ceiling, **Blancmange**

DH: They get a zero for originality. It's all the same. They all should make one big group; they're already using the same band and changing the names. These fuckers are stupid.
DJB: Wait a minute, I was getting into the lyrics. "I'm so tall, I'm so tall." That's fucking happening for tall people.

---

* *Source:* "Celebrity Rate A Record: Molly Hatchet," *Hit Parader*, September 1983, p. 23.

DH: Well then let's do a cover version for our next album. I'm thinking about all the good musicians out of work. I wouldn't even shit on this stuff. It really sucks. That's like puke on a record. (Breaks the record.)

Body Talk, **Kix**

DH: This is it, I like this song. It sounds like a speeded-up version of (I Am) Iron Man. That's the only part I like, the part "body talk," where it sounds like a heavy metal rubber duck. I can't break this one.

Gimme All Your Lovin', **ZZ Top**

DH: (cranks it very loud) I heard it a lot on the radio. I made sure it got a lot of radio—I paid the station managers.

DJB: Sounds like a real drum already.

DH: Drums by Mattel. Look at these three guys and call them faggots and they'll kick your ass. They are the most powerful three-piece band ever. I've been called narrow-minded, and that's one of the lighter comments, Great record. This is mine (puts it under his coat).

Windows, **Missing Persons**

DH: (breaks it) Oh. I was supposed to listen to it first.

Photograph, **Def Leppard**

DJB: Def is smoking. Let's hear that. They've done better.

DH: So Def Leppard did a cop on Boston's sound. You would think that Tom Scholz produced it because they've taken that sound. It's Boston for sure.

DJB: We're Skynyrd clones, so they've got to be something.

DH: This song deserves to be in the top 10. It worked for Boston for two years. Maybe we sound like the wrong people. I like this song. No wonder it's a hit.

Little Red Corvette, **Prince**

DH: That sound reminds me of Bette Davis Eyes. I knew somebody else would use it. If it was titled differently and the lyrics were different, I'd like the song. The music is different. I kind of like this. (Danny Joe Brown gets up to turn off the record.) Danny doesn't like it. How can I tell? Something about the record flying through the air.

DJB: When that guy grows up, he'll be Michael Jackson.

Mr. Soul, **Neil Young**

DH: That's not the Mr. Soul I knew.

DJB: This is great-I love this. I dig the shit out of this.

DH: We used to do this song. We wanted to record it because we all love Buffalo Springfield. I'm used to hearing the up tempo version. This is so much slower. Wait, this is his disco beat. I like it better the other way.

Saturday At Midnight, **Cheap Trick**

DH: That's Cheap Trick. They sold out. How do you top the Beatles? Frankly, I'm disappointed with Cheap Trick. We toured with them several times; we watched Bun E. Carlos get laid in Amsterdam. But c'mon Rick, Robin, get wise.

DJB: What a waste of talent.

DH: This is what happens when you do it yourself.

This Is For Real, **Aretha Franklin**

DH: It's Aretha. I love Aretha. As always, the champagne lady still serves champagne. This is timeless. She doesn't care about the trends. She's been there and will always be there. This is music. She gets an A+ on this.

DJB: I'd like to hear her and Lionel Richie together.

DH: That would be smoking.

Never Say Goodbye, **Yoko Ono**

DH: If she sounds as good as on the *White Album*, it should smoke. It sounds like an Uncle Ben's commercial. You notice her voice on the beginning of the record? That's her whining. She doesn't have an ounce of talent.

Put Angels Around You, **Maggie Bell and Bobby Whitlock**

DH: Bobby Whitlock … tried to steal my bass player and drummer.

DJB: He's trying to sound like Michael McDonald and it's not working.

DH: It's coming out like a drunk Joe Cocker and it's not happening. Bobby Whitlock doesn't know where he wants to go musically.

40

"The Cult of Violence"

TIPPER GORE

Few events involving rock music in the 1980s generated more media attention than the September 1985 congressional hearings instigated by the Parents Music Resource Center (PMRC). Led by Tipper Gore (born 1948)—the wife of Senator Al Gore—and a group of politically connected Washington, D.C. spouses dubbed the "Washington Wives," the PMRC persuaded the Senate to hear testimony on the questionable content and escalating influence of contemporary rock music and MTV videos. According to Gore, the organization's intent was solely to make information available for parents and consumers concerned about the contents of the records that their children were purchasing. While they initially sought a rating system similar to the MPAA's guidelines for films, the PMRC eventually prevailed on a more general scale when it convinced the recording industry to implement the "parental advisory–explicit content" sticker. At the time, such designs met with stiff resistance from respondents such as Frank Zappa, Dee Snider, and John Denver, all of whom claimed that the organization's endeavors would be tainted by ideological interpretations that would lead to censorship.

In her 1987 book *Raising PG Kids in an X-Rated Society*, Gore identifies five ways in which rock music has ostensibly forsaken the standards of societal decency: 1) abuse of drugs and alcohol, 2) portrayals of suicide, 3) graphic and misogynistic violence, 4) satanism and the occult, and 5) explicit sexual themes. As the following excerpt from the chapter on "The Cult of Violence" illustrates, no music drew more indignant responses from the PMRC than heavy metal. Gore's concerns revisit age-old debates over the relationship between music and society. Does heavy metal perpetuate America's most troublesome social ills or, as its advocates claim, is it simply "entertainment"? And where should the responsibility for society's troubles ultimately lie? Regardless of how one addresses these questions, it is worth noting that the PMRC's targets were selective. As Reebee Garofalo has pointed out, "country music, for example, remained largely untouched by the PMRC onslaught, even though it often deals with themes of sex, violence, and hard drinking."* Is it merely a coincidence that Gore's husband was at that time the senator from Tennessee, home to Nashville's thriving commercial country music industry?†

A conscientious man would be cautious how he dealt in blood.

—Edmund Burke

I like to drink blood out of a skull and torture females on stage.

—Blackie Lawless of the band W.A.S.P.[1]

---

* Reebee Garofalo, "Setting the Record Straight: Censorship and Social Responsibility in Popular Music," *Journal of Popular Music Studies*, vol. 6 (1994), p. 14.

† *Source*: Tipper Gore, "The Cult of Violence," from *Raising PG Kids in an X-Rated Society* (Nashville: Abingdon Press, 1987), pp. 47–59.

Blackie Lawless is anything but typical of rock musicians. Yet his disturbing message is a sign of the times. While Lawless and others like him may think they are merely entertaining impressionable youth with their shocking rituals, the country is witnessing more and more reports of youth violence and sexual assaults. As a nation, we remain somewhat isolated in our homes and places of work, and many of us are still unaware of the increasing number of violent acts, from murder to deadly assaults, being perpetrated by young people in every state. We simply cannot afford to ignore these mounting statistics any longer.

We live in a violent world, and America itself has a history of wars, civil strife, and crime. Humankind is a violent race and is host to aggressive impulses. But the real violence that we do to one another and must learn to control is of our own making, and as such is largely preventable. Its source lies in our families, neighborhoods, and communities, and we must effectively deal with all its causes and focus on its prevention, if we are to survive.

The violence that haunts our society has reached its extreme in the nuclear arms race. Our children grow up beneath a frightening nuclear shadow, the threat of annihilation hanging over them like the sword of Damocles. And all now live with the reality of international terrorism spilling the blood of the innocent. The violence in our lives is also often glorified and commercially exploited in the mass media, and unless we want to continue robbing, beating, maiming, and killing each other, that too presents all of us with a great and important challenge.

Just as it is imperative that we work intelligently to defuse the nuclear threat, so must we come to terms with the unfettered commercial exploitation of violence and violent messages throughout our culture. Overexposure to violent images is desensitizing us to violence. Because it now takes more and more violence to make us feel shock and revulsion, media violence has to become more and more graphic to be profitable. We are addicted—and we're about to overdose.

These disturbing messages are also reaching a larger and younger audience. The technological revolution has created home videocassette recorders, cable television, music videos, movie rental cassettes, compact discs, and satellite dishes providing a myriad of choices in home entertainment. Never before have such high-powered and diverse media been available to so many people, including the very youngest children. But these new marvels have a darker side. They can enhance educational and cultural opportunities—or they can spread new forms of graphic violence.

Parents should closely examine the smorgasbord of violent entertainment now offered to our children. The spread of simulated violence should be evaluated against the backdrop of steadily increasing violence in real life.

HEAVY METAL: THROBBING CHORDS AND VIOLENT LYRICS

Heavy metal and its loyal fan following represent a new phenomenon in rock music. Focusing on the darker, violent side of life, this brand of music was first played in England some twenty years ago as a vehicle for countercultural rebellion. Many of the songs were political. But the frustration and rebellion that is a normal part of the maturation process for many young people who are critical of adults and "the Establishment" seemed to turn to greater and greater despair. The music took an even darker turn and explored subjects like devil worship and the occult, sadistic sex, murder, rape, and suicide.

Defenders of such songs say that these things are occurring in the real world, that they are moving to the forefront of our consciousness, and that therefore the music should be seen as simply an artistic reflection of new realities. Others argue that emphasizing these themes in pop culture will in itself push them into the popular mind.

Perhaps the youth of the eighties have to go to new extremes such as these to get their parents' attention. It must be hard to rebel against a generation of adults who have broken quite a few taboos themselves.

The names of some of these bands imply a fascination with violence and evil: Venom, the Dead Kennedys, Suicidal Tendencies, W.A.S.P. (which, according to them, stands for "We Are Sexual Perverts"[2]), Judas Priest, Iron Maiden, Warlord, Metallica, Predator, the Scorpions, Slayer, and Black Sabbath. Certain of these heavy metal and punk rock bands make violence (particularly sexual violence), explicit sex, and the power of evil central themes in their concert performances and recordings.

Heavy metal does not yet receive a lot of Top Forty radio airplay, and MTV has reportedly cut back on the airing of some of their videos, although they do broadcast a heavy metal hour. But heavy metal songs are played regularly on many radio stations and college campuses, and heavy metal videocassette sales are surprisingly strong.

Most of the heavy metal bands record for small independent labels and will "only" sell perhaps 250,000 to 400,000 copies. These groups tour the country and can build up substantial numbers of fans by playing live concerts and selling their records by mail order. Increasingly, those independent labels are being distributed by the six major corporate record labels. This is a business decision which will further promote heavy metal to the public.

In concert, the most strident bands not only play their music at the highest decibels, but perform what they describe as "vaudeville acts" that glamorize explicit sex, alcohol and drug use, and bloody violence. Some depict the most extreme antisocial behavior imaginable. Most of their fans are adolescent boys between the ages of twelve and nineteen, although recently girls have made up a greater percentage of the audience. Some fans are younger still—aged eight, nine, and ten.

A male rock star, Alice Cooper, was one of the early proponents of "shock rock." He used props like guillotines and giant boa constrictor snakes to terrify and excite the audience. The band Kiss elaborated on Cooper's theatrical violence and drew nationwide protests and devoted fans. They were the first to use grotesque makeup and outrageous costumes. In England, Ozzy Osbourne, long-time lead vocalist for the heavy metal band Black Sabbath, horrified rock enthusiasts by biting off the head of a live bat during one frenzied performance. Heavy metal headliners are now competing with each other to be the most outrageous and socially unacceptable, which seems to assure them instant success among young fans.

PUSHING THE LIMITS

W.A.S.P. released an album of the same name that was replete with songs about death and sex. It included lyrics such as "Sex and pain the same,/ They're really the same."[3] The band's lead singer has convulsed audiences by throwing raw meat into the crowd. The band has also used skeletons, axes, blades, and gallons of fake blood as props. To promote their act, they have used a picture of a bloodied, half-naked woman chained to a torture rack. Past performances have included the simulated attack and torture of a woman. Reportedly, in the act lead singer Blackie Lawless wore between his legs a codpiece adorned with a circular saw blade. He pretended to beat a woman who was naked except for a G-string and a black hood over her head, and as fake blood cascaded from under the hood, he seemed to attack her with the blade.[4] In another version of the act, he pretended to slit her throat. As Adrianne Stone reports in the January 1985 edition of *Hit Parader*, "[W.A.S.P. are] the deranged demons who bind a loincloth-clad female onto a 'rack,' then 'slit' her neck until she shakes and convulses into oblivion."[5]

The cover of the W.A.S.P. twelve-inch single record *F**k Like a Beast* shows a close-up of a man holding his bloody hands on his thighs, with a bloody circular saw blade protruding from his genital area.[6] Although imported from England, this album was for sale in record stores throughout the U.S.

In an October 1985 article in the fan magazine *Hit Parader*, which advertised the band through a cover photograph of Blackie Lawless, blood running out of his mouth, holding up a bloody skull, the singer talked about his heavy metal exploits:

> To me rock is theater, electric vaudeville.... It's the place where you can do just about anything and get away with it. It's a zone where rules and restrictions are just totally thrown out the window. It's like controlled anarchy—if there is such a thing. We spit blood and throw raw pieces of meat into the crowd. We're not trying to make any great social statement; we're just trying to entertain and give the people who come to see us a good time.[7]

Thank goodness they're not interested in social statements. Not only does this package appeal to some children, it appealed to Capitol Records, who must have seen W.A.S.P. as just the band to promote to the nation's youth. The group signed a $1.5 million record deal with Capitol.[8]

Rock music fan magazines freely publicize this violent, gruesome entertainment, gleefully reporting and dramatizing the "fun." In September 1985 *Faces Rocks* carried a story about the "hot 'n' nasty" W.A.S.P. band. Band member Lawless told writer Keith Greenberg that "nastiness" is central to the W.A.S.P. performance. "I don't mean vulgar 'nasty,'" he said. "I mean violent. We sound like a tin can ripped open with your hands, that kind of nasty. It doesn't leave a clean cut."[9] Anger helps fuel the violence Blackie Lawless and other heavy metal rockers inject into their performances. "The anger is what helps you relate to the kids," he said in the same interview. "When you got adolescents and you put in a healthy dose of hostility, you got a lethal combination there. That's what makes rock 'n' roll what it is. You're pissed off. I'm still pissed off about a lot of things; thank God I haven't lost that. I think the worst thing that can happen to any rock 'n' roller is getting civilized."[10] Well, maybe rock doesn't have to get civilized in a middle-class sense, but it doesn't have to promote barbarism either.

* * *

Some heavy metal songs extol the virtues of torture, rape, and murder of women. They usually portray women as sexual playthings and as victims—objects of pleasure designed, like alcohol and drugs or fast cars, for men to use and abuse. Many of the album covers of heavy metal groups present glimpses of this anger-spurred violence.

The cover of Exciter's album *Violence & Force* depicts a homicidal attack; as a woman's hands desperately try to hold shut a door, a killer has thrust both hands, one holding a dagger, the other dripping blood, through the open crack.[11] Abattoir's *Vicious Attack* shows a woman's torso with a man's arms wrapped around her from behind. In one hand the man holds a dagger, in the other a sharpened meat hook which he presses to the woman's breast.[12] The album *Savage Grace* boasts a color photograph of a nude woman gagged and chained to a motorcycle,[13] and the album *Be My Slave* shows a scantily clad woman on her knees, holding sadomasochistic tools of the trade in her hands.[14]

This kind of message is spilling over into the musical mainstream. The cover of the album *Undercover*, by the Rolling Stones (not a heavy metal band), shows a nude woman lying on her back with a triangle placed over her pubic area. One song on the album is entitled "Tie You Up (The Pain of Love)."[15]

* * *

DOES IT REALLY MATTER?

Is all this just entertainment? A 1986 study by two professors at California State University at Fullerton concluded that teens don't listen to the words of songs, just to the beat. The researchers contend that parents hear more sophisticated themes in the songs than the children really understand.[16] However, common sense and virtually every other study on the topic suggest otherwise.

The healthy, mature personality may in fact be minimally affected by violent messages. But for many malleable teens and preteens who are searching for identity and who are beset by conflicts about authority, drugs, sex, religion, and education, a big dose of heavy metal messages like these can be extremely harmful.

Dr. Joseph Stuessy, professor of music at the University of Texas at San Antonio and author of *The Heavy Metal User's Manual,* holds that music does affect behavior. "Any kind of music affects our moods, emotions, attitudes and our resultant behavior," he says. "Music has both psychological and physiological effects on people. That's why we have choirs and organs in churches and synagogues, bands at football games, Muzak in business and doctors' offices, military marches, background music for movies and television programs, Jazzercise where legions of people are motivated to move by rock music, and most important, commercial jingles."[17]

Plato wrote that music had the power to shape society. Today, those who orchestrate the successful commercial jingle can certainly control social and commercial behavior. Advertisers would not spend billions annually if music and other messages were not persuasive. According to Dr. Stuessy, music aids retention of verbal messages; we are more likely to remember a message if it comes to us in a musical context. Repetition makes us more likely to internalize—and like—a message. The more senses the message involves—like sight, hearing, or touch—the more likely that message will have an impact on our conscious and subconscious minds. Dr. Stuessy warns that heavy metal music differs categorically from earlier forms of popular music and from mainstream rock and roll. With its celebration of extreme violence, substance abuse, explicit sex, and satanism, one of heavy metal's main themes is hatred. "I know personally of no form of popular music before which has had hatred as one of its central themes," he says.[18]

As radio consultant Lee Abrams allegedly stated, heavy metal may be "the music to kill your parents by." Teens who listen to heavy metal get that message of hate overtly or covertly. I've received many letters from teens who like heavy metal and who say, in effect, "Hey, I'm not gonna go out and kill someone just because that is in the lyrics." But while they will not go to that extreme, Dr. Stuessy points out that "anyone who says, 'I can listen to heavy metal, but it doesn't affect me,' is simply wrong. It simply affects different people in different degrees and different ways."

Another rock and roll expert cites examples of teen homicides, suicides, and other violent acts linked to a youth's involvement with, among other things, heavy metal music. Dr. Paul King, medical director of the adolescent program at Charter Lakeside Hospital, a psychiatric and addictive disease facility in Memphis, Tennessee, says that over 80 percent of the adolescent patients he treats have listened to heavy metal music for several hours a day. Dr. King notes that over 50 percent of them know the words to the songs and can write them down. A number of students spend school time writing and memorizing the words, he adds; "the lyrics become a philosophy of life, a religion."

Since we began the Parents' Music Resource Center, we have read many letters and reports indicating that the messages of violent hatred in the "religion" of heavy metal do influence and help corrupt; in some extreme cases, they even seem to play a part in ending young lives. Undoubtedly, there are other important factors in all these cases, but the messages of the music can be regarded, at the very least, as a symptom of some distress, if the young person is troubled. If more people understood that, they might be able to intervene and help the young person.

One such letter came from a mother in San Antonio, Texas. She has experienced a tragedy that she feels is directly related to the influence of music on behavior. This woman told me that in the summer of 1980, her sixteen-year-old son went into a trancelike state on a very hot summer night. He was listening to Pink Floyd's album *The Wall*. He had not been able to sleep because his allergies were acting up, and he had a severe headache. His aunt was asleep on the couch in front of the TV set, which was beaming a violent episode of "Starsky and Hutch" about a serial killer of prostitutes. The boy suddenly stabbed his aunt to death. He claims not even to remember the act.

According to the police report, there were no drugs involved, just the hot weather, the headache, the TV, and the music. Her son "believes the music itself can hypnotize you," she says. At this writing her son is now in prison, and she and her family have exhausted all means of appealing the case.

There are many other recent cases of children committing similar types of murders. In May 1986, the *Tacoma News Tribune* reported that a twenty-year-old boy murdered his mother with an ax and a pair of scissors, in the course of raping her. He was ruled sane for trial; the defense plans to plead that the influence of satanism and heavy metal music caused the boy to commit these acts. To date, however, no such defense has been successful in the courts.

We should be deeply concerned about the obvious cumulative effect of this cult of violence that has captured the public's imagination and pervaded our society. Few parents realize how much the angry brand of music that is part of it has presented suicide, glorified rape, and condoned murder. The message is more than repulsive—it's deadly.

NOTES

1.   An Exclusive Talk With A Shocking Performer—Blackie Lawless," *RockLine* (April 1985), p. 14.

2.   Don Mueller, "The Lawless Brigade Take Metal Outrage To New Heights," *Hit Parader* (November 1985), p. 46.

3.   W.A.S.P., "On Your Knees," WASP, Capitol/EMI ST-12343. Written by Blackie Lawless. Planetary Music Inc. Publishing controlled by Zomba Enterprises, Inc.

4.   Kandy Stroud, "Stop Pornographic Rock," *Newsweek* (May 6, 1985), p. 14.

5.   Adrianne Stone, "W.A.S.P., Rock and Roll Outlaws," *Hit Parader* (January 1985), p. 56.

6.   W.A.S.P., *Animal (F**k Like a Beast)*, Music for Nations 12-KVT-109.

7.   Andy Secher, "The Kings of Shock Rock," *Hit Parader* (October 1985), p. 33.

8.   Keith Greenberg, "W.A.S.P., Hot 'n' Nasty!" *Faces Rocks* (September 1985), p. 15.

9.   Ibid, p. 17.

10.   Ibid.

11.   Exciter, *Violence & Force*, Megaforce Records MRI 569.

12.   Abattoir, *Vicious Attack*, Combat Records MX8014.

13.   Savage Grace, *Master of Disguise*, Important Record Distributors RD-004.

14.   Bitch, *Be My Slave*, Metal Blade MBR 1007.

15.   Rolling Stones, *Undercover*, Rolling Stones Records RLS (S) 90120-1.

16.   Jill Rosenbaum and Lorraine Prinsky, "Sex, Violence and Rock 'n' Roll: Youths' Perceptions of Popular Music." Paper delivered at annual meeting of the Western Society of Criminology, Newport Beach, California, February 1986; Forthcoming in *Popular Music and Society*.

17.   Joe Stuessy, telephone interview with author, September 1985.

18.   Joe Stuessy, quoted from Senate Committee on Commerce, Science, and Transportation, Record Labeling, 99th Cong., 1st Sess., 1985, p. 117.

19.   Ethlie Vare, "Molten Hot Metal Flares Anew In Fad-Defying Fling At Pop Success," *Billboard* 96 (April 14, 1984), p. HM-3.

20.   Joe Stuessy, *The Heavy Metal User's Manual*, mimeographed handout, p. 1. Available from Dr. Joe Stuessy, College of Fine Arts and Humanities, Division of Music, University of Texas at San Antonio, San Antonio, TX 78285.

21. Paul King, "Heavy Metal: A New Religion," *Journal of the Tennessee Medical Association* 78, no. 12 (December 1985), p. 755.

22. "Ax-Scissors death trial date slated," *Tacoma* News Tribune, May 31, 1986.

41

Heavy Metal and The Highbrow/Lowbrow Divide

Robert Walser

Robert Walser, Professor of Musicology at UCLA, was one of the first academic scholars to attempt a serious and sympathetic analysis of the much-maligned genre of heavy metal in his landmark study *Running with the Devil: Power, Gender, and Madness in Heavy Metal* (Hanover: Wesleyan University Press, 1993). The essay reprinted here draws on material from his book, and was originally presented as part of a 1992 American Studies conference at Princeton University. At the time, few could have imagined two more polar opposites than the supposedly brutish power of "lowbrow" heavy metal and the sophisticated taste of "highbrow" classical music. But Walser complicates this assumed division, showing how heavy metal guitarists from Ritchie Blackmore (born 1945) to Eddie Van Halen (born 1955) have long "experimented with the musical materials of eighteenth- and nineteenth-century European composers," to the point where classical conventions are an essential component of the heavy metal style. Walser carefully demonstrates how classical's symbolic values and theoretical musical language has become imbued in heavy metal through such pedagogical forces as the widely influential magazine, *Guitar for the Practicing Musician*. Long after its commercial peak of the 1980s, heavy metal continues to thrive as a popular international style. To what degree does classical music figure into today's heavy metal?*

In his recent book on the emergence of cultural hierarchy in the United States, Lawrence Levine reminds us that when we use the terms "highbrow" and "lowbrow," we pay homage to the racist pseudoscience of phrenology.[1] Nineteenth-century phrenologists correlated moral and intellectual characteristics with brain size and skull shape, creating a hierarchy that conveniently placed themselves, white men, at the top. Subsequently, as "highbrow," "lowbrow" and "middlebrow" came into common usage to designate the relative worth of people and cultural activities, the social category of class was also mapped onto this hierarchy, and working-class culture acquired the aura of primitivity that nineteenth-century writers had projected onto non-white races. Levine's book is a valuable reminder that types such as "highbrow" and "lowbrow," or "classical" and "popular," do not simply reflect internal properties of texts or practices, but are, rather, invented categories that do cultural work. Like phrenology, cultural hierarchy functioned to naturalize social and cultural inequalities and deny the creative capacities of whole groups of people.

---

* *Source*: Robert Walser, "Highbrow, Lowbrow, Voodoo Aesthetics," in Andrew Ross and Tricia Rose, eds., *Microphone Fiends: Youth Music and Youth Culture* (New York: Routledge, 1994), pp. 235–49.

But Levine's topic does not belong to the nineteenth century alone; whether or not the same labels are used (and they often are), such essentializing categories are still at work at the end of the twentieth century, and they retain the power to affect millions of lives. People are constantly being typed by their cultural allegiances, respected or dismissed because of the music they like. Moreover, we internalize these categories; when I interviewed heavy metal fans, I found that while some of them regarded heavy metal music as the most important thing in their lives, they nonetheless completely accepted the conventional wisdom that classical music is categorically superior to any popular music. Many other people are similarly led to believe in their own inferiority because of the stories that are told about their culture. No one ever actually explains why classical music is better than all other musics, because no one ever has to explain; cultural hierarchy functions to naturalize social hierarchies through the circular reinscription of prestige—foreclosing dialogue, analysis and argument. Music historians are still writing textbooks of "Twentieth-Century Music" that omit popular musics entirely, without even explaining their exclusion of most of the music that people have actually heard and cared about during the last hundred years.[2]

But not everyone abides by the rules of cultural hierarchy. In the liner notes for his 1988 album, *Odyssey*, heavy metal guitarist Yngwie J. Malmsteen claimed a musical genealogy that confounds the stability of conventional categorizations of music into classical and popular spheres. In his list of acknowledgments, along with the usual cast of agents and producers, suppliers of musical equipment, relatives and friends, Malmsteen expressed gratitude to J. S. Bach, Nicolo Paganini, Antonio Vivaldi, Ludwig van Beethoven, Jimi Hendrix and Ritchie Blackmore.[3] From the very beginnings of heavy metal in the late 1960s, guitar players had experimented with the musical materials of eighteenth- and nineteenth-century European composers. But the trend came to full fruition around the time of Malmsteen's debut in the early 1980s; a writer for the leading professional guitar magazine says flatly that the single most important development in rock guitar in the 1980s was "the turn to classical music for inspiration and form."[4]

Throughout heavy metal's history, its most influential musicians have been guitar players who have also studied some aspects of that assemblage of disparate musical styles known in the twentieth century as "classical music." Their appropriation and adaptation of classical models sparked the development of a new kind of guitar virtuosity, changes in the harmonic and melodic language of heavy metal, and new modes of musical pedagogy and analysis. Of course, the history of American popular music is replete with examples of appropriation "from below"—popular adaptations of classical music. But the classical influence on heavy metal marks a merger of what are generally regarded as the most and least prestigious musical discourses of our time. This influence thus seems an unlikely one, yet metal musicians and fans have found discursive fusions of rock and classical musics useful, invigorating and compelling. Moreover, the meeting took place on the terms established by heavy metal musicians, at their instigation. That is, their fusions were not motivated by the desire for "legitimacy" in classical terms; rather, they have participated in a process of cultural reformulation and recontextualization that has produced new meanings. To those blinkered by the assumptions of cultural hierarchy, such reformulations are impossible to trace or understand because they step outside the dominant logic of cultural production.

Heavy metal appropriations of classical music are in fact very specific and consistent: Bach not Mozart, Paganini rather than Liszt, Vivaldi and Albinoni instead of Telemann or Monteverdi. This selectivity is remarkable at a time when the historical and semiotic specificity of classical music, on its own turf, has all but vanished, when the classical canon is defined and marketed as a reliable set of equally great and ineffable collectibles. By finding new uses for old music, recycling the rhetoric of Bach and Vivaldi for their own purposes, metal musicians have reopened issues of signification in classical music. Their appropriation suggests that, despite the homogenization of that music in the literatures of "music appreciation" and commercial promotion, many listeners perceive and respond to differences, to the musical specificity that reflects historical and social specificity. Thus the reasons behind heavy metal's classical turn reveal a great deal not only about heavy metal, but also about classical music. We must ask: if we don't understand his influence on the music of Ozzy Osbourne or Bon Jovi, do we really understand *Bach* as well as we thought we did?

* * *

Many rock guitarists have drawn upon classical techniques and procedures in their music; among the most important were Ritchie Blackmore in the late 1960s and 1970s, and Eddie Van Halen in the late 1970s and 1980s. Both had early classical training which familiarized them with that music; later, like most heavy metal guitarists, they turned to methodical study, emulation and adaptation. Blackmore took harmonic progressions, phrase patterns and figuration from Baroque models such as Vivaldi. As Blackmore himself has pointed out in numerous interviews, these classical features show up in many of the songs he recorded with Deep Purple: "For example, the chord progression in the "Highway Star" solo on *Machine Head* ... is a Bach progression." And the solo is "just arpeggios based on Bach."[5]

Eddie Van Halen revolutionized rock guitar with his unprecedented virtuosity and the "tapping" technique he popularized in "Eruption" (1978), which demonstrated the possibility of playing speedy arpeggios on the guitar. Van Halen also participated in the technological developments that helped make Baroque models newly relevant to heavy metal guitar players.[6] The electrification of the guitar, begun in the 1920s, and subsequent developments in equipment and playing techniques, particularly the production of sophisticated distortion circuitry in the 1960s, acquired for the guitar the capabilities of the premier virtuosic instruments of the seventeenth and eighteenth centuries: the power and speed of the organ, the flexibility and nuance of the violin. Increases in sustain and volume made possible the conceptual and technical shifts that led players to explore Baroque models.

Two guitarists of the 1980s, Randy Rhoads and Yngwie Malmsteen, brought heavy metal neoclassicism to fruition and inspired a legion of imitators. Like Edward Van Halen, Rhoads grew up in a musical household; he enrolled as a student at his mother's music school at the age of six, studying guitar, piano and music theory, and a few years later began classical guitar lessons, which he would continue throughout his career. In 1980, he landed the guitar chair in a new band fronted by ex-Black Sabbath vocalist Ozzy Osbourne; during his brief tenure with Osbourne's band (ending with his death at age twenty-five in a plane crash), Rhoads became famous as the first guitar player of the 1980s to expand the classical influence, further adapting and integrating a harmonic and melodic vocabulary derived from classical music. Among his early musical influences, Rhoads cited the dark moods and drama of Alice Cooper, Ritchie Blackmore's fusion of rock and classical music, Van Halen's tapping technique, and his favorite classical composers, Vivaldi and Pachelbel.[7]

Rhoads's and Osbourne's "Mr. Crowley" (1981) begins with synthesized organ, playing a cyclical harmonic progression modelled on Vivaldi. The minor mode, the ominous organ and the fateful cyclicism, culminating in a suspension, are used to set up an affect of mystery and doom, supporting the mocking treatment of English satanist Aleister Crowley in the lyrics.[8] The progression that underpins Rhoads's "outro" (closing) solo at the end of the song is a straightforward Vivaldian circle of fifths progression: Dm | Gm7 | C | F | Bb | Em7b5 | Asus4 | A. Until classically influenced heavy metal, such cyclical progressions were unusual in rock music, which had been fundamentally blues-based. The classical influence contributed to a greater reliance on the power of harmonic progression to organize desire and narrative, as well as the turn toward virtuosic soloing. Rhoads's solo on the live recording of "Suicide Solution" (1981) makes even more extensive use of Baroque rhetoric, including diminished chords, trills, sliding chromatic figures, a gigue and a tapped section that focuses attention on the drama of harmonic progression.[9] Like the tapping in Van Halen's "Eruption," such figuration leads the listener along an aural adventure, as the guitarist continually sets up implied harmonic goals and then achieves, modifies, extends or subverts them.

Not only the classical materials in his music, but also Rhoads's study of academic music theory influenced many guitarists in the early 1980s. Throughout the decade, years after his death, Rhoads's picture appeared on the covers of guitar magazines, advertising articles that discussed his practicing and teaching methods and analyzed his music. The inner sleeve of the *Tribute* album (1987) reproduces a few pages from Rhoads's personal guitar notebook, showing his systematic exploration of classical music theory. One sheet is titled "Key of C#"; on it, for each of the seven modes based on C# (Ionian, Dorian, Phrygian, and so on), Rhoads wrote out the diatonic chords for each scale degree, followed by secondary and substitute seventh chords. On another page, he composed exercises based on arpeggiated seventh and ninth chords.

Rhoads's interest in music theory was symptomatic of the increasing classical influence on heavy metal, but his success also helped promote classical study among metal guitarists. Winner of *Guitar Player's* "Best New Talent" Award in 1981, Rhoads brought to heavy metal guitar a new model of virtuosity which depended on patterns of discipline and consistency derived from classical models. Besides his classical allusions, and his methods of study and teaching, Rhoads's skill at double-tracking solos (recording them exactly the same way more than once, so that they could be layered on the record to add a sense of depth and space) was extremely influential on subsequent production techniques.[10] Rhoads's accomplishments also contributed to the growing tendency among guitarists to regard their virtuosic solos in terms of a division of labor long accepted in classical music, as opportunities for thoughtful composition and skillful execution, rather than spontaneous improvisation.

Classically influenced players such as Van Halen and Rhoads helped precipitate a shift among guitar players towards a new model of professional excellence, with theory, analysis, pedagogy and technical rigor acquiring new importance. *Guitar for the Practicing Musician,* now the most widely read guitarists' magazine, began publication in 1983, attracting readers with transcriptions and analyses of guitar-based popular music. Its professional guitarist-transcribers developed a sophisticated set of special notations for representing the nuances of performance, rather like the elaborate ornament tables of Baroque music. Their transcriptions are usually accompanied by various kinds of analysis, such as modal (for example, "The next section alternates between the modalities of Eb Lydian and F Mixolydian...."), stylistic (relating new pieces to the history of discursive options available to guitar players) and technical (detailing the techniques used in particular performances).

Swedish guitar virtuoso Yngwie J. Malmsteen continued many of the trends explored by Blackmore, Van Halen, and Rhoads, and took some of them to unprecedented extremes. Malmsteen was exposed to classical music from the age of five; his mother wanted him to be a musician, and made sure he received classical training on several instruments. Yet he claims to have hated music until television brought him a pair of musical epiphanies that, taken together, started him on the path to becoming the most influential rock guitarist since Van Halen. "On the 18th of September, 1970, I saw a show on television with Jimi Hendrix, and I said, 'Wow!' I took the guitar off the wall, and I haven't stopped since."[11] Malmsteen's first exciting encounter with classical music—his exposure to the music of Paganini, the nineteenth-century violin virtuoso—also took place through the mediation of television.[12] Thus the mass mediation of classical music makes it available in contexts that cannot be conventionally policed, for uses that cannot be predicted.

Upon the release of his U.S. debut album in 1984, which won him *Guitar Player's* "Best New Talent" award that year and "Best Rock Guitarist" in 1985, Malmsteen quickly gained a reputation as the foremost of metal's neoclassicists. He adapted classical music with more thoroughness and intensity than any previous guitarist, and he expanded the melodic and harmonic language of metal while setting even higher standards of virtuosic precision. Not only do Malmsteen's solos recreate the rhetoric of his virtuosic heroes, Bach and Paganini, but he introduced further harmonic resources and advanced techniques such as sweep-picking, achieving the best impression yet of the nuance and agility of a virtuoso violinist. Moreover, as I will show below, Malmsteen embraced the ideological premises of classical music more openly than anyone before.

Guitar for the Practicing Musician published a detailed analysis of Malmsteen's "Black Star," from his first U.S. album, *Yngwie J. Malmsteen's Rising Force* (1984). Such analytical pieces are intended as guides to the music of important guitarists, facilitating the study and emulation practiced by the magazine's readers. The following excerpts from Wolf Marshall's commentary can serve both as a summary of some technical features of Malmsteen's music and as a sample of the critical discourse of the writers who theorize and analyze heavy metal in professional guitarists' magazines:

> "Black Star" shows off the many facets of Yngwie's singular style. Whether he is playing subdued acoustic guitar or blazing pyrotechnics, he is unmistakably Yngwie—the newest and perhaps the most striking proponent of the Teutonic-Slavic *Weltsmerz* (as in Bach/Beethoven/Brahms Germanic brooding minor modality) School of Heavy Rock.... The opening guitar piece is a classical prelude (as one might expect) to the larger work. It is vaguely reminiscent of Bach's *Bourree* in Em, with its 3/4 rhythm and use of secondary dominant chords.... The passage at the close of the guitar's exposition is similar to the effect ... [of the] spiccato ("bouncing bow") classical violin technique. It is the first of many references to classical violin mannerisms.... This is a diminished chord sequence, based on the classical relationship of C diminished: C D# F# A (chord) to B major in a Harmonic minor mode: E F# G A B C D#.... The feeling of this is like some of Paganini's violin passages.... While these speedy arpeggio flurries are somewhat reminiscent of Blackmore's frenzied wide raking, they are actually quite measured and exact and require a tremendous amount of hand shifting and stretching as well as precision to accomplish. The concept is more related to virtuoso violin etudes than standard guitar vocabulary.... Notice the use of Harmonic minor (Mixolydian mode) in the B major sections and the Baroque Concerto Grosso (Handel/Bach/Vivaldi) style running bass line counterpoint as well.[13]

Marshall's analysis is quite musicological in tone and content; he deliberately compares Malmsteen's recorded performance to classical techniques, contextualizes it through style analysis, and translates certain features into the technical vocabulary of music theory. The style analysis situates "Black Star" with respect to two musical traditions: classical music (Bach, Paganini, Beethoven and so on) and rock guitar (Blackmore). Marshall simultaneously presents a detailed description of the music and links it to the classical tradition by employing the language of academic music theory: chords, modes, counterpoint, form. As rock guitarists have become increasingly interested in studying the history and theory of classical music, Marshall can safely assume that his audience is able to follow such analysis.[14]

Moreover, Marshall's analysis shows that metal guitarists and their pedagogues have not only adopted the trappings of academic discourse about music, but they have also internalized many of the values that underpin that discourse. Even as he carefully contextualizes Malmsteen's music, Marshall insists on its originality and uniqueness ("Yngwie's singular style," "unmistakably Yngwie"). The commentary emphasizes Malmsteen's precision of execution as well ("measured and exact," "tremendous ... precision"). Most tellingly, Marshall implicitly accepts the categories and conceptions of academic music analysis, along with its terms. For apart from the comment about "arpeggio flurries," Marshall deals exclusively with pitch and form, the traditional concerns of musicological analysis. And just as the discipline of musicology has drawn fire from within and without for ignoring or marginalizing musical rhythm, timbre, gesture, rhetoric and other possible categories of analysis, metal guitarists' own theorists and pedagogues could be criticized for the same restricted analytical vision.[15]

If they are to become effective musicians, metal guitarists must in fact learn to maneuver within musical parameters beyond pitch and form, just as their counterparts within conservatories and music schools must learn much that is not written down. In the academy, such learning is referred to as "musicality," and it is often the focal point of a mystification that covers up classical music's reliance on oral traditions. In both classical music and heavy metal, virtually the same aspects of music are far less theorized, codified and written; music students must learn by listening, emulating and watching the rhythm and gesture of bodily motion. Theorists of metal, like their academic counterparts, rarely deal with musical rhetoric and social meanings; one analysis of Van Halen's "Eruption" merely named the modes employed (E phrygian, A and E aeolian) and summed up with the blandness of a music appreciation text: "a well-balanced, thought-out guitar solo, which features a variety of techniques."[16]

Yngwie Malmsteen exemplifies the wholesale importation of classical music into heavy metal—the adoption of not only classical musical style and vocabulary, models of virtuosic rhetoric and modes of practice, pedagogy and analysis, but also the social values that underpin these activities. These values are a modern mixture of those that accompanied music-making of the seventeenth, eighteenth and nineteenth centuries, fused with the priorities of modernism. Along with virtuosity, the reigning values of metal guitar include a valorization of balance, planning and originality, a conservatory-style fetishization of technique and sometimes even a reactionary philosophy of culture—Malmsteen bemoans the lack of musicianship in today's popular music, and looks back on the "good old days" of the seventeenth century, when, he imagines, standards were much higher.[17] Malmsteen is particularly noted for his elitism, another value he derives from contemporary classical music, and which he justifies by emphasizing his connections with its greater prestige. In interviews, he constantly insists on his own genius, his links to the geniuses of the classical past, and his distance from virtually all contemporary popular musicians, whose music he regards as simple, trite and inept. Because he aspires to the universal status often claimed for classical music, he denounces the genre he is usually thought to inhabit, insisting "I do *not* play heavy metal!"[18]

While he has been known to claim that, as a genius, he never had to practice, Malmsteen also presents himself as one who has suffered for his art. A joint interview with bassist Billy Sheehan preserves an account of his early devotion to music, and its costs:

Yngwie: I was extremely self-critical. I was possessed. For many years I wouldn't do anything else but play the guitar.

Billy: I missed a lot of my youth. I missed the whole girl trip. I didn't start driving until I was 25.

Yngwie: I also sacrificed a lot of the social thing. I didn't care about my peers. To me, nothing else was even close in importance.

Such statements undoubtedly reflect the tendency toward self-aggrandizement and self-pity that have made Malmsteen unloved by his peers in the guitar world. But they also further reflect his virtually total acceptance of the model of music-making promulgated in classical music. Malmsteen, along with many other musicians, sees a need for music to "evolve" toward greater complexity and "sophistication." The pursuit of virtuosic technique usually requires many thousands of hours of patient, private repetition of exercises. To this end, many young players pursue a fanatical practice regime, a pursuit of individual excellence that often leaves little room for communal experiences of music-making, just as is the case in the training of classical musicians.[19]

The extreme extension of this set of ideological values is the complete withdrawal of the musician from his or her public, in pursuit of complexity and private meanings. This strategy, which had earlier been championed by academic composers such as Milton Babbitt, can now be recognized in some virtuosic guitar players. Steve Vai boasts of his most recent album:

> What I did with *Passion and Warfare* is the ultimate statement: I *locked* myself into a room and said, "To hell with everything—I'm doing this and it's a complete expression of what I am. I'm not concerned about singles, I'm not concerned about megaplatinum success, I'm not concerned about record companies." It was a real special time. All too often kids and musicians and artists just have to conform to make a living. I'm one of the lucky few and believe me, I don't take it for granted.[20]

Vai is trying to claim "authenticity" here, trying to prove his autonomy as an artist who is free of the influences of the very social context that makes his artistic statements possible and meaningful. When he goes on to describe his fasting, his visions, his bleeding on the guitar—and his compositional process of painstaking and technologically sophisticated multitrack recording—he presents himself as an updated, self-torturing, Romantic artist, reaching beyond the known world for inspiration. This individualism and self-centeredness unites classical music and heavy metal, and stands in stark contrast to many other kinds of music. For example, a bit later in the same issue of *Musician,* B. B. King says,

> What I'm trying to get over to you is this: ...when I'm on the stage, I am *trying* to entertain. I'm *not* just trying to amuse B. B. King. I'm trying to entertain the people that came to see me.... I think that's one of the things that's kind of kept me out here, trying to keep *pleasing* the audience. I think that's one of the mistakes that's happened in music as a whole: A lot of people forget that they got an audience.[21]

Malmsteen's work has convinced some that the classical influence is played out, even as it has been the leading inspiration for the eager experimentation of the avant-garde. He has helped turn many players to a fruitful engagement with the classical tradition, even as he has helped lead them toward the impoverishing regimes of practice and analysis that now dominate that tradition. Malmsteen's abrasive elitism contrasts with his attempt to forge links with the musical past and reinvigorate reified discourses for mass audiences. The new meritocracy of guitar technique he helped to create both encourages the fetishization of individual virtuosity and opens doors for female and African-American musicians, such as Jennifer Batten and Vernon Reid.[22] His music brings to light contradictions that add to our understanding of both heavy metal and classical music.

For heavy metal and classical music exist in the same social context: they are subject to similar structures of marketing and mediation, and they "belong to" and serve the needs of competing social groups whose power is linked to the prestige of their culture. The immense social and cultural distance that is normally assumed to separate classical music and heavy metal is in fact not a gap of musicality, but a more complex one constructed in the interests of cultural hierarchy. Since heavy metal and classical music are markers of social difference and enactments of social experience, their intersection affects the complex relations among those who depend on these musics to legitimate their values. Their discursive fusion provokes insights about the social interests that are powerfully served by invisible patterns of sound.

Heavy metal guitarists, like all other innovative musicians, create new sounds by drawing on the power of the old, and by fusing together their semiotic resources into compelling new combinations. They recognize affinities between their work and the tonal sequences of Vivaldi, the melodic imagination of Bach, the virtuosity of Liszt and Paganini. Metal musicians have revitalized eighteenth- and nineteenth-century music for their mass audience, in a striking demonstration of the ingenuity of popular culture. Although their audience's ability to decode such musical referents owes much to the effects of the ongoing appropriations of classical music by TV and movie composers, heavy metal musicians have accomplished their own adaptation of what has become the somber music of America's aristocracy, reworking it to speak for a different group's claims to power and artistry.

Metal musicians have appropriated the more prestigious discourses of classical music and reworked them into noisy articulations of pride, fear, longing, alienation, aggression and community. Their adaptations of classical music, while they might be seen as travesties by modern devotees of that music, are close in spirit to the eclectic fusions of J. S. Bach and other idols of that tradition. Metal appropriations are rarely parody or pastiche; they are usually a reanimation, a reclamation of signs that can be turned to new uses. Unlike art rock, the point is typically not to refer to a prestigious discourse and thus to bask in reflected glory. Rather, metal musicians adapt classical signs for their own purposes, to signify to their audience, to have real meanings in the present. This is the sort of process to which the linguistic philosopher V. N. Volosinov referred when he wrote that the sign can become an arena of class struggle; Volosinov and the rest of the Bakhtin circle were interested in how signs not only reflect the interests of the social groups that use them, but are also "refracted" when the same signs are used by different groups to different ends.[23] Thus heavy metal musicians and "legitimate" musicians use Bach in drastically different ways.

Like classical musicians, heavy metal musicians draw upon the resources of the past that have been made available to them through mass mediation and their own historical study. But it is precisely such predations that the musical academy is supposed to prevent. Bach's contemporary meanings are produced jointly by musicologists, critics and the marketing departments of record companies and symphony orchestras, and the interpretation of Bach they construct has little to do with the dramatic, noisy meanings found by metal musicians and fans, and everything to do with aesthetics, order, hierarchy and cultural hegemony. The classical music world polices contemporary readings of the "masterworks"; the adaptations of Randy Rhoads and Bon Jovi are ignored, while the acceptability of Stokowski's orchestral transcriptions is debated. Malmsteen's inauthentic performances fall outside the permissable ideological boundaries that manage to contain Maurice André and Glenn Gould. The drive to enforce preferred ideological meanings is, as both Bakhtin and Volosinov put it, "nondialogic." It is oppressive, authoritative and absolute.

> The very same thing that makes the ideological sign vital and mutable is also, however, that which makes it a refracting and distorting medium. The ruling class strives to impart a supraclass, eternal character to the ideological sign, to extinguish or drive inward the struggle between social value judgements which occurs in it, to make the sign uniaccentual.[24]

The social function of distinctions such as "highbrow" and "lowbrow" is precisely to stabilize signs, prop up automatic dismissals, and quash dialogue and debate. But since cultural hegemony is never absolute, appropriations such as those by heavy metal musicians constantly appear on the field of social contestation we call "popular culture."[25] Such disruptions are rarely even acknowledged by academics. In the histories they write and the syllabi they teach, most musicologists continue to define "music" implicitly in terms of the European concert tradition, ignoring non-Western and popular musics, and treating contemporary academic composers such as Milton Babbitt as the heirs to the canon of great classical "masters."

But Babbitt's claim to inherit the mantle of Bach is perhaps more tenuous than that of Randy Rhoads, and not only because Bach and Rhoads utilize, to some extent, a common musical vocabulary. The institutional environment within which Babbitt has worked (and which he helped create and vigorously championed) rewards abstract complexity and often regards listeners and their reactions with indifference or hostility; both Bach and Rhoads composed and performed for particular audiences, gauging their success by their rhetorical effectiveness. Babbitt's music demonstrates his braininess; Bach's and Rhoads's offer powerful, nuanced experiences of transcendence and communality. Despite their important differences, Bach and Rhoads have in common their love of virtuosic rhetoric and their willingness to seek to move people, to deploy shared musical codes of signification, to work in musical discourses that are widely intelligible, however complex.

In a recent journalistic defense of cultural hierarchy, Edward Rothstein begins by granting most of the usual objections to it—he admits that both high and low can be good or bad, simple or complex; that particular works of art cannot be considered innately high or low because they move up and down the ladder of cultural prestige as time passes; and that cultural categories are thus neither stable nor self-evident. In the end, though, Rothstein simply insists that the high/low distinction is necessary, falling back on some familiar mystical dogma about autonomy and timelessness, and implying that attacks on cultural hierarchy are attacks on culture. The idea seems to be that the worthy have high culture and the unworthy have popular culture and perhaps a bit of "music appreciation" to let them know what they're missing, a view I would characterize as "voodoo aesthetics" (after George Bush's derisive label for Reagan's trickle-down defense of economic hierarchy). Rothstein concludes by noting that classical composers have appropriated features of popular music, but seems unaware that the reverse has occured incessantly throughout the history of the split; he asserts that "while the high provides tools and perspectives which can comprehend the low, the low is powerless to comprehend the high."[26] Such a leap of faith, such imperial confidence, is prerequisite to voodoo aesthetics.

Rothstein's argument is of the sort that is common among those who know the fenced-in terrain of the so-called "high" much better than the vast, diverse spaces of the "low," for it depends upon denying the creative agency of those who inhabit the latter realm. Like musical phrenologists, critics such as Rothstein work to naturalize a hierarchy that privileges themselves and the culture they care about at the expense of everyone else. But heavy metal guitarists' creative appropriations of classical music rebut such attempts to ground cultural hierarchy in the inherent features of texts or practices. Metal musicians erupted across the Great Divide between "serious" and "popular" music, between "art" and "entertainment," and found that the gap was not as wide as we have been led to believe. As Christopher Small put it,

> The barrier between classical and vernacular music is opaque only when viewed from the point of view of the dominant group; when viewed from the other side it is often transparent, and to the vernacular musician there are not two musics but only one.... Bach and Beethoven and other "great composers" are not dead heroes but colleagues, ancestor figures even, who are alive in the present.[27]

Heavy metal musicians' appropriations of classical music help us to see "high culture" and "low culture" as categories that are socially constructed and maintained. Like "highbrow" and "lowbrow," the deployment of such terms benefits certain individuals and groups at the expense of others, and their power depends chiefly upon intimidation. By engaging directly with seventeenth-, eighteenth-, and nineteenth-century composers and performers, by claiming them as heroes and forebears despite contemporary boundaries that would keep them separate, and by mastering and recontextualizing the rhetoric and theoretical apparatus of "high" music, heavy metal musicians have accomplished a critical juxtaposition that undermines the apparent necessity and naturalness of cultural hierarchy. The specific meanings of metal's appropriations in their new contexts are of great importance, of course. But for cultural criticism, perhaps the most salient legacy of the classical influence on heavy metal is the fact that these musicians have "comprehended the high" without accepting its limitations, defying the division that has been such a crucial determinant of musical life in the twentieth century.

NOTES

1. Lawrence W. Levine, *Highbrow/Lowbrow: The Emergence of Cultural Hierarchy in America* (Cambridge: Harvard University Press, 1988), pp. 221–23. Theories of brows "scientifically" mapped onto the human body the more general concept of "high" and "low" culture, which had been most powerfully theorized earlier in the nineteenth century by German cultural nationalists. Sanna Pedersen has examined the extent to which the emergence of "autonomous" German instrumental music depended on the creation of a demonized other; see her "Enlightened and Romantic German Music Criticism, 1800–1850," Ph.D. dissertation, University of Pennsylvania, forthcoming.

2. See, for example, Robert P. Morgan, *Twentieth-Century Music: A History of Musical Style in Modern Europe and America* (New York: Norton, 1991); Robert P. Morgan, ed., *Anthology of Twentieth-Century Music* (New York: W. W. Norton, 1992); Glenn Watkins, *Soundings: Music in the Twentieth Century* (New York: Schirmer Books, 1988); and Bryan R. Simms, *Music of the Twentieth Century: Style and Structure* (New York: Schirmer Books, 1986). Of course, there is nothing wrong with writing about some kinds of music and not others; my point is that to use the grand title "Twentieth-Century Music" for a specialized repertoire is to make an implicit ideological argument that these authors neither admit nor defend.

3. Malmsteen's first U.S. album, *Yngwie J. Malmsteen's Rising Force* (1984), had offered "special thanks" to Bach and Paganini

4. John Stix, "Yngwie Malmsteen and Billy Sheehan: Summit Meeting at Chops City," *Guitar for the Practicing Musician* (March 1986), p. 59. To be sure, heavy metal, like all forms of rock music, owes its biggest debt to African-American blues. The harmonic progressions, vocal lines and guitar improvisations of metal all rely heavily on the pentatonic scales derived from blues music. The moans and screams of metal guitar playing, now performed with whammy bars and overdriven amplifiers, derive from the bottleneck playing of the Delta blues musicians, and ultimately from earlier African-American vocal styles. Many heavy metal musicians have testified that they learned to play by imitating urban blues guitarists such as B. B. King, Buddy Guy, and Muddy Waters, and those who did not study the blues directly learned it secondhand, from the British cover versions by Eric Clapton and Jimmy Page, or from the most conspicuous link between heavy metal and black blues and R & B, Jimi Hendrix. Glenn Tipton, guitarist with Judas Priest, offers a demonstration of the blues origins of heavy metal licks in J. D. Considine, "Purity and Power," *Musician* (September 1984), pp. 46–50.

5. Martin K. Webb, "Ritchie Blackmore with Deep Purple," in *Masters of Heavy Metal*, Jas Obrecht, ed., (New York: Quill, 1984), p. 54; and Steve Rosen, "Blackmore's Rainbow," in *Masters of Heavy Metal*, p. 62. Webb apparently misunderstood Blackmore's explanation, for what I have rendered as an ellipsis he transcribed as "Bm to a D$$ to a C to a G," a harmonic progression which is neither characteristic of Bach nor to be found anywhere in "Highway Star." Blackmore was probably referring to the progression that underpins the latter part of his solo, Dm | G | C | A. "Highway Star" was recorded in 1971 and released in 1972 on the album *Machine Head*.

6. This is described, among other places, in Jas Obrecht, "Van Halen Comes of Age," in *Masters of Heavy Metal*, Jas Obrecht, ed., (New York: Quill, 1984), p. 156.

7. See Wolf Marshall, "Randy Rhoads: A Musical Appreciation," *Guitar for the Practicing Musician* (June 1985), p. 57.

8. At the Princeton conference, I performed excerpts of Rhoads's solos on electric guitar, analyzing as I went. Since the printed format prevents me from using sounds and audience reactions as evidence for my arguments, my concern in this paper is more with the cultural significance of metal musicians' activities as appropriators rather than with the musical meanings of the resulting texts. For more on the latter, as well as theoretical discussions of how to ground musical analyses of affect, see my *Running with the Devil: Power, Gender, and Madness in Heavy Metal Music* (Hanover, NH: Wesleyan University Press, 1993); see also Susan McClary, *Feminine Endings: Music, Gender, and Sexuality* (Minneapolis: University of Minnesota Press, 1991), especially chaps. one and seven.

9. By "Baroque rhetoric," I mean the kind of transgressive virtuosity to be found in, for example, the cadenza of Bach's Brandenburg Concerto No. 5, or his E minor Partita. See Susan McClary's analysis of this Brandenburg in "The Blasphemy of Talking Politics During Bach Year," in *Music and Society: The Politics of Composition, Performance, and Reception*, Richard Leppert and Susan McClary, eds., (Cambridge: Cambridge University Press, 1987), pp. 13–62. The live recording of "Suicide Solution" appears on *Ozzy Osbourne/Randy Rhoads, Tribute* (CBS, 1987 [recorded in 1981]). For a fuller discussion of the song, see my *Running with the Devil*, chap. 5.

10. See Wolf Marshall, "Randy Rhoads," *Guitar for the Practicing Musician* (April 1986), p. 51.

11. Matt Resnicoff, "Flash of Two Worlds," *Musician* (September 1990), p. 76.

12. Joe Lalaina, "Yngwie, the One and Only," *Guitar School* (September 1989), p. 15

13. Wolf Marshall, "Performance Notes: Black Star," *Guitar for the Practicing Musician Collector's Yearbook* (Winter 1990), pp. 26–27.

14. In fact, in my experience, many metal guitarists (most of whom, like Bach and Mozart, never attended college) have a much better grasp of harmonic theory and modal analysis than most university graduate students in music.

15. Compare Janet Levy's cautious but valuable exposé of the values implicit in the writings of academic musicologists, "Covert and Casual Values in Recent Writings About Music," *Journal of Musicology* 6:1 (Winter 1987), pp. 3–27.

16. Andy Aledort, "Performance Notes," *Guitar for the Practicing Musician Collector's Yearbook* (Winter 1990), p. 6.

17. John Stix, "Yngwie Malmsteen and Billy Sheehan," p. 59. On the other side of his lineage, Malmsteen cites early Deep Purple as another moment of high musicianship (p. 64).

18. Fabio Testa, "Yngwie Malmsteen: In Search of a New Kingdom," *The Best of Metal Mania #2* (1987), p. 35.

19. Guitar players who are members of bands, however, are usually the leading composers of their groups, and the collaborative experience of working out songs and arrangements in a rock band is a type of musical creativity seldom enjoyed by classical musicians.

20. Matt Resnicoff, "The Latest Temptation of Steve Vai," *Musician* (September 1990), p. 60. Compare Milton Babbitt's "Who Cares If You Listen?" *High Fidelity* (February 1958), pp. 38–40, 126–127.

21. *Musician* (September 1990), p. 112.

22. Jennifer Batten, who has toured with Michael Jackson and others, is also a columnist for *Guitar for the Practicing Musician*. Vernon Reid, of Living Colour, has been featured on the cover and in the analyses of the same magazine.

23. V. N. Volosinov, *Marxism and the Philosophy of Language* (Cambridge, MA: Harvard University Press, 1986). Some authorities believe that this work was actually written by M. M. Bakhtin.

24. Volosinov, *Marxism and the Philosophy of Language*, p. 23. See also M. M. Bakhtin, *The Dialogic Imagination: Four Essays* (Austin: University of Texas Press, 1981), and Speech Genres and Other Late Essays (Austin: University of Texas Press, 1986).

25. See Stuart Hall, "Notes on Deconstructing 'The Popular,'" in *People's History and Socialist Theory*, Raphael Samuel, ed., (London: Routledge and Kegan Paul, 1981), pp. 227–240.

26. Edward Rothstein, "Mr. Berry, Say Hello to Ludwig," *New York Times* (April 5, 1992), p. H31.

27. Christopher Small, *Music of the Common Tongue: Survival and Celebration in Afro-American Music* (New York: Riverrun, 1987), p. 126.

42

"The Real Thing—Bruce Springsteen"

SIMON FRITH

Few writers since the 1970s, have helped bridge the gap between journalistic rock criticism and academic popular music scholarship more than Simon Frith. A longtime contributor to such publications as the *Village Voice* and *London Times*, he also is the author of such pioneering studies as *The Sociology of Rock* (London: Constable, 1978) and *Performing Rites: On the Value of Popular Music* (Cambridge: Harvard University Press, 1996). During the 1980s, Frith, like many others, was intrigued by the overwhelming popularity of Bruce Springsteen (born 1949), whose two mid-decade releases, *Born in the U.S.A.* and *Bruce Springsteen & the E Street Band Live 1975–85* combined to sell nearly 30 million records in the United States alone. As Frith points out, much of Springsteen's success can be attributed to the authenticity of his strong "populist anti-capitalism" image, which while carefully constructed, nonetheless expresses something tangible for his large fan base. Yet, according to Frith, this presents an inherent contradiction: Springsteen's appeal is that he appears to be so singularly "real," but this is also precisely why he is one of rock's best-selling commodities. And as a commodity Springsteen cannot dictate what his music means to his audiences. As a case in point, Springsteen's "Born in the U.S.A.," a bitterly ironic portrait of a rejected, disillusioned Vietnam veteran and a strident critique of the American dream, earned "The Boss" a Top 10 single. Yet much of its success hinged on its misperception as a patriotic anthem, an appropriated soundtrack that helped bolster Ronald Reagan's 1984 presidential campaign.*

INTRODUCTION

My guess is that by Christmas 1986 Bruce Springsteen was making more money per day than any other pop star—more than Madonna, more than Phil Collins or Mark Knopfler, more than Paul McCartney even; *Time* calculated that he had earned $7.5 million in the first *week* of his *Live* LP release. This five-record boxed set went straight to the top of the American LP sales charts (it reputedly sold a million copies on its first day, grossing $50 million 'out of the gate') and stayed there throughout the Christmas season. It was the nation's best-seller in November and December, when more records are sold than in all the other months of the year put together. Even in Britain, where the winter charts are dominated by TV-advertised anthologies, the Springsteen set at £25 brought in more money than the tight-margin single-album compilations. (And CBS reckon they get 42% of their annual sales at Christmas time). Walking through London from Tottenham Court Road down Oxford Street to Piccadilly in early December, passing the three symbols of corporate rock—

* *Source:* Simon Frith, "The Real Thing—Bruce Springsteen," *Musica E Dossier*, 1987. Reprinted in *Music for Pleasure: Essays in the Sociology of Pop* (New York: Routledge, 1988), pp. 94–101.

the Virgin, HMV and Tower superstores—each claiming to be the biggest record shop in the world, I could only see Springsteen boxes, piled high by the cash desks, the *safest* stock of the season.

Sales success at this level—those boxes were piled up in Sydney and Toronto too, in shop aisles in Sweden and Denmark, West Germany, Holland and Japan—has a disruptive effect on the rest of the rock process. American television news showed trucks arriving at New York's record stores from the CBS warehouses—they were immediately surrounded by queues too, and so, in the USA, Springsteen was sold off the back of vans, frantically, like a sudden supply of Levis in the USSR. Within hours of its release, the Springsteen box was jamming up CBS's works. In America the company announced that nothing from its back catalogue would be available for four months, because all spare capacity had been commandeered for Springsteen (and even then the compact disc version of the box was soon sold out—not enough, only 300,000, had been manufactured). In Europe the company devoted one of its three pressing plants exclusively to the box. Springsteen dominated the market by being the only CBS product readily available.

Whatever the final sales figures turn out to be (and after Christmas the returns of the boxes from the retailers to CBS were as startling as the original sales), it is already obvious that *Bruce Springsteen and the E Street Band Live* is a phenomenal record, a money-making achievement to be discussed on the same scale as *Saturday Night Fever* or Michael Jackson's *Thriller*. Remember, too, that a live record is cheaper to produce than a new studio sound (and Springsteen has already been well rewarded for these songs from the sales of previous discs and the proceeds of sell-out tours). Nor did CBS need the expensive trappings or promo videos and press and TV advertising to make this record sell. Because the Springsteen box was an event in itself (the only pop precedent I can think of is the Beatles' 1968 *White Album*), it generated its own publicity as 'news'—radio stations competed to play the most tracks for the longest times, shops competed to give Bruce the most window space, newspapers competed in speculations about how much money he was really making. The Springsteen box became, in other words, that ultimate object of capitalist fantasy, a commodity which sold more and more because it had sold so well already, a product which had to be *owned* (rather than necessarily used).

In the end, though, what is peculiar about the Springsteen story is not its marks of a brilliant commercial campaign, but their invisibility. Other superstars put out live sets for Christmas (Queen, for example) and the critics sneer at their opportunism; other stars resell their old hits (Bryan Ferry, for example) and their fans worry about their lack of current inspiration. And in these sorry tales of greed and pride it is Bruce Springsteen more often than not who is the measure of musical integrity, the model of a rock performer who cannot be discussed in terms of financial calculation. In short, the most successful pop commodity of the moment, the Springsteen Live Set, stands for the principle that music should not be a commodity; it is his very disdain for success that makes Springsteen so successful. It is as if his presence on every fashionable turntable, tape deck and disc machine, his box on every up-market living-room floor, are what enables an aging, affluent rock generation to feel in touch with its 'roots'. And what matters in this post-modern era is not whether Bruce Springsteen *is* the real thing, but how he sustains the belief that there are somehow, somewhere, real things to be.

FALSE

Consider the following:

Bruce Springsteen Is a Millionaire Who Dresses as a Worker

Worn jeans, singlets, a head band to keep his hair from his eyes—these are working clothes and it is an important part of Springsteen's appeal that we do see him, as an entertainer, working for his living. His popularity is based on his live shows and, more particularly, on their spectacular energy: Springsteen works *hard*, and his exhaustion—on our behalf—is visible. He makes music physically, as a *manual* worker. His clothes are straightforwardly practical, sensible (like sports people's clothes)—comfortable jeans (worn in) for easy movement, a singlet to let the sweat flow free, the mechanic's cloth to wipe his brow.

But there is more to these clothes than this. *Springsteen wears work clothes even when he is not working*. His off-stage image, his LP sleeves and interview poses, even the candid 'off duty' paparazzi shots, involve the same down-to-earth practicality (the only time Springsteen was seen to dress up 'in private' was for his wedding). Springsteen doesn't wear the clothes appropriate to his real economic status and resources (as compared with other pop stars), but neither does he dress up for special occasions like real workers do—he's never seen flashily attired for a sharp night out. It's as if he can't be seen to be excessive or indulgent except on our behalf, as a performer for an audience. For him there is no division between work and play, between the ordinary and the extraordinary. Because the constructed 'Springsteen', the star, is presented plain, there can never be a suggestion that this is just an act (as Elvis was an act, as Madonna is). There are no other Springsteens, whether more real or more artificial, to be seen.

Springsteen Is Employer-as-Employee

It has always surprised me that he should be nicknamed 'The Boss', but the implication is that this is an affectionate label, a brotherly way in which the E Street Band honour his sheer drive. In fact 'boss' is an accurate description of their economic relationship—Springsteen *employs* his band; he has the recording contracts, controls the LP and concert material, writes the songs and chooses the oldies. And whatever his musicians' contributions to his success (fulsomely recognized), he gets the composing/performing royalties, could, in principle, sack people, and, like any other good employer, rewards his team with generous bonuses after each sell-out show or disc. And, of course, he employs a stage crew too, and a manager, a publicist, a secretary/assistant; he has an annual turnover now of millions. He may express the feelings of 'little' men and women buffeted by distant company boards but he is himself a corporation.

Springsteen Is a 37-year-old Teenager

He is 20 years into a hugely successful career, he's a professional, a married man old enough to be the father of adolescent children of his own, but he still presents himself as a young man, waiting to see what life will bring, made tense by clashes with adult authority. He introduces his songs with memories—his life as a boy, arguments with his father (his mother is rarely mentioned)—but as a performer he is clearly *present* in these emotions. Springsteen doesn't regret or vilify his past; as a grown man he's still living it.

Springsteen Is a Shy Exhibitionist

He is, indeed, one of the sexiest performers rock and roll has ever had—there's a good part of his concert audience who simply fancy him, can't take their eyes off his body, and he's mesmerising on stage because of the confidence with which he displays himself. But, for all this, his persona is still that of a nervy, gauche youth on an early date.

Springsteen Is Superstar-as-Friend

He comes into our lives as a recording star, a radio sound, a video presence and, these days, as an item of magazine gossip. Even in his live shows he seems more accessible in the close-ups on the mammoth screens around the stage than as the 'real' dim figure in the distance. And yet he is still the rock performer whose act most convincingly creates (and depends on) a sense of community.

Springsteen's Most Successful 'Record' Is 'Live'.

What the boxed set is meant to do is reproduce a concert, an *event,* and if for other artists five records would be excessive, for Springsteen it is a further sign of his album's truth-to-life—it lasts about the same length of time as a show. There's an interesting question of trust raised here. I don't doubt that these performances were once live, that the applause did happen, but this is nevertheless a false event, a concert put together from different shows (and alternative mixes), edited and balanced to sound like a live LP (which has quite different aural conventions than an actual show). Springsteen fans know that, of course. The pleasure of this set is not that it takes us back to somewhere we've been, but that it lays out something ideal. It describes what we *mean* by 'Springsteen live', and what makes him 'real' in this context is not his transparency, the idea that he is who he pretends to be, but his art, his ability to articulate the right *idea* of reality.

TRUE

The recurring term used in discussions of Springsteen, by fans, by critics, by fans-as-critics is 'authenticity'. What is meant by this is not that Springsteen is authentic in a direct way—is simply expressing himself—but that he represents 'authenticity'. This is why he has become so important: he stands for the core values of rock and roll even as those values become harder and harder to sustain. At a time when rock is the soundtrack for TV commercials, when tours depend on sponsorship deals, when video promotion has blurred the line between music-making and music-selling, Springsteen suggests that, despite everything, it still gives people a way to define themselves against corporate logic, a language in which everyday hopes and fears can be expressed.

If Bruce Springsteen didn't exist, American rock critics would have had to invent him. In a sense, they did, whether directly (Jon Landau, *Rolling Stone*'s most significant critical theorist in the late sixties, is now his manager) or indirectly (Dave Marsh, Springsteen's official biographer, is the most passionate and widely read rock critic of the eighties). There are, indeed, few American rock critics who haven't celebrated Springsteen, but their task has been less to explain him to his potential fans, to sustain the momentum that carried him from cult to mass stardom, than to explain him to himself. They've placed him, that is, in a particular reading of rock history, not as the 'new Dylan' (his original sales label) but as the 'voice of the people'. His task is to carry the baton passed on from Woody Guthrie, and the purpose of his carefully placed oldies (Guthrie's 'This Land Is Your Land', Presley and Berry hits, British beat classics, Edwin Starr's 'War') isn't just to situate him as a fellow fan but also to identify him with a particular musical project. Springsteen himself claims on stage to represent an authentic popular tradition (as against the spurious commercial sentiments of an Irving Berlin).

To be so 'authentic' involves a number of moves. Firstly, authenticity must be defined against artifice; the terms only make sense in opposition to each other. This is the importance of Springsteen's image—to represent the 'raw' as against the 'cooked'. His plain stage appearance, his dressing down, has to be understood with reference to showbiz dressing up, to the elaborate spectacle of cabaret pop and soul (and routine stadium rock and roll)—Springsteen is real *by contrast.* In lyrical terms too he is plain-speaking; his songwriting craft is marked not by 'poetic' or obscure or personal language, as in the singer/songwriter tradition following Dylan, folk-rock (and his own early material), but by the vivid images and metaphors he builds from common words.

What's at stake here is not authenticity of experience, but authenticity of feeling; what matters is not whether Springsteen has been through these things himself (boredom, aggression, ecstasy, despair) but that he knows how they work. The point of his autobiographical anecdotes is not to reveal himself but to root his music in material conditions. Like artists in other media (fiction, film) Springsteen is concerned to give emotions (the essential data of rock and roll) a narrative setting, to situate them in time and place, to relate them to the situations they explain or confuse. He's not interested in abstract emotions, in vague sensation or even in moralizing. He is, to put it simply, a story-teller, and in straining to make his stories credible he uses classic techniques. Reality is registered by conventions first formulated by the nineteenth-century naturalists—a refusal to sentimentalize social conditions, a compulsion to sentimentalize human nature. Springsteen's songs (like Zola's fictions) are almost exclusively concerned with the working-class, with the effects of poverty and uncertainty, the consequences of weakness and crime; they trawl through the murky reality of the American dream; they contrast utopian impulses with people's lack of opportunity to do much more than get by; they find in sex the only opportunity for passion (and betrayal). Springsteen's protagonists, victims and criminals, defeated and enraged, are treated tenderly, their hopes honoured, their failure determined by circumstance.

It is his realism that makes Springsteen's populism politically ambiguous. His message is certainly anti-capitalist, or, at least, critical of the effects of capitalism—as both citizen and star Springsteen has refused to submit to market forces, has shown consistent and generous support for the system's losers, for striking trade unionists and the unemployed, for battered wives and children. But, at the same time, his focus on individuals' fate, the very power with which he describes the dreams they can't realize (but which he has) offers an opening for his appropriation, appropriation not just by politicians like Reagan but, more importantly, by hucksters and advertisers, who use him to sell their goods as some sort of *solution* to the problem he outlines. This is the paradox of mass-marketed populism: Springsteen's songs suggests there is something missing in our lives, the CBS message is that we can fill the gap *with a Bruce Springsteen record*. And for all Springsteen's support of current causes, what comes from his music is a whiff of nostalgia and an air of fatalism. His stories describe hopes-about-to-be-dashed, convey a sense of time passing beyond our control, suggest that our dreams can only be dreams. The formal conservatism of the music reinforces the emotional conservation of the lyrics. This is the way the world is, he sings, and nothing really changes.

But there's another way of describing Springsteen's realism. It means celebrating the ordinary not the special. Again the point is not that Springsteen is ordinary or even pretends to be, but that he honours ordinariness, making something intense out of experiences that are usually seen as mundane. It has always been pop's function to transform the banal, but this purpose was to some extent undermined by the rise of rock in the sixties, with its claims to art and poetry, its cult-building, its heavy metal mysticism. Springsteen himself started out with a couple of wordy, worthy LPs, but since then he has been in important ways committed to common sense. Springsteen's greatest skill is his ability to dramatize everyday events – even his stage act is a pub rock show writ large. The E Street Band, high-class professionals, play with a sort of amateurish enthusiasm, an affection for each other which is in sharp contrast to the bohemian contempt for their work (and their audience) which has been a strand of 'arty' rock shows since the Rolling Stones and the Doors. Springsteen's musicians stand for every bar and garage group that ever got together in fond hope of stardom.

His sense of the commonplace also explains Springsteen's physical appeal. His sexuality is not displayed as something remarkable, a kind of power, but is coded into his 'natural' movements, determined by what he has to do to sing and play. His body becomes 'sexy'—a source of excitement and anxiety—in its routine activity; his appeal is not defined in terms of glamour or fantasy. The basic sign of Springsteen's authenticity, to put it another way, is his sweat, his display of *energy*. His body is not posed, an object of consumption, but active, an object of exhaustion. When the E Street Band gather at the end of a show for the final bow, arms around each other's shoulders, drained and relieved, the sporting analogy is clear: this is a team which has won its latest bout. What matters is that every such bout is seen to be real, that there are no backing tapes, no 'fake' instruments, that the musicians really have played until they can play no more. There is a moment in every Springsteen show I've seen when Clarence Clemons takes centre-stage. For that moment he is the real star—he's bigger than Springsteen, louder, more richly dressed. And he's the saxophonist, giving us the clearest account all evening of the relationship between human effort and human music.

To be authentic and to sound authentic is in the rock context the same thing. Music can not *be* true or false, it can only refer to *conventions* of truth and falsity. Consider the following.

Thundering drums in Springsteen's songs give his stories their sense of unstoppable momentum, they map out the spaces within which things happen. This equation of time and space is the secret of great rock and roll and Springsteen uses other classic devices to achieve it—a piano/organ combination, for example (as used by The Band and many soul groups), so that melodic-descriptive and rhythmic-atmospheric sounds are continually swapped about.

The E Street Band makes music as a group, but a group in which we can hear every instrumentalist. Our attention is drawn, that is, not to a finished sound but to music-in-the-making. This is partly done by the refusal to make any instrument the 'lead' (which is why Nils Lofgren, a 'lead' guitarist, sounded out of place in the last E Street touring band). And partly by a specific musical busy-ness—the group is 'tight', everyone is aiming for the same rhythmic end, but 'loose', each player makes their own decision as to how to get there (which is one reason why electronic instruments would not fit—they're too smooth, too determined). All Springsteen's musicians, even the added back-up singers and percussionists, have individual voices; it would be unthinkable for him to appear with, say, an anonymous string section.

The textures and, more significantly, the melodic structures of Springsteen's music make self-conscious reference to rock and roll itself, to its conventional line-up, its cliched chord changes, its time-honoured ways of registering joys and sadness. Springsteen himself is a rock and roll star, not a crooner or singer/songwriter. His voice *strains* to be heard, he has to shout against the instruments that both support and compete with him. However many times he's rehearsed his lines they always sound as if they're being forged on the spot.

Many of Springsteen's most anthemic songs have no addresses (no 'you') but (like many Beatles songs) concern a third person (tales told about someone else) or involve an 'I' brooding aloud, explaining his situation impersonally, in a kind of individualised epic. Listening to such epics is a public activity (rather than a private fantasy), which is why Springsteen concerts still feel like collective occasions.

CONCLUSION

In one of his monologues Springsteen remembers that his parents were never very keen on his musical ambitions—they wanted him to train for something safe, like law or accountancy: 'they wanted me to get a little something for myself; what they did not understand was that I wanted *everything*!'

This is a line that could only be delivered by an American, and to explain Springsteen's importance and success we have to go back to the problem he is really facing: the fate of the individual artist under capitalism. In Europe, the artistic critique of the commercialization of everything has generally been conducted in terms of Romanticism, in a state of Bohemian disgust with the masses and the bourgeoisie alike, in the name of the superiority of the *avant-garde*. In the USA there's a populist anti-capitalism available, a tradition of the artist as the common man (rarely woman), pitching rural truth against urban deceit, pioneer values against bureaucratic routines. This tradition (Mark Twain to Woody Guthrie, Kerouac to Credence Clearwater Revival) lies behind Springsteen's message and his image. It's this tradition that enables him to take such well-worn iconography as the road, the river, rock and roll itself, as a mark of sincerity. No British musician, not even someone with such a profound love of American musical forms as Elvis Costello, could deal with these themes without some sense of irony.

Still, Springsteen's populism can appeal to everyone's experience of capitalism. He makes music out of desire aroused and desire thwarted, he offers a sense of personal worth that is not determined by either market forces (and wealth) or aesthetic standards (and cultural capital). It is the USA's particular account of equality that allows him to transcend the differences in class and status which remain ingrained in European culture. The problem is that the line between democratic populism (the argument that all people's experiences and emotions are equally important, equally worthy to be dramatized and made into art) and market populism (the argument that the consumer is always right, that the market defines cultural value) is very thin. Those piles of Bruce Springsteen boxes in European department stores seem less a tribute to rock authenticity than to corporate might.

'We are the world!' sang USA For Africa, and what was intended as a statement of global community came across as a threat of global domination. 'Born in the USA!' sang Bruce Springsteen on his last great tour, with the Stars and Stripes fluttering over the stage, and what was meant as an opposition anthem to the Reaganite colonization of the American dream was taken by large sections of his American audiences as pat patriotism (in Europe the flag had to come down). Springsteen is, whether he or we like it or not, an American artist—his 'community' will always have the Stars and Stripes fluttering over it. But then rock and roll is American music, and Springsteen's *Live 1975–1985* is a monument. Like all monuments it celebrates (and mourns) the dead, in this case the idea of authenticity itself.

43

Hip Hop Nation

Greg Tate

Originally published as the lead essay in a special *Village Voice* feature devoted to the "Hip Hop Nation," Greg Tate's 1988 article "It's Like This Y'all" provides a window into a style of music that at that time was enjoying its first true taste of commercial success.* Throughout the 1980s, rap music had been bubbling under as an exciting urban underground phenomenon. But by 1986 and 1987, breakthrough albums from Run D.M.C., L.L. Cool J, and others had made it clear that hip hop was crossing over into a much larger fan base. Addressing hip hop's African American culture as a whole, Tate provides a brief overview of its various dimensions—from graffiti and break dancing to DJ scratching and rapping—while also defending the music from its various critics. His writing style suits the subject, as he mirrors rap's rich wealth of allusions, slang, and playfully combative, boastful verse. Tate places the music within the roots of its urban environment; for example, recalling a conversation between two early 1980s downtown New York icons, graffiti/visual artist Rammellzee (born 1960) and East Village artist and critic Nicolas Moufarrege (1947–1985). Most of all, he situates hip hop within a long musical lineage stretching from the blues and jazz to funk and fusion. Nowhere, however, does he mention rock music. Which begs the question: exactly how *does* hip hop relate to rock?[†]

Where will rap end up? Where most postmodern American products end up: highly packaged, regulated, distributed, circulated and consumed. Upper-middle-class white students at Yale consume a lot of Run-D.M.C.

—Cornell West

Fuck hiphop. I don't define that shit. I define this, man: It's music. Let's not call it hiphop no more, Fred. We ain't writing graffiti on walls, we're trying to get paid.

—L.L. Cool J

Radio stations I question their blackness/They call themselves black/But we'll see if they play this.

—Public Enemy, "Bring the Noise"

---

* *Source:* Greg Tate, "It's Like This Y'all," *Village Voice*, January 19, 1988, pp. 21–22.
† Many of Tate's writings from this era are collected in his book *Flyboy in the Buttermilk: Essays on Contemporary America* (New York: Simon and Schuster, 1992).

We begin this benediction by sending out a message of love to the ancestors Kool Herc, Taki 183, and the Nigger Twins.

We know from her secretary that the Billie Holiday first wore gardenias to mask a bald spot made by an overzealous hot comb. Tell us, old muse, about the beauties bred from black disgrace. Had there never been discos, B-boys might have never become so engaged in class struggle, fashion rebels risen up to defy the Saturday night dress code, economically shamed into aggression. But hiphop in its manifold forms—rapping, scratch DJing, break dancing, graffiti—also emerges, in the twilight of '70s gang warfare, as a nonfratricidal channel for the B-boy's competitive, creative, and martial urges. All the aforementioned expressions flowered, like swing-era saxophone playing, *specifically*, in the hothouse of the cutting contest.*

Hiphop is the most modern example, after capoeira and basketball, of African culture's bent towards aesthetic combat—what the graffiti movement itself long ago defined as "style wars." We are reminded of an exchange between Rammellzee and Nicolas A. Moufarrege.

Moufarrege: Do you call your work total realism. Is this poster total realism? [Note: the images in Rammellzee's drawings do not resemble what is habitually referred to in art as realism; the drawing is cartoon, comic strip, pop, and science fiction related.]

Rammellzee: There's about 50,000 kids walking out the street who look just like that: Pumas, bell-bottom jeans—they have their pants hanging off their ass showing their underwear—shades and doo-rags.

What are doo rags? ... You say that this is real and that Picasso is abstract?

Yes.... The human body is abstracted; why do you want to abstract it even further? ... Man, on the street they'll burn it, they'll break it down. They'll say what is this shit? Are we your future too? No!

The battle flows in two directions—against the technique of rival virtuosos and against the city. The city fathers strike back, like that's their job. Ghetto blasters and bombed trains, might, as Jean Baudrillard proclaims, territorialize the urban bush, but they also invoke noise ordinances, razored barbed wire, and the patrolling of train yards by guard dogs. Rammellzee speaks of this as a war of symbols, but the execution of Michael Stewart was no symbolic gesture.† His death was status quo: another marginal man pushed into the marginality of the grave by the powerful for crimes surreal or imagined. Were Goetz's victims B-fashion victims too?‡ Do clothes make the man a target?

When the black-on-black crime that occurs before, during, and after (often blocks away) rap concerts is reported as "rap violence," the aging pontificators forget that hiphop is the flipside of being young, black, and urban-situated: the fun side, the funkyfresh side. Take out rap and one could go dying for a belly laugh in modern black pop. If drum sound is this music's heartthrob, humor is its blood vessels. The urge to snap, crack, jone, boast, toast, to stay forever anal, adolescent, and absurdist—to talk much, shit, in other words, and create new *slanguage* in the process—is what keeps the oral tradition's chuckle juices flowing through the rap pipeline. (If we have to, we can invoke holy tradition: the preacher goes "Huh!," James Brown goes "Unnhh!," George Clinton goes "Ho!," Bob Marley goes "Oh-oh-wo-oh-oh," and the DJs scratch their ecstatic ejaculations.)

Rap keeps alive the lineage of juke-joint jive novelty records that began with the first recorded black music—so-called classic blues. Here, too, we're talking your citified country Negro's mongrel sound, part jazz, part coonfoolery, part bawdy response to the man-woman question. Black vaudeville tent-show entertainment was best put to wax by heavy-duty womanists Ma Rainey and

---

* In jazz, the phrase "cutting contest" describes a competitive duel between two musicians, one of whom figuratively "cuts" off the other's head.

† Stewart was a train graffiti "tagger" who had been beaten to death in 1983 by the New York City Transit police.

‡ Tate is alluding to the subway vigilante Bernard Goetz, who in 1984 had shot and wounded four black youths on a New York City train.

Bessie Smith. Bringing us to the position of the sistuhs in rap. No, Stokely, not prone, but coming into their own, going beyond the first flurry of lubricated lip answer records to go stone careerist. Roxanne Shanté's jockin' *and* clockin'.

The minds behind the music's muscle are its DJs and producers—Russell Simmons, Eric B., Larry Smith, Teddy Riley, Rick Rubin, Dennis Bell, Hank Shocklee, Hurby Azor, Mantronik, Marley Marl, Terminator X. We continually marvel at this fraternal order of rhythm tacticians, this consortium of beat boppers, mega-mix researchers, sound-collage technicians, and rare-groove clerics. They think about electronic percussion orchestrally—voicings and shit—like any jazz drummer worth his African roots. We understand that analogies between hip-hop and jazz rankle the jazz police who believe harmonic improvisation on Western concert instruments is the measure of black genius. Partly because the beat-boppers' axes (save the wheels of steel) originate in the digital age—drum machines, sequencers, and samplers—the ears of the jazz police fly off the handle.

The suckers have yet to figure out the prototype—Miles Davis's 1972 *On the Corner*—so we can't expect them to listen to Eric B. & Rakim as Wynton Marsalis listens to Ornette Coleman, for his finesse with rhythmic changes. And it goes without saying that New Music America-type festivals don't consider these percussive melodists composers.* Probably because the beatboppers audience dances to the music.

The coordinated chaos of hiphop's dance component holds clues to the origin of the universe. You want to understand why the subatomic realm is so full of strange behavior? Look to the body language of the black teens. Their culturally acquired fluidity are new dance forms waiting to happen. Who can lament break dancing's faddish decline knowing such energy is never destroyed but transformed, in this case, into the Wopp, the Snake, the Cabbage Patch, and other spasms yet to be named.

For some, hiphop will always be "that chain-snatching music." We are reminded of a buppie party in Brooklyn where the hostess denied a request for Run-D.M.C. "This isn't a Run-D.M.C. kind of party." A Doritos and disco dipshit party is what it was. What can we expect from Philistines? Hiphop, Russell Simmons informs us, is an artform. To which we add, it's the *only* avant-garde around, still delivering the shock of the new (over recycled James Brown compost modernism like a bitch), and it's got a shockable bourgeoisie, to boot. Hiphop is not just Def Jam shipping platinum, but the attraction/repulsion of commodification to the black working class and po'-ass class. The music that makes like a saccharine pop ditty with a dopebeat today could be the soundtrack to a Five Per Cent Nation jihad tomorrow. Hiphop might be bought and sold like gold, but the miners of its rich ore still represent a sleeping-giant constituency. Hiphop locates their market potential and their potential militancy.

Public Enemy pointman Chuckie D wants to raise consciousness though his manifesto serves dreamers and schemers alike: "This jam may hit or miss the charts/But the style gets wild as state of the art/Dazzling in science/Bold in nerve/But giving my house what it deserves." Later for the revolution. For the here and now, hiphop's stance of populist-futurism is progressive enough. Is there any creative endeavor outside of recombinant gene technology whose shape to come is more unpredictable? Latter-day prophets predicting hiphop's imminent demise have already becomes extinct. Afrika Bambaataa sez rap will be around as long as people keep talking. You think we're gonna let 'em shut us up now? Sheee.

---

* The New Music America Festival was a yearly event devoted to contemporary art music composers.

44

"Madonna–Finally, a Real Feminist"

CAMILLE PAGLIA

Along with Michael Jackson, Madonna (born Madonna Louise Ciccone, 1958) established herself over the course of the 1980s as one of MTV's most dazzlingly innovative and risk-taking video stars. From the Marilyn Monroe homage of "Material Girl" (1985) and peep show eroticism of "Open Your Heart" (1986) to the daring religious and racial iconography of "Like a Prayer" (1989), Madonna constantly reinvented her glamorous image while wading into socially taboo waters. The controversy surrounding the singer reached a climax in the fall of 1990 with the release of the sexually suggestive "Justify My Love," the first Madonna video that MTV refused to air. On December 3, 1990, ABC's *Nightline* showed the unedited video for the first time, and spotlighted the singer in an interview. Madonna's appearance on *Nightline* generated a flurry of responses, among them Camille Paglia's editorial for the *New York Times*. Paglia (born 1947), an outspoken cultural critic and public intellectual, whose own controversial book *Sexual Personae: Art & Decadence from Nefertiti to Emily Dickinson* (New Haven: Yale University Press, 1990) had just been released, uses "Justify My Love" as an opportunity to proclaim Madonna's significant role in a new era of American feminism. Madonna's forays into issues of gender, sexuality, and identity would attract the interest of many other academics throughout the early 1990s, even leading to an *Inside Edition* exposé on "Madonna scholars.'"

Madonna, don't preach.

Defending her controversial new video "Justify My Love" on "Nightline" last week, Madonna stumbled, rambled and ended up seeming far less intelligent than she really is.

Madonna, 'fess up.

The video is pornographic. It's decadent. And it's fabulous. MTV was right to ban it, a corporate resolve long overdue. Parents cannot possibly control television, with its titanic omnipresence.

Prodded by correspondent Forrest Sawyer for evidence of her responsibility as an artist, Madonna hotly proclaimed her love of children, her social activism and her condom endorsements. Wrong answer. As Baudelaire and Oscar Wilde knew, neither art nor the artist has a moral responsibility to liberal social causes.

"Justify My Love" is truly avant-garde, at a time when that word has lost its meaning in the flabby art world. It represents a sophisticated European sexuality of a kind we have not seen since the great foreign films of the 1950's and 1960's. But it does not belong on a mainstream music channel watched around the clock by children.

---

* *Source:* Camille Paglia, "Madonna – Finally, a Real Feminist," *New York Times*, December 14, 1990, p. A39.

On "Nightline," Madonna bizarrely called the video a "celebration of sex." She imagined happy educational scenes where curious children would ask their parents about the video. Oh, sure! Picture it: "Mommy, please tell me about the tired, tied-up man in the leather harness and the mean, bare-chested lady in the Nazi cap." O.K., dear, right after the milk and cookies.

Mr. Sawyer asked for Madonna's reaction to feminist charges that, in the neck manacle and floor-crawling of an earlier video, "Express Yourself," she condoned the "degradation" and "humiliation" of women. Madonna waffled: "But I chained myself! I'm in charge." Well, no, Madonna the producer may have chosen the chain, but Madonna the sexual persona in the video is alternately a cross-dressing dominatrix and a slave of male desire.

But who cares what the feminists say anyhow? They have been outrageously negative about Madonna from the start. In 1985, *Ms.* magazine pointedly feted quirky, cuddly singer Cyndi Lauper as its woman of the year. Great judgment: gimmicky Lauper went nowhere, while Madonna grew, flourished, metamorphosed and became an international star of staggering dimensions. She is also a shrewd business tycoon, a modern woman of all-around talent.

Madonna is the true feminist. She exposes the puritanism and suffocating ideology of American feminism, which is stuck in an adolescent whining mode. Madonna has taught young women to be fully female and sexual while still exercising total control over their lives. She shows girls how to be attractive, sensual, energetic, ambitious, aggressive and funny—all at the same time.

American feminism has a man problem. The beaming Betty Crockers, hangdog dowdies and parochial prudes who call themselves feminists want men to be like women. They fear and despise the masculine. The academic feminists think their nerdy bookworm husbands are the ideal model of human manhood.

But Madonna loves real men. She sees the beauty of masculinity, in all its rough vigor and sweaty athletic perfection. She also admires the men who are actually like women: transsexuals and flamboyant drag queens, the heroes of the 1969 Stonewall rebellion, which started the gay liberation movement.

"Justify My Love" is an eerie, sultry tableau of jaded androgynous creatures, trapped in a decadent sexual underground. Its hypnotic images are drawn from such sado-masochistic films as Liliana Cazani's "The Night Porter" and Luchino Visconti's "The Damned." It's the perverse and knowing world of the photographers Helmut Newton and Robert Mapplethorpe.

Contemporary American feminism, which began by rejecting Freud because of his alleged sexism, has shut itself off from his ideas of ambiguity, contradiction, conflict, ambivalence. Its simplistic psychology is illustrated by the new cliché of the date-rape furor: "'No' always means 'no'." Will we ever graduate from the Girl Scouts? "No" has always been, and always will be, part of the dangerous, alluring courtship ritual of sex and seduction, observable even in the animal kingdom.

Madonna has a far profounder vision of sex than do the feminists. She sees both the animality and the artifice. Changing her costume style and hair color virtually every month, Madonna embodies the eternal values of beauty and pleasure. Feminism says, "No more masks." Madonna says we are nothing but masks.

Through her enormous impact on young women around the world, Madonna is the future of feminism.

45

"Can Madonna Justify Madonna?"

Barbara Grizzuti Harrison

For all the controversy that Madonna generated herself, what was perhaps more remarkable was the way in which the discourse *surrounding* her served to spark debates over the "true" meanings of feminism. Were Madonna's actions empowering or were they demeaning? Was she resisting patriarchal conventions or simply reinscribing them? In her editorial for *Mademoiselle* magazine, Barbara Grizzuti Harrison (1934–2002) responds to Camille Paglia's essay, as well as Caryn James's feminist reading of Madonna from the *New York Times*.* Harrison, a highly regarded author and one of the first contributors to *Ms.* magazine, addresses Paglia's claims from the perspective of someone who had been heavily involved with the formative years of the women's movement in the 1960s and 1970s.†

Is Madonna a feminist? Gimme a break. Do pigs fly?

There was a time that I didn't know the difference between Madonna and Cyndi Lauper. (I have these problems; it was a long time before I was absolutely sure which were flora and which were fauna.) Then, suddenly, I was reading and hearing about Madonna all over the place; and since I don't live in a cave, I'd seen her videos. It interested me to see how someone who was decidedly not beautiful could nonetheless manage, for seconds at a time, to project beauty. I thought it was a neat trick. Certainly a marketable trick. I thought: She's a sly one (I never for a moment thought: She's quite a feminist); and that was that…

Well, not *quite* that. I find Joan Rivers awfully persuasive (I can *so* tell the difference between her and Phyllis Diller); and when I heard Rivers' amusing speculation, on her TV talk show, that Madonna had a problem with body hair, I was no longer able to think of Madonna as a person who could project beauty, even for a few seconds. (I'm Italian, too; I know all about dark fuzz on the upper lip.)

The next thing I knew, magazine editors were standing in line to ask me to interview Madonna. Why? I said. Because, they (invariably) said, she invents herself and keeps on inventing herself. What does that mean, exactly? I said. Does it mean hiding behind flamboyant disguises? Coloring and recoloring your hair? (Have you noticed that you can't stop dark roots from showing on television? Pity.) And why is this inventing/reinventing business thought to be a good thing—as opposed, for example, to constancy? It had me beat.

---

* Caryn James, "Beneath All That Black Lace Beats the Heart of a Bimbo…and a Feminist," *New York Time*, December 16, 1990, H38,44.

† *Source:* Barbara Grizzuti Harrison, "Can Madonna Justify Madonna?," *Mademoiselle*, June 1991, pp. 80–82.

Then along came someone called Camille Paglia to explain to me, in the *New York Times*, the significance of Madonna's chameleonlike antics. She was a Real Feminist, *the* True Feminist, wrote Paglia, unlike all the other feminists who claimed to be feminists. Gosh. I never knew that all of us who call ourselves feminists have so much in common that it's possible for us to stand on one side of an ideological fault line, on the other side of which stands … *Madonna?* At first I thought it was a joke. (Paglia is the author of a book called *Sexual Personae: Art and Decadence From Nefertiti to Emily Dickinson*; at first I thought *that* was a joke, too; alas, it is not.)

Paglia rested much of her case for Madonna's feminism on her latest video, *Justify My Love*—which, as you of course already know, was banned by MTV on the grounds that it was too sexually explicit; and, as you also know, became a hit, in part because people always long to see what they are not permitted to see. If nobody had told me. I would have thought *Justify My Love* was a home movie. It's dumb. Like there's this parodic boneless male dancer—he looks like Gumby in silhouette—and he keeps popping up in the bedroom where Madonna lets her boyfriend—who wears more lipstick than she does—do lascivious things to her black underwear (she's in it). It's also decadent, druggy (well, everyone *tilts;* it looks like either everyone is stoned or Madonna needs a new camera for Christmas), and seems to include a lot of people in drag.

Madonna calls this "art." I heard her say so on *Nightline:* "Well, no, you know, with the wave of censorship being, you know—and the conservatism that is, you know, sort of sweeping over the nation…. It is my artistic expression … we're dealing with sexual fannies [sic]—fantasies, and being truthful and honest with our partner you know." In the video, she has a lot more than one partner; there are flash-cut references to multiple partners, voyeurism, leather, sadomasochism, dominance-submission, Nazi paraphernalia and Christ on the cross, an image Madonna evidently finds very turn-on-y. She also grabs her crotch a lot (she's always grabbing *something*—her breasts, her neck…). This, too, is supposed to be feminist: *Michael Jackson did it and so can she, ha ha ha, nyah, nyah, nyah.*

And what is the "feminist" message of a previous video, *Open Your Heart*, wherein Madonna sets up shop as a peepshow dancer? I hated that video like poison, not least because a little boy was in it—he played a would-be customer—and at the end he and a saucy Madonna skipped off into the sunset together, just two kids at play…. This is where sentiment becomes bilge, and this is where that which is silly becomes that which is dangerous.

In *Express Yourself*, another one of Madonna's works of so-called art, she is seen chained to a bed and crawling under a table—putrid images, you must admit. So here's what Madonna said on *Nightline:* "Okay, I have chained myself, though, okay? No—there wasn't a man that put that chain on me…. I was chained to my desires. [Come again? I thought it was a bed] … I'm in charge, okay. Degradation is when somebody else is making you do something against your wishes, okay?"

It really is not okay. Okay? It makes me inexpressibly weary to have to say the obvious—that the very worst degradation is that which we inflict upon ourselves. It won't do to say *I chose it, so it's okay.* What about self-laceration? Self-flagellation? Self-destruction? Whatever Madonna the producer may have chosen, Madonna the performer comes across as a dementedly cheerful masochist.

Nonetheless, Paglia says Madonna "has taught young women to be fully female and sexual while still exercising total control over their lives." The *Times's* Caryn James adds her voice: To Madonna, "feminism means the freedom to be sexy as well as sexual, to be in control of one's image as well as one's life…. Madonna [suggests] mastery of one's fate." But who in this green wide world has total control over her life? Beyond a certain point, mastery of one's fate is illusory. We *act* as if we have free will—that is what it means to be human; but we know that life acts upon us just as we act upon it.

Madonna has minor talent and major marketing skill. In her works the line between person and image has become hopelessly blurred, as has the line between responsibility and manipulation (both go by the name of *control*). Yes, an image can be manipulated; no, a life cannot be and *should* not be. We don't produce our lives as if they were videos; the script is not a one-woman exercise.

Madonna, her fan Paglia says, "embodies the eternal values of beauty and pleasure." Whereas traditional, no-fun-at-all feminists want to put an end to masks. "Madonna says we are nothing but masks." I find this scary beyond belief. Not the beauty-and-pleasure part; let's hear it for beauty and pleasure! Who's against it? Not I. The masks. In the '50s, when women wore the same push-up bras and high, high heels that Madonna postures in today, rebels against conformity spoke one word: *authenticity*. They knew that to wear a mask is an act of extreme defensiveness or aggression. What it is *not* is an act of existential courage.

As long as Madonna wears masks—and confuses the person with the image—there *is* no real person there (and no real risk). That's why, after a while, Madonna-adulation is dopey ... as in "Madonna loves real men" (Paglia). Yeah? Like Warren Beatty, he who is evidently incapable of commitment? Or, as in (James); "Her lyrics ... are a feminist anthem. 'Don't settle for second best, baby,' she sings.... 'You deserve the best in life...'" Oh, dear. That's as profound as a greeting card. Are we so starved for heroines that we have to make Madonna into one? We deserve better.

V

THE 1990S

46

Is As Nasty As They Wanna Be Obscene?

In 1990, 2 Live Crew's battles with the Florida judicial system brought the Miami-based rap group to national prominence as they faced prosecution on the grounds of obscenity for their album *As Nasty As They Wanna Be*. This was not the first time that musicians had been brought to trial on such charges. Four years earlier Jello Biafra, lead singer of hardcore punk band the Dead Kennedys and owner of the independent Alternative Records label, had been charged with distributing "harmful matter to minors," on the basis of a graphic poster included with the band's *Frankenchrist* album. *As Nasty As They Wanna Be*, however, moved the battle over obscenity to completely different grounds as the rappers were indicted solely for their music. The trial drew extensive commentary, including a special feature that appeared in *Reconstruction*, a Harvard-based journal devoted to issues of African American culture. Reprinted here from *Reconstruction* are two items: Judge Jose Gonzalez's ruling on the case and a response from Kathleen M. Sullivan, a professor of Constitutional Law. Both of their comments revolve around the three-pronged criteria for obscenity outlined in the 1973 *Miller v. California* ruling, a case that had involved the mass distribution of graphically illustrated advertisements for sex books. In his statement, Judge Gonzalez refutes the trial testimony of Carlton Long, a Columbia University political science professor who defended the band's music as part of such longstanding black cultural traditions as boasting and parody.* 2 Live Crew's music, Gonzalez declares, is inarguably obscene. Sullivan responds by questioning the very logic of *Miller v. California* itself. In the end, 2 Live Crew was vindicated when nearly a year and a half after their conviction, the U.S. Court of Appeals reversed the Gonzalez ruling. The Supreme Court upheld the decision, refusing to hear any further appeals.†

SKYYWALKER RECORDS INC. V. NICHOLAS NAVARRO (SHERRIF, BROWARD COUNTY, FLORIDA) UNITED STATES DISTRICT COURT, S.D. FLORIDA, JUNE 6, 1990

Judge Jose Gonzalez

This is a case between two ancient enemies: Anything Goes and Enough Already.

---

* An even more prominent scholar, Henry Louis Gates, Jr., took up the group's cause as well, in a *New York Times* editorial. See Gates Jr., "2 Live Crew Decoded: Rap Music Group's Use of Street Language in Context of Afro-American Cultural Heritage Analyzed," *New York Times*, 19 June 1990, op-ed., A23.
† *Source: Skyywalker Records Inc. v. Nicholas Navarro* (Sherrif, Broward County, Florida) United States District Court, S.D. Florida, June 6, 1990, and Kathleen M. Sullivan, "2 Live Crew and the Cultural Contradictions of *Miller*," *Reconstruction* 1, no. 2 (1990), pp. 16–20.

Justice Oliver Wendell Holmes, Jr. observed that the First Amendment is not absolute and that it does not permit one to yell "Fire" in a crowded theater. Today, this court decides whether the First Amendment absolutely permits one to yell another "F" word anywhere in the community when combined with graphic sexual descriptions.

Obscenity and the First Amendment

The First Amendment to the Unites States Constitution provides that "Congress shall make no law ... abridging the freedom of speech."

The First Amendment is one of our most sacred liberties since freedom of thought and speech are the key to the preservation of all other rights. Free speech plays a critical role in furthering self-government, in encouraging individual self-realization, and fostering society's search for truth via exposure to a marketplace of ideas."

To protect that sacred right, the judiciary carefully scrutinizes government regulation to determine if such regulation impermissibly infringes upon it. When legislative or executive action is directed at the content of one's speech, it will pass judicial review only upon a showing that the action is designed to further a compelling governmental interest by narrowly drawn means necessary to achieve the end.

Obscene speech has no protection under the First Amendment. The rationale is simple: the message conveyed by obscene speech is of such slight social value that it is always outweighed by the compelling interests of society as manifested in the laws enacted by its elected representatives. Sex has been called "a great and mysterious motive force in human life." Because of its power, both federal and state governments have chosen to regulate its abuse. The Florida Legislature enacted a statutory scheme [that] criminalizes the distribution, sale, or production of any obscene thing including a "recording" which can be "transmuted into auditory ... representations."

An argument underlying the plaintiffs' position is that obscenity or non-obscenity of any material should not be a concern of the criminal law, but rather should be left to the free market of ideas. Let each individual member of the public decide whether they wish to buy the material. This is the argument of those absolutists who believe all speech, regardless of its content, is protected by the First Amendment. Such individuals label all regulation of speech as "censorship" and "paternalism."

The absolutists and other members of the party of Anything Goes should address their petitions to the Florida Legislature, not to this court. If they are sincere let them say what they actually mean—Let's Legalize Obscenity! It is much easier to criticize the law, however, that it is to work to repeal it.

In an era where the law and society are rightfully concerned with the rights of minorities, it should not be overlooked nor forgotten that majorities also have rights.

Men and women in good faith may agree or disagree as to whether obscenity should be prohibited. They can argue that the obscenity statutes should or should not be repealed. In the meantime, however, the law must be obeyed and the Sheriff has a duty to enforce it.

The *Miller v. California* Test

In deciding whether a specific work is or is not obscene the court must apply the controlling test enunciated [by the Supreme Court] in *Miller v. California*. To be obscene, there must be proof of all three of the following factors: (1) the average person, applying contemporary community standards would find the that the work, taken as a whole appeals to the prurient interest, (2) measured by contemporary community standards, the work depicts or describes in a patently offensive way, sexual conduct, specifically defined by the applicable state law, and (3) the work, taken as a whole, lacks serious literary, artistic, political, or scientific value.

The Relevant Community

This court finds that in assessing whether this work is obscene, the relevant community is the area of Palm Beach, Broward, and Dade Counties. [T]his area is remarkable for its diversity. The three counties are a mecca for both the very young and the very old. Because of the beaches and the moderate year-round climate, this area includes young persons establishing homes and older residents retiring to enjoy life under the sun. There are both families and single individuals residing in the communities. Generally, the counties are heterogeneous in terms of religion, class, race, and gender.

The Average Person Standard

The next inquiry is more difficult because this court must determine what are the standard for determining prurient interest and patent offensiveness in Palm Beach, Dade, and Broward Counties.

This court finds that the relevant community standard reflects a more tolerant view of obscene speech than would other communities within the state. This finding of fact is based upon this court's personal knowledge of the community. The undersigned judge has resided in Broward County since 1958. As a practicing attorney, state prosecutor, state circuit judge, and currently, a federal district judge, the undersigned has traveled and worked in Dade, Broward, and Palm Beach. As a member of the community, he has a personal knowledge of this area's demographics, culture, economics, and politics. He has attended public functions and events in all three counties and is aware of the community's concerns as reported in the media and by word of mouth. In almost fourteen years as a state circuit judge, the undersigned gained personal knowledge of the nature of obscenity in the community while viewing dozens, if not hundreds of allegedly obscene film and other publications seized by law enforcement.

The *Miller* Test: Prurient Interest

This court finds, as a matter of fact, that the recording "As Nasty As They Wanna Be" appeals to the prurient interest. The Supreme Court has defined prurient as "material having a tendency to excite lustful thoughts." Appeals only to "normal, healthy sexual desire" are not adequate to meet the test. The material must exhibit a "shameful or morbid interest in nudity, sex, or secretion."

"Nasty" appeals to the prurient interest for several reasons. First, its lyrics and the titles of its songs are replete with references to female and male genitalia, human sexual excretion, oral-anal contact, fellatio, group sex, specific sexual positions, sado-masochism, the turgid state of the male sexual organ, masturbation, cunnilingus, sexual intercourse, and the sounds of moaning.

Furthermore, the frequency and graphic description of the sexual lyrics evinces a clear intention to lure hearers into this activity. The depictions of ultimate sexual acts are so vivid that they are hard to distinguish from seeing the same conduct described in the words of a book, or in pictures in periodicals or films.

It is also noteworthy that the material here is music. 2 Live Crew itself testified that the "Nasty" recording was made to be listened and danced to. The evident goal of this particular recording is to reproduce the sexual act though musical lyrics. It is an appeal directed to "dirty" thoughts and the loins, not to the intellect and the mind.

The Second *Miller* Test: Patently Offensive

The court also finds that the second element of the *Miller* test is satisfied in that the "Nasty" recording is patently offensive. The recording depicts sexual conduct in graphic detail. The specificity of the descriptions makes the audio message analogous to a camera with a zoom lens, focusing on the sights and sounds of various ultimate sex acts.

While the above facts are sufficient to support a finding that this material is patently offensive, there are additional considerations that support such a finding. First, the "Nasty" lyrics contain what are commonly known as "dirty words" and depictions of female abuse and violence. Secondly, the material here is music which can certainly be more intrusive to the unwilling listener than other forms of communication. Unlike a videotape, a book, or periodical, music must be played to be experienced. A person can sit in public and look at an obscene magazine without unduly intruding upon another's privacy; but, even according to the plaintiffs' testimony, music is made to be played and listened to. A person laying on a public beach, sitting in a public park, walking down the street, or sitting in his automobile waiting for the light to change is, in a sense, a captive audience. While the law does require citizens to avert their ears when speech is merely offensive, they do not have an obligation to buy and use ear plugs in public if the state legislature has chosen to protect them from obscenity.

The Third *Miller* Test: Social Value

The final factor under *Miller* is whether the "Nasty" recording, taken as a whole, lacks serious literary, artistic, political, or scientific value. This factor is not measured by community standards. The proper inquiry is whether a reasonable person would find serious social value in the material at issue. The plaintiffs correctly note that the value of a work can pass muster under *Miller* if it has serious merit, measured objectively, even if a majority of the community would not agree.

As a preliminary matter, it is again important to note what this case is not about. Neither the "Rap" or "Hip-Hop" musical genres are on trial. The narrow issue before this court is whether the recording entitled "As Nasty As They Wanna Be" is legally obscene. This is also not a case about whether the group 2 Live Crew or any of its other music is obscene.

This court must examine the "Nasty" recording for its content; the inquiry is objective, not ad hominem.

Finally, this court's role is not to serve as a censor or an art and music critic. If the "Nasty" recording has serious literary, artistic, political, or scientific value, it is irrelevant that the work is not stylish, tasteful, or even popular.

The plaintiffs themselves testified that neither their music nor their lyrics were created to convey a political message. The only witness testifying at trial that there was political content in the "Nasty" recording was Carlton Long, who was qualified as an expert on the culture of black Americans. This witness first stated that their recording was political because the 2 Live Crew, as a group of black Americans, used this medium to express themselves. While it is doubtless true that "Nasty" is a product of the group's background, including their heritage as black Americans, this fact does not convert whatever they say, or sing, into political speech. Professor Long also testified that the following passages from the recording contained political content: a four sentence phrase in the song "Dirty Nursery Rhymes" about Abraham Lincoln, the word "man" in the Georgie Porgie portion of the same song, and the use of the device of "boasting" to stress one's manhood. Even giving these isolated lyrics the meaning attributed by the expert, they are not sufficient in number of significance to give the "Nasty" recording, as a whole, any serious political value.

In terms of science, Professor Long also suggested that there is cultural content in 2 Live Crew's recording which rises to the level of serious sociological value. According to this witness, white Americans "hear" the "Nasty" recording in a different way than black Americans because of their different frames of references. Long identifies three cultural devices evident in the work here: "call and response," "doing the dozens," and "boasting." The court finds none of these arguments persuasive.

The only examples of "call and response" in the "Nasty" recording are portions where males and females yell, in repetitive verse, "Tastes Great—Less Filling" and, in another song, assail campus Greek-letter groups. The phrases alone have no significant artistic merit nor are they examples of black American culture. In the case of "Tastes Great—Less Filling," this is merely a phrase lifted from a beer commercial.

The device of "doing the dozens" is a word game composed of a series of insults escalating in their satirical content. The "boasting" device is a way for persons to overstate their virtues such as sexual prowess. While this court does not doubt that both "boasting" and "doing the dozens" are found in the culture of black Americans, these devices are also found in other cultures. "Doing the dozens" is commonly seen in adolescents, especially boys, of all races. "Boasting" seems to be part of the universal human condition.

Professor Long also cited to several different examples of literary devices such as rhyme and allusion which appear in "Nasty," and points to the song title "Dick Almighty" as an example of the literary device of personification. This, of course, is nonsense regardless of the expert's credentials. "A quotation from Voltaire in the fly leaf of a book," noted the Supreme Court in *Miller*, "will not constitutionally redeem an otherwise obscene publication."

Initially, it would appear very difficult to find a musical work obscene. As noted by the American Civil Liberties union, the meaning of music is subjective and subject only to the limits of the listener's imagination. Music nevertheless is not exempt from a state's obscenity statutes. Musical works are obscene if they meet the *Miller* test. Certainly it would be possible to compose an obscene oratorio or opera and it has probably been done.

Obscenity? Yes!

The recording "As Nasty As They Wanna Be," taken as a whole, is legally obscene.

* * *

2 LIVE CREW AND THE CULTURAL CONTRADICTIONS OF *MILLER*

Kathleen M. Sullivan

Miller v. California, decided in 1973, is the Supreme Court's last effort to draw a line between obscenity and protected speech. *Miller* denies First Amendment protection to a work that appeals to the "prurient interest," depicts sex in a "patently offensive" way, and lacks "serious" artistic or other value. Prurience and offensiveness are to be judged by the compass of the "average person applying contemporary community standards," while artistic value is to be assessed not by the local average but rather by the universal "reasonable" person. *Miller* was meant to build a categorical wall separating art from pornography, permitting hard-core material to be suppressed without throwing Joyce or Lawrence out with the bathwater.

But lately the art-porn boundary is breaking down. Obscenity law has come out of the porn shop and into the record store and the art museum. Federal Judge Jose Gonzalez made history when he declared 2 Live Crew's rap music obscene in *Skyywalker Records*. Never before had a record album been held to flunk the *Miller* test. Elsewhere too, obscenity law is overstepping its old Skid

Row boundaries. In another legal first, officials of a Cincinnati art museum have been charged criminally for exhibiting Robert Mapplethorpe's graphic photographs of homoerotic scenes and naked children. And efforts continue in Congress to legislate content restrictions on the National Endowment for the Arts that would bar public support for supposedly obscene art.

Against these imperial tendencies of the anti-obscenity movement, *Miller* is proving weak constraint. That is no surprise, for *Miller* sets forth an extraordinarily incoherent standard—as the 2 Live Crew case illustrates.

The first two parts of the *Miller* test pose a psychological contradiction. By requiring an obscene work to have *both* prurient appeal *and* patent offensiveness, *Miller* requires the audience, in vernacular terms, to be simultaneously turned on and grossed out. How can both conditions be satisfied at once?

There are two possible solutions. The first is to posit that every individual—even the average person applying contemporary community standards—has both a base and a noble side, or at least an id and a superego. An obscene work stimulates bodily sexual arousal that the higher faculties recognize as base. In other words, obscenity initially bypasses the brain and heads straight for the groin, but the brain quickly recognizes what has happened and overrides arousal with shame. This is the psychological dynamic the Supreme Court suggests when it seeks to define "prurient" interest in sex as "shameful or morbid" rather than "normal and healthy."

Judge Gonzalez's opinion, however, illustrates the problems with this approach. Human response to speech cannot be so readily subdivided into the high and the low, the cognitive and the physiological. Other areas of First Amendment law have long acknowledged that speech strikes chords both above and below the neck. The Supreme Court, for example, protected a person's right to wear a jacket emblazoned with the slogan "Fuck the Draft" on the ground that "words are often chosen as much for their emotive as their cognitive force." Great political speeches target both hearts and minds, prompting tears as well as thoughts. True, *Miller* tries to draw the line a little lower than the neck. But it is a psychological throwback to pretend that "the loins" any more than the heart are completely unconnected to "the intellect and the mind," as Judge Gonzalez, faithful to *Miller*, tries to do.

There is an additional problem with resolving the seeming contradiction in the first two parts of the *Miller* standard by assigning prurience to the id and offensiveness to the superego. What self-respecting decisionmaker wants to admit to being aroused by materials that are patently offensive? If shame is the name of the game, human instinct is to deny being turned on in the first place. Sure enough, Judge Gonzalez's opinion gingerly sidesteps just this point: it finds the "prurient interest" test satisfied *despite* evidence that, in the judge's words, "the Nasty recording did not actually physically excite anyone who heard it and indeed, caused boredom after repeated play." If that is the case, why ban it?

These problems suggest turning to a second, alternative method for finding prurient interest and patent offensiveness at the same time: subdivide the community rather than the individual psyche, and find the work sexually arousing to one subcommunity while patently offensive to others. This has the virtue of sparing the average decisionmaker the embarrassment of admitting any personal arousal. Not surprisingly, this is the escape hatch used by the Supreme Court to permit suppression of homoerotic, sadomasochistic, or other "deviant" pornography—deem it someone else's turn-on, but offensive to the community at large. And this may be the truest account of what is really going on in the 2 Live Crew case: the dominant culture is reining in a black male youth subculture whose portrait of its own sexuality offends those outside it.

The minute the case is described this way, however, its offense to free speech principles is made obvious. The Supreme Court has always disavowed that obscenity law has anything to do with suppressing the message or viewpoint conveyed—the cardinal sin forbidden by the First Amendment. Indeed, the Court has struck down state efforts to regulate sexually explicit speech whenever they could be characterized as viewpoint-discriminatory. The Court has invalidated, for example, right-wing efforts to suppress porn on the ground that it celebrates hedonistic promiscuity over monogamous marriage, and left-wing efforts to suppress porn on the ground that it constructs and reinforces unjust sexual hierarchy by eroticizing the domination of women by men.

Although Judge Gonzalez avoids any overt characterization of the case along these lines, distaste for 2 Live Crew's misogyny and sexual narcissism lurks as a subtext just beneath the surface of the opinion. It is not the judge's fault that he cannot be more direct. First Amendment law requires him to launder popular judgments of disapproval into judicial findings of low value.

Enter the third part of *Miller*—the "serious artistic value" test—which plays out in the 2 Live Crew case as farce. In an age where university literature departments teach "trash-lit" courses and where Madonna is a leading subject for doctoral dissertations, surely the serious/non-serious" boundary in art is at risk. Indeed, as a recent *Yale Law Journal* note argues, it is a boundary that postmodern aesthetics deliberately challenges. Nonetheless, the 2 Live Crew case suggests that the third part of the *Miller* test remains useful for at least one purpose: as a source of employment for academics willing to testify about such matters as the role of personification in "Dick Almighty." But it does nothing to reduce the tautological character of the decision. In the end, the late Justice Potter Stewart was right when he said that he couldn't define obscenity but that he knew it when he saw it: whether *Miller* switches a case onto the track of art or porn depends ultimately on a subjective hunch.

The 2 Live Crew decision should not survive appeal. You cannot take sex out of rock-and-roll or rhythm-and-blues. True, the quality of the mixture spans a wide range. 2 Live Crew's sexual lyrics are crude, vulgar, and blunt. They cannot hold a candle to the infinitely more clever double-entendre and subtle innuendo of earlier and greater sexually suggestive songs—there are no metaphorical "jellyrolls" or "handymen" in need of decoding in 2 Live Crew. But which is more "obscene"—sexual lyrics that are coded or blunt? No court should even start down the road toward an answer.

47

"Public Enemy's Bomb Squad"

Tom Moon

As we have seen in descriptions of such artists as Phil Spector and Brian Wilson, producers often obsess over the details of sound that comprise the musical "mix." In this respect, Hank Shocklee, the head of New York rap group Public Enemy's influential Bomb Squad production team, fits squarely into the history of rock's most musically innovative personalities. Hip-hop producers like Shocklee, however, broke with one of rock's most staunch traditions, substituting live musicians with backing tracks concocted out of samples. Consequently many critics and rock fans during the late '80s treated them more as plagiarists than composers. Shocklee convincingly dismisses such claims, explaining how the Bomb Squad (comprised of Shocklee, his brother Keith, Carl Ryder, and Eric Sadler) takes a songwriting approach to Public Enemy's music. As he shows, the Bomb Squad arranges their dense collage of layered samples with particular care and craft, and an awareness of earlier production techniques, such as those used by Motown. By deliberately highlighting elements of harmonic tension, placing samples slightly out of rhythm, and utilizing the potential of abrasive noise and dissonance, Shocklee's structures complement the political lyrics of Public Enemy's main rappers, Chuck D and Flavor Flav, in powerful ways.*†

Hank Shocklee's favorite word is "situation." As in "master of the recording studio situation." As in a man who enjoys problem solving. With his assertive, assaultive productions for Public Enemy and remixes for Ziggy Marley, Ralph Tresvant and others, Shocklee has become the sonic saint of hip-hop, the producer with the sound—that thickly layered noise-manipulation thing that defies transcription—most often imitated. He understands that situation: The eyes of the hip-hop world are on him. Everybody is going after his favorite samples. Everybody wants those same beats. Rather than keep his secrets secret, he's started SOUL (Sound of Urban Listeners) Records, and embarked on an ambitious roster of production projects (Son of Bazerk, the Young Black Teenagers, etc.).

When he talks about building a rap track, Shocklee gives credit to the other members of the Bomb Squad—his brother Keith, Carl Ryder and Eric Sadler. The group, which he describes as a band, has won critical praise; nonetheless, Shocklee's still sore about critics' distinction between trained musicians and so-called rap hacks. "People say we just copy, we can't make our own music," Shocklee says, lounging on the couch in the A room at Manhattan's Soundtrack Studios, where he's in the middle of mixing the frenetic Son of Bazerk record. "Let's be realistic here. There are only so many chords you can come up with. Everybody's copying variations anyway. The difference is

---

* For a particularly compelling musical analysis of Public Enemy's 1990 single "Fight the Power," see musicologist Robert Walser's Rhythm, Rhyme, and Rhetoric in the Music of Public Enemy," *Ethnomusicology* 39, no. 2 (Spring/ Summer 1995): 193–217.

† *Source:* Tom Moon, "Public Enemy's Bomb Squad: Hank Shocklee Explodes in Your Ear," *Musician,* October 1991, pp. 69–72, 76.

we're taking it from the record and manipulating it into something else. That's another type of musicianship. It would take less time to bring a band in and have them play this live than it does manipulating it our way, but what fun would that be?" he says, reaching over the console to punch buttons that isolate percussion tracks in his dense schemata. (Shocklee builds rap songs using as many as 48 tracks—far more than most rap producers.)

In fact, much of the Bomb Squad work is not very much fun. It's not a sweatshop, but it's close: The group cranks out beats and rhythm patterns and loops every day, whether there's a project or not. "It's not like an artist who leaves the piano if nothing's happening. We'll do something—a beat, some samples—and file it away. Then when we're thinking about a track, we'll call it up and try it out."

The business of building the tracks begins at "Demo World," the Squad's production studio in Hempstead, Long Island. "That's where we have our records and our sound libraries. We each have our specialties: My brother is amazing with computers, so he's always got sounds, and he knows records like an encyclopedia. Eric, I consider him a programming wizard. He knows drum machines backwards and forwards. They're like the builders and I'm the architect. I'm thinking about arrangements—putting in the chorus at times you don't really expect a chorus, coming up with that extra little interruption." Shocklee has become an executive architect now. Public Enemy's *Apocalypse '91: The Empire Strikes Black* credits him as executive producer, which means, Shocklee says, that he's "in and out, not as much hands-on, but not like a record company guy handling paperwork."

Assembling beats and loops from any number of sources, the Bomb Squad drafts a blueprint which is then used to match the sound with the message. "If the title of the album is *AmeriKKKa's Most Wanted*," Shocklee says, "your beat better sound like the most wanted, you know?* We look at that phrase and we've got darkness in our minds—rough streets, gloomy, hard, these are the things you have to put on tape. So once we get the outline, we think about trying to complement the vocal situation by making the backing tracks as aggressive as possible. Whatever you bring up as a sample, whatever beat you work with, has to be an exclamation point to the situation."

Shocklee can't stress this enough: "Music is a mood situation. As the Bomb Squad, we score to personalities. Nobody goes in and says, 'We're going to make the deffest record.' You know how you feel that day. Then you listen and say, this sounds like such-and-such emotion."

When they start really examining how the content fits the music, the Squad usually starts arguing. "It gets down to the very specifics of perception," Shocklee says, diving back onto the couch. "Here you've got a click on the one. Here you've got a snare drum that you want to put on the one with the click, right? How it's perceived depends on how it hits the one. For example, you rush something—a couple of seconds before the one—and there's a mood of emergency. Of uneasiness. On a lot of the early records we rushed the samples a bit. So you're constantly going, 'Why is this pushing me?' Now, if you bring it back a little bit, you're laying back. That's a whole other mood. You haven't changed the situation—you've still got a click and you've still got a snare, but now the perception is changed. That's the thing people feel. A loop is purposefully placed a little bit off, a little ajar, so that when it comes around again, it's like a wooosh against the snare.

"We fight to figure it out. Somebody'll say, 'I don't want this snare on the one, because instead of being laid-back it has the feeling of not doing anything.' That's what pop records do to you—it doesn't make you feel one way or the other. You went in the same way you come out. That's what we don't want. We want records that reach and transcend."

---

* The Bomb Squad had provided the production for *AmeriKKKa's Most Wanted*, the debut solo album from former N.W.A. rapper Ice Cube.

To get those records, the Bomb Squad has to do some fancy drum-machine footwork. Facing the limitations of the metrically rigid machines, Shocklee and Sadler work to create rhythm programs that swing—not the ricky-ticky new-jack style, but a deep and buoyant groove that automatically induces motion. It is a point of pride: "You'll hear three different kick drums, three snares, three hi-hats, and each has its own time frequency. This is because you've got to recreate all kinds of stuff. You've got to simulate that laziness—when the drummer hits the snare and gets a repeating note because he didn't lift the stick up. Also, a drummer's stick doesn't hit the skin in the same place all the time, but that happens with a machine. That right there adds the funk: We've got to take these machines and recreate mistakes on purpose."

Harmonic dissonances (listen to Public Enemy's "Bring the Noise") meet with the same debate. "Eric sings on key," Shocklee says, "while I'm like, fuck the key. I'm looking for a mood, a feeling. So some things are purposely out of key. Like Son of Bazerk, it's an R&B band, their stuff is in key. But I believe in complements, and Bazerk, he's meaner than anybody I've ever heard on wax. I work with him by having what's behind him in key, otherwise you lose Bazerk. If I put things in key behind Chuck D, you lose Chuck, because his vocal is smooth. So you have to put it against abrasion."

Today is a rare day in the studio: Shocklee usually observes a no-visitors policy. "If everybody is not focused on the same situation," says Hank, "we're not going to meet our goal. So I'm the leader, and I don't settle. There are no split decisions in music, no ties. It's either the right way or the wrong way. If somebody's walking around with that 'I don't give a fuck, let's just do this' attitude, that will come through. One negative can destroy the whole situation. People react to that, they know when it's not feeling good."

Once enough of the grooves and adornments are in place, the Bomb Squad leaves Demo World, transporting the not-so-basic tracks and programs to one of the large facilities in Manhattan (very occasionally, L.A.) for final touches and all-important mixing sessions.

The mix is everything. It doesn't matter how many cool sounds and structural surprises Shocklee and his crew put into the track—if the mix ain't happening, the magic's lost. So the Bomb Squad spends most of its time tweaking sounds, checking balances, carefully adjusting the dense collage so that every element comes through. Here, too, Shocklee has a renegade outlook. Operating on the assumption that most people don't sit in front of two speakers to listen to music, Shocklee puts his mixes through unusual tests. "Sometimes you hear three or four loops on the same track, all happening at different places with different levels and EQ settings. If one little thing is out of balance, everything is wack. That's why I'm here doing this now. There are certain things we want to cut through the track and other things we want in there, but not cutting through. For example, that string line we just heard, that little loop—if you have that too loud, you become too aware of it. It's got to be at a level where you still hear the line but you don't hear that it's repeating. We don't want it flat, like those old Motown songs, but if it's too high it's going to take away from the kick drum and everything else. So it's delicate. Sometimes we open up tracks to get more hiss. Hiss acts as glue—it fills in cracks and crevices so you get this constant wooooooffff. So you play around with everything, get to where you can hear it and what it's doing, and pretty soon the whole track is breathing.

"That's why I sit on the couch. Because music has to hit you. I don't want to hear it up close. I'll go listen in the hallway and decide whether the mix was pulling me in. I want to make records so that when a car is driving by and you hear the thing blaring, you could tell it was my record. Most of the time you just hear it as blaring. I want mine to be so distinct you want to stop and ask the guy, 'What was *that*?'"

48

"The Death of Sampling?"

MARK KEMP

By the early 1990s, hip-hop had become a major commercial force, and its producers were finally receiving recognition for their intricate use of samples. Given rap's increasing visibility, however, it was inevitable that hip-hop artists would eventually find the legality of their sampling practices questioned in a court of law. In December 1991, Judge Kevin Thomas Duffy ruled that rapper Biz Markie's song "Alone Again" was in copyright violation of the song it had sampled, Gilbert O'Sullivan's 1972 hit "Alone Again (Naturally)." Duffy's decision was forceful, but also vague; he did not state what amount of sampling *would* be permissible. As such, the ruling created a culture of fear within the music industry. It seemed implicit that any and all samples, regardless of their length, would require clearance. Mark Kemp's article for *Option* magazine captures in illuminating detail the debates that emerged in the wake of the Biz Markie case. Years later, many of the concerns that Kemp raises have come to be realized. On the one hand, since the early '90s most major hip-hop artists have taken a financially efficient approach to sampling, severely limiting their borrowing to only one or two prominently placed, and repeated, samples per song. On the other hand, many rap producers have worked around copyright restrictions by using obscure sources, or by deliberately altering samples to the point where the original is no longer recognizable. Whether or not the "Biz Markie case 'stole the soul' from rap music," as copyright expert and Fair Use advocate Siva Vaidhyanathan has maintained, is debatable. But its impact is impossible to ignore.*[†]

When a New York judge quoted the Bible in his decision to grant a temporary injunction barring further sales of Biz Markie's album *I Need a Haircut* last December, it sent a shock wave through the music industry.

"Thou shalt not steal" were the first words of Judge Kevin Thomas Duffy's ruling.

It was a reaction to Markie's use of a loop from the 1972 Gilbert O'Sullivan hit "Alone Again (Naturally)" in his rap song simply entitled "Alone Again." The Markie case marks the first time sampling has ever gone before a judge—earlier cases were settled out of court—and Duffy's words were chillingly clear and simple: if you're going to sample from another artist's work, you'd better get permission.

The ruling has caused a minor panic among some record companies. Top brass immediately sent down memos to the effect that all digital samples on all new albums would have to be cleared before release. But some artists who use digital samples in their work say such a requirement would

---

* Siva Vaidhyanathan, *Copyrights and Copywrongs: The Rise of Intellectual Property and How it Threatens Creativity* (New York: New York University Press, 2001), 144.

† *Source:* Mark Kemp, "The Death of Sampling?," *Option*, March/April 1992, pp. 17–20.

be virtually impossible to comply with; and as a legal precedent, it stands to threaten the creative process of contemporary pop music altogether.

"It's going to affect *everyone's* process," says Hank Shocklee of Public Enemy's production team, the Bomb Squad. "A whole chain of events will start happening: people are going to be trying like crazy to find all their sources, and records won't come out on time. It's impossible to keep up with every snippet of sound you use."

Shocklee should know. Unlike Biz Markie's song, in which a large portion of O'Sullivan's tune was sampled and looped throughout, the Bomb Squad's sound collages involve a veritable soup of samples. "You know how some people say. The Bomb Squad uses all these samples and I can't tell where they come from?'" Shocklee asks. "Well, *we* can't tell where they come from either. You change the sound, you alter them, and then you plug them into your mix; six months down the road, after you've been working with all these different samples, you have no idea where every one of them came from."

Los Angeles attorney Evan Cohen sees things differently. In 1989, Cohen represented Mark Volman and Howard Kaylan of the '60s pop group the Turtles in a landmark lawsuit against rappers De La Soul, who had used a sample of the Turtles' 1969 hit "You Showed Me" in their own "Transmitting Live From Mars" (the case was settled out of court). Cohen suggests that Judge Duffy's decision in the Biz Markie case is a milestone for copyright holders. "It should provide the final removal of doubt as to whether the Fair Use Doctrine applies to digital sampling," he says.

Cohen's reference is to the Fair Use Doctrine of 1972, an amendment to the copyright law which allows for various exceptions to the law, including appropriation of copyrighted materials for social comment, education, and other such purposes. Some observers, such as De La Soul's attorney Ken Anderson, feel that Fair Use should apply to certain instances of digital sampling. However, Cohen sees the judge's decision as definitive: "The judge in New York says sampling is stealing if one doesn't ask permission beforehand."

Anderson dismisses his colleague's observation, calling it premature. "The Biz Markie case doesn't even *refer* to Fair Use," Anderson says. "There has not yet been a case which analyzes the copyright issues relative to sampling. We're still waiting for that."

Since it made its way into popular music in the mid-'80s, digital sampling has been a highly charged issue of ownership, often pitting young, black, inner-city experimental hip-hop musicians against older, baby-boomer pop stars of the '60s and '70s. The Turtles, perhaps, were the symbolically perfect '60s group to sue for copyright infringement. They created perfectly happy melodies in a pure-pop structure. Side-by-side, the Turtles and De La Soul represented the past and future of pop music. "We weren't wanting to prohibit them from moving in a creative way," says Turtle Mark Volman. "No one I know wants to stop them from being creative, but at the same time you have to deal with legalities.

"It's important that artists receive their fair share and what's due. If someone's using music that's already been created and spent for, then they should pay for it. It was only a matter of time before the courts would say that.

"When Bob Dylan wrote that the times are a changing, hey, they still are," Volman adds. "Music is changing, too. Rock'n'roll takes on so many different ways, and rap is one of them."

Certainly, times have changed since popular groups penned simple verse-chorus-verse songs; with the advent of samplers and other technological advances, even the most mainstream popular music has become a more experimental medium. It's now common practice to incorporate snippets of prerecorded material into songs. But hip-hop has never been the only music built around electronic samples. In the early '80s, avant-garde musicians were playing around with sampling machines at about the same time, and since then all kinds of music, from R&B and dance music to heavy metal and alternative rock, have begun using samples.

But Judge Duffy's decision stands to put a damper on such experimentation. After the decision was handed down, record companies immediately instituted their new tougher policies. "It's much more stringent now than it had been," says Warner publicity head Bob Merlis. "We took a lot of stuff on faith before, but now we're demanding proof that these things are being cleared." Merlis admits that such policies "are going to slow things down." Lillian Matulic of Priority, N.W.A's label, agrees, saying, "We were issued a memo saying they have to clear all samples before we release anything." A spokesman for De La Soul's record company Tommy Boy, who agreed to talk on condition of anonymity, says it was the process of clearing all samples that caused the year-long delay of that group's second album, *De La Soul Is Dead*. "Here, we wait until *everything* is cleared—every drum beat, however small it is." he says. "It's like, why play around, right? The De La Soul vs. the Turtles situation really wised us up."

On the surface, this sort of caution may seem obvious: if you take from Gilbert O'Sullivan, you should get Gilbert O'Sullivan's permission. But there's a tremendous gray area in sampling. Markie's case indicated a clear breakdown in communication, and his attorney's argument that it's a common practice to go ahead and use non-cleared samples was not a real argument at all. Further evidence that Markie had sought O'Sullivan's permission beforehand, was denied it, and then released the song anyway, seemed to make the case clear-cut. After all, when MC Hammer released "U Can't Touch This," whose main hook was Rick James' 1981 hit "Super Freak," he had obtained James' permission, and even worked out a deal that gave James co-credit—and ultimately, big royalties.

The danger in Judge Duffy's decision is that sampling is still not a cut-and-dry issue. Duffy, who was so oblivious to pop music that he had to be told what the term "R&B" means, didn't address the more complex and subtle uses of sampling. As Anderson points out, sampling "is not the kind of thing that lends itself to the statement, 'Thou shalt not steal.' It's a little more sophisticated than that." Still, Anderson plays down the significance of the Markie case. "I don't think it has any legal impact at all because it doesn't analyze the copyright issues of whether sampling constitutes infringement."

"What this case *doesn't* answer are those borderline cases," says entertainment attorney Richard P. Dieguez, who distinguishes between what he terms *de minimis* sampling—a short horn blast, a James Brown scream, a kick or snare drum—from what he refers to in plainer English as "the primary hook of an actual master recording." For instance, Dieguez says, "if you deleted the sample from the Biz Markie song, you wouldn't have anything left but Biz kind of talking to himself. That's an obvious case. On the other hand, if you deleted any of the samples in a Public Enemy record, you'd still have a composition. I couldn't imagine anyone getting nailed for taking a snare. The difficulty is the stuff in the middle.

"Right now," says Dieguez, "there's no precedent. Some people want to believe that there's a set number of bars that's allowable, but that's just not true. It doesn't matter how many bars of a song are taken; it's an ad hoc judgment. No one can come up with a blanket rule."

"It's impossible," says Hank Shocklee of the possibility that he would have to account for all the sounds on a Public Enemy record. "I look at rap culture—and R&B culture, too—as becoming more of a scavenger culture," he says. "After a while, you start mixing it all together, mixing all the colors together, and you lose the source. I think that's what's *good* about it, the way it evolves into something else. I *like* that aspect of it."

Accordingly, Shocklee doesn't consider the Markie case a sampling issue, per se. "Biz did a cover of a song," he says. "People confuse that issue. A sample's when you take a snippet. Biz didn't just sample it, he took a hunk of it." Shocklee ultimately blames higher-ups for allowing the song to get out without clearance in the first place. "It goes to show how little record executives know about the music they put out. It shows that either they don't care about the music or that they don't know about it. And now that the Biz Markie song got past them, they're trying to cover their tails. Now, you're going to be asked to account for every snippet, and that's just not possible."

"I totally disagree," says DJ Daddy-O of Stetsasonic. "That's just a bunch of bullshit." Daddy-O has put his own group on hold for the moment because he has become a producer very much in demand lately, working on various hip-hop and R&B records, including Queen Latifah, as well as remixes for rock bands, such as Sonic Youth and the B-52s. Daddy-O feels the Biz Markie case should make DJs more responsible, that it should encourage those who sample to go beyond the mere looping of familiar songs. "Every DJ in the world knows what records he uses." Daddy-O says. "So for Hank to sit there and say, 'Six months down the road, when I'm working with the Bomb Squad, I don't know what I use,' that's bullshit. You're making records, you have to be responsible for where your material comes from."

But there's a distinction between Shocklee's technique and the approach taken by those who merely loop songs. And Daddy-O is somewhat sensitive to this. "I actually kind of understand what he's saying, though, because Public Enemy's music works in a different way, sort of like a painting," Daddy-O says. "What happens in the mix is the same thing that happens with paint—after a while some of the stuff starts blending together in the background, creating a foundation. So it's hard to tell what's there. It's like when you blend green with yellow: you get something very different. That's what happens in a PE mix. But I think people should still be aware of where their stuff is coming from.

"In fact, we as rap artists have got to start getting beyond what we've done in the past," he adds. "We need to think about making classic records, like all the classic rock and R&B records of the past. We need to be making records that people are happy with and not saying, 'Oh, all they're doing is stealing samples.' Look at what's happening in rock. Today, with the technology we have, you don't *need* guitars to make music. Yet look at what happened with the Nirvana record. And there's no reason that record should *not* have gotten as far as it did. It's a great record. Everything about it is right—it's got the melodies and it's got the power. It's just right. And it's regular old guitar rock. That's the level that our music should be going, and that's what we should be striving for.

"The Biz Markie situation was a stupid move," Daddy-O continues, "but everything happens for a reason. I think in a way it's good, because now it's going to make people start looking towards the future, looking towards that next level."

49

"Kurt Cobain and the Politics of Damage"

SARAH FERGUSON

When college rock favorites Nirvana and their front man Kurt Cobain (1967–1994) were thrust into the spotlight in 1991 on the strength of their major label debut *Nevermind*, the media quickly heralded them as the forerunners of a new alternative rock movement. While alternative came to encompass a number of styles—everything from Nine Inch Nails' industrial rock to Teenage Fanclub's power pop—its most popular manifestation was undoubtedly that of grunge. As a label, the term "grunge" seemed to fit perfectly the dirty, distorted guitars, metallic riffs, and hoarse, shouted vocals of groups like Pearl Jam, Mudhoney, and others. More than that, though, grunge became attached to a regional scene (Seattle), a fashion style, and, as Sarah Ferguson points out in her article for the *Utne Reader*, an attitude of alienation and victimization, crystallized in songs like "Smells Like Teen Spirit" and "Jeremy" and mirrored in the music's audience. Ferguson questions the reasons and social significance behind grunge's "politics of damage." If grunge is to be taken seriously as an authentic expression of the times, she argues, then it needs to be considered along lines of race, class, gender, and the place of youth within the American family.[*]

I came face to face with the essence of grunge culture last summer, when I was out in Seattle interviewing street punks. I was hanging out with a runaway vegan anarchist named Jackie and his street friend Anthony when we decided to go party with their friends from the band Suffocated. We took a shortcut to their house on the outskirts of the U district, tramping through the woods and under the bridge where the "trolls" (street kids) slept when they didn't have a squat to crash, then circling around the back of Safeway to scavenge for moldy sandwiches in the Dumpster.

Suffocated's lead guitarist received us nonchalantly, nodding at the 40-ouncers we'd picked up with Jackie and Anthony's panhandled change. Anthony said he wanted to try out his new piercing needle and disappeared into the bathroom upstairs. He said he wanted to pierce his scrotum, said he liked the experience of pain.

So Jackie and I sat there in the living room, watching the band members scarf down lines of speed and bong hits amid a blistering blur of crustcore and metal. At the end of the tape, the guitarist dug out a new one. "Mind if we listen to Nirvana?" he asked, almost apologetically, like he was 'fessing to being a Bon Jovi fan. "Sure," Jackie shrugged, but I just smiled. These were Kurt Cobain's people, the forgotten white trash he celebrated. If I'd asked them up front, they would have said

---

[*] *Source:* Sarah Ferguson, "The Comfort of Being Sad: Kurt Cobain and the Politics of Damage," *Utne Reader*, July/ August 1994, pp. 60–62.

they hated Nirvana for the same sellout reasons that Cobain hated himself. Yet even among this jaded crowd, Cobain's anguished wail offered a refuge of authentic despair.

Courtney Love said, "Every kid in America who's been abused loves Kurt Cobain's music." In fact, Nirvana made abuse his generation's defining metaphor. The hit "Smells Like Teen Spirit" was an anthem of powerless rage and betrayal. It was a resounding fuck you to the boomers and all the false expectations they saddled us with about rock 'n' roll revolution. And it made psychological damage—with all its concurrent themes of child abuse, drug addiction, suicide, and neglect—a basis for social identity.

Like Pearl Jam's "Jeremy," which tells the story of an alienated kid who blows his head off in school, Nirvana's "Teen Spirit," and indeed all of grunge culture, is rooted in the feeling of damage. Coming out of the get-ahead '80s, it's easy to understand the appeal. Being damaged is a hedge against the illusory promises of consumer culture. For grunge's primary audience, white male teens, damage offers a defense against the claims of gangsta rappers and punk rock feminists. It's a great equalizer at a time when multiculturalism seems to have devolved into competing schools of victimization. Grunge appeals to white kids because it tells them that they're not responsible for the evils of racism and injustices, that they are victims too.

The empowered feeling you get from listening to these songs lies in unearthing that essential nugget of shame. It's like going to a 12-step meeting. You stand up, announce the wrongs done to you as a child, your response (drugs, suicide attempts). Simply identifying and acknowledging your damage is empowering, because society seems to deny you the right to feel damaged.

What's frustrating is how the politics of the music remains so acutely personal. When the Sex Pistols screamed "No Future," they were condemning a society that gave young people no hope, no prospects for change. Yet underlying that nihilistic message was a vital rage at all the politicians and people in power who, they felt, had restricted their prospects. In other words, punk knew who the enemy was.

By contrast, grunge music seems more muddled. It's as if kids don't know who to blame: their parents, the media, the schools—or themselves. Even Cobain doubted the privilege of his despair. "I'm a product of a spoiled America," he once said. "Think of how much worse my family life could be if I grew up in a depression or something. There are so many worse things than a divorce. I've just been brooding and bellyaching about something I couldn't have, which is a family, a solid family unit, for too long."

In fact, the dissolution of the American family has exerted a tremendous torque on the members of Cobain's generation. And while they may not be growing up in the midst of the Great Depression, with the official unemployment rate for young people hovering at 13.2 percent, kids have reason to complain. The dwindling timber economy of Cobain's hometown, Aberdeen, Washington, was certainly no picnic. Yet Cobain and his fellow grunge balladeers never really aspire to protest, preferring to remain mired in their own sense of inadequacy. The inverted pose of the music mirrors the incoherence of the left and the replacement of class politics with self-help politics. In the absence of a viable counterculture, it's no wonder young people don't know who to blame.

Indeed, grunge expresses this generation's almost willful refusal to reach for larger truths. Instead, it engages in a kind of mournful nostalgia for a childhood without violation. Grunge sees the lie of consumer culture but still yearns for the manufactured suburban bliss of *Leave It to Beaver* and *Mayberry R.F.D.* (two of Cobain's favorite shows). It's an odd yet poignant stance, given rock's traditional aversion to the constraints of the nuclear family. "Daddy didn't give attention / To the fact that mommy didn't care," Eddie Vedder anguishes. Grunge is music for kids who grew up too fast. They keep reaching back for a childhood denied.

The contrast between Cobain's self-deprecation and his fans' adulation was jarring when I saw Nirvana play New York's Coliseum during their last concert tour. As the roadies wheeled out the hermaphroditic figurines and fiberglass trees for the *In Utero* stage set, I was struck by the band's unwillingness to indulge the audience's yearning for spectacle. Despite the corporate veneer of a big band setup, these hulking plastic dummies with their exposed innards had a kind of malevolent camp, like a twisted take on the witch's forest on *H.R. Pufnstuff*.

The crowd let out a dull roar as Dave Grohl's rapid-fire drumroll launched the band into the opening chords of "Breed." But Cobain steadfastly refused to play the role of a revered rock star, insulting his fans with sloppy chords and (apparently) drug-addled stupor. The overwhelmingly white, overwhelmingly male, overwhelmingly suburban crowd didn't seem to care. They sang along blithely to "Polly," a song about a girl being molested, and pogoed to "Rape Me," Cobain's angst-filled response to commercial fame.

The saddest moment came when the band played "Dumb": "I think I'm dumb, or maybe just happy. Think I'm just happy…" Cobain droned, underscoring the terribleness of not knowing the difference. The crowd stilled, grew listless, then restless, but Cobain kept intoning, "I think I'm dumb, I think I'm dumb." And for the first time it wasn't his audience's stupidity that he was railing at but his own, the horror of finding out that this was all his art could attract—people who stare back sheepishly, or worse, reverently, at your rage. He'd succeeded beyond his wildest dreams of combining punk and pop and created a Frankenstein that by its success seems to invalidate the thrust of its rebellion. You could hear him wanting to scoop it down the garbage disposal, nuke it in the microwave, except he couldn't. It just kept mutating into some yet more profitable venture.

What Cobain's suicide in April and the whole trajectory of his band's success prove is the inability of youth to own their own rebellion. The loop taken by a new musical style from the underground to the mainstream is now so compressed that there's no moment of freedom and chaos when a counterculture can take root. Even anti-corporatism can be rerouted into a marketing ploy. MTV makes fun of itself in order to ingratiate itself with its audience, but it's still one big extended commercial.

"There is no youth culture. It's like we've been robbed of culture," a street punk named Bones told me last summer as we were hopping freight trains through the South. A skinny 19-year-old with droopy brown eyes, he had covered his body with a latticework of tattoos tracing the different stages of his youth: skinhead, heroin addict, born-again Christian, skatepunk, acidhead, sous-chef. His latest "tat" was an almost photographic image of an Iraqi woman weeping over a skull.

Yet what struck me most was the battered *Sesame Street* Ernie doll that he'd sewn on the top of his backpack. It was meant to be goofy. But a flea-ridden high school dropout on food stamps tramping through train yards with this remnant of his childhood was a little like thrusting a stuffed animal into a propeller blade.

Nirvana's formula of Beatle-esque pop juxtaposed with bursts of harsh heavy metal captures the same dissonance. It recapitulates the violation of childhood innocence, the ultimate betrayal kids see in commercial culture, which promised *Brady Bunch* lives and gave them single-parent homes. The fact that this generation bought the *Brady Bunch* myth in the first place is testament to the totalitarian nature of commodity culture. Their dreams and desires have been manufactured and controlled at such an early age, they lack a clear sense of authentic experience. Perhaps that's why the theme of child abuse is so engaging. It's a visceral pain that adults produce but don't control.

And it's an accusation. In kids' eyes, it's the adults of America who are truly damaged. Their children are just collateral damage.

50

"The Problem with Music"

STEVE ALBINI

Renowned underground producer/engineer and post-punk musician Steve Albini (born 1962) issued the following eye-opening polemic against the mainstream music industry at a time in the early 1990s when many major labels were aggressively courting indie bands in the hopes of discovering the next Nirvana. Albini strips away the illusory trappings of financial fame to reveal the industry's devious machinations. As he explains, inexperienced bands often unwittingly assume the expenses of studio time, big name producers, and other numerous perks, while relinquishing the majority of their profits. And in the end these bands generally sacrifice much of their creative control as well. Albini's diatribe ultimately underscores the extent to which notions of "authenticity," in all its various guises (whether it's one's 'punk' credentials or the vintage instruments they play) circulate within the rock industry. The article's acerbic prose is typical of Albini's writings and interviews, and is equally matched by the music he has released with such abrasive bands as Big Black, Rapeman, and Shellac. Albini is equally well known for his extensive engineering credentials, a point he deliberately drives home during a lengthy detour in the middle of the article. All told, Albini has produced and recorded literally hundreds of independent bands, as well as major artists ranging from PJ Harvey and Nirvana to Jimmy Page and Robert Plant.[*]

Whenever I talk to a band who are about to sign with a major label, I always end up thinking of them in a particular context. I imagine a trench, about four feet wide and five feet deep, maybe sixty yards long, filled with runny, decaying shit. I imagine these people, some of them good friends, some of them barely acquaintances, at one end of this trench. I also imagine a faceless industry lackey at the other end, holding a fountain pen and a contract waiting to be signed.

Nobody can see what's printed on the contract. It's too far away, and besides, the shit stench is making everybody's eyes water. The lackey shouts to everybody that the first one to swim the trench gets to sign the contract. Everybody dives in the trench and they struggle furiously to get to the other end. Two people arrive simultaneously and begin wrestling furiously, clawing each other and dunking each other under the shit. Eventually, one of them capitulates, and there's only one contestant left. He reaches for the pen, but the Lackey says, "Actually, I think you need a little more development. Swim it again, please. Backstroke."

And he does, of course.

---

[*] *Source:* Steve Albini, "The Problem with Music," *The Baffler*, no. 5, 1993. Reprinted in Thomas Frank and Matt Weiland, eds., *Commodify Your Dissent: Salvos from The Baffler* (New York: Norton, 1997), pp. 164–76.

A&R SCOUTS

Every major label involved in the hunt for new bands now has on staff a high-profile point man, an "A&R" rep who can present a comfortable face to any prospective band. The initials stand for "Artist and Repertoire," because historically, the A&R staff would select artists to record music that they had also selected, out of an available pool of each. This is still the case, though not openly.

These guys are universally young (about the same age as the bands being wooed), and nowadays they always have some obvious underground rock credibility flag they can wave. Lyle Preslar, former guitarist for Minor Threat, is one of them. Terry Tolkin, former NY independent booking agent and assistant manager at Touch and Go is one of them. Al Smith, former soundman at CBGB is one of them. Mike Gitter, former editor of *XXX* fanzine and contributor to *Rip*, *Kerrang* and other lowbrow rags is one of them. Many of the annoying turds who used to staff college radio stations are in their ranks as well.

There are several reasons A&R scouts are always young. The explanation usually copped-to is that the scout will be "hip" to the current musical "scene." A more important reason is that the bands will intuitively trust someone they think is a peer, and who speaks fondly of the same formative rock and roll experiences.

The A&R person is the first person to make contact with the band, and as such is the first person to promise them the moon. Who better to promise them the moon than an idealistic young turk who expects to be calling the shots in a few years, and who has had no previous experience with a big record company. Hell, he's as naïve as the band he's duping. When he tells them no one will interfere in their creative process, he probably even believes it.

When he sits down with the band for the first time, over a plate of angel hair pasta, he can tell them with all sincerity that when they sign with company X, they're really signing with *him*, and he's on their side. Remember that great gig I saw you at in '85? Didn't we have a blast?

By now all rock bands are wise enough to be suspicious of music industry scum. There is a pervasive caricature in popular culture of a portly, middle-aged ex-hipster talking a mile-a-minute, using outdated jargon and calling everybody "baby." After meeting "their" A&R guy, the band will say to themselves and everyone else, "He's not like a record company guy at all! He's like one of us." And they will be right. That's one of the reasons he was hired.

These A&R guys are not allowed to write contracts. What they do is present the band with a letter of intent, or "deal memo," which loosely states some terms, and affirms that the band will sign with the label once a contract has been agreed on.

The spookiest thing about this harmless sounding little "memo," is that it is, for all legal purposes, a binding document. That is, once the band signs it, they are under obligation to conclude a deal with the label. If the label presents them with a contract that the band doesn't want to sign, all the label has to do is wait. There are a hundred other bands willing to sign the exact same contract, so the label is in a position of strength.

These letters never have any term of expiry, so the band remains bound by the deal memo until a contract is signed, no matter how long that takes. The band cannot sign to another label or even put out its own material unless they are released from their agreement, which never happens. Make no mistake about it: once a band has signed a letter of intent, they will either eventually sign a contract that suits the label or they will be destroyed.

One of my favorite bands was held hostage for the better part of two years by a slick young "He's not like a label guy at all," A&R rep, on the basis of such a deal memo. He had failed to come through on any of his promises (something he did with similar effect to another well-known band), and so the band wanted out. Another label expressed interest, but when the A&R man was asked to release the band, he said he would need money or points, or possibly both, before he would consider it.*

The new label was afraid the price would be too dear, and they said no thanks. On the cusp of making their signature album, an excellent band, humiliated, broke up from the stress and the many months of inactivity.

WHAT I HATE ABOUT RECORDING

1. Producers and engineers who use meaningless words to make their clients think they know what's going on. Words like "Punchy," "Warm," "Groove," "Vibe," "Feel." Especially "Punchy" and "Warm." Every time I hear those words, I want to throttle somebody.
2. Producers who aren't also engineers, and as such, don't have the slightest fucking idea what they're doing in a studio, besides talking all the time. Historically, the progression of effort required to become a producer went like this: Go to college, get an EE degree. Get a job as an assistant at a studio. Eventually become a second engineer. Learn the job and become an engineer. Do that for a few years, then you can try your hand at producing. Now, all that's required to be a full-fledged "producer" is the gall it takes to claim to be one.

   Calling people like Don Fleming, Al Jourgensen, Lee Ranaldo or Jerry Harrison "producers" in the traditional sense is akin to calling Bernie a "shortstop" because he watched the whole playoffs this year.

   The term has taken on pejorative qualities in some circles. Engineers tell jokes about producers the way people back in Montana tell jokes about North Dakotans. (How many producers does it take to change a light bulb?—Hmmm. I don't know. What do *you* think? Why did the producer cross the road?—Because that's the way the Beatles did it, man.) That's why few self-respecting engineers will allow themselves to be called "producers."

   The minimum skills required to do an adequate job recording an album are:
   - Working knowledge of all the microphones at hand and their properties and uses. I mean something beyond knowing that you can drop an SM57 without breaking it.
   - Experience with every piece of equipment which might be of use and every function it may provide. This means more than knowing what echo sounds like. Which equalizer has the least phase shift in neighbor bands? Which console has more headroom? Which mastering deck has the cleanest output electronics?
   - Experience with the style of music at hand, to know when obvious blunders are occurring.
   - Ability to tune and maintain all the required instruments and electronics, so as to insure that everything is in proper working order. This means more than plugging a guitar into a tuner. How should the drums be tuned to simulate a rising note on the decay? A falling note? A consonant note? Can a bassoon play a concert E-flat in key with a piano tuned to a reference A of 440 Hz? What percentage of varispeed is necessary to make a whole-tone pitch change? What degree of overbias gives you the most headroom at 10 kHz? What reference fluxivity gives you the lowest self-noise from biased, unrecorded tape? Which tape manufacturer closes every year in July, causing shortages of tape globally? What can be done for a shedding master tape? A sticky one?

---

* "Points" is industry lingo for the "percentage points" of retail profits that producers, labels, managers, and others can claim from the band … e.g. 10 percent = 10 points.

- Knowledge of electronic circuits to an extent that will allow selection of appropriate signal paths. This means more than knowing the difference between a delay line and an equalizer. Which has more headroom, a discrete class A microphone preamp with a transformer output or a differential circuit built with monolithics? Where is the best place in an unbalanced line to attenuate the signal? If you short the cold leg of a differential input to ground, what happens to the signal level? Which gain control device has the least distortion, a VCA, a printed plastic pot, a photoresistor or a wire-wound stepped attenuator? Will putting an unbalanced line on a half-normalled jack unbalance the normal signal path? Will a transformer splitter load the input to a device parallel to it? Which will have less RF noise, a shielded unbalanced line or a balanced line with a floated shield?
- An aesthetic that is well-rooted and compatible with the music, and
- The good taste to know when to exercise it.

3. Trendy electronics and other flashy shit that nobody really needs. Five years ago, everything everywhere was being done with discrete samples. No actual drumming allowed on most records. Samples only. The next trend was Pultec Equalizers. Everything had to be run through Pultec EQs.

   Then vintage microphones were all the rage (but only Neumanns, the most annoyingly *whiny* microphone line ever made). The current trendy thing is *compression*. Compression by the ton, especially if it comes from a *tube* limiter. Wow. It doesn't matter how awful the recording is, as long as it goes through a tube limiter, somebody will claim it sounds "warm," or maybe even "punchy." They might even compare it to the Beatles. I want to find the guy that invented compression and tear his liver out. I hate it. It makes everything sound like a beer commercial.

4. DAT machines. They sound like shit and every crappy studio has one now because they're so cheap. Because the crappy engineers that inhabit crappy studios are too thick to learn how to align and maintain analog mastering decks, they're all using DAT machines exclusively. DAT tapes deteriorate over time, and when they do, the information on them is lost forever. I have personally seen tapes go irretrievably bad in less than a month. Using them for final masters is almost fraudulently irresponsible.

   Tape machines ought to be big and cumbersome and difficult to use, if only to keep the riff-raff out. DAT machines make it possible for morons to make a living, and do damage to the music we all have to listen to.

5. Trying to sound like the Beatles. Every record I hear these days has incredibly loud, compressed vocals, and a quiet little murmur of a rock band in the background. The excuse given by producers for inflicting such an imbalance on a rock band is that it makes the record sound more like the Beatles. Yeah, right. Fuck's sake, Thurston Moore is not Paul McCartney, and nobody on earth, not with unlimited time and resources, could make the Smashing Pumpkins sound like the Beatles. Trying just makes them seem even dumber. Why can't people try to sound like the Smashchords or Metal Urbain or Third World War for a change?

THERE'S THIS BAND

There's this band. They're pretty ordinary, but they're also pretty good, so they've attracted some attention. They're signed to a moderate-sized "independent" label owned by a distribution company, and they have another two albums owed to the label.

They're a little ambitious. They'd like to get signed by a major label so they can have some security—you know, get some good equipment, tour in a proper tour bus—nothing fancy, just a little reward for all the hard work.

To that end, they got a manager. He knows some of the label guys, and he can shop their next project to all the right people. He takes his cut, sure, but it's only 15%, and if he can get them signed then it's money well spent. Anyway, it doesn't cost them anything if it doesn't work. 15% of nothing isn't much!

One day an A&R scout calls them, says he's "been following them for a while now," and when their manager mentioned them to him, it just "clicked." Would they like to meet with him about the possibility of working out a deal with his label? Wow. Big Break time.

They meet the guy, and y'know what—he's not what they expected from a label guy. He's young and dresses pretty much like the band does. He knows all their favorite bands. He's like one of them. He tells them he wants to go to bat for them, to try to get them everything they want. He says anything is possible with the right attitude. They conclude the evening by taking home a copy of a deal memo they wrote out and signed on the spot.

The A&R guy was full of great ideas, even talked about using a name producer. Butch Vig is out of the question—he wants 100 g's and three points, but they can get Don Fleming for $30,000 plus three points. Even that's a little steep, so maybe they'll go with that guy who used to be in David Letterman's band. He only wants three points. Or they can have just anybody record it (like Wharton Tiers, maybe—cost you 5 or 10 grand) and have Andy Wallace remix it for 4 grand a track plus 2 points. It was a lot to think about.

Well, they like this guy and they trust him. Besides, they already signed the deal memo. He must have been serious about wanting them to sign. They break the news to their current label, and the label manager says he wants them to succeed, so they have his blessing. He will need to be compensated, of course, for the remaining albums left on their contract, but he'll work it out with the label himself. Sub Pop made millions from selling off Nirvana, and Twin Tone hasn't done bad either: 50 grand for the Babes and 60 grand for the Poster Children—without having to sell a single additional record.* It'll be something modest. The new label doesn't mind, so long as it's recoupable out of royalties.

Well, they get the final contract, and it's not quite what they expected. They figure it's better to be safe than sorry and they turn it over to a lawyer—one who says he's experienced in entertainment law—and he hammers out a few bugs. They're still not sure about it, but the lawyer says he's seen a lot of contracts, and theirs is pretty good. They'll be getting a great royalty: 13% (less a 10% packaging deduction). Wasn't it Buffalo Tom that were only getting 12% less 10? Whatever.

The old label only wants 50 grand, and no points. Hell, Sub Pop got 3 points when they let Nirvana go. They're signed for four years, with options on each year, for a total of over a million dollars! That's a lot of money in any man's English. The first year's advance alone is $250,000. Just think about it, a quarter-million, just for being in a rock band!

Their manager thinks it's a great deal, especially the large advance. Besides, he knows a publishing company that will take the band on if they get signed, and even give them an advance of twenty grand, so they'll be making that money too. The manager says publishing is pretty mysterious, and nobody really knows where all the money comes from, but the lawyer can look that contract over too. Hell, it's free money.

Their booking agent is excited about the band signing to a major. He says they can maybe average $1,000 or $2,000 a night from now on. That's enough to justify a five-week tour, and with tour

---

* The "Babes" are Babes In Toyland, a Minneapolis band who had begun on Twin Tone records before signing with Warner Brothers.

support, they can use a proper crew, buy some good equipment and even get a tour bus! Buses are pretty expensive, but if you figure in the price of a hotel room for everybody in the band and crew, they're actually about the same cost. Some bands (like Therapy? and Sloan and Stereolab) use buses on their tours even when they're getting paid only a couple hundred bucks a night, and this tour should earn at least a grand or two every night. It'll be worth it. The band will be more comfortable and will play better.

The agent says a band on a major label can get a merchandising company to pay them an advance on t-shirt sales! Ridiculous! There's a gold mine here! The lawyer should look over the merchandising contract, just to be safe.

They get drunk at the signing party. Polaroids are taken and everybody looks thrilled. The label picked them up in a limo.

They decided to go with the producer who used to be in Letterman's band. He had these technicians come in and tune the drums for them and tweak their amps and guitars. He had a guy bring in a slew of expensive old "vintage" microphones. Boy, were they "warm." He even had a guy come in and check the phase of all the equipment in the control room! Boy, was he professional. He used a bunch of equipment on them and by the end of it, they all agreed that it sounded very "punchy," yet "warm."

All that hard work paid off. With the help of a video, the album went like hotcakes! They sold a quarter million copies!

Here is the math that will explain just how fucked they are:

These figures are representative of amounts that appear in record contracts daily. There's no need to skew the figures to make the scenario look bad, since real-life examples more than abound. Income is underlined, expenses are not.

Advance: <u>$250,000</u>
Manager's cut: $37,500
Legal fees: $10,000

Recording budget: $150,000
   Producer's advance: $50,000
   Studio fee: $52,500
   Drum, amp, mic and phase "doctors": $3,000
   Recording tape: $8,000
   Equipment rental: $5,000
   Cartage and transportation: $5,000
   Lodgings while in studio: $10,000
   Catering: $3,000
   Mastering: $10,000
   Tape copies, reference CDs, shipping tapes, misc. expenses: $2,000

Video budget: $30,000
   Cameras: $8,000
   Crew: $5,000
   Processing and transfers: $3,000
   Offline: $2,000
   Online editing: $3,000
   Catering: $1,000
   Stage and construction: $3,000

Copies, couriers, transportation: $2,000
Director's fee: $3,000

Album artwork: $5,000
Promotional photo shoot and duplication: $2,000

Band fund: $15,000
    New fancy professional drum kit: $5,000
    New fancy professional guitars (2): $3,000
    New fancy professional guitar amp rigs (2): $4,000
    New fancy potato-shaped bass guitar: $1,000
    New fancy rack of lights bass amp: $1,000
    Rehearsal space rental: $500
    Big blowout party for their friends: $500

Tour expense (5 weeks): $50,875
    Bus: $25,000
    Crew (3): $7,500
    Food and per diems: $7,875
    Fuel: $3,000
    Consumable supplies: $3,500
    Wardrobe: $1,000
    Promotion: $3,000

Tour gross income: $50,000
    Agent's cut: $7,500
    Manager's cut: $7,500

Merchandising advance: $20,000
    Manager's cut: $3,000
    Lawyer's fee: $1,000

Publishing advance: $20,000
    Manager's cut: $3,000
    Lawyer's fee: $1,000

Record sales: 250,000 × $12 = $3,000,000 gross retail revenue
Royalty (13% of 90% of retail): $351,000
    Less advance: $250,000
    Producer's points: (3% less $50,000 advance) $40,000
    Promotional budget: $25,000
    Recoupable buyout from previous label: $50,000
Net royalty: (−$14,000)

Record company income:
Record wholesale price $6.50 × 250,000 = $1,625,000 gross income
Artist royalties: $351,000

Deficit from royalties: $14,000
Manufacturing, packaging and distribution @ $2.20 per record: $550,000
Gross profit: $710,000

The Balance Sheet

This is how much each player got paid at the end of the game.

Record company: $710,000
Producer: $90,000
Manager: $51,000
Studio: $52,500
Previous label: $50,000
Agent: $7,500
Lawyer: $12,000
Band member net income each: $4,031.25

The band is now 1/4 of the way through its contract, has made the music industry more than 3 million dollars richer, but is in the hole $14,000 on royalties. The band members have each earned about 1/3 as much as they would working at a 7-Eleven, but they got to ride in a tour bus for a month.

The next album will be about the same, except that the record company will insist they spend more time and money on it. Since the previous one never "recouped," the band will have no leverage, and will oblige.

The next tour will be about the same, except the merchandising advance will have already been paid, and the band, strangely enough, won't have earned any royalties from their t-shirts yet. Maybe the t-shirt guys have figured out how to count money like record company guys.

Some of your friends are probably already this fucked.

51

"Feminism Amplified"

KIM FRANCE

The role of "women in rock" has long been a topic of serious contention for feminist critics. Writing in 1970, Patricia Kennealy-Morrison lamented the limited "male-specified" stereotypes assigned to female musicians. Folk singers and singer-songwriters aside, she argued that women were expected either to be a distant and brittle "ice princess" along the lines of Grace Slick or assume the passionate, sexy "down-home ball" stance of a Janis Joplin.[*] In the years that followed, punk, new wave, and indie introduced spaces where women could expand and move beyond these roles. But it was specifically the rise of 1990s alternative rock that finally pushed images of aggressive, confrontational female musicians fully into the mainstream. In 1993 Liz Phair's *Exile in Guyville* became the first album in almost two decades by a female artist to top the *Village Voice*'s prestigious "Pazz & Jop" poll, a feat which was duplicated in 1994 by Hole, and in 1995 by PJ Harvey. By the mid-90s, the notion of a strong, independent female rock musician no longer seemed an anomaly. Rock critic Kim France's 1996 article surveys the situation at that time, examining from a feminist perspective the conflicting opinions surrounding the liberating rise of these female performers. Her discussion begins with Alanis Morissette's *Jagged Little Pill*, which along with Shania Twain's *Come On Over* and Whitney Houston's soundtrack to *The Bodyguard* would eventually rank as one of the three best-selling albums of the decade—all by women. Near the article's end, however, France wonders if women have made any real progress. Indeed to what extent *have* feminist attitudes gained a hold or transformed rock since the 1990s?[†]

If the true test of social change is whether it's reflected in the marketplace, then this year's Grammy Awards were pretty compelling proof that feminism—at least a certain kind of feminism—is not dead at all. There was Mariah Carey—the type of standard-issue cream puff most commonly rewarded at this type of event—looking increasingly miffed as 21-year-old Alanis Morissette bounded onstage to receive five awards. Morissette's debut album, *Jagged Little Pill,* has spent almost a year on the *Billboard* charts. Her breakout single, "You Oughta Know," is a growly diatribe notable largely for stalkerlike lyrics that detail how she will make an ex-boyfriend pay for his betrayal. She is a woman who clearly has some issues with men, and she is beloved across the land.

Morissette's got little credibility with critics, who point out that she got her start as a fluffy, Debbie Gibson-style singer in her native Canada; that *Jagged Little Pill* was produced by cheesemeister Glen Ballard (whose résumé also includes such ultracommercial acts as Paula Abdul and Wilson

---

[*] Patricia Kennealy-Morrison, "Rock Around the Cock," in Evelyn McDonnell and Ann Powers, eds., *Rock She Wrote: Women Write about Rock, Pop, and Rap* (New York: Delta, 1995), 357–63.
[†] *Source:* Kim France, "Feminism Amplified," *New York*, June 3, 1996, pp. 34–41.

Phillips); that she represents little more than a corporate expropriation of the kind of female-rage music that had been all but ignored by the music industry and the public for years. Whatever her musical pedigree, Morissette has inarguably marked the arrival to the mass-market of an entirely new female-rocker persona. A woman moving so far beyond delicate, weepy declarations of loss and longing to express explicit rage in the context of a sexual relationship does not, traditionally, a Top 40 single make. Susan Faludi has often pointed out that while our culture admires the angry young man, who is perceived as heroic and sexy, it can't find anything but scorn for the angry young woman, who is seen as emasculating and bitter. That is, unless she is the kind of angry woman who, à la Camille Paglia, reserves her contempt for other women. Says Andrea Juno, editor of the forthcoming anthology *Angry Women in Rock*: "In the back of women's heads, they were gonna be delibidinized: You're unsexy, you won't be loved, and you won't get screwed."

But with the unrepentantly unscrewed Morissette of "You Oughta Know," a whole new palette of female emotions hitherto confined to college and alternative audiences has become acceptable— even admirable—to the lowest-common-denominator record buyers whose tastes are reflected by the Grammys and the *Billboard* charts. The Morissette persona harks back to *Fatal Attraction*, says Nina Gordon of the female-fronted band Veruca Salt, but with a difference: "Nobody identified with the Glenn Close character—she was clearly the villain—whereas people are like, 'You go girl!' to Alanis."

This does not mean that women everywhere can dance a happy jig to the end of the anti-feminist backlash. "But I think it probably reflects some growth in the consciousness of the audience, which translates into sales," says Mercury Records president and CEO Danny Goldberg, whose own label has done brisk business this year with the bluesy folk-rocker Joan Osborne. "There's no question that record companies, like any other business, are driven by business." Shirley Manson, lead singer of the band Garbage, puts it a bit more bluntly. "Alanis," she says, "has wiped the floor with the music industry, and I think that's phenomenally exciting. Because I know now that there's hundreds of A&R men running around trying to find the next Alanis."

There have been certain moments in the past few decades when rebellion has been expressed most acutely through popular music, when artists have provided more complicated, pointed answers to what's going on in the culture than self-styled thinkers. You don't "read" pop music the way you read *The Beauty Myth*, of course, but Liz Phair—by design and by example—happens to be a much more interesting feminist thinker than, say, Rebecca Walker. So it makes a lot of sense that the generation that came of age in the shadow of feminism—that both reaped its rewards and paid for its shortcomings—is using rock as a vehicle to make some powerful and nuanced statements about gender.

I was born in 1964, which is long enough ago for me to have formed a vague firsthand impression of suburban, middle-class seventies feminism. I remember consciousness-raising groups, and the few daring wives in the neighborhood who insisted on being called *Ms.* I remember a book that my mother's friend had given her husband as a joke: The title was *What I Understand About Women*, and all the pages were blank. What *I* didn't understand about women—who as far as I could tell spent their days playing tennis and carpooling—was what they needed liberation from, except possibly boredom.

I was way too young to get it, of course, and by the time I got to my lefty college, I was reading the Robin Morgan anthology *Sisterhood Is Powerful* and going to Take Back the Night marches. But after graduation, I dropped any pretense of being part of a movement. I went to a Women's Action Committee meeting once but was bored and annoyed by the main order of business, which was agreeing on the design of the T-shirt that the group would wear to the big pro-choice march on Washington. Outside of the collegiate petri dish, Big-F Feminism was revealed to be a pallid little affair, like American communism in the forties, that had little direct relevance to life as it is actually lived.

I didn't realize it at the time, but a lot of what I—and other young lapsed feminists—thought and felt was reflected in the complexity and contradictions of pop music. And after a while I understood that it didn't matter that my generation had no Gloria Steinems, Germaine Greers, or even Nancy Fridays or Erica Jongs. Because we have the Breeders, PJ Harvey, Liz Phair, Morissette, Courtney Love, Veruca Salt, Joan Osborne, Elastica, Tori Amos, and Tracy Bonham.

If these women constitute a movement, it's a helter-skelter one. The Breeders are pool-playing, beer-drinking tough chicks, and they make music that rocks in a hard and murky way and top it off with pretty harmonies. Courtney Love is all about anger, excess, obsession, confession, and great melodies. Polly Jean Harvey is restrained, theatrical, a diva. All of them are dealing with issues that feminism has traditionally claimed but without trafficking in constricting, sexless Women's Studies 101 dogma (and anyone who's ever puzzled over why the talent booked at pro-choice rallies is so consistently lame can attest to the necessity for that). Eschewing the usual angry platitudes, they give full symphonic vent to the particular pleasures and terrors of being female. This is very good news indeed to those of us who love Liz Phair's frisky, do-me lyrics and *still* think date-rape apologist Katie Roiphe is full of it.

"The future of rock belongs to women," Kurt Cobain predicted in 1994, and it is partly due to him that this is turning out to be true. He not only redefined the genre but also provided an updated guy-in-rock prototype. First of all, he wasn't a goon: He was inward, vulnerable—he sometimes wore dresses!—and he didn't seem to be in it for the money or the fame. And instead of dating models, Cobain married Courtney, showing himself to be the kind of man whose idea of masculinity involved loving a strong, opinionated woman, and carrying their baby in a Snugli.

"People like Kurt Cobain, Eddie Vedder, Michael Stipe, and Billy Corgan are very, very different as symbols of maleness for adolescents than Axl Rose or Steven Tyler and some of the other more muscle-bound, macho figures that immediately preceded them," says Danny Goldberg, who was a close friend of Cobain's. "And I think that created a sort of consciousness on the part of the audience. Kurt was very outspoken about the need for women to be respected, and he was passionate in his belief in Courtney. I think what happened in male rock and roll five years earlier broke up the macho hegemony over the rock part of the culture and gave the oxygen for some of the women to find an audience."

Nirvana also fired the final shot at that lumbering beast known as classic rock. No longer were radio listeners exclusively showered with music by way-past-their-prime peacocks like the Rolling Stones and Rod Stewart: Stations that shifted to modern-rock playlists were freed up to play bands like the Breeders or Hole—along with the now inevitable Soundgarden and Stone Temple Pilots—without worrying quite so much that listeners would switch stations once they heard female vocals. "Radio had always been a little afraid of that before," says Joan Osborne. "You know, they would play one Melissa Etheridge song in a four-hour slot and think that that was all they could do. Audiences I don't think ever really cared that much about those kind of distinctions. They just want something good. But it took a while for the programmers and people like that to catch up to that idea."

Furthermore, girls who loved music but had been too intimidated to pick up instruments—having somehow internalized the information that one had to possess some special boy gene in order to get behind a drum set—were inspired by Nirvana's punk-rock do-it-yourself ethos. "People who couldn't play anyway—boys—were doing it, and once that opened up, there was no reason not to be a girl and do it," says Phair, whose career started after a tape of songs she'd recorded in her bedroom scored her a record deal. The band Veruca Salt, which is fronted by Gordon and Louise

Post, inspired a major-label bidding war in 1994 when the single "Seether"—from a cheaply produced album on a tiny Chicago label—started getting radio play and heavy MTV rotation. They eventually signed with Geffen, which re-released the album and sold 700,000 copies. "It is much less expensive to make a record than do anything else in the media, other than fanzines, but that doesn't have the potential to plug into the mainstream culture the way a record can," says Goldberg. "It's not a moral thing, it's not an aesthetic thing, it's just an economic reality that that doorway exists in music. The nature of the medium is less top-down, it's more decentralized, it's more a vehicle for personal visions, and one of these visions has been women."

> When we first started getting written about, people kept saying we were 'angry post-feminists,' and we were like, 'Hmm … I guess, whatever.' It was like, 'Oh, thank you for reducing me to a little pat phrase that really means nothing to me.'
>
> —**Nina Gordon of Veruca Salt**

A few years ago, I met some rock-critic friends for dinner before going to see a show at Irving Plaza. It was around the time PJ Harvey—who is sort of the Maria Callas of rock—released her first record, and we were talking about a profile in which she'd said she didn't consider herself a feminist. As it happened, I had interviewed Miss America just that afternoon for a piece I was writing about how the pageant was trying to update its image, and we agreed that it is a strange world we live in, where Miss America will say she's a feminist and PJ Harvey won't.

Actually, though, it's not so ironic. Increasingly, feminism itself has become a meaningless term: You're now a victim feminist, a do-me feminist, a womanist. Then there are people like Miss America and swimsuit models who fashion themselves as feminists as a defense mechanism because the alternative would be too hard to countenance. Who can blame PJ Harvey for not wanting to sign herself up for that team?

Rock succeeds where textbook feminism has stalled for a variety of reasons. A huge question that sixties feminism failed to answer had to do with sex: Could a healthy heterosexual libido be reconciled with good movement politics? Were we tools of the patriarchy just because we enjoyed renting the occasional porno movie with our boyfriends? Or if we read *Vogue* and profoundly believed in the magic of Maybelline? The Big Thinkers famously recused themselves from such mundanities.

In the meantime, rock started providing ad hoc, provisional answers. The medium permitted contradiction; you could change your mind without having to justify it. And the more you broke the rules, the more likely you'd be rewarded. New images of strength and sexuality emerged out of the pop-cultural ooze. There was leather-clad, eyelinered Chrissie Hynde of the Pretenders, who beginning in the eighties projected a tough, almost-but-not-quite-bulletproof cool. "The thing I found so fascinating about Chrissie Hynde when I was growing up was that I found her incredibly sexy but she also embodied what I found attractive about men," says Shirley Manson of Garbage. "She wasn't wearing pretty skirts and being a victim and talking about love. She was standing at that microphone with her legs spread, she was playing her guitar, and she was the coolest sight I'd ever seen in my life. It was the first time I really connected with a woman like that."

Exene Cervenka of the Los Angeles band X made it cool to be a punk chick; Cyndi Lauper made it okay to be a goofy party girl. And Madonna made it okay to be entirely about sex and still be in control. Though the brazen, brassiere-by-Gaultier look she presented ten years ago looks quaint by today's standards, and her appeal never had much to do with her musicianship or songwriting abilities, it is amazing how many young rock women today proudly cite her as a role model.

The change Madonna wrought has been most visible on MTV. For the network's first decade, the women shown in videos tended to be either big-hair pop goddesses like Taylor Dayne, or heavy-metal video extras, or Apollonia humping Prince's thigh, or the zombie-ish Robert Palmer girls. "There are these sort of low moments—and there are plenty of them, believe me—at MTV," says Judy McGrath, the network's president and one of the handful of genuinely powerful women in an industry that is still largely run by men. She recalls a 1988 staff meeting during which a video for the song "Wild Thing"—in which Sam Kinison mud-wrestled a bikini-clad Jessica Hahn—was screened. "The level of despair on the faces of the women was beyond description," she says. "We haven't gotten a video in the door in years that made you feel that way.

"There's a certain exhilaration now, even from the guys here, about all these women," McGrath continues. "There's a guy in the music-programming department who is like, you know, he's Mr. Rock. And he always says, 'This rocks!' And if you go into his office, he has a nine-foot picture of PJ Harvey plastered to his wall. I've seen a change in that regard. It isn't like the Steven Tyler Hall of Fame in here anymore."

McGrath believes that the fact that so many of these artists are giving voice to so many different perspectives on the female experience—and not doing it under the banner of revolution—is precisely why fans are so attracted to it. "I think this is a watershed moment," she says. "When I was growing up, I knew the difference between Betty Friedan and Gloria Steinem and so on, and you had to line up in one of those camps or you weren't, you know, in the game. And now I think there are so many voices."

If a woman is acting dolled up and sexy in a video these days, chances are it's her own. But even when she's not dolled up and sexy, it's likely that she will be singing about sex in a way women have never sung about sex before. In one song, Elastica's Justine Frischmann, sounding very male, bemoans the guy who can't get it up when she's in the mood. Shirley Manson of Garbage vamped around the stage last month at Roseland with a pink feather puff attached to the mike stand at precisely crotch level. Tori Amos is famous for straddling the piano bench suggestively while she plays.

Not everyone is hailing this as tremendous social progress. "There was some article in one of the British magazines about one of our shows saying that we set feminism back ten years, because Louise [Post] applied lipstick onstage," says Veruca Salt's Gordon. "And I remember thinking, 'Who is this woman?'—it was a woman who wrote the article—'Who is this woman who thinks it's important to point that out?'"

She was probably a woman very much like Exene Cervenka, who doesn't understand why PJ Harvey performs in evening gowns, or why Liz Phair poses for pictures wearing nothing but a slip dress. "I kind of call it 'Rod Stewart Feminism,'" she says. "It's kind of the same mentality, which is if it's okay for guys to do it, it's okay for girls to do it. Tori Amos straddling a piano bench—is that empowering women or is that *Penthouse*-ing women? I don't know."

It's debatable whether men see this sexuality as edifying rather than merely hot. Writing about Maureen Dowd in *The New Yorker* a few weeks ago, James Wolcott bemoaned "one of the odd aftereffects of feminism . . . that it seems to have softened and juvenilized so much of women's journalistic swagger." He went on to cite other areas where he perceived the phenomenon to be occurring: "In pop music, a kooky singer-songwriter chick seems to surface every six months to be photographed barefoot for *Spin*." Wolcott, presumably, would prefer they pose in sackcloth and ashes or, alternatively, in nothing at all. Would that clear up the confusion?

Of course, women have been all over *Spin* recently, generally shod. Only one of the *Spin* cover girls, Tori Amos, could be considered kooky—she named her most recent album after the goddess of creation and destruction and has said she was a Viking in another life. But she has also never shied away from hard topics, writing smart, cant-free songs that deal with rape and the church's oppression of women. "Tori's no one to be messed or trifled with," says Phair, whose music could not possibly be more different from hers. "She's a goddess."

Amos is a minister's daughter; she's got a song, "Icicle," about being upstairs in her bedroom masturbating while the rest of the family is in the living room praying. The struggle to be at home with her sexuality has been too hard-won for her to care what anyone thinks about it. "Somebody made this really funny comment about me that I just giggled over: 'You can't fight the patriarchy in a tube top,'" she says. "So I went, 'Okay, so why don't I wait for that writer to fax me on what I should wear to fight the patriarchy?' To me, when you cut yourself off—mentally, emotionally, or physically—then you've just been dominated by somebody else's thought."

Joan Osborne, 33, is one of the few female rockers who go out of their way to call themselves feminists. She aligns herself with mainstream feminist causes like NARAL, and performed on *Saturday Night Live* in a CHOICE T-shirt. She's the most middle-of-the-road, VH-1–friendly artist of the group, and the sexuality she projects onstage and in videos is subdued. "Feminism as I always understood it—and I was somebody who read a lot of Germaine Greer and stuff like that—part of the manifesto was to find a way for women to reclaim their own sexuality, to not only be the object of male desire but discover what their own desire was about, and claim that for themselves," she says. "And of course, an ingredient of rock has always been this sexual display, and women have been more and more finding out a way that they can do that. Instead of just being the chick in the spandex with the teased-up hair that all the guys want to screw, it's more like, 'Yeah, this is how I'm going to project my sexuality, and these are my desires.'"

It's amazing how threatening that can still be to men. Liz Phair's first album was a godsend to female fans because it communicated so explicitly the ambivalent knot of feelings that coexist with sexual desire. That this clean-scrubbed college graduate from Winnetka could think as dirty as any man floored a lot of people. "I heard a lot of men saying that they were listening to my album because someone told them they should, then one day they suddenly heard the words and it flipped them out," says Phair. "They all expressed this powerful feeling of being both fired at and caught, like, for being what they are. And the women were like, 'Well, I heard the words from the beginning, and they made perfect sense to me.'" She says she was shocked that men were shocked. "For me what it highlighted was how very rarely they had felt that before. Because there wasn't anything that damning. And it just made me realize that women hadn't nailed them before."

Part of Liz Phair's appeal is how heady her lyrics are. She and many of the other women in rock right now are quite self-evidently overqualified for the job intellectually—though alternative rock these days seems increasingly to be performed by and for slumming grad students—and their songs have a truth-telling complexity and confidence that was hardly available on vinyl twenty years ago. Joni Mitchell was wonderful, but she has comparatively little to say to the proverbial just-dumped 16-year-old that Liz Phair cannot say better. Today's teenage girls simply have it over their elders in the tell-it-sister department. "I didn't have high self-esteem when I was a teenager," Morissette told the *New York Times*. "I used to think I was alone in that. Oh, man, I wish I had me to listen to when I was 14."

One of the best things about going to see PJ Harvey or Hole or Elastica or Veruca Salt is witnessing the hordes of teenage girls who force their way into the mosh pit. The fact that they're not climbing on their boyfriend's shoulders and whipping off their halter tops—but rocking out to a woman wailing on her guitar—changes everything. "It's like having someone in a movie that you can follow," says Phair. "It's like having a character you can live through. And for so long, they didn't. You go to a rock show because you want the guy to stare at you. You want to be noticed and singled out as an object. And this time, they are watching someone and pretending they are *her*. And that's a very good experience, I think, for the self-esteem of the young American girl."

Those looking for role models, however, will be as disappointed as basketball fans who wish Dennis Rodman would stop showing his butt to the kids. But since when have pop musicians had to be role models? (At precisely the same moment as women and rap stars started selling records, it would appear.) The personal has always made for better rock music than the straightforwardly political has, and that's a lesson these artists have taken to heart. "I don't want to be anyone's revolutionary," says Liz Phair. "I don't want to lead a movement. I mean, it turns me off so much. I never saw music as a way—and a lot of people do, especially riot grrrls—to make change happen. I never, ever saw it that way. I still don't. Anyone with any kind of sensitivity beyond their general age group knows you can't tidy life up like that."

No one is less tidy than Courtney Love. Experiencing Love, onstage or on CD, in the gossip pages or on the Internet (where, most recently, she has bitterly railed against Morissette), one can't help but notice that the line between her art and her life is hopelessly blurred. The raw, exposed manner in which she makes her music and conducts her affairs has made her the most loved/loathed figure in rock today. "I'm a huge admirer of Courtney Love," says Garbage's Manson. "She's vulnerable and I warm to that. She's incredibly intelligent and incredibly articulate and she's not afraid to open her mouth up and attack anybody and anything. She's neither black nor white and that's why, I think, she irritates a lot of people, but that's what I find endearing about her."

Cervenka, predictably, is not as impressed. "People who are pathologically insane don't interest me," she says. "Courtney has nothing to do with reality as far as I'm concerned. You've got to talk about people who are sober, who can raise their children, and who are not involved in all kinds of scandalous tabloid-style gimmicks in order to become famous."

Still, as wild as she's been, Courtney certainly hasn't done anything that would have raised eyebrows backstage at a Led Zeppelin show, and *those* guys just got inducted into the Rock and Roll Hall of Fame. Plus, she's a whole lot more interesting than Robert Plant. Love is a walking Rorschach test. Either a liberating angel or the Yoko Ono of alternative rock, she has quite improbably become an embodiment of all that is interesting, exciting, and depressing about being a young woman now. (Teenage boys in online chat groups, grossed out by her schizo aggressiveness and anti-pinup mien, often suggest that she has no right to be alive.)

Love is obviously well aware of her role. She has said that she was moved to name her band Hole by a line from Euripides' *Medea*: "There's a hole that pierces right through me." She once told a writer from *Spin* the band's name also refers to something her mother, a hippie feminist of the *Our Bodies, Ourselves* era, used to say: "You can't walk around with a big hole inside yourself."

Things are never that simple in Love-land. The song "Asking For It" was inspired, she told an interviewer, by the experience of stage-diving into the crowd at a show: "Suddenly, it was like my dress was being torn off me, my underwear was being torn off me, people were putting their fingers inside of me and grabbing my breasts really hard." The worst thing, she went on, was seeing a photograph of herself later "and I had a big smile on my face like I was pretending it wasn't happening. I can't compare it to rape because it isn't the same. But in a way it was. I was raped by an audience—figuratively, literally, and yet, was I asking for it?" The song is a more nuanced treatment than any ten essays about date rape of the way women can feel torn between the desire to be driven by their sexuality and the horror that the desire might ultimately degrade or even destroy them.

Love has also taken prototypically male gestures, transformed them into female ones, and made them powerful again and new. When a male artist, for instance, props his leg up on a monitor and launches into a guitar solo these days, he looks stupid—like he's playing in a Foghat cover band at some Bleecker Street tourist club. But when Love, wearing torn stockings, props a stiletto-heeled leg up on a monitor, the entire gesture changes—it is undeniably theatrical and brazen, but it's certainly interesting.

I share this theory of mine with Phair, who wonders whether I'm not getting a little carried away. "There is something that is rock itself, and it is an attitude that is genderless, and it is what is appealing about rock," she says. When Courtney does that thing with the monitor, she continues, "that's her just being infected with this thing called Rock. But probably I'm wrong, and she actually watched a million guys do that, sticking your foot up there, and she is saying, 'Fuck you, I'm the front guy; deal with my frontalness.'"

Phair pauses, then sighs. "I'm wondering, would Courtney Love really think about doing that gesture, or is it just like a way to really, you know, crunch into her guitar? … I'll bet she's just like, 'Why shouldn't I be right up at the edge of the stage?' She's just free in her mind. It's not so much that she has something. It's that she doesn't have something, which is the fear that traditionally keeps women in their place."

It's tempting, sometimes, to think that women are being allowed this moment only because we have seen every conceivable rock pose many times over from men, and the one thing that really feels fresh right now is a chick jabbing her stiletto heel into a monitor. And for all of their bravado, none of the artists I spoke to felt like a fundamental transformation had occurred; they thought the odds were about even that next year the charts will be ruled by guys again. "The industry still views bands fronted by women as novelties," says Nina Gordon. "It seems like to me that right now women are entitled to just one shining moment."

But Cervenka, the progressive-rock darling of 1982, was by far the most cold-eyed. "There's always some woman who is the new angry young woman," she said. "It was me, and it was someone else, and it was someone else. But as far as selling millions and millions of records, to me that's no validation whatsoever. It means nothing. If it means anything to me, it means it's *not* okay to be an angry young woman—it's cute to be an angry young woman; it's trendy to be an angry young woman." But is Love-ism really just the flavor of the month?

"I want to be the girl with the most cake," she sings on "Doll Parts." Women love that line; it's all about authorizing desire, and about winning, which remain as tricky as ever for a woman. And when I start thinking that *Ms.* magazine-era feminism has nothing to do with my life, I think about another person who wanted to be the girl with the most cake—Sylvia Plath's Esther, in *The Bell Jar.* There's that passage where she sees all of her options—wife and mother, famous writer, magazine editor—as figs on a tree. But she can choose only one, and she can't make up her mind, and the figs all wither and die.

Women, of course, have it better than they did when Plath wrote that book in 1963, but how much has really changed? You could argue that our culture still isn't rewarding women who try to stake out new territory. But Courtney Love is an object lesson in the punishments and rewards that come to a woman who tries. "Courtney's got the kind of ambition most people would associate with a male rock star," says Justine Frischmann. "One thing you have to admire her for is that she refuses—just refuses—to be overlooked in any way."

52

"Rock Aesthetics and Musics of the World"

Motti Regev

From its very beginnings rock 'n' roll has been perceived as a distinctly American (and soon there-after, Anglo-American) cultural product. At the same time, rock has circulated for decades around the world, where its presence has been felt as an influence on local music-making practices. While one could certainly see this spread of rock as yet another example of American cultural imperial-ism, Motti Regev argues against such a reading.* Regev, a sociologist at the Open University of Israel, instead emphasizes the way in which an international "rock aesthetic" has emerged, granting its participants a certain symbolic freedom. Drawing on the sociological studies of Pierre Bourdieu and Scott Lash, Regev suggests that those who take part in rock music making are figuratively "thrown" into two fields. From a spatial standpoint, they are members of a "local field," wherein they grasp some relationship to a larger national identity. At the same time, they are operating within the general "field of popular music," wherein rock has been accorded a privileged status of authen-ticity and innovation. "Thrown" into these fields, local musicians find a certain agency through rock's authenticity, one that allows them to explore the boundaries of national identity. In the fol-lowing excerpt from Regev's article, he outlines three different ways in which the "rock aesthetic" is articulated in the local field: Anglo-American pop/rock as such, "imitation," and hybridity.†

The uses and appropriations of rock by musicians and audiences around the world are far from homogeneous. The various styles could be easily described as completely different in pure musical terms. The point in discussing them together is, first, the relative sameness of meaning which is attributed to them, in the practices of listening or discursively and, second, the fact that they can all be shown to be influenced by and incorporate elements of the rock aesthetic.

The sameness of meaning is basically one: rock music is used to declare a 'new'—modern, con-temporary, young, often critical-oppositional—sense of local identity, as opposed to older, tra-ditional, conservative forms of that identity. The music patterns, however, differ in the extent to which rock music is used as-it-is, or subjected to appropriations, articulations and selective prac-tices that produce hybridity. Each one of these patterns represents a slightly different strategy for legitimizing rock within the local culture. Accordingly, I have divided these patterns into three

---

* On this debate, see Dave Laing, "The Music Industry and 'Cultural Imperialism' Thesis," *Media, Culture and Society* 8 (1986): 331–41.

† *Source:* Motti Regev, "Rock Aesthetics and Musics of the World," *Theory, Culture and Society*, 14, no. 3 (1997), pp. 131–36.

main categories: Anglo-American pop/rock as such; 'imitation' of foreign styles; and hybrids. Each is discussed below, with some examples. They are presented here as analytic 'ideal types'—in practice, they might be hard to distinguish.

ANGLO-AMERICAN POP/ROCK AS SUCH

Using Anglo-American rock itself as a cultural resource for constructing local identity is typically based on a logic which demands 'freedom of taste'. The interest in rock, and the desire to have (imported) records available or to have local concerts by Anglo-American rock stars—when denied—are formulated in terms of 'opening' the local culture to a modern, even liberating cultural form. This happens not only in the most obvious places and times like East Europe in the 1960s, but later on in industrial societies as well. Thus in Bulgaria, during the 1960s, British rock 'was seen not only as good music but also as a sort of symbol of freedom, of a liberated individuality and independent stand' (Levy, 1992: 211). Even in Italy, as late as 1982, concerts by the Rolling Stones had:

> provoked a bitter row between the leading political parties … accusing rock of being the transmitter of disorder, corruption, violence and drugs … [but the audience in these concerts responded with] … wonderful scenes in which joints and tricolors were juxtaposed for the first time ever, without incident and with a perfect sense of harmony. 'Viva l'Italia, viva rock'n'roll!'—a combination of slogans which was much more than the masses … could ever have expected. (Fiori, 1984: 261–2)

These are two examples to which others could easily be added. The point is that within conservative contexts or totalitarian regimes, attempts to prevent or just control the dissemination of Anglo-American rock, invoke the use of this music as a means to construct a local sense of autonomous identity.

Obviously, Anglo-American rock does not become, in the process, 'local authentic' music. It remains 'foreign' music. But it does become part and parcel of a generation's collective memory, of its different local/national sense of identity as opposed to that of an older generation (see Lou Reed's interview with Václav Havel, about the role of 1960s rock in general and that of the Velvet Underground in particular in Czech politics; Reed, 1991: 145–62). And in that regard, Anglo-American pop/rock does become an integral part of local/national cultures around the world, at least for some sectors within them.

'IMITATION'

The inverted commas indicate that although local, non-Anglo-American styles of punk, metal, rap, progressive or other sub-styles of rock can be understood as sheer imitations of the originals, they can also be interpreted as hybrids, be it only for their use of a language other than English. The main difference between this pattern of using rock music and listening to Anglo-American rock as such is the relative ease with which claims for legitimacy (within the local/national context) or interpretations of the music as 'locally authentic' can be made.

The turning point for the emergence of such claims is when local rock musicians move from 'covering', in English, hits by famous Anglo-American musicians, and from performing straight translations or other local-language versions of such songs, to producing original rock music. Indeed, beginning in the early 1960s, probably thousands of rock groups from Spain to Japan, from Scandinavia to South Africa and Latin America, have been performing rock hits. Starting with songs made famous by Elvis Presley, the Kinks or Otis Redding, later on some groups were performing music by Led Zeppelin or Pink Floyd. Gaining sufficient competence in the rock habitus, groups from non-English-speaking countries occasionally found success with an international hit in English (e.g., Spain's Los Bravos with 'Black is Black' in 1966, or Holland's Shocking Blue with 'Venus' in 1970).

But as much as these groups represent vivid local rock scenes, they do not supply the basis for legitimacy claims. Such claims emerge as rock groups start to produce original music, in a local language, even as they stick to Anglo-American rock sub-styles. One way of doing that is by appropriating styles associated mostly with African-Americans, for strengthening local ethnic or regional identity. Thus one strain of Italian hip hop has been used to distinguish Southern Italian identity, invoking in the process a supposed mythical affinity with Africa (whose northern shores are not too far away) and finding roots of rap in traditional folk music (Mitchell, 1995).

More typical is the attribution of 'artistic authenticity' to local versions of rock, and the emergence of a bohemian-oppositional 'counter-culture' which considers itself to be an avant-garde of the national or local conservative culture. This has been the case particularly under totalitarian regimes, where the local rock scene declared itself to be a site for the preservation of national artistic freedom. Producing original music, including lyrics in the local language, supports such claims and helps in making them into a cultural reality—despite the music itself being an 'imitation' of Anglo-American rock sub-styles.

Such is the case of Russian rock, which emerged during the Soviet regime in the 1970s and 1980s. Listening to historical recordings or even more recent records by leading Russian rock groups—Mashina Vremeni, Aqvarium, Alica, Kino, Aukzion and others—one gets to hear variations of hard rock or heavy metal. Indeed, as Kushman (1995: 53) points out, well into the 1980s 'Russian musicians continued to draw on those forms of rock music which were made available to them and to imitate and reproduce what they heard'. *Russification* of the music took place mostly through lyrics and singing, interpreting them as sung poetry. Regarding themselves as inheritors and carriers of a Russian tradition of poetry, Russian rock musicians perceive their art as a form of contemporary poetry. As Yuri, a prominent Russian rock musician who, according to Kushman (1995: 70) has been alternately referred to as 'a Russian Bruce Springsteen' and 'a second [Vladimir] Vysotsky' puts it:

> The main thing is that before … the poets like Bella Akhmadulina, Okudzhava, Voznesenskii read poems and drew huge audiences. Now poetry has sunk into rock-and-roll. Real poetry lives in rock-and-roll. In Russia that's for sure. Especially in the '80s, because the official youth poetry was not poetry at all. But the best, the finest poetry was in rock-and-roll music. That is, the best, the purest, most sincere of everything went into rock-and-roll in the '80s (quoted in Kushman, 1995: 105).

Another example is Argentinean rock. Its leading musicians—Charly García, Luis Alberto Spinetta, David Lebon (and their groups Sui Géneris, Almendra, Seru Girán), León Gieco, Fito Páez and others—since the mid-1970s have been sounding, more often than not, like Spanish versions of hard rock, progressive rock and singer/songwriters. During the 1976 to 1983 military dictatorship, the core of Argentinean rock music—as the *rock nacional* movement—became a focus of opposition to the regime. It:

> played an extremely important part in the socialization and re-socialization of broad sectors of Argentinean youth during the military period, restoring truthful communication regarding the real country.… The highly oppositional content of the songs, the frankly critical attitude of the audiences, and the gathering together in public places to express opposition to the military regime … [created] popular and communal channels of participation.… (Vila, 1987: 147–8).

Thus, although not sounding 'genuinely Argentinean' (except for the lyrics), *rock nacional* gained, in the eyes of its members, something which has been inscribed in its name: national legitimacy, Argentinean-ness. That this trait has been of primary importance to rock fans, can be learnt from this prominent Argentinean rock commentator, who insists that:

> The pioneers of [our] native rock did not step down here from a flying saucer, they emerged from the grain of the people, like the folklorists and the tango-ists before them. Our rock is already part of the Argentinean musical tradition, despite those who view it solely as 'foreign penetration'. The [acoustic] guitar and the bandoneon were also imported to these pampas and it occurs to nobody to consider them aliens (Grinberg, 1993: 18; my translation).

Indeed, later on, as Argentinean rock became the herald of a much larger phenomenon of *rock en español* in Latin America and Spain, defense of rock in general and in other national contexts grew broader (De Garay Sanchez, 1993).

Although in a better position to claim national legitimacy than Anglo-American rock as such, rock musicians and audiences practicing the 'imitation' pattern in various countries, are often forced to justify the 'local authentic' quality of their music. One way of doing this is by elaborating a specific genre of rock as a 'national' one—like the emphasis on local progressive rock in some European countries during the 1970s. The point I want to stress here is the spontaneous commitment to such justifications. As much as musicians and fans believe in the general artistic qualities of rock, they are also strongly committed to localizing rock, to produce its meaning as national music.

HYBRIDITY

Very different, in this regard, is the position of music scenes in which rock elements are selectively adapted and mixed with traditional-local styles to produce hybrids. Practitioners of such hybrid musics sometimes do not even have to claim their 'local authenticity'. It is inscribed in the essence of the sonic texture and affective impact of their music to begin with. These are typically the 'rock' substyles that garner the most enthusiastic response within the Western, Anglo-American rock establishment—probably because of their readily perceived 'exoticism', 'otherness' and 'authenticity'—and which are collectively labeled 'world music' (together with non-rock styles, see Mitchell, 1993).

Many of the contemporary 'world music' rock styles that found sympathetic audiences in Western countries are African—and they barely need introduction. Senegalese *mbalax*, South African *mbaqanga*, Nigerian *juju*, Ghanaian *highlife*, Zairean *soukous*, Zimbabwean *chimurenga* and *jit* are the most prominent. While some of these hybrids embody early influences of Western music, dating back to the 19th century (Collins and Richards, 1989), most of them took a turn into rock aesthetic during the 1970s—or indeed came into their own being in the wake of rock's presence in their countries. Musicians in these genres incorporate not only typical rock instrumentation (electric guitars, bass and organs, synthesizers, drumkits), but most often also rock sound texture like fuzz, distortion, shouting, etc. Mixing these with traditional instruments, vocal styles and 'ethnic' rhythms, they create musics that sound as much 'rock' as planted in the local culture.

Thus *soukous* (probably the most widespread style in Africa), after being consolidated by Franco and Tabu Ley as a relatively 'sweet' and polished electric mixture of rumba and Zairean elements, became much rockier during the 1970s with the group Zaiko Langa Langa:

> They were wild. It was like the Sex Pistols coming on to the scene. They twisted everything around ... Zaiko were uncompromising. They challenged the old established musical norms of Zaire, and the youth followed (Mwana Musa, Sierra-Leonean musician, quoted in Stapelton and May, 1990: 173).

The group 'blew a rude, rough-house blast of folk rhythms, hard snare drums, wild guitars and rough vocals' (Stapelton and May, 1990: 174). In a similar manner, the Zimbabwean group the Bhundu Boys followed Thomas Mapfumo's already rocky hybrid of traditional music (which he called *chimurenga*) with a rockier style called *jit.*

Another example of hybridity can be found in (former) Yugoslavia, and in particular in the music of the group Bijelo Dugme, led by Goran Bregovic. Blending Balkan touches of melody, female harmonies and poetic imagery with dramatic metallic-distorted electric guitars, and soaring vocals commenting on Yugoslav social reality, during the 1970s and 1980s Bijelo Dugme produced rock anthems that made them the most popular and acclaimed group of the country. Bregovic (born in Bosnia to a Serb mother and a Croat father), insisting on his general Yugoslav identity and taking Anglo-American rock as his artistic reference point, demonstrates clearly the dual character of 'ethnic rock':

> Our big advantage is that we are really Yugoslav. There is a Yugoslav character to our music. But by the same virtue, our music is a little bit too rude and too primitive for the outside world. So you can say we are a rock 'n' roll band, but we are popular in the way that a country and western band would be in the United States.... For me, the future of rock music, not just in Yugoslavia but in the world, is ethnic music. Some really fine rock records in the last few years are really close to ethnic music, like Paul Simon, like Peter Gabriel, like U2. They all draw upon ethnic elements. I am doing this too, and I have been doing this from the beginning. After all, there is no point just copying American rock 'n' roll (Goran Bregovic, in 1989, quoted in Ramet, 1994: 133–9).

One last example of hybridity is Algerian *(pop-)rai*. It emerged in the 1970s, when synthesizers, drum-machines and electric guitars, as well as rock rhythmic and melodic elements had been added to the traditional instruments and rhythms of *rai*. The leading musicians—Chaba Zahouania, Chaba Fadela, Cheb Sahraoui, Cheb Mami and Cheb Khaled (chabas and chebs are general appellations for youth)—became, with their sound and often erotic-hedonistic lyrics, national exponents for young people who 'challenged official puritanism and patriarchal authority ... [and] who were chafing at traditional social constraint' (Gross et al., 1994: 7).

Nevertheless, *rai* signifies the ethnic-national identity as well, as is evident from its use (together with Arab *rap*) by Franco-Maghrebis (Algerians, Moroccans, Tunisians) 'to carve a space for themselves in France ... [and] identify simultaneously with French and Arab cultures' (Gross et al., 1994: 25).

This last function exemplifies the use of rock hybrids among contemporary diaspora communities. There, the rock aesthetic becomes a tool for constructing an identity and claiming legitimacy in the 'host' culture as well. Thus, the emergence of *bhangra-rock* within the British-Asian community expresses claims for contemporary British as well as South-Asian identity (Banerji, 1988).

The list of local rock hybrids, as well as of 'imitations', which are used as tools to construct contemporary local identities, is far from exhausted—more could be added. And in a sense this is only part of the story of 'rock in the world'. The rest of it has to do with the fact that musicians and others within the Western, Anglo-American rock establishment, upon 'discovering' rock hybrids from various countries, import them and make them yet another 'scene' within rock culture. Perceived as another frontier of 'authenticity' (Garofalo, 1992) or artistic innovation, some of these styles are incorporated into the work of major musicians, and then distributed to additional parts of the world and influence them. Reggae, which emerged as a Jamaican hybrid of rock, and then influenced musicians all over the world, is the prime example. Another practice which should be noted in this regard is the mixing of sampled 'ethnic' musics with electronic, mostly dance-rhythms, which is done by Western musicians and then distributed to the whole world.

BIBLIOGRAPHY

Banerji, Sabita (1988) "Ghazals to Bhangra in Great Britain," *Popular Music* 7: 207–14.

Collins, John and Paul Richards (1989) "Popular Music in West Africa," pp. 12–46 in Simon Frith (ed.) *World Music, Politics and Social Change*. Manchester: Manchester University Press.

De Garay Sanchez, Adrián (1993) *El Rock También es Cultura*. Mexico: Universidad Iberoamericana.

Fiori, Umberto (1984) "Rock Music and Politics in Italy," *Popular Music* 4: 261–78.

Garofalo, Reebee (ed.) (1992) *Rockin' the Boat*. Boston, MA: South End Press.

Grinberg, Miguel (1993) *Como Vino la Mano*. Buenos Aires: Distal.

Gross, Joan, David McMurray and Ted Swedenburg (1994) "Arab Noise and Ramadan Nights; Rai, Rap, and Franco-Maghrebi Identity," *Diaspora* 3: 3–39.

Kushman, Thomas (1995) *Notes from the Underground: Rock Music Counterculture in Russia*. Albany: State University of New York Press.

Levy, Claire (1992) "The Influence of British Rock in Bulgaria," *Popular Music* 11: 209–12.

Mitchell, Tony (1993) "World Music and the Popular Music Industry," *Ethnomusicology* 37: 309–38.

———. (1995) "Question of Style: Notes on Italian Hip Hop," *Popular Music* 14: 333–48.

Ramet, Sabrina Petra (ed.) (1994) *Rocking the State: Rock and Politics in Eastern Europe and Russia*. Boulder, CO: Westview Press.

Reed, Lou (1991) *Between Thought and Expression*. New York: Hyperion.

Stapelton, Chris and Chris May (1990) *African Rock: The Pop Music of the Continent*. New York: Obelisk/Dutton.

Vila, Pablo (1987) "Rock Nacional and Dictatorship in Argentina," *Popular Music* 6: 129–48.

53

Fat Boy Slim Explains Electronic Dance Music

MICHAEL GELFAND

When British electronic dance music (EDM) groups like The Prodigy and Chemical Brothers began attracting attention in America throughout 1996 and 1997, the U.S. rock press was quick to herald the arrival of a new movement, the dubiously titled "electronica." For all the anticipation, however, many questioned whether a style like electronica, which deviated from many of rock's traditional trappings, could succeed with American rock audiences. As with disco, many of the criticisms revolved around the movement's seeming *lack* of rock authenticity: where rock strove for artistry (listening), electronica's goals were primarily functional (for dancing); where rock employed 'real' instruments, electronica relied on samplers; where rock was structured around stable verse/chorus forms and lyrical innovation, electronica's primarily instrumental songs emphasized flow and flexibility; and where the music press promoted rock musicians as larger-than-life personalities, electronica's DJs were relatively anonymous figures. Like many of the musicians involved with electronica, Norman Cook (born 1963) had a background in rock music, having played bass for the mid-1980s group The Housemartins before eventually adopting the Fatboy Slim moniker a decade later. Coming from this background, Cook understands the objections leveled against electronica, and in fact embraces the music's supposed disposable nature. At the same time, Cook is also aware that much like writing rock songs, composing with samplers involves specific, intuitive aesthetic decisions. Cook offers *Musician* magazine's Michael Gelfand a closer look into this process, as he gives him a sneak preview of "Rockafeller Skank," a song that would become one of the best known EDM singles of the late 1990s.*

You've got to admire the foolhardy tenacity of anyone who appears at the front door of their house dressed in nothing but a bathrobe and slippers in the dead of winter—particularly in the cold and damp seaside town of Brighton, England—but that's Norman Cook's way. Cook (a.k.a. Fat Boy Slim) is all the rage in the U.K.'s exploding breakbeat dance music scene, but the demand for his talent as a recording artist, DJ, and remixer have driven him to a life of excess, which on this day translates into a bad case of the flu and an unmistakable need for sleep.

After apologizing for his mid-afternoon lethargy, Cook runs upstairs to change into some clothes, leaving me alone in his dimly lit living room—save for the company of a squirrely truffle hound named Pickles—to ponder the surroundings. Various kitsch items are strewn about, such as a plastic Japanese tongue scraper, neo-psychedelic paintings of a bleary-eyed woman and a cherubic

---

* *Source:* Michael Gelfand, "The Art of the Gag," *Musician*, May 1998, pp. 18–19.

space alien, numerous Keith Haring prints, and dozens of framed yellow smiley faces of all sorts and sizes. But before the situation can become too much like a walk through Willy Wonka's chocolate factory, a reinvigorated Cook returns, his hands shaking in anticipation of the day's first cigarette, and we settle down over tea to discuss my main fascination with his music: his ear for turning layers of disparate samples into seamlessly hooky, rock-friendly dance hits.

According to Cook, the difference between rock music and dance music is that the former is steeped in analysis while the latter is purely instinctual. "Dance music is primarily there to get your hips moving," he says. "There's nothing to sit and listen to. It's the soundtrack of your nights out rather than anything that's supposed to be heard or discussed at home at great length. It's like the difference between seeing a Martin Scorsese film and an advert [on TV]: One is meant to be there for years, the other just does what it does. And that's a bit what dance music is like. I'm not expecting that in ten years' time anyone will be listening to the songs I'm making today."

Stalwart rockers, ever quick to draw negative conclusions about the music that Cook and his peers create, might agree with his assessment. But Cook is actually less likely to call what he does music; his preference is to compare it to pop art. "It's just like Andy Warhol not painting his own paintings," he insists. "It's all how you put it together. A lot of people say the sampler isn't an instrument, that it could kill music as we know it. I say if it's placed in the wrong hands, the sampler is just the same as a guitar being used to play some horrible twelve-bar blues riff, or 'Smoke On the Water,' or trying to rewrite 'Smells Like Teen Spirit.' A sampler can be just as useless as a guitar. You've just got to learn the noises—and they are just noises."

The talent, he says, is to compose something that other people want to hear. After twenty years of DJing, watching people dance and watching what bits of a record they respond to best. Cook believes he's developed a feel for what sections of a record—gags, as he calls them—people like. "It's really all about gags," he explains, "Has anyone written a song with that chord, or that sort of mix? Like that Nirvana gag: good cop, bad cop, quiet bit, noisy bit. But it's a great gag. Some bands make a whole career out of one gag, some are always looking for the next gag, and some are always listening to someone else's gag. That's what it is—it's what turns you on about a tune.

"I'll hear a groove on someone's record and I'll ask myself, 'What can I do with this?'" he says. In the event of an epiphany, Cook keeps an extensive library of personalized samples carefully catalogued by type—*i.e.*, drum breaks or power riffs—on computer disks, and mixes and matches them like pieces of a puzzle to hear which ones sound best together.

That's not the case with "Going Out of My Head," the third song on *Better Living Through Chemistry* (Astralwerks), which is built around Pete Townshend's seminal riff from "Can't Explain," along with some time-stretched John Bonham beats for good measure. The song is unquestionably catchy, but the blatant theft of that hook could suggest that Cook is simply reducing time-honored anthems into sutured soundbites of disposable pop—or, as Cook likes to call it, "Nirvana with breakbeats."

"Some musicians would say I'm a complete charlatan, and what I do is nick other people's stuff. 'This isn't a new form of music: It's just an amalgamation of house music, rap music, funk music, whatever.' Well, that's all I ever said it was. I never said it was high art. I never said I was going to put it on a pedestal. I've been in bands where we've tried to make real proper music"—Cook was the bassist in the Housemartins—"and tried to make records that had substance, where people could hang onto every word. But I'm better at doing this side of it. I'll leave the other side to Radiohead, who are very good at it."

For proof, we go upstairs to Cook's makeshift studio, where he's neatly packed racks of gear and thousands of obscure records into a highly organized factory for churning out hits. Admitting that *Better Living* was written and recorded in two weeks. Cook is taking a little more time on his next project to create, record, and deal with the complexities of sample clearance with his British and American lawyers.

Turning to his equipment, he plays me his latest work-in-progress, which is based around a vocal sample: a rapper saying "Right about now, the funk soul brother, check it out now," lifted from an underground vinyl release.* As Cook explains it, the entire song sprang from the way the rapper says the word "now": "There's almost a note in it, and when you play it with music behind it, you can infer the note."

Instead of harmonically correlating the spoken phrase to an assigned note, Cook works out the tempo of the phrase—in this case 160 bpm—via the fifteen-year-old Creator software on his Atari 1040ST, and then goes about adding sampled beats here and there according to the vibe he's divining.† "The fact that it's 160 bpm is interesting to me because it's not a tempo I normally work at. It's a bit twisting," he says, gyrating his hips. "It's a bit like *Hawaii Five-O* or something."

Feeding off this tropical inspiration, Cook chops up and reorders a resonant kick-and-snare beat he's chosen to blend in with an incessant hi-hat sound, only to later stack an offset hi-hat clutch and a techno kick on top of the initial hi-hat sound. As the sounds begin to coalesce and combine into a singularly rousing drum sound, he rounds out the mix by throwing in a couple of divergent, mutated Sixties surf guitar licks and an equally retro, time-stretched I-IV-V guitar progression. The scratches and low fidelity of each sample are blatant when played alone, but when they're thrown together, one hears only the sum of the parts, and each sample's sonic imperfection becomes lost in the majesty of the whole.

I'm amazed by the groove, so orthodox and yet so organic. It *must* be the bass, I say to myself, but when I broach the subject Cook gleefully reveals, "I haven't picked up the bass in eight years." At that moment, the bassist in me feels the delight of pure understanding tempered by a sense of my own imminent demise.

---

* The vocal sample comes from the 1972 funk single "Sliced Tomatoes" by The Just Brothers.
† bpm stands for "beats per minute," a common reference point for dance music DJs.

54

Nü Metal and Woodstock '99

Barry Walters

As rock entered its fourth decade in the mid-90s, the celebration and canonization of its now lengthy history escalated on numerous fronts. The Rock and Roll Hall of Fame and Museum opened its doors in 1995, new glossy British magazines such as *Mojo* (1993) and *Uncut* (1997) devoted extensive coverage to "classic" rock history, and a nonstop parade of CD reissues and box sets united listeners across generations. Given this climate, it was perhaps to be expected that the collective memory of one of rock's most enduring symbols, Woodstock, should entice promoters to restage the festival on its 25th anniversary in 1994 and then again in 1999. Woodstock '99, however, differed dramatically from its famous forebear. Tickets for the three-day event cost $150 and rock's strong capitalist allure attracted festival vendors selling water for $4 a bottle. Most of all, Woodstock's historic message of communal harmony was lost on a young audience clamoring for angry, aggressive music. By the festival's end, destructive riots and reports of rape and sexual assault had cast a dark shadow over the event. As journalist Barry Walters writes in his Woodstock review, at the center of the maelstrom lay the music of headlining acts like Limp Bizkit, Korn, and Kid Rock. Mixing together elements of grunge, rap, and a resuscitated heavy metal style, these groups were generally lumped together under the label of "nü metal." Given the attitudes towards women that seemed to surface at the festival, it is worth asking how far rock had progressed (or regressed) in the three decades since feminists lamented the oppressive nature of "cock rock."[*]

Just as history has looked back on the original Woodstock with grainy footage of body-painted hippies, Woodstock '99 will undoubtedly be remembered by the bonfires that raged out of control as concertgoers rioted and looted. But the more pervasive recurring image in the 65 hours of pay-per-view coverage was of shirtless young women floating above a sea of male bodies, waiflike teens struggling to maintain strained smiles for the camera as they swatted away unwanted hands.

Singer Sheryl Crow described Woodstock '99 as "the most disconcerting audience and worst performing experience I've ever had." Crow, who also performed at the 1994 Woodstock festival, said that this year's event was different. "This year was much more focused on young, white, male America—an aggressive, macho energy full of discontentment, and I think that's where rock is about right now.

"These people were so full of rage and totally unappreciative of the music, kids raised without any pride in themselves. I'm still really [angry] about the event and regret being a part of it," she said.

What was it about this year's Woodstock that created such tension?

---

[*] *Source:* Barry Walters, "The Arson is Blowin' in the Wind: Why Woodstock '99 Devolved into a Frat-Style Free-For-All," *The Washington Post,* August 8, 1999, p. G1.

Although each day started with veterans and unknowns, acts that have had hits or may someday have hits, each night climaxed with performances by bands that are happening right now—Korn, Limp Bizkit, Rage Against the Machine, Metallica and Red Hot Chili Peppers. All are exclusively male, excessively loud, defined by a diffuse wrath against anything resembling authority, and driven more by rhythm and fury than melody. In other words, they're classic rock groups.

Which means boy rock groups. Right now, the music industry is running scared from the future. The rise of the Internet, the threat of unprofitable music duplication via digital downloads, the predicted demise of the conventional record store, and the commonplace buying and selling of record labels by multinationals have fostered a panicked corporate mentality that frowns on artistic development and looks for quick hits. The promised electronica revolution didn't instantly happen, so American music bizzers have fallen back on what they know—teeny-bop pop and boy rock.

Although reigning sugar harmony kings the Backstreet Boys, their solo female counterpart Britney Spears and Latin heartthrob Ricky Martin will most likely score the year's best-selling albums, the teen-pop backlash began soon after these acts topped the charts. The typical male rock fan *hates* this stuff with a vehemence that hasn't been seen since the "disco sucks" days of Donna Summer and the Village People, and although the music industry is much more attentive to female and African American audiences than it's ever been, its primary allegiance will always be to college-age white boys.

And rap-influenced hard rock is what college-age white boys like these days.

This is not necessarily a bad thing. When the last technological media upheaval occurred—at the beginning of the '80s with MTV—rock and black pop were seen as mutually intolerant opposites. Eager to shake off its recent disco past, black popular music was either smoothing out in the easy-listening balladry of Kool & the Gang, or roughing up in the form of rap, a sound ignored by major record companies in its crucial developmental years. Despite the fact that plenty of New Wave acts drew on disco and reggae rhythms, black pop was shut out of the rock world, and it took performers on the charismatic level of Michael Jackson and Tina Turner to break down the color barrier of MTV and rock-leaning radio.

Not since rock-and-roll's infancy have white musicians drawn so explicitly and so consciously on contemporary black sounds. And unlike the '50s Pat Boone fan who could fall in love with sanitized renditions of R&B hits and remain unaware of their black origins, today's Korn, Limp Bizkit and Kid Rock fan knows that his heroes are paying tribute to the rhythms and attitudes of hip-hop poets from Run-D.M.C. to Snoop Dogg. Many of the same kids sending Limp Bizkit to the top of the charts have also made possible the mainstream success of such ghetto-centric talents as Jay-Z and the Wu-Tang Clan. Today's typical white male rocker is somewhat supportive of R&B acts like TLC, Ginuwine or Lauryn Hill.

This is progress.

The flip side of rock's current openness to African American culture is that black pop's most positive elements are not always what's most successfully crossing over. Woodstock '99 favorites Limp Bizkit, Kid Rock and Insane Clown Posse all mimic the misogyny that hard-core hip-hop seems incapable of shaking off, and although their more introspective compatriots in Korn and Rage Against the Machine address topics like gay-bashing and modern-day imperialism, their delivery is often so ham-fisted that any thoughtful intent is lost on the kids who need to hear it most.

It was telling that the final words of Rage Against the Machine's Saturday night set—an anti-war chant of "[Expletive] you, I won't do what you tell me"—was appropriated the next night by arsonists and looters facing off with police.

While pop celebrates girl power, rock is once again all about boy power. The inroads made by grunge guy softies wary of thuggish heavy metal and female renegades from Liz Phair to Bjork seem lost to fashion. While VH1 honors the women of rock, hoisting Aretha Franklin and Tina Turner to the top of its honors list, MTV negotiates the divided desires of its young audience by pumping up the rap-rock bad boys so that college-age males don't turn the channel at the mere sight of their younger sisters' goody-goody favorites.

The problem with this strategy is that it leaves out much of the most innovative, soul-searching, potentially lasting music happening right now, and that lack was reflected in Woodstock '99. Not every female musician is busy with Lilith Fair right now, and although Sleater-Kinney, Drain S.T.H. or even Courtney Love and Missy Elliott don't sell the same numbers as Korn and Limp Bizkit, their presence certainly could've helped defuse the male rage that characterized much of the festival.

Although Crow only had Jewel and Alanis Morissette for female company on Woodstock '99's vast three-day lineup, she feels the bill's gender demographics—which included mellow afternoon performances by such summer festival senior standbys as Los Lobos, Bruce Hornsby and George Clinton—were irrelevant: It was the festival's pervasive bullying tone culminating in several rapes that allegedly took place in the mosh pits and on the campgrounds that mattered.

During Crow's set, males in the audience repeatedly asked her to take off her shirt. "At first, I thought it was in fun," says Crow. "But then I saw all these young women who had their tops off being disrespected by the guys, and everyone's bad behavior was exacerbated by the constant presence of the pay-per-view cameras. There is absolutely no justification for rape. None. But I think girls were taking their tops off and the guys were groping them just so they could get on TV."

Crow's sentiments are echoed by Brian "Dexter" Holland of the Southern California punk band Offspring, who was one of two rockers who tried to curb his fans' cop-a-feel free-for-all. (The other was repentant bad boy bassist Flea of the Red Hot Chili Peppers.)

"I stopped our show and reminded the crowd that girls should not have to fear being assaulted just because they are girls," Holland says. "We hate to see anyone bullied, guys or girls. It is not what live music is about. But then you look around at the TV cameras and all they are focusing on is girls with their tops off. So more girls take their tops off. No problem, right? Except then there are girls who don't want to take off their tops and they start getting ridiculed."

A smaller point: At a time when much of rock and pop's creativity is coming from overseas, the fact that few non-North American performers were featured on the main stage is inexcusable. The late-night programming of electronica acts Moby and Fatboy Slim meant no pay-per-view coverage, and techno's Chemical Brothers—the one major act that managed to plug into the original Woodstock's euphoric togetherness—had to go up against Metallica.

"I played in the rave tent late at night to about 40,000 to 50,000 people, and the crowd was very good-natured, gregarious, fun-loving. I personally had a great performance experience, even if $5,000 worth of my T-shirts went up in flames Sunday night," says Moby.

"But the rest of what I witnessed at Woodstock had a frat party vibe that was totally oppressive. Now I personally like testosterone-driven rock—I've played it myself. Yet it's got to be balanced by something else, and that something else was hardly there. Instead they had one aggressive band after the other because aggressive bands are selling records right now," Moby says. "But I don't think the outcome should've surprised anyone."

55

Indie Pop Goes Twee

Joey Sweeney

In theory, "indie" is one of the easiest words in the rock lexicon to define. The term is simply short for "independent" record labels. Yet beyond this initial designation, indie opens onto an entire realm of attitudes, audience formations, and musical genres—all of them set in some way against the mainstream of musical values. Joey Sweeney's *Salon.com* review of the Expo 2000 Athens, a five-day festival hosted by the local-based Georgia label, Kindercore Records (one of the most prominent American indie labels of the late '90s) offers a unique window into the indie pop world. Sweeney, a music critic and indie musician himself, bases his description of Kindercore and their roster of artists on the style of "twee," a subgenre that at the time enjoyed one of the indie underground's most devoted fan followings. Sweeney draws attention to the distance separating twee from rock 'n' roll's rebellious pose. And indeed, comparing Sweeney's account of the Expo with Barry Walters' review of Woodstock '99's "frat-style free-for-all," it is hard to imagine a sharper contrast at the turn of the millennium than between indie pop and alternative nü metal audiences.*

If you're not of a certain age or social subset—as director Hal Hartley once put it, "white, middle-class, college-educated" and on and on—you might not know a thing about this thing called twee. And if you're not obsessed by music, obscurantist, willfully infantile and smitten with all things Japanese, you probably don't even care.

But this loose subculture lives among you, in English-speaking countries and abroad (especially in Spain and Japan). Twee music and the twee lifestyle—such as there is one—are a refutation of all that we know about rock 'n' roll. For twee kids, who use the term with equal parts reverie, disdain and cheek, the subculture doesn't really have anything to do with actually, you know, rebelling or anything. Twee kids listen to an emasculated version of rock ' n' roll. They don't care much for sex or drugs. They favor puppy love over scary sex, prefer Japanese candy over beer and pot and like looking at postcards instead of going out into an intimidating, rainy world.

They clad themselves in tight T-shirts with "Brady Bunch" stripes and mix-and-match corduroy. They wear unfortunate bedhead hairstyles and thick glasses rescued, almost always, from the bottom of a cardboard box at the local Lenscrafters.

Twee kids are a lot like the punk rockers before them, but you could say that twee, since its erstwhile inception in the '80s, has always rebelled against punk. Back then, cornerstone twee acts like the Smiths and Marine Girls (an outfit featuring Tracey Thorn, who went on to become the singer in Everything But the Girl) eschewed the gutteral reactionism of punk in favor of the sweetness and

* *Source:* Joey Sweeney, "We're the Younger Generation," *Salon.com*, August 31, 2000, http://archive.salon.com/ent/music/feature/2000/08/31/kindercore/

light (and yes, craft) of naive '60s pop groups such as the Mamas and the Papas or the Association. At the same time, twee cops several of punk's do-it-yourself moves: There are twee magazines, twee all-ages shows, twee record labels and twee local music scenes filled with bands that can't really play their instruments—or at the very least, bands that aspire to radically unlearn what has gone immediately before them.

And in that radical unlearning, that nostalgia for the great pop eras of the past, there's the one major and defining difference between punk and twee: Twee kids love Mom and Dad. In fact, if they could, they'd stay with them forever. I've seen several twee shows at family homes. Twee kids, instead of defining themselves against their parents, embrace a Jonathan Richman worldview: The Old World was better; love was pure and, more than that, less confusing.

Today, Belle and Sebastian, the dainty Scottish pop band, are the Beatles of twee, and their influence looms large over just about every group in the subgenre.

The Kindercore record label is the biggest purveyor of twee music and happiness in the United States. First an Athens, Ga., label, then a New York one and then very shortly thereafter based in Athens again, Kindercore enjoys a generous patronage through a manufacturing deal with California's Emperor Norton label and, as a result, has put out more high-quality twee product, pound for pound, than probably any of its competitors worldwide: March Records, Siesta (based in Spain), Matinee and a handful of others.

And there's apparently an audience for it, although it's hard to tell unless you do the books for an independent record store. Besides Belle and Sebastian, whose last record debuted in the '80s on the Billboard chart, no twee band moves the number of records it would take to, say, be even mildly attractive to a major label. But if you put all the bands into a genre, they can earn a small pile of cash for a little record store, just as punk bands do by hobbling along on word of mouth. In terms of whether twee bands and labels register on SoundScan, the service that tracks record sales, well, they don't. Moneywise, it isn't very much. But then again, the rock underground has rarely made millions for anyone until it ceased being underground.

And that's exactly why Kindercore was able to pull off Expo 2000 Athens, a five-day celebration of the label's take on twee. With 50 releases in all, Kindercore is big enough to have something like this and know that people will come to it, but still small enough to know that it'll know most of the folks who do.

That's because Kindercore, like so many of its successful punk and twee predecessors, keeps close tabs on fans. The Kindercore expo, with its $30 passes, was as much about thanking those 300 or so fans as it was about celebrating its own achievements (neither of the label's co-heads is even close to being out of the 20s) and showing off some new signings. All told, 30 bands played over the five nights, all but one of which were held at Athens' legendary 40 Watt Club—the same club (although now in a different location) where bands like R.E.M., Pylon and the B-52's put Athens on the map more than 15 years ago. Of the 30 bands, roughly half hailed from or had significant ties to Athens. That made the Athens of Expo 2000 a rare sight in rock 'n' roll: a faded boomtown booming once again. The coffee shop a few doors down from the 40 Watt bore a handwritten sign, knowingly saying, "Welcome Indie Rockers!"

The four nights of music I attended revealed a group of awkward, beat-phobic kids getting turned on to what most of us in the world of pop music have known for a while: Dance music is really fun! They also demonstrated a label on the cusp of growing out of its Garanimals, and bittersweetly relishing every minute of it. Because as much as Kindercore's pop jones invites dinky, jangly twee bands, it was only a matter of time before the label invited in featherweight pop as a whole. And from the crowd, it looked like Kindercore at long last was stretching out its hands and accepting what it for so long had hinted at: a genuine love for pop in all its forms.

The 40 Watt looks like a lot of rock clubs in the South. It's a big, airy dive (way bigger than the dives you have to patronize to see rock bands in the North) that's part converted auto garage, part church basement—and thanks to a tenuous tiki, Christmas lights and disco-ball décor—part *M*A*S*H* canteen. Budweiser and Shiner are only two bucks a bottle, and the bartenders look like Wilco: rock-scene lifers, and damn proud of it. It doesn't sound like much, but if your town doesn't have at least one place like this, you should probably move.

Pulling into Athens late, I caught the tail end of Wednesday night's Expo acts, including Japancakes, a local five-piece that is currently doing for the lap steel what Stereolab did for the Moog a few years back. Japancakes are one of the more hypnotic, sublime and even mature acts on the Kindercore label, which might explain why they pulled in a way smaller crowd than they deserved. As the band ran through a handful of the eight-minute epics that make up their *I Can See Dallas* LP and *Down the Elements* EP, a large video display at stage left revealed loops of silhouetted trees and telephone wires, shot from below at dusk in a passing automobile.

They were pretty good, but for my money, they didn't even touch the 8-Track Gorilla.

Simply put, the 8-Track Gorilla is just that: some guy in a gorilla suit with an old portable eight-track player around his neck, singing along in a deadpan Ben Stein voice over whatever tape happens to be catching his fancy at the moment. On this particular night, that meant some old Kinks stuff (including, appropriately enough, "Ape Man"), a rousing rendition of the Stones' "Happy" and a sexy duet of some "Pina Colada Song"-esque '70s tune with a saucy blond Goth chick that veered from strangely tender to nearly queasy making. The 8-Track Gorilla was not so much a proper Kindercore act as a joke that seems to have mutated far beyond whatever stoned fantasy provoked him into existence in the first place. Audience reactions to the guy—whose set ran a full 40 minutes, just like the sets of the rest of the Kindercore artists—vacillated wildly, but to me, watching a guy in a gorilla suit sing along with Keith Richards after being in a car for 13 hours seemed just about right.

I loved it, couldn't get enough of the guy—I mean, Gorilla. And I wasn't alone. All week, my traveling companion, Martin, would wander around the 40 Watt Club, secretly staring at the hands of men to see if they revealed the 8-Track Gorilla's telltale black nail polish. It became something of a collective obsession for the both of us. Which, I suppose, is why we went down to Athens in the first place.

TWISTING, IN THE WIND, BY THE POOL

Sooner or later, even Martin and I knew that as our snickering about the man in the ape suit fell away we were going to have to socialize with our own kind. For once in our lives, we were in a town overrun with indie, a town where, at least for this week, striped T-shirts flew like freak flags and the stars in the sky from any direction spelled twee. For maybe the first time ever, soaked in the mid-August heat, there was a confederacy of twee. It was nerve-racking even just walking down the street and seeing people who looked just like me.

So imagine our surprise on Thursday afternoon when we went to take a dip in the hotel's pool and found, to our mutual shock, titillation and dismay, some kind of twee pool party. This made sense when you thought about it; unlike South by Southwest or the CMJ music conference, the Expo held no daytime events. Where else were we going to go during the day? Still, this was alarming. One, twee kids have little, tiny bodies well into their 20s and carry for them a kind of skinny shame usually reserved for anorexics, which makes it hard to catch any sun at all. Two, to venture into the pool, which would mean at least in part removing the two layers of coverup clothing just about all of us wore, you had to strip quickly and quietly down to your swimsuit and get into the pool in deep enough water before anyone noticed you. This was all but impossible.

Instead, most of us just sat by the pool, inspecting the badges on each other's backpacks, pretending to read and simultaneously praying for and dreading the moment when we'd all finally introduce ourselves on this, the first day of indie-pop summer camp.

THE RUSHMORE PLAYERS, A.K.A. OF MONTREAL

On most nights of the Expo, a band called Of Montreal appeared onstage as either themselves or as the backing band for another project on an average of twice a night. We saw principal members of the Athens group participating in sets by the Marshmallow Coast, Summer Hymns and the Great Lakes—as well as during their own set, which bridged the gap between *Magical Mystery Tour*-era Beatles and dadaist high school theater. The band is part of the second wave of groups in the Elephant 6 collective of neo-retro pop bands. Engineered by the Apples in Stereo, the Olivia Tremor Control and Neutral Milk Hotel, the E6 collective is split mostly between Denver and Athens and is to indie pop today what Death Row was to hip-hop in the mid-'90s.

The omnipresent Of Montreal were both a blessing, when they worked and the bands they helped came off as something more than the total of their influences, and a curse, when it just seemed that Of Montreal's loopiness was getting spread thin. But either way, the Of Montreal bands seemed to be the most succinct statement of the brand of fresh-faced (if only marginally inventive) guitar pop Kindercore has been going after. In stark relief to the willfully juvenile stuff the label has been passing off for a few years with bands like Masters of the Hemisphere and Kincaid—the former of which, for instance, has offered a free comic book with its new album, a concept piece that seems like a direct lift of the Jim Henson show *Fraggle Rock*—Of Montreal delivered that kind of exuberance without any of the cringe-worthy infantilism that makes this kind of thing so hard to take for so many people. What's more telling about the level of craft in Of Montreal's flights of fancy is that, note for note, the music sounds even more youthful than that of their contemporaries, "Partridge Family" tambourines, junior-high nasal vocals and all. And yet, it doesn't grate; during their set, even the old farts in the crowd like me had to pogo just a little. I mean, these days, how many chances do you get?

And if the new signings are any indication, the label seems to be getting better and better. Norway's Kings of Convenience took the stage like a Euro Smothers Brothers, punctuating quiet, winsome tunes in the manner of Simon and Garfunkel or Nick Drake with a snappy stage presence that suggested, for the first time on the Expo stage, that here was a pair of guys actually interested in craft. Another new signing that debuted on Saturday night was San Francisco's Call and Response (C.A.R.), which invoked the Jackson 5 and the Mamas and the Papas way more than, say, early twee prototype groups like Heavenly or Beat Happening. Self-assured, sassy and with the chops and harmonies to match, Call and Response turned the earnest, honest approach Kindercore has been hammering away at for years into something that was heartbreaking, uplifting and pretty all at once: pure pop for now people.

BUT DOES TWEE KNOW HOW TO PARTY?

On any given night of the Expo shows, in my immediate surroundings I would see at least two girl flutists, two people curled up on any of the 40 Watt's gross couches, obsessively, manically "journaling," and one table full of people playing Mad Libs.

This does not a party make, and even though reports of kids filing into the bathrooms to vomit after drinking too many Red Bull energy drinks shot through with vodka were many, the Expo kids seemed seriously laid-back, verging on what I saw in some eyes as downright despondency. This fell in line with the collective message I was getting after seeing so many of the Kindercore bands: Kindercore records are the records Belle and Sebastian fans are listening to when they're not listening to Belle and Sebastian.

But how much of this is a pose? It seemed as if any chance the kids got to rage, they took it on, no questions asked. I saw it during Of Montreal's raucous (if cute) set, during the Four Corners' big-rock pastiche and even—although I could be reading too much into this—during what I saw as the 8-Track Gorilla's glorious (and apt) rewrite of rock history. Something in twee bubbles under, and that something is the sex and freedom of rock that twee so coyly tries to repress.

So on Friday night, when attention turned to Kindercore's two new groups—groups that you could actually dance to—it wasn't hard to imagine a block-rockin' beat falling in the forest. I imagined twee kids like the guy one of my friends called Badge Museum—with his perfectly symmetrical display of buttons bearing the logos of his favorite bands—politely acting as though they couldn't hear the beat. But it was just the opposite. The five-piece guitar-house band called VHS or Beta took the stage in blue plastic suits, staring indie pop in the face while brandishing a vocoder and electronic drums—the kind the guy in New Order used to play. A quiet descended over the crowd and people started to nod at first. Within a few minutes I swear I could see feet moving and one massive thought bubble hovering over the crowd: "Oh, we get it. And, just between us, we are so very glad to finally get it."

A dance party sponsored by Electronic Watusi Boogaloo, an Amsterdam breakbeat label, opened up a few doors down an hour or so later. The Expo crowd all but ran into the warehouse space. A wall broke and twee went dance; Kindercore turned a corner and you could feel the kids turning with it.

THE MADDENING CROWD

So far, Kindercore has been able to sell a fairly idiosyncratic vision of what it considers valuable music. And to move along in this strange epoch of the music industry, the label has been pretty adept at consistently refining what it is and what it is not.

As noble as those efforts are, in the meantime it is stuck with a lot of deadwood, bands lacking the same kind of inspiration. Unfortunately, just about all of them played at Expo 2000, right alongside the bands that could help the label make something of lasting importance for people who don't work at record stores or at college radio stations.

But while those bands allowed the Expo to be a more complete event, by the last night my head began to hurt. When that headache split open and I had left the club, a fairly obvious realization hit me: There is nothing that I've heard on the Kindercore label that has made much of an effort to touch me on an emotional level. For as nakedly ambitious as the label is, it still adheres pretty rigorously to the tenets of twee: that nothing should make you cry unless it is in the name of sheer sentimentality, and furthermore, in no circumstances does the music want to make you do what rock 'n' roll is supposed to want you to do: to fight or fuck.

Kindercore is a label with plenty of Herman's Hermits and no Rolling Stones. But it's trying.

HOW TO MAKE FRIENDS AND CONFOUND PEOPLE: BOY-BAND REVISIONISM

In all of this, if you didn't care about the music; if you thought these pasty white kids and their bullshit bands were repellent; if you didn't see the sense in all the hoo-ha about what a genius Brian Wilson was and saw no need for so much inept tribute laid at his feet, here and now in the summer of 2000; if, not to put too fine a point on it, you were a bartender at the 40 Watt Club and just wanted to make your money and go home, thank you; and if you were not really looking for entertainment, you had to hand it to Kindercore for at least one thing: When it invited anyone in the whole pop world who wanted to have a look-see into its home and head, it had the balls on the biggest night of its shindig to pull a total goof on itself.

Especially for the Expo, Kindercore constructed its own stable of boy bands. Not some retro goofiness like the Wonders in the Tom Hanks movie *That Thing You Do!* but the real, sweaty, icky, present-day faux-sexy thing. Adding to a world of Backstreet Boys and 'N Syncs, Kindercore presented on Friday night From U 2 S (pronounced "from you to us") and N2 Her (pronounced, uh, "into her"). It was one of the most hilarious things I've ever seen in my life.

Starting out by clearing the stage and setting up a movie screen to show a "Making the Band"/ "Behind the Music"-styled mockumentary on how the groups came into existence, label co-head Ryan Lewis approached the mike to introduce the proceedings as if they were yet another band on the label. "Well, we know a lot of people have been dying to see these guys, so without further ado..."

And that quickly, the Spinal Tap of boy bands took the stage: There was a clean-cut one, a dirty one, a half-naked one, a tiny one. And they had dance routines! Like so much teen pop, the music tracks accompanying the boy bands were a weird mix of Celica-thumping Miami bass and synth-driven, up-tempo trip-hop—until you realized that the songs they were singing were misappropriated indie anthems: Unrest's "Make-Out Club," for From U 2 S, and for N 2 Her, Pavement's "Summer Babe," with sections of Stephen Malkmus' deadpan lyrics recast into a Jay-Z-esque rhyme.

Everything Kindercore wanted to or could have said about itself got said on Friday night: that it was above all, like the Immediate label that put out fresh, sunshiny pop in the '60s, simply "happy to be a part of the industry of human happiness," and that, once in a while, sweating the details pays off.

VI

THE 2000S

56

"My Week on the Avril Lavigne E-Team"

Chris Dahlen

From the late 1990s through the early 2000s, teen pop was one of the most pervasive of popular music genres. Following the groundbreaking success of Britney Spears and Christina Aguilera, the industry welcomed a wave of young female artists, ranging from the R&B pop sounds of Pink and Nelly Furtado to the more rock-oriented styles of Michelle Branch and Avril Lavigne. In his 2002 article "My Week on the Avril Lavigne E-Team," music critic Chris Dahlen examines the rapid rise up the charts of the 17-year-old Lavigne (born 1984), whose debut *Let Go* would finish as the third best-selling album of the year. Joining the Avril Lavigne "E-Team" under an assumed identity, Dahlen offers a revealing glimpse into what it means to be a pop music fan in an era of message boards, chat rooms, online communities, and interactive television programs like MTV's video countdown show *Total Request Live* (TRL). In the process, he raises intriguing questions about the mechanisms of the industry's star-making machinery and the measurement of popularity in the Internet age. As a side note, it is worth pointing out that Dahlen's article, which originally appeared on the influential Web magazine *Pitchfork Media*, is itself indicative of rock music's move toward an increasingly online discourse.*

I saw a lot of girls at my bachelor party in Montréal, but the one I was sober enough to remember was Avril Lavigne. We were watching Canadian cable in our hotel room, polishing off a case of Molsons before we went out for lunch, and as we flipped through the music stations we stumbled across Avril Lavigne's "Complicated." None of us knew who she was, and most of the guys didn't care, but I made us stop and watch.

At first glance, Avril's just another cute teen-pop star. But rather than dancing in choreographed formation with gay New Yorkers, she whizzes around on a skateboard; she's a female pop singer, but she plays with a rock band, cops a wholesome mid-80s punk look, and acts like a tomboy. She probably hangs with the outsiders at school—the kids who smoke weed, hate football and try to read Camus. No, her music isn't great, and no, she's not as punk as her record label claims. But she's spunky, sharp, and comes off as a real teen instead of a creepy blow-up doll. If I could go to school with these girls—and don't think I don't dream about it—Britney Spears is the girl I'd ogle, but Lavigne's the one I'd knock myself out to impress.

* *Source:* Chris Dahlen, "My Week on the Avril Lavigne E-Team," *Pitchforkmedia.com*, September 12, 2002, http://www.pitchforkmedia.com/watw/02-09/avril.shtml.

One day I was skimming through her website (because, um, I'm a rock critic, and I have to keep up on this stuff) and I found a weird ad: "Join the official Avril eTeam!" Lavigne's handlers have hired a company called the Hype Council to start a grassroots marketing effort: they're getting fans to sign up and spread the word about Avril, online. It's the same concept as a street team, where a label gets kids to blanket the city with posters and bumper stickers to promote a show or a record release. Street teams are a time-honored way to get free labor out of dedicated fans. But eTeams are more efficient, more powerful—and just as cheap.

But exactly how does it work? What's in it for us? A free t-shirt? Concert tix? Maybe, dare I dream, a chance to meet Avril? It had to be checked out.

MY LIFE AS A TEENAGE GIRL

I knew I couldn't go into this thing as a grizzled 28-year-old music snob. So step one was to create a cover for myself: I became Kate Thompson, born on July 4th, 1984, and currently living in Allston, Massachusetts (a.k.a. "Rock City!!"). All I know about being a girl is what I've learned from Judy Blume novels and the WB, but I figured I could bluff it well enough to get in the door. I set up a fake e-mail address in Kate's name and then sent in my application for TeamAVRIL.

While I waited to hear back, I also got a copy of her album, *Let Go*, and listened to it a few times. Listening as a teenage girl and not as a critic, I've got to say, it's not bad—half heartfelt angst, half high-energy spaz pop. The songs come off as honest, genuine teenage mood swings, from the crashing guitars and angst-drenched cries of "Losing Grip" to whimsical and hyper-poppy tracks like her latest hit, "Sk8er Boi." Expect to see the lyrics from "Anything but Ordinary" scribbled all over yearbooks across America's junior high schools: "To walk within the lines would make my life so boring!!/I want to know that I have been to the extreme...I'd rather be anything but ordinary." Lavigne's voice is pretty strong, too, as she started out singing country music, where weak pipes will get you nowhere. (But don't tell anyone about the country connection—if the kids find out, it'll be worse than if she had VD.)

And now it's my job to help push her record as far up the charts as it'll go.

MICHELLE BRANCH, YOU WANNABE, YOU'RE GOING DOWN

Within days I got—that is, Kate Thompson got—marching orders from TeamAVRIL, in a four-page long e-mail from someone named "Wag."

Wag runs TeamAVRIL on behalf of the Hype Council, and at last count, she's in charge of over 60,000 rabid Avril fans. I couldn't find a biography or a profile of her (if Wag is even a woman), but I would guess that she's an early-to-mid-twentysomething with dotcom marketing experience who was once: 1) a camp counselor; 2) on the prom committee; or 3) the plane crash survivor who ate everyone else.

Wag's there to keep the kids in line with a friendly but firm hand, encouraging us to finish our tasks and helping us through the frequent site outages and relaunches that plague the TeamAVRIL site. Every week, Wag sends us the latest news on Avril, and then gives us a list of ways to help her. From the first update, it didn't look like Lavigne needed much help: *Let Go* went double platinum the last week of August and hit #3 on the *Billboard* 200 (behind the Dixie Chicks and Eminem). The video for "Sk8er Boi" hit full rotation on MTV and made #1 on "Total Request Live," that critical gauge of teen pop fame. And best of all, as Wag wrote: "Avril won the VMA [Video Music Award] for Best New Artist!!! What an absolutely COOOOOOL night that was!"

But as Wag reminded us, "the competition wants #1. Let's heat it up!!!" And it's true: as big as Avril gets, a dozen other wannabes vie for her spot—for example, porcelain doll Michelle Branch, who, like Avril, claims she writes her own songs and never uses a stylist. Branch won MTV's 2002 Viewer's Choice and her song "Goodbye to You" is climbing the charts. Wag didn't need to spell it out: we had to put that bitch down.

So how do you help Avril? TeamAVRIL focuses on three kinds of targets: online polls, message boards, and "Total Request Live." The polls are the easiest. Many pop websites run some kind of survey where you vote for your favorite new artist; Wag has listed them all, and told us to hit them early and often. The most critical is CosmoGIRL.com's, where we're voting for nothing less than the CosmoGIRL of the Year. If Avril wins, you'll see her raccoon-eyed, necktie-sporting Canadian visage on the cover of the November issue.

I had to register on the CosmoGIRL site to vote, which means CosmoGIRL gets my (fake) registration and demographics info. But at least they send me helpful make-up and fashion tips. They've narrowed the poll options to Sarah Michelle Gellar, Gwen Stefani, Katie Holmes, Shirley Manson, and our girl Avril. Now, you may think CosmoGIRL would only give one vote to each registered visitor. Instead, they encourage you to vote up to one hundred times a day. So naturally, that's how many times I voted. I thought about tossing a couple votes to Gellar because I dig "Buffy," but she's been phoning it in for the past couple of years. In the end, all my votes went to Avril.

The next task is to look for message boards and chat rooms and barrage them with Avril propaganda. In case you're not familiar with these forums, the basic idea is that anyone in the world can go to a website with a message board or a chat room, and just start typing. For example, you may create a subject titled, "Avril RAWKS," and post a few comments about why. Then a dozen other people will come in and post messages saying, "Avril SUX." Then you write back telling them to blow themselves. This can go on for days.

There are many message boards that focus on music, and all of them, from the poppiest to the snobbiest, have at least a couple threads about Avril. Most of them are negative, taking her to task for not being "real" and not being "punk." Cocky teenagers with hit singles have to expect some amount of flak, but Avril inspires profound hatred. On the "Total Request Live" boards, punk-drummergirl15 writes: "I would love to wack her in the head with a tennis racket (the one she should be holding!) she is a freaking yuppie wannabe!!" Or from RapSmirk: "Avril Lavigne looks worse than an adult diaper with semen in it."

As an upstanding member of the team, I just kept posting back, trying to turn the tide. "She's not trying to be anything! She does what she wants—she doesn't sing songs about being a punk, she sings about being alone, or depressed, about being lonely but not wanting to act just like everyone else in her class..." I ended each post with, "AVRIL RAWKS! Nobody's gonna talk trash about my girl!"

THE MOST IMPORTANT FORUM IN POP—AND IT'S RUN BY IDIOTS

At the end of the week I sent in a detailed two-page status report. And then I waited, until this Monday, when I got another update and found out how we were doing. *Let Go* still holds the #3 spot on the *Billboard* 200—no movement there, but at least it hasn't slipped. Nothing much else had changed. But there was one way I could watch our progress: sit through "Total Request Live" and see if Avril's video stayed at #1.

From what I can tell, "Total Request Live" is the most important forum in teen music. It's a daily show that broadcasts live right after school, from 3:30 to 4:30. They rank and play the top ten videos of the day, ostensibly chosen by you the viewer, who can call in or vote online for your favorite music. In the days of street teams, labels encouraged the fans to call radio stations and request songs. But TeamAVRIL doesn't even bother mentioning the radio: it's too local, and no station can touch "TRL"'s influence. In addition, radio stations barely take requests, while "TRL" claims to work strictly from your votes. Granted, you only get 60 videos to choose from, but if you want to write in a vote for some weirdo indie band, there's a form for that, too.

Usually, Carson Daly hosts "TRL," but today the second stringers were in charge: up in the studio was Quddus, a bland guy who kept saying "bro" and "man" to remind us that he's black, and working the crowds on the street was a featureless twig named Hilarie. These dopes made Daly look like Cronkite.

I waded through eight crappy videos before it came down to Eminem and Avril fighting for the top spot. And Avril won! Eminem got the #2 spot with that whiny song about how his mom didn't love him as a child. Listen, Em, you goddamn bleached weasel, I've got problems, too—I don't need to hear about yours. "Sk8er Boi" topped the charts once again and we got to watch the video, where Avril flies around on a dirt bike, hangs with her band, and runs around with that silly necktie she's always wearing. I clapped and cheered. Maybe it was my 500 votes that put her over the top! Every little bit helps.

IT'S ONLY CHILD LABOR IF YOU PAY THEM

Now, this is all pretty exciting, until you look at the big picture.

What do the members of TeamAVRIL get for all their hard work and trouble? Nothing. That's right, nothing. Not even a t-shirt. At best, you're entered in a contest to *win* a t-shirt, or an autographed CD. The hardest working team member, out of all 60,000, wins an autographed guitar. But the rest of us don't get shit—not a discount, not advance orders on tickets, nothing.

The site does promise 'exclusive content' that only TeamAVRIL members can see. This might be cool for the dedicated fans that typically sign up for this kind of stuff, but when I joined, nothing was up there but a clip from the song "My World" (which is already on the album) and a personal message of thanks from Avril: "Thank you for all of your e-mails and calls to 'TRL' and [Canadian music channel] 'MuchMusic' which helped me get to #1 on both, which in turn increased record sales…" Wow, that came from the heart.

The only real perk is that as soon as you're accepted as a member of TeamAVRIL, you get access to their 'backstage area', where you can check your TeamAVRIL e-mail (yourname@teamavril. com—prestigious!), or access the message board. This message board seems to be the only one in the world where nobody makes fun of Avril, thereby making it some kind of refuge.

I had a blast hanging around the board. You probably want me to quote some of the funny things I read, in some kind of "16-year-old Avril Lavigne fans say the darndest things!" expose. But I won't, mainly because I wasn't any smarter or cooler at their age. Besides, apart from some arguments over whether Avril *really* plays guitar or whether she's *really* punk, it was a pretty average board. It has male and female fans, from their pre-teens to early twenties. Kids wrote in to complain about the first day of school, or make plans to meet after Avril concerts; they talked about music and posted links to their home pages.

And even though I could rant about how TeamAVRIL is scamming us, I'm willing to bet that most of the thousands of TeamAVRIL members just signed up to hang out and use the board. After all, if everyone followed orders, Avril would have 60,000 votes on the RollingStone.com "Who's Gonna Win the Pop Pack Race?" poll; instead, she got a mere 4,000, putting her far behind Anastacia and Dropline. Maybe TeamANASTACIA hands out free shirts.

CONCLUSION: WHAT A SCAM

A lot of energy gets wasted on this. It's free labor, with kids like me as the suckers who click these stupid polls and chat up Avril. And it's even worse because the company's not just after your time:

they want to use you as marketing data. Even the members who do nothing have handed the Hype Council their names, ages and addresses. It never hurts to have 60,000 people come to you with their personal information, so whether or not TeamAVRIL makes a difference, the Hype Council and the record company still win.

But if the fans like Avril that much, more power to them: you can't really choose the music you like. Heck, I'll admit even I've got a soft spot for Avril after doing so much work for her. Maybe it's true what they say about missionaries: if nothing else, you end up converting yourself.

57

"Punk's Earnest New Mission"

Michael Azerrad

Emo, screamo, pop-punk: no matter what the label, it was clear by the early 2000s that more and more punk-related bands were beginning to deal with themes of despair and loneliness. As we have seen, such emotions have been a part of punk and alternative history for some time, appearing in the music of bands from Black Flag to Nirvana. In particular, the 1990s witnessed a widespread rise of indie label "emo" bands, whose "emotional" music conveyed an intensely introspective and con-fessional quality best captured in the title of Sunny Day Real Estate's influential 1994 debut, *Diary*. With the popular 2002 and 2003 major label releases of groups like Good Charlotte and Thursday, punk and emo witnessed a stronger mainstream presence than ever before. Surveying the current scene, music critic Michael Azerrad delves into the various issues of "adolescent mental health" populating the music of these bands, focusing specifically on the topics of depression and suicide. Azerrad, the author of the 1993 Nirvana biography *Come As You Are* (Doubleday), brands the trend toward self-examination in this music as a form of "therapy rock." For all the statistics and testimo-nials that Azerrad uses as support for his argument, it is curious that he mostly avoids discussions of race, class, and gender. At one point, however, he does allude to therapy rock's roots in suburbia. To what extent is this connection important to understanding the music and its audience?*

Among the many gripping moments in the video for Good Charlotte's recent single "Hold On," the most gripping of all may well be a close-up shot of an ordinary-looking middle-aged man—not a band member or an actor but Bob Burt, a high school coach who lost his 19-year-old daughter to suicide. "It's not the right order of things," he says, his face creasing in grief. "You're not supposed to bury your children, they're supposed to bury you." The "Hold On" video is an avowed attempt by this double-platinum pop-punk band to talk suicidal kids back from the brink. "Hold on if you feel like letting go/Hold on, it gets better than you know," the singer Joel Madden keens as the black-clad, heavily tattooed band plays in a dilapidated little house whose walls are scrawled with words like "fear," "lonely" and "pain." The music breaks for a series of other heart-rending sound bites from friends and relatives of those who have committed suicide.

Made in conjunction with several suicide prevention organizations, the video closes as a tearful young woman, her voice breaking, says: "It's O.K. to get help. You're going to miss out on so much." A black screen lists hot line phone numbers and the Web address of the American Federation for Suicide Prevention.

"It's almost like a public service announcement," Mr. Madden recently told MTV.com. If so, it's a hugely popular one: "Hold On" is a big hit on MTV, played heavily and featured on the channel's

---

* *Source:* Michael Azerrad, "Punk's Earnest New Mission," *New York Times*, January 4, 2004, Section 2, pp. 1, 32.

"Total Request Live," which showcases viewers' favorite videos. (It's not the only song on Good Charlotte's latest album, "The Young and the Hopeless," that addresses suicide; another is called "The Day That I Die.")

"Hold On" is a perfect specimen of a new strain of teenage-oriented music—call it therapy rock—that uses the language of punk music to address, and sometimes even attempt to assuage, many adolescents' powerful feelings of alienation and despair. Of course rock has long addressed itself to the emotionally wounded teenager. What's new is this genre's astonishing frankness, its wide popularity and its active, earnest attempt to lend troubled fans a helping hand.

Musicians from a few different punk-related genres are exploring therapy rock: the up-and-coming "emo" genre, which features hyperdramatic, almost mawkish rock delving deeply into personal upheaval; rap-metal, an aggressive hybrid that has lately turned more introspective; and pop-punk, a slick version of punk that's deceptively up-tempo and not generally noted for its profundity. But it is bands in the last category—like the hugely popular Good Charlotte, Sum 41 and Blink-182—whose songs most often amount to vivid case studies in adolescent mental health issues. The group A Simple Plan, who are also receiving heavy play on MTV, might have expressed pop-punk's attitude most directly: "I'm just a kid/And life is a nightmare."

Consider Blink-182. With more than 10 million albums sold, it's one of the biggest bands in the country. Its new self-titled release is punctuated by evocations of depression like "I'm so lost, I'm barely here/ I wish I could explain myself but words escape me/ It's too late to save me."

"Adam's Song," from Blink-182's previous album, was based on a fan's suicide note; it profiled a character struggling to overcome hopeless thoughts. (Unlike the real-life inspiration, the song's protagonist survives his crisis.) With their messages of care and support, these bands give the lie to the hoary stereotype of the nihilistic punk rocker. And not only do some of them make videos that are specifically designed to serve a public health function; they've found other novel ways to guide their fans through emotional troubles.

The annual Take Action Tour, mostly featuring punk-derived "screamo" bands, raises depression and suicide awareness and benefits the National Hopeline Network (which oversees the anti-suicide hot line 800-784-2433). This summer the network sent a gleaming new semi full of information on the popular Warped Tour, which featured Rancid, the Used and AFI among many major acts. (The benefit album "Take Action, Volume 3" includes multimedia content based on "Suicide: The Forever Decision," a book by Dr. Paul Quinnett, as well as a self-test for depression.)

Some songs in this genre are downright prescriptive, counseling kids to be patient and tenacious through the lonely, bewildering years of adolescence. (Many other tracks merely depict depression, in hopes that teenagers might at least find comfort in knowing someone else understands what they're going through).

In "Hang On" (not to be confused with Good Charlotte's "Hold On") the pop-punk band Smashmouth exhorts, "Things are getting' weird/Things are getting' tough/Nothing's makin' sense/But you keep on lookin' up." Virtually every song on the bad-boy pop-punks Sum 41's hit record "Does This Look Infected?" is about profound alienation, depression or imminent emotional breakdown, but on "Hell Song" the band urges listeners to look for solutions, instead of wallowing in despair: "Everybody's got their problems/It's just a matter how you solve them/And knowing how to change the things you've been through."

Other songs recommend solidarity: "I was confused/And I let it all out to find/that I'm not the only person with these things in mind," Linkin Park's Chester Bennington sings on the band's hit single "Somewhere I Belong." In 1967 the Beatles sang "Getting Better All the Time," whose lyrics now read like a gentler version of the prototypical therapy rock song. (Sure enough, Smashmouth covers the song on "The Cat in the Hat" soundtrack.) Four years later the Who famously sang, "Don't cry, don't brace your eye/It's only teenage wasteland" on the classic rock staple "Baba O'Riley." Heavy metal and industrial rock have profiled psychological imbalance for decades, and many current bands worship the 80's mope-rockers the Cure. (Robert Smith of the Cure even sings a tune on the new Blink-182 album.)

But therapy rock has its most direct roots in the genesis of American punk rock, a movement founded by a tiny coterie of troubled misfits and outcasts. The pioneering Southern California punk band Black Flag's landmark 1978 debut EP was called "Nervous Breakdown" and themes of insanity, alienation and depression have been a hallmark of punk lyrics ever since.

The first stirrings of therapy rock's introduction to a mass audience came in the early 90's, when alternative rock, inspired by punk music and led by Nirvana, apotheosized a generation of disaffected and confused latchkey kids. "Lots of music now comes from Nirvana, and a lot of people identify with what Kurt Cobain was saying," said William, 16, of New York City. In what many interpreted as the defining event of a generation, Cobain killed himself with a shotgun blast in April 1994.

The tuneful punk revivalists Green Day picked up the ball of teen angst in the mid 90's, and thereafter various pop-punk bands ran with it all the way to commercial glory. American youth welcomed songs about the emotional difficulties of being a teenager. The audience for therapy rock was always there, it was just waiting for punk rock's popularity to catch up with it.

Since commercial success and punk credibility are virtually antithetical, the new pop-punk bands embrace themes of emotional distress as a way of asserting their authenticity and musical lineage. (They cleave to punk orthodoxy musically as well, having progressed remarkably little from early Southern California punk bands like the Descendents and Bad Religion.)

As a result therapy rockers fetishize depression like gangsta rappers fetishize the thug life, publicizing their plight while asserting their credibility. Just as the group Public Enemy once called rap the "CNN of the streets," therapy rock claims to report from the front lines of suburbia. In other words, it's cool to be bummed out. And it sure sells records.

The popularity of therapy rock may in part be a reaction to the shallow kiddie-pop and testosterone-addled "nu metal" of recent years, making sincerity and relentless introspection the new rebellion. But even considering the adolescent penchant for magnifying ordinary personal woes into downright apocalyptic melodrama, therapy rock addresses some sober realities. According to the National Center for Injury Prevention and Control, the adolescent suicide rate has about tripled since the 1950's, and suicide is the third-leading cause of death for people 15 to 24 (behind accidents and homicide).

Each year about 5,000 young people kill themselves, and several times that number try. The numbers have tailed off somewhat in recent years but only, some experts say, because of the rise in antidepressant prescription drugs. "If all the bands are singing about this, I can't see how you can't see it as a voice for what the youth are thinking," says the Blink-182 singer-guitarist Tom DeLonge.

It may be the very fact of pop success that's spurring bands to write these songs. With huge sales figures comes a deluge of needy fans, some of whom say they literally owe their lives to the band. "Every day we read letters from fans saying that the stress of life, the pressure with family and losing love is too much to bear," Mr. Madden of Good Charlotte noted in a recent news release.

"Once you actually start selling records, and you actually figure out that people are listening to you," says Mr. DeLonge, who recently became a father, "then you start thinking about it, going, 'Wow, you don't want to influence them in a bad way.'"

Performers like Marilyn Manson, Ozzy Osbourne and Judas Priest have faced public condemnation and even legal action after accusations of influencing kids' behavior adversely, so rock musicians know that, whether it's appropriate to do so or not, the public holds them accountable. But these musicians' motivations run deeper than that. Punk is a vast support group for misfits, a community united by alienation. That strong sense of community is the same impulse that leads even the most hardened body-slammers to help up those who have fallen in the mosh pit. Likewise, punk bands—and even bands who merely grew up on punk—look out for their fans. The difference now is that they enjoy a vastly bigger community than ever, and that the bands have cast themselves more directly as trusted peers. And adolescents seem more than ready to listen. Raised in a culture of therapeutic self-examination, the current generation of teenagers may be more alert to—and articulate about—their troubles than their predecessors. "I think it's just becoming less of a taboo subject and more people are talking about it and being aware of it," said Saara, 16, from Rockville Centre, N.Y. "Everyone knows someone who's gone through it." Steve Pedulla, of the emo band Thursday—whose recently released "War All the Time" is virtually a concept album about coping with suicidal urges—agrees. "Kids are more self-aware now," he said.

Suicide and depression may also, however, be among the few remaining dangers that still bear a sense of romantic fascination. In the late 50's, for example, when teenagers first became a major presence on the road, there was a profusion of car crash songs—so many that the songs constituted a subgenre of their own. The 60's and 70's saw a host of anti-drug songs; in the 80's fear of AIDS manifested itself in pop music. Those are no longer the cutting-edge topics of youth culture. But partly as a result of school shootings, depression and its consequences retain their edge.

Even for kids who aren't severely troubled, pop-punk has become a medium for ritual soundings of distress. Like a high-school version of the blues, it's a cathartic shout-out to the hellhounds on one's trail. "A lot of kids are depressed about school and friends, and instead of hearing happy music they'd rather hear something that's sadder than they are—it makes them feel better," says 16-year-old William. "They don't want to hear about why things are so great."

The bands say they hope that this new line of pop discourse will have an actual effect on kids' lives. "It's good that it's out there," the Blink-182 bassist-singer Mark Hoppus says. "It opens dialogue. It makes people able to talk to one another about things. And hopefully it makes things better, you know?"

Dr. Dan Romer, research director of the Adolescent Risk Communication Institute of the Annenberg Public Policy Center, says no significant studies have been made of whether this music has a therapeutic effect. "Not enough attention has been paid to the stuff that's actually pretty valuable to young people," he said. "Unfortunately most of the time we spend trying to find out if it's bad for people."

Indeed, there is some concern that songs decrying suicide could actually encourage it. A 1999 Surgeon General's report concluded that "suicide can be facilitated in vulnerable teens by exposure to real or fictional accounts of suicide." Much to Blink-182's horror, the ultimately life-affirming "Adam's Song" was found playing on repeat when Greg Barnes, a teenage survivor of the Columbine massacre in Colorado, hanged himself in May 2000. "It affected us really strongly because that song was a song of hope," Mr. DeLonge said, the pain still clear in his voice. "When we were writing it, we knew specifically that we did not want kids to think it was something that we thought was cool or rad. We didn't endorse it in any way."

Judging by a visit to the Good Charlotte online message board (http://www.goodcharlotte.com/board/index.php?s=), however, plenty of other teenagers are getting valuable support from songs like "Adam's Song" and "Hold On." "Just a week or so ago my friend was going to kill herself, then she saw the 'Hold On' video," said a Good Charlotte fan named Ann, 14, of Columbus, Ohio. "It stopped her from slitting her wrists. I just don't want to think about what would have happened if that video didn't come on." Kelly, 15, of Grove City, Ohio, said in an interview conducted via

Instant Message, "As disappointing as it is, most kids listen to famous people a lot more than their parents or a teacher."

Lee Huff, president-elect of the National Association of School Psychologists, said that although he devoutly wished parents and schools were more involved, he approved of rock bands counseling young people about depression and related issues. "Bless their hearts," he said. "It certainly goes a long way from talking about killing bitches and whores and cops and everything else doesn't it? If kids listen to rock music more than they listen to a teacher in a classroom, God bless us that they're getting the message."

58

"Rip. Burn. Die."
The Music Industry Sings the Blues

DAVID SHEFF AND ROB TANNENBAUM

As rock music entered its fifth decade in the mid-2000s, talk amidst the recording industry continually returned to the crisis facing record labels in an age of rapidly declining CD sales and rampant peer-to-peer file sharing. While these developments were often framed in apocalyptic terms, the industry has survived many such perilous moments throughout its history. Between 1942 and 1944, for example, the powerful American Federation of Musicians issued a devastating ban on recordings, largely to protest the intrusion of "canned music" and jukebox sales into an industry that had been thriving on live performances. In the early 1980s, faced with the threat of blank cassettes and illicit duplication, the industry unleashed the memorable slogan "home taping is killing music." Like these earlier instances, the turmoil of the 2000s arose from the unforeseen consequences of changing technologies. Specifically, an industry that had been based for so long around the sale of physical objects such as CDs had not properly planned for the shift to music downloading. This issue is but one of many that the participants assembled for *Playboy*'s 2004 music panel address in their discussion of the music industry's overwhelming woes. Prodded by the questions of journalists David Sheff and Rob Tannenbaum, who appear as the anonymous voice of *Playboy*, the panelists voice their opinions on topics ranging from industry-artist relationships to iTunes and the future of record stores.*

THE PANEL

- Simon Renshaw (managing partner, the Firm; manager, Dixie Chicks and others)
- Moby (recording artist)
- Ron Shapiro (former co-president, Atlantic Records)
- Rick Rubin (producer, Johnny Cash, Red Hot Chili Peppers and others; co-founder, Def Jam Recordings)
- Liz Brooks (vice president of marketing, BuyMusic.com)
- Jason Flom (chairman and CEO, Atlantic Records)
- Marc Geiger (senior vice president, William Morris Agency; co-founder and former CEO, ArtistDirect)

* *Source:* David Sheff and Rob Tannenbaum, "Rip. Burn. Die.," *Playboy*, October 2004, pp. 84–86, 148–58.

- Sharon Osbourne (manager, Ozzy Osbourne; overseer of Ozzfest)
- Perry Farrell (recording artist, Jane's Addiction; founder, Lollapalooza)
- Chuck D (recording artist, Public Enemy; producer)
- David Benveniste (manager, System of a Down, Deftones)
- Andy Gould (manager, Rob Zombie)
- Aimee Mann (recording artist, former leader of 'Til Tuesday)
- Michael Hausman (manager, Aimee Mann)
- Russ Solomon (founder and chief executive, Tower Records)
- David Draiman (recording artist, Disturbed)
- John Mayer (recording artist)
- Joe Fleischer (vice president of sales and marketing, BigChampagne, a research firm)
- Chris Bell (director of product marketing, iTunes)

What Went Wrong—by the Numbers

845 million: overall music sales (in units) in 2000

803 million: overall music sales in 2001

693 million: overall music sales in 2002

687 million: overall music sales in 2003

1.8 billion: number of blank CDs sold each year

$3.5 billion: worldwide sales of ring tones in 2003

1.7 million: number of iPods Apple sold in the first six months of 2004

4.4 million: number of iPods Apple has sold since they were introduced in October 2001

70 million: number of songs sold by iTunes in its first year

2.6 billion: number of songs that are illegally shared online each month, according to Recording Industry Association of America testimony to Congress

29 percentage of Americans surveyed who admitted to using free file-sharing services before the RIAA lawsuits were announced

14 percentage of Americans surveyed who admitted to using free file-sharing services after the RIAA lawsuits were announced

260 approximate number of stores closed in 2003 by Musicland Group

294 number of stores closed by Wherehouse last year, out of a total of 405

PART 1: DESPARATE TIMES: HOW DID THE MUSIC BUSINESS LOSE SO MUCH MONEY AND PISS OFF SO MANY FANS?

Playboy: Irving Azoff, who manages the Eagles and Christina Aguilera, recently said of the music business, "This is about as bad as it gets. These are desperate times." Is he right?

Simon Renshaw (managing partner, the Firm; manager, Dixie Chicks and others): He is. From 1982 to 1997 the record industry enjoyed a free ride. People basically restocked their libraries, replacing vinyl and cassettes—and even eight-tracks, God forbid—with CDs. Huge profits passed to record labels. For 15 years the record companies' coffers swelled and swelled—and then this crisis started.

Playboy: Everything from downloading to the price of CDs to the quality of music has been blamed. What's the real story?

Moby (recording artist): This is a very unpopular thing to say, but the record companies themselves are at fault. In the late 1980s and early 1990s big corporations started buying them up. Their sole criterion for determining success was how a company did on a quarterly basis. A friend of mine who ran a big record label said that because of the pressure put on him by the corporation, all he cared about was an album that delivered one hit single. A lot of what succeeded was simple, formulaic, lowest-common-denominator stuff. If the record companies don't value the music, why should the consumer?

Playboy: Successful labels such as Island, Geffen and A&M have been purchased by large corporations. After the Sony/BMG merger, there will be only four major labels. How does consolidation affect musical quality?

Ron Shapiro (former co-president, Atlantic Records): Corporations want irrational growth, but the music business has historically worked on long-term artist development. Now there is an incredible lack of patience for developing artists. Where you program for your parent company's immediate gratification, you sign stuff that's easy to digest, not what you consider brilliant. We're not selling boxes of cereal; we're selling musicians, and musicians almost never live their lives to the rhythm of Wall Street.

Rick Rubin (producer, Johnny Cash, Red Hot Chili Peppers and others; co-founder, Def Jam Recordings): It stopped being about music. The business became all about marketing and promoting singles. Radio doesn't care what the rest of the album sounds like, so the labels stopped caring too. And they taught bands to think that way. If you're in a band, you don't really know anything. You sign to a label and you're told to make a hit single. Then kids go out and buy the album for one song, and the rest of it sucks. The kids get burned and don't want to get burned again.

Liz Brooks (vice president of marketing, BuyMusic.com; former Napster employee): Customers look at an $18 CD, and there may be one or two songs on it they want to own. That's not value for their entertainment dollar.

Jason Flom (chairman and CEO, Atlantic Records): I have a very difficult time with all these generalizations. No one ever told bands to put a bunch of bad songs on an album. I mean, that's a ridiculous concept.

Playboy: Why are consumers so alienated from the music business today?

Ron Shapiro: There's been a shameless lack of self-evaluation. Labels did all kinds of crazy things to succeed, to make the most money and to have the most hits—to win at all costs. It gives consumers the sense that they've been fucked with.

Moby: If Bruce Springsteen had been signed to a major label in the 1990s, he would have been dropped three months after his first record. And the same with Fleetwood Mac, Bob Seger and Prince. Their first records were not successful.

Marc Geiger (senior vice president, William Morris Agency; co-founder and former CEO, ArtistDirect): Bigger is not better. The entrepreneurial spirit that made the music business has disappeared. People once cared about the music and not about "I've got to file my 10-K and my 10-Q." That's the result of mergers.

Playboy: But we keep reading about Norah Jones selling 8.5 million records and 50 Cent selling 6.5 million. How can labels be losing money?

Ron Shapiro: The record business is a bit like Las Vegas. You throw acts against the wall and hope a few will stick—to pay for everything.

Simon Renshaw: Five percent of records make money, and the other 95 percent lose money. If Ford Motor Company failed 95 percent of the time, it would be out of business. The business model doesn't work—it doesn't make sense. Mergers are the reward for bad management.

You screw up so badly there's only one thing to do: merge with another screwed-up business and perpetuate this bullshit for another couple of years. All you're doing is bilking shareholders.

Sharon Osbourne (manager, Ozzy Osbourne; overseer of Ozzfest): Ozzy is signed to Sony, but we don't want to be with them, so we're not delivering anything. We're in a stalemate, firing angry faxes and e-mails to each other. The music people are gone, and the suits who've come in don't understand music. They have a fucking calculator on their desk, and that's all they care about.

Perry Farrell (recording artist, Jane's Addiction; founder, Lollapalooza): Musicians have been treated like dirt. It's sort of like boxing these days: There may be a few champions making money, but most of them are getting their head kicked in. That's what has happened to artists since Wall Street came into the music industry and bankers and accountants took the place of producers and A&R people. When Jane's Addiction started, Warner Bros. Records was run by people who loved music. They produced great groups. Those men were pushed out and replaced with accountants.

Chuck D (recording artist, Public Enemy; producer): When businessmen start to think they know what this business is about, we're dead. They start trying to tell artists what to do. No one told Picasso what to paint. He didn't paint a picture and wonder if people would think it was hot.

Playboy: Can we conclude that music today is worse than it was in the past?

David Benveniste (manager, System of a Down, Deftones): I don't know. I'm 32 years old. I was just a kid when the industry was energized by Led Zeppelin, Pink Floyd, Fleetwood Mac, the Grateful Dead, the Doors and Crosby, Stills, Nash & Young. This wasn't just music. It was a culture. Compare that with the songs we hear on radio today. Big conglomerates own radio. They're concerned only with selling ads. They play songs for 15 seconds and call their focus groups. If the song researches well—great. If not, they take it off the air. What do we get as a result? Limp Bizkit. You can't compare Limp Bizkit to Led Zeppelin. You can't compare the All-American Rejects to the Doors. At the age of 75, when I'm talking to my grandkid, I'm not going to say, "I lived during the Strokes era!" Where's the music that will save the day now?

Ron Shapiro: We all sort of smell the stink of commercialism and consolidation perverting the music. In the 1960s and 1970s, a time of great change in this country, music helped you define who you were—and it changed lives. Rock is no longer antiestablishment; now it speaks for the establishment. It reflects the powers that be, the things that make people feel powerless.

Jason Flom: Are we just a bunch of old guys sitting on a bench reminiscing about the old days? I don't think so. There really was a golden age. But by the way, has anybody made *The Godfather* lately? Have you seen anything as good as that? The quality of the movies coming out every week in the 1970s was ridiculous. Yet the movie industry is doing better than ever with these sensationalistic, dumb movies. Our whole culture seems to have become disposable.

Playboy: Do record labels really deserve all the blame?

Rick Rubin: Artists aren't blameless. You have to be willing to write 40 songs to put out only 12. You have to push the limits of your ability. Some artists are lazy. Their album takes off, they tour, they take some time off, and they go back into the studio. They push out an album to a schedule rather than take as long as they need to make a record great. Also, since

MTV, music has become much more image-driven. Image should have nothing to do with it.

PART 2: THE INEPTITUDE IS MIND-BOGGLING: WHY DO CDS COST SO MUCH?

Playboy: CD sales have been declining since 1999, but the average cost of a CD has kept increasing. Are consumers right to complain that CDs cost too much?

Moby: It's pure greed. Maybe the record companies could save themselves if they stopped charging $20 for a record that costs very little to make, if they stopped spending millions on corrupt indie promotion, if they stopped giving themselves millions of dollars in bonuses and if they stopped spending a million dollars on a music video. A video should never cost more than a house in West Virginia.

Jason Flom: I think it's ridiculous. You'd be hard-pressed to find anything that has risen less in price over the past 30 years, whether it's movie tickets or bus fare. I don't know why people are willing to pay $3.49 for a ring tone but think $13 is too much for an album. Maybe it goes back to Napster—for a while music was free. It still is, if you're willing to break the law.

Sharon Osbourne: The ineptitude is mind-boggling. These people!

Andy Gould (manager, Rob Zombie): I'm not saying that I don't like some of the people in the industry. I do. And some of them must be smart. It's like no matter what you hear about George W. Bush, you think, he must be kind of smart. I mean, he did become president. He must be smarter than I am; I ain't fucking president. The same thing goes in the record business. I'm sure some people out there are smarter than they appear, but they do seem to have forgotten something essential to the music business. It's become all business, and they've forgotten about music.

Playboy: What's wrong with putting businessmen in charge of the music business? We keep hearing about these huge recording and video budgets. Shouldn't someone be telling bands not to overspend?

Sharon Osbourne: The guys in suits spend all their time at lunch and have no idea what's going on in the streets. We had signed with Sony and suddenly they were all up in arms about downloading, while they themselves were creating the software to make it possible. Talk about out of touch. They didn't care. They were making millions even though the record companies were losing a fortune.

Simon Renshaw: Without a doubt, some executives are grossly overpaid. If you have an executive whose company is losing $200 million a year, why would you pay him $20 million?

Moby: It makes me want to scream. People from the record company fly first-class, and the artist flies economy. They stay at the Four Seasons while the artist is at the Days Inn. But what really galls me is that everyone who works at a record company has health insurance, yet none of the musicians do. It's so profoundly unethical that it's unconscionable. Record companies have mistreated artists for 50 years, and now they expect sympathy from us?

PART 3: IT'S PAYBACK: WILL ARTISTS ABANDON THE MAJOR LABELS?

Playboy: Consumers are obviously unhappy. What about the musicians?

Marc Geiger: As the labels became all-powerful, the artists became powerless. They were at the bottom of the food chain, but now it's payback: Artists who can reject labels are doing so.

Playboy: Will more artists go out on their own and work around the labels?

Andy Gould: Pearl Jam has no record label. Other big names don't want to be part of the industry. They would rather do it themselves. Why not? They can cut out the middleman.

Sharon Osbourne: If we get out of our contract with Sony, we will do it ourselves. We would probably make an album and give it away on the Internet for free. Then we'd have another one that you could purchase on the road.

Playboy: Aimee, you were on three major labels before starting your own independent one. How much money were you making on a major label?

Aimee Mann (recording artist; former leader of 'Til Tuesday): That's easy—none. I made a little bit on the first 'Til Tuesday record but only a little.

Michael Hausman (manager, Aimee Mann): Let's put it this way: I was in 'Til Tuesday, and I had part of the songwriting royalties. We probably sold 800,000 CDs with our first record, and I never earned more than $35,000 a year. Now we make a lot more money. We ship 200,000 of Aimee's records to a distributor at a little over $9 each. That leaves us with about $1.8 million. We can make the record and do the marketing and promotion for $1 million. After costs, that puts our profit at $4 or $5 a CD.

Aimee Mann: There's this mythology among artists that you can't do it without a major label. One of the first things Michael said to me after we got up and running was, "It's not that hard."

PART 4: THE ENEMY INVADES THE SHORELINE: HOW DID NAPSTER OVERTHROW THE RECORD COMPANIES?

Playboy: What role did Napster play in the music-business crisis?

Ron Shapiro: The day the Napster story broke on the front page of the *New York Times*—March 7, 2000—the executives at Atlantic Records gathered in a conference room to read it together. I'll never forget that day as long as I live. The enemy had just invaded the shoreline, and we hadn't seen them coming. Everybody knew instantly that things were going to change forever.

Russ Solomon (founder and chief executive, Tower Records): There's no question about that. One morning we woke up and realized how much Napster was affecting the business.

Andy Gould: If I hear one more record executive say, "Oh, the problem is downloading," I'll fucking punch him. I'm just sick of it. It's such an excuse.

Ron Shapiro: People spent a lot of time being outraged about Napster. But there were 100 million people using the service every day who loved music and shared it. Shouldn't we have found a way to monetize that?

Perry Farrell: They all say downloading killed the industry, but maybe people started downloading because the industry wasn't giving them what they wanted—good music at a fair price.

Simon Renshaw: The average kid thinks, I'm not stealing from the bands; I'm stealing from the record companies, and the bands say the record companies steal from them already. They could care less.

Rick Rubin: When you abandon your audience, you can't be surprised when it finds another way to get what it wants.

Playboy: The RIAA has prosecuted people for illegally downloading music. Metallica has sued downloaders. Do you support the prosecutions and lawsuits?

David Draiman (recording artist, Disturbed): [Sarcastically] Real smart. Turn your customers into enemies. Demonize them.

Perry Farrell: It's pathetic.

Andy Gould: Suing your customers? Have you ever heard of anything so fucking stupid?

John Mayer (recording artist): The RIAA suing its customers is akin to my getting onstage and making fun of overweight people in the crowd.

Chuck D: It's like a Roman emperor busting into a house and raiding the kitchen because the family grew the food on land that was considered imperial property. Besides everything else, suing over downloading doesn't address the real problem, which is burning CDs. Yeah, Sony is against downloading music, but the company also makes blank CDs and sells burners. What the hell? The corporations are trying to get it from all sides.

Moby: It's incredibly hypocritical and disingenuous for record companies to go after file sharing but leave CD burning alone. CD burning is a much greater threat. But a lot of parent companies also make CD burners and blank CDs. They go after file sharing because they don't have any financial stake in it.

John Mayer: You can go into a Comp-USA—I don't recommend it, but you can—and buy 50 CD-Rs for $10. I guarantee you, most of my lost sales come from kids going, "Oh, I already bought it; don't worry about it" and then burning a copy for a friend.

Playboy: When fans download your songs or burn a copy of your CD, are they stealing from you?

Moby: When I make music, I want people to hear it. I don't really care if they pay for it or not.

John Mayer: If you have the dedication to sit at your computer for two hours and queue up on some kid's connection at Penn State while he's serving one of my songs, then maybe your time is worth getting that song for free. I make an incredibly good living. Not as good as Dave Matthews, but I'm not in a race.

Moby: I've downloaded my own music just to tweak the nose of the RIAA. Are they going to sue me for illegally downloading my own music? I hope they do.

Liz Brooks: They blame Napster, but long before it the industry was out of touch with its consumers, who were already alienated when Napster arrived. It wasn't just the free music. Napster brought this incredible sense of access, a smorgasbord of any record you could have dreamed of: one you heard when you were a child, a B side you liked or the obscure Norwegian remix you hadn't been able to find in your local store. Not only could you find it on Napster, if you had a high-speed connection you could get it in a few minutes from another person, which is very empowering. Every business that has had massive Internet success, such as eBay or AOL, has been based on community.

Simon Renshaw: Technology had a staggering effect. No one saw it coming, and we responded with our usual mentality: We put our heads in the sand and denied it existed. Record companies had always controlled the system by which music reaches the public, but the Internet leveled that playing field.

John Mayer: You can't fight technology. You have to adapt to it. But record companies aren't known for being crafty. They're inflexible; they can't react quickly. It's a slow-moving industry, and it's been slow to respond to technology, which moves like a fire hose.

Marc Geiger: Blaming technology for the industry's problems is like blaming the weatherman for a hurricane. My forehead is flat from the number of times I've hit my head against the wall trying to tell record industry executives that technology was coming and would change things forever. Napster founder Shawn Fanning was the bad guy, but if he hadn't written Napster, someone else would have. And the technology isn't popular because people want to steal. That's the biggest bullshit the industry will tell you. You don't want to pay? You bought a burner for $299. You upped your bandwidth because it was painful sucking a song over a 56kbps connection, so your ISP fee went from $21.99 a month to

$40. You may have bought an iPod for $500. You bought cool Cambridge SoundWorks speakers, and those are a couple hundred bucks. Then your old four-gigabyte hard drive filled up with music and porn and other stuff you downloaded, so you replaced it with a new $1,800 computer and a 20-gigabyte hard drive. Don't tell me people don't want to pay for music.

Liz Brooks: There's no going back. When I was at Napster, it was the most exciting thing I had seen since I was 14 and discovered punk rock. Napster offered me a job and I seized the opportunity. Maybe seven people worked at the company. We had pizza stuck to the ceiling, cereal boxes and engineers sleeping in the server room. It was wonderful. It was the fastest-growing application in the history of the Internet. Napster's first six months surpassed Hotmail's first six months, when Hotmail signed up 18 million users. It made Hotmail look like a Yugo on the autobahn.

Playboy: The labels sued Napster, and the company went out of business. Did that put a stop to file sharing?

Joe Fleischer (vice president of sales and marketing, BigChampagne, a research firm that monitors file sharing): Kazaa has been downloaded more often than any instant-messaging program.

Andy Gould: We could have made Napster a subscription service and embraced it, but we didn't and drove everybody to a million different places. Now it's going to be really hard to get them all back.

Liz Brooks: There's no way to stop what Napster started. Look at how much good it did to squash Napster: Peer-to-peer isn't going away.

Playboy: There's some evidence that downloading can help record sales. Perhaps the most file-shared artist of 2003 was 50 Cent, but he also had the year's best-selling record. Is downloading a good form of promotion?

Chuck D: I don't think it hurts anyone. It's great exposure, especially in a business in which big companies co-opt and buy exposure. Downloading is just the new radio. Norah Jones is one of the most downloaded new artists of all time, and her second album sold a million units in its first week on sale. In the end, downloading does not hurt this business; it helps it.

Moby: My album *Play* wouldn't have sold 10 million copies worldwide without file sharing. People came up to me and said, "I read an article about you, so I went to Napster and downloaded a song, and then I bought your record."

David Draiman: I say free file sharing is great as long as there is some measure of control. You want it for marketing reasons. You want to get your music out there. There's no greater tool for massive exposure with little effort and cost.

Perry Farrell: We always had free downloads on our site, and we had a website early on. We've always been involved online in trying to keep a close connection to our fans. They get music for free, but they'll pay because they want digital quality from a reliable source. The more tunes are made available for a price that seems fair, the more people will accept it. They won't stop just because you tell them it's wrong. So make it easy and cheap to get the real thing. iTunes does i.

PART 5: THE INNOVATION: CAN ITUNES SAVE THE MUSIC BUSINESS?

Playboy: How big of a success has iTunes been?

Jason Flom: This is the first year that downloads are having a noticeable impact on the labels' bottom line.

Ron Shapiro: I have a 12-year-old son who lives for music, and he's been in a record store only four or five times in his life. He spends almost all his leisure hours using iTunes, and every night it's, "Daddy, can I buy one more song?"

Aimee Mann: It's amazing that an online download store is such a recent development. I mean, how could you not have seen that coming? Major labels just clung to this attitude of "We do it one way and it's always worked for us, and the wolf apparently is not at the door. We don't have to worry about that."

Chris Bell (director of product marketing, iTunes): A number of artists are still unwilling to make their music available for individual song downloads. We respect that. It's their creative decision. They're pretty much hanging up a sign that says, KAZAA: THIS WAY.

Playboy: Apple has sold more than 3 million downloads in a week, plus 4.4 million iPods since October 2001. Is it surprising that such a successful way to profit from digital music came from outside the music business?

Andy Gould: We have no brains in this industry. In 1979 we were up in arms about home taping—it was going to kill music. The industry was in free fall. Two things saved us: CDs were invented, and MTV came on the air. We had nothing to do with creating either of them. The last time there was a free fall, in the 1960s, at least we came up with FM radio and new ways of touring, which pulled us out. Now we are bankrupt of ideas. Everything that has come along recently to give the industry some life—Napster, iTunes—came from outside it. We don't have anyone with a fucking original idea. If you're making $10 million a year, why bother?

John Mayer: In the music world, there's so much room for cleverness—which is where Steve Jobs comes in. He knows how to be clever. He's prospering now because he's clever in an industry that is just so well-known for not being clever.

Simon Renshaw: If you look back in history, innovation tends to surface during moments of crisis. But it comes from outside the core affected industry. Steve Jobs wasn't concerned about musicians, and now he's selling iPods. Forget the 99-cent download. That's irrelevant. Music is just something that goes on his iPods. Apple will continue to do well, but the record companies have lost because now everyone is a distributor. BestBuy.com, WalMart.com—they're all selling downloads.

Liz Brooks: Depending on which analyst you believe, Jobs's margin on the iPod is between $70 and $175. He can afford to lose money on music. Technology once again drives the transformation of an industry. Everyone is following Apple.

Playboy: What will the long-term impact of iTunes be?

Chris Bell: Think about the ways people discover music: Market research shows that you hear about it through word of mouth or on the radio. You may see an artist on TV, on *Letterman* or *Saturday Night Live.* You scribble the name on a matchbook cover and look for it online or at a record store. And iTunes has just broken down a lot of those barriers. You can see a band on *SNL* and have its music on your iPod in the morning. We also provide a way to release music between official album releases and to keep the relationship with the audience very vibrant and rich.

David Benveniste: iTunes is cool because you can download whatever song you want, but it doesn't necessarily kill CDs. At the end of the day, U2 and the Chili Peppers and Dave Matthews—bands that have real music and a real message—are still making money.

Playboy: Steve Jobs recently called the album obsolete. Many people think it won't exist in 10 years. Do you agree?

Simon Renshaw: It'll be sooner.

Chris Bell: Customers have a choice, and 45 percent of the songs of iTunes are still sold as part of an album. The much-predicted deconstruction of the album has not happened. But a song economy has been evolving during the past five or six years, and people want the choice. iTunes is all about choice.

Playboy: There are still plenty of online file-sharing services. Will people choose to pay 99 cents when they can get songs for free?

David Draiman: It's worth spending the measly 99 cents on a download instead of spending all that time trying to get the frigging thing for free.

Chris Bell: The first thing I'd say is that all the music we sell on iTunes reflects a pent-up demand to get it digitally. A lot of customers have said for a long time that they're willing to buy music if given a viable alternative to stealing it. In addition, we're getting to people who are shopping for music and discovering it online for the first time, because it's so easy to get CD-quality music.

PART 6: THE REFRIGERATORS TAKE OVER: WILL RECORD STORES VANISH?

Playboy: If iTunes and Kazaa are replacing record stores, will Tower and other brick-and-mortar businesses become things of the past?

David Draiman: We don't know what will happen. Tower has filed for protection under bankruptcy law. If you can get something online, why should you leave home?

Russ Solomon: I obviously feel all these changes. However, Tower is reorganizing and will open more stores, if I have anything to say about it. We're not ignoring the Internet, either.

Playboy: But what about Draiman's point? Why go to a record store if you can get music online?

Russ Solomon: I think stores will complement online outlets. They're going to exist side by side. Why go to a record store? Many people still find it easier to buy music in a packaged form, and many like going to stores to browse.

Andy Gould: When I was growing up, a record store fostered a sense of community, which is long gone. Tower is not a great place to buy records, but Amoeba—a music store in L.A., San Francisco and Berkeley—is and it's doing great. You can ask the guy behind the counter, "Do you know Captain Beefheart?" and he'll go, "Yeah. If you want to check him out, listen to this." Tower has all these little nerds in fucking Marilyn Manson T-shirts. You think they're going to know?

Russ Solomon: The problems we and the industry have had are making us look at everything we do. We have to do better. We know that.

Andy Gould: If a music store can be made to feel like a community environment again, maybe you'll have a culture that hangs out there.

David Benveniste: The experience of going into a record store has to become much more exciting. There's a reason Marilyn Manson sells out shows across the country but sells only 300,000 records. His performances are like Broadway shows—they're stimulating. Tower has to make its stores as exciting.

Russ Solomon: We have to figure out a way to attract young people. The strongest thing, of course, is price. The industry has to do better and offer more. We're also looking at ways to make the experience more fun. Crazily enough, I'm experimenting now with soda fountains.

We're going to put one in our Atlanta store. I got to thinking, What would happen if we put a soda fountain and a jukebox in a record store?

Marc Geiger: The record stores—whether Tower or Amazon.com or any of the others—aren't going away. Everyone said movie theaters would disappear because of the VCR, but they didn't. Movie theaters actually got better. Many old theaters were run-down mom-and-pops that sold Jujyfruits and didn't have THX sound or stadium seating. Instead of disappearing, they became Cineplex 10s with a Starbucks and good food and THX and 92 movies to choose from. It's Darwinian. For movies, I may be a pay-per-view guy. The guy next to me may like Blockbuster. The next guy may like Netflix. The next may subscribe to HBO. The next loves to go out to see movies. Are we all jerks? No. Music will be the same. For some, record stores. For some, downloading. For some, music by cable. For some, satellite radio. For many, all of the above.

Russ Solomon: There will be many ways to buy music. In addition, you can do more things in a record store than just buy records. We're exploring them. The fastest-growing part of the business right this minute is music video on DVD. We sold $20 million worth last year. We'll also look at selling downloaded products in stores. However, at this point the number of songs being downloaded is still infinitesimal compared with the total number of songs sold on CD. In one recent week, 1.6 million downloaded songs were legitimately paid for, and 12 million units of CDs were sold. Multiply that times 12 songs on each CD and you get 144 million songs. People bought 144 million songs in packaged form, as opposed to the 1.6 million downloaded. I'm not writing off packaged goods.

Simon Renshaw: I don't think music stores will disappear; I just think refrigerators will take over more space. You'll see CD departments in Barnes & Noble and Borders decrease in size. The chains—Tower, Virgin—are becoming increasingly irrelevant. We'll see fewer titles physically released; the vast majority will be distributed and sold in non-physical form, and CDs will be just for big-artist releases, sold with convenience and price in mind by the Wal-Marts, Targets and Costcos. Sad, huh?

PART 7: THE LOWEST COMMON DENOMINATOR: IS CLEAR CHANNEL THE ENEMY?

Playboy: Now that we have so many ways to discover music, is radio as important as it used to be?

David Draiman: It's a massive factor. Your average Joe still has an average car stereo—with a CD player if he's lucky—but no satellite radio, no streaming audio and no Internet radio. And teenagers' lives revolve around the car. Radio is at the center of it all. I'm sure many programming directors all over the country will be very happy to hear me say that.

Simon Renshaw: Most North American radio is owned by a few large corporations. Clear Channel is by far the largest. All it cares about is ratings and selling advertising. Radio has become the lowest common denominator: "What 20 songs does our audience like most?"

Playboy: Clear Channel owns more than 1,200 radio stations, and its concert division sold more than 27 million tickets in 2001, nearly seven times as many as the closest competitor. Some Clear Channel stations banned the Dixie Chicks after the group denounced President Bush, and this year it knocked Howard Stern off its stations for supposed indecency. What's your view of the company?

John Mayer: It's really hip right now to hate Clear Channel. The company's been good to me, and I don't think you can be a performing artist and not have a relationship with it.

Sharon Osbourne: Right. Some people think Clear Channel is the bad guy, but not us. As a sponsor of Ozzfest, Clear Channel built this house.

Joe Fleischer: I think the idea that Clear Channel or MTV controls the music business is false. Clear Channel is not in the music business. Clear Channel is in the advertising business, and it is incumbent upon them to play what people want. Instead of whining, artists should make better music.

Playboy: Clear Channel is one of President Bush's and other Republican politicians' biggest supporters. Is that why the government doesn't regulate it more closely?

Simon Renshaw: [Sarcastically] That would be saying that big business has some sort of influence over the government, wouldn't it? I can't believe you'd suggest something like that. Big business gets its will done by exerting financial muscle in the elective process. Hopefully Clear Channel's importance will decrease. Satellite and Internet radio are growing.

Ron Shapiro: The issue for me is the current lack of healthy competition in our country in general. How has it happened that a handful of corporations control most of the basics of our lives? It's capitalism gone wild. Where's the competition? That worries me more than sales going down. One major company, Viacom, owns virtually all the video networks. One or two major companies own all the radio stations. It's harder and harder for David to go up against Goliath, because our leaders have focused on letting Goliath get bigger and bigger.

PART 8: TICKET SALES FELL OFF THE CLIFF: WHY IS THE CONCERT BUSINESS STUMBLING?

Playboy: From 1996 to 2001 the average price of a concert ticket increased by 61 percent. Why?

Simon Renshaw: Consolidation within the concert business drove up ticket prices. Ticketmaster has a near-monopoly, which allows it to add surcharges of unbelievable proportions—often $7 to $9 a ticket.

Playboy: Does Ticketmaster get that money?

Simon Renshaw: Ticketmaster, the venue and the promoter get it. Ticketmaster says to a building, "We'll guarantee you X million dollars a year for the right to be your exclusive ticketing agent." The only people who get nothing are the public and the artists. Is it worth it? I guess we'll find out when people stop buying tickets.

Playboy: Hasn't that started to happen? Lollapalooza was canceled this summer because of bad ticket sales.

Jason Flom: Ticket sales are terrible.

Playboy: Marc, as co-founder of Lollapalooza, do you blame high ticket prices?

Marc Geiger: Some people blame ticket prices or service fees, but last year was a record year with the same or higher prices. Others blame the lineup, saying there was too much indie rock and too few commercial bands—but who knows, because the entire touring business died this summer. Unlike the record business, in which you can blame a lack of good records or piracy, it's difficult to pinpoint a cause. All we know is that ticket sales suddenly fell off a cliff. I actually think it's an aberration, but we'll see.

Sharon Osbourne: Ozzy's catalog used to sell constantly. Now his sales are horrid in America, though not in Europe. Touring is our cash cow, along with merchandising. As a result, the major record companies are trying to get new artists to sign away their touring and merchandising, which is insane.

John Mayer: We charge around $40 for a ticket, which isn't a lot of money. Twenty-three-year-old kids have $40 to spend on a concert. They may say they don't, but they do. Probably 80 percent of my income comes from concerts. I've never seen anybody rip and burn a concert ticket. But if you make your money selling singles, you'd better put on your best suit and go before Congress.

Sharon Osbourne: We could charge more, but with what's going on with unemployment in this country, we want to keep ticket prices down. The fact that kids still come out to shows tells you one thing: They want music. Music is still important in their lives. They may not be that interested in CDs, but they want music.

PART 9: THE FUTURE: HOW DOES THE MUSIC INDUSTRY SAVE ITSELF?

Playboy: Can the music industry be saved?

Simon Renshaw: It's time to burn it down. It's time to get rid of the system. The whole business is so hopelessly antiquated that companies will have to reinvent themselves from top to bottom.

Chuck D: People still buy good records. That's the message of Norah Jones's success. But they are no longer going to tolerate something that is microwaved and put out for mass consumption.

Andy Gould: The business needs to look at other opportunities. I saw a band the other day—kind of a cross between Everlast and Sugar Ray, good-time rock-rap. The guy said, "Most of my songs are about drinking and fucking, so why don't we put ads for Budweiser and Trojan between the tracks?" Holy fucking mackerel, I had never thought of it. Now, is that a good idea? Probably not. But maybe you could go to Budweiser and get it to sponsor the back of a CD. It's not the worst idea I've ever heard.

Playboy: What are some other changes we'll see in the future?

David Draiman: There could be direct billing when you download through ISPs. A pop-up window would say, "You're about to be charged 99 cents to your account," whether it's AOL, Earth-link or MSN. "Do you accept the charge?" Click, boom, no credit card. Half goes to the ISP, half goes to the label, and everybody makes money.

Rick Rubin: The way we get music might look a lot more like the way we get cable TV—a monthly bill for all the music you want. You want the equivalent of Showtime and HBO? You pay a little more.

Liz Brooks: There may be a new type of record company, too. Some alternative labels are showing that labels can still work. Vagrant has Paul Westerberg, Dashboard Confessional, Alkaline Trio and No Motiv. Through consistency of brand and word of mouth, it has created a wildly successful business. Vagrant isn't living a poor punk-rock life. It's probably making more money than most of the major-label entities.

Andy Gould: Do you notice how much video games still sell? Do you notice how much that industry has embraced television? You can't watch a hip TV show without seeing a video-game ad. When was the last time you saw a music ad on TV? Everything we do—the Tylenol we take, the Coca-Cola we drink, the films we see—is advertised on TV. I can come home and see a guy spraying fake hair color on his hair, but I can't come home and see an ad for Metallica. Don't you think we should wake up?

rick rubin: So much will be decided by the music itself. Who will make something that will blow everyone away? Where will it come from?

Simon Renshaw: Music is alive and well. BMI, the songwriters' royalty-collection agency, announced that its revenue was up. There is still a large amount of money in music, but less is flowing to the record companies—they still think it's about selling pieces of plastic.

John Mayer: Ten years from now, software will allow you to go online and get any record you want. The guy who makes that software is going to get the money, not the record companies.

Liz Brooks: The companies still have a role. They've been good at finding talent and making records. Artists need to be discovered by somebody. A&R and production are still needed.

Jason Flom: Ring tones could be tremendous business for us. Soon you'll be able to download songs wirelessly onto your cell phone. I've done this; you plug headphones into the phone, and the sound is just as good as an iPod. There are a lot of mobile phones—more than 136 million in the U.S.—so that creates an incredible new market. At the same time, there's a danger from Symbian phones, which allow you to download ring tones illegally. That's a concern.

Marc Geiger: The winners in this? Consumers. They'll get more music, the way they want it, at fair prices. One big downside to all the choices: the white noise of available content. Filters will be more crucial than ever. A filter can be radio but also critics, websites, TV, everything. The new list of filters has to mature. It's just starting.

Perry Farrell: If you want to make music because it's your passion, you have to think of it in different terms. The old idea—that a company will sign you, there'll be champagne backstage, and you'll run around out of your mind and not pay attention to the business—is over. Instead you have to come from a different place: I love to make music. I'm going to allow the music to be spread around on the Internet as a calling card. I'm not looking for big advances. I want to perform for people year-round. I'm not going to wait five years until my next recording. It's healthier.

Russ Solomon: At least we know that music is no less important than it ever was. Maybe it's more important.

Jason Flom: Yeah, the good news is that music is more popular than ever. More people are spending more time listening to music and playing with their new musical devices than ever before. As an industry, we're going to survive.

Ron Shapiro: Music is everywhere. People never see a movie without music. They never get married without it.

Perry Farrell: People will get music one way or another. That's all we know. Danger Mouse put out *The Grey Album* using samples from the Beatles' "White Album" and Jay-Z's *Black Album*—what we call a mash-up. Danger Mouse can't sell it because of all the licensing issues; he'd be sued if he did. But he plays it live. People are digging this music. They will look at whatever he does next.

Jason Flom: I don't know if anybody is smart enough to say what the industry will look like even two years from now. Things are changing so fast.

Simon Renshaw: In this business, whatever we say now will be irrelevant in six months.

David Benveniste: I think it's going to get worse before it gets better. Lots of faceless music. No message, no art, no cultural value, no ethical value. Things will change, but we don't know when. Kids are smarter now than when we were kids, and they have access to the Internet. They can hit SEND on their computer and disseminate information anywhere in the world in 10 seconds—a song, an image, a phrase, a religion, a word. So when the next thing comes, it will hit hard and big.

59

"The Rap Against Rockism"

Kelefa Sanneh

Few articles in the mid-2000s caused greater debate among popular music critics and bloggers than Kaleefa Sanneh's deliberately inflammatory *New York Times* essay "The Rap Against Rockism." As Sanneh defines it, "rockism" is a form of criticism that reduces rock music to a narrow set of aesthetic values which can then be used to dismiss commercially successful artists ranging from Ashlee Simpson to Mariah Carey. Rockism's authority is never questioned, for its power has accrued over time through the efforts of countless rock critics. Its critical standards are assumed to be normative. For Sanneh, rockism clearly is a pejorative label, and in the 2000s, its presence is particularly problematic because it blinds critics to a mainstream popular music landscape more open than ever to pop, hip hop, country, and dance. Many who have responded to Sanneh's polemical piece have pointed out that he seems simply to be suggesting that critics ought to suspend their judgment altogether. Music critic Jody Rosen has even labeled this reflexive action as a form of "poptimism," an anti-rockist urge to reject the idea of "guilty pleasures" and willfully embrace any and all music as worthy of serious consideration.[*] Rosen's is doubtlessly not the last word in the debate, as rockism will likely continue to be a point of contention for years to come.[†]

Bad news travels fast, and an embarrassing video travels even faster. By last Sunday morning, one of the Internet's most popular downloads was the hours-old 60-second .wmv file of Ashlee Simpson on "Saturday Night Live." As she and her band stood onstage, her own prerecorded vocals—from the wrong song—came blaring through the speakers, and it was too late to start mouthing the words. So she performed a now-infamous little jig, then skulked offstage, while the band (were a few members smirking?) played on. One of 2004's most popular new stars had been exposed as....

As what, exactly? The online verdict came fast and harsh, the way online verdicts usually do. A typical post on her Web site bore the headline, "Ashlee you are a no talent fraud!" After that night, everyone knew that Jessica Simpson's telegenic sister was no rock 'n' roll hero—she wasn't even a rock 'n' roll also-ran. She was merely a lip-synching pop star.

Music critics have a word for this kind of verdict, this knee-jerk backlash against producer-powered idols who didn't spend years touring dive bars. Not a very elegant word, but a useful one. The word is "rockism," and among the small but extraordinarily pesky group of people who obsess over this stuff, rockism is a word meant to start fights. The rockism debate began in earnest in the early

---

[*] Jody Rosen, "The Perils of Poptimism: Does Hating Rock Make You a Music Critic?," *Slate.com* May 9, 2006, http://www.slate.com/id/2141418/nav/tap1/.

[†] *Source:* Kelefa Sanneh, "The Rap Against Rockism," *New York Times*, October 31, 2004, Section 2, pp. 1, 32.

1980's, but over the past few years it has heated up, and today, in certain impassioned circles, there is simply nothing worse than a rockist.

A rockist isn't just someone who loves rock 'n' roll, who goes on and on about Bruce Springsteen, who champions ragged-voiced singer-songwriters no one has ever heard of. A rockist is someone who reduces rock 'n' roll to a caricature, then uses that caricature as a weapon. Rockism means idolizing the authentic old legend (or underground hero) while mocking the latest pop star; lionizing punk while barely tolerating disco; loving the live show and hating the music video; extolling the growling performer while hating the lip-syncher.

Over the past decades, these tendencies have congealed into an ugly sort of common sense. Rock bands record classic albums, while pop stars create "guilty pleasure" singles. It's supposed to be self-evident: U2's entire oeuvre deserves respectful consideration, while a spookily seductive song by an R&B singer named Tweet can only be, in the smug words of a recent VH1 special, "awesomely bad."

Like rock 'n' roll itself, rockism is full of contradictions: it could mean loving the Strokes (a scruffy guitar band!) or hating them (image-conscious poseurs!) or ignoring them entirely (since everyone knows that music isn't as good as it used to be). But it almost certainly means disdaining not just Ms. Simpson but also Christina Aguilera and Usher and most of the rest of them, grousing about a pop landscape dominated by big-budget spectacles and high-concept photo shoots, reminiscing about a time when the charts were packed with people who had something to say, and meant it, even if that time never actually existed. If this sounds like you, then take a long look in the mirror: you might be a rockist.

Countless critics assail pop stars for not being rock 'n' roll enough, without stopping to wonder why that should be everybody's goal. Or they reward them disproportionately for making rock 'n' roll gestures. Writing in The Chicago Sun-Times this summer, Jim DeRogatis grudgingly praised Avril Lavigne as "a teen-pop phenom that discerning adult rock fans can actually admire without feeling (too) guilty," partly because Ms. Lavigne "plays a passable rhythm guitar" and "has a hand in writing" her songs.

Rockism isn't unrelated to older, more familiar prejudices—that's part of why it's so powerful, and so worth arguing about. The pop star, the disco diva, the lip-syncher, the "awesomely bad" hit maker: could it really be a coincidence that rockist complaints often pit straight white men against the rest of the world? Like the anti-disco backlash of 25 years ago, the current rockist consensus seems to reflect not just an idea of how music should be made but also an idea about who should be making it.

If you're interested in—O.K., mildly obsessed with—rockism, you can find traces of it just about everywhere. Notice how those tributes to "Women Who Rock" sneakily transform "rock" from a genre to a verb to a catch-all term of praise. Ever wonder why OutKast and the Roots and Mos Def and the Beastie Boys get taken so much more seriously than other rappers? Maybe because rockist critics love it when hip-hop acts impersonate rock 'n' roll bands. (A recent Rolling Stone review praised the Beastie Boys for scruffily resisting "the gold-plated phooey currently passing for gangsta.")

From punk-rock rags to handsomely illustrated journals, rockism permeates the way we think about music. This summer, the literary zine The Believer published a music issue devoted to almost nothing but indie-rock.* Two weeks ago, in the New York Times Book Review, Sarah Vowell approvingly recalled Nirvana's rise: "a group with loud guitars and louder drums knocking the whimpering Mariah Carey off the top of the charts." Why did the changing of the guard sound so

---

* Sanneh is likely referring to the June 2004 issue of *The Believer*, which did indeed come with a compact disc consisting primarily of recent indie rock. What Sanneh does not mention is that the magazine itself contained interviews with folk musicians Ani DiFranco and Joanna Newsom, hiphop veteran Q-Tip, David Byrne, and others.

much like a sexual assault? And when did we all agree that Nirvana's neo-punk was more respectable than Ms. Carey's neo-disco?

Rockism is imperial: it claims the entire musical world as its own. Rock 'n' roll is the unmarked section in the record store, a vague pop-music category that swallows all the others. If you write about music, you're presumed to be a rock critic. There's a place in the Rock and Roll Hall of Fame for doo-wop groups and folk singers and disco queens and even rappers—just so long as they, y'know, rock.

Rockism just won't go away. The rockism debate began when British bands questioned whether the search for raw, guitar-driven authenticity wasn't part of rock 'n' roll's problem, instead of its solution; some new-wave bands emphasized synthesizers and drum machines and makeup and hairspray, instead. "Rockist" became for them a term of abuse, and the anti-rockists embraced the inclusive possibilities of a once-derided term: pop. Americans found other terms, but "rockist" seems the best way to describe the ugly anti-disco backlash of the late 1970's, which culminated in a full-blown anti-disco rally and the burning of thousands of disco records at Comiskey Park in Chicago in 1979: the Boston Tea Party of rockism.

That was a quarter of a century and many genres ago. By the 1990's, the American musical landscape was no longer a battleground between Nirvana and Mariah (if indeed it ever was); it was a fractured, hyper-vivid fantasy of teen-pop stars and R&B pillow-talkers and arena-filling country singers and, above all, rappers. Rock 'n' roll was just one more genre alongside the rest.

Yet many critics failed to notice. Rock 'n' roll doesn't rule the world anymore, but lots of writers still act as if it does. The rules, even today, are: concentrate on making albums, not singles; portray yourself as a rebellious individualist, not an industry pro; give listeners the uncomfortable truth, instead of pandering to their tastes. Overnight celebrities, one-hit-wonders and lip-synchers, step aside.

And just as the anti-disco partisans of a quarter-century ago railed against a bewildering new pop order (partly because disco was so closely associated with black culture and gay culture), current critics rail against a world hopelessly corrupted by hip-hop excess. Since before Sean Combs became Puff Daddy, we've been hearing that mainstream hip-hop was too flashy, too crass, too violent, too ridiculous, unlike those hard-working rock 'n' roll stars we used to have. (This, of course, is one of the most pernicious things about rockism: it finds a way to make rock 'n' roll seem boring.)

Much of the most energetic resistance to rockism can be found online, in blogs and on critic-infested sites like ilovemusic.com, where debates about rockism have become so common that the term itself is something of a running joke. When the editors of a blog called Rockcritics Daily noted that rockism was "all the rage again," they posted dozens of contradictory citations, proving that no one really agrees on what the term means. (By the time you read this article, a slew of indignant refutations and addenda will probably be available online.)

But as more than one online ranter has discovered, it's easier to complain about rockism than it is to get rid of it. You literally can't fight rockism, because the language of righteous struggle is the language of rockism itself. You can argue that the shape-shifting feminist hip-pop of Ms. Aguilera is every bit as radical as the punk rock of the 1970's (and it is), but then you haven't challenged any of the old rockist questions (starting with: who's more radical?), you've just scribbled in some new answers.

The challenge isn't merely to replace the old list of Great Rock Albums with a new list of Great Pop Songs—although that would, at the very least, be a nice change of pace. It's to find a way to think about a fluid musical world where it's impossible to separate classics from guilty pleasures. The challenge is to acknowledge that music videos and reality shows and glamorous layouts can be as interesting—and as influential—as an old-fashioned album.

In the end, the problem with rockism isn't that it's wrong: all critics are wrong sometimes, and some critics (now doesn't seem like the right time to name names) are wrong almost all the time.

The problem with rockism is that it seems increasingly far removed from the way most people actually listen to music.

Are you really pondering the phony distinction between "great art" and a "guilty pleasure" when you're humming along to the radio? In an era when listeners routinely—and fearlessly—pick music by putting a 40-gig iPod on shuffle, surely we have more interesting things to worry about than that someone might be lip-synching on "Saturday Night Live" or that some rappers gild their phooey. Good critics are good listeners, and the problem with rockism is that it gets in the way of listening. If you're waiting for some song that conjures up soul or honesty or grit or rebellion, you might miss out on Ciara's ecstatic electro-pop, or Alan Jackson's sly country ballads, or Lloyd Banks's felonious purr.

Rockism makes it hard to hear the glorious, incoherent, corporate-financed, audience-tested mess that passes for popular music these days. To glorify only performers who write their own songs and play their own guitars is to ignore the marketplace that helps create the music we hear in the first place, with its checkbook-chasing superproducers, its audience-obsessed executives and its cred-hungry performers. To obsess over old-fashioned stand-alone geniuses is to forget that lots of the most memorable music is created despite multimillion-dollar deals and spur-of-the-moment collaborations and murky commercial forces. In fact, a lot of great music is created because of those things. And let's stop pretending that serious rock songs will last forever, as if anything could, and that shiny pop songs are inherently disposable, as if that were necessarily a bad thing. Van Morrison's "Into the Music" was released the same year as the Sugarhill Gang's "Rapper's Delight"; which do you hear more often?

That doesn't mean we should stop arguing about Ms. Simpson, or even that we should stop sharing the 60-second clip that may just be this year's best music video. But it does mean we should stop taking it for granted that music isn't as good as it used to be, and it means we should stop being shocked that the rock rules of the 1970's are no longer the law of the land. No doubt our current obsessions and comparisons will come to seem hopelessly blinkered as popular music mutates some more—listeners and critics alike can't do much more than struggle to keep up. But let's stop trying to hammer young stars into old categories. We have lots of new music to choose from—we deserve some new prejudices, too.

Index